GUIDE TO *Asian Studies* IN EUROPE

The IIAS is a postdoctoral institute, established jointly by the Royal Netherlands Academy of Arts and Sciences (KNAW), the Vrije Universiteit Amsterdam (VUA), the University of Amsterdam (UvA), and Leiden University (RUL).

The main objective of the iias is to encourage the pursuit of Asian Studies in the Humanities and Social Sciences, nationally as well as internationally.

To achieve this end, the constituent institutes have agreed upon the following activities, which were defined in the *Agreement on National Co-operation in Asian Studies* signed by all parties in 1993.

1. to set up and execute a post-doctoral programme for Dutch and foreign researchers;
2. to organize international scientific gatherings;
3. to act as a national centre for Asian Studies in order to improve international co-operation in the European context;
4. to develop other activities in the field of Asian Studies, such as the publication of a newsletter and the establishment of a database, which should contain up-to-date information on current research in the field of Asian studies.

INTERNATIONAL INSTITUTE FOR ASIAN STUDIES

Main Office:
NONNENSTEEG 1-3, LEIDEN
P.O.BOX 9515, 2300 RA LEIDEN
THE NETHERLANDS
TELEPHONE: +31-71-527 22 27
TELEFAX: +31-71-527 41 62
E-MAIL: IIAS@RULLET.LeidenUniv.NL

Branch Office:
SPINHUIS, O.Z. ACHTERBURGWAL 185
1012 DK AMSTERDAM
THE NETHERLANDS
TELEPHONE: +31-20-525 36 57
TELEFAX: +31-20-525 36 58
E-MAIL: IIAS@pscw.uva.NL

www: http://iias.leidenuniv.nl

International Institute
for Asian Studies

GUIDE TO
Asian Studies
IN EUROPE

CURZON

First published in 1998
by Curzon Press
15 The Quadrant, Richmond
Surrey, TW9 1BP

and International Institute for Asian Studies
P.O. Box 9515, 2300 RA Leiden
The Netherlands
Telephone: +31-71-527 22 27
e-mail IIAS@RULLET.LeidenUniv.NL
www: http://iias.leidenuniv.nl

© 1998 IIAS

Typeset by IIAS

All rights reserved. No part of this book may be reprinted or reproduced or utilised in any form or by any electronic, mechanical, or other means, now known or hereafter invented, including photocopying and recording, or in any information storage or retrieval system, without permission in writing from the publishers.

British Library Cataloguing in Publication Data
A catalogue record for this book is available from the British Library

Library of Congress in Publication Data
A catalogue record for this book has been requested

ISBN 0–7007–1054–X

Table of Contents

List of Advertisers

Acknowledgements

This Guide has been produced on behalf of the European Science Foundation Asia Committee. We would like to thank that Committee for entrusting us with this task. We also should like to thank all Asianists who have co-operated with us by sending in their questionnaires without which this first edition of the *Guide to Asian Studies in Europe* could not have been produced.

In the course of this project, quite outside the ongoing activities at the IIAS, several initiatives were undertaken by either institutes or individuals to collect information on Asian Studies in specific countries such as Russia, Spain, and France. These activities have accentuated the European dimension of the project to an even greater extent.

The gathering of information on Russian Asianists was done under the supervison of Prof. R.B. Rybakov, Director of Institute of Oriental Studies (IOS) in Moscow, while Dr L.I. Chernorutskaya, Head of the Information Department of that same institute, acted as editor of the information compiled by research fellows of the Information Department A.I. Cuprin, V.P. Kabarikho, L.D. Kalashnikova, and M.L. Nikolaeva. They also gathered information about scholars of the Arab world. In view of the geographical definition of Asian Studies used by the IIAS (Asia east of the Indus), unfortunately these latter scholars could not be included in this Guide.

On the initiative of Dr F. Rodao, an inventarization of the Spanish Asianists was conducted in that country at the end of 1996, and in France Drs M. Schaling compiled a list of French Asianists and Institutes in the field of Asian Studies.
Over the past two years data entry at the IIAS has been entrusted to Drs Helga Lasschuijt, Marianne Langehenkel, Gabrielle Landry, Tina Titahena, Christina Tsagkaraki, Oscar Navarro, and Afelonne Doek, who are or have been attached to the IIAS. Drs Didi Karni acted as an advisor to the project and as a liason officer with the National Bureau of Asian Research in Seattle. Dr Rik Hoekstra, who is at present attached to the IIAS, acted as the proverbial whizz kid dealing with all technical matters relating to the database.

Funding in financial or other forms for this project was received from the Chiang Ching-kuo Foundation (Taipei), the Institute of Oriental Studies (IOS) of the Russian Academy of Sciences (Moscow), the Institute RED IRIS Complutense (Madrid), Microsoft (Seattle), and the KITLV (Leiden). Without this support this project could not have been executed in anything like the form in which it now appears.

Drs. P.G.E.I.J van der Velde
Supervisor GASE Project

Foreword

We are pleased to be able to present you with the first edition of *the Guide to Asian Studies in Europe* which has been produced on behalf of the European Science Foundation Asia Committee. This publication aims to provide a survey of the researchers, institutes, university departments, museums, and newsletters in the field of Asian Studies in Europe. We hasten to clearly state that the regional subdivision used in this guide mirrors a scholarly concept, not a political one.

We also ask you to keep in mind that this guide is something new and therefore will suffer from various teething problems. Information was obtained from all over Europe. It reached us not only in different languages, but also in varying degrees of legibility, completeness, and form. If data are lacking this can mostly be laid at the door of the fact that questionnaires were not returned. Undaunted, this did not stop us from doing what we had been asked to do. The result can be found in this Guide which, notwithstanding the fact that we aimed at conciseness, grew into what it has become: a Guide of more than 300 densely printed pages.

When we compare the number of 500 Asianists which was included in the Preliminary Guide to Asian Studies in Europe '95 to the approximately 5000 contained in this guide, we regard this tenfold rise as an incontrovertible sign of the growing awareness amongst Asianists in Europe that co-operation and transparency in the field of Asian Studies is of crucial importance. We venture to believe that the 5000 Asianists contained in this guide represent more than 60% of all Asianists in Europe. Furthermore, we are convinced that nearly 90% of all institutes, university departments, museums, and newsletters are included in this guide. The results presented form a good basis for a second, improved edition scheduled to appear in 1999. The second phase of this project will concentrate on the entry of the data gained from the replies to the questionnaire enclosed in this guide in which more detailed information about researchers and their activities is asked. Needless to say, we are always open to suggestions as to how a future edition of this guide may be improved.

We realize that in this fleeting world information is quickly outdated. We are convinced, however, that this first edition of the *Guide to Asian Studies in Europe* will enhance the cooperation of the scholarly community of Asianists in Europe.

The IIAS is at your service!

Prof. W.A.L. Stokhof
Director IIAS

Introduction

This Guide cannot be seen as an abstraction, divorced from developments over the past few years which have influenced the field of Asian Studies in Europe. Therefore, before turning to this *Guide to Asian Studies in Europe* itself, it is necessary to set the stage with a brief sketch of those developments which have generated the growing awareness in Europe that intensive co-operation is a vital key to unlock new research areas and deal with the new realities of present-day Asia and of the world at large. An awareness which is to be found at all levels among Asianists, institutes, organizations, and associations in the field of Asian Studies.

The foundation of the European Science Foundation (ESF) Asia Committee in 1994 can be seen as marking the beginning of the intensification of institutional co-operation in Europe. On its board are twenty members representing all the important European institutes in the field of Asian Studies. The Committee has set itself three main goals. The first of these is to reinforce Asian Studies by setting up an ESF fellowship programme, which has so far been supported by the governments of France, the Scandinavian countries, and the Netherlands.
The second goal on which the ESF Asia Committe has set its sights is the organization of international scholarly meetings to increase mobility and co-operation among Asia scholars. So far thirty meetings of this kind have been organized, pertinently generating new impulses for Asian Studies in Europe. In a further attempt to stimulate co-operation and mobility the Committee also allotted a budget to the regional associations for Asian Studies in Europe in the field of Korean, Japanese, Chinese, and Southeast Asian Studies, which had already been founded, and stimulated the foundation of the European associations for South Asian and Central Asian Studies in 1996.
The third goal identified by the Committee as necessary to the achievement of its purpose was to create a European Database for Asian Studies [EDAS], which should initially help to identify the quantative spread of Asian Studies in Europe and later their professional content. The publication of this edition of the *Guide to Asian Studies in Europe* can be regarded as the outcome of that first quantitative phase of the project. Now this project is poised to enter upon its second phase in which more qualitative information will be added to the EDAS by means of a more elaborate questionnaire. This does not mean that the quantitative gathering of information will not continue. If all works well, the second edition of this Guide will be published in 1999.

The Guide to Asian Studies in Europe (GASE) Project

Anyone who has ever had the pleasure of compiling or supervising a project of this kind knows that he or she is fully dependent on the co-operation of the people who are candidates for inclusion in the Guide. Certainly when it is the first time that such a guide is put together, a lot of water has to flow under the bridge before such potential candidates are convinced of the necessity for the guide. The purpose of this publication is to present as concisely as possible the outcome of a project which has spanned a two-year period. The cataclyst was a similar line of research conducted in the Netherlands in 1994-1995, resulting in the *Guide to Asian Studies in the Netherlands '95*.

The GASE Project commenced in 1995 with an announcement in the IIAS Newsletter, which included a questionnaire requesting professional data and information from Asianists about region and discipline. By appending their signature, the respondents declared that they agreed that the information they had supplied us could be used for this publication. The response to this mailing was condensed in the *Preliminary Guide to Asian Studies in Europe '95* which was sent as an insert to all readers of the IIAS Newsletter. The primary reason behind this earlier publication was to act as a stimulus to generate more response. In this we were not disappointed. In Russia, Spain, and France national initiatives were undertaken to inventorize the field of Asian Studies, a move which expanded the European dimension of the project. In June 1996 a letter, which also contained a print-out of the data then in our possession, was sent to all respondents and, as an encouragement, to all non-respondents. This initiative created a very sizeable response which, taken in conjunction with questionnaires received up to June 1997, seemed to justify the decision to go ahead with the publication of this guide, now that nearly 5,000 respondents or approximately 60% of the European Asianists are represented in it. These figures would indicate that the total number of Asianists in Europe is in the region of 8,000.

Quantative Data

The *Preliminary Guide to Asian Studies in Europe '95* contained information on 300 institutes and about 500 Asianists. The Netherlands was not included because the *Guide to Asian Studies in the Netherlands '95* alone contained more than 500 Dutch Asianists. In September 1995, a presentation detailing the GASE Project was made to a meeting of the ESF Asia Committee. By that time slightly more than 2,000 Asianists had responded. About 40% of them were Dutch. It was therefore no wonder that the area most studied turned out to be Southeast Asia, taking account of the strong Dutch tradition in that field. South Asia was in the second place, and third place was taken by East Asia. Central and Insular Southwest Asia were virtually virgin territories. Discipline-wise there was a clear preponderance of anthropology and history. French, German, and British Asiansts were already well-represented whereas the Mediterranian countries and Russia went almost unrepresented.

In this Guide almost 5,000 Asianists are listed, which is a tenfold increase in comparison with the Preliminary Guide. There is still a Dutch bias, but in all the precentage of Dutch Asianists has dwindled from 50% to a little more than 20%. Although the Netherlands emerges as the country with the most Asianists, we are convinced that in the second edition of this publication this number will be proportionally more representative. Countries with more than 500 Asianists are Germany, Russia, France, and Great Britain. All other countries have fewer than 200 Asianists. Fortunately Italy, Spain, Portugal, and Greece can now account for more than 300 Asianists between them. This number is comparable to the number of Scandinavian Asianists.

In the presentation in September 1995, South and Southeast Asia were the most studied regions. Now we can note that East Asia has stolen the march as the most studied area followed by Southeast and South Asia. Interestingly a remarkable growth of Central Asian Studies can also be discerned. Countries attracting the most attention from Asianists are China, Indonesia, India, and Japan, each with on average 1,000 specialists. A middle category is formed by countries and regions such as Thailand, Korea, Malaysia, Pakistan, The Philippines, Taiwan, Tibet, and Vietnam which are studied by on average 400 scholars.

By far the largest discipline in the field of Asian Studies is history followed by anthropology, both fields with more than 1000 scholars. Cultural studies and religion attract about 800 researchers. Noteworthy is the rise of researchers in the field of political science, international relations, and economics. Each of these disciplines has more than 500 practitioners.

The Second Phase of the GASE Project

In the second phase of the GASE Project our aim will be to collect more detailed information on the professional content of the work of the European Asianists. The instrument we have chosen to accomplish our aim is a more elaborate questionnaire. We would ask our contributors to this second phase to be fairly reticent in filling in their regional and disciplinary specialization. If there is one thing we have learned from the first phase questionnaires it is that Europe has a fair percentage of Asianists who feel competent in a variety of disciplines and regions. Of course, it is hard to qualify when it is possible to claim to be a specialist in a certain field but a minimum requirement should be that one has to have at least written three articles on the topic or a book. This should not stop young scholars from filling in the questionnaire, because it can also be seen as a statement of aspiration. Those who have already filled in the first phase questionnaire will receive a print-out of the information already provided. They then have to fill in only the remaining part. Please note that there is a separate entry in the questionnaire which is from the National Bureau of Asian Reserach (Seattle). If you fill out this questionnaire we will relay this information to this Bureau which will include it in its directory which tends to concentrate on specialists in policy studies.
We hope for your continued support in this project and please do not hesitate to comment on this Guide so that we will be able to improve the second edition.

Drs. P.G.E.I.J. van der Velde
Supervision GASE Project

How to use this Guide

The *Guide to Asian Studies in Europe* contains four directories:

Directory A Asianists in Europe

The Directory of Asianists in Europe lists the Asianists in alphabetical order. The following information is given: surname - title (s) - initial(s) - address if not institutionally affliated - country of residence - acronym of institutional affiliation - e-mail address if any - regional specialization indicating countries (abbreviated) studied - disciplinary specialization (abbreviated).

Directory B Asianists by Region and Country of Interest and Discipline

The Directory by Region and Country of Interest and Discipline is listed in alphabetical order. There are five regions: Central Asia, East Asia, Insular Southwest Asia, South Asia, Southeast Asia. Each region has sub-headings of country in the region and sub-sub-headings of countries in Europe. The specialists and their disciplines (abbreviated) are registered alphabetically under these headings.

Directory C Universities, Insitutes, Organisations, and Museums

The Directory of Universities, Institutes, and Museums lists the institutes in alphabetical order per country. These are preceded by the acronym of the institution. The name of the institution - address - tel/fax and e-mail addresses. In most cases an English translation is given of the names of the institution so as to increase the accessibility.

Directory D Newsletters on Asia in Europe

The Directory of Newsletters on Asia in Europe lists newsletters in the field of Asian Studies in Europe in alphabetical order and gives information about their editors, circulation, format, language used, contact persons - address - tel/fax and e-mail addresses.

DIRECTORY A

ASIANISTS

IN EUROPE

Aalto, Prof. dr P.
Topeliuksenkatu 21 B 41
00250 Helsinki 25
Finland
[IN, MN][His, DevS]

Aase, Prof. dr T.H.
UB,DSA Norway
tor.aase@nhh.no
[IN, NP, PK][DevS, Geo, Ant]

Abbiati, Prof. M.
UTT,HMLIT Italy
[CN][Lin]

Abbink, Dr J.
RUL,ASC Netherlands
[MO][Lin]

Abdulsomad, K.
UL,NASEAS Sweden
[MY, TH][DevS, Eco]

Abe, Dr J.
INALCO,DASHA France
[JP][Lit]

Abou-Zahab, M.-P.
39 rue Ernest Renan
92130 Issy les Moulineaux
France
[PK][Lit]

Abud, M.
CNRS,EHESS,BIB France
[CN][Lit]

Abud, Drs M.
CNRS,CRLAO France
[CN, JP][Phi, Lin, His, Lit, CuS, His, AHis]

Ackermann, Dr A.
KI Germany
[ID, MY, SG][Ant, CuS, Soc]

Ackooy, C.S. van
Malderburchstraat 30
6581 AK Malden
Netherlands
[IN, JP][AHis, CuS, Arch, Rel, Phi]

Adamo, S.A.
CNRS,CEIAS France
[BD, IN, NP, PK, LK][AHis, CuS, His, Rel, Soc]

Adamova, Dr A.T.
Russia
[AHis]

Adams, N.
60 avenue des Saisons
1050 Brussel
Belgium
[LA, VN][GenS, His, DevS]

Adriaensens, Drs G.M.J.E.
ATD France
[ID][Soc]

Aelst, Drs A. van
EUR,BIB Netherlands
vanaelst@ubib.eur.nl
[CN, ID, JP, VN][His]

Agajanyan, Dr A.S.
RASP,IOS Russia
[Rel]

Aganina, Dr L.A.
RASP,IOS Russia
[NP][Lit]

Agergaard, J.A.
UC, CIG Denmark
ja@geogr.ku.dk

Ahmed, Dr I.
ILO Switzerland
[BD, IN, NP, PK, PH, LK, TH][Env, Agr, Eco]

Ahrens, Prof. Dr T
UHAM,IMOR Germany
[CN, IN, PI, PG,][Rel]

Ahuja, R.
Karl-Metz-Str. 15
69115 Heidelberg
Germany
[IN][His]

Aijmer, Dr L.G.
GU,IASSA Sweden
Aijmer@iassa.gu.se
[CN, HK, LA, MO, PG, TW][Ant]

Aithal, Dr P.
RKU,SI,DI Germany
[IN][Lit, Lin, CuS, Rel]

Ajimamudova, Dr V.S.
RASP,IOS Russia
[CN][Lit]

Akamatsu, P.
CNRS,JAP France
[JP][Eco, PolS]

Akiner, Dr S.
SOAS,CARF United Kingdom
ab8@soas.ac.uk
[CuS, Rel, Lin, His, Lit]

Akkermans, Dr H.A.
Lauwers 2
5032 ZD Tilburg
Netherlands
[JP][Eco, His, IR]

Akkitham, N.
7 Rue Ricaut
75013 Paris
France
[IN, JP][His, Eco, IR]

Aktor, M.
UC, IHR Denmark
aktor@coco.ihi.ku.dk
[IN][Ant, Lin, Rel, Lit, His]

Alayev, Prof. dr L.B.
NPH,VJ Russia
[IN, PK, LK][His]

Albanese, M.
ISIAO Italy
[KH, IN, MM, LK][His, AHis, Rel, Phi]

Albarrán Serrano, Antonio
[KH, HK, IN, JP, LA, MN, NP, LK, TW, TH, TI, VN][Lit]

Albino, M.
FAU,IVIS Germany
[IN][Lin]

Albis, R.
UP7,UAO France
[CN, JP, KR, VN][Eco]

Albrecht, E.W.
Triftstrasse 5
13353 Berlin
Germany
[CN, HK, IN, MO, SG, LK, TW][Eco]

Aldis, L.
BVFS United Kingdom
[VN][Eco]

Alejano Monge, M.
Carmen Cobeña N§3 2§D
28005 Madrid
Spain
[JP][Eco, Lin]

Alejo, Prof. A.E.
SOAS,DAS United Kingdom
aa2@soas.ac.uk
[PH][Ant]

Alekseeva, Dr E.A.
MSU,IAAS,CIBS Russia
[IN][Lin]

Aletton, V.
la Huberdiere
72500 Jupilles
France
[CN][Ant]

Alexakhina, Dr S.N.
RAS,IFES,FEB Russia
[CN, TW][Eco, Agr]

Alexakhina, Prof. dr A.
IL,DEAL Russia
[CN, HK, SG, TW, VN][Edu, Lin]

Alexander, A.
Schwartzkopff Str. 9
10115 Berlin - Mitte
Germany
[TI][Lin, Edu]

Ali, Dr K.A.
URO,DA United Kingdom
knar@uhura.cc.rochester.edu
[BD, IN, PK][CuS, Ant]

Alibux, R.F.
Allendestraat 10
1314 SE Almere
Netherlands
[IN, PK][IR, His]

Aliev, Prof. S.M.
RAS,IOS,AL Russia
[AF, IR, TJ][His, CuS, Rel]

Alieva, Dr N.F.
RAS,IOS,AL Russia
[ID, MY, PH, VN][Lin, Lit]

Alikhanova, Dr Yu.M.
MSU,IAAS,CIBS Russia
[IN][CuS, Lit]

Alimov, I.A.
IAS Russia
alimov@petrost.spb.su
[CN][CuS, Lit, Rel]

Aliyeva, Dr N.F.
RASP,IOS Russia
[PI][Lin]

Allen, Dr N.J.
UO,ISCA United Kingdom
[NP][Ant]

Alleton, Dr V.A.
CNRS,ARCHIPEL France
all@ehess.fr
[CN, HK, TW][Lit, Lin]

Allibert, Dr C.
INALCO France
[MG][Ant, His, Arch]

Allinger, Dr E.
UW,ITBS Austria
[AF, BD, AF, BD, BT, IN, ID, MN, MM, NP, PK, LK][Rel, His, CuS, Arch, AHis]

Allioux, Y.-M.
UTM,CUP France
[JP][Lit]

Allott, Drs A. J.
SOAS,DLCSEA United Kingdom
[MM][PolS, Lit, Lin, His, Rel, Edu]

Allwood, Prof. J.
GU,GESEAS Sweden
[CN, JP, MY][Lin, Phi]

Almeida Teles e Cunha, Drs J.M. de
Av. Amadeu Duarte, 249
2775 Parede
Portugal
[IN, PK][His]

Alosina, Dr I, E.
RAS,IL Russia

Alpatov, Dr V.M.
RAS,IOS,DC Russia
[JP][Lin]

Alphen, J. van
ME Belgium
[AF, BT, IN, KZ, NP, TJ, TI, UZ][AHis, Ant, Lin, His]

Alt, Drs B.
UB,ZA Germany
[IN, MN, TI][Rel, Lin, Phi]

Altenburger, R.T.
HIO Cambridge
[CN][CuS, Lin, Lit]

Alwis Perera, D.R. De
DPDJ France
[IN, LK][Lin, IR, Eco]

Ambar, I.
Bloemgracht 74-A
1015 TL Amsterdam
Netherlands

Amemiya-Lombard, H.
UR2, LCER France
[JP][Lit]

Amen, W.J. van
Bulgersteijn 7117
3011 AB Rotterdam
Netherlands

Amer, Dr R.
UU,DPCR Sweden
ramses.amer@prc.uu.se
[BN, KH, CN, IN, ID, JP, KR, LA, MY, MM, PH, TW,][IR, PolS, His]

Ammerlaan, Drs R.P.J.
Boomkwekerij 11
2635 KC Den Hoorn (Z-H)
Netherlands
[ID][Lit, Rel, Lin, Law, Psy]

Ammerlaan, Dr A.A.
KUN,PW Netherlands
t.ammerlaan@maw.kun.nl
[Lin]

Amorés Gonell, F.
UB,FGH,CEHI Spain
[PI][Ant, Arch, Lin]

Anbäcken, E.M.
SSE,EIJS Sweden
[JP][Rel, Phi]

Anbeek, Dr C.W.
VU,GW Netherlands
[JP][Phi, Rel]

Andersen, A.H.
UC, IA Denmark
[CN, TI][DevS, Ant]

Andersen, Dr P.B.
UC, IHR Denmark
peterba@coco.ihi.ku.dk
[IN][Ant, Lit, Soc, Rel]

Andersen, H.
SSE,ASTRA,EAST Sweden
[VN][Eco]

Anderson, Drs M.
SOAS,DL United Kingdom
[IN][Env, Law, DevS]

Ando, V.
Spotzova 1, \Dolni Liboc
16100 Prague 6
Czech Republic
[CN][Law, Env, DevS]

André, Y.
1, rue de Mirbel
75005 Paris
France
[CN][Lit]

André-Pallois, Dr N.
EFEO France
[VN][His, AHis]

Andreeva, V. A.
RAS,IL Russia
[VN][Lin]

Andrès, Dr E.
13, rue des Carrières
78740 Evecquemont
France
[IN][Ant, Phi, Rel]

Andrews, Dr A.Y.
UD,RRC,,SESS United Kingdom
a.y.andrews@derby.ac.uk
[BD, IN, PK][Soc, CuS, Rel]

Andrews, Dr B.J.
SOAS,DH United Kingdom
bja1000@hermes.cam.ac.uk
[CN][His]

Andreyev, A.I.
SPCF Russia
[TI][CuS, Rel, Soc]

Andronov, Dr M.S.
RASP,IOS Russia
[IN][Lin]

Androssov, Dr V.P.
RASP,IOS Russia
[IN][Rel, Phi]

Ang, Dr I.
SA France
[CN][Rel, His, Ant]

Angerler, Drs J.
RUL,CNWS Netherlands
hansangerler@rullet.leidenuniv.nl
[ID][His, Ant]

Angot, M.
INALCO France
[IN][Lit]

Annerstedt, Prof. J.O.E.
LU,NCI Sweden
[PH, VN][His, Eco, IR, PolS]

Anrooy, Drs F. van
AR Netherlands
[ID][His]

Ansorge, Drs C.A.
NCOLR,FOS,BIB United Kingdom
caa1@cus.cam.ac.uk
[CN, IN, JP, MN, PK, TW][His, Arch, CuS, Rel, Lit, Phi]

Antikainen-Kokko, Dr A.
AA,CSEAS Finland
annamari.antikainen-kokko@abo.fi
[ID, JP, MY, PH, SG, TH][IR]

Anton Burgos, Dr F.J.
UCM,GH,GF Spain
[CN, JP, TW][Geo]

Antoni, Prof. dr K.
UT,FAP Germany
[JP][Ant, Phi, Rel, His]

Antonian, Dr K. V.
RAS,IL Russia
antonian@iling.msk.su
[CN][Lin]

Antonova, Dr Ye.V.
RASP,IOS Russia
[CuS]

Antunes Dias, L.F.
IICT,CEAA Portugal
[IN][His]

Antweiler, Prof. dr C.
UT,CEAPS Germany
[ID, MY][DevS, Ant]

Antypa, U.
LPI France
[KH][His]

Arapova, Dr T.B.
Russia
[AHis, CuS]

Ardley, Drs J.C.
KU,CBPU United Kingdom
pod05@cc.keele.ac.uk
[CN, IN, TI][PolS]

Arens, Drs J.F.
RUL,CNWS Netherlands
arens@rullet.leidenuniv.nl
[BN, ID, MY, SG][Lit, His, CuS]

Arghiros, Dr D.
UHU,DSEAS United Kingdom
D.Arghiros@seas.hull.ac.uk
[TH][Ant, DevS]

Aristova, Dr L.B.
RAS,IOS,AL Russia
[AF, KZ, PK, TJ][Eco, Edu]

Ariyasajsiskul, Drs S.
RUL,TCZOAO Netherlands
[TH][IR, His]

Ark, Dr B. van
RUG,VAE Netherlands
h.h.van.ark@eco.rug.nl
[Eco]

Arkhipov, Dr V.Ya.
RASP,IOS Russia
[Eco, IR]

Arnaud, V.
CNRS,LASEMA France
[Lin]

Arnaud, M.A.
CNRS,CEIAS France
[IN][Ant, Rel, Eco, Edu, Soc]

Arnold, M.
RKU,KI,AA Germany
arno@gw.sino.uni-heidelberg.de
[CN, HK, JP, KR, TW][Arch, His, AHis]

Arnold, Prof. D.J.
SOAS,DH United Kingdom
da2@soas.ac.uk
[IN][His]

Arnoldus-Schröder, Drs V.
VMGVL Netherlands
v.arnoldus-schroder@theol.rug.nl
[IN, ID, PI, PG, VN][Edu, Ant, CuS]

Arom, S.
CNRS,LACITO France
[ID][Ant, CuS, Edu]

Aronstein, M.
UC, IS Denmark
[CN, JP, KR][PolS]

Arps, Prof. dr B.
RUL, VA/AVMI Netherlands
arps@rullet.leidenuniv.nl
[ID][Lit, Lin, CuS]

Arras, Th.C. van
Postbus 876
2501 CW The Hague
Netherlands
[AHis]

Arrault ., Dr A.
CNRS,IHEC France
Alain.Arrault@ulg.ac.be
[CN][Rel, Soc, PolS, CuS, His]

Arskaya, Dr L.P.
IWEIR Russia
[JP][Eco]

Arunova, Dr M.R.
RASP,IOS Russia
[AF][His]

Asadullin, Dr F.
Rublevskol St. 38 \copn. 2, flat 195
121609 Moscow
Russia
[PolS, Soc, Rel, His, CuS]

Asari, M.
INALCO France
[JP][Phi, Lit]

Aschoff, Prof. dr J.C.
UU Germany
juergens.aschoff@medizin.uni-ulm.de
[IN, NP, TI][CuS]

Asher, Prof. R.E.
UE,DAS United Kingdom
[IN][Lit, Lin]

Ashkenazy, Drs I.
Gentsestraat 110-A
2587 HX The Hage
Netherlands
[CN, TI][Ant, His]

Ashrafyan, Dr K.Z.
RASP,IOS Russia
[IN][His]

Asim, Dr I.A.
UW,IS Germany
ina.asim@rzhub.uni-wuerzburg.de
[CN][Arch, CuS, His]

Asmussen, Drs V.M.S.
AU,FH,DESA Denmark
etnovma@moes.hum.aau.dk
[ID][Ant, Rel]

Aspengren, E.
ULP,DSS Sweden
evasp@ipp.liu.se
[ID][Edu, His]

Asselbergs, Drs G.
EUR, SEO Netherlands
[CN, ID, MY, MN, NP, PK, SG,][Agr, Eco, Edu]

Asten, C. van
Netherlands

Astuti, Dr R.
LSEPS United Kingdom
r.astuti@lse.ac.uk
[MG][Ant, GenS]

Atabaki, Dr T.
ESCAS Netherlands
Atabaki@Let.Ruu.nl
[KZ, TJ, TM, UZ][PolS, His]

Athari, Drs D.
72 Cours des Roches
77186 Noisiel
France
[AF, TJ][Ant, Soc, DevS]

Atknine, V.D.
ILR Russia
[KR][Lin]

Atman, Dr R.E.
HIS Netherlands
[ID, LK, TH][DevS]

Attema, Drs Y.
RM,OC&W Netherlands
[IN, ID, MY, SG, LK][AHis, CuS, His]

Aubert, Dr C.
INRA,ES France
[CN, TW][DevS, Agr, Ant, Eco, Soc]

Aubin, F.
CERI,FNSP France
[CN, MN, TI][Soc, Law, His]

Aubriot, Dr O.
CNRS,MSCH France
[NP, TI][Ant]

Aufray, M.
INALCO France
[Lin]

Augustin, R.
Netherlands
gmde@euronet.nl
[BT, IN][Edu, PolS]

Aussedat Maitrise, AV
INALCO,JK France
[JP,][IR]

Auty, Dr R.M.
ULC,DG United Kingdom
r.auty@lancaster.ac.uk
[BD, CN, HK, IN, ID, KR, MY, PK, PG, PH, SG][DevS, Env, Eco]

Auwera, J. van der
UIA, L Belgium
auwera@uia.ua.ac.be
[Lin]

Avé, J.
CNRS,IRSEA France
[ID][Lin]

Avilla Gomez, S.
CASESA Spain
[IN][Lit, Phi, His, Ant, His, AHis, Rel]

Axel, Dr M.
FUB,OS,JAP Germany
[JP, TH][Psy, Ant, PSYCHIATRY]

Aylmer, C.A.
CU,FOS United Kingdom
ca22@cam.ac.uk
[CN][Rel, Phi, Lin, Arch, His, IR, Lit]

Aymard, M.
MSH France
aymard@msh-paris.fr

Azovsky, Dr I.P.
RASP,IOS Russia
[, MM][Eco]

Baak, Dr P.
UvA,ASSR,CASA Netherlands
[IN, ID][PolS, His, Soc, Eco, Agr]

Baardewijk, Drs F.G. van
RUL,TCZOAO Netherlands
BAARDEWIJK@RULLET.LeidenUniv.nl
[ID][Agr, Eco, His, Soc]

Baark, Dr E.
TUD, ITSS Denmark
itseb@unidhp.uni-c.dk
[CN, HK, IN, MN, TW, VN][His, DevS, Env, CuS]

Baars, M.
Heeper Str. 107
33607 Bielefeld
Germany
[ID][Soc]

Baas, Prof. dr P.
RUL,OR/HB Netherlands
[BN, ID, MY, PG, PH, SG][Env]

Babic, Prof. B.
UB, ISF Yugoslavia
[CN][DevS, Eco]

Babing, Dr F.
HUB,AA,SOA,SL Germany
frank=babing@asa.hu-berlin.de
[IN][Rel, His]

Bacqué-Grammont, Dr J.
INALCO,CGD France
[UZ][Rel, His]

Bady, Prof. P
UP7,UAO France
[CN][Lit]

Baetens-Beardsmore, Drs H.
ULB, FPL Belgium
hbaetens@unet3.vub.ac.be
[BN, HK, SG][Edu, Lin]

Baffie, Dr J.
CNRS,IRSEA France
[TH][His, Soc, PolS, CuS]

Bagdassarov, Dr S.B.
RASP,IOS Russia
[CuS, Eco, His]

Baille, B.
CNRS,IRSEA France
[CN, HK, MO, SG, TW][Ant]

Baird, Drs C.J.
NM,GM United Kingdom
[CN, HK, MO, SG, TW][AHis]

Bakaya, A.
INALCO France
[IN][Edu, CuS, GenS, Env, Lit, DevS, Soc, Lin]

Bakel, Dr M.A. van
RUL,CA/SNWS Netherlands
[His, PolS, Ant]

Bakels, Drs J.
RUL,CNWS Netherlands
[ID][AHis, Ant]

Baker, Dr P.W.
SOAS,DL United Kingdom
bakerpw@link.org.uk
[CN][Law]

Baker, Prof. dr H.D.R.
SOAS,DLCSEA United Kingdom
[CN, HK, TW][Law, Lin, Ant, His, CuS, Lit, Rel]

Bakewell, Mr A.D.
Grimsduke Cottage, Nufficed Ln. Crowmarsh Oxford
OX10 6QW Wallingford, Oxon
United Kingdom
[CN, IN, KG, MG, PK, LK, TI][]

Bakken, Dr B.
NIAS Denmark
bakken@nias.ku.dk
[CN][Soc]

Bakker, Prof. dr H.T.
RUG,IIS Netherlands
bakker@let.rug.nl
[IN][Arch, Rel, Phi, His, CuS, AHis, Lit]

Bakker, Drs M.E.
RUL,TCZOAO,PD Netherlands
bakkerm@rullet.leidenuniv.nl
[ID][Lit]

Bakker, Dr W.A.
RUL,LISWO Netherlands
BakkerJ@rulfsw.LeidenUniv.nl
[PH][Soc, Ant]

Bakker, Dr P.J.
AU, DL Denmark
linpb@hum.aau.dk
[IN, ID, PI, LK][His, Lin, Ant]

Bakker, Dr F.L.
Jan van Bergenstraat 17
1962 VH Heemskerk
Netherlands
[ID][Rel]

Baks, Dr Ch.
La Croix
24388 St. Chamassy
France
[IN, ID][Agr, Ant, Law]

Bal, Drs E.W.
EUR,HK Netherlands
bal@fmgs.fhk.eur.nl
[BD, IN][His]

Balaize, C.
ICP, FA France
[CN, HK, JP, KR, TW, VN][Ant, Agr, CuS, Rel]

Balan, L.
UB,FL,OL Romania
[CN][CuS, Soc, Lin]

Balasubramanyam, Prof. V.N.
ULC,DE United Kingdom
[IN, MY][DevS, Eco]

Balbir, Prof. N.
CNRS,LACMI France
[IN][Lit, Rel, Lin]

Balland, Dr D.
UP,G France
[AF][Agr, Ant, Geo]

Ballegeer, J.
MFA Belgium
[CN, IN, ID, JP, KR, PK, PH, TH, VN][PolS, Law]

Baloch, Dr I.
RKU,SI Germany
[AF, IN, IR, KZ, MY, PK, TJ, TI, TM][PolS, CuS, His]

Balyuk, Dr I.A.
RAS,IFES,FEB Russia
[CN][Eco]

Balzar, Dr D.M.
Invalidenstr. 11
1033 Vienna
Austria
[KH, ID, LA, MO, TH][CuS, His, AHis]

Banaschak, Drs P.
An der Wallhecke 7
48167 Munster
Germany
[JP, KR][Ant, His, CuS]

Bandilenko, Dr G.G.
MSU,IAAS,CIBS Russia
[ID][AHis, CuS, Ant, His]

Bangoer, N.
OHM Netherlands
[IN][Lit]

Banks, Dr M.J.
UO,ISCA United Kingdom
marcus.banks@anth.ox.ac.uk
[IN][Ant]

Bansat-Boudon, Dr.L.
UL3,CREO France
[IN][Lit, Phi, Lin, Rel]

Banti Pereira, Dr J.
V. Nicolò Tartaglia 46
00197 Rome
Italy
[CN, JP][His, CuS, His, AHis]

Barbiche, Prof. dr J.-P.
UH,FIA,IO France
[BN, KH, CN, HK, IN, ID, JP, KZ, KR, LA, MY,][Law, IR, His, PolS, Eco, DevS, CuS, Edu, Soc]

Barbier-Kontler, Dr C.
UP,CREOPS,AA France
[CN, IN][Phi, Rel]

Bardon, I.M.E.

Pelikaanhof 162-B
2312 EJ Leiden
Netherlands

Bareja-Starzynska, Drs A.

UW,OIS,MS Poland
bareja@plearn.edu.pl
[MN, TI][Rel, Lin, His, Lit]

Baren, H. van

ISRIC Netherlands
[Agr, Env]

Barend-van Haeften, Dr M.L.

UvA,VHNTL Netherlands
m.barend@let.uva.nl
[ID][Lit]

Barendregt, Drs B.A.

RUL,CA/SNWS Netherlands
barendregt@rulfsw.leidenuniv.nl
[ID][AntAnt]

Barends, F.

Tartinistraat 120
5049 CZ Tilburg
Netherlands
[ID][Agr, Phi, His, AHis, Rel, Law, IR, His, Edu, Arch, Ant, CuS,]

Barendse, Dr R.J.

Van der Kunstraat 6-II
1097 LV Amsterdam
Netherlands
[IN, KZ, MG, TJ][His, Eco]

Barker, Dr N.H.

USTA,DA United Kingdom
[PH][Ant, Rel]

Barkhuis, Dr R.

RUG,IIS Netherlands
[IN][Rel, CuS]

Barnes, Prof. G.L.

UDU,BAKS United Kingdom
Gina.barnes@durham.ac.uk
[CN, HK, JP, KR, TW][Arch]

Barnes, Dr R.H.

OU,SAME United Kingdom
rhbarnes@vax.ox.ac.uk
[ID][Ant]

Barnett, Drs R.

7, Beck Road
E8 4RE London
United Kingdom
[TI][Arch]

Barraud, C.

CNRS,CRLAO France
barraud@msh-paris.fr
[ID][Ant]

Barres-Kotobi, F.

EFEO,BIB France
[ID][Phi, Psy, PolS, Rel, Soc, Lit, Lin, IR, His, Arch, Ant, CuS,]

Barrett, Prof. T.

SOAS,DH United Kingdom
[CN, JP][Rel, His]

Barron, Dr T.J.

UE,IO United Kingdom
tom.barron@ed.ac.uk
[LK][His]

Barth, Dr F.

UO,FSS,EM Norway
[AF, BT, CN, IN, ID, PK, PG][DevS, Ant]

Bartstra, Dr G.J.

RUG,BAI Netherlands
[Arch]

Baryshnikova, Dr O.G.

RASP,IOS Russia
[IR]

Bass, Dr H.H.

UBR,FW Germany
[CN, JP, MM, VN][DevS, Eco, IR]

Bassa, Dr Z.

HAS,IWF,JESRC Hungary
zbassa@vki3.vki.hu
[P, KR, VN][Eco]

Bassilov, Dr V.N.

RAS,IEA Russia
[Ant]

Bastiaansen, Drs A.C.G.M.

Adenl Netherlands
[CN, HK, IN, ID, JP, KR, MO, MY, PH, SG, TW,][IR, Eco, Edu]

Bastid-Bruguière, M.

EACS France
bastid@canoe.ens.fr / bastid@ehs.fr
[CN, TW][His]

Basu, Dr H.

FUB,PSW,IE,A Germany
basu@zedat.fu-berlin.de
[IN, PK][Ant, Rel]

Bates, Dr C.N.

UE,DH United Kingdom
crispin.bates@ed.ac.uk
[IN][His]

Battum-v.d.Horst, M. van

P. Verhagenstraat 10
1333 JJ Almere
Netherlands
[IN][His]

Baud, Dr I.S.A.

UvA,VPD Netherlands
ibaud@isg.frw.uva.nl
[IN, PH][DevS, GenS, Eco, Soc]

Baud Berthier, Dr G

MAK,DHS France
[CN, JP, KR][Eco, His]

Bauer, Prof. dr C.H.R.

HUB,AA,SOA Germany
h0198kaq@rz.hu-berlin.de
[KH, CN, IN, ID, LA, MY, MM, LK, TH, VN][Lit, Rel, Ant, Lin, His, Arch]

Baumann, Dr G.

EKUT,DOS,BIB Germany
[BD, BT, IN, NP, PK, LK][Lit, Rel, Lin]

Bavinck, Drs J.M.

UvA,VSG Netherlands
bavinck@isg.frw.uva.nl
[IN, LK][DevS, Ant]

Bax, Drs M.Th.

BA Netherlands
[IN, ID, JP,][His, CuS, Phi, Rel, AHis]

Bayard-Sakai, A.

UL3,ETROM,C France
[JP][Lit]

Baye, Dr E.B.

EH France
[CN, ID, JP, PH, SG][DevS, Env, Eco]

Bayly, Prof. dr C.A.

SCC United Kingdom
[IN][His]

Bayou, H.

MNAAG France
[JP][AHis, Arch, Lit]

Bazhanova, Dr N.Ye.

RASP,IOS Russia
[KR][Eco, His]

Bazhenova, E.S.

Golubinskayastr. 25-2-306
117463 Moscow
Russia
[CN][Eco, Env, Soc, Agr, GenS]

Bazin, N.

MNAAG France
[NP, TI][AHis]

Beatty, Dr A.W.

UO,WC United Kingdom
[ID][Ant]

Beaujard, Dr P.

70, rue du Faubourg Poissonnière
75010 Paris
France
[MG][Ant]

Bechert, Prof. H.H.

GAUG,SIB Germany
[IN, MM, LK][His, Lit, Rel, CuS]

Beck, Prof. dr H.L.

TU, FT Netherlands
h.l.beck@kub.nl
[ID][Rel]

Becka, Dr J.

ASCR,OI,SA Czech Republic
[MM][Rel]

Becque, .

UO,FL France
[JP][Rel]

Bedner, Mr A.W.
RUL,VVI Netherlands
jfvviab@ruljvr.leidenuniv.nl
[ID][Soc, Law]

Beek, Drs J.E.F. ter
KITLV Netherlands
beek@rullet.leidenuniv.nl
[ID][Lit, Lin]

Beek, Dr M. van
AU,FH,DESA Denmark
etnomvb@moes.hum.aau.dk
[IN, NP, TI][DevS, Soc, PolS, Ant]

Beek, Mr T.J. van
MVW, BS-G Netherlands
[CN, IN, ID, TH, VN][PolS, IR]

Beek, Dr A.G. van
UvA,ASC,CASA Netherlands
[PG][Ant]

Beek, E. van de
CKE Netherlands
[IN, NP, TI][AHis, Lit, Edu, CuS, His]

Beekes, Prof. dr R.S.P.
RUL,CNWS Netherlands
[CN, IN, PK,][Lin]

Beer, Dr B.
UHAM,IE Germany
[PG, PH][Ant]

Beer, Drs J.H. de
Luthershofje 4
6822 Arnhem
Netherlands
[Ant]

Beermann, Drs R.E.
GMU,IO,J Germany
[JP][Lin]

Beers, Mr H.A.J.J. van
ASSR Netherlands
[IN, PK, PH, TH][Law, DevS, GenS]

Beers, Dr G.G. van
Les Quatre Ours \Rue Septentionales \Taradeau
83460 Var
France
[ID][DevS, Eco, Soc]

Béguin, G.
MC France
[CN, JP, NP, TI][GenS, Law, DevS]

Behnam, .
Druckerstraat 1-B
2312 VB Leiden
Netherlands
[DevS, Law, GenS]

Beije, Drs C.F.
Sumatrastraat 256
2585 CW The Hague
Netherlands
[ID][Lin]

Beillevaire, Dr P.
CRMJ, EHESS France
[JP][His, Rel, Ant]

Beitis Hanso, M.
UE Portugal
[IN][His]

Bekius, Drs R.A.
ISS,BIB Netherlands
bekius@iss.nl
[AF, KZ, TJ, TM][Agr, Ant, Env, DevS, Eco]

Bekmann-Appelqvist, Dr R.
AA,S Finland
[Env, Agr, Eco, Ant, DevS]

Bektimirova, Prof.dr N.N.
MSU,IAAS,CIBS Russia
[KH][Rel, His, PolS]

Beletskaja, Dr A. A.
RAS,IL Russia
[TI][His, Lin]

Belkov, Dr P.L.
PGMAE,K Russia
[PI][Ant]

Bellassen, Dr J.B.
UP7,UAO France
[CN][Lin]

Bellemans, R.L.L.
Netherlands
[CN][Ant, Edu, CuS]

Bellen, Drs M.W.
RUL,ICB Netherlands
bellen@rullet.leidenuniv.nl
[ID][His, AHis]

Bellers, Prof. dr J.
UGS,PW Germany
[CN][Eco]

Belokrenitsky, Dr V.Y.
RAS,IOS,AL Russia
[AF, KZ, PK, TJ, UZ][Soc, PolS, His, IR]

Belov, Dr Ye.A
RASP,IOS Russia
[CN][His]

Belova, Dr N.K.

[His, PolS]

Belshaw, Prof. D.G.R.
UEA,ODG,SDS United Kingdom
[CN, IN, MG, MY, NP, PK, PG, PH, SM, LK, TH][DevS, Env, Agr, Eco,]

Belt, Drs J.H.J.
Gen. Spoorlaan 19
2111 WS Aerdenhout
Netherlands
[CN, TI][Ant, AHis, CuS, His, Rel, His]

Beltran Antolin, Dr J.
UPF, FH Spain
[CN, HK, MO, PH, TW][Soc, Ant]

Beltz, J
RKU Germany
[IN,][Ant, Rel]

Bem, Dr K.Yu.
RASP,IOS Russia
[PI][His]

Benda Beckmann, Mr dr K. von
SI,VSW Netherlands
vonbendabeckmann@soc.frg.eur.nl
[ID, NP,][Law, Env, Ant]

Benda Beckmann, Prof. dr F. von
LW,DDE Netherlands
franz.vonbenda-beckmann@alg.ar.wau.nl
[IN, ID][DevS, Law, Ant]

Bensaou, B.
INSEAD,EAC,BIB France
[JP][Rel]

Benthem van den Bergh, Prof. dr G. van
ISS Netherlands
[IR]

Bentinck, Drs J.V.
RUG,FRW Netherlands
j.v.bentinck@frw.rug.nl
[IN][Geo, Env]

Benz, Drs M.
HKR,FH,IH Sweden
[IN][Lit, Lin, CuS]

Bercea, R.
SAGIOS Romania
[IN, TI][Rel, Phi]

Berceló Mezquita, Dr J.L.
REMF Spain
[KZ, KG, MN, TJ, TI, TM][Env, His, PolS, Soc]

Berezina, Dr Yu.I.
IWEIR Russia
[JP][Soc]

Berezny, Prof. dr L.A.
SPU, FOS Russia
[CN][His]

Berg, Dr M.E. van den
RUL,SI Netherlands
vandenberg@rullet.LeidenUniv.nl
[CN, HK, TW][Lin]

Berg, R. van den
SILI United Kingdom
rene.vandenberg@sil.org
[ID][Lin]

Berg, Dr D.D.
UDU,DEAS United Kingdom
d.d.berg@durham.ac.uk
[CN, HK, TW][Lit, His, GenS]

Berg, Drs G.R. van den
RUL,CNWS Netherlands
grvdberg@rullet.leidenuniv.nl
[TJ][Lin, Rel, Lit]

Berg, Dr E. van den
USC,PD Philippines
edberg@usc.edu.ph
[ID, PH][Edu]

Berge, Dr T. v.d.
RUL,TCZOAO Netherlands
tvdberge@rullet.leidenuniv.nl
[ID, JP][PolS, Lit, His]

Berge, H.
General Birchgatan 32
0454 Oslo
Norway
[CN][His, PolS, Lit]

Berger, Drs C.I.
AVRO Netherlands
[MG][Ant]

Bergerot, H.
INALCO France
[JP][Ant]

Bergersen, A.
HSF Norway
ane.bergersen@alu.hisf.no
[ID][GenS]

Bergink, Drs D.
Lindenstraat 67 B
1015 KW Amsterdam
Netherlands
[ID, TH][Rel, Psy, Lin, His, Edu, Ant, GenS, CuS]

Berinstain, Dr Vallerie
INALCO,DAS France
[AF, IN, PK,][AHis, His]

Berkel, P. van
Hoevestraat 7-A
3033 GA Rotterdam
Netherlands
[Ant]

Berkel, Ir C.W.M. van
UvA,IVAM Netherlands
ruberkel@ivambv.uva.nl
[CN, IN,][Env]

Berkemer, Dr G.
RKU, SI Germany
gberkemer@t-online.de
[IN][His, CuS, Ant, Rel]

Berkhof, J.A.
Netherlands
[IN][AHis]

Berlinguez-Kono, N.
INALCO,CIV France
[JP][Soc]

Bernard, J.A.
16 Rue de l'Université
75007 Paris
France
[BD, IN, PK][IR, His, Eco, PolS]

Bernede, F.
CNRS,MSCH France
[NP, TI][PolS, IR, His, Eco]

Berner, Dr E.
UBI,FS,SDRC Germany
Erhard.berner@post.uni-bielefeld.de
[PH][Soc, Ant]

Bernier, X.
CNRS,MSCH France
[NP, TI][Geo]

Bernot, D
CNRS,IRSEA France
[MM][Lin]

Bernot, D.
47, Avenue du Bois-de Verrieres
92160 Antony
France
[MM][Lin]

Berque, Prof. A.
CNRS,CRJC France
[JP][Phi]

Berra, A.B. Annette
4 Louis Armand
30600 Vestric + Candiac
France
[ID,][]

Berthier, A.
BNF,MO France
annie.berthier@bnf.fr
[AF, KZ, MN, TJ, TM][His, Rel, Phi, CuS, Lit, His, AHis, Lin]

Bertille, Drs .
CNRS,AAC France
[AF, TJ, UZ][Arch]

Bertrand, R.
CERI,FNSP France
[ID][PolS]

Bertrand, Dr D.
UTM,CUP France
[KH, LA, VN][Psy, Rel, Ant]

Bertsch, Drs H.B.
EUR,EW,BO Netherlands
bertsch@intorg.few.eur.nl
[JP, MY, SG, TW][Soc, Eco]

Bertuccioli, Dr G.
URLS,DOS Italy
[CN, TW][Lit, His]

Besenval, R.
CNRS,AAC France
[AF, PK, TJ][Arch]

Beukering, P.J.H. van
VU,IM Netherlands
beukering@ivm.vu.nl
[CN, IN, NP, PH,][IR, Eco, Env, DevS]

Beukers, Prof. dr H.
RUL,VM Netherlands
[ID, JP][His]

Beumer, Drs W.G.M.
UvA,BIB Netherlands
beumer@uba.uva.nl
[IN, LK][AHis]

Beusch, Drs D.
Jordanstraáe 1
60486 Frankfurt
Germany
[KH, LA, TH][PolS, IR]

Bevir, Dr M.
UNC,EAC United Kingdom
mark.bevir@ncl.ac.uk
[IN][His, Phi]

Bevis, G.G.
SOAS,DE United Kingdom
[PH][His, Lit, AHis]

Bezançon, P.
UP7 France
[KH, LA, VN][Edu, His]

Bhatt, Prof. dr B.
WWUM,II Germany
[IN][Rel, Lit, His]

Bhattacharja, S.
INALCO France
[BD, IN][Rel, Lit, His]

Bhattacharya, Prof. F.
UL3,CREO France
[BD, IN][CuS, Ant, Lit, Rel]

Bhattacharya, Dr B.
RUL,KERN Netherlands
[IN, ID][His]

Bhola, R.
Loosduinseweg 649
2571 AK The Hague
Netherlands
[IN][Rel, LitAnt, CuS]

Biardeau, M.
UL3,CREO France
[IN][Phi, Ant]

Bichler, Mr
Zeltweg 30
8032 Zürich
Switzerland
[CN][Ant, Phi]

Biervliet, Drs W.E.
NUFFIC,DESC Netherlands
wbvliet@nufficcs.nl
[BD, CN, IN, ID, PH][Edu]

Bigger, A.
UZ,SI Switzerland
[BD, IN, NP, PK,][CuS, His, Lit, Rel]

Bijlert, Dr V.A. van
RUL,KERN Netherlands
bijlert@rullet.leidenuniv.nl
[BD, IN][Phi, Rel, Lin, CuS, His]

Billeter, Prof. J.F.
UG,FAH,DOLL Switzerland
[CN, HK, TW][Lit, His, Phi, Rel]

Billion, T.
UMMB,DEEO,DU France
[JP][Lit, Phi, Lin, IR, His, Edu]

Billion, R.
UMMB,DEEO,DU France
billion@montaugne.u-bordeaux.fr
[CN, HK, TW][His, Phi, Lit, Lin, IR, Edu]

Birkin, I.
UO,ISCA United Kingdom
isabella.birkin@anthro.ox.ac.uk
[CN, IN, ID, JP,][Ant]

Birks, L.
NETI Hungary
[JP, KR, PH, SG, TW, TH][Eco, DevS, Env, Agr, IR]

Biros, N.
INALCO,CIV France
[Ant]

Birrell, Prof. A.M.
UC,CH United Kingdom
[CN][CuS, Lit, GenS]

Birtalan, Dr A.
ELU,DJS Hungary
[CN, IN, JP, KZ, KR, MN, NP, TW, TI][AHis, Rel, Phi, Lit, Lin, His, Arch, GenS]

Birwé, Prof. R.
Schnepfenlucht 10
5090 Leverkusen 1 (Rheindorf)
Germany

Bischoff, F.
Morziplatz 1/18
1010 Vienna
Austria
[TI][His, Lin, GenS, Phi, Rel, Arch, AHis, Lit]

Bissat, V.
INALCO France
[CN][Lit]

Björkman, Prof. dr J.W.
ISS Netherlands
Bjorkman@iss.nl
[BD, BT, IN, NP, PK, LK][PolS, DevS]

Blaay, L.A.C. de
BLAAY Netherlands
[ID][DevS, Env]

Blamont, Dr D.
CNRS,MSCH France
[IN, NP][Agr, DevS]

Blanc, Dr M.E.
CNRS,IRSEA France
[VN][Soc, GenS]

Blanc-Pamard, Chantal
France
cpb@ehess.fr
[MG][Agr, DevS, Env]

Blanchard, F.
INALCO,CIV France
[ID, MY][PolS]

Blanchon, Dr F.
UP,CREOPS,AA France
[CN, TW][His, Arch, His, AHis]

Bläsing, Dr U.
RUL,VTW Netherlands
blaesing@rullet.leidenuniv.nl
[KZ, MN, TJ, TM, UZ][Lit, Lin]

Blavignac, L.O.
13 rue des Muriers
75020 Paris
France
[Arch, His, AHis]

Blayac, A.A.
UPV France
relinter@sig.univ-montp3.fr
[KH, CN, JP, LA, VN][Lit, His, Phi, Edu, Psy, Soc]

Blazy, Dr H.
UK,OS Germany
[ID, MY, PI, PH][Lin, Psy, CuS, Phi, Lit]

Blazy, S.
MG France
[KH, CN, ID, TH][His]

Bleie, T.
CMI,DSHR Norway
toneb@a,amadeus.cmi.no
[BD, BT, IN, LA, MM, NP, VN][Env, Ant, GenS, DevS, CuS]

Bloch, Prof. M.
LSEPS United Kingdom
[MG][Ant, DevS, GenS, CuS, Env]

Bloembergen, M.
Fr. Halsstraat 106-III
1072 BZ Amsterdam
Netherlands
[ID][His]

Blom, H.W.
TGF Netherlands
[CN, HK, TW][His]

Blotkamp, Prof. dr C.
VU,FL Netherlands
[CN, HK, TW][His, AHis]

Blumkhen, S.I.
RAS,IOS,DC Russia
[CN][CuS, His, Phi, Rel, Arch]

Blussé, Dr J.L.
RUL,VG Netherlands
[CN, ID, JP, TW][IR, His]

Bock-Raming, Dr A.
[IN, NP][His, CuS, Lit, Rel, AHis]

Bocking, Prof. B.
BCHE,SRD United Kingdom
bbocking@bathe.ac.uk
[JP][Rel]

Bode, Drs M.
Jacob van Lennepkade 148-C
1053 MV Amsterdam
Netherlands
[Ant, Psy]

Boden, J.
Karel de Stoutestraat 49
9000 Gent
Belgium
[CN, HK, TW, TI][Lin, AHis, Lit, His]

Bodewitz, Prof. dr H.W.
RUL,KERN,DC Netherlands
iias@rullet.leidenuniv.nl
[IN][Lin, Lit, Rel]

Boelaars, Dr J.H.M.C.
p/a Huize De Stenenberg
\Tooropstraat 41
6813 KS Arnhem
Netherlands
[ID][Rel, Ant]

Boelaars, Dr H.J.W.M.
Korvelseweg 165
5025 JL Tilburg
Netherlands
[ID][Soc, Rel]

Boele van Hensbroek, P.
RUG,BU Netherlands
p.boele.van.hensbroek@bureau.rug.nl
[ID, VN][Law, Eco]

Boelhouwer, R.H.
Palestrinalaan 11
2253 HA Voorschoten
Netherlands
[ID, MY, SG, VN][Eco, Lit, IR]

Boender, Dr C.J.B.
EUR,FR,DSES Netherlands
boender@soc.frg.eur.nl
[ID][Soc, Law, Env]

Boer, E. de
VWU,AR Netherlands
[ID, MY, PH, TW][Soc, Ant, CuS]

Boeren, Drs A.J.J.M.
NUFFIC,DESC Netherlands
aboeren@nuffics.nl
[ID, PH, TH][Edu, Ant]

Bogaerts, Drs E.M.
RUL, SAP Netherlands
elsbogaerts@rullet.leidenuniv.nl
[IN, ID, MY, LK, TH][Phi, IR, AHis, Rel, Lit, Lin, His, Ant]

Bogart, K.J.
Chaussée de Roodebeek 128/21
1200 Brussel
Belgium
[HK, ID, JP, MY, SG, TH][Edu, CuS]

Bogdan, E.
CNRS,IRSEA France
[TH][Art]

Bohle, Prof. H.G.
RKU,SI,AG Germany
[IN, NP, PK, LK][CuS, GenS, Agr, Env, DevS]

Boikova, Dr E.V.
RAS,IOS,AL Russia
[CN, MN][IR, His, CuS]

Boikova, Dr Ye.V.
RASP,IOS Russia
[MN][His, CuS]

Boin, Drs M.M.O.
RUL,ASC Netherlands
[CN, ID, JP, TW][His]

Boisguerin, R.
BAMEP France
[CN][Lit]

Boitsov, Dr V.V.
MSU,IAAS,CIBS Russia
[MM, ID, PH][DevS, Eco, Geo, IR]

Bokshchanin, Dr A.A.
RAS,IOS,DC Russia
[CN][His]

Bollée, Prof. W. B.
RKU,SI,DI Germany
[IN][Rel, Lit, Lin]

Bolukbasi, Dr S.
Turkey
suhab@rorqual.cc.metu.edu.tr
[KZ, KG, TM][IR, PolS]

Bolyatko, Dr A.V.
RAS,IFES,FEB Russia
[IR]

Bompard, J.M
LBT France
[ID, LA, MY, PI][Agr, Env]

Bongard-Levin, Prof.dr G.M.
RASP,IOS Russia
[, IN, LK][CuS, His]

Bonneff, Dr M.
EFEO,ID Indonesia
[ID][CuS]

Bonnithon, H.
UB2,SSP France
[ID][Ant]

Bonouvrié, Drs N.C.
RUL,KERN Netherlands
bonouvrie@rullet.leidenuniv.nl
[IN][Rel]

Boogaart, Drs E. van den
Keizersgracht 802b
1017 ED Amsterdam
Netherlands
[IN][His]

Booij, Prof. dr G.E.
VU,VT Netherlands
booij@let.vu.nl
[IN][Lin]

Boomgaard, Prof. dr P.
KITLV,EUROSEAS
Netherlands
boomgaard@rullet.leidenuniv.n
l
[ID, MY][His, Env]

Boon, Drs H.
LIW Netherlands
[IN][Geo]

Boon, M.B.
STT Netherlands
[PI][CuS, His]

Boon, D.
R. Anslo straat 22/II
1054 KV Amsterdam
Netherlands
[CN, IN, JP, NP, TI][AHis, Rel, CuS, Phi, His]

Boon, Drs G.J.
Ringdijk 32-huis
1097 AD Amsterdam
Netherlands
[PI][Ant, His]

Boot, Prof. dr W.J.
RUL,TCJK Netherlands
boot@rullet.leidenuniv.nl
[JP][His, Phi, Lit]

Booth, Prof. A.E.
SOAS,DEPS United Kingdom
ab10@soas.ac.uk
[ID, MY, PG, PH, SG, TH, VN][Agr, Eco, Edu, GenS, His, DevS]

Bootsma, Dr N.A.
Philippuslaan 6
6564 AM Heilig Landstichting
Netherlands
[ID, PH][His, IR]

Bor, Dr J.
RC,VWM Netherlands
[IN][IR]

Borchers, Drs D.
Schlesierring 2
37085 Göttingen
Germany
[IN, MM][CuS, Lin]

Bordahl, Dr V.
UC,FH,DAS Denmark
[CN][Lin, Lit]

Bordone, Prof. S.
UP,DPSS Italy
[CN, MM][His]

Borevskaya, Dr N.Ye.Ye.
RAS,IFES,FEB Russia
[CN][CuS]

Bórinstain, V.
INALCO France
[CuS, Rel, Psy, Lin, His, Edu, Ant, GenS]

Borkent, Drs H.
Lindenplein 2
2201 JJ Noordwijk
Netherlands
[ID][Ant, Soc]

Borner-Mouer, Dr E.J.
YB Switzerland
[JP][GenS, Soc]

Borokh, Dr O.
RAS,IFES,CRC Russia
[CN, TW][Eco]

Borokh, Dr L.N.
RASP,IOS Russia
[CN][His]

Boronina, Dr I.A.
RAS,IWL Russia
[JP][Lit]

Borotov , Drs L.
CU,FF,DEAS Czech Republic
lucie.borotova@ff.cuni.cz
[CN, TW][Lit, His, AHis]

Borovkova, Dr L.A.
RASP,IOS Russia
[CN][His]

Borreguero Sancho, E.
Tutor 31, 1-A
28008 Madrid
Spain
[IN, NP, PK, LK][Soc, Rel, PolS, His, AHis]

Borsboom, Dr A.O.
KUN,CPS Netherlands
a.borboom@maw.kun.nl
[Rel, Ant]

Borsboom, Dr A.P.
Fagot 37
6644 AZ Ewijk
Netherlands
[PI, PG][Rel, Ant]

Borstlap, Drs A.V.
Stellingenweg 25
8421 DA Oldeberkoop
Netherlands
[CN, JP, KR, TH, VN][His, AHis]

Boscaro, Prof. A.
UV,DSIEO,J Italy
boscaro@unive.it
[JP][Lit]

Boselie, Drs D.
KUN,CPS Netherlands
[VN][Ant]

Bosma, Drs U.T.
SEPHIS Netherlands
bosma@sephis.fhk.eur.nl
[ID][His]

Bosse, F.
IFA Germany
ifahn@rrz.uni-hamburg.de
[JP][GenS, Eco, Soc, Agr]

Bossé, Dr.
INALCO,CIV France
[IN][GenS, Soc, Rel, Lin, Ant]

Botsch, A.A.
TUAC France
[KH, CN, HK, IN, ID, JP, KR, MY, PK, PH, SG,][Eco, DevS, IR, Edu, Law]

Bottema, Prof. dr S.
RUL,VA Netherlands
[KH, CN, HK, IN, ID, JP, KR, MY, PK, PH, SG,][Arch]

Bottero, F.
CNRS,CRLAO France
[CN][Lin]

Bouamrane, M.
UP1,LES France
[Lin]

Boubault, D.
UO,FL France
[JP][Lin]

Bouchez, Dr D.
E-1, Résidence les Tilleuls
91240 St. Michel sur Orge
France
[KR][His, Lit]

Bouchy, A.-M.
EFEO,BB France
[JP][Rel]

Boudarel, G.
6-A rue des Fontaines
93230 Romainville
France
[KH, LA, VN][IR, PolS, CuS, His, Ant, GenS]

Bouillier, Dr V.B.
3, rue des Petits Carreaux
75002 Paris
France
[NP][Ant, Rel, Ant]

Bouissou, J.-M.
INALCO,CIV France
ceri@msh-paris.fr
[JP, KR][Soc, IR, PolS, His]

Boully, J.L.
BML,FC France
boully@bmserveur.univ-lyon1.fr
[CN, HK, TW][Lit]

Boulnois, Dr L.
CNRS,MSCH France
[NP, TI][His, Geo]

Bourdier, Dr F.
UB2 France
claude.ragnaut@u-bordeaux2.fr
[KH, IN,][CuS, Ant, Env, DevS]

Bourdier, Dr ir M.J.F.
CNRS,CRJC France
[JP][CuS]

Boussemart, M.-S.
INALCO France
[TI][CuS]

Bouteiller, E.
HEC,EI France
[CN, HK, ID, MO, MY, SG, TW, TH][DevS, Eco]

Bouvier, Dr H.
CNRS,IRSEA France
[ID][AntAnt, PArt]

Bouwers, Drs A.
RNW Netherlands
[CN][Soc, PolS, Eco]

Bowie, Mr N.J.G.
FOC United Kingdom
[KR][His, Phi]

Bowman, Drs M.I.
BCHE,SRD United Kingdom
exxmib@bath.ac.uk
[HK, MY][Rel]

Bowring, Prof. R.J.
CU,FOS United Kingdom
rb101@cam.ac.uk
[CN, JP][Rel, Lit]

Boyd, Dr R.A.
Libellenveld 5
2318 VE Leiden
Netherlands
[JP][PolS]

Br†ten, E.
UB,DSA Norway
eldar.braten@sosantr.uib.no
[ID][Ant, CuS]

Braadbaart, Dr O.
Netherlands
okb@ihe.nl
[ID][Ant, Env, Eco]

Braarvig, Prof. dr J.
UO,FA,CS Norway
jens.braarvig@iks.uio.no
[CN, IN, NP, TI][Lit, Rel, Phi, DevS, His, CuS, Lin]

Brac de la Perriere, Dr B.
CNRS,LASEMA France
brac@ext.jussieu.fr
[MM][Ant]

Bradnock, Dr R.W.
SOAS,CSEAS United Kingdom
rb3@soas.ac.uk
[BD, IN, NP, PK, LK][Env, Agr, IR, Geo, DevS]

Braeunlein, Dr P.J.
UBR,DRS Germany
braeunl@uni-bremen.de
[PH][Rel, Ant, CuS]

Bragdon, J.
Rechtboomsloot 39
1011 CS Amsterdam
Netherlands
[CN, HK, TI][AHis, Phi, AHis]

Braginsky, Prof. V.I.
SOAS,CSEAS United Kingdom
[BN, ID, MY, SG][Rel, Lit]

Braguinskaya, Dr L.I.
RASP,IOS Russia
[TJ][Lit]

Brailey, Dr N.J.
UBRI,DHS United Kingdom
[JP, TH][His]

Brakel, Drs J.H. van
KIT Netherlands
[IN, ID][His, AHis, Arch, Ant]

Brakel-Papenhuyzen, Dr C.
Prins Bernhardlaan 133
2274 HW Voorburg
Netherlands
[Rel, LitAnt, Part]

Bramijn, I.
SAS,OI Netherlands

Brammer, H.
6 Barrington House \South Acre Park
CB2 2TY Cambridge
United Kingdom
[BD][Lit, PArt, Rel, Ant]

Brandtner, Drs M.
CAUK,GA Germany
[IN][Arch, His]

Brantas, Drs G.C.
Zaadmarkt 87
7201 DC Zutphen
Netherlands
[ID][Lit, His]

Bras, Drs C.H.
KUB, VV Netherlands
C.H.bras@kub.nl
[ID][Ant]

Bratthall, Prof. D.
LU,COHS Sweden
douglas.bratthall@odcariol.lu.se
[KH, CN, ID, JP, LA, SG, LK, TH, VN][Eco]

Brauen, Dr M.
VMUZ Switzerland
[TI][Eco]

Braun, Dr H.
GAUG,SIB Germany
[IN, MM, LK][His, Lit, Rel]

Braun, W.H.
St. Anna Str. 11
54295 Trier
Germany
[CN, HK][Ant]

Brauns, Drs T.
JLUG,GI Germany
thorsten.brauns@geo.uni-giessen.de
[ID, MY, PH, TH][DevS, Env, Agr]

Bray, Drs J.N.
CRIS United Kingdom
[BT, IN, MM, PK, TI][His, IR, PolS]

Bree, D.M. de
Utrechtsestraat 79-4
6811 LW Arnhem
Netherlands
[ID, PG][CuS]

Breet, Drs J.A. de
Aert van Neslaan 139
2341 HJ Oegstgeest
Netherlands
[IN, TI][Rel, Lin, His]

Breman, Prof. dr J.C.
UvA,ASSR,CASA
Netherlands
A723all@hasara11.bitnet
[IN, ID][DevS, His, Eco, Ant, Soc]

Bremen, Dr J.G. van
RUL,TCJK Netherlands
vanbremen@rullet.leidenuniv.nl
[JP][Ant, His]

Brenier, J.
CNRS,IHEC France
[CN][His]

Brentjes, Prof. dr B.
MLU,KAW,OA Germany
[KZ, TJ, TM][AHis, Arch, Env]

Brentjes, Dr S.
[IN, PK, TJ][Phi]

Breslin, Dr S.G.
UNC,EAC United Kingdom
shaun.breslin@uk.ac.newcastle
[CN][Eco, PolS]

Bressan, Dr L.
UM,IFL Italy
[CN][Lin, Edu]

Breton, Dr S.
CNRS,ARCHIPEL France
[ID, PG][Geo, Ant]

Breugel, Drs J.E.M. van
Grote Beerstraat 71
7521 XJ Enschede
Netherlands
[ID, PG][Ant, DevS]

Briend, M.
MBAPSP France
[JP, KR, MO][AHis]

Briggeman, T.
Martin Luther King 129
4102 GT Culemborg
Netherlands

Brinke, Ir H.W. ten
Netherlands
[CN, IN, ID, KR, PH, TW, TH, VN][Agr, Edu]

Brinkhaus, Prof. dr H.
CAUK,SO,AI Germany
hbrinkhaus@indo.uni-kiel.de
[IN, NP][CuS, Lit, Rel]

Brinks, Drs H.
Prinsenstraat 9
7121 AE Aalten
Netherlands
[ID][His]

Broch, Dr H.B.B.
UO,FSS,SA Norway
harald.beyer-broch@ima.uio.no
[ID][Psy, CuS, Ant]

Brocheux, Prof. P.B.
UP7, GHSS France
[VN][His]

Brochlos, Dr H.
HUB,AA,KI Germany
[KR][Lit, Lin]

Brochlos, Dr A.
HUB,AA,IJ Germany
[JP][His]

Brockington, Dr J.L.
UE,DS United Kingdom
j.l.brockington@ed.ac.uk
[IN][Lin, Rel, Lit]

Brocquet, S.
UP3,EI France
[IN][Lin]

Brodsgaard, K.E.
UC,FH,DAS Denmark
keb@coco.ihi.ku.dk
[Lin]

Brommer, A.B.
Amsteldijk 123-III
1078 RS Amsterdam
Netherlands
[ID][Eco, CuS, His]

Bronger, Prof. D.
RUB,GI Germany
[CN, IN, KR, PH, TH, TI][DevS]

Bronkhorst, Prof. dr J.
UL,DOLC Switzerland
Johannes.Bronkhorst@orient.unil.ch
[Phi, Rel, Lit]

Broquet, J.
UP3,EI France
[IN][Rel, Phi, Lit]

Broschart, Dr J.
UK,IDSL Germany
am004@rs1.rrz.uni-koeln.de
[Lin]

Brouwer, A.A.
GRA Netherlands
[CN, HK, IN, JP, KR, MO, PK, TW, VN][CuS, Eco, His, IR, PolS, Psy, Rel, Phi]

Brown, Dr N.D.
OU,FI,PS United Kingdom
nick.brown@plants.ox.ac.uk
[BN, ID, MY, LK][Env]

Brown, Prof. J. M.
OU,BC,MHF United Kingdom
judith.brown@history.ox.ac.uk
[IN][Rel, GenS, His]

Brown, Dr I.G.
SOAS,CSEAS United Kingdom
[ID, MY, MM, PH, TH, VN][His]

Brückner, Prof. dr H.
EKUT,SIVRW Germany
[IN][Phi, Lit, Rel]

Brug, Ir dr P.J. van der
Iepenlaan 6
2243 GE Wassenaar
Netherlands
[ID][His]

Bruggraaff, Drs W.
Maredijk 111
2316 VW Leiden
Netherlands
[ID, PG][His]

Bruguière, Dr Ph.
MM France
[IN][Soc, His, AHis, Ant]

Bruhn, Prof. dr K.
FUB,AW,IPKG Germany
[IN][AHis]

Bruijn, Dr T. de
Zuster Meijboomstraat 81
2331 PE Leiden
Netherlands
[IN, PK][Rel, His, Lit]

Bruijn, E.J. de
UT,DTM Netherlands
[CN, HK, ID, MY, SG, LK, TW, TH][His]

Bruijn, Prof. dr J.R.
RUL,VG Netherlands
[ID][His]

Bruijn, Prof. dr J.T.P. de
RUL,VTCIMO Netherlands
brujtp@rullet.leidenuniv.nl
[IN, PK, TJ][Lit, Rel]

Bruijn, Drs J.E. de
5 Carleton Gardens,
\Brecknock Road
N19 5AQ London
United Kingdom
[CN, JP, KR][His, AHis, CuS]

Bruijn, Drs B. de
NIDI,BIB Netherlands
[IN, LK][DevS, Soc, Psy, Ant]

Bruijn, Drs I.D.R.
Europaplein 91 III
1098 GZ Amsterdam
Netherlands
[ID][His]

Bruijn., P.J.J. de
Kogeldistel 3
3068 NH Rotterdam
Netherlands
[IN, LK][His, AHis]

Bruijne, Prof. dr G.A. de
UvA,VPD Netherlands
debruyne@isg.frw.uva.nl
[IN][Geo]

Bruijninckx, Drs W.P.M.
FIO Netherlands
bruii@ezh.amsterdam.nl
[CN, HK, IN, SG, TW, VN][Eco, IR]

Bruin, Ir D. de
MIN,VW,RWS Netherlands
[BD, CN, IN, ID, LA, MY, NP, TH, VN][DevS, Env]

Bruinessen, Dr M.M. van
UU,VOTC Netherlands
martin.vanbruinessen@let.ruu.nl
[AF, ID, MY, UZ][Rel, His, Ant]

Brumann, Drs Chr.
UK,IV Germany
Christoph.Brumann@Uni-koeln.de
[JP][Ant]

Brummelhuis, Dr H.C.F. ten
UvA,ASC,CASA Netherlands
[TH][Ant]

Brun, Dr C. le
INALCO,DASHA France
[HK, JP, KR, MY, PH, SG, TW][Eco, IR, PolS]

Brun, Prof. V.
UC,FH,DAS Denmark
Brun@coco.ihi.ku.dk
[TH][Lin, Lit, Rel]

Bruneau, Dr M.
CNRS,REGARDS France
[KH, MM, TH][PolS, DevS, CuS, Geo, Agr]

Brunet, Y.
UP7,UAO France
[JP][Lit]

Brunner, Dr H.
16 Route des Joyeuses
2016 Cortaillod
Switzerland
[IN][Rel]

Bruns, A.
Neue Hoch str. 42
1000 Berlin 65
Germany
[MM][Rel]

Brunt, Prof. dr L.
UvA,FPSCW Netherlands
Brunt@sara.nl
[HK, IN, JP, PH, SG, TW][Ant, Soc]

Bruschke-Johnson, Drs L.
RUL,TCJK Netherlands
bruschke@rullet.leidenuniv.nl
[CN, JP, KR][AHis]

Brustinow, Dr A.
UW,UCS,CDS United Kingdom
a.brust@swansea.ac.uk
[BD][DevS]

Bruun, Drs O.
UC, IA Denmark
ob@nias.ku.dk
[CN, MN][Ant]

Bruyn, E.
Anton Mauwestraat 20
3817 DL Amersfoort
Netherlands
[TI][Psy, Rel]

Bry, M.-F.
CNRS,EHESS France
[ID, MY][Rel, Psy]

Bryan, Drs D.
6 Southgate Lane
NR1 2DB Norwich
United Kingdom

Bryant, Dr R.L.
KCL,DG United Kingdom
[ID, MM, PH, TH][Geo, PolS, DevS, Env]

Bryder, Dr H.P.
LU,DH Sweden
[CN, HK, JP, KR, LA, MN, TW][Ant, Rel]

Bubandt, Dr N.
AU,FH,DESA Denmark
ethnonob@moes.hum.au.dk
[ID][Ant]

Bubentsov, Dr Ye.V.
RAS,IFES,FEB Russia
[CN][Eco]

Bucherer-Dietschi, P.
SBA Switzerland
[AF, TJ, TM, UZ][His, CuS, IR]

Buchholt, Dr H.
UBI,FS,SDRC Germany
Helmut.Buchholt@post.uni-bielefeld.de
[ID, PH][CuS, DevS, Geo, Soc, His]

Budde, Drs A.
HUB,ITKK Germany
[CN][CuS, Soc, DevS, Geo, His]

Buddingh, P.
Fagotstraat 9
4241 CC Arkel
Netherlands
[ID][Edu]

Buddruss, Prof. G.A.
JGU,II Germany
[AF, BD, AF, BD, IN, NP, PK, LK, TJ, TI][His, Rel, Lin, Ant, CuS, Lit]

Buen, J.
FNI, NCF Norway
[CN, HK, TW, TI][PolS]

Bugge, Dr H.
UC, IH Denmark
[IN, LK, TH][Rel, His]

Bui, V.Q.
Urkhovenseweg 380
5641 KR Eindhoven
Netherlands
[VN][His, Eco, Lin, Soc, EduAgr]

Bui, X.Q.
126 rue Nationale
75013 Paris
France
[Soc, Agr, Eco, Edu, Lin, His]

Bulfoni, C.
UM,IFL Italy
[CN,][Eco, Lin]

Bunder, Drs M.A.
Deensestraat 24-C
3020 GY Rotterdam
Netherlands
[ID][His]

Bundgaard, Dr H.
UC, IA Denmark
helle.bundgaard@anthro.ku.dr
[IN][Ant]

Bunin, Dr V.N.
RAS,IFES,FEB Russia
[JP][PolS, IR]

Bunnin, Dr N.F.
ICS United Kingdom
nick.bunnin@cmcs.ox.ac.uk
[CN][Phi]

Bunt, Dr G.
UWL,DTRIS United Kingdom
g.bunt@lamp.ac.uk
[MY, PK, SG,][CuS, Ant, Law, Rel]

Burdman, M.M.
SCHI,DEA Germany
marymb@eirna.com
[CN, IN, ID, TI][His, Eco, DevS]

Burg, B. & C. von der
32 Exeter House, \Putney Heath
SW15 3SX London
United Kingdom
[CN, JP][His, AHis]

Burg, Drs C.J.G. van der
VU,GW Netherlands
[IN][Ant, Lit, Rel, Soc]

Burgers, Dr A.B.
Louis Pregerkade 268
3071 AZ Rotterdam
Netherlands
[JP][Lin, Eco]

Burght, Prof. dr Gr.
VU,FR Netherlands
grburght@xsuall.nl
[CN, HK, ID, MO, TH][Law]

Burgler, Dr R.A.
Pythagorasstraat 101/boven
1098 EZ Amsterdam
Netherlands
[KH, LA, TH, VN][Ant, PolS, His]

Burkert, Prof. W.
Switzerland

Burlet, S.D.
UBR,DPS United Kingdom
[IN][His, PolS, Ant]

Burman, Dr A.D.
RASP,IOS Russia
orient@ieos.spb.su
[MM][His, CuS, Lit, AHis]

Burmann, P.E.M.
Buiten Bantammerstraat 15
1011 AX Amsterdam
Netherlands
[MG][Arch, Ant, His, CuS, AHis]

Burns, M.
CIIR United Kingdom
[PH][Arch, His, AHis, CuS, Ant]

Burton, Drs J.A.
Providence Green \Green Hammerton
4058 DP York
United Kingdom
[AF, IN, KZ, TJ, TM, UZ][His, IR]

Buskens, Dr L.P.H.M.
RUL,VTCIMO Netherlands
lphmbuskens@rullet.leidenuniv.nl
[AF][Ant, His, Law, AHis, Rel]

Busser, Drs R.B.P.M.
RUL,TCJK Netherlands
[JP, TH][IR, Eco]

Bussotti, M.
121 Avenue d'Ivry
75013 Paris
France
[CN][AHis, CuS]

Bustelo, Dr P.
UCM,ICA Spain
[BN, KHCN, HK, ID, JP, KR, LA, MO, MY, MM, PH][DevS, Eco]

Busuttil, J.
CNRS,CRLAO France
[CN][Lin]

Buuren, Drs B.L.M. van
St. Willibrordusstraat 51-D
1074 XK Amsterdam
Netherlands
[IN, LK][Ant, DevS]

Buyze, Drs A.
Weteringschans 117-II
1017 SC Amsterdam
Netherlands
[ID][AHis, Ant, Rel, Lit, CuS, IR]

Bykova, Dr S.A.
MSU,IAAS,CIBS Russia
[JP][Lin]

Bylinyak, Dr S.A.
RASP,IOS Russia
[IR]

Byster, Drs E.D.
Gal.10&2K Netherlands
[BD, IN, PH, LK][IR, CuS, His, Lit, Phi, AHis]

Cabañas, P.
IJ Spain
[JP][AHis]

Cabanes, M.
CNRS,EHESS France
[His, AHis]

Caboara, Drs M.
Via Byron 4/2
16145 Geneva
Italy
[CN][His, Agr, Ant]

Cadart, Drs C.E.A.
CERI,FNSP France
[CN][PolS, IR, His]

Cadene, Prof. Ph.
UPV France
[IN][DevS, Geo]

Cadier, S.
ASEMI,BIB,SL France
[DevS, Geo]

Cailleau, Y.
12 avenue des Fauvettes
78380 Bougival
France
[His, AHis]

Cain, Dr H.
MVB Germany
[ID, MG, PI, PH][Rel, Lin, Ant]

Cairó I Céspedes, G.
Escoriol 18, 3er 1a
08024 Barcelona
Spain
gcairo@riscc2.eco.ub.es
[IN,][Eco]

Callewaert, Dr W.M
KUL,DAS Belgium
Winand.callewaert@arts.kuleuven.ac.be
[IN][Lit, CuS, Rel]

Calvetti, Prof. P.
UIO,DAS Italy
calvett@unina.it
[JP][Lin]

Calvo-Platero, M.
INALCO France
[His]

Cambon, P.
MNAAG France
[AF, KR][His]

Cameron, Mr J.
UEA,ODG,SDS United Kingdom
john.cameron@uea.ac.uk
[BD, IN, MM, NP, PI, PK, SG,][Edu, Env, Phi, Eco, CuS, DevS]

Campagnolo, H.
194 rue du Chateau des Rentiers
75013 Paris
France
[Phi, DevS, Edu, Eco, Env, CuS]

Campana, Dr A.
UF,DSS Italy
[CN, HK, JP, KZ, KR, MN, SG, TJ, TW][His, IR, PolS]

Campbell, Dr G.R.
UAPV,SLA France
gcampb3195@aol.com
[His]

Campo, Dr J.N.F.M. A'
PI,IESG Netherlands
acampo@mgs.fhk.eur.nl
[ID][IR, PolS, His]

Camroux, Dr D.F.
CHEAM France
[BN, MY, PI][His, IR, Soc, PolS]

Cannell, F.
LSEPS,DE United Kingdom
[PH][His, IR, PolS, Soc]

Cannon, Dr T.G.
UGR,SH United Kingdom
t.cannon@greenwich.ac.uk
[CN][DevS, Env]

Canova, Dr G.
BIL Italy
[JP][Lit]

Cantlie, Dr J.
CS United Kingdom
[CN][CuS, AHis]

Canto, Dr P.
UD,SE Spain
[CN, HK, ID, JP, KR, MY, PH, SG, TW, TH][DevS, IR, Eco]

Cantwell, Dr C.
UWL,DTRIS United Kingdom
[TI][Ant, Rel]

Cao, Dr T.L.
CNRS,IRSEA France
[MM, VN][Lin]

Caplan, Prof. dr L.
SOAS,DAS United Kingdom
lc3@soas.ac.uk
[IN, NP,][Ant]

Captain, Drs E.S.J.
UU,DH Netherlands
[ID][IR, His, GenS]

Caracchi, Dr P.
Italy
CARACCHI@CISI.UNITO.IT
[IN,][Lin, Lit, Rel]

Cardena, M.
Gietersstraat 33
1015 HB Amsterdam
Netherlands
[ID, JP, PI, SG, TH][AHis]

Cardholm, M.
Förbindelsevägen 7
340 41 Kullavik
Sweden
[CN, ID][IR]

Cardinaud, M.-H.
INALCO,DASHA France
[MM][Lan]

Carey, Dr P.B.R.
OU,TC,FMH United Kingdom
[KH, ID, MM, PH][His, IR, CuS, Lit, Rel]

Carino, J.
PRC United Kingdom
[PH][CuS, Rel, Lit, His, IR]

Carioti, Dr P.
UIO,DSO Italy
[CN, JP][His]

Carle, Dr R.
UHAM,SIS Germany
indons@phil.philosopie.uni-hamburg.de
[ID, MY, PH][Lit]

Carnogurska, Dr M.
SAS,IOAS Slovak Republic
[CN, TW][Rel, Phi]

Carpano, R.
EC, DG I-J Belgium
[BD, KH, IN, ID, MY, MM, NP, PH, SG, LK, TH][Eco, IR]

Carrithers, Prof. dr M.
UDU,DA United Kingdom
[IN, LK][CuS, His, Rel, Soc, Ant]

Carstens, Dr R.
FSUJ,BOS,IND Germany
[BN, ID, MY, PI, PH, SG][His, Edu, CuS, AHis, Lin, Lit, DevS, PolS, Rel]

Carswell, Prof. J.W.
S,ID United Kingdom
[CN, IN, KZ, MG, MY, MV, MN, PG, PH, SG,][AHis, CuS, His]

Carter, Dr L.J.
UC,CSAS United Kingdom
ljc10@cam.ac.uk
[BD, BT, BN, KH, HK, IN, ID, LA, MY, MM, NP,][His]

Carter, Dr M.D.
92 Greenfield Road
N15 5ER London
United Kingdom
[IN, LK][His]

Casado-Fresnillo, Dr C.
UNED,FF,DLE Spain
[PI, PH][Lin]

Casares Vidal, D.
Muntavez 373-1°-2°
08021 Barcelona
Spain
[HK, JP, SG, TW][Eco]

Casero Fernandez, E.J.
Perez de Ayala 1-4°F
33007 Oviedo
Spain
[JP][]

Casevitz, Prof. M.H.
UP10,GREC France
[BD, IN,][Arch, Lin, Rel]

Casie Chetty, C.D.C.
8 Avenue Hamoir
1180 Brussel
Belgium

Casimir, Prof. dr M.J.
UK,IV Germany
[AF, IN, PK,][Psy, Arch, Ant, His, GenS, Agr]

Casparis, Prof. dr J.G. de
RUL,KERN Netherlands
[IN, ID, MY, PH, LK][AHis, Rel, His, Arch, His]

Cassen, Prof. R.H.
OU,FE United Kingdom
robert.cassen@qeh.ox.ac.uk
[IN][Env, DevS, Eco, Edu, POPULATION]

Castillo Rodriguez, S.
c/ Mc Lopez - No 41-6
28015 Madrid
Spain
[KH, CN, HK, JP, KR, LA, MO, MY, MN, MM, PI, PH,][IR]

Catalan Aguila, J.
UB,FB,DE Spain
catalan@porthos.bio.ub.es
[JP][Env]

Cauquelin, Drs C.J.
CNRS,LASEMA France
[CN, TW][Rel, Ant]

Cavalieri, Dr R.C.
UP,CEUP Italy
[CN, HK, TW][Law, IR, PolS]

Cayley, J.
Wellsweep Press, \1 Grove End Hse \150 Highgate Rd.
NW5 London
United Kingdom
[CN][Lit, CuS]

Cayrac-Blanchard, F.
CNRS,FNSP France
blanchar@msh.paris.fr
[ID][PolS, IR]

Cedercreutz, S.J.T.
LSEPS,DSA United Kingdom
cedercre@lse.ac.uk
[ID, PH][Ant]

Cederlöf, G.
UU,DS,DG Sweden
gunnel.cederlof@uland.uu.se
[His, DevS]

Cederroth, Dr S.
NIAS Denmark
sven@nias.ku.dk

Centlivres, Prof. P.
UN,IE Switzerland
[AF, PK, TJ, TM][CuS, Ant]

Ceplak-Mencin, Dr R.
MNEC Slovenia
[CN, MN, TI][CuS, Ant]

Ceresa, Dr M.
UV,DSIEO,C Italy
ceresa.unive.it
[CN][Ant, Lit, CuS]

Ceruera Fernández, I.
UCM, GH,HAC Spain
[CN, HK, IN, JP, MO,][AHis, His]

Chaballe, M.
UH,FAI France
[PolS]

Chagnaud, F.J.
14 Rue de la Corderie
75003 Paris
France
[KH, CN, LA, MM, TH, VN][Eco, Agr, Env, DevS]

Chai, Drs M.
Govert Flinckstraat 130 II
1072 EM Amsterdam
Netherlands
[MY][CuS]

Chalmers, Dr M.
UBR,DPS United Kingdom
mgchalme@bradford.ac.uk
[ID, MY, SG, TH, VN][IR]

Chambard, Prof. J.-L.
UL3,CREO France
[IN][Ant]

Champion, C.
UL3,CREO France
[IN][Lit]

Chan, M.Y.
KUL,OAB Belgium
mei-Yee chang@bib@lw.ac.be
[CN, JP][CuS]

Chan, Drs Y.W.F.
UvA,ASSR,CASA
Netherlands
[ID][PolS, GenS, Ant, Lit, His]

Chanda, T.
INALCO France
[Ant, His, GenS, Lit, PolS]

Chandramohan, Dr B.
ULU,KLCC United Kingdom
bala.chandromohan@luton.ac.u
k
[BD, IN, PK, LK][Lit, DevS, Edu, IR, Lin, CuS]

Chang, I.-B.
CNRS,CRLAO France
[KR][Lin]

Chang, I.
UJML3,FL France
[CN][Edu, IR, Lin, DevS, CuS, Lit]

Chant, Dr S.
LSEPS,DG United Kingdom
[PH][DevS, GenS]

Chao, J.
INALCO France
[CN][GenS, DevS]

Chapman, G.
72 Mallinson Road
SW11 1BP London
United Kingdom
[BT, KH, CN, HK, IN, ID, MO, MN, MM, PI, TW, TH][His, AHis, CuS]

Chapman, Prof. G.P.
ULC,DG United Kingdom
g.chapman@lancaster.ac.uk
[BD, IN, LK][Geo, Agr, Env, DevS]

Chaponniere, Dr J.R.
UPMF,CA France
jchapon@grenet.fr
[HK, ID, KR, PG, PH, SG, TW, TH][IR, Eco, PolS, DevS]

Charbonnier, Dr J.
128 Rue de Bac
75007 Paris
France
[CN][CuS, Rel, Phi, His]

Chard, Dr R.
ICS United Kingdom
robert.chard@orienst.ox.ac.uk
[CN, TW][His, Rel]

Charon de Saint Germain, Drs E. de
1ste Jan Steenstraat 9-I
1072 NA Amsterdam
Netherlands

Charpentier, Dr J.M.
CNRS,LACITO France
[PI, PG, VN][Ant, Lin, Edu, CuS]

Charras, S.
655 avenue du Rigaud
83240 Cavalaire
France
[Ant, Geo, DevS, Env]

Charras, M.
CNRS,LASEMA France
[ID][Geo, Env, DevS, Ant]

Charsley, Dr S.R.
UG,DS United Kingdom
[IN][Ant]

Chavagneux, Chr.
France
[Ant]

Chavushian, Dr A.N.
RASP,IOS Russia
[Eco]

Chayet, A.
16 Place Henri Bergson
75008 Paris
France
[TI][Ant]

Chegodar, Dr N.I.
RASP,IOS Russia
[JP][CuS, Lit]

Chelintseva, Dr N.P.
RASP,IOS Russia
[PI][His, IR]

Chemparathy, Prof. dr G.
UU,FL Netherlands
[BT, IN, NP, SM, LK, TH, TI][Rel, Phi]

Chen, L.
INALCO France
[CN][Soc, His]

Chen, Dr F.
UMAN,HIS Germany
feng@rummelplatz.uni-mannheim.de
[CN][Soc, His]

Chen, C.
UP7,UAO France
[CN][Lit]

Cheng, Dr S.
IIAS Netherlands
cheng@rullet.leidenuniv.nl
[CN, TW][His]

Cheng, Dr A.L.
LPI France
[CN, HK, TW][CuS, His, Phi]

Cheng, Prof. F.
CNRS,CRLAO France
[TW][AHis, Lit, Phi, His]

Cheng, S.H.
CNRS,AAC France
[CN, , JP, KR, MO, MY, MN, SG, TW, TI][AHis, CuS, Rel]

Cheng, Dr Y.
CNRS,CM France
[TW][Soc, Ant]

Cheng-Cadart, Dr Y.X.
CERI,FNSP France
[CN][PolS, CuS, His, IR]

Cheng-Wang, A.
INALCO France
[CN][Lin]

Cherepneva, Dr Ye.A.
RASP,IOS Russia
[CuS, PolS]

Cherepnyova, Dr E.A.
RAS,IOS,CIS Russia
[ID][His, PolS]

Cherevko, Dr Yu.M.
RASP,IOS Russia
[JP][Eco, IR]

Chernyshev, Dr V.A.
RASP,IOS Russia
[IN][Lin]

Cherrington, Dr R.L.
Bulgaria
[CN, HK][Soc, CuS, PolS]

Cherry, J.A.
USH,EARS United Kingdom
[KR][Eco]

Cheutching, L.C.
HUB,AA,SOA Germany
[LA][Phi, His]

Chevrier, Y.
INALCO France
[CN][His]

Chhachhi, Drs A.
ISS Netherlands
100020.3354@compuserve.com
[BD, IN, PK, LK][GenS, Soc]

Chhim, K.
HUB,AA,SOA Germany
[KH][His]

Chiao, Prof. dr W.C.
UT,SIN Germany
[CN, TW][Phi, Lin, His, Eco]

Chiche, .
INALCO France
[Eco, His, Phi, Lin]

Chicherov, Dr A.I.
RASP,IOS Russia
[IN][Eco, His]

Chilson, Mr C.U.D.
ULC,DJS United Kingdom
c.chilson@lancs.ac.uk
[TI][Rel, Ant]

Chin, Dr J.
MU,SHP United Kingdom
j.chin@mdx.ac.uk
[BN, ID, MY, PI, SG][PolS, DevS, His]

Chinnabutr, W.
Akanapolku 2 C 285/1
01370 Vantaa
Finland
[PolS, His, DevS]

Chlenova, Dr N.L.
Russia
[Arch]

Cho, Dr M.Y.
IFA Germany
[KR][PolS]

Choenni, Dr C.E.S.
Kennemerplein 23
2011 MH Haarlem
Netherlands
[IN, MY, PK, SG, LK][His, IR, Phi, PolS, Rel, Lit, DevS, Soc]

Choi, D.-J.
3 Anne Carver Lodge \Stanley Ave.
HA0 4LB Wembley ,Middlesex
United Kingdom
[ID, KR, MY, SG, VN][PolS]

Choi, S.-U.
UP7,UAO France
[KR][His]

Choi-Chaballe, E.-S.
UH,FAI France
[KR][Lin]

Cholley, J.
UJML3,FL France
[JP][Lin]

Chong, Mr G.
SIBF United Kingdom
[MY][Env]

Choron-Baix, Dr C.
CNRS,LAU France
[LA, TH][Ant, Rel]

Chou, Dr C.
IIAS Netherlands
chou@Rullet.LeidenUniv.nl
[ID, SG][Ant]

Choudodeyev, Dr J.V.
RAS,IOS,DC Russia
[CN, TW][His]

Christiaans, P.A.
CBG Netherlands
[ID, LK][His]

Christiansen, Dr F.
5 Grosvenor Court \Alexandra Road South
M16 8GZ Manchester
United Kingdom
[CN][PolS, Env, DevS]

Christin, Prof. A.-M.
ecriture@paris7.jussieu.fr
[CN, JP, KR, LA, TW, VN][Ant, AHis, CuS, Lin, Lit, Psy, Soc]

Chufrin, Dr G.I.
RAS,IOS,AL Russia
[IN, ID, KR, MY, SG,][IR, Eco]

Chung, Dr Y.-S.
HUB,AA,KI Germany
[KR][His]

Chung, Dr Kim Le
[JP][Lit]

Chung, Dr H.J.
UE,DAS United Kingdom
[CN][Lit, GenS]

Chutiwongs, Dr N.
RMV Netherlands
[BD, BT, KH, IN, ID, LA, MY, NP, SM, LK][Rel, His, Arch, AHis]

Chvyr, Dr L.A.
RASP,IOS Russia
[CuS, Ant]

Chylinski, Dr E.A.C.
ESCAS Denmark
[TJ, TM, UZ][Soc, DevS, Eco, Rel, PolS]

Ciapparoni La Rocca, Dr T.
URLS,DOS Italy
[JP][Lit]

Ciarla, Dr R.
ISLAO Italy
[CN, HK, KR, LA, MN, MM, PH, TW, TH, VN][His, AHis, CuS, Arch, Ant]

Citro, M
UIO,DAS Italy
[ID, MY,][CuS, Lit]

Claessen, Prof. dr H.J.M.
RUL,CA/SNWS Netherlands
[PI][Ant, His]

Clair, Dr S.A.
COA France
[KH][His]

Clancy, Dr J.S.
TUE,DTDS Netherlands
j.s.clancy@TDG.utwente.nl
[IN][Env]

Clarence-Smith, Dr W.G.
SOAS,DH United Kingdom
wc2@soas.ac.uk
[KH, ID, MO, MY, PH, VN][His]

Clarke, Dr G.
UW,UCS,CDS United Kingdom
G.Clarke@swansea.ac.uk
[PH][PolS, DevS]

Clarke, Dr J.W.
VAM,ISEAD United Kingdom
[TI][His, AHis]

Clarke, G.
42 Lantern Close
HA0 2JT Wembley (M-Essex
United Kingdom
[PH][His, AHis]

Clarke, S.J.G.
UW,UCS,DSPASS United Kingdom
[PH][DevS]

Clason, Prof. dr A.T.
RUG,BAI Netherlands
[IN, ID][DevS]

Clausen, Drs S.C.
AU,DEAS,OI Denmark
Ostsc@hum.aau.dk
[CN][Soc, PolS, His]

Claver, Drs A.
VU, DCA Netherlands
a.claver@scw.vu.nl
[ID][His]

Clayton, Dr D.W.
UY,DE United Kingdom
Durci@ac.york.uk
[CN, HK][His, IR, DevS, Eco]

Clegg, Dr J.R.
EUC,SMSS,AA United Kingdom
cleggj@admin.ehche.ac.uk
[CN][DevS]

Clementin-Ojha, C.
EFEO France
[IN][Ant, Rel]

Clemmensen, J.
Ndr Fasanvej 52, 3.tv
2000 Frederiksberg
Denmark
[Ant, Rel]

Clotte, M.
INALCO France
[IN, LA][Lin]

Clunas, Dr C.
USUS,SCCS United Kingdom
c.clunas@sussex.ac.uk
[CN, HK, TW][His, Arch, His, AHis, CuS]

Cobbi, J.
CNRS,JAP France
[JP][Ant]

Cockburn, Mr R.C.
UY,IAAS United Kingdom
[CN, IN, ID, JP, KR, MY, TH][DevS, CuS]

Coelen, Drs M.
ESCAS Netherlands
[IN][His, Rel]

Cohen, M.
BNF,MO France
monique.cohen@bnf.fr
[CN][His, Rel]

Colas Doctorate, G
CNRS,CEIAS France
CEIAS@ehess.fr
[IN,][CuS, His, Lit, Phi, Rel]

Coleman, Drs P.H.
ULEED,SE United Kingdom
p.h.coleman@education.leeds.ac.uk
[ID][Edu]

Coleman, Drs G.
UEA,ODG,SDS United Kingdom
G.coleman@uea.ac.uk
[IN, MN, MM, NP, PK][DevS]

Coll Compte, X.
Via Augusta 185-AT-B
08021 Barcelona
Spain
[IN, NP, LK][Psy, Phi, Rel]

Collin, H.
38, Rue de L'Alma
92400 Courbevoie
France
[CN, HK, ID, JP, MO, MN, NP, SG, TJ, TW, TH][Law, Soc, PolS, Eco, IR]

Collins, Dr P.S.
USTR,DH United Kingdom
p.s.collins@strath.ac.uk
[IN][His]

Collotti Pischel, Prof. E
UM,IFL Italy
[KH CN, VN][His, PolS]

Colombijn, Dr F.
KITLV Netherlands
[ID][Soc, Env, Ant, His]

Comas Montoya, Dr R.
UCM, GH,HAC Spain
[BH, IN, KZ, KG, LD, MN, NP, CN, SK, TJ, TI, TM][AHis, His]

Condominas, G.
UAM1,LSH France
[JP][Lan]

Coningham, Dr R.A.E.
UBR,NAS,AS United Kingdom
r.a.e.coningham@bradford.ac.uk
[AF, BD, AF, BD, IN, PK, LK][Arch, Ant, CuS, His, AHis]

Conti, Dr G.
Via Monterotondo 17
20162 Milan
Italy
[BN, ID, MY, PG][Lin, Rel, Law]

Conway, Dr B.M.
CLP,LGU,FB United Kingdom
[ID, MY, SG, TH][Edu]

Conzelmann, Dr E.
FUB,PSW,IE,A Germany
[IN][Ant, Rel, Soc]

Cook, M.
NCSB United Kingdom
[KH, CN, HK, JP, KR, MM, PH, TH][Eco]

Cook, Dr A.S.
IOLR United Kingdom
andrew.cook@bl.uk
[BD, IN, MM, PK,][His]

Copans, M.
CNRS,EHESS France
[Eco]

Copley, Mr A.R.H.
KU, RC United Kingdom
[IN][Rel, His]

Cordier, Mr B. de
Ten Stroom, 29
9890 Gavere (Vurste)
Belgium
[AF, KZ, MN, TJ, TM, UZ][IR, His, PolS]

Corlin, Dr C.G.
GU,DSA Sweden
Claes.corlin@sant.gu.se
[LA, TH, TI, VN][DevS, Ant]

Cornet, C.
CNRS,IAO France
[CN][His]

Cornilleau, K.
UTM,CUP France
[JP][His]

Cornillet, M.
UP8, France
[IN][His]

Corradini, Prof. P.
URLS,DOS Italy
Corradin@itcaspur.Caspur.it
[CN, JP, TW][Law, IR, His]

Cospedal, Drs R.
UCM,ICA Spain
ialz0@sis.vcm.cs
[ID][DevS]

Cossio, Dr C.
UV,DEAS Italy
[IN][Lit]

Couderc, P.
CNRS,IRSEA France
[MM][AntAnt]

Coulie, Prof. dr B.R.R.
KUL,IO Belgium
[CN, HK, IN, JP, PK, TW][AHis, Soc, Lin, Phi, DevS, Ant, Eco, His, Lit]

Coursey, R. de
KITLV Netherlands

Courtens, Drs I.A.M.
KUN,CPS Netherlands
[ID][GenS, Ant]

Cousins, Drs L.S.
35 Burlington Road \Withington
M20 4QA Manchester
United Kingdom
[IN, LK, TH][His, Rel, Lit]

Coutinho, Dr V.
EMTG Portugal
[JP][His]

Couto, Dr D.
CNRS,EPHE,SHP France
[HK, IN, ID, INSULAR SOUTHWEST IN, MO,][Arch, His, PolS]

Cowan, Drs F.M.
KIT Netherlands
[BD, BT, KH, CN, IN, ID, LA, NP, PK, PH,][GenS, DevS, CuS, Ant, Env, LinAgr]

Coyaud, Dr M.
CNRS,LACITO France
[CN, JP, KR, MN, MM, PH, TW, TH, TI, VN][Ant, Lin]

Crespi Reghizzi, Prof. G.
PAV Italy
[CN, IN, KZ, MN, NP, TJ, TW, TM][PolS, DevS, IR, Law]

Cribb, Prof. R.B.
NIAS Denmark
cribb@nias.ku.dk
[ID][PolS, His, Env]

Crince le Roy, E.A.W.
Achtergracht 9
1017 WL Amsterdam
Netherlands
[IN, ID][DevS, AHis, Edu]

Crombe, V.
4 rue du Sergent Hoff
75017 Paris
France
[CN, IN, JP,][His, CuS, AHis, Rel, His, Arch]

Crosbie, Dr A.J.
UE,DG United Kingdom
[BD, BNCN, HK, IN, ID, JP, KR, LA, MY, PI][IR, Env, Eco, Geo, DevS]

Crowe, Dr P.R.
ESEM France
[PI, PG][Rel, His, Ant, AHis, Ant, Psy, Arch, Soc]

Crump, Dr S.T.
Twentestraat 4
1079 PV Amsterdam
Netherlands
[JP][Ant]

Crump, Drs T.M.
12 Wenlock Drive \Escrick
YO4 6JB York
United Kingdom
[JP][CuS, Lit]

Crump, Prof. J.D.
UY,DP United Kingdom
[JP][PolS, His]

Crunelle, G.
CDIL France
[LA][Ant, Lit, Lin, Law, IR, Psy, Rel, Soc, Edu, PolS, Arch, His,]

Cruz Alcaide, J.M.
UNEDC,FP Spain
[JP][Edu, Phi, Rel]

Cseh, É.E.
FHMEAA Hungary
[JP][AHis, Rel]

Cuesta Garcia, Antonio
Trias Giro, 21
08034 Barcelona
Spain
[PH][His]

Cuhls, Drs K.E.
UFK,FI Germany
cu@isi.fug.de
[JP][Env, Eco, PolS, CuS]

Cummings, I.
SOAS,CSEAS United Kingdom
[PH][Eco, CuS, PolS, Env]

Cunin, P.
Trébons sur Grasse
31290 Villefranche-Lauragais
France
[VN][Ant, Soc, Eco]

Curien, Dr A.
CNRS,CM France
[CN][Lit]

Custers, Dr P.J.J.M.
BPSC Netherlands
[BD][Eco, GenS, PolSAgr]

Cwiertka, Dr K.J.
RUL,TCJK Netherlands
[JP][Soc, His, Ant]

Cyrzyk, Drs L.M.
PIIA,DSID Poland
[CN, HK, KR, TW][His, IR]

Daan, K.
Brouwersgracht 196
1013 HD Amsterdam
Netherlands
[CN, JP][Env, CuS]

Daane, Dr ir J.R.V.
ICD Netherlands
[MY][Soc]

Daberkow, R.
Neuwiesen Str. 9
60528 Frankfurt
Germany
[CN, HK, TW][CuS, Lit]

Dagens, Prof. B.
UP3,EI France
[IN][Rel, His]

Dahl, Dr O.
CIC Norway
od@misjonshs.no
[MG][Ant]

Dahles, Dr H.
KUB, VV Netherlands
H.dahles@kub.nl
[ID][Ant, CuS]

Dahlgren, Drs T.
Liisankatu 16 B 15
00170 Helsinki
Finland
[His]

Dahlgren, Drs T.
SSE,EIJS Sweden
[JP][His]

Dahlhausen, Drs S.
Ossastrasse 7
12045 Berlin
Germany
[JP][His]

Dahm, Prof. dr B.
Bischof-Wolfger-Strasse 32
94032 Passau
Germany
[ID, MY, PH, TH, VN][Rel, His, CuS]

Dahm, H.
UP,SEAS Germany
p4dahm01@fsrz1.rz.uni-passau.de
[VN][IR, Eco]

Daiber, Prof. dr J.H.
JWGU,IOOP,SOAW
Germany
[VN][Rel]

Daillie, F.-R.
En Tilhomme
71250 Donzy Le National
France
[MY][Lit, CuS]

Dakpa, N.
INALCO France
[TI][Lan]

Dalen, Prof. J.Chr. van
LW,VB Netherlands
[CN, ID, VN][DevS, Edu, Soc, Eco, IR, PolS, Env]

Dalla Chiesa, Drs S.
UV,DSIEO,J Italy
[JP][Lin, Rel, Ant]

Dallidet, M.
CNRS,CRLAO France
[CN][Lin]

Dalmia, Dr V.
EKUT,SIVRW Germany
vasudha.dalmia@uni-tuebingen.de
[IN][CuS, Rel, His, Lit]

Daluwa Thumul, G.J.
INALCO France
[IN, LK][Lan]

Dam, Dr J.E. van
MIN,OCW,OWB Netherlands
[CN, ID, MY, SG][]

Damen, Ir P.J.C.
BIL,AD Netherlands
pda@bilance.antenna.nl
[Eco, DevS, Agr]

Damon, Dr F.Y.
UL3,ETROM,C France
[CN][DevS, His]

Damshäuser, Drs B.
UB,OS,AI Germany
[ID][Lin, Lit, PolS, Phi]

Damsteegt, Dr Th.
RUL,KERN Netherlands
[IN][Lit, Lin]

Dang, T.
UP7,UAO France
[VN][Lit]

Dang, Dr D.B.
Uiterste Gracht 17
2312 TB Leiden
Netherlands
[VN][CuS]

Daniel, A.D.
9 rue de Suisses
75014 Paris
France
[KH][Lin, Lit]

Daniel, V.
UNSA,LSH,S France
[VN][Soc]

Daniels, Ch.
5A, Belsize Square
NW3 4HT London
United Kingdom
[TI][Soc]

Dannecker, Drs P.
UBI,FS,SDRC Germany
[BD, IN, TH][PolS, GenS, DevS, Soc, Eco]

Darma Palguna, Drs I.B.M.
RUL,TCZOAO Netherlands
[ID][Lit]

Das, Prof. dr R.P.
MLU,KAW,II Germany
[BD, IN][CuS, Lin, Rel]

Daszenies, Drs J.
UK,IV Germany
[ID][Rel, Ant]

Datshenko, Dr G.M.
MSU,IAAS,CIBS Russia
[IN, PK][Lin]

Daudet, M.
5 rue Thouin
5005 Paris
France
[Ant, Rel]

Dauphin, A.
LPI France
[VN][Lit]

Davidovich, Prof.Dr Ye.A.
RASP,IOS Russia
[His]

Davis, Drs C.E.
LSVCHE,SS United Kingdom
[ID][DevS, GenS, Ant]

Davydov, Dr A.D.
RASP,IOS Russia
[AF][Eco]

Dawson, R.
Highfields, 4 Pettiwell
\Garsington
OX44 9DB Oxford
United Kingdom
[CN][Lin, Phi, His]

De Coppet, Prof. D
CRMJ, EHESS France
[ID, PI, PG, PH][Ant, Soc]

De Llanos Isidoro, P.
Lluis Companys 42-2-1°
08921 St^a Coloma de Gramanet, Barcelona
Spain
[CN, JP, KR, TW][His, Lin, Lit, Phi]

De Prado Yepes, C.
Italy
deprado@datacomm.iue.it
[JP,][Eco, IR]

Deacon, Mr A.G.
ULEED,DP United Kingdom
[CN, TW][His, Phi]

Debaine-Francfort, Dr C.
CNRS,AAC France
[CN, KZ][Arch]

Debnicki, Dr K.
UW,IOS,DFES Poland
[AF, IN, NP, PK,][PolS, IR, His]

Debono, F.
20 rue André del Sarte
75018 Paris
France
[TH][Lit, Soc]

Dechering, Dr W.H.J.C.
RUL,CA/SNWS Netherlands
dechering@rulfsw.leidenuniv.nl
[LK][DevS, Soc, Ant]

Deckers, Drs W.
RC,PS United Kingdom
deckerw@staff.richmond.ac.uk
[CN, JP, TW][IR, DevS, PolS]

Deelstra, T.
IIUE Netherlands
[BT, CN, HK, IN, ID, JP, MM, NP, TH, TI][Env]

Defoort, Dr C.M.G.
KUL,SIN Belgium
Carine.defoort@artskuleuven.ac.be
[CN][Phi]

Dege, Prof. dr E.
CAUK,GI Germany
dege@geographie.uni-kiel.de
[CN, KR][Eco, Agr]

Degener, Dr A.C.
JGU,II Germany
[AF, IN, PK, TI][Rel, Lin]

Degryse, Dr K.M.
Eduard Arsenstraat 64
2640 Mortsel
Belgium
[CN, IN][His]

Delacour, C.
MNAAG France
[CN][His]

Delage, F.
Padilla, 6
28006 Madrid
Spain
[CN, JP, TW][IR, PolS]

Delahaye, Dr H.
CF,IEO France
delahaye@ext.jussieu.fr
[CN, JP][His, CuS, AHis]

Delanghe, H.
Nationalestraat 81
2000 Antwerp
Belgium
[CN, JP][IR, His, PolS]

Delaune, Dr F.
UL,FS,ECS France
[MY, SG][Eco, DevS]

Delden, Drs M.C. van
Kon. Julianaweg 23
3628 BN Kockengen
Netherlands
[ID][Ant, His, Soc]

Delemarle-Charton, M.
INALCO France
[CN][Ant, His, Soc]

Deliege, Dr R.
KUL,DAS Belgium
[IN][Ant]

Delire, J.M.
ULB Belgium
[IN][His]

Delissen, Dr A.R.
CNRS,EC France
delissen@ext.jussieu.fr
[KR][His]

dell'Anglese, Dr E.
UM,IILP Italy
[ID][PolS, Env, Geo]

Della Pietra, B.
16, Av. Marcel Thriy Bte 22
1200 Brussel
Belgium
[CN, HK, MO, SG, TW][IR, His, CuS]

Dellaert, J.E.M.
ISS,BIB Netherlands

Delouche, Prof. G.
LPI France
[TH][Lit, Lin]

Delsol, Ch.
CNRS,MSCH France
[NP, TI][Ant]

Delteil, Dr A.F.
UAM1,ERLAOS,J France
[JP][Lit]

Demetrio, M.
INALCO,PHIL France
[Ant, Arch, His, CuS, AHis]

Demidioek, Dr L.N.
Universitetsky Prospect 4-285
117333 Moscow
Russia
[ID, MY][Lin]

Demidiuk, Dr L.N.
MSU,IAAS,CIBS Russia
[ID][Lin]

Demin, L.M.
Komsomolsky Prospect 23/7
\Flat 27
119146 Moscow
Russia
[BN, ID][His, AHis]

Demmers, S.
Van 't Hoffstraat 39-A
2313 SN Leiden
Netherlands

Deng, T.
ISS Netherlands
[CN, HK, TW][PolS, Soc, DevS, CuS]

Dengel, Dr H.
RKU,SI Germany
[ID, MY, SG][Rel, AHis, Eco, Arch, DevS, His]

Denissov, Dr
RASP,IOS Russia
[JP][Eco]

Deol, Mr J.S.
UC,STC United Kingdom
jod25@com.ac.uk
[IN, PK,][AHis, His, Lit]

Deopik, D.V.
MSU,IAAS,CIBS Russia
[ID, VN][Arch, CuS, Rel, Ant, His]

Derichs, Dr C.
GMU,IO,PS Germany
derichs@uni-duisburg.de
[JP][IR, PolS]

Derks, Dr W.A.G.
IIAS Netherlands
derks@rullet.leidenuniv.nl
[ID, MY][Lit]

Derveld, Dr F.E.R.
RUG,VBE Netherlands
[CN, HK, ID, JP, KR, SG, TW][Eco]

Desai, Prof. M.J.
LSEPS,DE United Kingdom
[BD, BT, IN, NP, PK, LK][DevS, Eco]

Desaintes, Prof. J.
UCL,EU Belgium
desaintes@rehu.ucl.ac.be
[Eco, IR]

Desirat, M.
CNRS,CRLAO France
[CN][Lin]

Despeux-Fays-Long, Prof. C.
INALCO,CIV France
[CN][CuS]

Desroches, J.-P.
MNAAG France
[CN][CuS]

Dessaint, Prof. W.L.
CNRS,CASCIP France
[BT, LA, MM, NP, TH, TI, VN][Ant]

Dessein, Dr B.
RUG,SIN Belgium
[CN][Phi]

Deuchler, Prof. M.
SOAS,CKS United Kingdom
md3@soas.ac.uk
[KR][His]

Deugd, Drs J.E. de
Netherlands

Deuve, J.
LPI France
[LA][His]

Devedjieva, Dr E.
BAS, ICSS Bulgaria
[CN][IR, His, CuS]

Devlet, Dr M.A.
Russia
[Arch]

Dewall, Dr M.V. von
Am Mühlrain 18
69151 Neckargemünd
Germany
[CN, HK, TW, VN][His, CuS, Arch, Ant, AHis]

Dewey, Dr C.J.
United States of America
[IN, PK][His]

Dharampal-Frick, Dr G.
UA,MCH Germany
gita.dharampal-frick@phil.uni-augsburg.de
[IN][Rel, His, Ant]

Dhogon, S.D.
94 Av. Victor Hugo
75016 Paris
France
[TI][Lan]

Diaconscu, Drs B.
Route de Bertigny 16
1700 Fribourg
Switzerland
bogdan.diaconescu@unifr.ch
[IN,][CuS, Lin, Lit, Phi, Psy, Rel]

Diakonova, Dr N.V.
Russia
[AHis, CuS]

Diakov, Dr N.N.
SPU, FOS Russia
[His, PolS, Soc, Rel]

Diana, Dr I.P.F. de
UT,FEST Netherlands
diana@edte.utwente.nl
[CN][Psy, Edu]

Diaz Fernandez, Dr B.A.
UO,FEII Spain
adenso@etsiig.unioui.es
[JP][Eco]

Didier B.A., Drs B.J.
CU,DSA United Kingdom
[IN][Edu, Ant, Phi]

Diemberger, H.
Via Crispi 134
21100 Varese
Italy
[TI][Ant, Phi, Edu]

Dienstag, C.
UP,CREOPS,AA France
[CN][Arch]

Diény, J. P.
11, rue de la Pacaterie
91400 Orsay
France
[CN][His, Lit]

Dietrich, Dr S.
[ID][Ant, Rel, His]

Dietz, Dr A.J.
UvA,VPD Netherlands
[IN][Agr]

Dietz, Dr S.
SW Germany
[TI][Agr]

Diez Faixat, V.
Asturias, 20-5°B
33206 Gijon
Spain
[JP][]

Díez Galán, Dr J.
Santa Inés 4-3°
28012 Madrid
Spain
[CN, IN, JP][AHis, Lit]

Diglio, Prof. S.
UIO,DAS Italy
[MY][IR, Eco, DevS, CuS]

Dijk, Drs T. van
Jac. van Deventerstraat 23
7412 ES Deventer
Netherlands
[ID][His, Rel, AHis, Ant]

Dijk, Drs W.O.
Rigolettostraat 18
2555 VS The Hague
Netherlands
[CN, IN, JP, KR, MM,][Rel, CuS, His, Lin]

Dijk, Prof. dr C. van
KITLV Netherlands
[ID, MY][His, Rel]

Dijkman, K.
RUL,TCJK Netherlands
dijkman@rullet.leidenuniv.nl

Dijksterhuis, C.
Hoofdstraat 25
9921 PA Stedum
Netherlands
[ID, PK][GenS, Ant, CuS, Soc]

Dijkstra, Drs G.H.
GDH Netherlands
[CN, HK, IN, ID, JP, KR, PI, PH, SG, LK, TW][Soc, Rel, Phi, Eco, His, IR, Psy, PolS]

Dikarev, Dr A.D.
RASP,IOS Russia
[CN][His]

Dikötter, Dr F.
SOAS,DH United Kingdom
[CN][His, CuS]

Dinety, J.-C.
UMMB,DEEO,DU France
[CN][Geo]

Dinh, T.H.
UP7,UAO France
[VN][Soc]

Dinkevich, Dr A.I.
RASP,IOS Russia
[JP][Eco]

Dirkse, Drs J.P.
Min.BuZa Netherlands
[CuS, DevS, IR, His, AHis]

Dirkzwager, Drs M.H.
HKI,BIB Netherlands
[ID][Ant]

Dishoeck, Drs E.R. van
RUL, BB Netherlands
[CN, , JP, MO, SG, LK, TW][Eco, Edu, Phi, CuS]

Dixon, Dr C.J.
CLP,LG,DG,CH United Kingdom
c-dixon@tvax.lgu.ac.uk
[LA, MY, PH, SG, TH, VN][Geo]

Djajadiningrat-Nieuwenhuis, Drs M.
FNI Netherlands
[ID][His, GenS, Ant, IR]

Djajasoebrata, Drs A.M.L.R.
MVROT Netherlands
[ID][Ant, AHis]

Djalili, Dr M.R.
GIIS,IHP Switzerland
[AF, IR, KZ, TJ, TM, UZ][CuS, Soc, His, IR, DevS, PolS]

Djamouri, Dr R.
CNRS,CRLAO France
djamouri@ehess.fr
[CN][Lin]

Djindjian, F.
CNRS,AAC France
[Arch]

Djumaini, Dr M.
Douwes Dekkerstraat 63
2273 SP Voorburg
Netherlands
[ID][PolS, Law]

Djurfeldt, Dr G.
LU,DS Sweden
Goran.djurfeldt@soc.lu.se
[IN, LA][Soc, Agr, DevS]

Dobbelaer, R.
BAMEP France

Dobronravin, Dr N.A.
SPU,FOS,DAS Russia
[KZ, MG, SC, TJ, TM][Lin, Rel, Lit, His, Ant]

Dobrovits, Drs M.A.
ELU,DJS Hungary
[AF, KZ, MN, TJ, TI, TM, UZ][Rel, Lit, CuS, His, Ant]

Doderlein de Win, E.F.
SEASP Netherlands
[BN, ID, MY, PH, SG, TH, VN][Law, IR, Edu, Eco, Agr, DevS]

Dodin, T.
UB,ZA Germany
dodin@uni-bonn-de
[BT, NP, TI][Phi, Lit, Rel, Soc, Lin, IR, His, Ant, DevS, CuS, PolS]

Doel, Dr H.W. van den
RUL,VG Netherlands
vddoel@Rullet.LeidenUniv.nl
[ID][His]

Doering, Drs O.
IAA Germany
ifahh@ttz.uni-hamburg.de
[CN, HK, TW][Phi]

Dol, Drs P.H.
RUL,TCZOAO,PD Netherlands
phdol@rullet.leidenuniv.nl
[ID][Lin]

Dolce, Dr L.D.M.
RUL,TCJK Netherlands
dolce@rullet.leidenuniv.nl
[JP][CuS, Rel, Phi]

Dolcini, Dr D.M.
UM,IFL Italy
[IN][His, Lin, Lit, Rel, CuS]

Dolin, Dr A.A.
RASP,IOS Russia
[JP][Lit]

Dolinski, M.
UAM1,LSH France
[CN][Lan]

Dolk, Dr E.C.
UP7,FEG,DEN France
[ID, MY][Lit, His]

Dollfus, P.
CNRS,MSCH France
[NP, TI][Ant]

Dolnikova, Dr V.A.
MSU,IAAS,CIBS Russia
[TH][His]

Domenach, Dr J.L.
FNSP France
[CN, JP, TW][IR, PolS]

Domenig, Ir G.
RUL,CA/SNWS Netherlands
domenig@rulfsw.leidenuniv.nl
[ID, JP][Rel]

Domes, Prof. dr J.
US,IP Germany
[CN, HK, MO, TW, TH][Soc, PolS, DevS]

Dommanget, F.
74 rue Nationale
75013 Paris
France
[DevS, PolS, Soc]

Domroes, Prof. dr M.R.J.
JGU,DG Germany
[IN, LK][Agr, Geo, Env]

Donald, S.
USUS,MS United Kingdom
[CN, HK, TW][PolS, GenS, CuS, His, AHis]

Dong, C.
NIAS Denmark
Dong@coco.ihi.ku.dk
[CN][Soc]

Dongen, Drs A.M. van
IME Netherlands
[CN, ID][Ant]

Dongen, Drs P.L.F. van
RMV Netherlands
[CN, HK, SG, TW, VN][His, Ant, AHis]

Donker Duyvis, Drs P.
Haarlemmerdijk 7
1013 JZ Amsterdam
Netherlands
[CN, HK, JP, KR, TW][AHis, Arch, Ant, His]

Donkers, J.K.J.
MF Netherlands
[ID][AHis, Ant, Arch]

Doop, J.V.
RUL,VTW Netherlands
[ID][Lin]

Doornbos, Prof. dr M.R.
ISS Netherlands
doornbos@iss.nl
[IN, PI,][DevS, PolS, Soc]

Doortmont, Dr M.R.
RUG,VG Netherlands
m.r.doortmont@let.rug.nl
[ID][His]

Dor, Prof. Dr R
INALCO,CGD France
dor@moh.paris.fr

Dore, A.
CNRS,CASCIP France
[CN, LA, TH][DevS, CuS, Ant]

Dorofeeva, Dr T.V.
MSU,IAAS,DSEAP Russia
[ID, MY][Edu, Lin]

Dorofeeva-Lichtmann, Dr V.V.
RAS,IOS,AL Russia
[CN][Geo, CuS, His]

Dosch, Drs J.
JGU,IP Germany
[ID, MY, PH, SG, TH][IR, PolS]

Douglas, Prof. M.
UCL,DA United Kingdom

Dournon, Dr G.
CNRS,EM France
[IN][AntAnt]

Douw, Dr L.M.
UvA,MAG Netherlands
douwl@jet.let.vu.nl
[CN][CuS, IR, Soc, Ant, His, DevS]

Douwes, Dr D.
RUL,TCZOAO,PD
Netherlands
Douwes@rullet.leidenuniv.nl
[ID][His, Rel]

Dr¡nek, Dr V.
Europsk 674/156
16000 Prague 6
Czech Republic
[CN, HK, MO, TW][IR]

Draguhn, Dr W.
DUI Germany
ifahh.draguhn@rrz.uni-hamburg.de
[CN, IN, ID, JP, MY, SG, TW, TH, VN][PolS, IR, Eco, DevS]

Drakakis-Smith, Prof. D.
LUI,FSES,DG United Kingdom
drakis@liverpool.ac.uk
[HK, LA, MY, SG, VN][DevS]

Drège, Prof. J.-P.
CNRS,EPHE France
[CN][CuS, His, Edu]

Drexler, Christian
Hellweg 28-30
44787 Bochum
Germany
[CN, HK,][His, Lit]

Driem, Dr G.L. van
RUL,VTW Netherlands
driem@rullet.leidenuniv.nl
[BT, CN, IN, NP, SM, TI][DevS, Lin, Ant, His]

Driessen, Drs B.
Overtoom 390
1054 JS Amsterdam
Netherlands
[CN, HK][Edu, CuS]

Driessen, Drs J.M.C.
Van Vollenhovenlaan 213
3527 JE Utrecht
Netherlands
[IN][Psy, Lit, Lin]

Drifte, Prof. R.
UNC,EAC United Kingdom
r.f.w.drifte@newcastle.ac.uk
[JP][PolS, IR]

Drint, Drs A.
Netherlands
[Lin]

Drocourt, Z.T.
INALCO France
[CN][Lin]

Drooglever, Prof. dr P.J.
Netherlands
pieter.drooglever@inghist.nl
[ID][PolS, IR, His]

Drugov, Dr A.Y.
RAS,IOS,AL Russia
[ID][PolS, IR]

Druijven, Dr P.C.J.
RUG,FRW Netherlands
p.c.j.druyven@frw.rug.nl
[CN, IN, PH,][Geo, Env, Agr, DevS]

Dryburgh, Dr M.E.
USH,EARS United Kingdom
m.e.dryburgh@sheffield.ac.uk
[CN, JP][His]

Dubanchet, R.
31 La Roseraie \12 avenue de Porchefontaine
78000 Versailles
France
[His]

Dubbeldam, Prof. dr L.F.B.
NUFFIC,DESC Netherlands
cesosecr@nufficcs.nl
[CN, ID, PH, TH][Ant, Edu]

Dubianski, Prof. A.M.
[IN,][Ant, Lit, Rel]

Duc-Reynaert, M.J.
UG,MARC Switzerland
[KH][Edu, Ant]

Ducaru, S.
KCL,CNR,JNRP United Kingdom
s.ducaru@kcl.ac.uk
[JP][GenS, Ant, Rel]

Ducor, Dr J.
EM,A Switzerland
jerome.ducor@ville.ge.ch
[CN, IN, JP, MN, NP, TI][Rel, Ant, GenS]

Dudbridge, Prof. G.
ICS United Kingdom
dudbridge@vax.ox.ac.uk
[CN][Rel, Ant, GenS]

Dudink, Dr A.C.
KUL,SIN Belgium
[CN][Rel, His]

Dudrah, R.K.
UB,DCS United Kingdom
r.kumar.1@bham.ac.uk
[BD, IN, PK, LK][CuS, Soc]

Duermeijer, Ir A.J.
Wim Sonneveldlaan 137
3584 ZR Utrecht
Netherlands
[ID, MY, NP, PK, PH, SG, LK, TH][AHis, Arch, DevS]

Dumas, Drs R.M.
A. Paulownastraat 2-A
2316 NP Leiden
Netherlands
[ID, MY, SG, TH][PArt, Lit, CuS]

Dumont, Prof. R.
2, Avenue Pres. Roosevelt
94120 Fontenay sur Bois
France
[BD, CN, IN, VN][Agr, Env, DevS]

Dumont, Prof. L.
UL3,CREO France
[IN][His]

Dumont, M.
CNRS,EHESS France
[Lit, PArt, CuS]

Dumoulin-Genest, M.-P.
20, rue de Grenelle
75007 Paris
France
[CN][His]

Dunand, F.
BC Switzerland
[CN, JP, KR][His, AHis]

Dundas, Drs P.
UE,DS United Kingdom
P.dundas@ed.ac.uk
[IN][Lit, His, Lin]

Dung, Drs T.T.
INALCO,VIET France
[LA, PI, VN][Rel, Lin, Edu, Ant, CuS]

Dungkar Lobzang, T.
Rue Goffart 1
1050 Brussel
Belgium
[TI][Lin, Rel, Edu, Ant, CuS]

Dunham, Dr D.M.
ISS Netherlands
[IN, LK][CuS, DevS, Agr]

Dunn, Prof. J.M
KCL,DG United Kingdom
[KH, JP, MY, TH, VN][PolS]

Dunn, Mr A.J-J.
23 St. Peter's Street \Islington-Angel
N1 8JP London
United Kingdom
[KH, JP, MY, TH, VN][IR, Edu, CuS, Ant]

Duppel-Takayama, Drs M.
Lenaustrasse 91
60318 Frankfurt
Germany
[JP][Lit]

Durand, Dr F.B.
UTM,GA France
[KH, ID, MY, VN][Env, Agr, Lit, DevS]

Durand-Daste, Mr F.
UL3,CREO France
[IN][Geo]

Durand-Dastès, V.
BILO France
[CN][Lit]

Durey, Ms.
MBAPSP France
[JP, KR][His, AHis]

Dürr, Prof. dr H.B.
RUB,GI Germany
[ID][Ant, Env, DevS, Soc, PolS, CuS]

Durrans, Dr B.
BM,MM United Kingdom
b.durrans@mailbox.ulcc.ac.uk
[ID][CuS, Ant]

Dury, Drs S.
INRA,ESR France
dury@msdos.montpellier.inra.fr
[ID][Agr, Eco]

Dusseldorp, D.B.W.M. van
RAWOO Netherlands
[ID, NP, PH, LK][Ant, Agr, DevS, PolS, Soc]

Dutrait, N.
UAM1,LSH France
[CN, HK, TW][Lit]

Dutta, S.
INSEAD,EAC,BIB France
[IN][Lit]

Duuren, Drs D.A.P. van
KIT,TM Netherlands
[ID, PG][Ant, CuS]

Duus, K.D.
RU,IIDS Denmark
[NP][His, DevS, PolS, Soc, CuS]

Duxbury, Drs K.E.
Brooke House \Ashdon Road
CB10 ZAA Saffron Waldon, Essex
United Kingdom
[CN][PolS]

Duy-Tu, Prof. dr V.
UHAM,SKC,VIET Germany
[VN][Lit, Lin, His]

Duyker, Drs M.
S. van Drielstraat 13
2435 XP Zevenhoven
Netherlands
[ID][Arch]

Dvorak, Drs J.
CU,FF,IND Czech Republic
Dvorakj@dec59.ruk.cuni.cz
[IN, LK][Lit, Lin]

Dwyer, Prof. D.J.
KU,DG United Kingdom
[CN, HK, MY][DevS]

Dwyer, Dr R.M.J.
SOAS,DSA United Kingdom
rd3@soas.ac.uk
[IN][Lit, Lin, CuS]

Dybo, Dr Prof. A. V.
RAS,IL Russia
dybo@iling.msc.su
[JP, KZ, KG, MN, CN, TJ, TM][Ant, Lin]

Dyck, A.M. van
59 rue de la Chine
75020 Paris
France
[DevS]

Dylykova, Dr V.S.
RASP,IOS Russia
[TI][Lit]

Dyson, Prof. T.P.G.
LSEPS,DPS United Kingdom
t.dyson@lse.ac.uk
[IN][DevS, Agr]

Ebbatson, Dr P.
Gussau 33
22359 Hamburg
Germany
[IN, NP, LK, TI][Lin, Rel, Phi, Lit]

Eberspaecher, Drs C.
Hundsmuehler Str. 68
26131 Oldenburg
Germany
[CN, JP][PolS, His]

Eberstein, Prof. dr B.
UHAM,SKC,KTV Germany
[CN, HK, TW][Lit, Eco]

Ebner von Eschenbach, Dr S.
UW,IS Germany
[CN][His, Ant, Rel]

Ebsen, Drs L.
Marstalsgade 17, 4.th.
2100 Copenhagen 0
Denmark
[JP][Edu]

Eches, R.
Saint-Honest \Appartment 25 \37 Boulevard Matabiau
31000 Toulouse
France
[Edu]

Edelman, Dr J.I.
IL,DEAL Russia
[TJ][Lin]

Eden, Dr N.A.S.W.
GU,DEH Sweden
[BD, IN, PK][His, IR, Rel, His, DevS, Agr, Ant]

Edmonds, Dr R.L.
SOAS,CCI United Kingdom
[CN, HK, JP, MO, TW][Env, Geo]

Edouard, N.
1, rue du Pont-de-Lodi
75006 Paris
France
[IN][Lin, Rel]

Edström, Dr B.
SU,CPAS Sweden
bert.edstrom@orient.su.se
[JP][IR]

Edwards, C.L.C.
VA United Kingdom
[JP][AHis, CuS]

Eeuwijk, Drs P. van
UB,ES Switzerland
[ID, PG][Ant]

Efimova, Prof. L.
MSIIR,DOS Russia
[ID, MY][His, Rel, PolS]

Egden, S.E.
UO,FSS,SA Norway
[IN][Ant]

Egenter, Ir N.
DOFSBT Switzerland
negenter@worldcom.ch
[IN, JP][Rel, Ant, CuS, His, AHis]

Eggers-Lura, A.M.A.E.
Nygade 71
4690 Haslev
Denmark
[TH][His]

Eggert, Dr M.
LMU,IOAK Germany
ucc02bd@sunmail.lrf.muenchen.de
[CN][Lit, CuS]

Egorin, Prof. A.Z.
RAS,IOS,DHO Russia
[His]

Ehmcke, Prof. dr F.
UK,OS,AJ Germany
[JP][Rel, Soc, His, CuS, Phi, Lit]

Ehrensperger, A.
CS Switzerland
albi@gfeu.unibe.ch
[ID, LA][Ant, Env]

Ehrhard, Drs F.K.
WWUM,II Germany
[NP, TI][Rel, Phi, Lit, CuS]

Ehrlich, Prof. E.
HAS,IWF,JESRC Hungary
h10760ehv@ella.hu
[CN, HK, ID, JP, KR, MY, SG, TW, TH, VN][Eco, DevS]

Eichenberger, C.A.
UB,ES Switzerland
[PI, UZ][CuS, Ant, Soc]

Eichinger Ferro-Luzzi, Dr G.
UIO,DAS Italy
[IN][CuS, Ant, Lit, Rel]

Eichner, U.
Adolf-Wagner Str. 36
41063 Munichgladbach
Germany
[CN, JP, KR][AHis]

Eifring, Prof. H.
UO,FA,EOS Norway
Halvore@hedda.uio.no
[CN, TW][Lit, Lin, CuS]

Eigenhuijsen, J.Th.N.
Prolan Netherlands
[CN, HK, ID, KR][Eco]

Eijnsbergen, E. van
JVBD Netherlands
[JP][AHis, Lin]

Eikemeier, Prof. dr D.
EKUT,SSK Germany
[KR][His, Rel, Ant, CuS, Lit]

Eimer, Dr H.
UB,SI Germany
[IN, NP, LK, TI][Lit, His]

Eindhoven, Drs J.D.R.
UvA,ISA,CC Netherlands
eindhoven@pscw.uva.nl
[ID][IR]

Eisenbruch, M.
CNRS,CASCIP France
ime@msh-paris.fr
[KH][Psy, Ant]

Eisma, Prof. dr D.
NISR Netherlands
[CN, ID][Env]

Ekstrand, Prof. L.H.
DEPR,SE Sweden
[IN][Psy, DevS, CuS]

Elands, Drs M.
KMM Netherlands
[ID][IR, His]

Elbers, Dr C.T.M.
VU,VOAE Netherlands
elbers@econ.vu.nl
[ID, NP][Eco]

Elías de Tejada Lozano, Diplomat F.

[AF, CN, HK, IN, ID, JP, MY, PK, PH, SG, TH, VN][Eco, Lit, PolS]

Eliasson, Prof. S.S.E.
JGU,IAVS Germany
Eliasson@mzdmza.zdv.uni-mainz.de
[PI][Lin]

Eliëns, Prof. dr T.M.
FHM Denmark
[CN, JP][AHis]

Elisséeff, Dr D.
CNRS,CEIAS France
[CN, JP][Arch, His, AHis]

Elizalde Perez-Grueso, Dr D.
UCSIC, CEH, DHMC Spain
[JP, PI, PH][His, IR]

Elkanidze, Dr M.M.
RAS,IOS,AL Russia
[IN, LK][Arch, His, Phi, Psy, Ant, His, Rel, Soc, AHis, CuS]

Ellen, Prof. R.F.
UK,EC,DSSA United Kingdom
rfe@ukc.ac.uk
[BN, ID, PG][Env, Ant]

Elliott, D.
MMAO United Kingdom
[CN, IN, ID, JP, TW, TH][AHis]

Ellis, Dr S.D.K.
RUL,ASC Netherlands
[MG][His]

Ellman, Prof. dr M.J.
FIS Netherlands
Ellman@fee.uva.nl
[VN][Eco, DevS]

Elorza Domíngoez, Antonio
UCM,PS Spain
[PolS]

Elsenhans, Prof. dr H.
UL,IP Germany
helsen@server1.rz.uni-leipzig.de
[BD, IN][DevS]

Emelianenko, Dr T.G.

[UZ, TJ][Ant]

Emmer, Prof. dr P.C.
RUL,VG Netherlands
Emmer@Rullet.LeidenUniv.Nl
[HK, IN, ID, PI,][His]

Emst, Dr P. van
De Hooghlaan 2
3723 GS Bilthoven
Netherlands
[ID][Ant, His]

Engel, Drs M. van den
Netherlands

Engelbert, Dr J.T.
HUB,AA,SOA Germany
thomasengelbertsuedostasien@hub-afrikaasien
[KH, VN][His, IR]

Engelenhoven, Dr A.Th.P.G. van
RUL,TCZOAO Netherlands
engelenhoven@rullet.leidenuniv.nl
[ID][Lin]

Engelfriet, Drs P.M.
Rooseveltlaan 53-2
1079 AD Amsterdam
Netherlands
[CN, TW][His]

Engelhardt, Dr I.
Fuchsbichl 22-A
82057 Icking
Germany
[TI][His]

Enghardt, F.C.A
Prinsegracht 61
2512 EX The Hague
Netherlands

Enk, E.M.C. van
Paulus Potterstraat 27
7204 CP Zutphen
Netherlands
[ID][His]

Ensering, Drs E.
Langswater 239
1069 TS Amsterdam
Netherlands
[ID][Rel, His, Soc]

Enskat, Drs M.
RKU,SI Germany
[IN][DevS, PolS]

Epskamp, Dr C.P.
NUFFIC,DESC Netherlands
[ID, TH][AHis, Ant]

Eriksson, Drs I.E.
Dalagatan 35A
11323 Stockholm
Sweden
[LA][DevS]

Ermakov, Dr M.E.
RASP,IOS,DSSEAS Russia
[Lit, Rel]

Ermakova, Dr T.V.
RASP,IOS,DSSEAS Russia
[TI][CuS, Rel]

Erpecum, I.L. van
MIN,J Netherlands
[IN, ID][Lit, Law, CuS, AHis]

Erve, Dr H.J. van der
VU,DOS,PI Netherlands
[ID][Ant, Soc]

Es, Dr A.J.H. van
Westkaap 16
8224 EE Lelystad
Netherlands
[CN, HK, IN, ID, KZ, KR, TW, TI][Agr]

Escaich, J.C.
47 rue Marx Dormoy
75018 Paris
France
[Agr]

Eschbach-Szabo, Prof. V.A.
EKUT,JAP Germany
eschbach
japanologie@mailserv.zdv.uni-tuebing
[JP][Lin, His, CuS, Phi, Ant]

Esche, Dr A.
Immersee Str. 2
1570 Potsdam
Germany
[MM][Lin, Lit]

Escurriola Sans, Jordi
Avgda. Meridiana, 320 -5è.5ª
08027 Barcelona
Spain
[JP, MY, PI,][His, Lin, Lit, Phi, Soc]

Esmein, Dr J.C.
CFJM France
[JP][Eco]

Esparrago Rodilla MA, Luis
CSCC,CEHC Spain
[CN, HK, IN, MO, TW, VN][Agr, PolS]

Esperança, J.P.
UL,FL,TA Portugal

Esposito, Dr M.
UV,DSIEO Italy
[CN][Rel]

Etienne, Prof. G.
UG,MARC Switzerland
Etienne@hei.unige.ch
[AF, BD, AF, BD, CN, IN, PK,][His, Agr, Eco, PolS, DevS]

Etty, Drs B.
MIN,OCW,OWB Netherlands
[CN][IR]

Evans, Dr K.K.
UL,DRS United Kingdom
[BD, CN, IN, PK, LK, TI][AHis, Rel, GenS, His]

Evans, Dr H.
UWE,CS United Kingdom
[CN][GenS, His]

Even, M.-D.
INALCO France
[MM, TI][His, GenS]

Everding, K.-H.
Mirecourt Str. 2
53225 Bonn
Germany
[TI][GenS, His]

Evers, Drs B.H.
KUB, IVO Netherlands
[BD, CN, PK, TJ][DevS, Env, Eco, Agr]

Evers, Drs S.J.Th.M.
Burg. van Leeuwenlaan 72-4
1064 KZ Amsterdam
Netherlands
[MG][Ant]

Everts, Drs N.
RUL,VG Netherlands
everts@rullet.leidenuniv.nl
[TW][His]

Evison, Dr G.A.
OU,IIBIB,BBIB United Kingdom
gae@bodley.ox.ac.uk
[His]

Ewers, K.
Sten 4-1 \Galgebaken
2620 Albertslund
Denmark
[BD, IN, LA, MM, NP, TH, VN][Ant, Env, DevS]

Eyck van Heslinga, Dr E.S. van
NSMA Netherlands
[ID][His]

Eykhoff, P.
TUE Netherlands
P.Eykhoff@ele.tue.nl
[CN][His]

Eyre, Dr A.
CU, SBE United Kingdom
[MY][Rel, Soc]

Fabre, Prof. A.J.J.
INALCO,JK France
[JP, KR][Lin, Lit]

Fabre, Prof. G.F.
UH,FAI France
[CN][CuS, Env, Eco, DevS, Soc]

Faccaro, F.
UF,IGOLT Italy
[JP][Lit]

Fadeeva, Dr E.Y.
RAS,IFES,FEB Russia
titarenk@ifes.msk.su
[CN, HK, TW][Phi, Soc, CuS, Rel, Lit]

Fahner, Dr Chr.
Arnhemseweg 66
6739 BT Otterlo
Netherlands
[ID][Ant, Rel, Lin]

Faircloth, Drs A.L.
Fiolstr'de 36 A, 2
1171 Copenhagen K
Denmark
[PG][Ant]

Falk, Prof. dr H.
FUB,AW,IPKG Germany
Falk@zedat.fu-berlin.de
[IN][CuS, Lit, Rel]

Fan, F.
INALCO France
[CN][Lit]

Fang, Dr S.-S.
TRO,CD Belgium
[CN, HK, SG, TW][CuS, Edu]

Fanger, E.-B.
Oscars Ellingersvej 8
2000 Frederiksberg
Denmark
[Edu, CuS]

Fanin, C.
Via G. Pascoli 10
00040 Lavinio/Anzio (RM)
Italy
[CN, JP][IR, Lin, His, Lit]

Fanjul, Dr E.
ITR Spain
efanjul@tecnicasreunidas.es
[CN][Eco]

Fanjuz Martin, E.
ITR Spain
[CN][Eco]

Farizov, Prof.dr I.O.
MSU,IAAS,CIBS Russia
[IN][Ant, DevS, His, IR, Lin]

Farooqi, Drs K.H.
ISS Netherlands
[AF, PK,][Rel, CuS, Soc, His, GenS, Env, DevS]

Fasseur, Prof. dr C.
RUL,TCZOAO Netherlands
Fasseur@Rullet.LeidenUniv.nl
[ID][His]

Faure, Dr G.L.
CNRS,IAO France
Guy.faure@mrash.fr
[JP][PolS, Eco]

Faure, Dr D.W.
ICS United Kingdom
faure@server.orient.ox.ac.uk
[CN][His]

Faust, Dr H.
GAUG,GI Germany
hfaust@gwdg.de
[IN, PI][DevS, CuS]

Fauzia, Drs A.
Rijnsburgerweg 124
2333 AG Leiden
Netherlands
[ID][His]

Fava, P.
44, rue Vivienne
75002 Paris
France
[CN, JP, TI][Psy, Lit, CuS, Ant, His, Arch, AHis, Soc, Rel, Phi]

Favre-Le Van Ho, M.
72 rue de Tolbiac
75013 Paris
France
[Ant, Rel, Psy, Phi, Soc, CuS, Arch, AHis, Lit, His]

Feddema, Drs R.
UvA,MAG Netherlands
[KH, KR, VN][PolS, IR, His, Eco]

Fédensieu, Dr A.
UNSA,LSH,E France
[ID][Ant]

Federlein, Drs D.
Wichernstrasse 18
91052 Erlangen
Germany
[, CN, HK, JP, MO, MN, TW, TI][His, Lin, Rel]

Fedorenko, Dr N.T.
RASP,IOS Russia
[CN][Lit]

Fedotoff, Prof. dr A.
US,COLC Bulgaria
[BT, CN, IN, KR, MN, NP, SM, TI][Rel, Lit, CuS]

Feillard, Drs A.
CNRS,CEIAS France
[BN, ID, MY][IR, GenS, His, Soc, PolS, Rel, Eco]

Feistel, Dr H.O.
SBIBB,OA Germany
[IN, MM,][CuS, Lit, Rel, Lin]

Felber, Prof. R.
HUB,AA,IS Germany
[CN][PolS, CuS, IR, His]

Feldbaek, Prof. O.
UC,IEH Denmark
[PolS, CuS, His, IR]

Fendler, Dr K.
IOCFT Hungary
[KR][His, PolS, IR, Eco]

Fenés Folch, E.
Av. Sant Jordi, 33-7-4
43201 Reus
Spain
[JP][DevS]

Feoktistov, Dr V.F.
RAS,IFES,FEB Russia
[CN][Phi]

Ferdinand, Drs C.I.P.
UWA,DPIS United Kingdom
posan@csv.warwick.ac.uk
[CN, HK, ID, JP, KZ, KR, MY, TJ, TW, TH, TM,][PolS, DevS, His, Eco, IR]

Ferdinand, K.
AU,FH,DESA Denmark
[AF, MN, PK][DevS, Ant, CuS]

Feriyanto, F.
Goeman Gorgesiuslaan 16-I
3515 ES Utrecht
Netherlands
[ID][His, AHis]

Ferlus, M.
CNRS,CRLAO France
ferlus@crlao.msh-paris.fr
[KH, CN, LA, MY, MM, TH, VN][Lin]

Fernandez Lommen, Dr Y.
CERI Spain
[CN, MN][Eco]

Fernández Miguélez, J.
Luis Buñuel, 12, 6°B
28038 Madrid
Spain
[CN, HK, IN, JP, KZ, KG, MY, PH: SG, SOUTHEASTASIA,][IR]

Fernández Salido, J.M.
Av. Visley, 21
11407 Jerez
Spain
salido@mura.comp.kyutech.ac.jp
[JP][]

Fernandez-Del-Campo Barbadillo, E.
UCM, GH,HAC Spain
[IN, PK,][AHis]

Fernández-Shaw Baldasano, C.M.
Claudio Coello 60
28001 Madrid
Spain
[ID, PI, PG, PH,][]

Ferraro, Dr F.
UIO,DAS Italy
[AF, IR, PK, TJ][Lin, Ant]

Ferro Payero, M.J.
UCM, GH,HAC Spain
[IN,][AHis, His]

Fessen-Henjes, Dr I.
Murtzaner Ring 17
12681 Berlin
Germany
[CN, TI][Lit, CuS]

Fets, K.A.
RASP,IOS Russia
[IN][His, PolS]

Feuchtwang, Dr S.
LCU,DS,CRU United Kingdom
s.feuchtwang@city.ac.uk
[CN, TW][Ant, Soc, Rel, His, DevS, CuS, PolS]

Fiévé, Dr N.B.
CNRS,CJ France
nfieve@docsrvr.mrash.fr
[JP][Ant, His, Rel, Soc, CuS, DevS, PolS]

Figuière, C.
CNRS,IAO France
[JP][Eco]

Fijneman, Drs Y.
Karmelietenstraat 36
5042 BE Tilburg
Netherlands
[IN][Psy, DevS]

Filimonova, T.N.
MSU,IAAS,DSEAP Russia
[VN][Lin, Lit]

Filippini, Prof. C.M.
UC,ISESAO Italy
[JP][Eco]

Filipsky, Dr I.
ASCR,OI Czech Republic
filipsky@orient.cas.cz
[IN, LK][Rel, Lin, His]

Filliozat, J.
EFEO,BIB France
[KH, IN, LA, MM, LK, TH][Rel, Lit]

Findeisen, Dr R.D.
UZ,AS,OS Switzerland
RDF@oas.unizh.ch
[CN, HK, JP, TW][Phi, GenS, Lit]

Fisac Badell, Dr T.
UAM,CEAO Spain
tfisac@ccuam3.sdi.uam.es
[CN, TW][Lit, GenS]

Fischer, Dr P.
SBIBB,OA Germany
[CN, JP][His, Rel]

Fischer, D.
GMU,IO,E Germany
hg460fi@unidui.uni-duisburg.de
[CN, HK, TW][PolS, Eco]

Flacelière, M.-H.
UAM1,LSH France
[IN][Lin]

Fleetwood, J.E.V.
SJFRD Sweden
[JP][Eco, Edu]

Fleming, Prof. D.E.B.
RU,IIDS Denmark
fleming@iv.ruc.dk
[ID, MY, SG][Soc, DevS]

Flessel, Prof. dr K.
FAU,IASK,SJ Germany
fp151@fim.uni-erlangen.de
[CN, TW][Soc, Lin, His, CuS]

Flitsch, Dr M.
FUB,OS Germany
[CN][Agr, CuS, Ant, Rel]

Flood, Dr G.D.
UWL,DTRIS United Kingdom
floodg@lampeter.ac.uk
[IN][CuS, Rel]

Flores, Dr J.
ULU,DRI Portugal
[HK, MO, LK][His, IR]

Flüchter, Prof. dr W.
GMU,IO,G Germany
w.fleuchter@uni-duisburg.de
[CN, HK, JP, KR, MO, SG, TW, TI][Geo, Env]

Foekema, Drs G.M.M.
Wouwermanstraat 38
1071 MA Amsterdam
Netherlands
[IN][Arch, His, AHis]

Folch Fornes, Dr D.
UPF, FH Spain
folch@upf.es or eo@upf.es
[CN][His]

Fold, N.F.
UC, CIG Denmark
nf@geogr.ku.dk
[MY][DevS]

Foljanty-Jost, Prof. dr G.

MLU,HPS,JAP Germany
foljanty-jost@japanologie.uni-halle.de
[JP][PolS, Env]

Fomicheva, Dr M.F.

[TH][Lin]

Fomicheva, Dr Y.A.

RASP,IOS Russia
[TH][PolS, IR]

Fomina, Dr N.I.

RASP,IOS Russia
[CN][His]

Fontinelle, Dr J. de la

E12 "Les Grandes Coudraies"
91190 Gif-sur-Yvette
France
[Lin]

Foot, Dr R.J.

OU,FOS,ICS United Kingdom
rosemary.foot@sant.ox.ac.uk
[CN, KR, TW][IR]

Fóray, Dr J.-C.

INSERM France
feray@univ-paris12.fr
[LA, TH, VN][Lin, His]

Ford, Dr N.J.

UEX,DG United Kingdom
[ID, MY, PH, TH][Geo, GenS, DevS, CuS]

Forest, Dr A.

LPI France
[KH, TH, VN][His, Rel]

Forest, Drs M.H.

SP,IO Finland
Merja.Forest@cc.spt.fi
[KR][Lin]

Forfar, D.J.

UES,DS United Kingdom
[CN, JP, KR][Ant, Soc, CuS, Rel]

Formanek, S.

OAW,IKGA Austria
formanek@oeaw.ac.at
[JP][Rel, CuS, His, Lit]

Formoso, Dr B.

UP10,LESC France
[CN, LA][Rel, Soc, Ant]

Forrer, Dr M.

RMV Netherlands
[JP][AHis]

Forssman, Prof. dr B.

FAU,IVIS Germany
[IN, IR,][Lin]

Fortin, N.

5 rue Thouin
75005 Paris
France
[Lin]

Fossati, Prof. G.

UG,IMMAH Italy
[CN, JP][His, AHis]

Fosse, Drs L.M.

UO,FA,EOS Norway
fosse@hedda.uio.no
[IN][Lin, Lit]

Foucher, Dr M.

EG France
[IN, PK, SG,][IR, PolS, Eco]

Fouquin, M.F.

France
m.fouquin@cep11.fr
[HK, ID, JP, KR, MY, SG, TW, TH][Eco]

Fourcade, Dr M.

UL3,CREO France
[IN][His, GenS]

Fourniau, Prof. Ch.

CNRS,IRSEA France
[VN][His]

Fourniau, C.

INALCO France
[GenS, His]

Fournié, Prof. M.

INALCO,CRI France
fournie@citi2.fr
[His]

Fradera, Dr J.M.

UPF, FH Spain
[PH][His]

Fradera Barceló, J.N.

UPF, FH Spain
[PH][His]

Fragner, Prof. B.G.

OFU,IR Germany
bert.fragner@split.uni-bamberg.de
[AF, IR, KZ, TJ, TM, UZ][Lin, Lit, His, CuS]

Francfort, H.P.

CNRS,AAC France
francfor@centrasie.msh-paris.fr
[AF, KZ, TJ, TM, UZ][Arch]

Francis, Mr.S.

27 Whitehall Gardens
\Chiswick
W4 3LT London
United Kingdom
[BN][His, DevS, IR]

Francisco, E.

INALCO France
[PH][IR, DevS, His]

Franck, M.

23, Rue de Cronstadt
75015 Paris
France
[ID][Geo]

Francois, Dr I.M.

France
[KH][IR, PolS]

Frank, Drs E.

HIS Netherlands
[IN, ID][Eco, Soc]

Frank, B.

CNRS,JAP France
[JP][Lit]

Franke, Prof. dr H.

BAWS,KZAS Germany
[CN][His]

Franke, Prof. dr W.

Carl-Heinr.-Becker-Weg 12
12165 Berlin
Germany
[CN, ID, MY, SG, TH][His, Rel]

Frankenhauser, Dr U.

GAUG,STZA Germany
[CN, MN, TW][Phi, CuS, His, Rel]

Franse-Hagenbeek, A.A.

Koraalstraat 6-C
6217 EM Maastricht
Netherlands
[CN, HK, TW][Lin]

Frasch, Drs T.

RKU,SI,AG Germany
[IN, MM, LK][His]

Fraser, Prof. T.G.

NUU,CDH United Kingdom
tg.fraser@ulst.ac.uk
[IN][His]

Frederic, L.F.

54 rue des Roses
94520 Perigny
France
[BT, KH, CN, IN, ID, JP, KR, MM, TI][AHis, CuS, Arch, Rel, His]

Freedman, Prof.dr L.A.

MSU,IAAS,CIBS Russia
[DevS, Eco, Ant, His, Soc]

Freitag, Dr G.J.

HUB,AA,SOA Germany
[IN][Eco]

French, Mr P.R.

The Flat, Madbrook Farm
\Westbury
Ba 13 3RB Wiltshire
United Kingdom
[BD, BT, IN, MM, PK, LK, TI][His, Lit]

Frenger, M.

Linden Str. 62
53227 Bonn
Germany

Frenzel, R.F.

Wolfgang-Heinz-Str. 44
13125 Berlin
Germany
[CN][Eco]

Fresnais, J.

UJML3,FL France
[CN][Eco]

Friebel, M.

Am Konebusch 12
41469 Neuss
Germany
[CN, HK, SG, TW, TI][Eco]

Friedlander, D.
8 rue Popincourt
75011 Paris
France
[TI][Eco]

Friedrich, Dr M.K.A.
UHAM,SKC,KTV Germany
[CN][Phi, CuS]

Frolova, Dr O.B.
SPU, FOS Russia
[Lit, Phi, Lin]

Froustrey, M.-M.
9 rue des Chevrefeuilles
91270 Vigneux sur Seine
France
[Lin, Phi, Lit]

Frühstück, Drs S.
UW,IJS Austria
sabine.fruehstueck@univie.ac.at
[JP][Soc, GenS, His, Ant, CuS]

Fuchs, Dr M.
Reichensteinstr. 48
69151 Neckargemünd
Germany
[IN][Rel, Ant, Soc, CuS]

Fuehrer, Dr B.
SOAS United Kingdom
BF3@soas.ac.uk
[CN][Phi, Lin, CuS, Lit]

Fuentes, Alicia
Spain
interart@pangea.org
[CuS]

Fujimori, B.
INALCO France
[JP][Phi, Lin, CuS, Lit]

Fujimoto, E.
UMMB,DEEO,DU France
[JP][Lit]

Fukae-Watanabe, M.
RUL,TCJK Netherlands

Fukasawa, Dr Y.
NRI,EAHSL United Kingdom
[CN, JP, KR, MN][CuS, Soc, Ant, Arch, His, Lin]

Fukuda, K.
UMMB,DEEO,DU France
[JP][CuS, Ant, Arch, Lin, Soc, His]

Fuller, Prof. C.J.
LSEPS,DA United Kingdom
c.fuller@lse.ac.uk
[IN][Ant]

Furundzic, V.
UB, DOS Yugoslavia
[CN, HK, ID, KR, PK, TW, TI][Psy, Rel, Lit, Lin, Edu, His, Phi, AHis]

Furundzic, M.F.
UB, FA Yugoslavia
[Eco, Agr]

Fynes, Dr R.C.C.
DMU,SII United Kingdom
[IN][His, Rel, Lit, CuS]

Gaanier, C.
INALCO France
[JP][Lin]

Gaastra, Dr F.S.
RUL,VG Netherlands
gaastra@Rullet.LeidenUniv.Nl
[CN, IN, ID, JP,][His]

Gaay Fortman, Prof. B. de
ISS Netherlands
fortman@iss.nl
[BD, IN, LK][Eco, Law]

Gaborieau, Dr M.
UL3,CREO France
mgb@ehess.fr
[IN, NP, PK][His, Ant]

Gadiot, M.M.P.E.H.
Singel 289-G
1012 WH Amsterdam
Netherlands
[ID][Ant, AHis, GenS, Arch, His, IR, Psy, Soc, DevS]

Gaenszbauer, Dr M.
CI Germany
[CN, HK, TW, TI][Lit, GenS, CuS, Rel]

Gaenszle, Dr M.
RKU,SI Germany
martin.gaenszle@urz.uni-heidelberg.de
[IN, NP][Rel, Lin, Ant, CuS]

Gafurova, Dr N.B.
RASP,IOS Russia
[IN][Lit]

Gai, J.
UMMB,DEEO,DU France
[CN][Lan]

Gaibov, Dr V.A.
Russia
[Arch]

Gail, Prof. dr A.
FUB,AW,IPKG Germany
[IN, NP, LK][His, AHis]

Gaillard, Dr C.
IPH France
[IN, PK][Arch]

Gaillard, Drs H.C.J.J.
TUE,TWIM Netherlands
[IN, PK][CuS]

Gajentaan, Mr H.
MIN,Buza,DGIS Netherlands
[BD, IN, MY, LK][PolS, IR, DevS]

Gal, M.S.

Galan, Ch.
UTM,DJ France
[JP][Edu]

Galenovitch, Dr Y.M.
RAS,IFES,FEB Russia
[CN][His]

Galey, Dr J.C.
UL3,CREO France
[IN][Soc, Rel, CuS, Ant]

Galindo, Drs A.
ISS Netherlands
galindo@iss.nl
[ID, PH][Eco, GenS, DevS]

Galinski, C.
INFOTERM Austria
[CN, JP][Edu, Lin]

Galizia, Dr M.
UBE,IE Switzerland
[ID, MY][Soc, PolS, Law, His, DevS, CuS]

Galjart, B.F.
RUL,CA/SNWS Netherlands
galjart@rulfsw.leidenuniv.nl
[ID, MY][DevS, Soc]

Gall, Dr H.C.
RUL,VRV Netherlands
jfhohg@ruljur.leidenuniv.nl
[ID, LK][His, Law]

Gallego Fresnillo, C.
Pza. Urdanibia, 2,2° izq
Irún
Spain
[PI, PH][His]

Gallio, Dr R.
Dussano 41
32030 Meano (BL)
Italy
[CN, HK, TW][Law, His]

Gallop, Drs A.T.
BL,OIOC United Kingdom
annabel.gallop@london.bl.uk
[BN, ID, MY, SG][Lit, His, AHis]

Galvan, A.
Paseo Colón 41, 5D
20301 Irun
Spain

Galy, L.
INALCO France
[CN][His, Lit, AHis]

Gamage, J.
18, rue Thiebault
94220 Charenton le Pont
France
[IN, ID, PG, LK][Env]

Gamman, L.
CSM United Kingdom
[IN, ID, PG, LK][AHis, CuS, GenS]

Gammeltoft, Drs T.
UC, IA Denmark
tine.gammeltoft@anthro.ku.dk
[VN][GenS, Ant]

Gangaram Panday, A.J.
Wildemanakker 2
1541 VM Koog a/d Zaan
Netherlands
[IN][Art]

Gankovsky, Prof.dr Yu.V.
RASP,IOS Russia
[His]

Ganshin, Dr G.A.
RAS,IFES,FEB Russia
[CN][Eco]

Gantès, G. de
LPI France
[VN][His]

Gao, J.
UU,AD Sweden
jianping.gao@estetik.uu.se
[CN, TW][AHis, Phi, Lit, CuS, His]

Garbutt, .
INALCO France
[AHis, Lit, CuS, His, Phi]

Garceran Piqueras Roas Maria, Rosa
UCM, BA, DD Spain
[JP][]

Garci -Ab solo, Dr A.
UC,FL,CHA Spain
[PI, PH][His, Ant, CuS]

Garcia, Fernando
Ramon Gomez de la Serna 79 (6°C)
28035 Madrid
Spain
[CN, HK, JP, KR, TW, TI][AHis, Geo, His, IR, PolS]

Garcia Erviti, J.
Jose Maria Peman, 22-D
47008 Valladolid
Spain
[CN, JP, TW][ECONOMIA]

García Gutiérrez Lic.Fil., F.
Trajano, 35A
41002 Sevilla
Spain
[JP][AHis, Rel]

Garcia Weda, R.
Jaquinto Verdager, 36
28019 Madrid
Spain
[JP,][Lin]

Garcia-Borron Martínez, M.-D.
UG,FFL, DLGTL Spain
[CN][Lin, Lit]

Garcia-Ormaechea Quero, C.
UCM, GH,HAC Spain
[AF, BD, BH, KH, HK, IN, ID, JP, KR, LD, LA, M][AHis, Geo, His, Lit, Rel, Phi]

Garforth, Prof. dr C.J.
UR,DAERD United Kingdom
c.j.garforth@reading.ac.uk
[BD, IN, MY, NP, PK, TH][Agr, Edu]

Garmendia Herrero, E.
Filipinas s/n Apartado de Corres 26
20240 Ordizia
Spain
[CN, JP, TW][His]

Garrigues Areiczo, M.
Apartado 460/3
28080 Madrid
Spain
[JP,][Eco]

Garushyants, Dr Yu.M.
RASP,IOS Russia
[CN][His]

Gasper, Dr D.R.
ISS Netherlands
gasper@iss.nl
[IN][Eco, Phi, PolS, DevS]

Gassmann, Prof. dr R.H.
UZ,AS,OS Switzerland
[CN][Phi, Lit, Lin]

Gastllo Martinez, J.V.
Adv. Peris y Valero 112-PTA 5
46006 Valencia
Spain
[CN, HK, TW, TI][Eco, Geo, Lin]

Gatzlaff, Dr M.
UL,IIZAW Germany
[BD, IN, NP, PK,][Lit, CuS, Lin]

Gaucher, J.
EFEO,BIB France
[KH, IN,][Art]

Gautam, Dr M.K.
RUL,KERN Netherlands
gautam@rullet.leidenuniv.nl
[BD, BT, IN, KZ, MG, MM, NP, PK, SM,][Rel, Soc, Lit, Lin, His, Ant, CuS, PolS, Env]

Gauthier, A.
LI France
[IN][Rel]

Gavin, Dr T.
UHU,DSEAS United Kingdom
[ID, MY][Ant]

Gavrilova, Dr A.G.
MSU,IAAS,CIBS Russia
[MM][His, Ant]

Gavryushina, Dr N.D.
RASP,IOS Russia
[IN][Lit]

Gay, B.
LPI France
[LA][His]

Gazano, A.
UNSA,DEG France
[BN, ID, MY, PH, SG][Law]

Ged, F.
93 Rue Monge
75005 Paris
France
[CN][CuS, DevS]

Geense, Drs P.H.A.M.
Edisonplein 11
5621 HV Eindhoven
Netherlands
[CN, HK, TW][Edu, Soc]

Geer, Drs A.A.E. van der
RUL,CNWS Netherlands
heijstee@rullet.leidenuniv.nl
[IN][Lin]

Geiser, Dr U.
UZI,DG Switzerland
ugeiser@geo.unizh.ch
[IN, PK, LK][DevS, Geo, Env]

Geisler, Drs G.H.S.
Hofer Strasse 49
95213 Muenchberg
Germany
[KH, CN, HK, JP, KR, LA, TW, VN][Geo, Env, DevS]

Geisler, T. Ch.
UW,ITBS Austria
[TI][Geo, DevS, Env]

Gelbras, Dr V.G.
MSU,IAAS,DSEAP Russia
[CN, HK, TW, TI][PolS, Eco, Soc]

Gelder, Drs R. van
Netherlands
[IN, ID, JP, LK][CuS, His, IR]

Geluk, M.C.
1e Weteringdwarsstraat 37
1017 TL Amsterdam
Netherlands
[TI][Edu, IR, CuS, AHis]

Gemeren, Drs A.J.G. van
Korenmolen 130
3481 AX Harmelen
Netherlands
[BD][His]

Generalsekretär, Der
Germany

Gengnagel, Dr J.P.
EKUT,SIVRW Germany
[IN][Rel, CuS, Phi]

Gentelle, Dr P.P.
CNRS,AAC France
gentelle@centrasie.msh-paris.fr
[AF, CN, TM, UZ][Env, Arch, Geo]

Genugten, Drs Y.A. van
RUL,TCZOAO,PD
Netherlands
genugten@rullet.leidenuniv.nl
[ID][Lin, Lit]

Georg, Dr S.
UB,ZA Germany
[MN, NP][Lin]

George, Drs S.
Godetiaweg 28
2555 RV The Hague
Netherlands
[IN][Ant, Agr, Soc]

Georgieva, Drs V.
RUL,SI Netherlands
[CN][His, Rel]

Gerasimovich, Prof. dr L.K.
SPU,FOS,DAS Russia
[MN][His, Rel]

Gerbault, D.P.
19, rue du Saleve \Prénépla
01210 Ornex
France
[KH, LA, MM, TH, VN][CuS, Lin]

Gerganova, Drs K.M.G.
Bulgaria
[CN, JP, KR][Ant, Rel, Phi, His]

Gerke, Prof. dr S.
UB,OS,AI Germany
Solvay.Gerke@t-online
[ID, MY, SG, VN][CuS, Soc, DevS]

Germeraad, Dr ir P.W.
Korhoenlaan 7
3161 TD Rhoon
Netherlands
[MN, NP][Env, Ant, CuS]

Gernet, Prof. J.
CNRS,IHEC France
gernet@ext.jussieu.fr
[CN][Rel, Phi, Law]

Gerrits, Drs A.C.M.
FIA Netherlands
[IN][AHis]

Gertsch, Drs L.J.
BLF Netherlands
[IN, MY, SG, TH][CuS, DevS]

Gethin, Dr R.M.L.
UBRI,DTRS United Kingdom
rupert.gethin@bristol.ac.uk
[KH, IN, LA, MM, LK, TH][Rel]

Getreuer-Kargl, Dr I.
UW,IJS Austria
ingrid.getreuer-kargl@univie.ac.at
[JP][Ant, CuS, GenS]

Geurtsenberg, Prof. dr L.G.
SPU,FA,DGL Russia
herzenbg@lgg.usr.pu.ru
[TJ][His, Lin]

Ghose, M.
31 Ridgmount Gardens
WC1E 7AS London
United Kingdom
[AHis, Arch]

Ghosh, Dr D.
USTI,DE United Kingdom
dipakghosh@stir.ac.uk
[BD, IN, MY][DevS, Eco]

Giambelli, Dr R.A.
Via G.B. Tiepolo N.30
20092 Cinisello Balsamo - Milan
Italy
[ID, MY, NP, SG,][Soc, Ant,]

Gianto, Prof. A.
PI,BANES Italy
gianto@agora.stm.it
[ID][Lin, Rel]

Gibson, C.
United Kingdom

Giel, Mr P.
MST Netherlands
[CN, IN, ID, MG, MY, PK, PH, SG, VN][Env, DevS]

Giele, Drs E.
FUB,OS Germany
egiele@fub46.zedat.fu-berlin.de
[CN, JP, KR, TW][His, Arch]

Giès, J.
MNAAG France
[CN][His, Arch]

Giesbers, Dr H.W.M.
KUN,ALMB Netherlands
[ID][Edu, Lin]

Gijsbers, Drs D.J.
Cannerweg 117
6213 BA Maastricht
Netherlands
[CN, IN,][Env, Eco]

Gijsen, Drs R.P.E.M.
Rembrandtlaan 32
2102 BS Heemstede
Netherlands
[IN, NP][His]

Gil, Prof. J.
US,FF Spain
[CN, JP, MN, PI, PH][His, Lit]

Gile, D.
INALCO France
[JP][Lit, His]

Gimm, Prof. M.
UK,OAS,SM Germany
amao1@uni-koeln.de
[CN][His, AHis, Lit, Rel]

Gimpel, D.
PUM,SIN Germany
gimpei@mailer.uni-marburg.de
[CN][Lit, CuS]

Ginkel, Drs M. van
Netherlands

Ginkel, Prof. dr J.A. van
UU,CB Netherlands
rector@cvb.ruu.nl
[ID, JP, MY, TH][Geo, DevS]

Ginkel, Drs W.T. van
Varkenmarkt 31
3511 BX Utrecht
Netherlands
[KZ, MN, MM, TJ, TI, TM, UZ][His, Geo, IR]

Gipoulon, C.
UP7,UAO France
[CN][Lin]

Gipouloux, Dr F.
CNRS,CM,BIB France
[CN, HK, JP, KR, TW][Eco, Soc]

Gippert, Prof. J.
JWGU,VS Germany
gippert@em.uni-frankfurt.de
[BD, IN, NP, LK, TJ][His, Lit, Phi, Lin, CuS, Rel]

Girard, F.
EFEO,BIB France
[JP][Rel]

Girdner, Dr E.J.
UEM,IR North Cyprus
[IN, PK][IR]

Girgis, Dr M.
UZ,AS,OS Switzerland
girgis@oas.vuizh.ch
[CN][CuS, His]

Girich, L.M.
RAS,IFES,FEB Russia
[CN][Eco]

Giroux, M.S.
USHS,LLCE France
[JP][Lit]

Giustozzi, A.
LSE,DIR United Kingdom
giustozz@lse.ac.uk
[AF][PolS, IR, His]

Gladdines, N.
ASU Netherlands
[AF][CuS, His, Env]

Glanville, Drs J.J.M.
Ferens Hall \Northgate
HU16 5SE Cottingham, E. Yorkshire
United Kingdom
[VN][Ant, GenS, His]

Glatzer, Dr B.
CMOS Germany
[AF, KR, PK, TJ, TM][GenS, DevS, CuS, Soc, Ant]

Glazachev, Dr M.V.
RASP,IOS Russia
[Eco]

Glebov, N.V.
RASP,IOS Russia
[IN, PK][Lin, Lit]

Glombitza, J.G.
DFG Germany
[Ant, CuS, DevS, GenS, Soc]

Glover, Dr I.C.
IA United Kingdom
ian.glover@ucl.ac.uk
[KH, IN, JP, TH, VN][Arch]

Glunin, Dr V.I.
RAS,IFES,FEB Russia
[CN][His]

Gmoser, K.
KFU,IS Austria
[TI][Arch]

Gnoli, Prof. Gh.
ISIAO Italy
[IR][Rel]

Go, M.A.
SW,A Netherlands
[CN][Soc, Ant, CuS]

Gobalakchenane, Dr M.
UN,LSH France
[KH, IN, ID, MY, MM, LK, TH][CuS, His, Rel, Soc]

Godement, Prof. dr F.L.

IFRI France
[CN, HK, JP, KR, SG, TW][His, IR]

Goderbauer, Drs J.P.L.

RUL,VPW Netherlands
[ID][PolS]

Godman, Dr A.

UK,EC United Kingdom
[HK, MY][Lin, Edu]

Goebel, Prof. E.

DNA Denmark
[CN, IN,][His]

Goes, Drs B.A. van der

Rietschans 38
2352 BB Leiderdorp
Netherlands
[ID][Ant]

Goettingen, Drs D.

[BD, BT, CN, HK, IN, JP, KR, MN, MM, TW][PolS, IR]

Goetzfried, Dr F.X.

DWZP Germany
[KH, CN, LA, TH, VN][His, Phi, Ant, Rel]

Goldblum, Ch.

14 rue des Tournelles
75004 Paris
France
[Soc, PolS, DevS]

Golden, Prof. S.

DSC,EB,LV Belgium
IUTS0@cc.uab.es
[CN, HK, TW][CuS, Phi, Lit]

Golman, Dr M.I.

RASP,IOS Russia
[MN][His]

Golovnin, Prof.dr I.V.

MSU,IAAS,CIBS Russia
[JP][Lin]

Golubeva, Dr Ye.V.

RASP,IOS Russia
[PolS]

Golubeva, Dr H.

RAS,IOS,AL Russia
[ID][PolS]

Golyghina, Dr K.I.

RASP,IOS Russia
[CN][Lit]

Gombrich, Prof. R.F.

OU,BC,MHF United Kingdom
richard.gombrich@balliol.ox.ac.uk
[IN, LK][Rel, Lin, Ant]

Gombrich-Gupta, Dr S.

OU,OI United Kingdom
[BD, IN][Rel, GenS, CuS, Phi, Lit]

Gomez Candela, Monica

UCM, BA, DE Spain
[JP,][AHis, Rel]

Gomez Pradas, Muriel

MEB Spain
[JP, PH][AHis, Ant]

Gommans, Dr J.J.L.

RUL,KERN Netherlands
[AF, IN, PK,][His]

Gomperts, Drs A.T.

Willemsparkweg 147-I
1071 GX Amsterdam
Netherlands
[ID][AHis]

Gonsalves, Drs C.M.

Fabiaanspoort 4
2312 BV Leiden
Netherlands
[CN, JP][Law]

Gontscharoff, C.

J. Bontelaan 21
2015 EH Haarlem
Netherlands
[HK, IN, ID, JP, VN][IR, DevS]

Gonzales de Orduña Criado, Silvia

[CN, IN, ID, MY, PK, TH][DevS]

González Valles, J.

USTM, IT Spain
[JP][Phi, Rel]

Gonzalo Castellanos, Dr A.

Belgium
Ana.Gonzalo-Castellanos@dg1b.cec.be
[AF, BD, BN, KH, IN, ID, LA, MG, MM, NP, PH, SG, LK][IR]

Good, Dr A.

UE,DSA United Kingdom
a.good@ed.ac.uk
[BD, IN, LK][DevS, Rel, His, GenS, Ant]

Goody, Prof. J.

CU,DSA United Kingdom

Gooptu, Dr N.

OX,IDC United Kingdom
ngooptu@vax.ox.ac.uk
[IN, PK, LK][PolS, DevS, His]

Goor, Dr J. van

UU,VG Netherlands
elsbeth.locher-scholten@let.ruu.nl
[IN, ID, LK, TH][His, IR]

Goossaert, V.

CNRS,EPHE,SR,T France
[CN][His, Rel]

Gooszen, Dr A.J.

Hugo de Grootstraat 10
3581 XS Utrecht
Netherlands
[ID][His, Geo]

Goralski, Prof. dr

PIIA Poland
[KH, ID, JP, LA, MY, MM, PH, VN][PolS, His, IR]

Gorbunova, Dr S.A.

RAS,IFES,FEB Russia
titarenk@ifes.msk.su
[CN, TI][Rel, His]

Goregliad, Prof. dr V.N.

RASP,IOS Russia
[JP][Lit, Rel]

Gorelik, Dr M.V.

RASP,IOS Russia
[His]

Gorelova, Dr L.M.

RAS,IOS,AL Russia
[CN][Edu, His, Lin]

Gorely, Dr I.O.

RAS,IFES,FEB Russia
[KR][His]

Gorter, Dr P.L.H.M.

Kirchstrasse 78
12277 Berlin
Germany
[IN][Eco, Agr, DevS, Ant, Soc, PolS]

Goryacheva, Dr A.M.

RASP,IOS Russia
[IN][Eco]

Goryayeva, Dr L.V.

RASP,IOS Russia
[, MY][Lit]

Goscha, Chr.

LPI France
[LA][His]

Gossot, A.

UL3,ETROM,C France
[JP][His, AHis]

Gossot, Dr Anne

UMMB3,FL,DOS France
[JP][Arch, AHis]

Goto, T.

INALCO France
[JP][AHis]

Gottowik, Dr

JGU,IEAS Germany
gottowik@mail.uni-mainz.de
[ID][Ant]

Goudsblom, Prof. J.

PISW Netherlands

Gournay, A.

UP,CREOPS,AA France
[CN][Arch, His, AHis]

Gouzalez Molina, A.

Plaza Doctor Laguna, 8.6 B
28009 Madrid
Spain
[KH CN, ID, JP, TH, VN][IR, Soc]

Graaf, T. de

ABN,HA Netherlands
[ID][His]

Graaf, Dr T. de
RUG,VTW Netherlands
degraaf@let.rug.nl
[JP][Lin]

Graaff, Drs B.G.J. de
Netherlands
bob.degraaff@inghist.nl
[ID, JP][His, IR]

Graas, Drs A.F.W. van
CSJN Netherlands
[ID, JP][AHis]

Graevenitz, Prof. dr A. von
UK,OS Germany
[CN, HK, ID, JP, KR, TI][Phi, AHis]

Graf, Drs A.W.
UHAM,SIS Germany
[ID][Lit]

Graff, Dr V.
UL3,CREO France
[IN][PolS]

Graivoronsky, Dr V.V.
RASP,IOS Russia
[MN][His]

Gransow, Dr B.
RUB,FOAW Germany
bettina.gransow@rz.ruhr-uni-bochum.de
[CN, HK, TW][Eco, Soc, GenS, PolS, DevS]

Grant, Dr M.E.
MGP Netherlands
[KH, CN, JP, TW, VN][Lit, IR, His, AHis, Rel]

Grathwohl, J.U.
Azaleavej 35
2000 Frederiksberg
Denmark
[MY, SG][Ant, Law]

Gravers, Dr M.
AU,FH,DESA Denmark
[MM, TH, VN][Env, His, Rel, PolS, Soc, CuS, Ant]

Grayson, Dr J.H.
USH,EARS United Kingdom
[KR][Rel, Ant]

Greatrex, R.G.
LU,FA,DEAL Sweden
roger.greatrex@ostas.lu.se
[CN][Law, His]

Greck, F.
LPI France
[LA][His]

Green MA, A.R.
MEAA United Kingdom
[CN, MM][AHis]

Gren-Eklund, Prof. G.
UU,DI Sweden
Gunilla.Gren-Eklund@afro.uu.se
[IN, MM, LK][Lit, Lin, Phi, Rel, CuS]

Grent, P.C.M.
TIDC Netherlands
[BT, CN, IN, MN, NP, TI][CuS, Lin, Lit, Rel, Phi]

Gricourt, Drs M.R.
INALCO,JK France
[IN][Lit]

Grigoriev, Dr A.M.

[CN][His]

Grigoriev, Dr S.E.
RAS,IFES,FEB Russia
[AF][CuS, IR, PolS]

Grigorieva, Dr G.M.

[IN][PolS, Soc]

Grigorieva, Dr T.P.
RASP,IOS Russia
[JP][Rel]

Grigorieva, N.V.
SPU,FOS,DAS Russia
vladimir@orient.lgu.spb.su
[VN][Ant, Rel]

Grijns, Dr C.D.
Nieuwstraat 202
3011 GM Rotterdam
Netherlands
[ID, MY, SG][Lin]

Grijp, Dr P. van der
UU,VCA Netherlands
Grijp@fsw.Ruu.nl
[PI][DevS, Eco, Agr, His, Ant]

Grijpstra, Dr ir B.G.
Netherlands
[BN, ID, MY, PK,][Env, DevS, Agr, Ant]

Grikurov, Dr S.S.
RAS,IOS,AL Russia
[TH][Eco, IR]

Grimaud-Hervé, D.
IPH France
[ID][Arch]

Grimm, Drs C.
UK,OS,AJ Germany
[JP][Rel, His, Soc, Phi, CuS, Lit]

Grintser, Dr P.A.
RAS,IWL Russia
[IN][Lit]

Griolet, P.
INALCO France
[JP][Lin]

Grishina, Dr V.A.
MSU,IAAS,CIBS Russia
[JP][Lit, Phi]

Grist, N.
13 Wingmore Road \Herne Hill
SE24 0AS London
United Kingdom
[TI][Lin]

Grivnin, Prof.dr V.S.
MSU,IAAS,CIBS Russia
[JP][Lin, Lit, PolS]

Groen, Prof. P.M.H.
KMM Netherlands
[ID, JP][His]

Groenen, Drs I.G.M.E.
KIT Netherlands
[ID][CuS]

Groenendael, Dr Clara van
Spuistraat 253-III
1012 VR Amsterdam
Netherlands
[IN, ID][Ant, Rel, Lin]

Grönbold, Dr G.C.
BSBIB,OABT Germany
[BT, IN, NP, LK, TI][CuS, Rel, Lit]

Grönning, Dr T.
UO, FSS,ESST Norway
Terje.gronning@esst.uio.no
[JP][Soc]

Groot, Drs I. de
J. Verhulststraat 27 hs
1071 MR Amsterdam
Netherlands
[IN][Ant, GenS]

Groot, Dr A.H. de
RUL,VTCIMO Netherlands
[KZ, TM, UZ][Lit, IR, Rel, His]

Groot, J.J.R.
AB-DLO Netherlands
[CN][Agr, Env]

Groot, W.T. de
RUL,CESP Netherlands
[ID, PH][Env, Ant, DevS]

Groot, Drs G.A. de
KUB, IVO Netherlands
g.a.de.groot@kub.nl
[IN][Eco]

Groot, Drs G.P. de
Frans Halskade 237
2282 TZ Rijswijk
Netherlands
[JP][PolS, Eco, Ant]

Groot, Drs H.U. de
Joh. Willem Frisolaan 40
1412 AJ Naarden
Netherlands
[ID][Rel, Lin, Lit]

Gropp, Dr G.C.A.
UHAM,SGKVO,AI Germany
[AF, IN, ID, KZ, MN, NP, PK, TJ, TM][Phi, Lit, His, Rel, Arch, AHis, CuS, Ant, Lin]

Gröpper, Drs D.
Kirchplatz 9
59199 Bönen
Germany
[BN, ID, MY, MM, PG, SG, TH][CuS, AHis, Arch, His, Ant]

Gros, Prof. F.E.
CNRS,EPHE,SHP France
[IN, LK][CuS, Lit, Rel]

Grossheim, Dr M.
UP,SEAS Germany
pqgroso@fsrz1.tz.uni-passau.de
[VN][His]

Grotterud MA, Kari
UB,DSA Norway
kari.grotterud@sosantv.vib.no
[ID,][Ant, Rel]

Grötzbach, Prof. dr E.
KUE,KG Germany
[AF, IN, PK,][Rel, Geo, CuS]

Grounina, Prof.dr E.A.
MSU,IAAS,CIBS Russia
[UZ][Lin]

Gruberova, Drs I.M.
CU,FF,DEAS Czech Republic
[KR][Lit, Rel]

Grünendahl, Drs R.
GAUG,BIB,IND Germany
gruenen@mail.sub.uni-goettingen.de
[IN, NP][Rel, Lin]

Gruner, Prof. dr
Unter den Linden 5
04880 Trossin
Germany
[CN][Lit]

Grünfelder, Mr A.
Weiselpfad 16
12527 Berlin
Germany
[CN, HK, TI][Lit]

Grunsven, Dr L.M.J. van
UU,VSGO Netherlands
l.grunsven@frw.ruu.nl
[MY, SG, TH][DevS, Eco, Geo, IR]

Gryaznov, Dr G.V.
RASP,IOS Russia
[KR][Eco]

Gude, R.
BAMEP France

Gudoshnikov, Prof. dr L.M.
RAS,IFES,CRC Russia
[CN, HK, TW][PolS, Law]

Gudowski, J.
UW,FGRS,IDC Poland
Jgudikr@plearn
[IN, MY, NP, VN][Eco, Agr, DevS]

Guedes, Drs M.A.M.
UNL,CHAM Portugal
[MM][His]

Guelbras, Prof.dr V.G.
MSU,IAAS,CIBS Russia
[CN][Eco, His, PolS, Soc]

Guelle, F.
CNRS,IAO France
fguelle@mrash.fr
[JP][IR, Eco]

Guen, H. le
CNRS,IRSEA France
[BN, PH][AHis, CuS, Env, Ant, Arch, His, Soc, Rel, His]

Guénel, A.
INSERM France
[VN][CuS, His]

Guerassimoff, Dr C.
IIAS Netherlands

Guerassimova, Dr A.S.
RASP,IOS Russia
[AF][Lit]

Guerassimovich, Dr L.K.

[MN][Lit]

Guermonprez, Dr J.F.
CNRS,LASEMA France
[Soc]

Guerreiro, Dr A.
CNRS,IRSEA France
[ID, JP][Ant]

Guichard, A.S.
UP,G France
[JP][Ant, AHis, CuS, His, Rel]

Guiheux, Dr G.
UA,SIN France
[CN, JP, TW][Eco, Soc, His]

Guillaume, X.
INALCO France
[VN][His, ArchAgr, Env]

Guillemin, A.
CNRS,IRSEA France
[VN][Soc]

Guillemoz, Dr A.L.
UP7,UAO,C France
[KR][GenS, CuS, Ant, Rel]

Guillon, Dr E.
CNRS,CASCIP France
[IN, MM, LK, TH, VN][Ant, AHis, Arch, Rel, His]

Guillot, C.
CNRS,EHESS France
[ID, MY][Rel]

Guimaraes, Ir J.P.C.
ISS Netherlands
[BD, LK][Eco, Env, DevS]

Guimaraes, Prof. dr A.L.
ISCTE,DH,AA Portugal
angela.guimaraes@iscte.pt
[CN, MO][His]

Guirich, Dr L.M.
RAS,IFES,FEB Russia
[CN][Eco]

Gulik, Prof. dr W.R. van
RUL,TCJK Netherlands
cjgall@Rulcri.LeidenUniv.nl
[Ant, AHis]

Gullestrup, Prof. H.
AU, RCDIR Denmark
gullestrup@34.auc.dk
[CN, JP, KR, PI][His, Soc, IR, Eco, Ant, DevS, CuS, PolS]

Gunawan, Dr B.
Treiler 12
1276 ED Huizen (N-H)
Netherlands
[ID, MY][His, Soc, DevS]

Gunning, Prof. dr J.W.
VU,VOAE Netherlands
jgunning@econ.vu.nl
[ID, MY][Eco, DevS]

Gurbindo Lambán, N.
Azalea, 69
28109 Alcobenas (Madrid)
Spain
[CN, JP,][Ant]

Gurevich, Dr E.M.
RAS,IOS,AL Russia
[HK, KR, MY, SG, TW][His, PolS, Phi]

Gusev, Dr M.N.
RAS,IOS,AL Russia
[MY][Eco, IR]

Gussev, Dr M.N.
RASP,IOS Russia
[Eco]

Gustafsson, Drs J.E.
KTH,CEE Sweden
[CN, TI][Env]

Guterres, A.
Rua Bento de Jesus Caraça, 7
1495 Cruz Quebrada
Portugal
[Ant]

Gütinger, E.
Belszstrasse 97
12249 Berlin
Germany
[CN, HK, TW][His, PolS]

Guy, Drs J.S.
VAM,ISEAD United Kingdom
[KH, IN, MM, TH][His, AHis]

Guyt, Drs H.J.
Goudsbloemstraat 137-A
1015 JM Amsterdam
Netherlands
[AF, BT, KH, IN, IR, KZ, LA, MN, MM, NP, PK][His, IR, AHis, Lin, CuS, DevS]

Gyss-Vermande, C.G.V.
LPI France
[CN][Rel, His, AHis]

Haahr, T.
LU,ICR,FRS,DI Sweden
[IN, ID, PK, PH][Lit, Rel, CuS]

Haan, C.L. de
Netherlands

Haan, Dr A. de
USUS,AFRAS United Kingdom
[BD, IN][Soc, DevS, His]

Haar, Prof. dr B.J. ter
RKU,OAW,SIN Germany
bth@gw.sino.uni-heidelberg.de
[IN, PK][Lit, Rel]

Haar, Dr J.G.J. ter
RUL,VTCIMO Netherlands
TERHAAR@RULLET.Leiden Univ.nl
[IN, PK][Rel, Lit]

Haas-Lambert, A.-M.
10 rue de la Filassière
78121 Crespières
France
[IN, ID, TI][His]

Haberland, Dr D.
UK,IDSL Germany
[JP][CuS, Lit]

Habiboe, Drs R.R.F.
RUL,CNWS Netherlands
HABIBOE@Rullet.LeidenUniv.nl
[ID][His]

Hacourt, B.J.H.
KUL,ANTR Belgium
[BD, IN, MY, PK,][DevS, Ant]

Haffner, Prof. dr W.N.
JLUG,GI Germany
[IN, ID, NP, LK, TH, TI][Env]

Haft, Dr L.L.
RUL,SI Netherlands
[CN][Lit]

Haftmann, Drs A.K.
RUB,FOAW,KOR Germany
[KR][CuS, Lin, Lit]

Hagenaar, Dr E.P.G.
Korte Spaarne 29
2011 AJ Haarlem
Netherlands
[CN][Lit]

Hagendoorn, Prof. dr A.
UU,CB Netherlands

Hagendoorn, Prof. dr A.J.M.W.
UU,VASW Netherlands
hagendoo@fsw.ruu.nl
[BT, CN, IN][His]

Hager, D.
H&PWP Germany
[CN, IN, ID, KR, PH, TH, VN][Eco, IR, PolS]

Hagers, Drs S.J.
RUL,TCJK Netherlands
[JP][Lin]

Hai, Mr N.
MMU, DS United Kingdom
n.hai@mmu.ac.uk
[Rel, Soc]

Haidrani, Dr S.
Flat 3 \223 North Gower Street
NW1 2NR London
United Kingdom
[PK][CuS, His, Lit]

Haikonen, Dr J.
EVA Finland
[MY, SG][DevS, Eco, PolS]

Haitsma, T.J.
KLM Netherlands
[HK, IN, ID, MY, SG][IR]

Hajnal MA, L
ELTE\HSJS
[CN, JP, KR, MN, TW, TI][Ant, AHis, CuS, Edu, His, Lin, Lit, Rel]

Halbeisen, Dr H.
RUB,FOAW,POA Germany
[CN, TW][PolS]

Haldar, Mr A.
Van Ruysdaallaan 78
2264 TM Leidschendam
Netherlands
[IN][PolS]

Hall, Dr A.R.
RAD,FCO,FES United Kingdom
[BD, BT, IN, MM, NP, LK][Ant, IR, PolS]

Haller, Dr F.
UBE,DLHC Switzerland
felix.haller@isw.unibe.ch
[TI][Lin]

Hallett, Mr D.J.
UWO,WBSSC United Kingdom
j.hallet@wlv.ac.uk
[JP][Eco]

Halsberghe, Dr N.M.
KUL,SIN Belgium
[CN][His]

Halsema, W.B. van
D,GKN Netherlands
[ID][Rel]

Hamayon, Dr R.N.
UP10,LESC France
hamayon@u-paris10.fr
[MN][Rel, Lin, Ant]

Hamel, Dr B.R.
CAC Netherlands
[MN][AHis, Psy]

Hamelink, Prof. dr C.J.
UvA,VCW Netherlands
hamelink@antenna.nl
[BD, IN, ID, JP, KR, MY, NP, PH, SG, LK, TH][IR, Law]

Hammar, U.
Rackarbergsgatan 56
75232 Uppsala
Sweden
[TI][AHis, Ant]

Hammargren, Drs H.A.
SIDA Sweden
henrik.hammargren@sida.se
[AF, KH, , KZ, KR, LA, MN, MM, TJ, TH, TI,][PolS, IR, DevS]

Hamon, C.
UP7,UAO France
[CN, JP][Eco]

Hamonic, G.
CNRS,LASEMA France
[Soc]

Han, M.
UAM1,LSH France
[CN][AHis]

Han, S.-I.
INALCO France
[KR][AHis]

Hana, Dr K.
PUM,SIN Germany
[CN, HK, JP, TW][PolS, His, DevS]

Hande, B.E.
Rubensstraat 207
2526 MA The Hague
Netherlands
[IN][Phi, AHis, Arch, Lit]

Hanibal, Mr J.
Emb.Mong. Belgium
[MN][IR, PolS]

Hanisch, Prof. dr R.
UHAM,IB Germany
[ID, MY, PH, SG, TH][IR, DevS, PolS]

Hanneder, Drs J.
PUM,IOAS,ASKU Germany
hanneder@mailer.uni-marburg.de
[IN][Phi, Rel, Lin, Lit]

Hannibal, Dr A.S.
Otto Hahn Strasse 26
53117 Bonn
Germany
[LK][Arch]

Hansen, Dr M.H.
UO,EACS Norway
mettehh@extern.uio.no
[CN][Ant, Edu]

Hansen, J.Chr.K.
UO, IH Denmark
JCKH@HIST.OV.DK
[VN][His]

Hanssen, Drs L.M.
MVROT Netherlands
[AF, KHIN, ID, KR, PK, TJ, TM, VN][Ant, CuS]

Hansson, Prof. I.L
LU,FA,DEAL Sweden
inga.lill.hansson@ostas.lu.se
[CN, TH][Lin, Rel]

Hansson, E.
SU,DPS Sweden
eva.hansson@statsvet.su.se
[KH, ID, LA, VN][PolS]

Hansson, Dr A.
UE,DAS United Kingdom
anders@hansson@ed.ac.uk
[CN][His]

Harangi, Dr L.
HAS,SA Hungary
[JP][Soc, Edu]

Harbsmeier, Prof. dr M.
UO, IH Denmark
harbsmeier@hist.ou.dk
[CN, MY, SG][His, CuS, Rel, LitAnt]

Harbsmeier, Prof. dr C.
UO,FA,EOS Norway
harbsmei@hedda.uio.no
[CN, MY, SG][His, Phi, Lit, Lin, CuS, AHis]

Hardiman, Dr T.P.
IBMITS,IFSC United Kingdom
thardiman@vnet.ibm.com
[JP][IR, Eco]

Harding, Dr A.J.
SOAS,DL United Kingdom
ah9@soas.ac.uk
[ID, MY, SG][Law, Env]

Hardon, Dr A.P.
UvA,ASC,CASA Netherlands
a71506ah@horus.sara.nl
[PH][Ant, GenS]

Haringhuizen, Drs W.
UvA,MAG Netherlands
[BN, KHCN, HK, ID, JP, KR, LA, MY, MM, PG, PH][PolS, Ant, IR]

Harrer, H.
HHM Austria
[TI][Ant, PolS, IR]

Harries, Dr P.T.
OU,OI United Kingdom
phillip.harries@queens.ox.ac.uk
[JP][Lit]

Harris, Drs W.N.
BRC,RC United Kingdom
[PolS]

Harris, Drs N.
UCL,DPU United Kingdom
nigel.harris@vcl.ac.uk
[CN, HK, IN, ID, KR, MY, MM, NP, PK, SG, TW,][DevS, Eco]

Harris, Drs F.M.
UE,DSA United Kingdom
f.m.harris@sms.ed.ac.uk
[MY][Ant]

Harrison, Dr R.V.
SOAS,CSEAS United Kingdom
rh6@soas.ac.uk
[TH][Lit, CuS, GenS]

Harriss, Dr J.C.
LSEPS,DDS United Kingdom
[AF, BD, AF, BD, IN, ID, NP, PK, LK, TJ][DevS, Ant]

Harriss-White, Dr B.
OU,FE United Kingdom
[BD, IN][Eco, DevS, Agr, GenS]

Harsono, S.
Postbus 22245
1100 CE Amsterdam
Netherlands
[ID][Agr, GenS, Eco, DevS]

Harst, Dr J.F. van der
Mr P.N. Arntzeniusweg 64
1098 GS Amsterdam
Netherlands
[ID][Lit, Phi]

Hart, R.F.
WP,IC United Kingdom
[CN, HK, JP,][His, PolS, IR]

Hart, Prof. T.G.
SU,CPAS Sweden
tom.hart@orient.su.se
[CN, TI][IR, His, PolS]

Hart-van den, Drs H.J. 't
RUL,KERN Netherlands
HJHART@Rullet.LeidenUniv.nl
[PolS, IR, His]

Harteveld, Ir K.
KIT Netherlands
[BD, CN, ID, MY, TH][Agr, Eco, IR, Soc, DevS]

Hartevelt, Drs J.H.W. van
KIT,BIB Netherlands
[DevS, His, Agr, Ant, Eco, Soc, Edu, PolS, GenS, Env, IR]

Hartkamp-Jonxis, Drs E.
RMA Netherlands
[IN, ID][His, AHis]

Hartmann, Prof. J.-U.
HUB,AA,ZA Germany
[IN, TI][Rel, Lit]

Hartog, Dr A.P. den
LW,DHN Netherlands
adel.denhartog@et3.voed.wau.nl
[ID, MY, SG][Ant, DevS]

Hartveld, Drs ing A.J.
Stephensonstraat 42
2561 XW The Hague
Netherlands
[ID][Agr, Eco, DevS, Soc]

Hartveldt, Dr D.
Gravelandsewijk 8
9354 VK Zevenhuizen
Netherlands
[ID][Lin]

Hartwell, S.
18, Avenue Clara
94500 Champigny sur Marne
France
[TI][Lin]

Hasselgren, J.H.
UU,TI Sweden
johanhas@teol.uu.se
[ID][His, Rel]

Hasunuma, R.
JFK Germany
[JP][His, Rel]

Hatalov , Dr H.
SAS,IOAS Slovak Republic
[CN, TW][PolS, His]

Hatano, Y.
INALCO France
[JP][His, PolS]

Hatti, Prof. N.
UL,NASEAS Sweden
Neelambar.hatti@ekh.lu.se
[IN][Agr, DevS, Ant, His]

Haude, Dr D.K.H.
KUN,IDS Netherlands
d.haude@maw.kun.nl
[LK, TH][DevS, Eco]

Hauser, B.
Lerchenstrasse 81
22676 Hamburg
Germany
[IN][Rel, Ant, DevS, CuS]

Haute, Dr L. Van
MHOV,JS Belgium
[JP][CuS, Lit, Soc]

Havnevik, Mr H.
UO,FA,CS Norway
hanna.havnevik@iks.uio.no
[TI][Rel]

Hawthorn, Mr G.P.
CU,FSPS United Kingdom
[ID, JP, KR, SG][IR, DevS, PolS]

Hayashi, O.
INALCO France
[JP][DevS, IR, PolS]

Hayward, Dr K.
SOAS,CSEAS United Kingdom
kh3@soas.ac.uk
[ID][Lin]

Hazod, Dr G.
UW,IV Austria
[TI][Ant, Rel]

Headley, Dr S.C.
CNRS,IRSEA France
[ID][Ant, Rel]

Healy, Dr D.
SOAS,CSEAS United Kingdom
[VN][Lit, Lin]

Heberer, Prof. dr Th.
UT,CEAPS Germany
heberer@pcmail.uni-trier.de
[CN, HK, KR, LA, MY, MN, MM, PH, SG, TJ, TW,][Ant, Rel, DevS, GenS, Eco, PolS, Soc]

Heemskerk, Dr M.T.
KUN, VTCMO Netherlands
[PH][Rel]

Heemst, Drs J.J.P. van
ISS Netherlands
[KH, ID, PK, LK][Eco]

Heer, Dr P. de
Netherlands

Heering, Drs E.L.
NIDI,BIB Netherlands
heering@nidi.nl
[ID][GenS, DevS]

Heerink, Dr N.B.M.
LW,DDE Netherlands
nico.heerink@alg.oe.wau.nl
[CN][Env, Agr, DevS, Eco]

Heersink, Dr C.G.
Uilenstede 102-A
1183 AM Amstelveen
Netherlands
[ID, MY, SG][His]

Heeschen, Dr V.
Prinzenweg 22B
82319 Starnberg
Germany
[ID, PI, PG][Lin, CuS, Ant, Phi, Rel]

Heesterman, Prof. dr J.C.
RUL,KERN Netherlands
[IN][His, Rel]

Heide, Dr S. von der
UNESCO France
[AF, BD, AF, BD, BT, KH, CN, IN, NP, PK, SM, LK][Ant, DevSAHis, Env, CuS, Rel, PolS]

Heidrich, Dr P.
CMOS Germany
[IN][Soc, Agr, His]

Heidrich, Prof. dr J.
CMOS Germany
[IN,][His, IR]

Heidt, Dr E.U.
UBI,FS,SDRC Germany
[MY, SG][CuS, Edu]

Heiduk, Dr G.
GMU,FE Germany
iwbheiduk@uni-duisburg.de
[CN, JP][Eco]

Heij, Dr C.J.
Meidoornsingel 75
3053 BK Rotterdam
Netherlands
[ID][Edu, Env, DevS]

Heijer, Dr J. den
RUL,VTCIMO Netherlands
[His, Lit]

Heijn, Drs A.
II Netherlands
[IN][IR, Eco]

Heikkilä-Horn, M.L.
UH,TT,U Finland
[Eco, IR]

Heikkinen, V.
UH,VT,S Finland
[CN][Soc, Ant]

Heilmann, Dr S.
IFA Germany
[CN, HK, SG, TW, TI][Soc, PolS, IR, His]

Heinemeijer, Prof. dr W.F.
Victorieplein 21-A
1079 KL Amsterdam
Netherlands
[ID][Env, Geo]

Heins, Dr E.L.
UvA, ECJK Netherlands
[ID][Ant]

Heins, Drs J.J.F.
VU,VTDM Netherlands
[BD, IN, ID, LK, VN][Env, DevS]

Heinschke, Dr M.
UHAM,SIS Germany
[ID][Lit]

Heinzig, Dr D.
BI Germany
[CN, HK, JP, KZ, KR, MN][His, PolS, IR]

Heissig, Prof. dr W.
Heideweg 43
55494 Rheinböllen
Germany
[MN][Lit, Rel, His]

Heitkoetter, Drs M.
RKU,SI,AG Germany
ag1@ik.urz.uni-heidelberg.de
[IN][PolS, DevS, GenS, Geo]

Helffer, M.
CNRS,IRSEA France
[NP, TI][Ant]

Helgesen, Dr G.H.
NIAS Denmark
geir@nias.ku.dk
[KR][PolS, Soc, CuS]

Hell, S.
Germany
stefan.hell@uni-tuebingen.de
[, TH][His, IR]

Heller, Dr A.
38 Lignolet
1260 Nyon
Switzerland
[CN, MN, NP, TI][CuS, AHis, Rel, His]

Heller, Y.J.
G,AB Netherlands
[BN, ID, JP][Rel, CuS, His, AHis]

Helliwell, Drs D.J.
OU,BL United Kingdom
djh@bodley.ox.ac.uk
[CN, HK, TW][AHis, CuS, Rel]

Hellmann, J.
GU,DSA Sweden
jorgen.hellman@sant.go.se
[ID][Ant]

Helmes, B.J.
Kinderdijk 16h
4331 HG Middelburg
Netherlands

Hemery, Dr D.
UP7 France
[KH, LA, VN][His]

Hemmann, M.
UK,OAS,MCS Germany
[CN, HK][Law, His, Eco, Env]

Hemmet, Ch.
MH,LE France
[LA, TH, VN][Ant]

Hemmingsen, H.
Finsensvej 8 d, 3.tv
2000 Copenhagen F
Denmark
[Ant]

Hendrawan, Drs S.
Il Cisitu Indah III/5
40135 Bandung
Indonesia
[ID][DevS, PolS]

Hendriks, Drs A.P.C.
KIT Netherlands
[CN, HK, TW][PolS, IR, Eco, CuS, His]

Hendriks, Drs M.B.
M.S. Trassi Westerdoksdijk t/o 20
1013 AE Amsterdam
Netherlands
[PH][Ant]

Hendriks, M.
UvA,ASSR,CASA
Netherlands
[PH][Ant]

Hendry, Prof. R.J.
OBU,SSS United Kingdom
[JP][Ant]

Heng, J.W.M.
19 Gainsborough Court
\Wellesley Road
W4 4BD London
United Kingdom
[BN, KH, ID, MY, MM, PH, SG, TH, VN][His, Arch, AHis]

Hengel, Drs A. van
van Kempensingel 3
3443 AL Woerden
Netherlands
[ID, TH][Eco, IR]

Henke, Drs R.F.W.
NSSEPR Netherlands
r.f.w.henke@fsw.ruu.nl
[IN, NP][Psy, Ant, DevS, Soc]

Henley, Dr D.E.F.
KITLV Netherlands
Henley@Rullet.LeidenUniv.nl
[ID][Geo, His]

Hennig, A.
HUB,AA,IJ Germany
[JP][CuS]

Henns, M.
ABD Switzerland
[TI][CuS]

Henriksen, Drs M.A.
Esplanaden 18-4
1263 DK Copenhagen
Denmark
[CN, TH][Arch, CuS]

Henriot, Chr.
CNRS,IAO France
christian.henriot@mrash.fr
[CN][His]

Henry, Dr J.C.K.
OBU,SBMSNFS United Kingdom
jhenry@brookes.ac.uk
[IN, MY, PH, LK, VN][His]

Henry, R.
12 Bis, Boulevard Edgar Quinet
75014 Paris
France
[HK, ID, LA, MO, MG, SG, LK, TW][Lin, GenS, Env, CuS, AHis, Arch, IR, Lit, Phi, Psy]

Henss, Michael
ABD Switzerland
[Ant, Arch, AHis, Rel]

Henze, Prof. J.
HUB,IAP Germany
juergen=henze@rz.hu-berlin.de
[CN, HK, ID, MY, MN, PH, SG, TW, TH, VN][Edu]

Herbers, H.
FAU,IS Germany
hherbers@geographie.uni-erlangen.de
[BD, IN, PK][GenS, Agr, CuS]

Herbers-Lee, S.
Hustadtring 141/8.OG
44801 Bochum
Germany
[CN, KR, TW][PolS]

Herbert, Drs P.M.
BL,OIOC United Kingdom
patricia.herbert@bl.uk
[MM][AHis]

Herdick, R.
Daiser Str. 3
81371 Munich
Germany
[TI][AHis]

Heringa, R.
Pieter de la Courstraat 23
2313 BP Leiden
Netherlands
[ID][Rel, His, Ant]

Hermanov, Dr Z.
Sumberova 12
16200 Prague 6
Czech Republic
[CN][Lit, Lin]

Hermans, Dr J.W.M.
LW,PR Netherlands
jeanine.hermans@doffs.sz.wau
[CN][Agr, Env, IR]

Hermens, B.
Cor. Gehrelslaan 25
5626 HB Eindhoven
Netherlands
[CN, IN, ID, JP, KR, TH, VN][Agr, Env, IR]

Hermiyono, D.
CNRS,EHESS France
[Agr, IR, Env]

Hermse, Drs M.A.A.
Borneolaan 302
1019 KL Amsterdam
Netherlands
[IN][CuS, Phi, His, Rel, GenS, Lit, Lin, AHis, Psy]

Hernádi, Dr A.
HAS,IWF,JESRC Hungary
ahernadi@vki3.vki.hu
[JP][DevS, IR, Eco, Env]

Hernandez, Alberto
Rodriguez san Pedro 13
28015 Madrid
Spain

Herno, Drs R.
RU,IIDS Denmark
rolf@geo.ruc.dk
[VN][IR, PolS]

Heroldov, Mgr. H.
CU,FF,DEAS Czech Republic
[CN][His, Edu]

Heron, Dr C.P.
UBR,DAS United Kingdom
c.p.heron@bradford.ac.uk
[TH, VN][Arch]

Herrmann, Dr W.
HUB,AA,KI Germany
[JP, KR][Lin]

Herry-Priyono, B.
LSEPS United Kingdom
herryprb@lse.ac.uk
[ID][DevS, His, Phi, PolS]

Herst, Drs D.
Reguliersgracht 17B
1017 LJ Amsterdam
Netherlands
[ID][His, GenSAHis]

Hessel, E.
Berg. Land Str. 276-A
40629 Düsseldorf
Germany
[TI][GenS, His, AHis]

Hesselink, N.D.
SOAS,CMS United Kingdom
nh@soas.ac.uk
[JP, KR][Ant]

Hessing, Ir E.L.P.
Netherlands
[IR, DevS]

Heuser, Prof. R.
UK,OAS,MCS Germany
[CN, HK, JP, KR, MO, TW, TI][Law]

Heuvel, Ing T. van den
Westerse Drift 53
9752 LC Haren
Netherlands
[ID, MY, PI, PG, TH, VN][Agr]

Heuven, Dr V.J.J.P. van
RUL,ATW Netherlands
heuven@rullet.leidenuniv.nl
[ID][Lin]

Heuze-Brigant, Dr G.L.D.
UL3,CREO France
[IN, PK,][DevS, Env, Soc, Ant, Eco]

Heyndrickx, J.J.
KUL,FV Belgium
[CN, HK, TW][Rel]

Hidas, Mr S.
Honvéd u. 97
1185 Budapest
Hungary

Hidasi, Prof. J.
IOCFT Hungary
h5339hid@ella.hu
[CN, JP, KR][Lin, IR, Edu, Soc, CuS]

Hijiya-Kirschnereit, Prof. I.
FUB,OS Germany
dijtokyo@mb.tokyo.infoweb.or.jp
[JP][CuS, Lit, Lin]

Hildebrandt Diplom, Sabine
UMMB3,FL,DOS France
[CN, ID][]

Hill, Mr L.G.
UHU,CSEAS United Kingdom
[DevS, Eco]

Hillege, G.
UU,VASW Netherlands
hillege@fsw.ruu.nl
[CuS, Psy]

Hillenius, J.
Zomerdijkstr. 24
1079 XC Amsterdam
Netherlands

Hillock, M.
BRC,RC United Kingdom

Hilton, Drs I.
27 Corsica Street
N5 1JT London
United Kingdom
[CN, TI][IR]

Hintzen, Drs G.H.
RUL,CNWS Netherlands
[CN, HK, JP, TW][IR, Law, Phi, PolS, His]

Hinüber, Prof. dr O. von
[IN, LA, MM, NP, PK, LK, TH][His, CuS, Arch, His, Law, Lit, AHis, Phi, Rel, Lin]

Hinüber, Dr H. von
ALU,OS,IND Germany
[CN, IN, JP, NP, PK, LK, TI][Law, His, Rel, Lin, Phi, Lit]

Hinzler, Dr H.I.R.
RUL,TCZOAO Netherlands
hinzler@rullet.leidenuniv.nl
[ID][Lit, Arch, AHis, Ant]

Hiorth, Dr F.
Kirkehaugsveien 3
0283 Oslo
Norway
[ID][Soc, Rel, Phi]

Hisyam, Drs M.
RUL,TCZOAO,PD
Netherlands
[ID][Soc, Rel, His]

Hitchcock, Dr M.J.
UNL,BS United Kingdom
m.hitchcock@vnl.ac.uk
[CN, ID, MY][Soc, Ant, DevS]

Hitipeuw-Palyama, E.J.
MHMSM Netherlands
[ID, PG][Ant, Lit, Edu]

Hjellum, T.
UB,DCP Norway
Torstein.Hjellum@isp.uib.no
[CN][DevS, PolS, His]

Ho, K.-C.
UJML3,FL France
[CN, HK, TW][Lit]

Hoa, M.
UH,FAI France
[CN][Lin]

Hoadley, Prof. dr M. C.
LU,FA,DEAL Sweden
Mason.Hoadley@ostas.lu.se
[ID][His]

Hoare, Dr J.E.
RAD,FCO,FES United Kingdom
[CN, HK, JP, KR, MO, MN, TW, TI][IR, His, PolS, CuS]

Hoareau, D.
France
Denise.Hoareau@ujf-grenoble.fr

Hobart, Dr P.M.
SOAS,DAS United Kingdom
mh5@soas.ac.uk
[ID][CuS, Ant]

Hockx, Dr M.L.L.G.
SOAS,DEA United Kingdom
mh17@soas.ac.uk
[CN][Lit]

Hodgkinson, E.
E,IU United Kingdom
[PH][Eco]

Hoebink, Dr P.R.J.
KUN,IDS Netherlands
[ID, LK][DevS, PolS, CuS]

Hoedt, S.
KLI United Kingdom
Selma.Hoedt@kli.wkap.nl
[ID, LK][Law, IR]

Hoefnagels, Ir H.A.M.
Bergen en Dalseweg 54
6522 BM Nijmegen
Netherlands
[BD, BT, KH, CN, HK, IN, ID, JP, LA, MY][Agr, Eco, Law]

Hoeij Schilthoven Pompe, Mr S.
RUL,VVI Netherlands
[ID, MY][Law]

Hoek, Drs A. van der
Laan van Ouderzorg 24
2352 HV Leiderdorp
Netherlands
[ID][Rel]

Hoek, Drs A.W. van den
RUL,CNWS Netherlands
[IN, NP][Rel, Ant, Lin, CuS]

Hoekema, Dr A.G.
UvA,TDI Netherlands
Theouva@sara.nl
[CN, HK, ID][Rel]

Hoekstra, Drs H.F.M.F.
NVM Netherlands
f.hoekstra@MAW01.kun.nl
[ID, PI, PG][Ant]

Hoeppe MSc, G
Germany
[IN, ID, PI, PG,][Ant, Env]

Hoesel, Drs R. van
EUR,EW Netherlands
Hoesel@cvd.few.eur.nl
[KR, TW][Eco]

Hoetjes, Dr B.J.S.
Bank B. Indonesia
[BD, BT, IN, MO, NP, PI, PK, SM, LK, TI][PolS, IR, Agr, DevS]

Hoffmann, J.
Klisto Str. 29
1000 Berlin 37
Germany
[MM][Eco, His, PolS]

Hoffmanns, Drs P.R.
Steenbakkerslaan 30
2352 AM Leiderdorp
Netherlands
[ID, LK][AHis, Arch]

Hofland, J.C.
Willem de Zwijgerlaan 16
3116 HX Schiedam
Netherlands
[IN][Rel]

Hofmann, Drs Z.S.
UW,RG Germany
[IN, ID, KR][Ant, Rel, Phi, CuS]

Hohlova, Dr L.V.
MSU,IAAS,CIBS Russia
[IN][Lin, Soc]

Hohnholz, Prof. J.
IWZ Germany
[CN, HK, IN, MY, PK, PH, SG, TH][DevS, Agr, Geo]

Hojgaard, Mr F.C.
37 Tollosevej
2700 Bronshoj
Denmark
[IN, PK][His]

Holdstock, Prof. T.L.
VU FPPW Netherlands
len@psy.vu.nl
[IN, JP][Psy]

Holle, A.
CNRS,MSCH France
[NP, TI][Geo]

Hollup, Dr O.
Sri Lanka
[LK][DevS, Ant]

Holm, N.G.
Sirkkalog 26 A 17
20700 Åbo
Finland
[Ant, DevS]

Holm, S.
UB,DSA Norway
sholm@sasantr.uib.no
[ID][GenS, Ant, CuS]

Holmström, Dr M.
UEA,ODG,SDS United Kingdom
[IN][DevS, Ant]

Holodovich, Dr L.A.
US,COLC Bulgaria
[JP][Rel, Lit]

Holtrot, Prof. D.N.
TUK Netherlands
[ID][CuS, Ant, His, Lit, Rel, Phi]

Holzman, D.
UL3,CREO France
holzman@ehess.fr
[CN][Lit]

Holzner, Dr B.M.
ISS Netherlands
[ID][GenS, Psy, DevS]

Hómery, M.
UP7,UAO France
[CN][Lit]

Hommes, Prof. dr E.W.
UT,DTM Netherlands
[BD, IN, ID, LK, VN][DevS, Ant]

Hong, Dr E.P.
Niederhein strasse 8
40474 Düsseldorf
Germany
[CN, JP, KR][His, IR]

Hoogenhout, Drs S.
D. Defoelaan 3
1102 ZD Amsterdam
Netherlands
[CN, HK, TW][AHis]

Hoogerbrugge, J.
Paulus Potterlaan 35
2902 GN Capelle a/d IJssel
Netherlands
[ID, PG][AHis, CuS]

Hooghe, Drs I.M.A.
c/o Ministerie van BuZa
\Postbus 20061
2500 EB The Hague
Netherlands
[CN][IR]

Hoogland, Drs J.G.D.
K.P. van der Mandelelaan 11
3062 MB Rotterdam
Netherlands
[CN, ID, PK, VN][Eco, DevS, Env]

Hook, Dr B.G.
ULEED,DEAS United Kingdom
[CN, HK, MO, SG, TW][IR, DevS]

Hook, Prof. G.D.
USH,CJS United Kingdom
g.hook@sheffield.ac.uk
[JP][PolS, IR]

Hoppal, Dr M.
HAS,EIF Hungary
[Rel, Ant]

Hor, Mr N.H.
RCE France
[KH][Law, His, IR, PolS, Soc, CuS]

Hor kov , Drs D.
PU,FF,JS Czech Republic
[CN, JP][Lit, Rel]

Hórail, Dr F.
CNRS,EPHE,SHP France
[JP][His]

Horlemann, B.
c/o Dr Isrun Engelhardt
\Fuchsbichl 22-A
82057 Icking
Germany
[TI][Lit, Rel]

Horn, Drs N.A. van
DNB Netherlands
[ID][His, Eco]

Hornby, J.E.
NMD Denmark
[CN, JP, KR, TW][CuS, AHis]

Horst, Dr J. van der
Plantage Doklaan 42-III
1018 CN Amsterdam
Netherlands
[LK][PolS, Rel]

Horuichi, A.
CNRS,IHEC France
[CN, JP][His]

Hospes, Dr ir O.
LW,DDE Netherlands
[IN, ID,][Soc]

Hossain, M.
UH,VT,KI Finland
mhossain@cc.helsinki.fi
[BD, BT, IN, NP, PK, LK][DevS, IR, PolS]

Hottinger, Prof. dr L.C.
UB,GPI Switzerland
[IN, ID, PK, PG][IR, DevS, PolS]

Houben, Dr J.E.M.
RUL,KERN Netherlands
jhouben@rullet.leidenuniv.nl
[IN, PK, LK][Rel, His, Lin, Lit, Phi]

Houben, Dr V.J.H.
UP,SEAS Germany
[ID][His]

Hout, Prof. dr Th.P.J. van den
UvA,AHI Netherlands
[CuS, Lin, Lit]

Hout, Drs I.C. van
KIT Netherlands
[ID][Rel, CuS, CuS, Ant]

Hout, Dr W.
KUN, VP Netherlands
w.hout@bw.kun.nl
[PolS, IR, DevS]

Houtman, Dr G.
RAI United Kingdom
rai@cix.compulink.co.uk
[MM, TH][Ant, Lit, Rel]

Hovemyr, Dr A.P.
Stureparken 5
114 26 Stockholm
Sweden
[LA, MM, TH][Rel, His, CuS]

Howard, Dr K.D.
SOAS,CSEAS United Kingdom
kh@soas.ac.uk
[KR, TH][Ant, Rel]

Howe, Dr L.E.A.
CU,DSA United Kingdom
[ID][Ant]

Howell, Dr J.A.
UEA,ODG,SDS United Kingdom
[CN, HK, IN,][DevS, PolS, GenS]

Hoy, Dr C.S.
ULEED,SG United Kingdom
c.noy@geog.leeds.ac.uk
[CN][GenS]

Hruska, Prof. dr B.
ASCR,OI,DANE Czech Republic
[AF, IR][Agr, His, Lit, Rel, Arch]

Hsu, E.
CU,BASAS United Kingdom
elh25@hermes.cam.ac.uk
[CN][Ant]

Hu Sun, P.-S.
Salado 1, (El Bosque)
28679 Villaviciosa de Odon
(Madrid)
Spain
[CN, TW][Lit]

Hu-Sterk, F.
139, Rue de la Chapelle Ste Anne
78830 Bullion-Moutiers
France
[CN][Lit]

Huang, Dr P.Z.Z.
UH,HT,AA Finland
ejkettun@vipunen.hut.fi
[CN][Rel, His, Arch, Ant, CuS, Phi]

Huang, Dr W.
Netherlands
[CN][DevS, IR, Eco]

Huang, M.
UP7,UAO France
[CN][Lit]

Huang, R.
UMMB,DEEO,DU France
[CN][Lan]

Hubinger, Prof. dr V.
ASCR, IE Czech Republic
[ID, VN][PolS, Ant, Soc]

Hübsch, Prof. B.
UCL,THM France
[MG][His, Rel]

Hudcovicova, A.
Bruynssteeg 47
7411 LS Deventer
Netherlands
[IN, ID, JP, MG, NP, TH, TI][CuS]

Huff, Dr W.G.
UG,DPE United Kingdom
w.g.huff@socsci.gla.ac.uk
[IN][DevS, Eco]

Hugenholtz, Drs W.R.
NIAS Netherlands
[ID][His]

Hughes, Dr D.W.
SOAS,CMS United Kingdom
Dh6@soas.ac.uk
[ID, JP][Ant]

Hughes-Freeland, Dr F.A.
UW,UCS,DSA United Kingdom
f.hughes-freeland@swansea.ac.uk
[ID][Ant]

Huisman, Dr H.
UU,VSGO Netherlands
h.huisman@frw.ruu.nl
[ID][Geo, DevS]

Huizer, Prof. dr G.J.
KUN,IDS Netherlands
[CN, IN, ID, PH, LK, TH][Rel, IR, Env, DevS]

Huizinga, Drs F.
Graaf Janlaan 21
1181 EC Amstelveen
Netherlands
[ID][His]

Huldt, Prof. B.
SIIA Sweden
[CN, IN, ID, JP, KR, PK,][IR, His]

Hulec, Dr O.
ASCR,OI,SC Czech Republic
[CN, HK, IN, ID, JP, KR, MG, MY, MN, MM, NP, PK,][His, AHis, CuS, Arch, IR, Eco, Phi, Lit, Lin]

Hulin, M.
UL3,CREO France
[IN][Phi]

Hull, Mr S.J.
SOAS,DL United Kingdom
sh12@soas.ac.uk
[KZ, TJ, TM][Law]

Hulsbergen, T.

Rustenburgenstraat 423/2
1072 GX Amsterdam
Netherlands
[JP][IR, AHis, Edu, CuS, His, Soc]

Hulsman-Vejsov, Drs M.

Bezuidenhoutseweg 67
2594 AC The Hague
Netherlands
[JP][Eco]

Hulst, W.A.

3e Looiersdwarsstraat 59
1016 VD Amsterdam
Netherlands
[AF, IN, ID, IR, KZ, MY, PK, SG, TJ, TM][Eco]

Hummel, Dr H.

TUCW,PS Germany
h.hummel@tu-bs.de
[JP][PolS, IR]

Humphrey, Dr C.

CU, KC United Kingdom
[CN, MN, NP, TI][Ant, Env, Rel, Soc]

Hundius, Prof. H.

UP,SLTL Germany
[LA, TH][Lit, Lin]

Hunter, Dr J.E.

LSEP,STICERD United Kingdom
j.e.hunter@lse.ac.uk
[JP][His, Eco]

Hunter, Drs H.J.

Japan
[JP][AHis, Rel, His]

Hurpré, Dr J.F.

4 Rue Du Viel renverse
69005 Lyon
France
[IN, ID][AHis, Arch]

Hurtig, Ch.

CERI,FNSP France
[IN][PolS]

Hüsken, Prof. dr F.A.M.

KUN,CPS Netherlands
f.husken@mailbox.kun.nl
[ID][DevS, Ant, His]

Hussain, W.

Martktgasse 11
8001 Zürich
Switzerland
[AF, BD, IN, PK, TJ, TM][CuS, Eco, His, IR, PolS, Rel]

Hussein, Dr A.

LSEP,STICERD United Kingdom
[PK][PolS, CuS, Edu, DevS, Rel, Soc]

Husson, Dr L.

CNRS,IRSEA France
[ID][Soc, His, Ant]

Hutt, Dr M.J.

SOAS,DLCSEA United Kingdom
mh*@soas.ac.uk
[BT, IN, NP][AHis, CuS, Lit]

Hutter, Dr I.

RUG,FRW Netherlands
i.hutter@frw.rug.nl
[IN][Ant]

Huurman, J.

MCNV Netherlands
mcnv@nld.toolnet.nl
[IN][]

Huxley, Dr T.J.

UHU,DSEAS United Kingdom
t.j.huxley@seas.hull.ac.uk
[BN, CN, ID, MY, MM, PH, SG, TH, VN][IR, PolS]

Huxley, Mr A.D.

SOAS,DL United Kingdom
ahg@soas.ac.uk
[LA, MM, TH][Law, His]

Huyser, Drs G.L.J.

Van Polanenpark 81
2441 SG Wassenaar
Netherlands
[ID, MY, TW][IR]

Hylkema, S.

Mariëracker 71
8711 CE Workum
Netherlands
[ID][Rel, Ant, Lin]

Iannaccone, Prof. I.

UIO,DAS Italy
[CN][His]

Idema, Prof. dr W.L.

RUL,SI Netherlands
[CN, HK, TW][Lit]

Ignatovich, Dr A.N.

MSU,IAAS,CIBS Russia
[JP][Rel, His]

IJiri, Drs Y.

RUL,KERN Netherlands
[CN, IN, ID][Rel, AHis, Phi, CuS]

Iljic, R.

CNRS,CRLAO France
[CN][Lin]

Illionnet, D.

Calle Cabeza 29
28012 Madrid
Spain
[VN][Lin]

Illyefalvi-Vitez, Prof. Z.

BME,DEE Hungary
illye@ett.bme.hu
[CN, KR, PH, LK, TW, TH][Edu]

Ilyushenko, V.I.

IWEIR Russia
[MM, ID][His]

Imaeda, Y.

12, chemin de la Bourrellerie
18100 Thénioux
France
[TI][Edu]

Imamovic, E.

UB, ISF Yugoslavia
[ID, JP, TH][His, CuS, AHis]

Immig, Drs O.I.

NISAS Netherlands
[AF, IN, PK, TJ, TM][Soc, His, IR, Rel, Eco, PolS]

Indro Nugroho-Heins, Drs M.

Javastraat 20-III
1094 HH Amsterdam
Netherlands
[ID][PArt, His, Ant]

Ing, E. van den

Schutveldstraat 22
5402 LS Uden
Netherlands
[JP][His, CuS, Lit, AHis]

Inoue, F.

EUR,DSVJ Netherlands
[JP][AHis, CuS, Lit, His]

Inthamone, L.

INALCO France
[LA, TH][Lan]

Ioanesian, Dr S.J.

RAS,IOS,AL Russia
[LA][Edu, DevS, IR, Agr, Eco]

Ioanesyan, Dr S.I.

RASP,IOS Russia
[LA][Eco]

Iongh, Ir H.H. de

RUL,CESP Netherlands
Iongh@rulcml.leiden.univ.nl
[ID][Env]

Ionova, Dr Yu.V.

PGMAE,K Russia
[JP, KR][Ant]

Ipatova, Dr A.S.

RAS,IFES,FEB Russia
[CN][His]

Iqbal, Dr Z.

Pakistan
[PK][DevS, Eco]

Irisa, J.I.

BL,OS,DS United Kingdom
jane,irisa@bl.uk
[JP][DevS, Eco]

Ishaja, Drs F.A.

EUROSEAS Netherlands
[CN, ID, VN][His]

Ishizuki, H.

INALCO France
[JP][His]

Iskoldsky, Dr V.I.

RASP,IOS Russia
[Eco]

Issayeva, Dr N.V.

RASP,IOS Russia
[IN][Rel, Phi]

Ito, Y.

INALCO France
[JP][Edu, GenS]

Ivanoff, Dr I.J.
CNRS,IRSEA France
[TH][Soc, Arch, Ant]

Ivanov, Dr A.A.
Russia
[AHis, His]

Ivanov, Dr B.A.
MSU,IAAS,DSEAP Russia
ivan@polit.iaas.msu.su
[BT, IN, NP][CuS, Ant, His, Rel]

Ivanov, Dr S.M.
SPU, FOS Russia
[BT, IN, NP][Eco, IR, His]

Ivanov, Dr P.M.
[CN HK, TW][His, IR, PolS]

Ivanov, Dr V.B.
[TJ][Lin]

Ivanova, Dr E.V.
PGMAE,K Russia
[TH][Ant]

Ivanovic, S.
IRMO Croatia
snjezana@mairmo.irmo.hr
[BT, IN, NP][PolS, CuS, Env, IR, Eco]

Ivarsson, Dr S.
UC,EAI Denmark
ivars@coco.ihi.ku.dk
[LA, TH][His]

Ivnyi, Dr Z.
Dayka G bor u. 19/A, III./13
1112 Budapest
Hungary
[CN, VN][IR, PolS]

Iwanaga, Dr K.I.
SSE,EIJS Sweden
kazuki.iwanaga@orient.su.se
[JP][PolS, IR]

Iyer, Dr A.
11 Eton House \Leigh Road
N5 15R London
United Kingdom
[ID][AHis, Arch]

Jaarsma, Dr S.R.
UU,VCA Netherlands
s.r.jaarsma@fsw.ruu.nl
[ID, PI, PG,][Ant]

Jackson, Dr E.M.
UD,RRC,,SESS United Kingdom
e.jackson@derby.ac.uk
[IN, PK, LK][Rel]

Jackson, Prof. D.P.
UHAM,KGIT Germany
[TI][Rel, Lit]

Jacobs, Dr H.K.
RUG,FL Netherlands
[IN][His]

Jacobs, Drs E.M.
RUL,VG Netherlands
jacobs@rullet.leidenuniv.nl
[CN, IN, ID, JP, MY, LK][His]

Jacobsen, Dr M.
NIAS Denmark
jacobsen@nias.ku.dk
[ID, PG][PolS, CuS, IR, Ant]

Jacobsen, Prof. dr K.A.
UB,DHR Norway
knut.jacobsen@ikrr.uib.no
[IN][Rel]

Jacq-Hergoualc'h, Dr M.
LPI France
[BN, KH, IN, ID, LA, MY, PH, SG, LK, TH, VN][Rel, His, Arch, His, AHis]

Jacquemin, A.R.A
ULB, CP Belgium
ajacquem@vub.ac.be
[IN][Soc, DevS, PolS]

Jacques, C.
CNRS,EPHE,SHP France
[KH, TH][His]

Jaeger, Drs H.
UT,SIN Germany
[CN, JP][CuS, Rel, Phi]

Jaffer, Dr A.K.H.
VAM,ISEAD United Kingdom
[IN, MO, PK, LK][CuS, His, AHis]

Jaffrelot, Dr Ch.
MSH France
ceri@msh-paris.fr
[IN][PolS]

Jager, Drs Y.M. de
KITLV Netherlands
[ID, MY][Lit]

Jager, Drs L.M.H. de
Waverstraat 105
1079 VK Amsterdam
Netherlands
[PK][His]

Jagtenberg, Dr R.W.
EUR,R Netherlands
jagtenberg@rrj.frg.eur.nl
[CN, HK, JP, MO, TH, VN][Law]

Jahnke, M.
Auf Pastorsfeld 10
47918 Tönisvorst
Germany
[CN, HK, MO, SG, TW][Law, Eco, CuS]

Jakobi, Drs S.
UT,CEAPS Germany
jakobi@uni-trier.de
[CN, KR, MM][GenS, PolS]

Jalagin, Drs S.
UO,H Finland
seija.jalagin@oulu.fi
[JP][His]

James, Drs D.
SOAS,DH United Kingdom
dj3@soas
[BD, IN, NP, PK, LK][PolS, His]

James, Dr J.
KuB, VBSO Netherlands
[ID][DevS, Eco]

Jameson, Drs A.L.
United Kingdom
a.jameson@lancaster.ac.uk
[CN, JP][CuS, His]

Jami, C.
CNRS,REHSEIS France
[CN][CuS, His]

Jamsheer, Prof. H.
UL,IH Poland
[AF, BD, AF, BD, IN, KZ, PK, TJ, TM][IR, His, PolS, Rel]

Janhunen, Prof. dr J.A.
UH,HT,AA Finland
[CN, JP, KR, MN][AHis, CuS, Ant, Arch, Lin]

Jankowski, Prof. H.
AMU,COBS Poland
[KZ, MN, TM][Lin]

Jansen, Dr K.
ISS Netherlands
[TH][Eco, DevS]

Jansen, Drs M.H.M.
UvA,VISTA Netherlands
[MM, NP, TH][Ant]

Jansen, Prof. dr W.H.M.
KUN, CvV Netherlands
[Ant, GenS]

Jansen, Drs A.
RD Netherlands
[Env, Agr, Eco, DevS, Rel, Soc, PolS, Phi, IR, His, Ant, CuS]

Jansen, Drs T.E.
UvA,BZI Netherlands
[ID, MY, SG][DevS, GenS, His]

Janssen, M.
Van Leeuwenhoekstraat 104
2516 GH The Hague
Netherlands
[CN, JP][Phi, His]

Janssen, Prof. dr R.H.C.
Laan van Arenstein 8
2341 LT Oegstgeest
Netherlands
[CN, JP][Psy]

Janssen, Drs A.M.
Marnixkade 15-III
1015 XN Amsterdam
Netherlands
[Ant]

Janssen, Drs F.H.P.M.
Mariaplaats 17
3511 LJ Utrecht
Netherlands
[IN][His, AHis, Arch]

Janssens, Dr R.V.A.
UvA,INDRA Netherlands
ruud.janssens@let.uva.nl
[JP][His, IR]

Janz, K.E.
Forstweg 56
13465 Berlin
Germany
[CN, LA, LK][Ant, Agr, GenS, DevS]

Jaquet, Drs F.G.P.
Maanvlinder 4
2317 JM Leiden
Netherlands
[ID][His]

Jarrige, J.F.
MNAAG France
[AF, BT, KHIN, ID, JP, KR, NP, PK, SG,][His, CuS, Arch, AHis]

Jarylgassinova, Dr R.Sh.
RAS,IEA Russia
[CN JP, KR][Ant]

Jaussaud, Dr J.
UP,IAE France
[CN, HK, ID, JP, KR, MY, SG, TW, VN][Eco, IR]

Javed, M.A.
OW Denmark
[AFCN, IN, PK, TI][CuS, Rel, IR, Soc]

Jayasinghe, M.A.
INALCO France
[IN, LK][Lan]

Jeanne, S.
UMMB,DEEO,DU France
[JP][Eco]

Jebens, Drs H.J.
JGU,IEAS Germany
[ID, PI, PG][CuS, Rel, Phi]

Jeffery, Dr R.
UE,DS United Kingdom
r.jeffery@ed.ac.uk
[BD, IN, PK, LK][DevS, Soc, Ant, GenS, Env]

Jeffery, Dr P.M.
UE,DS United Kingdom
p.jeffery@ed.ac.uk
[BD, IN, PK][DevS, GenS, Ant, Soc]

Jehle, Dr E.
SIFO Netherlands
[CN, IN, ID, JP, KZ, KR, LA, MY, MM, PK, PH][IR, DevS, Eco, Edu, Law]

Jelsma, Drs J.
RUG,BAI Netherlands
[ID][Arch]

Jepma, Prof. C.J.
RUG,VBE Netherlands
c.j.jepma@eco.rug.nl
[BT, IN, LK][Env, DevS, Eco]

Jeppesen, L.
UC,FH,DAS Denmark
[JP][Soc, Ant]

Jerndal, Drs R.
GU,GESEAS Sweden
[LA][Geo, DevS]

Jerneck, Dr A.
UL,NASEAS Sweden
[CN, HK, VN][DevS, Eco]

Jest, C.
CNRS,MSCH France
[BT, CN, NP, TI][DevS]

Jeudy-Ballini, Dr M.
LAS France
[PG][Ant, CuS]

Jevremovic, Dr P.
UB, ISF Yugoslavia
[IN, PK, LK][IR, Law, PolS]

Jimenez Blanco, I.
OJM Spain
[JP][Eco]

Jimenez Valentin, J.M.
ACEF Spain
[KH CN, ID, JP, KR, MO, MY, PI, PG, PH, TH, TW,][Eco, Env, IR]

Jing Li, A.
GIIS,IHP Switzerland
li8@hei.unige.ch
[CN, HK, JP, MO, SG, TW, TI, VN][IR, PolS]

Jirström, Dr M.
LU,DSEG Sweden
Magnus.jirstrom@kulekgeo.lu.se
[MY][Agr, DevS]

Johansen, Prof. dr O.K.
KTM,IPACH Norway
[ID][Arch]

Johansson, Drs J.H.
GU,DSA Sweden
[BD][Ant]

Johansson, Drs P.J.
SU,IOL,CD Sweden
Perry.Johansson@orient.su.se
[CN, HK, TW][CuS, His]

Johnson, Dr G.
UC,CSAS United Kingdom
[AF, BD, AF, BD, IN, PK, LK][His]

Johnson, M.
UCL,DA United Kingdom
[PH][Ant]

Jokinen, Drs J.J.
UTU,SSPH Finland
janvoki@utu.fi
[KH, CN, LA, MM, TH, VN][DevS, IR, PolS]

Jolivet, A.
12 rue du Ruisseau
75018 Paris
France
[PolS, IR, DevS]

Jones, Dr R.M.
UCL,DA United Kingdom
r.m.jones@ucl.ac.uk
[AF, IN, PK, LK][Ant]

Jones, Dr S.
OU,PRM United Kingdom
skye.jones@prm.ox.ac.uk
[AF, TI][Ant]

Jones, Dr R.
Little Antron \Antron Lane, Mabe \Penryn
TR10 9JD Cornwall
United Kingdom
[CN, ID, MY, SG][Lin, Lit, Rel]

Jones, Mr S.C.
PO Box 144 \Bourne
CB3 7SL Cambridge
United Kingdom
[BD, IN, ID, PI, PK,][Eco, DevS]

Jong, Dr C.G.F. de
HKI,BIB Netherlands
[ID][Rel, His]

Jong, Prof. dr F. de
ESCAS Netherlands
fred.dejong@let.ruu.nl
[IN, IR, PK,][CuS, Rel]

Jong, Dr J. de
RUG,VG Netherlands
janny.de.jong@let.rug.nl
[ID, JP][CuS, IR, His]

Jong, Dr J.J.P. de
BuZa, DAO/ZO Netherlands
[ID][IR, His]

Jong, Dr S.C.N. de
EUR,VS Netherlands
[ID][CuS, DevS]

Jong, Dr W. de
UZ,ES Switzerland
wdj@athno-unizh.ch
[ID][Ant, GenS]

Jong, Drs A.H.
D. Defoelaan 183
1102 ZG Amsterdam
Netherlands
[IN, ID][His, GenS]

Jong, J. de
William Boothlaan 4
3012 VJ Rotterdam
Netherlands

Jong Boers, Drs B.D. de
KITLV Netherlands
Bernice@Rullet.LeidenUniv.nl
[ID][Ant, His]

Jonge, Dr H.M.C. de
KUN,CPS Netherlands
hdejonge@man.kun.nl
[ID][Ant, DevS]

Jonge, Drs ing J.D. de
Glazeniershorst 103
7328 TH Apeldoorn
Netherlands
[ID][Soc, Agr]

Jonge, Drs N.C. de
Luttik Oudorp 66
1811 MZ Alkmaar
Netherlands
[ID][Soc, Rel, Ant, His, AHis]

Jongeling, Dr M.C.

Kievitstraat 6
2352 HH Leiderdorp
Netherlands
[ID][Rel, His, GenS, Ant]

Jongeling, Dr K.

RUL,VTW Netherlands
[Lin]

Jongsma-Blanche Koelensmid, Drs H.T.

CFA Netherlands
[CN, HK, JP, SG][AHis, Arch, CuS, His]

Jordaan, Dr R.E.

Onder den Bomen 2
6871 CH Renkum
Netherlands
[ID][His, AHis, Ant, Arch]

Jorgensen, F.V.

Avenue des Arts 18
1040 Brussel
Belgium
[ID, SG][IR, DevS, Env, PolS, Law]

Jorgensen, B.D.

PG Sweden
B.jorgensen@padrigu.gu.se
[IN][IR]

Josephs, Drs N.C.

Keizerottostraat 69-A
1402 VN Bussum
Netherlands
[ID, SG][DevS, Eco, IR, Soc]

Joshi, S.

INALCO France
[IN][Lan]

Joshi, Drs R.R.

UW,IIA Austria
[IN][Lit, Lin]

Josselin de Jong, Prof. dr P.E. de

Willem de Zwijgerlaan 33
2341 EH Oegstgeest
Netherlands
[ID, MY, SG][Ant]

Joukov, Dr A.

RAS,IOS,CJS Russia
[JP][His, PolS, Soc]

Jousse, C.

INALCO France
[CN][Lan]

Joyaux, F.

INALCO France
[His]

Jullien, F.

UP7,UAO France
[CN][Lit]

Jung, Drs J.I.

HESR,ID Netherlands
[ID, MY][Edu, His, Lin, CuS]

Jungmann, Prof. dr B.

RKU,KI Germany
[CN, JP, KR, TW][AHis]

Junne, Prof. G.C.A.

UvA,VVIB Netherlands
[CN, HK, IN, JP, KR, MY, PH, SG, TH][IR, DevS, PolS, Env]

Jutil, Drs S.

AU,DEAS,OI Denmark
[CN][Arch, His]

Jüttner, Prof. Dr G.

Germany
[CN, HK, JP][AHis, CuS, His]

Kaa, Prof. dr D.J. van de

NOW Netherlands
[PG][His]

Kaartinen, Dr T.A.

UH,VT,S Finland
takaarti@valt.helsinki.fl
[ID][Ant]

Kabir, Dr M.R.

KuB, VBSO Netherlands
m.r.kabir@kub.nl
[BD][Eco]

Kaden, Dr M.

MPZ Germany
mkaden@rz.uni-potsdam.de
[ID][Eco]

Kaden, Prof. dr K.

HUB,AA,IS Germany
klaus=kaden@asa.hu-berlin.de
[CN, JP][Lin]

Kahlen, Prof. W.

Germany
[BT, MN, TI][Rel, Ant, AHis]

Kaikkonen, Dr M.

SU,IOL,CD Sweden
marja.kaikkonen@orient.su.se
[CN, HK, TW][Lit]

Kainu, A.

Pilopolku 3 E 27
02130 Espoo
Finland
[Lit]

Kaiser, Drs M.

UBI,FS,SDRC Germany
mrkaiser@post.uni-bielefeld.de
[AF, KZ, TJ, UZ][DevS, Ant, Soc, PolS]

Kal, Drs W.H.

KIT Netherlands
[BD, BT, KH, CN, IN, ID, LA, NP, PK, PH,][Env, Lin, DevS, Agr, CuS, Ant, CuS, GenS]

Kalashnikov, Dr N.I.

RASP,IOS Russia
[PolS]

Kalinnikova, Dr Ya.

RASP,IOS Russia
[IN][Lit]

Kalinovskaya, Dr K.P.

RAS,IEA Russia
[Ant, Soc]

Kalinowski, M.

CNRS,IHEC France
[CN][Lit, His]

Kállay, Dr I.

ELU,CHL Hungary
[JP][His, Lin, Phi, Law, Eco]

Kalpana Kartik MA,

13 rue Ruhmkorff
75017 Paris
France
[IN, ID, MY, PI, PG, TH][Ant, AHis, CuS, Rel]

Kalvodov , Prof. dr D.

Ser¡kov 10
11800 Prague 1
Czech Republic
[CN, IN, JP][Eco, Phi, Law, His, Lin]

Kalyuzhnaya, Dr N.M.

RASP,IOS Russia
[CN][His]

Kamenarovic, Dr I.P.

96, rue Pierrè Demours
75017 Paris
France
[CN][Phi]

Kames, Drs P.

HUB,ITKK Germany
[CN, HK, TW][Lit, AHis, CuS, His]

Kamp, E.P. van der

Hoofdweg 273-III
1057 CX Amsterdam
Netherlands
[KH, ID, LA, VN][His]

Kampen, T.

Goerlitzer str. 70
10997 Berlin
Germany
[CN][PolS, IR, His]

Kamphorst, Drs J.

Oude Veenendaalseweg 6
3911 NL Rhenen
Netherlands
[IN][His, GenS]

Kamstra, Prof. dr J.H.

Peppinghof 37
1391 BB Abcoude
Netherlands
[JP][Rel]

Kan, Dr Q.

ULC,SML,DCS United Kingdom
q.kan@lancaster.ac.uk
[CN][CuS, Lin]

Kannen, B.

Lochner Strasse 22
50674 Cologne
Germany
[ID, MY, TH][CuS, Ant, Rel, Soc]

Kano, M.

INALCO France
[JP][Ant, Rel, Soc, CuS]

Kapp, M.

Bennogasse 17/11
1080 Vienna
Austria
[MM][CuS, Ant, Soc, Rel]

Kaptein, Dr N.J.G.
RUL,TCZOAO,PD
Netherlands
nkaptein@rullet.leidenuniv.nl
[ID][Rel]

Kaptein, L.
RUL,CNWS Netherlands
[Rel]

Karapetiants, Prof.dr A.M.
MSU,IAAS,CIBS Russia
[CN][Ant, Lin, Lit, Phi, Rel]

Kardinaal, Drs A.H.
NSMA Netherlands
[ID][His, PolS, IR]

Karelova, Dr L.B.
RAS,IP,DOP Russia
[JP][His, Phi, Rel]

Kark, M.
UT,DH,COS Estonia
[BT, IN, MN, NP, TI][CuS, Lin, Phi, AHis, Rel, Edu]

Karl, Dr I.
Hans Beimlerstr. 31
10178 Berlin
Germany
[CN][Lin]

Karlsson, Drs K.
NME Sweden
[MM, TH][Rel]

Karlussov, Dr V.V.
RAS,IFES,FEB Russia
[CN][Eco]

Karmay, S.
UP1,CECD,IEDES France
karmay@u-paris10.fr
[CN, NP, TI][His, Lit, Phi, Ant, Rel]

Karmysheva, Dr B.Kh
RAS,IEA Russia
[Ant]

Karpen, Dr A.P.
Kastrupvej 98-A
2300 Copenhagen S
Denmark
[IN][CuS]

Karssen, Dr C.M.
LW,PR Netherlands
[CN, ID, MY, NP, PH, LK, VN][DevS, Env, Agr, Eco, Edu, Soc, GenS]

Karttunen, Dr K.J.
UH,HT,AA Finland
kalus.karttunen@helsinki.fi
[IN, NP, PK, LK][CuS]

Karunaratne, Dr J.A.
VU,DEG Finland
jka@uwasa.fi
[BD, HK, IN, ID, MY, NP, PI, PH, SG, LK,][DevS, Eco]

Kashin, Dr V.P.
RASP,IOS Russia
[IN][His]

Kasi-Henkus, C.
UL3,CREO France
[BD, BT, IN, NP, PK, LK][Eco, DevS]

Katassonova, Dr Y.L.
RASP,IOS Russia
[JP][CuS]

Kater, Dr A.
Heidestein 2
3971 ND Driebergen
Netherlands
[ID, TH, VN][Ant, DevS]

Katkova, Dr Z.D.
RASP,IOS Russia
[CN][His]

Kaul, C.
OU,NC United Kingdom
ckaul@vax.ox.ac.uk
[IN][His]

Kaushik, S.Ch.
INALCO France
[BT, NP,][His]

Kautz, Dr U.
GI,Z Germany
[CN][His, Lin, AHis, Lit]

Kawanami, Dr H.
UL,DRS United Kingdom
h.kawanami@lancaster.ac.uk
[JP, MM][Ant, Rel]

Kazaryan, Dr R.S.
RASP,IOS Russia
[Lit]

Kazer, K.
FCO,NAPRG United Kingdom
[PH][Rel, Ant]

Keck, Dr V.
UB,ES Switzerland
[ID, PI, PG][Ant]

Keijser, Drs A.S.
RUL,SI Netherlands
keijser@rullet.leidenuniv.nl
[CN, HK, TW][Lit]

Keld, L.
AU,DEAS,OI Denmark
[JP][CuS, His]

Kellner, B.
UW,ITBS Austria
[TI][CuS, His]

Kemner, Ir R.
PMS Netherlands
rkemner@mswe.dnet.ms.philips.nl
[ID][CuS, His]

Kemp, Prof. J.H.
UK,EC United Kingdom
[TH][Ant, CuS, Rel]

Kempen, M. van
TGD Netherlands
[ID][Ant, Rel, CuS]

Kennedy, Dr L.A.
UL3,CREO France
kennedy@ehess.fr
[IN][Eco, PolS, DevS]

Keppy, Drs P.J.
UvA,ASSR,CASA Netherlands
[ID, MY, SG][His, Ant]

Kerde, Drs O.
PUM,JZ Germany
[JP][PolS]

Kerloque, Drs F.G.
UHU,DSEAS United Kingdom
f.g.kerloque@seas.hull.ac.uk
[ID][CuS]

Kersale, P.
2 Rue des Trois Freres
75018 Paris
France

Kersenboom, Dr S.C.
UvA,ASC,CASA Netherlands
[IN][Rel, Lin, Ant]

Keskinen, Dr E.O.
UTU Finland
eskeski@utu.fi
[JP][Psy]

Kessel-Hagesteijn, Dr R.R. van
WOTRO Netherlands
kessel@nwo.nl
[KH, ID, LA, MM, TH, VN][His, Ant]

Kester, Drs J.J. van
Vijf Meilaan 29
2321 RH Leiden
Netherlands
[ID][DevS, GenS, Ant, Rel, Soc]

Keurs, Dr P.J. ter
RMV Netherlands
[ID, MY, PG, PH][Ant, CuS, His, AHis]

Kevenhörster, Prof. dr P.K.
WWUM,ISP Germany
kevenho@uni-muenster.de
[CN, ID, JP, MY, PH, TH][PolS]

Keysers, Drs L.
ISS Netherlands
keysers@iss.nl
[BD, IN, NP, PK, PH][GenS, DevS]

Khan, Mr S.M.
Netherlands
[PK][IR]

Kharatischoily, G.S.
SPU, FOS Russia
[AF][His]

Kharatishvilly, H.S.
[AF][His]

Khashimbekov, Dr Kh.
RASP,IOS Russia
[AF][His]

Khazanov, Prof.dr A.M.
RASP,IOS Russia
[IR]

Khin, S.
INALCO France
[His]

Khin, M.S.
HUB,AA,SOA Germany
[MM][His]

Khing, Dr H.D.
LPI France
[KH, TH][Lin, Rel, His, Lit]

Khlynov, Dr V.N.
RAS,IFES,FEB Russia
[JP][PolS, Eco]

Khmelevsky, Dr K.A.
kabanoff@kam.east.spb.ru
[AF, BD, BH, BN, KH CN, HK, IN, ID, JP, KZ, KG,][CuS, Edu, His, Law, Lit, Phi, PolS, Psy, Rel, Soc]

Khokhlov, Dr A.N.
RASP,IOS Russia
[CN][His]

Khokhlova, Dr L.V.
MSU,IAAS,DIP Russia
[IN][Lin]

Khomenko, Dr I.Ye.
RASP,IOS Russia
[IR, PolS]

Khoo, Drs M.J.
United States of America
michael.kuoo@uscu.colorado.edu
[BT, MN, NP, PK, TI][Rel, Arch, Ant]

Khoros, Dr V.G.
IMEMO Russia
[IN][His, PolS, DevS, CuS]

Khosla, Dr A.
RUL,TCJK Netherlands
Khosla@rullet.leidenuniv.nl
[IN, JP][DevS, Eco]

Khrenov, Dr Yu.Ph.
RASP,IOS Russia
[DevS]

Khryashcheva, Dr N.M.
RASP,IOS Russia
[IR]

Kidd, Mr J.B.
AU,ABS United Kingdom
j.b.kidd@aston.ac.uk
[CN, JP, MY][CuS, Edu]

Kieniewicz, Prof. J.
UW,IH Poland
[IN][His]

Kievid, Drs J. de
Leidsekade 101-bis
3531 HC Utrecht
Netherlands

Kikuchi, Y.
CCAD United Kingdom
[JP, KR][His, AHis, CuS]

Kiligbeyli, E.H.
Leninsky Prospekt, \Dom. 37, Flat 16
Moscow
Russia
[PolS, Eco, IR]

Killingley, Dr D.H.
UNC,DRS United Kingdom
d.h.killingley@ncl.ac.uk
[IN][Lin, Rel]

Kilpatrick, Dr H.
155, Avenue de Cour
1007 Lausanne
Switzerland
[IN][Lit]

Kilpatrick MA Dphil, Dr Hilary
Avenue de Cour 155
1007 Lausanne
Switzerland
[Lit]

Kim, Drs S.-H.
IECE Spain
[CN, JP, KR, MN, NP, TW, TH, TI][Arch, Rel, Phi, Lit, His, AHis]

Kim, H.-M.
UH,FAI France
[KR][Lin]

Kim-Lee, B.
UMMB,DEEO,DU France
[KR][Lan]

King, Prof. U.
UBRI,DTRS United Kingdom
[CN, IN, JP, KR, MN, NP, PK, PH, LK, TW,][Phi, His, Edu, Ant, GenS, CuS, Rel, Soc]

King, Prof. V.T.
UHU,DSEAS United Kingdom
[BN, ID, MY][DevS, Soc, Ant, Env]

Kinzelbach, Prof. dr W.K.H.
EPZ,VWHG Switzerland
kinzelbach@ihw.baum.ethz.ch
[CN, TW][Env]

Kirabaev, Dr N.S.
RPFU,DP Russia
[KZ][Phi]

Kirillova, O.B.
Academica Anonima Street 6-3-444
117602 Moscow
Russia
[JP,][Edu, Lin]

Kirkby, Dr R.J.R.
LUI,FSES,DCD United Kingdom
twpred@liv.ac.uk
[CN, HK, TW][Eco, DevS, Env]

Kirkpatrick, Prof. C.H.
UBR,DPPC United Kingdom
colin.kirkpatrick@man.ac.uk
[IN, ID, MY, PH, SG][Env, Eco]

Kisliakov, Dr V.N.
PGMAE,K Russia
[Ant]

Kiss, A.
CNRS,IRSEA France
[CN, TW, VN][Ant, Phi, Psy]

Kistanov, Dr V.O.
RASP,IOS Russia
[JP][Eco]

Kitayama, S.
INALCO France
[JP][Psy, Ant, Phi]

Kittlaus, Drs M.
RUB,FOAW,POA Germany
Martin.Kittlaus@rz.ruhr-uni-bochum.de
[CN, HK, TW][PolS, GenS]

Kiuchi, Prof. Miyako
US, II, DJ Spain
[JP][]

Kiva, Dr A.V.
RASP,IOS Russia
[PolS]

Kivimäki, Dr T.A.
UH,VT,Y Finland
timo.kivimaki@helsinki.fi
[CN, HK, ID, PH, TW][PolS, IR, DevS]

Kjaerholm, L.
AU,FH,DESA Denmark
[DevS, IR, PolS]

Kjellgren, Drs B.
SU,IOL,CD Sweden
bjorn.kjellgren@orient.su.se
[CN, HK][CuS, Soc, Psy, Rel]

Klamer, Dr M.A.F.
VU,VL Netherlands
Klamerm@jet.let.vu.nl
[ID][Lin]

Klaschka, Dr S.J.
FAU,IASK,SJ Germany
sdklasch@phil.uni-erlangen.de
[CN][Lit, Soc, PolS]

Klausing, Andreas
Meisenweg 10
4564 Obergerlafingen
Switzerland
[ID, MY,][IR, PolS, Soc]

Klein, Prof. dr P.W.
RUL,CNWS Netherlands
[ID, JP][His]

Kleinen, Dr J.G.G.M.
UvA,ASC,CASA Netherlands
jgk@sara.nl
[KH, PH, VN][Ant]

Kleinpenning, Prof. dr J.M.G.
KUN,SES Netherlands
[KH, PH, VN][DevS]

Klenner, Prof. Dr Wolfgang
RUB,FOAW Germany
Wolfgang.Klenner@rz.ruhr-uni-bochum.de
[CN, ID, JP, KR, TW][DevS, Eco]

Klerk, B.A.S. de
UNESCO,NC Netherlands
bklerk@nufficcs.nl
[Edu, Soc, DevS, GenS, Env, CuS]

Klerk, N. de
Netherlands

Kliashtorina, Dr V.B.
RAS,IOS,AL Russia
[IR][PolS, Soc, Lit, Rel, Edu, CuS]

Klimburg-Salter, Dr D.
UW,ITBS Austria
[TI][CuS, Lit, Edu, Soc, Rel, PolS]

Klimova, Dr T.N.
RASP,IOS Russia
[IN][Eco]

Kloet, Drs ir B.J.
UvA,ASSR Netherlands
[CN, HK, TW][CuS, Ant, PolS, Soc]

Kloetzli, Prof. dr F.A.
EPZ,GBI Switzerland
[BT, CN, IN, MG, NP, PK][Agr]

Klokke, Dr A.H.
Oude Larenseweg 28
7214 PC Epse
Netherlands
[ID][Lin, Rel]

Klokke, Dr M.J.
RUL,BIB Netherlands
abiaklokke@rullet.leidenuniv.nl
[ID][Arch]

Kloos, Prof. dr P.
VU, DCA Netherlands
p.kloos@scw.vu.nl
[LK][Ant, DevS]

Klooster, Dr H.A.J.
Koningin Emmakade 35-D
2518 RK The Hague
Netherlands
[ID][His]

Kloosterman, J.
IISG,IISH Netherlands
jkl@iisg.nl

Klopfenstein, Prof. E
UZ,IEAS,DJ Switzerland
[JP][Lit]

Kloppenborg, Prof. dr M.A.G.T.
UU,FG Netherlands
mkloppenbo@ggl.ruu.nl
[IN, NP, LK, TH, TI][His, Lin, Lit, Rel]

Klöpsch, Dr V.
UK,OAS,MCS Germany
[CN][Lit, Lin]

Klöslov , Zd.
N Petrin ch 1896/31
16200 Prague
Czech Republic
[KR][His, Lit]

Klotz, Drs S.
RKU,SI,DPS Germany
[KH, ID, LA, MY, NP, PI, PG, PH, LK, VN][PolS, IR]

Klovth, Th.
Görlitzer Str. 39
1000 Berlin 36
Germany
[MM][IR, PolS]

Klugkist, Drs C.W.
NUFFIC, DIAR Netherlands
klugkist@nufficcs.nl
[ID, MY, TW][Edu, CuS, His]

Klyuyev, Dr B.I.
RASP,IOS Russia
[IN][His, Lin, PolS]

Knaap, Dr G.J.
KITLV Netherlands
[ID, MY, LK][His]

Knall, Prof. B.R.
RKU,SI Germany
[IN, MY, NP, PK, SG, LK, TH, VN][IR, Edu, PolS, Eco, DevS]

Knapen, Drs J.J.
KITLV Netherlands
Knapen@Rullet.LeidenUniv.nl
[ID][Ant, His, Env]

Kneib, A.
UAM1,LSH France
[CN][AHis]

Kniffka, Prof. dr H.
UB,SI Germany
[CuS, Lin]

Knight, Dr J.P.
IIAS Netherlands
jknight@rullet.leidenuniv.nl
[JP][Ant]

Knippenberg, Drs L.W.J.
KUN,IDS Netherlands
l.knippenberg@maw.kun.nl
[TH][His, DevS, Env, PolS]

Knödel, Dr S.
HMV,SOA Germany
[CN, TW][CuS, GenS]

Knorringa, Dr P.
ISS Netherlands
knorringa@iss.nl
[IN, ID][Eco, DevS]

Knutsen, Drs H.M.
UO,FSS,HG Norway
h.m.knutsen@sgeo.uio.no
[IN, LK][DevS, Env]

Knyazhinskaya, Dr L.A.
IWEIR Russia
[IN][Eco]

Ko, Prof. dr S.S.
FDILA Netherlands
koswansik@sta.frg.eur.nl
[IR, Law]

Kobayashi, Dr M.B.
UKON,SF,KVMJ Germany
[JP][Psy, Edu, CuS]

Kobelev, Dr E.V.
RAS,IOS,AL Russia
[KH, LA, VN][PolS, His, IR]

Kobzev, Dr A.I.
RASP,IOS Russia
[CN][Phi]

Kockum, K.
LU,FA,DEAL Sweden
[TI][PolS, IR, His]

Koerbs, C.
HUB,AA,IS Germany
christoph=koerbs@rz.hu-berlin.de
[CN, JP, TW][His, Edu, Phi]

Koesoebjono, R.H.S.I.
EUR Netherlands
[AF, ID, JP, LA, MM, PI, LK, TH, VN][DevS, GenS, Eco]

Koesoebjono-Sarwono, Dr S.
Rozeveldlaan 18
2241 NT Wassenaar
Netherlands
[ID][DevS, Psy, Soc, GenS, Ant]

Koessel, P. van
Netherlands

Koester, Drs K.
FAU,IASK,SJ Germany
[CN, HK, JP, TW][Eco]

Kohl, Prof. dr K.-H.
JWGU,VK Germany
[ID, PG][Rel, His, Ant]

Kohl MA, Arko
UT,CEAPS Germany
Kohla@uni-trier.de
[AF, VN][His, PolS, Soc]

Kok, Drs J.T. van de
RNW Netherlands
[ID][His, Ant, CuS]

KöK, Dr H.
ULEED,DP United Kingdom
h.kök@leeds.ac.uk
[KZ, KG, MN, TJ, TM,][IR]

Kokko, Dr A.O.
SSE,DE Sweden
gak@hhs.se
[VN][Eco, DevS]

Koktvedgaard Zeitzen, M.
CU,DSA United Kingdom
[ID, MY, SG,][Ant, Arch, GenS]

Kol, Prof. dr J.
EUR,EW,EC Netherlands
[HK, ID, JP, SG, TW][DevS, Eco, Agr]

Kol Torov , Dr H.
IIPE,BIB Czech Republic
[DevS, IR, PolS]

Kolff, Prof. dr D.H.A.
RUL,KERN Netherlands
kolff@rullet.leidenuniv.nl
[IN, PK, LK][His, Ant, Law]

Kolko, Dr G.
Wittenburgergracht 53
1018 MX Amsterdam
Netherlands
[PH, VN][Eco, PolS]

Kollmar-Paulenz, K.
UB,ZA Germany
[MN, TI][His, Ant, Lit, Rel, CuS]

Kolmas, Prof. dr J.
ASCR,OI Czech Republic
kolmas@orient.cas.cz
[CN, TI][Phi, CuS, Ant, His, Lit, Rel]

Kolontayev, Dr A.P.
RASP,IOS Russia
[Eco, Soc]

Komarov, Dr E.N.
RAS,IOS,DHO Russia
[BD, IN, PK, LK][Soc, His, PolS]

Komarova, Dr I.N.
IL,DEAL Russia
asialang@iling.msk.su
[TI][Soc, PolS, His]

Komarova, Dr I. N.
RAS,IL Russia
[Lin]

Kommers, Dr J.H.M.
KUN,CPS Netherlands
[PI][Ant]

Kondo, Dr.E.
CSFEA Italy
[JP][CuS, His, AHis]

Kondo, K.
Lomanstraat 83
1075 PX Amsterdam
Netherlands

Kondrashkina, Dr E.A.
RAS,IL Russia
[CN, ID, MY][Lin]

Konge Nielsen, Drs M.
AU,FH,DESA Denmark
etnomkn@moes.hum.aau.dk
[CN][Lin]

Koniahin, Dr V.A.
MSU,IAAS,CIBS Russia
[JP][His, Lin]

Koning, Dr J.B.M.
LW,SS Netherlands
koning@pscw.uva.nl
[ID][GenS, Ant]

Koningh, R.T.M. de
Lessinglaan 3
3533 AM Utrecht
Netherlands
[IN, IR][His, IR, AHis]

Konings, Dr P.J.J.
RUL,ASC Netherlands
[IN, IR][PolS, Soc]

Konings, P.
KUL,DOS Belgium
patricia.konings@arts.kuleuven.al.be
[CN][His]

Kontsevich, Dr L.R.
RASP,IOS Russia
[KR][Lin, Lit]

Konttinen, Dr A.
UTU,DS Finland
ankont@utu.fi
[JP][Env, Soc, GenS]

Konttinen, Drs T.P.
Vaha-Hameenkatu 3A
20500 Turku
Finland
[JP][PolS, His]

Kooij, Prof. dr K.R. van
RUL,KERN Netherlands
krvankooy@rullet.leiden.univ.nl
[IN, NP, PK, LK][Arch]

Kooiman, Dr D.
VU, DCA Netherlands
d.kooiman@scw.vu.nl
[His, Ant]

Koolen, Dr G.M.J.M.
Noordmolenwerf 97
3011 DC Rotterdam
Netherlands
[ID, TW][Edu, CuS, His, Rel]

Koolhof, Drs S.
RUL,CNWS Netherlands
Koolhof@Rullet.LeidenUniv.nl
[ID][Lit, Lin]

Kooyman, Dr S.
Willem de Zwijgerlaan 10
2341 EJ Oegstgeest
Netherlands
[PI, PG][AHis]

Korchaguina, Dr T.I.
MSU,IAAS,CIBS Russia
[JP][Lin]

Korff, Dr H.R.
UBI,FS,SDRC Germany
Ruediger.korff@post.uni-bielefeld.de
[TH][DevS, CuS, Soc]

Korff, Dr R.
UBI,FS Germany
[MM][CuS, DevS, Soc]

Korgun, Dr V.G.
RASP,IOS Russia
[AF][His]

Korimushin, Prof. dr I. V.
RAS,IL Russia
sysop@iling.musc.su
[KZ, KG, MN, CN, TM][Ant, Arch, Lin]

Kornev, Dr V.I.
RASP,IOS Russia
[Rel]

Kornicki, Dr P.F.
CU,FOS United Kingdom
[CN, JP, KR][CuS, His]

Kortlandt, Prof. dr F.H.H.
RUL,VTW Netherlands
fklan@rullet.leidenuniv.nl
[CN, IN, JP, KR, MN, MM, NP, TH, TI, VN][Lin]

Kortteinen, Dr T.
UH,VT,S Finland
Timo.kortteinen@helsinki.fi
[MY][Agr, Soc, DevS]

Korwenski, N.
CNRS,LASEMA France
[VN][Soc]

Korzec, Dr M.
RUL,VPW Netherlands
Korzec@rulfsw.leidenuniv.nl
[CN, JP][PolS]

Koshelenko, Dr G.A.
Russia
[Arch]

Kostic, Dr S.
CU,FF,IND Czech Republic
[BD, IN, NP, PK, LK][Rel, Lin, Phi]

Kostyayeva, Dr A.S.
RASP,IOS Russia
[CN][His, PolS]

Kotanski, Prof. dr W.
UW,IOS,DFES Poland
[JP][Lin, CuS]

Kothari, Dr U.
VUM,IDPM United Kingdom
[BD, IN][CuS, GenS, Agr, DevS]

Kotilainen, Dr E.-M.E
AF Finland
[ID][Ant, GenS]

Kotova, Dr A.F.
MSU,IAAS,CIBS Russia
[CN][Lin]

Kott, D.
GAUG,OAS,SIN Germany
[CN, MM, TW, TI][CuS, His, Law]

Koubi, J.
CNRS,LASEMA France
[ID][Soc]

Kourbanov, Dr S.O.
IOS, FED Russia
[KR][Soc, CuS, Edu, His, Rel, PhiAgr]

Kouwen, H.J.

Min-Buza,DCH/HH
Netherlands
[ID, KZ, MN, TJ, TM, UZ][His, IR, DevS, Ant]

Kouwenhoven, F.

CHIME Netherlands
[CN][Ant, CuS]

Kouwenhoven, Drs A.P.

Morsweg 60-B
2312 AE Leiden
Netherlands
[MG][Ant]

Kovrizhkin, Dr S.V.

RASP,IOS Russia
[JP][Eco]

Kozhekina, Dr M.T.

RASP,IOS Russia
[His, IR]

Kozhin, Dr P.M.

RAS,IFES,FEB Russia
[CN][His]

Kozlov, Dr A.A.

RAS,IFES,FEB Russia
aakozlov@ifes.msk.su
[CN, HK, ID, JP, PH, SG, TW, TH][His, Eco]

Kozlova, Dr M.G.

RASP,IOS Russia
[His]

Kozlovsky, Dr Yu.B.

[JP][Phi]

Kraas, Dr F.

UB,GI Germany
kraas@geo.bn.evnet.de
[BN, KH, CN, HK, KZ, LA, MO, MY, MN, MM, SG,][Ant, DevS, CuS, Geo]

Kraatz, Dr M.

PUM,RS Germany
[IN, JP][Rel]

Kracht, Prof. dr K.

HUB, ZSKJ Germany
klaus.kracht@rz.hu-berlin.de
[JP][Ant, His, Phi, Rel, CuS]

Kramarovski, Dr M.G.

Russia
[Arch, CuS]

Kramers, Prof. dr R.P.

Laan van Cattenbroeck 53
3703 BJ Zeist
Netherlands
[CN, HK, TW][Phi, Rel]

Kranenburg, Drs L.G.

CBTG United Kingdom
[CN][IR, Eco]

Krása, Dr M.

ASCR,OI Czech Republic
[BT, IN, NP][His]

Krasnodembskaya, Dr N.G.

PGMAE,K Russia
[IN, LK][Ant, Lit]

Krasser, Dr H.

IATS Austria
[TI][His]

Kratz, Dr E.U.

SOAS,DLCSEA United Kingdom
uk1@soas.ac.uk
[BN, ID, MY][Lit, CuS]

Kraus, Dr W.

UP,SEAS Germany
[ID, MY][AHis, Rel]

Krause, C.

UHAM,SKC,KTV Germany

Krause, Prof. E.D.

UL,OAI Germany
[BN, ID, MY, SG][Lin]

Krauskopff, Dr G.

CNRS,MSCH France
kraus@u-paris10.fr
[NP][Ant]

Kravtsevich, Dr A.I.

RAS,IOS,CJS Russia
[JP][Eco]

Kravtsova, Dr M.E.

RASP,IOS,DSSEAS Russia
[Rel, CuS, Lit]

Krebs, Dr G.

E.C. Diltzstrasse 6
14163 Berlin
Germany
[CN, ID, JP, KR][Edu, His, PolS, IR]

Krebs, C.

MVL,IA Germany
[IN, NP, LK][Ant, Env]

Kreiner, Prof. dr J.

UB,JAP Germany
[JP][His, Ant, CuS]

Kreiser, Prof. Dr Klaus

OFU,TUR Germany
LSKREISER@SPLIT.UNI-BAMBERG.DE
[KZ, KG, TJ, TM][AHis, CuS, His]

Krengel, Dr M.

RKU,SI,AG Germany
[IN, NP, UZ][Soc, Edu, Ant, DevS]

Kretzschmar, A.E.

L. Boisotstraat 15-III
1057 ZM Amsterdam
Netherlands
[ID][His]

Kreutzmann, Prof. dr H.J.

FAU,DG Germany
hkreutzm@geographie.uni-erlangen.de
[AF, BT, CN, NP, PK, TJ, UZ][Agr, DevS, Ant]

Krieg, Dr R.E.

Maassenstr. 5
10777 Berlin
Germany
[CN][GenS, DevS]

Kriegeskorte, Dr M.

UT,SIN Germany
[CN, JP][His, CuS]

Krijnen, Drs H.G.

RUG,VBE Netherlands
[ID][Eco]

Krische, S.

HHU,GI Germany
stephan.krisch@r7.ruhr-uni.bochum.de
[PH, LK][DevS, Env, Geo]

Kristiansen, Prof. K.

UO,FA,EOS Norway
[AF, BD, AF, BD, IN, NP, PK, LK][Rel, CuS, Lin, Lit]

Kroell, Dr A.

CNRS,EPHE,SR France
[AF, IN, PK, TJ, TM][His]

Kroes, Drs G.C.

RUL,CNWS Netherlands
Kroes@rullet.leidenuniv.nl
[ID, MY][Ant, Rel]

Kroll, Y.L.

RASP,IOS Russia
[CN][Phi, His, CuS]

Kronsteiner, K.

UW,ITBS Austria
[TI][CuS, His, Phi]

Krowolski, N.

CNRS,LASEMA France
[VN][Ant]

Kruessmann, Dr I.K.

DFG Germany
kruessmann@ch.dfg.d400.de
[CN, HK, TW][IR, CuS, Edu, Lit]

Krüger, Prof. dr H.

UK,IIFPL Germany
[AF, ID, KZ, MY, PK, SG, TJ, TM][IR, Law, Rel, Soc, Eco]

Kruidenier, Drs J.H.

Van Imhoffstraat 57
3531 HV Utrecht
Netherlands
[CN][His]

Kruijk, Drs J.L. de

EUR,EW,CDP Netherlands
[PK][DevS, Eco]

Kruijswijk, M.F.

SK Netherlands
[ID][AHis, CuS, His]

Kruip, Drs D.

Hemonystraat 53-III
1074 BM Amsterdam
Netherlands
[ID][Ant]

Kruk, Prof. dr R.

RUL,VTCIMO Netherlands
[Phi]

Krupyanko, Dr M.I.
RASP,IOS Russia
[JP][IR]

Krushinsky, Dr A.A.
RASP,IOS Russia
[CN][Soc]

Krylov, Dr A.B.
RASP,IOS Russia
[PolS]

Kryukov, Dr V.M.
RASP,IOS Russia
[CN][His]

Krzyzanowski, Dr L.K.
ul. Grzybowska 39/814
00-855 Warsaw
Poland
[KH, VN][AHis]

Ksenofontova, Dr G.A.
PGMAE,K Russia
[JP, KR][Ant]

Kubin, Prof. dr W.
UB,SS Germany
[CN][Lit, Phi, Rel]

Kubitscheck, Prof. H.D.
HUB,AA,SOA Germany
[ID, MY, MM][His, Ant]

Kuckertz, Prof. dr J.
Achenseeweg 41
12209 Berlin
Germany
[KH, CN, IN, JP, LA, TH, TI][His, Ant]

Kucukcan, Dr T.
UWA,CRER United Kingdom
erraj@csv.warwick.ac.uk
[Soc, Rel]

Kuczera, Dr S.R.
RASP,IOS Russia
[CN][His]

Kudriavtsev, A.V.
RAS,IOS,AL Russia
[His, PolS, Rel, Soc]

Kudryavtsev, Dr A.V.
RASP,IOS Russia
[Rel, Soc]

Kuehner, Dr H.
JGU,ICSK Germany
[CN][Lit, Phi, His, PolS]

Kuethe, Mr F.Ph.
Wmag. Netherlands
[LK][PolS, Phi, Lit, His]

Kügelgen, Dr A. von
RUB,SOI Germany
anke.d.vonkuegelgen@rz.ruhr-uni-bochum.de
[AF, KZ, TJ, UZ][Rel, Lit, His, Edu, CuS, Phi]

Kuhl, Drs M.
EKO Germany
[CN, IN, JP, KR,][Lin, Phi, CuS, His, AHis, Lit, Rel]

Kuhn, Prof. D.
UW,IS Germany
[CN][CuS, His, Arch]

Kühne, Drs C.
UZ,AS,OS Switzerland
kuehne@oas.unizh.ch
[CN][Lit]

Kuhnt-Saptodewo, Dr S.T.
UP,SEAS Germany
sri.kuhnt@uni-passau.de
[ID][AHis, Lin, Lit, Rel, CuS, GenS, Ant]

Kuijper, Drs J.J.P.
Ben Websterstraat 58
3069 XJ Rotterdam
Netherlands
[CN, HK, TW][Eco]

Kuijpers, E.
JvEA Netherlands
[CN, HK, TW][AHis, GenS, Lit, PolS, Edu, His, Phi, Lin]

Kuiken, Drs C.J.
CIP Netherlands
[HK, MO][Rel, Law, CuS]

Kuiper, Drs P.N.
RUL,SI Netherlands
[CN][Lit]

Kulig, Prof. J.
PAN,IES Poland
[CN, HK, ID, JP, KR, MY, TW, VN][Eco, IR]

Kulik, Dr B.T.
RAS,IFES,FEB Russia
[CN][His]

Kulikov, Dr L.J.
RAS,IOS,AL Russia
kulikov@rullet.univ.nl
[IN, MV,][Lin]

Kulikova, Dr L. V.

[JP, KR][Edu, His]

Kulke, Prof. dr H.
CAUK,GA Germany
[KH, IN, ID, LK][His, Soc, Rel]

Kullanda, Dr S.V.
RAS,IOS,AL Russia
[ID, MY][His, Lin]

Kullberg, Dr A.I.
LU,DL Sweden
anders.kullberg@limnol.lu.se
[LA][Edu, Env]

Kulpin, Dr E.S.
RASP,IOS Russia
[CN][His]

Kummer, Dr M.E.F.
LLC Germany
[BN, KH, ID, LA, MY, MM, SG, TH, VN][Psy, RelAgr, Phi, Soc, Lin, IR, Eco, His, Ant, PolS, Env, E]

Kundu, Dr A.
UBR,DSES United Kingdom
a.kundu@bradford.ac.uk
[BD, BT, IN, NP, PK, LK][DevS, IR, PolS, His]

Künzi, A.
Holzhacker Str. 39
3113 Rubingen
Switzerland
[PH][PolS, Eco, DevS]

Kuo, Dr L.
EFEO,BIB France
[CN, JP][Rel]

Kupfer, Dr P.
JGU,FAS Germany
[CN][Lin, CuS]

Kurbatov, Dr V.P.
RASP,IOS Russia
[CN][Eco, His]

Kurian, Dr R.
ISS Netherlands
[IN, MY, PH, LK][Eco, DevS]

Kurylev, Dr V.P.
PGMAE,K Russia
[KZ][CuS, Ant]

Kurz, Dr J.L.
RKU,OAW,SIN Germany
[CN][His]

Kusin, Prof. dr J.A.
KIT Netherlands
[BD, IN, ID, PH, LK, TH][GenS]

Kutsenkov, Dr A.A.
RASP,IOS Russia
[IN][His, PolS]

Kuypers, Drs S.A.M.
IIAS Netherlands
kuypers@rullet.leidenuniv.nl
[ID][Soc, Ant]

Kuypers, E.E.M.
Van der Oudermeulenlaan 13
2243 CR Wassenaar
Netherlands

Kuyvenhoven, Prof. dr A.
LW,DDE Netherlands
kuyvenhoven@nei.nl
[ID][DevS, Eco]

Kuzes, Dr V.S.
RASP,IOS Russia
[CN][His]

Kuznetsov, Dr V.S.
RAS,IFES,FEB Russia
[CN][His]

Kvaerne, P.
UO,FA,CS Norway
[BT, NP, TI][Rel]

Kwantes, Drs R.C.
Segbroeklaan 410-N
2565 EC The Hague
Netherlands

Kwee, Ir H.G.
Kipstraat 197
3011 ZX Rotterdam
Netherlands
[CN, ID][Art]

Kyamilev, S.Kh.
RASP,IOS Russia
[Env, Lin, Rel]

Kychanov, Dr E.I.
RASP,IOS,DSSEAS Russia
[, CN][Ant, His, Law, Lin, Rel]

Laamann, Mr L.P.
SOAS,DH United Kingdom
lars.laamann@bl.uk
[CN, ID][Rel, Phi, His, CuS]

Laar, Drs H.M.F.M. van de
RUL,VTW Netherlands
hvandelaar@rullet.leidenuniv.n
l
[IN, ID][Lin]

Laar, Dr A.J.M. van de
ISS Netherlands
vdlaar@iis.nl
[IN, ID][Eco, DevS]

Labat, A.
UJML3,FL France
[CN][Lin]

Labbal, V.
CNRS,MSCH France
[NP, TI][Agr]

Labrousse, Prof. dr P.
CNRS,EHESS France
[ID][Agr]

Labrousse-Soemargono, F.
Tour Jade 29 \16, rue
Vandrezanne
75644 Paris Cedex 13
France
[ID][Agr]

Labrune, L.
UMMB,DEEO,DU France
[JP][Lin]

Labus, U.L.
HHU,BIB Germany
labus@ub.uni-duesseldorf.de
[Lin]

Lackner, Prof. dr M.
GAUG,OAS,SIN Germany
mlackne@gwdg.de
[CN, HK, TW][Phi, His]

Lafont, Prof. dr P.B.
CNRS,EPHE,SEP France
[LA, MM, TH][His, Rel]

Lagashova, Dr B.-R.
RAS,IEA Russia
[AF][Ant]

Lagaune, E.
CNRS,IRSEA France
irsea@romarin.univ.aix.fr
[CN, HK, MO, SG, TW][Ant]

Lamant, Prof. P.L.
LPI France
[KH, ID, LA, MY, MM, PH,
SG, TH, VN][SocAHis, CuS,
Arch, Rel, His]

Lamba, Drs J.K.
Bailiffs House \Yeaton
SY4 2HY Shropshire
United Kingdom
[IN][AHis, CuS, His]

Lambert, Prof. B.H.
SSE,EIJS Sweden
Japan@hhs.se
[IN, JP, PI][PolS]

Lambourn, Dr E.A.
13 Robin's Dale
GU21 2LQ Knaphill, Surrey
United Kingdom
[IN, ID, MY,][AHis, Arch]

Lambrecht, M.
KMKG,HCS Belgium
[VN][AHis]

Lamers, Drs J.P.
RUL,TCJK Netherlands
jplamers@rullet.leidenuniv.nl
[JP][His]

Lammerts van Bueren, Dr E.M.
TF Netherlands
[ID][Eco, Env, Soc]

Lamouroux, Ch.
EFEO,BIB France
[CN][His]

Lamshukov, Dr V.K.
RASP,IOS Russia
[IN][Lit]

Lamsweerde, F. van
KIT Netherlands
[IN][Ant]

Lamvieng Inthamone, M.
INALCO,LAO France
[Ant]

Lamvik, G.M.
UTR,SAI Norway
gunnar.lamvik@sv.utnu.no
[PH][Ant]

Lancashire, Prof. R.D.
15 Cecil Avenue
EN1 1PT Enfield, Midox
United Kingdom
[CN, HK, TW][Lit, Rel]

Lancee, Mr L.E.
RUL,CILC Netherlands
[ID][Law]

Lanciotti, Prof. L.
ISIAO Italy
[CN, TW][Rel, Lit]

Lancret, N.
CNRS, IPRAUS France
[ID][Art]

Landa, Dr L.Y.
RAS,IOS,AL Russia
[KZ, TJ][His, Soc, PolS]

Landa, Prof. Dr. R.G.
RASP,IOS Russia
[Soc]

Lande, A.
Netherlands
[ID, JP][His, PolS, Soc]

Landman, Dr N.
ESCAS Netherlands
nico.landman@let.ruu.nl
[ID, JP][Rel]

Landsberger, Dr S.R.
RUL,SI Netherlands
Landsberger@rullet.leidenuniv.
nl
[CN, HK][PolS, IR]

Landy, Dr F.
UL3,CREO France
[IN][Agr, DevS, Geo, Eco]

Lange, Dr L.H. de
RUL,SI Netherlands
[CN][His]

Lange, Dr C.
128 rue du Bac
75341 Paris Cedex 07
France
[KH, LA, MO, TH, VN][His,
Rel, Ant, His, AHis, Soc]

Lange, Drs ir Ph.G. de
Diakenhuisweg 112
2033 AS Haarlem
Netherlands
[ID, PG][Env, Ant]

Langlet, Dr P.
UP7,UAO France
[VN][His]

Langlet-Quach, T.T.
CNRS,EPHE,SHP France
[His, Lit, Rel, CuS]

Lanjouw, Dr G.J.
RUG,VBE Netherlands
g.j.lanjouw@eco.rug.nl
[VN][Eco, Edu]

Lannoy, Drs M. de
Nieuwstraat 25-C
2312 KA Leiden
Netherlands
[IN][His]

Lanzaco Salafranca, Drs F.
[JP][Eco, Lin, Phi, Psy, Rel,
Soc]

Lapina, Prof. Dr. Z.M.
MSU,IAAS,CIBS Russia
[CN][CuS, Ant, His, Law,
PolS]

Laping, Dr J.
Christophstr 31
69214 Eppelheim
Germany
[IN][PolS, CuS, DevS, Env,
Ant, IR, Rel, Soc, His]

Larcher, A.
UP7 France
[IN, VN][His]

Lardinois, R.
UL3,CREO France
[IN][Soc, His]

Large, Dr S.S.
CU,FOS United Kingdom
[JP][His]

Larin, Dr A G
RAS,IFES,CRC Russia
aakozlov@ifes.msk.su
[CN, TW][His, IR]

Larsen, Dr A.K.
UTR,SAI Norway
Ankala@sv.ntnu.no
[MY][Ant]

Laseur, Dr W.J.J.
RUG,VBB Netherlands
[ID][DevS]

Lasic, H.
OAW,IKGA Austria
[TI][DevS]

Laskewicz, Drs Z.A.L.
Rogierlaan 283
1030 Brussel
Belgium
[ID][CuS, Lin, Ant]

Lasschuijt, Drs I.D.
IIAS Netherlands
lasschuyt@rullet.leidenuniv.nl
[JP][IR, PolS]

Lasserre, Ph.
INSEAD,EAC,BIB France
[PolS, IR]

Latter, Dr R.
WP,IC United Kingdom
[IR]

Latyshov, Dr I.A.
RASP,IOS Russia
[JP][IR, PolS]

Lau, W.Y.
EUR,HK,KW Netherlands
142112WL@student.eur.nl
[CN, HK, JP, KR, SG, TW][SocAHis, CuS]

Laube, Prof. J.
LMU,IOAK,JAP Germany
[JP][CuS, Edu, Phi, Rel]

Laubscher, Prof. dr M.S.
LMU,IVA Germany
[IN, ID][Rel, Ant]

Lauer, Drs U.
RKU,KI,AA Germany
[CN, JP, MN][AHis]

Laureillard, Dr M.
UP,CREOPS,AA France
[CN][His, AHis]

Laurent-Perrey, I.
CNRS,MSCH France
[NP, TI][AHis]

Lauridsen, Prof. L.S.
RU,IIDS Denmark
lsl@ruc.dk
[TW, TH][DevS]

Lautenbach, Drs H.
RUG,FRW Netherlands
h.lautenbach@frw.rug.nl
[ID, PK, LK][His]

Lavoix, V.
INALCO France
[CN][His, Lin, Lit]

Lawson, Drs Y.B.
KI Netherlands
[ID][Soc, Ant, IR]

Lazerson, Prof. M.
Via Versigliami
58050 Catabbio
Italy

Le Bonheur, A.
MNAAG France
[Law]

Le Failler, Dr Ph.
CNRS,IRSEA France
[VN][His]

Le Nestour, P.
CNRS,CRLAO France
[JP][Lin, Lit]

Le Nouëne, P.L.N.
MP France
[CN, JP][AHis, Arch]

Le Och-Mach, T.-C.
INALCO France
[VN][Lan]

Lê Thành Khôi, Prof. dr
15 rue Georges Pitard
75015 Paris
France
[VN][His, CuS, Edu]

Lebail, A.
5 rue Taillepied
95200 Sarcelles
France
[His, Edu, CuS]

Lebedev, Prof. Dr. K.A.

[AF][Lin, Lit]

Lebedeva, Dr N.B.
RASP,IOS Russia
[PI][IR]

Lebedeva, Dr I.P.

[JP][Eco]

Lebreton, A.-S.
CNRS,MSCH France
[NP, TI][Art]

Lecher, Drs H.E.
UW,IS Austria
hanno.lecher@univie.ac.at
[CN, TW][His, Soc]

Lechervy, Chr.
MD,DAS France
[BN, KH, JP, KR, MY, MM, PH, TH, VN][IR, PolS]

Lecomte-Tilouine, Dr M.
CNRS,MSCH France
[NP, TI][Ant]

Ledovsky, Dr A.M.
RAS,IFES,FEB Russia
[CN][His]

Lee, Dr S.-K.
UW,IJS Austria
A7611dae@awiuniii.edvz.univie.ac.at
[CN, IN, ID, JP, KR][CuS, Lit]

Lee, Drs J.T.
SOAS United Kingdom
jl21@soas.ac.uk
[CN][His]

Lee, H.
USG,MITM Switzerland
[IN, JP, KR][Env, Eco, Edu, CuS]

Lee, B.-J.
INALCO France
[KR][Ant]

Lee, Drs W.-S.
RUB,FOAW,KOR Germany
weon-sook.lee@rz.ruhr-uni-bochum.de
[KR][Phi]

Lee Jen, W.-T.
EOI Spain
[TW][Lin]

Leemann, Prof. dr A.
UZI,DG Switzerland
[ID, TH][Agr, DevS, CuS]

Leenhouts, Drs M.A.
RUL,CNWS Netherlands
maleenhouts@rullet.leidenuniv.nl
[CN][Lit]

Leeuw, Dr K.L. v.d.
UvA,FW Netherlands
leeuw@philo.uva.nl
[CN][Phi]

Leeuw, Drs E.J.
Heemraadssingel 184-M
3021 DM Rotterdam
Netherlands
[DevS]

Legrand, Prof. J.
36, rue Louis Talamoni
94500 Champigny s/ Marne
France
[MN][Lin, His]

Lehmann, Dr T.
RKU,SI,DI Germany
d53@ix.urz.uni-heidelberg.de
[IN][Lin]

Lehrmann Rasmussen, Dr J.
DCHR Denmark
jlr@dcmr.dchr.dk
[IN, NP, LK][Eco, Phi, DevS]

Leibold, M.
UW,IS Germany
michael.leibold@rzhub.uni-wuerzburg.de
[CN][Rel, Phi, His]

Leider, J.P.
Route de Bissen, 3
9173 Michelbuch
Luxemburg
[MM][His]

Lein, Dr A.
KSG Germany
[KR][DevS, PolS, IR, Eco]

Leinss, Dr G.L.
EKUT,JAP Germany
[JP][CuS, His]

Lelyukhin, Dr D.N.
RASP,IOS Russia
[IN][His]

Lemarechal, Dr A.
USHS,ISESA France
[PI, PH][Lin]

Lemoine, Dr J.
CNRS,CASCIP France
lemoine@msh-paris-fr
[CN, JP, LA, TH, VN][CuS, Ant, GenS, His, Psy, Rel]

Lengerke, Dr H.J. von
V-SD Germany
[BD, IN, LK][Env, Agr, Geo]

Lenman, Prof. B.P.
USTA,DMH United Kingdom
bl@standrews.ac.uk
[BD, IN, ID, MM, PK, LK, TH][His]

Leothaud, G.
CNRS,LACITO France
[ID][His]

Lercari, C.
INALCO France
[Lin]

Leschenko, Dr N.
RAS,IOS,CJS Russia
[JP][Lin]

Lesger, Dr C.
Netherlands

Leshchenko, Dr N.F.
RASP,IOS Russia
[JP][His]

Lesseur, C.
MP France
[CN, JP][AHis]

Lesslauer, Drs C.
Birken Str. 29
4055 Basel
Switzerland
[CN, JP][Ant]

Lesthaeghe, Prof. R.
ULB, CP Belgium
[CN, IN, ID, PK, LK][DevS, Soc]

Leszczynski, Prof. L.
UMCS Poland
lesles@ramzes.umcs.lublin.pl
[CN, IN, JP, KR][Soc, PolS, Law, Eco]

Lethiaghin, Dr D. V.
RAS,IL Russia
[VN][]

Letsch, Drs M.
UvA,ASC,CASA Netherlands
[IN][Ant]

Leukart, Dr A.P.
UG,FL,DSA Switzerland
[IN][Lin]

Leung, Drs A.
Op den Toren 140
6361 VH Nuth
Netherlands
[CN, HK][Lin]

Leutner, Prof. dr M.
FUB,OS,SIN Germany
mleutner@zedal.fu-berlin.de
[CN, TW][GenS, CuS, His]

Levelt, Prof. dr W.J.M.
MPIP, CARG Netherlands
pim@mpi.nl

Levin, Dr Z.I.
RASP,IOS Russia
[Phi, Rel]

Levinson, Prof. S.C.
MPIP, CARG Netherlands
levinson@mpi.nl
[IN, PG][Psy, Lin, Ant]

Levtonova, Dr Y.O.
RAS,IOS,AL Russia
[PH][His, PolS, IR]

Levtonova, Dr Yu.O.
RASP,IOS Russia
[PH][PolS]

Lévy, Ch.
UMMB,DEEO,DU France
[JP][His]

Lévy, Dr A.
UMMB,DEEO,DU France
[CN, TW][Lit]

Lévy, A.-M.
UMMB,DEEO,DU France
[IN][Lan]

Levy-Ward, Dr A.
CNRS,LASEMA France
award@ext.jussieu.fr
[LA, TH][Ant, Lin]

Lew, Dr R.
36, avenue F. Roosevelt
94300 Vincennes
France
[CN][Soc, PolS]

Lewis, Dr D.C.
160 Southwood Road \Rusthall
TN4 8UX Tunbridge Wells, Kent
United Kingdom
[JP, KZ, MN, TM][Rel, Ant, CuS]

Lewis, Dr J.B.
OU,OI United Kingdom
jay.lewis@oriental-institute.ox.ac.uk
[JP, KR][His]

Lewis, Dr M.E.
CU,FOS United Kingdom
mel1000@hermes.cam.ac.uk
[CN, TW][Arch, His, Lin, Ant]

Li, X.
AU, RCDIR Denmark
xing@i4.auc.dk
[CN, HK, TW][DevS, PolS, IR]

Li, R.
LJMU,SSS,CPRS United Kingdom
r.y.li@livjm.ac.uk
[CN, HK, JP, KR, TW][PolS, IR]

Li, Drs X.F.
Muntendamstraat 23
1091 DR Amsterdam
Netherlands
[CN][AHis]

Li, Y.
AMU,COBS Poland
[CN][Soc, Ant, CuS]

Li, Dr Y.
RUL,VVI Netherlands
[CN, HK, TW][Law]

Li, Dr W.
UNC,DS United Kingdom
li.wei@ucl.ac.uk
[CN, HK, SG, TW][Lin, Edu, Psy]

Li, D.C.S.
UJML3,BIBS France
[CN][Lit]

Li, Dr O.
UP7,UAO France
[KR][His, Rel]

Liang, Prof. dr J.C.P.
RUL,SI Netherlands
liang@rullet.leidenuniv.nl
[CN][Lin]

Liao, R.
NI Norway
[CN, HK, JP, TW, TI][IR, DevS, PolS, AHis]

Lichtveld, A.
Rozenstraat 131b
1016 NP Amsterdam
Netherlands
[JP][AHis]

Lidin, Prof. O.G.
UC,FH,DAS Denmark
[JP][Phi, CuS]

Lidova, Dr N.
RAS,IWL Russia
[IN, LK, TI][AHis, CuS, His, Lit, Phi, Rel]

Lie, Prof. R.K.
UB,DP Norway
reidar.lie@fil.uib.no
[ID, LK][Phi, DevS]

Lie, Drs H.
Hoofddorpplein 9
1059 CV Amsterdam
Netherlands
[CN, HK, SG, TW][Eco, Ant]

Liegl, Dr M.
Grüner Weg 49
12359 Berlin
Germany
[KR][His, PolS]

Lieshout, Drs W.D.C. van
BOT Netherlands
[BT, BN, ID,][Arch, AHis, Ant, His]

Lieshout, Ir M. van
LW,DHN Netherlands
machteld.vanlieshout@eti@voed.wau.nl
[ID][Agr]

Lieten, Dr G.K.
UvA,ASC,CASA Netherlands
g.k.lieten@mail.uva.nl
[IN, NP, PK][Soc, DevS, Agr]

Liew-Herres, Dr F.M.
UHAM,SKC,TBI Germany
[CN, MY][His]

Lightfoot, Drs S.
Unicorn House
28 East St. Helen Street
OX14 5EB Abingdow
Oxfordshire
United Kingdom
[CN, TW][AHis]

Ligthart, Drs M.J.H.M.
Prinseneiland 331
1013 LP Amsterdam
Netherlands
[ID, MY, PH][Env, PolS, DevS]

Lim, Dr P.
KUL, FSW Belgium
paullim100710.323@compuserv.com
[MY, SG][DevS, Soc, PolS]

Lin, C.-W.
Alpmechrain 6
4143 Dornach
Switzerland
[CN, HK, TW][CuS, Psy, Ant]

Lin, X.
Netherlands

Linck, Drs F.C.
Sumatrastraat 60-II
1094 NG Amsterdam
Netherlands
[IN, ID][Ant]

Lindberg Falk, M.L.F.
GU,DSA Sweden
monica.lindberg.falk@sant.gu.se
[TH][CuS, Rel, Ant, GenS, Soc]

Lindberg-Wada, Prof. K.G.
SSE,EIJS Sweden
Gunilla.lindberg-wada@orient.su.se
[JP][Lit]

Lindblad, Dr J.T.
RUL,VG Netherlands
lindblad@rullet.leidenuniv.nl
[ID][His, Eco]

Lindell, Drs K.
LU,DLP Sweden
[KH, LA, TH, VN][Lin, CuS, Env]

Linden, F.J.W.T. van der
Doesburgermolenweg 7
6718 TR Ede
Netherlands
[BT, CN, HK, LA, MO, TW, TI][IR, PolS]

Linden, B. van der
Raamstraat 42
1016 XM Amsterdam
Netherlands
[IN, PK][CuS, His, Rel]

Linden, Dr J.J. van der
IISG,IISH Netherlands
jj.vd_linden@scw.vu.nl
[IN, PK][DevS]

Linder Sabine, Drs L.
LMU,AIS Germany
[CN, ID, MN, MM, NP, TH, TI, VN][Ant, Arch, Soc]

Lindhoud, Drs P.C.
CHW Netherlands
pc.lindhoud@chw.nl
[CN, ID, JP][His]

Lindskog, E.I.M.
JPCAB Sweden
[VN][Soc, DevS, GenS, Ant, CuS]

Lindved Madsen, J.
Nordre Fasanvej 120, 4.tv
2000 Frederiksberg
Denmark
[CuS, DevS, GenS, Ant, Soc]

Ling, Prof. T.O.
Flat 3
14 Clifton Terrace
BN1 3HE Brighton, East Sussex
United Kingdom
[MY, SG, TH][Rel]

Lingen, Ing J.
Albert Schweitzerstraat 29
2861 XZ Bergambacht
Netherlands
[AF, IN, ID, MY, PK, LK][His]

Lingen, Drs B.M. van der
6 Carol Court
143 Auckland Road
SE19 2RR London
United Kingdom
[JP][CuS, GenS]

Linhart, Prof. dr S.
UW,IJS Austria
[JP][His, Soc]

Link, Drs U.A.
Stettiner Str. 33
32427 Minden
Germany
[CN, TW][Lit, His, Phi]

Linkenbach, Dr A.
CMOS Germany
[IN][Soc, Ant, Env]

Linn, Drs R.E.
Hugo de Grootstraat 17-A
2518 EA The Hague
Netherlands
[ID][His, PolS, DevS, Soc]

Linschooten, Drs R.
Pieter Saenredamstraat 175
7312 RA Apeldoorn
Netherlands
[ID][IR, PolS, Lin, CuS, Eco, His]

Linz, Drs J.
EKUT,JAP Germany
[CN, JP][CuS, His]

Liperovsky, Dr V.P.
RASP,IOS Russia
[IN][Lin]

Lipinsky, Drs A.
Hohe str. 94 / Hurst
51570 Windeck
Germany
[CN, HK, TW][GenS, Law, DevS]

Lipovsky, Dr K.Yu.
RASP,IOS Russia
[PI][Eco]

Lippe-Fan, Dr Y.Q. von der
Laupendahler weg 23a
42579 Heiligenhaus
Germany
[CN, HK, TW][CuS, Lin]

Lippert, Prof. W.L.
FAU,IASK,SJ Germany
[CN][Lin, His]

Lippiello, Drs T.
UV,DSIEO,J Italy
[CN][Rel]

Lipton, Dr M.
USUS,FE United Kingdom
[BD, IN, PK, LK][DevS, Agr, Eco]

Liscák, Dr V.
ASCR,OI Czech Republic
[CN, JP, MN, TI][Rel, His, Phi, Lin, CuS]

Lisiakova, L.
RAS,ICPS Russia
[CN][Eco, Soc, Agr]

Lissevich, Dr I.S.
RASP,IOS Russia
[CN][CuS, Rel]

Lissevitc, I.S.
IOS,DCR Russia
[CN][Phi, Rel, Lit]

Litamahuputty, Drs B.H.J.
RUL,CNWS Netherlands
Bathseba@rullet.leidenuniv.nl
[ID][Lin]

Littrup, Dr L.
Frb. Bredegade 13 A-1
2000 Frederiksberg
Denmark
[CN, HK, TW][His, Edu]

Litvinsky, Dr B.A.
RASP,IOS Russia
[His]

Liu, Dr J.-K.
IFA Germany
[CN][PolS, Law, IR]

Liu, Drs B.S.
UO,FA,EOS Norway
[CN][IR, PolS, Law]

Liu, R.
INALCO France
[CN][Lan]

Liu, Drs T.T.
ICS United Kingdom
[CN, TW][Lit]

Liu-Sun, H.
INALCO France
[CN][Lan]

Liushnea, Dr D.S.
RA,IWE,EEA Romania
[CN, HK, KZ, MN, TJ, TW, TM, VN][DevS, Eco, IR, PolS]

Livshits, Prof. Dr. V.A.
[AF][His]

Liyanaratne, J.
INALCO,CIV France
[IN, LK][IR, Eco, DevS, PolS]

Lo, Dr A.H.B.
SOAS,DEA United Kingdom
[CN][Lit]

Lo, X.-X.
INALCO France
[CN][Lan]

Lobato, Dr M.L.M.
CEHCA Portugal
[ID, MY][His]

Lobo, Dr W.
MVB Germany
[BD, BT, BN, KH, IN, ID, LA, MY, MM, NP, LK][AHis, Ant, Arch]

Loch, P.
INALCO France
[KH][Lan]

Lochen, C.
UAM1,LSH France
[CN][Lan]

Locher-Scholten, Dr E.B.
UU,VG Netherlands
elsbeth.locher.scholten@let.ruu.nl
[ID][IR, GenS, His]

Loewe, Prof. dr M.A.N.
CU,FOS United Kingdom
[CN][His]

Loh, Min Ling
Gudenauer Weg 128
53127 Bonn
Germany

Loke-Schwalbe, Dr P.M.L.
SMVD,DSA Germany
[BD, BT, IN, JP, LK, TI][CuS, Ant]

Lomanov, Dr A.V.
RAS,IFES,FEB Russia
Alomanov@ifes.msk.su
[CN, TW][Phi]

Lombaers, Drs H.A.
Westeinde 8
1017 ZN Amsterdam
Netherlands

Lombard, Prof. dr D.
CNRS,DAC France
[CN, ID][His]

Lommel, Dr A.
Bad Brunnthal 4
80 Munich
Germany
[PI, VN][His, AHis, CuS]

Lomov , Dr O.
CU,FF,DEAS Czech Republic
lom@ruk.cuni.cz
[CN][Lit]

Long, Dr Seam
RASP,IOS Russia
[Lin]

Loon, Prof. dr P. van der
Old Boars Hill \Midhurst
OX1 5JQ Oxford
United Kingdom
[CN][His, Lin]

Loop, Dr T.H.M. van der
ISS Ethiopia
[IN, ID][Env, DevS, Eco]

Loosli, Dr U.
UZ,IEAS,DJ Switzerland
loosli@oas.unizh.ch
[JP][Lin, CuS, PolS]

Lopez, Drs S.
UvA,VKG Netherlands
[IN, ID, MY, SG, TH][CuS, His, AHis]

Lopez Navalon, J. A.
Avda Pablo Iglesias N° 94 6°E
28039 Madrid
Spain
jlopez@ugdna.aena.es
[JP][Eco, Lin, IR]

Lopez Sastre, G.
UCLA,CSH,DF Spain
[CN, HK, TW][Phi]

Lorenz, J.
HUB,AA,SOA Germany
[MM][AHis, CuS, His]

Lorenz, Prof. D.
FUB,W,IW Germany
ls-lorenz@ccmailer.wiwiss.fu-berlin.de
[CN, HK, IN, ID, JP, KR, LA, MY, MM, SG, TW,][Eco]

Loseries, Dr A.S.
Franck Str. 31
8010 Graz
Austria
[BD, BT, IN, MN, NP, TI][His, Rel, CuS, Phi, His, AHis, DevS, Ant]

Lostragine, Mr V.N.
3 Likhachowski per 7/1, fl. 67
125438 Moscow
Russia
[ID, MY][Lin, His]

Louis, B.
10 square du Dragon
78150 Le Chesnay
France
[His, Lin]

Loureiro, Prof. dr R.M.
ULHT,PP Portugal
[CN, JP, MO][His, CuS]

Loven, Drs K.
RUL,CNWS Netherlands
Loven@rullet.leidenuniv.nl
[ID][Lit]

Lowe, Dr P.C.
VUM,DH United Kingdom
[KH, CN, HK, JP, KR, LA, MY, MN, MM, TW, TH, TI][IR, His]

Lowira, C.
CNRS,IRSEA France
[TH][Ant]

Loyré, Dr G.
CNRS,IRSEA France
[PH][His, Rel, PolS, Ant]

Lozerand, E.
INALCO France
[JP][Lit]

Lu, S.
INALCO France
[CN][Lan]

Lu, Drs H.
CNRS,CASCIP France
luhui@dmi.ens.fr
[CN][Ant]

Lu, Dr L.
CNRS,CASCIP France
[CN][Ant]

Lubeigt, G.
LPI France
[MM, TH][His, AHis, Agr, DevS, Ant, PolS, Env, Arch, Eco, CuS, Geo, H]

Lubo-Lesnichenko, Dr.o E.I.
[Arch, CuS]

Lubotsky, Dr A.
RUL,VTW Netherlands
Lubotsky@Rullet.Leidenuniv.n l
[IN][Lin]

Lubrano di Ciccone, C.
8, Rue de L'Alboni
75016 Paris
France
[His, Lin, CuS, Ant]

Lucardie, Drs G.R.E.
BIL,AD Netherlands
grl@bilance.antenna.nl
[ID, MY, PI, PG][Ant, DevS]

Lucas, Dr N.
CNRS,CJ France
LUCAS@KIMSI.FR
[JP][Lin]

Lucas, A.
CNRS,CRLAO France
[CN][Lin]

Luczanits, Dr Ch.
UW,ITBS Austria
[IN, PK, TI][His, AHis, Rel, Arch]

Ludwar-Ene, Dr G.
UBAY,KW,E Germany
[Ant, Rel, DevS, GenS]

Ludwig, D.
Herengracht 24
2312 LD Leiden
Netherlands

Lüem, B.
UB,ES Switzerland
Lueem@ubaclu.unibas.ch
[ID][Ant, CuS]

Luesink, Drs A.W.M.
GO,IP Netherlands
Post@nvgom.nl
[KZ, TJ, TM][Eco, Lin, Lit]

Lukàs, É
Fehérv ri £t 147
1119 Budapest
Hungary
[CN, HK, JP, MO, SG, TW][AHis, IR, His, CuS]

Lukaszuk, Dr L.B.
UW,FJPS,IIR Poland
[BN, KH, ID, LA, MY, MM, PH, SG, TH, VN][Law, Eco, IR, DevS]

Lukoyanov, Dr A.K.
RASP,IOS Russia
[CuS, Rel]

Lulei, Prof. W.
HUB,AA,SOA Germany
[MM][DevS, IR, Law, Eco]

Lummer, Drs E.
Mannsfelder Strasse 17
50968 Cologne
Germany
[BN, ID, MY, PH, SG][His, Ant, CuS, Lit]

Lund, Prof. R.
UTR,DG Norway
[MY, LK, TH][GenS, Geo, DevS]

Lundström, S.H.I.
MCM Sweden
hakan.lundstrom@mhm.lu.se
[JP, LA][Geo, GenS, DevS]

Lundström-Burghoorn, Dr W.S.Y.M.C.
GU,DSA Sweden
wil.lundstrom@sant.gu.se
[BD, ID, MY, VN][Ant, DevS, GenS]

Lunsing, W.M.
President Steinstraat 36-A
2312 ZS Leiden
Netherlands
[JP][Ant, CuS, GenS, PolS]

Lunsingh Scheurleer, Drs P.
RMA Netherlands
[IN, ID][AHis, Arch]

Lunyov, Dr S.I.
RASP,IOS Russia
[IN][IR]

Luova, Drs O.E.
UTU,SSPH Finland
outi.luova@utu.fi
[CN, KR][IR, PolS]

Lushnikova, Dr L.I.
RASP,IOS Russia
[Eco]

Lütkes, Dr C.
WWUM,IE Germany
[CN, KR][Ant]

Lütt, Dr J.K.
HUB,AA,SOA Germany
[IN][His, Rel]

Luttik, Drs J.
HKI,BIB Netherlands
[ID][His]

Lutz, P.
SC Switzerland
[ID, MG, NP, PK, PH, LK, VN][Eco, GenS, Env, Edu]

Lyonnet, B.
CNRS,AAC France
[PK, TJ][Arch]

Lysenko, Dr V.G.
[IN][Phi]

Lyssenko, N.
UP7,UAO France
[CN][Lin]

Maaker, Drs E. de
RUL,CA/SNWS Netherlands
maaker@rulfsw.leidenuniv.nl
[IN][Ant]

Maan, Drs E.E.
HIS Netherlands
[ID, TH][Soc, DevS]

Maanen, G.H.O. van
Netherlands
gert.edcs.nl
[BD, KH, IN, ID, LA, NP, PI, PH, LK, TH,][Rel, GenS, DevS, Law, Eco, Agr]

Maaren, F. van
RUG,FB Netherlands
f.van.maaren@rcondw.rug.nl
[PH][IR, Eco, DevS]

Maas, C.H.J.M.
H. Verheeslaan 47
5283 CR Boxtel
Netherlands
[PK][His, AHis]

Maas, Dr A.J.J.
EUR, RSCM,DOPS
Netherlands
amaas@fac.fbk.eur.nl
[IN][His, AHis]

Mac Dowal, Prof. dr D.W.
Admont, Dancers End, Tring
HP23 6JY Herts
United Kingdom
[AF, IN, PK, LK][Arch, AHis]

Macaista Malheiros, Drs J.
UL,FL,CEG Portugal
[IN, PK][Geo]

Macdonald, Prof. A.W.
UP,LESC France
[IN, NP, TI][Ant, Rel]

Macdonald, Dr C.J.H.
CNRS,IRSEA France
mcdonald@romarin.univ-aix.fr
[ID, PH, VN][CuS, Ant, Lin, Rel]

Macé, M.
CNRS,IHEC France
[JP][His]

Macé, F.
INALCO France
[JP][Rel]

MacFadyean, Dr N.J.
IREES United Kingdom
[CN, HK, TW][Eco, His]

Machetzki, Dr R.
IFA Germany
[CN, HK, ID, KR, MY, SG, TW, TH][DevS, Eco, PolS]

Mackay, Drs C.H.
Groenburgwal 40
1011 HW Amsterdam
Netherlands
[ID][Ant, His, IR]

Mackenzie, Prof. dr J.L.
VU, VE Netherlands
lachlan@let.vu.nl
[PG][Lin]

MacMorran, I.
UP7,UAO France
[CN][His]

Macouin, F.
MNAAG France
[CN, KR][His, AHis]

Maderdonner, Dr M.
UW,IJS Austria
[JP][Soc]

Madsen, Dr S.T.
RU,IIDS Denmark
stigtm@mail.ruc.dk
[BD, IN, NP, PK, LK][Soc, PolS, DevS, Env, Rel, Ant, IR, Law, His]

Madsen, A.M.
CDR Denmark
[Soc]

Maestro Yarza, Irene
Ermengarda 3, Casa 2, 1° 1°
08014 Barcelona
Spain
imaestro@riscd2.eco.ub.es
[PH,][ECOMICS, DEVELOPMENT STUDIES]

Magannon, E.
CNRS,IRSEA France
[PH][Ant]

Mager, Drs E.M.C.
Jac. v. Lennepkade 368-C
1053 NL Amsterdam
Netherlands
[Ant]

Maggi, Dr M.
ISLAO Italy
[Lin]

Magnussen, Drs T.
RU,IIDS Denmark
[KH, KR, LA, MN, MM, VN][DevS, IR, PolS]

Magnusson, J.A.
LU,RDSSW Sweden
jan.magnusson@soch.lu.se
[IN, NP, PK, TI][PolS, Soc]

Magone, R.P.
FUB,OS Germany
magone@zedat.fu.berlin.de
[CN][Lit, Edu]

Mahdi, Ir W.
FHI Germany
waruni@fritz-haber-institut.mpg.de
[ID, MG][Lin]

Mahias, Dr M.-C.
CNRS,TC France
[IN][Ant]

Mahkamov, Dr M.
RASP,IOS Russia
[AF][His]

Mahmoodi, A.
RU,IIDS Denmark
[IN, ID, MY, TJ][Soc, PolS, His, Eco, DevS, CuS]

Mahn, Dr S.
Alfred-Schurig-Strasse 1
04318 Leipzig
Germany
[BD, BT, IN, NP, PK, SM, LK][His, AHis, CuS, Arch]

Maier, Prof. dr H.M.J.
RUL,TCZOAO Netherlands
maier@rullet.leiden.univ.nl
[ID, MY][Lit]

Maillard, M.
CNRS,AAC France
[AHis, Arch]

Maing-van der Werff, Drs H.I.
KUN,CPS Netherlands
[ID][GenS, Ant]

Maitre, E.
UP7,UAO France
[CN][His]

Majewicz, Prof. dr A.F.
AMU,COBS Poland
[CN, JP, PI, PG, TH, VN][Lin, Ant]

Majstorac, Drs A.
UB, DOS Yugoslavia
[JP][CuS, His, Lit, Rel, AHis]

Mak Phoeun, Dr
LPI France
[KH][His]

Makarenko, Prof. dr V.A.
Apt. 9, 93 Vernadskogo
Prospekt \V-526
117526 Moscow
Russia
[IN, ID, MY, PH, SG, LK][Lin, Lit, His, Ant, Edu, CuS, Rel]

Malakhovsky, Prof.dr K.V.
RASP,IOS Russia
[PI][His, PolS]

Malamoud, Mr Ch.
UL3,CREO France
[IN][Lin]

Malashenko, Prof. A.V.
RAS,IOS,AL Russia
[KZ, TJ, TM, UZ][Rel, PolS]

Malcontent, Drs P.A.M.
UU,VG Netherlands
[IN, ID, VN][His]

Malik, Dr J.
UB,OKG Germany
jamal.malik@ibm.rhrz.uni-bonn.de
[BD, IN, KZ, PK, TJ][His, Rel, CuS, Edu, His, Lit]

Malik, Dr I.H.
BCHE,SH United Kingdom
imalik@bathhe.ac.uk
[PK][His]

Malinar, Dr A.
EKUT,SIVRW Germany
[IN][Rel, Phi, Lit, GenS, CuS]

Mallee, Drs H.P.
RUL,CNWS Netherlands
mallee@rullet.leidenuniv.nl
[CN][Ant, DevS, Agr, Soc]

Mallick, Drs S.
UHAM,II Germany
mallick@orientalistik-uni-hamburg.de
[BD, IN, PK][Rel, Lit, Law, His]

Mallison, Dr F.
CNRS,EPHE,SHP France
[IN][Rel, Lin, Lit, His, CuS]

Malmqvist, Prof. N.G.D.
Odengatan 23
11424 Stockholm
Sweden
[CN, HK, TW][Lin, CuS, Lit]

Maloney, Dr B.K.
QUB,SG,PC United Kingdom
b.maloney@qub.ac.uk
[ID, PG, TH][Env]

Malyarov, Dr O.V.
RASP,IOS Russia
[IN][Eco]

Malyavin, Dr V.V.
RAS,IFES,FEB Russia
[CN][His]

Mamayeva, Dr N.L.
RAS,IFES,FEB Russia
[CN][His]

Mamedova, Dr N.M.
RAS,IOS,AL Russia
[IR][Eco, His, Edu]

Manandhar, Drs S.
CNRS,MSCH France
[NP, TI][Ant]

Manceron, G.
LDH France
[His, CuS]

Mancini, J.-M.
CNRS,IRSEA France
[VN][His]

Mann, Dr M.
FU,ESGW Germany
[IN, PK, LK][His, Env]

Manning, Dr C.M.
10 Durham Place
SW3 4ET London
United Kingdom
[IN][His]

Manor, Prof. J.G.
UL,ICS United Kingdom
jmanor@sas.ac.uk
[BD, IN, LK][PolS]

Manschot, Drs E.B.
EUR, RSCM,DOPS
Netherlands
emanschot@fbk.eur.nl
[ID][PolS, Eco]

Manso, L.
UCM, INE Spain
[VN][Agr, Edu, Env, His, IR]

Manthey, B.
UB,JAP Germany
manthey@uni-bonn.de
[JP][Lin]

Mantienne, F.
LPI France
[KH, CN, MM, TH, VN][His, Eco]

Manuhutu, Drs W. Chr.
MHMSM Netherlands
[ID][His]

Manurung-Boekhoudt, C.M.A.
Govert Flinckstraat 199hs
1073 BV Amsterdam
Netherlands
[ID][Ant]

Manzenreiter, Drs W.
UW,IJS Austria
Wolfram.manzenreiter@univie.ac.at
[JP][Ant, Soc]

Marco Mart¡nez, Dr C.
UCM,FF Spain
[CN, TW][Lin]

Marco Martínez, Consuelo
UCM,FF,FEI Spain
[CN, TW][Lin]

Marek, Dr J.
CU,FF,IND Czech Republic
jan.marek@ff.cuni.cz
[IN, PK][CuS, Lit]

Mares Petr, PM
Hlavacova 1163
18200 Prague
Czech Republic
[CN,][Rel]

Maretina, Dr S.A.
PGMAE,K Russia
[IN][Ant]

Marett, Dr P.
20 Barrington Road
\Stoneygate
LE2 2RA Leicester
United Kingdom
[CN, IN, ID, SG,][Rel, Law]

Marey, A.J.F.
A. Schweitzerlaan 201
2552 PG The Hague
Netherlands
[ID, PI, PG][Rel, Law]

Margolin, J.L.
CNRS,IRSEA France
[KR, SG, TW][IR, Eco, His, PolS]

Marinelli, Dr M.M.
Via Lemonia 47
40133 Bologna
Italy
[CN, HK, ID, JP, MY, PH, SG, TW, TH, VN][His, IR, PolS, DevS]

Markariants, Dr S.B.
RASP,IOS Russia
[JP][Eco]

Markov, Dr A.P.
RAS,IFES,FEB Russia
[JP][His]

Markov, Prof.dr G.Ye.

[Ant, Soc]

Markov , Dr D.
ASCR,OI Czech Republic
[IN][Soc, Lit, Rel, GenS, CuS]

Markovits, Prof. C.
UL3,CREO France
[IN][His]

Marks, Dr A.F.
Netherlands

Marques Gvedes, Prof. dr A.
UNL,CHAM Portugal
[PH][Ant]

Marquet, Ch.
INALCO France
[JP][His, Lit]

Marr, Dr J.R.
BVB United Kingdom
[AF, IN, ID, KZ, MY, MM, NP, PK, SM, SG, LK][Lin, His, CuS, Arch, His, Phi, Rel, AHis, Lit]

Marschall, Prof. dr W.
UBE,IE Switzerland
marschall@abeclu.unibe.ch
[ID, MG][Arch, Agr, Ant]

Marshak, Dr B.I.
Russia
[Arch, AHis, CuS]

Marszewski, Dr T.
UJ,IOP,CP Poland
[AntAnt]

Martchenko, S.D.
MSU,IAAS,DSEAP Russia

Martel, G.
9 rte de Gif Villiers Le Bacle
91190 Gif sur Yvette
France
[AntAnt]

Martin, Prof. dr B.
ALU,HS Germany
[CN, JP][His]

Martin, Prof. H.
RUB,FOAW Germany
[CN, HK, TW][CuS, Lit]

Martin, Dr
UP,CREOPS,AA France
[Agr, His, Ant]

Martin, A.E.
101 Warnham Court Road
SM5 3ND Carshalton Beeches
Surrey
United Kingdom
[CN][Lin]

Martinell Gifre, E.
Aribau 255, 5° 2°
08021 Barcelona
Spain
martinell@lingua.fil.ub.es
[PI, JP, MO, MY,][Lin]

Martinez Peinado, Javier
UB,FEE, DPEEEM Spain
[ECONOMIA]

Martinussen, Prof. dr J.
RU,IIDS Denmark
johnm@iu.ruc.dk
[BD, IN, MY, NP, PK, LK, TH][Eco, DevS, PolS]

Martokusumo, Ir W.
UGK,SL Germany
[ID][Art]

Martyshin, Dr O.V.
IWEIR Russia
[IN][PolS]

Martzel, G.
INALCO France
[JP][]

Marx, C.
HUB,AA,IJ Germany
[JP][Lin]

Mas Murcia, A.
O. Namon de la Cruz N° 98
28006 Madrid
Spain
[CN, HK, ID, KR, MO, MY, PH, SG, TW, VN][Eco]

Masachs Castell, J.
Pav Picasso, 59, 2n
08304 Mataró
Barcelona
Spain
[CN, JP][Eco, Geo, His, IR, Soc, PolS]

Masala, F.
Via Asiagno no. 5
09122 Cagliari
Italy
[ID, MY, PH][Edu]

Mascarenhas, J. A. S.
UNL,CHAM Portugal
[IN][His]

Mash, M.J.
MU,SHP United Kingdom
Mezindaz@mdx.ac.uk
[ID, MY, PH][AHis, GenS, His]

Masi, Dr E.M.
Moscova 60
20121 Milan
Italy
[CN][His, Lit]

Masina, P.P.
RU, DSS Denmark
pietro@ruc.dk
[CN, VN][DevS, His, IR]

Masini, Dr F.
URLS,DOS Italy
[CN][Lit, Lin]

Maslov, Dr G.M.

[VN][His]

Maslov, Dr Yu.N.
RAS,IFES,FEB Russia
[LK][Eco]

Maslov, Dr A.A.

[CN][His]

Massard-Vincent, Dr J.
CNRS,LASEMA France
[MY][Ant]

Massier, Drs A.W.H.
RUL,VVI Netherlands
[ID][DevS, Lin, Law, His]

Massonnet, P.
CNRS,MSCH France
massonne@cnrs.bellevue.fr
[BT, IN, NP, TI][His, IR, Soc, Rel, PolS, AHis, DevS, Law, Env, CuS, Lin, His]

Maters, Drs M.J.
UU,VG Netherlands
[ID][His]

Mathou, Th.
CNRS,MSCH France
[NP, TI][His]

Matringe, Dr D.
UL3,CREO France
matringe@msh-paris.fr
[IN, PK][Lin, Lit, Soc, Ant, CuS, Rel]

Matrussova, Dr T.N.
RASP,IOS Russia
[JP][Eco]

Mattila BA, M.M.
Rauduntie 11 C
0213 Espoo
Finland
[CN, JP][AHis, Lit]

Maucuer, M.
MC France
[CN, JP][AHis, Phi]

Maue, Dr D.
Moeserstrasse 56
35396 Giessen
Germany
[CN, IN,][Rel, Lin, Lit, Phi]

Maull, Prof. H.W.
UT,CEAPS Germany
maull@uni-trier.de
[JP, KR][IR]

Maurice, A.-M.
225 rue de Vaugirard
75015 Paris
France
[VN][Rel, Ant]

Maury, F.
CNRS,CRLAO France
[CN][Lin]

Mawet, Prof. F.
ULB Belgium
[IN][Lin]

Maximov, Dr A.A.
RASP,IOS Russia
[Eco]

Maxwell, Prof. dr T.S.
UB,OKG Germany
[IN][His, AHis]

Mayer, Dr R.D.S.
12 Clyde Street
CT1 1NA Canterbury, Kent
United KIngdom
[IN, TI][Rel]

Mayer, Dr A.L.
RKU,OAW,SIN Germany
[CN, IN, JP][Rel, Phi]

Mayer, Drs M.
RKU,SI,AG Germany
[IN, LK][Soc, Env, DevS]

Mayer, Prof. A.C.
112 Highgate Hill
N6 5HE London
United Kingdom
[IN, PK][Ant]

Mayer-König, Dr B.H.
MLU,KAW,II Germany
[IN, NP, PK][Phi, Rel, Lit]

Mayevski, Dr E.V.
MSU,IAAS,CIBS Russia
[JP][Lin]

Mayoux, Dr L.C.
61 Cheney Way
CB4 1UE Cambridge
United Kingdom
[IN][DevS, Ant, GenS]

Mazaudon, M.
CNRS,LACITO France
[MM, NP, TI][Lin]

Mazgani, M.
Willem de Zwijgerlaan 28
2252 VR Voorschoten
Netherlands
[IR, TJ][Lin, Soc, His, Rel, CuS]

Mazourik, Dr V.P.
MSU,IAAS,CIBS Russia
[JP][Rel, Lit]

Mazur, Dr Yu.N.
MSU,IAAS,CIBS Russia
[KR][Lin]

Mazure, F.J.M.
Icarusstraat 11
1829 DC Oudorp (Z-H)
Netherlands

Mazurov, Dr V.M.
RASP,IOS Russia
[KR][His]

McCargo, Dr D.J.
ULEED,DP United Kingdom
d.j.mccargo@leeds.ac.uk
[JP, TH][PolS]

McClellan, Dr T.M.
UE,DAS United Kingdom
t.mcclellan@ed.ac.uk
[CN][Lit]

McDonaugh D.Phil, C.E.
OBU,DA United Kingdom
cemcdonaugh@brookes.ac.ku
[IN, NP,][Ant]

McDonnel, Dr J.G.
UBR,DAS United Kingdom
j.g.mcdonnel@bradford.ac.uk
[IN, TH][Arch]

McDougall, Prof. dr B.S.
UE,DAS United Kingdom
Bonnie.s.Mcdougall@ed.ac.uk
[CN, HK][Lit, GenS]

McGrail, Prof.dr S.F.
United Kingdom
[BD, IN, PK, LK][Ant, Arch]

McGregor, Dr C.D.
The Spinney
Hamerton Road
Alconbury Weston
PE17 5JD Huntingdon, Cambridgeshire
United Kingdom
[KH, CN, VN][IR]

McGregor, Dr J.A.
UBA,SSS United Kingdom
[BD, TH][DevS, Ant, His]

McGregor, Dr R.S.
CU,FOS United Kingdom
rsm3@hermes.cam.ac.uk
[IN][Rel, Lit, Lin, His]

McKay, Dr A.C.
Kaiserstraat 5A
2311 GN Leiden
Netherlands
[IN, TI][His, Rel]

McKillop, Drs E.D.
BL,OIOC United Kingdom
beth.mckillop@bl.uk
[CN, KR][AHis, CuS, Rel, Lit, His]

McMullen, Prof. D.L.
CU,FOS United Kingdom
[CN][His]

McVey, Dr R.T.
Il Picciolo
53020 Montisi
Siena
Italy
[ID, TH][PolS, His]

Medeiros uno Gaspar, Dr C. de
UL,ICS Portugal
[ID][IR, PolS]

Medina Bermejo, R.
Avenida Castelao 79, 2B
36209 Vigo
Spain
[JP][AHis, His, IR, Lin]

Meer, Dr ir C.L.J. van der
Min.LNV Netherlands
[ID, JP, TH][DevS, Agr]

Meer, Drs M.G. van der
RUL,SI Netherlands
mgvdmeer@rullet.leidenuniv.nl
[CN][Lit]

Meer, N.J. van der
UvA,MAG Netherlands
[ID, TH][His]

Meer, Drs R. van der
HHM,HM Netherlands
[ID, TH][Soc]

Meerman, J.M.M.
VENJB Netherlands
[CN, JP][His]

Meij, Drs Th. C. van der
RUL,TCZOAO,PD
Netherlands
tcvdmeij@rullet.leidenuniv.nl
[ID][Lit, His, AHis, Lin]

Meij, Prof. J.M. de
UvA,VS Netherlands
[ID, JP][His, Law]

Meijer, Drs E.N.
Netherlands
evert@geodan.nl
[CN, IN,][Env, Geo]

Meijer, Dr H.
Parallelweg 37-A
9717 KS Groningen
Netherlands
[ID][IR, His]

Meijeraan, Drs H.
Frans Halslaan 223
2343 EE Oegstgeest
Netherlands
[JP][Geo, Env]

Meijl, Dr A.H.M. van
KUN,CPS Netherlands
t.vanmeijl@mailbox.kun.nl
[PI][His, DevS, Ant]

Meijs, Drs M.A.G.
M.H. Trompstraat 27 II
1056 HW Amsterdam
Netherlands
[AF, BD, AF, BD, CN, ID, KZ, PK, TJ, TM][IR, Rel, Ant, CuS]

Meiracker, Drs C.H. van den
MVROT Netherlands
[ID, PI, PG][Ant]

Mekking, Prof. dr A.J.J.
RUL,VKA Netherlands
[ID, PI, PG][AHis]

Melanowicz, Prof. M.
UW,IOS,DFES Poland
[JP][Lit]

Melby, E.
Eilert Sundgt. 25
4010 Stavanger
Norway
[BD, MM,][DevS, CuS]

Melixetova, Dr I.M.
RASP,IOS Russia
[Soc]

Mellen Blanco, F.
AEEP Spain
[ID, JP, PI, PG][Ant, Arch, AHis, His]

Menick, Drs R.H.
RUL,TCZOAO,PD
Netherlands
[ID][Lin]

Menon, Dr A.G.
RUL,KERN Netherlands
menon@rullet.leidenuniv.nl
[IN, LK][Rel, Lit, Lin]

Menshikov, Lev.
RASP,IOS Russia
[CN, TW][His, Rel, Lit]

Menshikov, Dr L.N.
RASP,IOS,DSSEAS Russia
[CN][Arch, His, Lit]

Mensink, Drs O.H.
FHM Denmark
[BN, KH, ID, JP, KR, LA, PH, TH][AHis, Ant, CuS, His]

Menski, Dr W.
SOAS,DL United Kingdom
[BD, BT, HK, IN, NP, PK, LK][CuS, Rel, Law, Edu]

Menzel, Prof. U.
TUCW,PS Germany
ulrich.menzel@tu-bs.de
[CN, HK, ID, JP, KR, TW][IR, PolS]

Mercier, L.M.
MH,BIB France
[Soc, GenS, Ant, Rel, His, CuS, AHis]

Mercier, N.
CNRS,MSCH France
[NP, TI][Soc]

Meredith, Mr P.I.
RMV, FECC Netherlands
[CN, JP, KR][Art]

Merinero Martin, M.J.
UE,FL,DH Spain
[CN, IN, JP,][His, PolS]

Merrett, Drs N.M.
Flat 3, Courtenay Lodge
Courtenay Terrace
Kingsway
BN3 2WF Hove, E. Ssx
United Kingdom
[CN, HK, MO, TW][Lin, Law, Eco, DevS]

Mertz, M.
UP,CREOPS,AA France
[JP][AHis]

Merz, Drs R.M.
UBI,FS,SDRC Germany
rmerz@hrz.uni-bielefeld.de
[IN, PK, LK][His, Agr, Soc, Eco, DevS, PolS]

Meshcheryakov, Dr A.N.
RASP,IOS Russia
[JP][CuS, His]

Meshkov, Dr K.Yu.
RAS,IEA Russia
[PI, PH][Ant]

Mesquita, Dr R.A.C.
UW,IIA Austria
[IN][Rel, His, Phi]

Messing, Mr A.J.
J.P. Sweelinklaan 8
1401 CD Bussum
Netherlands
[CN, ID, JP][Law]

Messner, Drs A.
CAUK,SO,AS Germany
messner@sino.uni-kiel.de
[CN][His, Soc, Ant, CuS, Law]

Métaillé, M.-H.
UP7,BFDEEO France
[CN][Lit]

Metzger-Court, Dr S.F.
AU,DML,JS United Kingdom
s.f.metzger-court@aston.ac.uk
[JP][Eco, His]

Meuldijk, Drs I.M.
MH Netherlands
[BD, ID, KR, PK, VN][Soc, Agr, GenS, Env, Ant, DevS]

Meulenbeld, Dr G.J.
De Zwaan 11
9781 JX Dedum
Netherlands
[IN][Lin, Lit]

Meulenbeld, Drs B.C.
KIT Netherlands
[AF, BT, IN, ID, NP, PK, TI][CuS, His, Ant, AHis, Rel, Arch]

Meunier, P.
INALCO France
[JP][His, Rel, Arch, Ant, AHis, CuS]

Mevissen, Drs G.J.R.
FUB,AW,IPKG Germany
[IN, NP, TI][His, AHis]

Mey, Dr L.M. van der
RUL,VPW Netherlands
[PI][IR, PolS]

Meyer, A. de
INSEAD,EAC,BIB France
[JP][PolS, IR]

Meyer, Dr E.P.
INALCO,DAS France
eric.meyer@inalco.fr
[IN, LK][His]

Meyer, Dr J.A.M. de
RUG,SIN Belgium
[CN, TI][Lit, Rel, His, Phi]

Meyer, Drs S.
UT,SIN Germany
meyerst@netwareserver.uni-trier.de
[CN, TW][CuS, Eco]

Meyer, E.-M.
UT,FAP Germany
emmeyer@uni-trier.de
[JP][His]

Meyer, F.

CNRS,MSCH France
[BT, NP, TI][Ant, Rel, His, CuS]

Meyer-Tran, E.

UBI,FS,SDRC Germany
erland@hrz.uni-bielefeld.de
[ID, TW, VN][DevS, Agr, His, Soc, Eco]

Meynert, Drs M.J.

LU,PI Sweden
[IN][GenS, Edu]

Mez, Dr H.

SOAS,DL United Kingdom
[CN][Law]

Mezentseva, O. V.

RAS,IP,DOP Russia
[IN,][CuS, Phi, Rel]

Mézerov , I.

SAS,IOAS Slovak Republic
[CN][GenS, Lit]

Mézin, L.

MNCI France
[CN, IN,][His, AHis]

Michael, Drs H.

WWUM,ISO Germany
Michaeh@uni-muenster.de
[Phi, Lit, Arch, His, Lin, Rel, His, AHis, CuS]

Michaels, A.

Overtoom 539-A
1054 CK Amsterdam
Netherlands

Michaelsen, Dr H.

ZKM-M Germany
[TH][CuS, His, AHis]

Michailovsky, B.

CNRS,LACITO France
boydm@lacite.msh-paris.fr
[BT, IN, NP, TI][Lin]

Micollier, Dr E.

CNRS,IRSEA France
[CN, TW][Ant]

Middleton, Dr K.

25 Aston Street
OX4 1EW Oxford
United Kingdom
[MG][Ant]

Miedema, Drs B.J.

Noordeinde 54
1141 AN Monnickendam
Netherlands
[BD, IN, ID][DevS, Eco, Agr]

Miedema, Dr J.

RUL,TCZOAO,PD
Netherlands
miedema@rullet.leidenuniv.nl
[ID, PG][CuS, Rel, His, Ant, DevS, Soc]

Mierlo, Drs H.W.R. van

FF Netherlands
[CN, HK, JP, KR, MN, TW, TI, VN][Lin, CuS, AHis]

Miert, Dr H. van

St. Stephanusstraat 10
6512 HT Nijmegen
Netherlands
[ID][His]

Mijn, Ir F.E. van der

KNAW,IRQA Netherlands
frank.van.der.mijn@bureau.knaw.nl
[ID][DevS, Env]

Mijnssen, Mr W.G.C.

Schubertstraat 12
1077 GS Amsterdam
Netherlands

Mikamo, S.

6C Greenwich South Street
SE1D 8TY London
United Kingdom
[PH][Env, DevS]

Mikkelsen, Prof. dr E.

UO,FSS,EM Norway
egil.mikkelsen@iakn.uio.no
[IN, MV, LK][Rel, Arch]

Mikkelsen, G.B.

AU,DEAS,OI Denmark
ostgm@hum.aau.dk
[CN][His, Phi, Rel, CuS]

Milbert, Dr I.M.

UL3,CREO France
milbert@uniza.unige.ch
[IN, NP, PK][PolS, Law, GenS, Soc, Env]

Milcinski, Prof. dr M.

UL,FF,OAAS Slovenia
majalmulcinski@uni.lj.si
[CN, JP][Phi, Rel]

Miles, M.

4 Princethorpe Road
B29 5PX Birmingham
United Kingdom
[AF, IN, PK,][DevS, Edu]

Milewska, I.

UJ,IOP,CP Poland
[IN][Edu, Lin, Lit, CuS]

Millan Gomez MBA, Yomi

Apolonio Morales, 8-10 Apto. B-405
28036 Madrid
Spain
[JP][]

Miloslavsky, G.V.

RASP,IOS Russia
[Rel, Soc]

Milton, Dr A.

USH,DH United Kingdom
a.milton@sheffield.ac.uk
[ID][Rel, PolS]

Milwertz, Dr C.N.

ICS United Kingdom
cecilia.milwertz@chinese-studies.oxtwd.ac.uk
[CN][CuS, GenS]

Min Tjoa, Prof. dr A.

TUW, IST Austria
tjoa@ifs,tuwien.ac.at
[CN, ID, JP, MY, TH, TI][Edu]

Minde, Dr D. van

RUL,TCZOAO Netherlands
dvanminde@rullet.leidenuniv.nl
[ID, MY][Lin]

Minnee, Drs P.

HH Netherlands
pmi@hh5a.hsholland.nl
[CN, ID, KR, MY, TW][CuS, IR, Eco, Edu]

Minnema, Mr H.E.

RUL,CILC Netherlands
[CN, KZ, MN, TJ, TM][Law]

Minnigh, Ir P.E.

Eefdese Enkweg 21
7211 LK Eefde
Netherlands
[ID, VN][DevS, Env]

Mira Borges, M.C.

Av. Cristofei,
20-1-E
2800 Almada
Portugal
[ID][His]

Mirage, M.

Sarphatistraat 338
1018 GW Amsterdam
Netherlands
[JP, NP, TI][CuS]

Miranda, Dr A.

CMI,DSHR Norway
[BD, IN, LK][DevS]

Miranda, E.M.

URLS,DOS Italy
[CN][Eco, His]

Miroshnikov, Dr L.I.

RASP,IOS Russia
[CuS, His]

Mirsky, Dr G.I.

IWEIR Russia
[PolS, Soc]

Mirza, Prof. H.R.

UBR,MC United Kingdom
h.r.mirza@bradford.ac.uk
[CN, JP, KR, MY, SG][DevS, Eco]

Mischung, Prof. R.

UHAM,IE Germany
[KH, CN, IN, LA, MM, TH, VN][Ant, Soc, Rel]

Mishio, S.

UJML3,FL France
[JP][Ant, Soc, Rel]

Mitrokhin, Dr L.V.

RASP,IOS Russia
[IN][CuS, His]

Mittag, Dr J.H.

IIAS Netherlands
[CN][His, CuS, Rel]

Mitter, Dr P.

USUS,AFRAS United Kingdom
p.mitter@ac.uk
[IN][His, AHis, CuS]

Mittler, Dr B.
RKU,OAW,SIN Germany
barbara@gw.sino.uni-heidelberg.de
[HK, TW][His, Lit, CuS]

Moberg, P.
GU,IOL,JS Sweden
pia.moberg@japan-gu.se
[JP][CuS, Lit, His]

Moeller, Dr K.
Boschetsrieder Str. 51 A
81379 Munich
Germany
[BN, KHCN, HK, ID, KR, LA, MO, MY, MN, MM, PI][IR, PolS]

Moeshart, Drs H.J.
RUL,PK Netherlands
Moeshart@rullet.leidenuniv.nl
[JP][His, IR]

Moffett, J.P.C.
NRI,EAHSL United Kingdom
jm10019@cus.cam.ac.uk
[CN][His, Rel, Lit]

Mohammad, A.T.
CNRS,ARCHIPEL France
[BD, IN, PK][His, Soc, Rel]

Moharir, Dr V.V.
ISS Netherlands
moharir@iss.nl
[BD, IN, NP, PH,][PolS, DevS, Edu]

Mohkamsing, Drs N.
RUL,CNWS Netherlands
mohkamsing@rullet.leidenuniv.nl
[AF, BD, AF, BD, BT, IN, NP, PK, LK, TI][Rel, AHis, Lit, Phi]

Moilanen, Dr I.A.
Emännäntie 31 B 8
40740 Jyväskylä
Finland
[MM][Ant, His, AHis, Rel]

Mojzes, Prof. I.
BME,DEE Hungary
mojzes@ett.bme.hu
[JP][PolS, Edu]

Molen, Dr W. van der
RUL,TCZOAO Netherlands
[ID][Lit]

Molina Memije, A.
Florestan Aguilar, 7-1° Dcha
28028 Madrid
Spain
[PH][His, Lit]

Molinga, Dr P.P.
LW,DISWC Netherlands
Peter,Molinga@Users.TCT.WAU.NL
[IN][Agr, DevS]

Moll, Dr Ir. H.A.J.
LW,VAS Netherlands
henk.moll@alg.de.wau.nl
[IN, ID][Eco, Agr]

Molodyakova, Dr E.V.
RASP,IOS Russia
[JP][His]

Molteni Corrado, Dr C.M.
UC,ISESAO Italy
[JP][Eco]

Molto Garcia, T.
UB,FEE,DEPHP Spain
[CN][Eco]

Moltzer, Drs R.
Torenlaan 39
1217 RV Hilversum
Netherlands
[ID, MY][Ant]

Momdjian, K.
Kerkweg 45
2481 KB Woubrugge
Netherlands

Momounbaeva, Dr M.I.
EK Belgium
[IR, Law, Eco, CuS, PolS]

Moncé Rebollo, Dr B.
UCM,PS Spain
[MO][Ant]

Monclés, Dr A.
UCM,FE,DD Spain
[CN, IN, MY][Env, Edu]

Monfils, Drs V.
Maaswijkstraat 27
2586 CB The Hague
Netherlands

Mong, A.
INALCO France
[CN][Lan]

Mong, Drs A.
12 Ellerdale Road
NW3 6BB London
United Kingdom
[PolS]

Monnet, N.
BNF,MO France
[CN][Lit]

Monogarova, Dr L.F.
RAS,IEA Russia
[Ant]

Montaut, A.
INALCO France
[IN][Lit]

Montero Moreno, J.
Manuel Aguilar Muno 2, 26
28042 Madrid
Spain
[CN, JP, TW][His, Lit, Rel]

Montessoro, F.
UM,IILP Italy
[VN][His]

Montoya, M.
INALCO,DASHA France
[IN][IR]

Montyn, J.
1e Jan Steenstraat 122
1072 NS Amsterdam
Netherlands
[KH, ID, JP, LA, MM, PH, TH, VN][Phi, AHis, CuS, Lit]

Moodley, Mr D.
UGR,SH United Kingdom
d.moodley@greenwich.ac.uk
[IN][His]

Mooij, Dr ir J.E.
ISS Netherlands
mooij@iss.nl
[IN][DevS, PolS]

Moonen, Drs E.M.B.
Hoogte Kadijk 143a II
1018 BH Amsterdam
Netherlands
[PH][Env, Agr]

Moor, Dr E.C.M. de
KUN, VTCMO Netherlands
[Rel, CuS, Lit]

Moor, Drs J.A. de
RUL,VG Netherlands
[ID][His]

Moore, Dr E.H.
SOAS,CSEAS United Kingdom
em4@soas.ac.uk
[KH, MM, TH][AHis, Arch]

Moore, Dr O.J.
259b Lewishamway
SE4 1XF London
United Kingdom
[CN][Arch, His, AHis]

Morch, M.J.V.
Vejsmarkvej 16
7870 Grattrup
Denmark
[AF, MM, TH][Ant]

Moreau, P.
2 rue Graverol
30000 Nîmes
France
[KH, CN, LA, PK, TI, VN][Art]

Morena Martin, T. de la
UCM, FE, DM Spain
[JP,][Edu]

Moreno Garcia, Dr J.
UCM, GH,HAC Spain
[CN, JP][His, IR, PolS]

Moreno Garcia, J.
UCM,GH,DHC Spain
[CN, JP][His, IR, PolS]

Moreno Marcos, A.
IEdCE Spain
[JP][Eco, IR]

Morev, Dr L.N.
RAS,IOS,AL Russia
[LA, TH][CuS, Lin]

Móriot, Prof. CH.
MEUB France
[KH, ID, JP, KR, LA, MG, PI, VN][Ant]

Morozova, Dr M. Yu
RAS,IOS,AL Russia
[KZ, PK, TJ, TM][GenS, Agr, Eco, Env]

Morris-Jones, Prof. W.H.

95 Ridgway
SW19 4SX London
United Kingdom
[BD, IN, PK][PolS]

Mortarivergaracaffarelli, Prof. P.

UG,IMMAH Italy
[BT, CN, MN][Arch, AHis]

Mosca, Prof. L.

UN FII,FPS Italy
[MG][His, PolS]

Mosch, Dr N.

Kaiser-Ebersdorferstr. 90/11/66
1110 Vienna
Austria
[CN, HK, JP, KR, SG, TW][CuS, Phi]

Moser, Dr R.

UBE,IE Switzerland
[IN, NP][Ant]

Moskalenko, Prof. V.N.

26 Kutuzovsky Prospekt, Flat 582
121165 Moscow
Russia
[AF, BD, IN, PK, LK, TJ, TM][His, IR]

Moskalyov, Dr A.A.

RAS,IFES,FEB Russia
[CN][Soc]

Mosyakov, Dr D.V.

RAS,IOS,AL Russia
[KH][Eco, PolS, His]

Motzki, Dr H.H.

KUN, VTCMO Netherlands
[His, Law, GenS]

Moucuer, M.

MC France
[CN, JP][Law, GenS, His]

Mourer, R.

MGHN France
[KH, TH][AHis, Ant]

Moussay, G.

LPI France
[MY][Lit]

Moutal, P.

CNSM France
[IN][Ant]

Mozaffari-Mehdi, Prof. M.M.

AU, DPS Denmark
ifskmehdi@ps.aau.dk
[IR, KZ, MN, PK, TI, TM][PolS, Rel, IR]

Mozheiko, Dr I.V.

RASP,IOS Russia
[CuS, His, PolS, Rel]

Mozheylo, Dr I.

RAS,IOS,AL Russia
[CuS, His]

Much, Dr M.T.W.

UW,ITBS Austria
michael.torsten.much@univie.ac.at
[BT, IN, MN, NP, SM, LK, TI][Phi, Rel]

Mückler, Drs H.N.

UW,IV Austria
Hermann.mueckler@univie.ac.at
[PI][PolS, His, Ant]

Mugruzin, Dr A.S.

RAS,IFES,FEB Russia
[CN][His]

Muijzenberg, Prof. dr O.D. van den

UvA,ASC,CASA Netherlands
vandenmuijzenberg@pscw.uva.nl
[IN, ID, MY, PH, SG, VN][Soc, DevS, Ant, His]

Muir, J.C.

CU,FOS United Kingdom
[CN][His]

Mukhamedova, Dr D.M.

IWEIR Russia
[IN][His]

Mukhherjee, Dr P.

CNRS,LACITO France
[BD, IN, PK][His, Lit, Phi, Rel, AHis, Soc, His]

Mukimjanova, Dr R.M.

RASP,IOS Russia
[His, IR]

Mulder, Dr N.

Postbus 53211
1007 RE Amsterdam
Netherlands
[ID, PH, TH][Soc, Ant]

Muller, Drs G.W.

KNAW,IRQA Netherlands
[CN, HK, TW][Lin, AHis, Lit, His]

Muller, Drs H

Havanastraat 1
2622 HH Delft
Netherlands
[ID][His, Rel]

Müller, S.

LMU,IVA Germany
muellesh@cip.ub.uni-muenchen.de
[CN, MN, TW][AHis, Ant, CuS, His, Arch]

Müller, Dr T.J.

FS Germany
[IN][His, Rel]

Müller, Drs B.

Frans Halsstraat 68
7021 DN Zelhem
Netherlands
[ID][Ant, GenS]

Müller, M.

UK,AHI,DEAA Germany
[KH, CN, IN, ID, JP, KR, MN, NP, PK, TW, TH][His, AHis]

Müller, W.

KFU,IPB Austria
[TI][AHis, Ant, CuS, His, Arch]

Müller, Prof. dr E.

HUB,AA,IS Germany
[CN][Lit, GenS, CuS]

Müller, K.

RKU,SI Germany
[KH, HK, IN, ID, JP, LA, MY, MM, NP, SG, VN][PolS, CuS, His]

Müller, Dr R.

Moosdorfstrasse 4
12435 Berlin
Germany
[CN, HK, TW][His, DevS, PolS, Env]

Müller, Prof. J.

HPM,IG Germany
[ID, PH][Soc, Rel, Phi, DevS, CuS, IR]

Müller, Prof. K.

HHU,JAP Germany
kmueller@uni-duesseldorf.de
[JP][His]

Muller-Boker, Dr U.

UZI,DG Switzerland
boeker@geo.unizh.ch
[IN, NP, PK][GenS, Agr, CuS, DevS, Env]

Müller-Hofstede, Drs C.

OWK Germany
[CN, HK, IN, ID, JP, KR, SG, TW, VN][PolS, Soc, His, IR, CuS, DevS]

Müller-Saini, Dr G.

FF,VSIB Germany
[CN, HK, JP, TW][His, CuS, Ant, Phi, Rel]

Munier MA, M.C.

32/34 ave Fontarabie
75020 Paris
France
[KH LA, MY, MM, TH][Arch, AHis, CuS, Rel]

Munshi, Dr S.

[IN][His, CuS, GenS]

Munthe, Prof. L.

Adrew Smithgt. 17
4024 Stavanger
Norway
[ID, MG][CuS, His, Rel]

Muranova, Dr A.P.

RASP,IOS Russia
[Eco]

Murasheva, Dr G.F.

RAS,IOS,AL Russia
[VN][His, IR]

Mürer, O.H.A.

SOAS,DHAA United Kingdom
[KH, CN, IN, ID, JP, KR,][Arch, His, AHis]

Murr, Dr S.

UL3,CREO France
[IN][Phi]

Musayev, Prof. dr K. M.

RAS,IL Russia
sysop@iling.msc.su
[KZ, KG, TM][Lin]

Mussayev, Dr K.M.
IL,DEAL Russia
[Lin]

Myasnikov, Prof.dr V.S.
RAS,IFES,FEB Russia
[CN][His, IR]

Mydel, Prof. R.
UJ,DG Poland
rmydel@grodzki.phils.vj.edu.pl
[JP][Eco]

Mylius, Prof. K.
Bergstrasse 13
79288 Gottenheim
Germany
[IN][CuS, Lin, Lit, Rel]

Myrman, Y.
SU,DPS Sweden
yngve.myrman@statsvet.su.se
[IN, ID][PolS]

Naastepad, Drs C.W.M.
EUR,EW,CDP Netherlands
Naastepad@cvo.few.eur.nl
[IN][Eco]

Nabers, D.
WWUM,ISP Germany
nabers@uni-muenster.de
[JP, KR][PolS]

Nadal Uceda, F. de
Altingastraat 5
2593 SP The Hague
Netherlands
[CN, IN, ID, JP, PH,][Ant, Arch, Lin, Phi, Psy, Rel]

Nadirov, Dr Sh.G.
RASP,IOS Russia
[MN][IR, PolS]

Naerssen, Dr A.L. van
KUN,SES Netherlands
[MY, PH][DevS, Geo]

Nagashima, Prof. dr Y.
UC,FH,DAS Denmark
Yoichi@coco.ihi.ku.dk
[JP][Lit, IR, His, CuS]

Nagel, Dr B.M.J.
UvA,FW Netherlands
nagel@philo.uva.nl
[IN, JP][Rel, Phi]

Nagel-Angermann, Drs M.
WWUM,ISO Germany
Nagelm@uni-muenster.de
[CN][His, Phi, AHis, Lit, Lin, Arch, Rel]

Nagtegaal, Dr L.W.
KITLV Netherlands
Nagtegaal@Rullet.LeidenUniv.nl
[ID][His, Env]

Nahser, Dr S.
MVB Germany
[JP][AHis]

Nakamura, N.
UP7,UAO France
[JP][Lin]

Nalesini MA, Oscar
NMOA Italy
[ID, MY,][Arch]

Nam, Dr S.G.
RASP,IOS Russia
[KR][CuS]

Naour, .
UL3,ETROM,C France
[CN][His]

Nardin, D.
16 rue Sainte Cécile
75009 Paris
France
[PolS, IR]

Närhi, Drs P.
Martilankatu 24 B 6
04260 Kerava
Finland
[VN][His, CuS, Rel, Ant]

Narmaev, Dr B.M.

[MN, TI][Rel, Lit]

Narten, Prof. dr J.
FAU,IVIS Germany
[IN][Lin]

Nas, Dr P.J.M.
RUL,CA/SNWS Netherlands
nas@rulfsw.leidenuniv.nl
[ID][Ant, DevS, Soc]

Nass, O.
TUCW,WW Germany
[ID, JP, MY, SG, TH, VN][Eco]

Nastich Ph.D.Ph.D., V.N.
RASP,IOS Russia
[CuS, His]

Natschläger, H.
UW,IS Austria
[CN][Arch, AHis, GenS, His]

Naudou, E.
UAM1,LSH France
[IN][Lan]

Naumkin, Dr V.
RAS,IOS,DHO Russia
zviagel@glas.apc.org
[KZ, TJ, TM][Rel, PolS, IR, His, Ant]

Naumov, Dr I.N.
RAS,IFES,FEB Russia
[CN][Eco]

Navarro Celada, F.
Clara del Rey 35° 7° Dcha, B
28002 Madrid
Spain
[KH , HK, ID, JP, KR , LA, MY, MM, PI, PG, PH, SG,][]

Navasquillo Sarrjon, C.
Alberto Villalba, 2
46292 Masacaves
Spain
[PH,][His]

Navlitskaya, Prof.dr G.B.
MSU,IAAS,CIBS Russia
[JP][CuS, His]

Nawas, Dr J.A.
UU,VG Netherlands
john.a.nawas@let.ruu.nl
[JP][Phi, His]

Nayak, Prof. A.
UF,FT,IMSR Switzerland
anand.nayak@unifr.ch
[CuS, Rel, Ant, Phi]

Nazirova, Dr N.N.
RASP,IOS Russia
[His]

Neary, Prof. I.J.
UES United Kingdom
ianj@essex.ac.uk
[JP, KR, TW][PolS]

Nederveen Pieterse, Dr J.P.
ISS Netherlands
nederveen@iss.nl
[IN][Ant, Soc, Rel, PolS, Phi, DevS]

Nelson, Drs E.N.
UU,DA Sweden
enid.nelson@antro.uu.se
[ID][Ant]

Nemchinov, Dr V.M.
RASP,IOS Russia
[Eco]

Nepomnin, Dr O.Ye.
RASP,IOS Russia
[CN][His]

Népote, J.
10 avenue Dubonnet
92400 Courbevoie
France
[BN, KH, LA, TH, VN][Ant, Rel, PolS, Lit, Eco, His]

Nespital, Prof. dr H.
FUB,AW,IPKG Germany
nespital@zedat.fu-berlin.de
[BD, IN, NP, PK, LK][Lit, CuS, His, Lin]

Netshaewa, Dr L.

[JP][Lin]

Nettleton, G.
PRC United Kingdom
[PH][Lin, CuS, His, Lit]

Neuser, Drs J.
Stiglitzweg 9-B
85591 Vaterstetten
Germany
[KH, LA, MM, TH][Lit, Lin, CuS, Rel]

Neuss, J.
FUB,AW,IPKG Germany
jneuss@zedat.fu-berlin.de
[IN][Rel, His, Lin, His, AHis]

Neve, Drs R.G. de
Melis Stokezijde 189
2543 GL The Hague
Netherlands
[ID][His]

Newalsing, R.N.
NM,STC Netherlands
[IN][PolS]

Newman, Dr R.K.
UW,UCS,DH United Kingdom
[BD, IN, PK][His]

Ngo, T.T.L.
KITLV Netherlands
ngo@rullet.leidenuniv.nl
[VN][Lin]

Ngo, Drs T.-W.
RUL,SI Netherlands
twngo@rullet.leidenuniv.nl
[CN, HK, MO, TW][PolS, DevS]

Nguyen, Drs U.
HUB,IAP Germany
nguynaic@sp.zrz.tu-berlin.de
[VN][Edu]

Nguyen, Dr X.L.
CNRS,MSH,CAS France
[VN][Rel, Ant]

Nguyen, Dr V.K.
8, rue Saint Ambroise
75011 Paris
France
[VN][His]

Nguyen, T.
CNRS,LASEMA France
[VN][Soc]

Nguyen, Prof. X.H.
CVC Netherlands
[VN][CuS, Agr, Arch, Lit]

Nguyen, Dr M.H.
HUB,AA,SOA Germany
[VN][Lin]

Nguyen, M.H.
INALCO France
[VN][Lan]

Nguyen, Dr T.-H.
Germany
[KH, LA, VN][AHis, Rel, CuS, His, Arch, Ant, Soc]

Nguyen, Dr P.P.
CNRS,CRLAO France
pnguyen@crlao.paris-msh.fr
[VN][Edu, Lin, Lit]

Nguyen, Dr N.L.
ISS Netherlands
[CN, PH, TH, VN][CuS, DevS]

Nguyen, Dr D.N.
UP7, GHSS France
[LA, VN][Soc, Ant, DevS, Edu]

Nguyen, Q.
INALCO France
[VN][Lan]

Nguyên, Prof. dr T.A.
LPI France
[KH, LA, VN][IR, CuS, His, Rel, Lit]

Nguyen-Tri, Ch.
Bâtiment B, Entrée C \140,
avenue R. Salengro
94500 Champigny sur Marne
France
[CN][Ant, DevS]

Nibbio, N.
EPFL,IMT Switzerland
[JP][Ant, DevS]

Nicholson, Drs M.
UHU,BJL United Kingdom
m.nicholson@lib.hull.ac.uk
[Ant, DevS]

Nickel, Drs L.R.
RKU,KI,AA Germany
lnickel@urz-mail.urz.uni-heidelberg.de
[CN][His, AHis, Arch]

Nicolaisen, I.
NIAS Denmark
nicolaisen@nias.ku.dk
[Arch, His, AHis]

Nicolas, Drs P.J.M.
OCCP Belgium
[CuS]

Nicolini, Dr B
UCSC Italy
bibl02@simised.mi.unicart.it
[AF, KZ, KG, PK, TADZIKHISTAN, TM,][His, PolS]

Niederer, B.
28 Rue Pierre Leroux
75007 Paris
France
[CN, VN][Lin, His, Ant]

Nieh, Dr Y.H.
IFA Germany
[CN, HK, MO, TW][PolS, Law, IR, Eco, His]

Niehof, Prof. dr A.
LW,VH Netherlands
[ID, PH][Ant, Soc]

Nielen, Dr J.E.
BIL,AD Netherlands
[IN, TH, VN][DevS]

Nielsen, Prof. B.
UC,FH,DAS Denmark
bentn@coco.ihi.ku.dk
[CN][Phi, Rel]

Nielsen, J.
RU,IIDS Denmark
[DevS]

Nielsen, Drs H.A.
AU, RCDIR Denmark
han@i4.auc.dk
[BD, NP, VN][PolS, DevS]

Niemeijer, Drs H.E.
TUK Netherlands
[ID][Rel, His]

Niemöller, Dr B.
UvA,FPSCW Netherlands
niemoller@pi.net
[ID][Rel, His]

Niessen, Mr N.J.A.P.B.
RUL,CNWS Netherlands
niessen@rullet.leidenuniv.nl
[ID][Law, DevS]

Nieto Piñeroba, Dr. J.A.
UNED,FPS,DS Spain
[PI][Ant]

Nieto-Sandoval Millan, V.
UCM, GH,HAC Spain
[IN,][His]

Nieuwenhuijsen, Drs J.W. van
Vermeerlaan 3
1412 JX Naarden
Netherlands
[PI, PG][Ant]

Nieuwenhuijsen-Riedeman, Dr C.H. van
Vermeerlaan 3
1412 JX Naarden
Netherlands
[PI, PG][Ant]

Nieuwenhuijze, Prof. dr C.A.O. van
de Mildestraat 34
2596 SX The Hague
Netherlands
[ID][Rel, Soc, DevS, CuS]

Nieuwenhuys, Dr O.
UvA,INDRA Netherlands
onindra@ivp.frw.uva.nl
[IN][Ant, DevS, GenS]

Nihom, Dr M.
IATS Austria
max.nihom@oecw.ac.at
[TI][DevS, Ant, GenS]

Nijenhuis, Dr E. te
Verlengde Fortlaan 39
1412 CW Naarden
Netherlands
[IN][Part]

Nijland, Dr C.
NINO Netherlands

Nijs, Drs C.F. de
RUL,TCZOAO Netherlands
[ID][Lin, Lit]

Nijziel, M.J.
Bachplein 12
3603 CK Maarssen
Netherlands
[CN, HK, IN, ID, JP, KR, MY, MM, PI, PK, PH][IR, Agr]

Nikitin, Dr A.V.

[VN][Phi]

Nikkilä, Drs P.S.
UH,TT,U Finland
[HK][Rel, Phi]

Nikolaeva, M.L.
RAS,IOS,CIS Russia
[PK][PolS, Soc]

Nikolayev, Dr V.P.
RASP,IOS Russia
[PI][IR, PolS]

Nikulin, Prof. N.I.
RAS,IWL Russia
[VN][Lit]

Nikulina, Dr L.V.
RAS,IEA,SEAAO Russia
[BN, ID, MY][DevS, CuS, Ant, Env, Edu, His, Rel, Arch]

Nimerius, P.
SU,CPAS Sweden
[CN][PolS]

Ninomiya, Prof. M.
UG,FAH,DOLL Switzerland
ninomiya@uniza.unige.ch
[JP][Phi, Lit]

Nish, Prof. I.H.
33 Charlwood Drive
KT22 0HB Oxshott
United Kingdom
[JP, KR][PolS, His, IR]

Nishide, M.N.
Oukoopsedijk 13
2811 NE Reeuwijk
Netherlands
[JP][IR, PolS, His]

Nishimoto, Dr K.
IGCR Italy
[JP][Lit, Edu]

Nivard, J.
CNRS,EHESS,BIB,S France
[CN][GenS, Soc]

Niyazi, Dr A.
RAS,IOS,DHO Russia
[BD, IN, KZ, PK, TJ, TM][Env, Rel, PolS]

Njammasch, Prof. dr M.
HUB,AA,SOA,SL Germany
marlene=njammesch@asa.hu-berlin.de
[IN][His]

Noda, S.
INALCO France
[JP][His]

Nodot, E.
UP,CREOPS,AA France
[CN][Arch, His, AHis]

Noël, H.
UTM,CUP France
[JP][AHis, Arch]

Noer, Drs F.L.
Rijnsburgerweg 124
2333 AG Leiden
Netherlands
[JP][Edu]

Noesberger, Prof. J.
EPZ,IPS Switzerland
noesber@ipw.agrl.ethz.ch
[BT][Agr]

Noirbusson-Soubra, S.S.
UP,CREOPS,AA France
[CN][AHis]

Nolten, Drs H.M.
NOVIB Netherlands
[ID, MY, SG][GenS, Geo]

Nooijens, Drs A.I.
Ness 99
1012 KD Amsterdam
Netherlands
[MN][IR, PolS, His]

Nooy, Drs C.I.
UvA,FPSCW Netherlands
[ID][PolS, Env, IR, DevS]

Nooy-Palm, Prof. dr C.H.M.
'La Conaque'
24510 Paunat
France
[ID, PI][Arch, AHis, Env, Ant, Rel]

Norbury, P.
JL United Kingdom
[CN, JP, KR][AHis, Rel, Env, Ant, Arch, His]

Nordenhake, S.C.M.
LU,FA,DEAL Sweden
[CN][Lin]

Nordman MA, G.M.
Merimiethenkatu 33A 21
00150 Helsinki
Finland
[PI, PG][CuS, Lit]

Norlund, Dr I.M.
NIAS Denmark
irene@nias.kv.dk
[PH, VN][His, GenS, DevS]

Nossiter, Prof. T.J.
ULEED,DP United Kingdom
[BD, HK, IN, MY, PK, SG, LK, TW, VN][Soc, PolS, IR, DevS, His]

Nothofer, Prof. dr B.
JWGU,IOOP,SOAW
Germany
nothofer@em.uni-frankfurt.de
[BN, ID, MY][Ant, Lit, Lin, CuS]

Novakova, Dr O.V.
MSU,IAAS,CIBS Russia
[VN][Geo, His, Soc, Edu]

Novaky, Dr G.W.
UU,DH Sweden
gyorki.novaky@hist.uu.se
[BN, ID, MY][His]

Novgorodova, Dr E.A.
RASP,IOS Russia
[Arch, His]

Novgorodskaya, Dr N.Y.
SD,SCIA Russia
[CN][His, PolS, IR]

Novoselova, Dr L.V.
RAS,IFES,CRC Russia
titarenk@ifes.msk.su
[CN][DevS, Eco, IR]

Novossyolova, Dr L.V.
RAS,IFES,FEB Russia
[CN][Eco]

Nowak, Prof. B.K.
UW,IH Poland
[Ant, His, Rel]

Nugteren, Dr A.
TU, FT Netherlands
[IN][Phi, Rel]

Nuijten, Drs I.G.
MPV Netherlands
[CN, HK, MO, TW][Phi, Rel]

Núnez Garcia-Sanco, Antonio
MAE Spain
[Eco, IR, PolS]

Nyiri, Drs P.D.
Költö utca 2-4 A16
1121 Budapest
Hungary
[CN, MY, MM, SG, TW][Ant, PolS]

O'Connor, Drs K.
KPIL United Kingdom
[JP, PI][CuS, Ant, Soc]

O'Hanlon, Dr R.
CU,CC United Kingdom
[IN][His, GenS]

Oberhammer, Prof. dr G.
UW,IJS Austria
[IN][Rel, Phi]

Obi, Drs L.
LMU,IVA Germany
[CN, TW][Rel, CuS, Ant]

Obringer, Dr F.O.
CNRS,IHEC France
[CN, TW][Ant, His, CuS]

Oda, Prof. H.
UCL,FL United Kingdom
[JP][Law]

Odé, Dr C.
RUL,TCZOAO,PD
Netherlands
ode@rullet.leidenuniv.nl
[ID][Lin]

Odegaard, S.E.
UO,FSS,SA Norway
s.e.odegaard@ima.uio.no
[IN, NP][Ant]

Odgaard, Drs K.
AU,FH,DESA Denmark
[KZ][Ant]

Oei, K.L.
Ceintuurbaan 145
1072 GB Amsterdam
Netherlands
[Art]

Oesterheld, Dr J.
HUB,AA,SOA Germany
[BD, BT, IN, NP, PK, LK][Soc, His, PolS]

Oetke, Prof. dr C.
SU,IOS,DI Sweden
claus.oetke@orient.su.se
[IN, TI][Lin, Phi]

Offredi, Prof. M.
UV,DEAS Italy
[IN][His, Lit, AHis]

Ogarek-Czoj, Dr H.
UW,IOS,DFES Poland
[KR][Rel, Lit]

Ogloblin, Prof. A.K.
SPU,FOS,DAS Russia
vladimir@orient.lgu.spb.su
[ID, MY][Lin]

Oguibenine, Prof. B.
USHS,ISESA France
oguibeni@monza.u-stasb.fr
[IN, TI][Lit, CuS, Lin, Rel]

Ogura, M.
UAM1,LSH France
[JP][Lan]

Oh, K.Y.J.
Ganzenstraat 4
3815 JD Amersfoort
Netherlands

Oinas-Kukkonen, Drs H.T.
UO,H Finland
htok@cc.oulu.fi
[JP][IR, His]

Ojeda, Dr A.
UCM,FEE Spain
[KR][Law, PolS]

Ojeda Marin, Prof. Dr A.
UCM,FEE,DDA Spain
[HK, KR, TW][IR, Law]

Okada, A.
MNAAG France
[IN][His, AHis]

Okell, Mr J.W.A.
SOAS,DLCSEA United Kingdom
jo@soas.ac.uk
[MM][Lit, Lin]

Okhuizen, Drs E.
UU,DC Netherlands

Olalla Cuervo, MA I.
Villanueva, 19-5° Izq.
28001 Madrid
Spain
[IN, ID, LK][AHis]

Olbrys, Drs M.
SACCP Poland
[KH, IN, LA, MN, VN][Lin, Lit]

Olden, Drs J.F. van
CIJS Netherlands
BURFBP@RULMVS.LeidenUniv.NL
[ID][Ant, Law]

Oliveira, Prof. L.S.
FO Portugal
[IR, His]

Oliveira e Costa, Dr J.P.
UNL,CHAM Portugal
[CN, IN, JP, MO, PH, TW][His, Rel]

Olle Rodriguez, M.M.
Congell de Cent 456 31a
08013 Barcelona
Spain
manuel .olle@human.upt.es
[CN, PH, TW][His]

Olof, Drs A.M.
RUL,TCJK Netherlands
olof@rullet.leidenuniv.nl
[KR][Rel, Lit]

Olsson, I.
LU,ICR,FRS,DI Sweden
[TI][Ant, Rel]

Ommen, Drs A.F. van
MVW, BS-G Netherlands
[CN, HK, IN, ID, JP, KR, MO, MY, PH, SG, TW,][IR, PolS]

Onderdenwijngaard, Drs T.A.
Admiralengracht 287-I
1056 EA Amsterdam
Netherlands
[LK][Ant]

Ondracek, Drs W.F.J.
Korte Velterslaan 3
1393 PB Nigtevecht
Netherlands
[JP, KR][Lit, Soc]

Onikienko, Dr A.
IWEIR Russia
[CN, TW][Eco, DevS]

Onkalo, P.A.M.
UO,NSG Finland
ponkalo@phoenix.oulo.fi
[ID][PolS, Geo, DevS, IR]

Ooi, Drs K.B.
SU,IOL,CD Sweden
Keebeng.ooi@orient.su.se
[CN, MY][PolS, His, Phi]

Ooi, Drs K.G.
UHU,DSEAS United Kingdom
[MY][His]

Oomen, Dr C.P.C.M.
Waldeck Pyrmontlaan 14
2341 VB Oegstgeest
Netherlands

Oonk, Drs G.
EUR,HK,G Netherlands
oonk@mgs.fhk.eur.nl
[BT, IN, NP, PK, TI][DevS, His, Ant]

Oonk, G.J.B.
LIW Netherlands
[IN][DevS, IR]

Oordt, P. van
RBK Netherlands
[IN][AHis]

Oort, Drs M.S.
RUL,KERN Netherlands
kernlibort@rullet.leidenuniv.nl
[IN][Lit, Rel, Lin, Phi]

Oorthuizen, Ir H.J.M.
LW,DISWC Netherlands
joost.oorthuizen@users.tct-wan.nl
[BD, PH][Agr, DevS]

Oosten, Dr J.G.
RUL,CNWS Netherlands
[Ant, Rel]

Oosterhout, Drs D.W.J.H. van
RUL,TCZOAO,PD
Netherlands
oosterhout@rullet.leidenuniv.nl
[ID][Ant]

Oosterwijk, A.J.
RD Netherlands
[BD, BN, HK, IN, ID, KR, LA, MO, MG, MM, PI][His, Ant, Arch]

Opdam, Drs J.H.M.
TUE,DTDS Netherlands
[BD, IN, NP, LK, VN][DevS]

Openshaw, Dr J.
UC,CSAS United Kingdom
jo10005@cam.ac.uk
[Rel, Ant]

Opgenort, Drs J.R.M.L.
RUL,VTW Netherlands
[ID][Lin]

Opitz, Prof. P.J.
Josef Snellriederweg 10
82515 Wolfratshausen
Germany
[CN, HK, SG][Phi, His, IR]

Oppitz, Prof. M.
UZ,MCA Switzerland
[CN, MN, NP, TI][Rel, Ant]

Orange, Dr M.
CNRS,EC France
[KR][Lit, His, IR, Law]

Orberger, Dr B.
UP7,LGSP France
orberger@ipgp.jussieu.fr
[BN, KHCN, HK, ID, JP, LA, MO, MY, MM, PH, SG][Lin, Lit, Geo]

Ordonnadu, G.
EIP France
[BN, KHCN, HK, ID, JP, KR, LA, MO, MY, MN,][IR, Eco]

Orduna Diez, L.
UCM,FEE,HIE Spain
[JP][Eco, Law, PolS]

Origas, J.-J.
INALCO France
[JP][Lit]

Orioli, Dr H.
Via Fattiboni 11
47023 Cesena-Fo-
Italy
[KH, CN, HK, LA, MY, MM, SG, TW, TH, TI, VN][Ant, His, Arch, AHis]

Orlovskaya, Dr M.N.
RASP,IOS Russia
[MN][Lin]

Orsi, Prof. M.T.
URLS,DOS Italy
[JP][Lit]

Ortiz, E.
INALCO France
[PH][Lit]

Ortiz Armengol, P.
Paseo de la Castellana 122 (7° Dcho) 28
28046 Madrid
Spain
[PH][Geo, His, IR, Lit]

Oshima, H.
UH,FAI France
[JP][Lin]

Oshima, Hi.
INALCO France
[JP][Lin]

Osipov, Prof. dr Y.M.
SPU,FOS,DAS Russia
[LA, MM, TH][Lit, Rel]

Ossipova, Dr O.A.
RASP,IOS Russia
[Ant, Soc]

Ostergaard, Dr C.S.
AU, DPS Denmark
clemens@ps.aau.dk
[CN, HK, JP, KR, MO, MN, SG, TW, TI, VN][Agr, Soc, PolS, IR, DevS]

Osterhammel, Dr J.K.
FU,ESWG,DH Germany
diana.schulz@fernuni-hagen.de
[CN][IR, His]

Ostrovskaya, Dr E.P.
RASP,IOS,DSSEAS Russia
[Rel, CuS, Phi]

Ostrovskaya, E.A.
RASP,IOS,DSSEAS Russia
[MN, TI][Rel, Phi, Soc]

Ostrovski, Dr B.Ya.
MSU,IAAS,CIBS Russia
[Lin, Lit]

Ostrovski, Dr A.V.
RAS,IFES,FEB Russia
[CN][Soc, Agr, PolS, Eco]

Ostrovsky, Dr A.V.
RAS,IFES,FEB Russia
[CN][Eco]

Osvath, G.
IOCFT Hungary
[KR][Rel, CuS, Lin, Lit, Soc]

Otto, Prof. dr T.H.A.H.
AU,FH,DESA Denmark
ton.otto@moes.hum.aau.dk
[PG][Ant]

Otto, Drs S.S.
WHU,KSCM,CJS Germany
sisuotto@whu-koblenz.de
[JP][Eco]

Otto, Dr J.M.
RUL,VVI Netherlands
j.otto@law.leidenuniv.nl
[CN, ID][DevS, Law, Env]

Ouden, Dr J.H.B. den
LW,DS Netherlands
[BD, IN, ID, MY, PK, LK, VN][DevS, Ant, Agr, GenS]

Oudheusden, Drs O.M.
van Boetzelaerstraat 67-I
1051 EA Amsterdam
Netherlands
[IN, ID][His]

Outer, Drs M. den
Hoofdstraat 39
6061 CA Posterholt
Netherlands
[His]

Overweel, Drs J.A.
RUL,TCZOAO,PD
Netherlands
[ID][DevS, His]

Paardekooper, M.J.L.
Netherlands
mpaard@worldacess.nl

Paasman, Dr A.N.
VU,FL Netherlands
[ID][Lit]

Paderni, Dr P.
UIO,DAS Italy
[CN][GenS, His]

Padolecchia Polo, Prof. S.P.
RU,CCAS Denmark
[CN, HK, IN, KZ, MO, MY, MN, PI, SG, TI,][DevS, PolS, Rel, Edu, Eco, Soc, Env, IR, CuS]

Padoux, Dr A.
CERI,FNSP France
[IN, NP][CuS, Rel, Phi, Lin, Ant]

Pagel, Prof. U.
UW,DALL United States of America
[BT, IN, SM, TI][Lin, Rel]

Paia, M.
INALCO France
[Lin]

Paik, Dr S.
EKUT,SSK Germany
[KR][Rel, Lit, His, CuS]

Pairault, Prof. dr Th.
CNRS,CM France
pairault@ehess.fr
[CN, TW][Eco, Soc, Ant]

Pairoux, Prof. S.
CCBC Belgium
[CN, HK][His, IR, CuS, Soc]

Pajares Ruiz, J.M.
UAM,CEAO Spain
[KH, IN, JP, LA, MY, MM, TH, VN][AHis, Eco, Geo, Soc]

Pak, Dr Y.S.
SOAS,DAA United Kingdom
yo@soas.ac.uk
[CN, JP, KR][Arch, His, AHis]

Pakhomova, Dr L.F.
RASP,IOS Russia
[Eco, Soc]

Palazuelos Manso, A.
UCM,PS Spain
[JP, KR, TW][Eco, Soc]

Palmgren, I.
UL,NASEAS Sweden
ingela.palmgren@ekh.lu.se
[MY][DevS]

Palmier, L.H.
9 St Catherine's Close
BA2 6BS Bath
United Kingdom
[Soc, PolS]

Palmujoki, E.A.
UTA,PT,PRDS Finland
pteepa@uto.fi
[VN][PolS, IR]

Paludan, A.
Low Town Farm
Upper Denton
Gilsland
CA6 7AG Nr. Carlisle
United Kingdom
[CN][Arch]

Pampusé Philé, Dr K.H.
JWGU,VK Germany
[ID][CuS, Lin]

Panarin, Dr S.A.
RASP,IOS Russia
[IR, PolS, Soc]

Panattoni, E.A.
UP,DL Italy
[IN][Lin, CuS, Lit, Rel]

Pang, T.A.
RASP,IOS,DSSEAS Russia
[CuS, Lit]

Panglung, Dr J.L.
BAWS,KZAS Germany
[IN, TI][CuS, Phi, Rel]

Pant, M.R.
CNRS,MSCH France
[NP, TI][His]

Pape, Mr W.
EC, CDP Belgium
wolfgang.pape@edp.cec.be
[CN, JP, TW][IR, Law, Eco, PolS]

Papeté, Drs J.F.
CNRS,AAC France
[CN, LA, TW, TH][Ant, Lin, Rel]

Parikh, Prof. A.
UEA,SESS United Kingdom
a.parikh@uea.ac.uk
[BD, IN, ID, MY, PK, SG][Eco, DevS, Agr]

Paris, Dr M.C.
UPVII,UFRL France
marie.claude.paris@linguist.jussieu.fr
[CN, HK, TW][Lin]

Park, S.S.
EUK,P United Kingdom
[KH, CN, HK, IN, ID, JP, KZ, KR, LA, MO, MY, MN][Psy, PolS, Phi, SocAHis, DevS, Env, Edu, IR, Law]

Park, H.S.
UJML3,FL France
[KR][Eco, PolS]

Park, Dr S.-C.
GU,GESEAS Sweden
sang-chul.park@geography.gu.se
[CN, JP, KR, TW][Eco, PolS]

Parker, H.S.E.
UE,EAS,ACJS United Kingdom
helen.parker@ed.ac.uk
[JP][GenS, CuS, His]

Parliter-Renault, A.
UP,CREOPS,AA France
[IN][His, AHis]

Parnickel, Prof. dr B.B.
IMLI Russia
[ID, MY, SG][Lit]

Parnikel, Dr B.B.
RAS,IWL Russia
[ID, MY][Lit]

Parnwell, Dr M.J.G.
UHU,DSEAS United Kingdom
m.j.parnwell@seas.hull.ac.uk
[ID, MY, TH][DevS, Env, Geo]

Parpola, Prof. A.
UH,HT,AA Finland
asko.parpola@helsinki.fi
[IN, PK][Lit, Arch, Rel, CuS, Lin]

Parpola, Prof. S.K.A.
UH,HT,AA Finland
simo.parpola@helsinki.fi
[ID, MY, TH][CuS, His, Lin, Rel]

Parru, Dr J.P.
LSEPS,DA United Kingdom
[IN][Ant]

Partecke, M.P.
LMU,IVA Germany
mparteck@cip.ub.uni-muenchen.de
[ID][Ant, Lin, Rel]

Partenheimer-Bein, A.
Paul Ehrlichstrasse 26
97218 Gerbrunn
Germany
[IN, ID, JP][His]

Parthasarathi, Dr P.
IISG,IISH Netherlands
[IN][Eco, His]

Pasch, Drs J.P.M. van der
RUL,TCZOAO Netherlands
[ID][Lin, Lit]

Pascha, Prof. dr W.
GMU,EAES Germany
[JP, KR][Eco]

Pasquel Rageau, Dr Ch.
INALCO,DAS France
[VN][CuS, His]

Pastor, J.C.
UMMB,DEEO,DU France
[CN][Phi]

Pastrano, Dr F.
Ramon Gomez de la Serna 79
28035 Madrid
Spain
[CN, HK, JP, KR, MO, TW, TI][His, IR, Rel, Soc]

Pasveer, Drs J.M.
RUG,BAI Netherlands
j.m.pasveer@let.rug.nl
[ID][Arch]

Patel, Drs D.
VAM,ISEAD United Kingdom
[AHis]

Patel, Drs B.
OPWL.LD Netherlands
[BD, BT, IN, NP, PK, LK][Law, PolS, IR]

Patella, Drs P.E.
CELSO Italy
[CN][AHis, Phi, His]

Patmo, Drs S.
NUFFIC, DIAR Netherlands
[KH, CN, HK, ID, LA, MY, PH, SG, TH, VN][Edu, Soc, Ant, DevS]

Pattiruhu, M.
Celsiusstraat 17
1097 PC Amsterdam
Netherlands
[ID][Lan]

Patty-Noach, Dr
UHU,DSEAS United Kingdom
m.a.patty-noach@seas.hull.ac.uk
[ID][Ant, GenS]

Pauer, Prof. dr E.
PUM,JZ Germany
[JP][His]

Paul, Dr W.
CNRS,CRLAO France
wpaul@ehess.fr
[CN][Lin]

Paulus, A-G.
FF,VSIB Germany
[CN, HK, TW,][CuS, DevS, Eco, IR, Lin]

Pavlyatenko, Dr V.N.
RAS,IFES,FEB Russia
[JP][IR, PolS, Eco]

Pazasz-Rutkowska, Dr E.
UW,IOS,DJLC Poland
rutewa@plearn.edu.pl
[JP][His]

Pchelina, Dr (Ruzova) M.L.
Russia
[AHis, CuS, Rel]

Peach, Dr C.
OU,SG United Kingdom
[BD, IN, JP, PK,][Geo, Soc]

Pechaczek, Drs M.J.A.
Zurbano 25 \at. 6a
28010 Madrid
Spain
[BD][GenS, Soc, Edu, DevS, CuS]

Pedersen, Prof. dr P.
AU,FH,DESA Denmark
[BT, IN, KZ, MN, NP, PK, LK, TJ, TI, TM][His, CuS, Ant, Phi, Psy, Rel, Env]

Pederson, Drs E.W.
MPIP, CARG Netherlands
pederson@mpi.nl
[IN][Lin]

Peeters, Dr J.C.M.
van Swietenstraat 11
2334 EA Leiden
Netherlands
[ID][His]

Peh, G.-K.
CNRS,EHESS,BIB France
[CN][Lit]

Pei, X.
UL,NASEAS Sweden
ekhpxi@luecfou.ec.lu.se
[CN][Eco, Agr, PolS, His, DevS]

Pekka Ruohom,,ki, O.
UH,HT,E Finland
[PolS, His, Eco, Agr, DevS]

Pelevin, Dr M.S.
SPU, FOS Russia
[AF, PK][Lin, Lit]

Pelkmans, Prof. dr J.
EURASIA Belgium
[HK, MY, PH, SG, TH][IR, Eco]

Pellard, S.
MBAHN France
[CN, IN, ID, JP, PG, TH][His, Arch, AHis]

Pels, Dr P.J.
UvA,GM Netherlands
[IN][Ant, His]

Peltenburg, Drs M.E.
HIS Netherlands
[IN, TH][DevS]

Pemwieser, M.
IATS Austria
[TI][Lit]

Penent, J.
MGL France
[CN, JP][His]

Pennarz, Dr J.P.
TUB,IEM Germany
[CN, TW, TI][Ant, DevS]

Perelomov, Dr L.S.
RAS,IFES,FEB Russia
[CN][His]

Perez Miguel, A.
Saliente N° 10
28007 Madrid
Spain
aurora@h.asociacion.fulbright.es
[CN, IN, MY,][Ant, GenS, His, IR]

Perlas, Dr Ch.
CNRS,LASEMA France
[ID, MY, SG,][Ant, CuS]

Perrey, Ch.
CNRS,MSCH France
[NP, TI][Lin]

Persoon, Dr G.A.
RUL,CESP Netherlands
[ID, PH][DevS, Ant, Env]

Persoons, Dr M.A.
MVG, DGHO Belgium
[CN, IN, ID, TW][AHis, Edu, IR, Lin, Phi]

Pesch, H.J. von
BuZa, DAO/ZO Netherlands
[CN, IN, ID, TW][PolS, Soc]

Pesch, L.
Korte Geuzenstraat 414
1056 KV Amsterdam
Netherlands
[IN][Edu, CuS]

Peters, Prof. dr J.R.T.M.
Netherlands
[BN, ID, MY, PG, SG][Rel, Lin, Phi]

Peters, Drs F.H.
R.J. Schimmelpennincklaan 18-G
2517 JN The Hague
Netherlands
[BN, ID, MY, PG, SG][DevS, His]

Petersen, J.O.
UC,FH,DAS Denmark
oesterg@coco.ihi.ku.dk
[CN][His]

Petersen, C.I.
GU,DSA Sweden
[BN, ID, MY, PG, SG][Ant]

Petitmengin, S.
CNRS,JAP France
[JP][Lit]

Petrikovskaya, A.S.
RASP,IOS Russia
[PI][CuS, Lit]

Petrov, Dr A.M.
RASP,IOS Russia
[Eco]

Petrov, Dr A.I.
RAS,ICPS Russia
[CN, KR, TW][His]

Pettigrew, Dr J.M.
QUB,DSA United Kingdom
[IN][Ant]

Peverelli, Dr P.J.
Molenstraat 25
2611 JZ Delft
Netherlands
[CN][Eco]

Pews, Dr H.U.
Esplanade 48
13187 Berlin
Germany
[KR, MN, NP, TI, VN][Eco, DevS, Geo]

Peyraube, A.
CNRS,CRLAO France
[CN][Lit]

Pfeiffer, Dr M.
Brunowstrasse 19, 335
13473 Berlin 27
Germany
[IN][Lin, Rel, Lit, CuS]

Pfennig, Dr W.
FUB,OS,CEAP Germany
[CN, KR, PH, TH][His, PolS, DevS, IR]

Pfister, Drs B.
UZ,IGS Switzerland
[IN][DevS, His, PolS, IR]

Pfister, R.
Aaraver Str. 74
4600 Olten
Switzerland
[CN][His, CuS, AHis, Ant]

Pham Dan Binh, .
UP7,UAO France
[VN][Lin]

Pham Dinh Tieu, N.-A.
INALCO France
[VN][Lan]

Phan Thanh Thuy, Dr
UP7,UAO France
[VN][Lin]

Philipp MA, H.M.
PUM,JZ Germany
[JP][Env, Law]

Phillips, Dr N.G.
SOAS,DLCSEA United Kingdom
[ID, MY][Lit, Lin]

Piacentini, Dr P.M.
URS Italy
piacentini@vaxca1.unica.it
[CN, JP, KR][Eco, DevS]

Piano, Prof. S
UT,IOS Italy
PIANO@rs950.cisi.unito.it
[IN,][CuS, Lin, Lit, Rel]

Picard, Dr F.
37 rue Piat
75020 Paris
France
[CN][Rel]

Picard, Dr M.
CNRS,LASEMA France
[ID][Ant, Rel, Soc, CuS]

Picavet, Drs R.T.C.M.
KUB, IVO Netherlands
ruud.picavet@kub.nl
[PK][Eco, DevS]

Pichard, Ir L.
CNRS,IRSEA France
[MM, TH][Lit, Soc]

Pichikyan, Dr I.R.
RASP,IOS Russia
[CuS]

Picken, Dr L.E.R.
Jesus College
CB5 8BL Cambridge
United Kingdom
[AF, BT, KH, CN, ID, JP, KZ, KR, LA, MY, MN,][CuS]

Picone, Drs M.J.
CNRS,CRJC France
[JP][Ant, Rel]

Picornell Marti, P.
Son Armadams N° 8 III-1A
07014 Palma de Mallorca
Spain
[IN, ID, PH,][Eco, Env, His]

Piek, Drs J.G.
Jacobastraat 204
2512 JE The Hague
Netherlands
[CN][IR, DevS, PolS]

Pieke, Dr F.N.
ICS United Kingdom
pieke@server.orient.ox.ac.uk
[CN, HK, TW][Ant]

Pigeot, Prof. dr J.
CNRS,JAP France
[JP][Lit]

Pigler, Drs K.
Elõpatak u 9/B1
1118 Budapest
Hungary
[IR]

Pigulla, Dr A.
RUB,FOAW,POA Germany
[CN, HK, JP, KR, TW][His, PolS, IR]

Pijl-Ketel, Ch. van der
RBK,BIB Netherlands
[CN, JP, KR][AHis]

Pilot-Raichoor, Dr C.
CNRS,LACITO France
[IN][Lin]

Pilz, Prof. dr E.
UW,IS Austria
erich.pilz@univie.ac.at
[CN, TW][His]

Pimpaneau, Dr J.
INALCO,MKO,CD France
[CN][Lit]

Pinault, G.-J.
UP3,EI France
[IN][Rel]

Ping, Q.
Jahnstrasse 5
10967 Berlin
Germany
[CN][His, CuS, AHis]

Pink, Prof. P.
UK,OS,MA Germany
[ID, MY][Rel, Phi, Lit]

Pinkers, Ir M.J.H.P.
ILRI Netherlands
[BD, IN, KZ, MY, PK, TJ, VN][IR, DevS, EduAgr]

Pinney, Dr C.
SOAS,DAS United Kingdom
cp2@soas.ac.uk
[IN][His, AHis, Ant, CuS]

Pinto Da Costa, Mr R.M.
Rua da Milharada, Lte B 1B
Massam
2745 Queluz
Portugal
[MG][His]

Pinto de Sousa, P.J.C.
UNL,CHAM Portugal
[ID, MY][His]

Pinto Leite, Drs P.
IPJET Netherlands
[Law]

Pinxteren, Drs M.H.M. van
RUL,SI Netherlands
[CN][CuS]

Piontek-Ma, Drs E.
UW,IS Germany
elke.piontek-ma@rzbox.uni-wuerzburg.de
[CN, HK, TW][His, CuS, Soc, GenS]

Piper, Dr N.
USH,SEAS United Kingdom
n.piper@sheffield.ac.uk
[JP][Soc, GenS]

Piquard, B.
KUL,ANTR Belgium
[BD, IN, ID, MY, PK,][Rel, PolS, Ant]

Pirazzoli-t'Serstevens, Dr M.
CNRS,EPHE,SHP France
[CN][Arch, AHis]

Pirogov, Dr G.G.
IWEIR Russia
[JP][Eco]

Pissarev, Prof.dr A.N.
MSU,IAAS,CIBS Russia
[CN][His, PolS]

Pistilli, Drs G.M.
UV,ECSG Italy
Peergynt@unive.it
[IN, LK][Lit, His]

Pitoëff, P.
CNRS,EM France
[IN][Ant]

Pitoun MA,
11 rue Alphand
75013 Paris
France
[BD, KH IN, PK,][Arch, AHis, Lit]

Piurbeer, Prof. G. T.
RAS,IL Russia
[MN][Lin]

Pivovarova, Prof. dr E.P.
RAS,IFES,FEB Russia
titarenk@ifes.msk.su
[CN][Edu]

Plaeschke, Dr I.
MLU,KAW,OA Germany
[AF, BD, AF, BD, BT, IN, NP, PK, LK][His, Arch, AHis]

Plaeschke, Dr H.
Rathenauplatz 21
4020 Halle
Germany
[AF, BD, AF, BD, BT, IN, NP, PK, LK][AHis, Arch]

Plaisier, Drs H.
RUL,VTW Netherlands
plaisier@rullet.leidenuniv.nl
[BT, CN, NP, SM, TI][Lin]

Planas, Prof. R.
EOIM,DJ Spain
[JP][Lin, CuS]

Plantema, Drs E.P.
RC,VWM Netherlands
[ID][Lin, CuS]

Plantier, F.
UJML3,FL France
[CN][CuS, Lin]

Plastun, Dr V.N.
RASP,IOS Russia
[AF][His]

Plate, Drs P.A.
IFA Germany
[JP][Env, Edu]

Platenkamp, Prof. dr J.D.M.
WWUM,IE Germany
platenk@uni-muenster.de
[ID, LA, PG][CuS, Soc, Ant, Rel]

Plempe, Drs D.
RKU,OAW,SIN Germany
[CN][Rel]

Pleshov, Dr O.V.
RASP,IOS Russia
[, PK][His]

Pleshova, Dr M.A.
RASP,IOS Russia
[IN][His, PolS]

Plessis, Drs F.
INALCO,CRI France
[PI, PH, TW][Lin, Ant]

Ploeg, Dr A.
Slagmanstraat 9
7217 SE Harfsen
Netherlands
[ID, PI, PG][Ant]

Plomp, Drs M.
RUL,KERN Netherlands
plomp@rullet.leidenuniv.nl
[ID, MY][Lit]

Plukker, Dr D.F.
IndI Netherlands
d.plukker@inter.nl.net
[IN][Lin, Lit]

Plumbe, A.J.
UBR,DPPC United Kingdom
[IN, ID, MY, SG, LK, TH][DevS]

Pluvier, Dr J.M.
Heideweg 5
3768 BA Soest
Netherlands
[KH, ID, LA, MY, MM, PH, SG, TH, VN][His, DevS, IR]

Po Dharma Quang, Dr
EFEO,BIB France
[KH, MY, VN][Lin, Lit, His]

Pochta, Dr Y.M.
RPFU,DP Russia
[Phi, Soc, Rel]

Podest, Dr M.
Corso Sempione 38
20154 Milan
Italy
[AF, CN, KZ, TJ, TW, TI][Lin, Rel]

Podlesskaya, Dr V.I.
RASP,IOS Russia
[JP][Lin]

Podzeit, Dr U.
UW,IIA Austria
utz.podzeit@univie.ac.at
[IN][Rel]

Poeze, Dr H.A.
KITLV,Press Netherlands
kitlv@rullet.leidenuniv.nl
[ID][His, PolS, IR]

Pogadaev, Dr V.
Nachimovski Pr. 7-1-148
113149 Moscow
Russia
[ID, MY][His, CuS]

Pohl, Prof. dr K.H.
UT,SIN Germany
pohlk@uni-trier.de
[CN, TW][His, CuS, AHis, Phi, Lit, Rel]

Pohl, Prof. dr M.
UHAM,SKC,TBI Germany
[JP, KR, SG][PolS, His]

Pol MA, C.M.
Netherlands
[ID][AHis, GenS, His, CuS]

Poley, Drs U.M.
UB,SI Germany
[IN, TI][Rel, His, CuS, Arch, Phi, AHis, Lin]

Politon, S.
Grote Bickersstraat 333
1013 KR Amsterdam
Netherlands
[CN, ID, TI][AHis, Arch, Phi, Lin, CuS, His, Rel]

Pollmann-Schlichting, Drs M.T.
RM,OC&W Netherlands
tesselp@worldonline.nl
[ID][Ant, His, Lit]

Polonskaya, Dr L.R.
RAS,IOS,CIS Russia
[AF, BD, AF, BD, IN, PK][Rel, His]

Pols, Dr A.
RUL, JIP Netherlands
[JP][Lit, Lin]

Pomerantseva, Dr L.E.
MSU,IAAS,CIBS Russia
[CN][His, Lit, Phi]

Pommaret, Dr F.
CNRS,IRSEA France
pommaret@univ-aix.fr
[BT, TI][Rel, His, CuS, His, Ant, AHis]

Pompe, Mr S.
RUL,VVI Netherlands
[ID][Law]

Pompe, Dr J.H.
RUG,FPPSW Netherlands
[BN, ID, MY, PH, SG][PolS, DevS, Env, IR, Agr, Ant, Eco, Soc, CuS, Edu, Phi, Law,]

Poncini, G.
Inst.I Netherlands
[JP][His, AHis, Arch]

Pont Ferrer, Beatriz
UCES,DGE Spain
beatriz.pont@ces.es
[JP][Eco, Edu, IR, PolS]

Pooput, W.
INALCO France
[TH][His, Arch, AHis]

Poorter, Dr E.G. de
RUL,TCJK Netherlands
[JP][Lit]

Poortinga, Dr F.H.
KUB, FSW, P Netherlands
poort@kub.nl
[IN, ID][Psy]

Pope, Dr A.D.
Margarethenstra. 37
23558 Lübeck
Germany
[IN][His]

Popov, Dr A.V.
RASP,IOS Russia
[Eco, IR]

Popov, Dr G.V.

[, MM, TH][Eco, IR]

Porcher, M.-C.
UL3,CREO France
[IN][Lit, Lin]

Porciò, Drs T.
JAU,DAS Hungary
porcio@hung.u-szeged.hu
[IN, MN, TI][Lit, Rel, CuS]

Porter, Dr R.
KU,CBPU United Kingdom
[CN][Rel, Lit, CuS]

Portier, Dr M.K.
KUN,IV Netherlands
h.slaats@jur.kun.nl
[ID][Ant, Law]

Portier-Lehmans, Dr A.P.L.
UMMB,DEEO,DU France
[JP][His, CuS]

Portyakov, Dr V.Ya.
RAS,IFES,FEB Russia
[CN][Eco]

Pospisilova, Dr D.
NMP Czech Republic
[BD, BT, KHIN, ID, NP, PK, LK, TH][Rel, AHis]

Post, Dr P
VU, DCA Netherlands
[ID, JP, SG][IR, Ant, His]

Postel-Coster, Prof. dr E.
Van Leyden Gaellaan 1
2343 HE Oegstgeest
Netherlands
[ID][DevS, Ant, GenS]

Posthumus Meyjes, Drs H.C.
Ravetsmaar 1
6373 AK Landgraaf
Netherlands
[JP][Ant, DevS, GenS]

Postrelova, Drs T.A.
RASP,IOS Russia
[CN][His, AHis]

Potabenko, Dr S.I.
RASP,IOS Russia
[IN][CuS, His]

Potet, Dr J.P.G.
CNRS,CRLAO France
[PH][Lin]

Potter, J.M.
USUS,FI,SIM United Kingdom
j.m.potter@bton.ac.uk
[CuS]

Pottier, M.
INALCO France
[PH][]

Pou-Sykes, Dr S.
1, Rue Molière, \Appl. 118
94000 Créteil
France
[KH][Lit, Lin, CuS]

Pouchepadass, Dr J.
UL3,CREO France
[IN][His]

Pouvatchy, Dr J.R.
USHS France
[KH, MY, VN][Rel, His, PolS, IR]

Pouwer, Prof. dr J.
Nieuwe Veenendaalseweg 229
3911 MJ Rhenen
Netherlands
[ID, PG][Ant]

Powell, Dr B.W.F.
OU,OI United Kingdom
[JP][Ant]

Pozner, P.
LPI France
[VN][His]

Pozner, Dr P.V.
RASP,IOS Russia
[VN][CuS, His]

Pozzana, Dr C.
UB,IG Italy
[CN][Phi, Lit, CuS, Lin, His]

Prag, J.
DCM Denmark
[VN][DevS]

Prager, Drs S.
RKU,OAW Germany
[MM][Rel, PolS, His, CuS]

Prakash, Drs A.
SOAS,DEPS United Kingdom
ap@soas.ac.uk
[IN][DevS, PolS]

Prall, J.
6 Link House
37 Lower Teddington Road
KT1 4HQ Kingston-upon-Thames
United Kingdom
[PH][PolS, DevS]

Prasad, Drs S.
UWA,DS United Kingdom
[JP, MY, PI][Soc, Ant, Eco, DevS]

Pratt, Prof. K.L.
UDU,BAKS United Kingdom
keith.pratt@durham.ac.uk
[AHis, CuS, His]

Prazauskas, Dr A.A.
RAS,IOS,DSPS Russia
[BT, IN, KZ, NP, TM][Rel, His, PolS]

Prchal, Drs M.
HKU,M Netherlands
[BT, CN, HK, ID, JP, KR, MY, PH, SG, TW, TH, VN][PolS, His, Rel]

Pregadio, Dr F.
FGC,IVO Italy
pregadio@unive.it
[CN][Rel]

Preisendanz, K.
UHAM,KGIT Germany
[TI][Rel]

Preston, Dr D.A.
ULEED,SG United Kingdom
d.a.preston@leeds.ac.uk
[ID, MY, PH][Geo, Agr, DevS, Env]

Preston, Dr P.W.
UB,DPS,IS United Kingdom
prestonp@css.bham.ac.uk
[SG][PolS, DevS]

Prets, Dr E.
IATS Austria
[TI][DevS, PolS]

Pretzell, Dr K.A.
IFA Germany
[MY, TH][Rel, CuS, PolS, Ant]

Prevosti Monclus, Dr A.
UB,DFTP Spain
prevosti@trivium.gh.ub.es
[CN][Phi]

Prévot, M.
UP7,UAO France
[VN][Lin]

Price, Dr P.G.
UO Norway
p.g.price@hi.uio.no
[IN][His]

Prigarina, Dr N.I.
RASP,IOS Russia
[IN][Lit]

Primel, Drs A.-G.
23, Rue Chandigarh
94310 Orly
France
[CN][His]

Prince, Drs G.H.A.
RUG,VG Netherlands
g.h.a.prince@eco.rug.nl
[ID][His]

Prins, Prof. dr H.H.T.
WAU,TE Netherlands
herbert.prins@staf.ton.wag.nl
[ID][Env]

Prins, Dr W.J.M.
Zandbos 3
2134 DA Hoofddorp
Netherlands
[IN][DevS]

Prins, B. de
Platanenlaan 29
1820 Steenokkerzeel
Belgium
[IN, ID][His]

Probojo, Dr L.
UBI,FS,SDRC Germany
prbojo@sozjur.uni-bielefeld.de
[ID][Soc]

Prodolliet, Dr S.
CS Switzerland
[ID][GenS, His, Ant]

Promés, Drs H.J.A.
Rijnsburgerweg 4-B/41
2215 RA Voorhout
Netherlands
[ID][His, Lin, Rel, LitAnt]

Prost, M.
CNRS,CRLAO France
[KR][Lin]

Provine, Prof. dr R.C.
UDU,MS United Kingdom
r.c.provine@durham.ac.uk
[CN, JP, KR, VN][Lin]

Prüch, Dr M.M.
Schlossheide 73 A
65366 Geisenheim-Johannisberg
Germany
[CN][Arch, His, AHis]

Prunner, Dr G.
HMV,SOA Germany
[CN, IN, JP, KR, MM, PK, TW, TI][Ant, Rel, CuS]

Pungor, Prof. dr E.
Hungary
pungor@bzaka.hu

Pusey, Dr J.G.
OU,BL United Kingdom
jgp@bodley.ox.ac.uk
[ID][Lin]

Put, Drs M.
UvA,VPD Netherlands
[IN, ID, NP][Agr, Env, Soc, DevS]

Put, I.H.A. van
KUL,DOS Belgium
imeke.vp@arts.kuleuven.ac.be
[JP][CuS]

Putilov, Dr B.N.
PGMAE,K Russia
[PI][Ant]

Putten, Drs J. van der
RUL,TCZOAO Netherlands
[ID, MY, SG][Lin, His]

Putten, Drs F.P. van der
RUL,VG Netherlands
itinerario@rullet.leidenuniv.nl
[CN, ID, SG][His, IR, PolS, Eco]

Putz, Drs O.P.
EKUT,JAP Germany
[JP][Lit]

Putzel, Drs J.J.
LSEPS,DDS United Kingdom
j.putzel@lse.ac.uk
[ID, MY, PH, TH, VN][DevS, Env, PolS]

Puyraimond, G.
INALCO France
[CN][PolS, DevS, Env]

Pyatt, Prof. F.G.
ISS Netherlands
[Eco, DevS]

Pye, Prof. E.M.
PUM,FR Germany
pye@mailer.uni-marburg.de
[JP][Rel]

Quarles van Ufford, Dr J.J.
Anna Paulownalaan 24
3818 GD Amersfoort
Netherlands

Quarles van Ufford, Dr Ph.
VU, DCA Netherlands
[Ant, DevS]

Quilis, Antonio
UNED,FF,DLE Spain
[PI, PH][Lin]

Quiquemelle, M.-C.
SA France
[CN, HK, TW][His, CuS]

Quirin, Dr M. Th.
Lisztstrasse 19
53115 Bonn
Germany
[CN][His, PolS, Phi, CuS]

Quispel, Drs C.I.
RUG,VOTI Netherlands
[HK, JP][PolS, Phi, CuS, His]

Quist, Drs C.
c/o Winschoterdiep 67-B
9724 GK Groningen
Netherlands
[LK][GenS, DevS]

Raben, Dr R.
RIOD Netherlands
[ID, LK][His, Ant]

Rabusseau, M.
10 rue Marieau - Auger
92270 Bois-Colombes
France
[CN, TW][Eco]

Rabut, I.
INALCO,CRESCIC France
[CN][Lin, Lit]

Racine, Drs J.-L.
UL3,CREO France
racine@msh.paris.fr
[IN, PK][DevS, PolS, IR]

Rackwitz-Ziegler, Drs N.
PUM,SIN Germany
[CN, HK, TW][Lit, CuS, His]

Raczka, Prof. W.
9, rue de l'Observatoire
67000 Strasbourg
France
[AF, KZ, MN, TJ, TM, UZ][DevS, Eco, His, PolS, IR]

Radicchi, Prof. dr A.
UC, DCP Italy
[IN, ID][Lin, Lit, Rel]

Radtke, Prof. dr K.W.
RUL,TCJK Netherlands
k.radtke@rullet.leidenuniv.nl
[CN][PolS, Lit, IR, His]

Radvanyi, Prof. dr J.
INALCO,RUS France
radva@ext.jussieu.fr
[KZ, UZ][Eco, Geo]

Raendchen, Drs O.
SEACC,TC Germany
Olivertaic@aol.com
[LA, TH, VN][CuS, Ant, Lin, Lit]

Raffi, G.
CNRS,IRSEA France
[VN][His]

Raghuraman, K.
Spiegheldreef 9
2353 BJ Leiderdorp
Netherlands

Ragvald, Prof. L.R.
LU,FA,DEAL Sweden
lars.ragvald@ostas.lu.se
[CN][Lin, Lit, Rel]

Rahim, Dr E.
USTR,DE United Kingdom
[PK][DevS, Eco]

Rahman, Drs S.
ITIM Netherlands
[ID][CuS]

Rahman-Steinert, U.
MVB Germany
[His, AHis]

Rai, Dr S.S.
Uhlenkruggarten 7
45133 Essen
Germany
[CN, IN,][PolS, IR]

Raibaud, M.
UMMB,DEEO,DU France
[CN][His]

Raillon, Dr F.
CNRS,EHESS France
[BN, ID, MY, PH, SG][Soc, Eco, IR, His, PolS, DevS, Rel]

Raison, Prof. F.
UP7, GHSS France
[MG, PI][Rel, AHis, Ant, CuS]

Raitza, Dr K.
HUB,AA,SOA Germany
kathrin=raitza@rz-hu-berlin.de
[VN][Lin]

Raj, Dr K.
CSI France
raj@univ-lille3.fr
[IN, PK, TI][Geo, His]

Rajala, Drs T.M.
Kakkospesankatu 2C 21
40520 Jyväskylä
Finland
[JP][Lit, CuS]

Rajaonarimanana, Prof.
INALCO France
[MG][CuS, Lit]

Rajapakse, Drs D.A.
48 Tile Kiln Hill
Blean
CT2 9EE Canterbury, Kent
United Kingdom
[LK][Agr, DevS, Eco, GenS, Ant]

Rakotofiringa, Prof. H.
USG France
[ID, MG, MY][Lin, Lit]

Ramat, Prof. P.
UP,DLFL Italy
paoram@ipv36.unipv.it
[MG][Lin]

Ramirez, Dr P.
CNRS,MSCH France
himal.res@cnrs-bellevue.fr
[KH, NP,][Ant, His, PolS, Soc]

Rammandanlall, Drs J.
Haïtidreef 3e
3563 HC Utrecht
Netherlands
[IN, PK][Ant]

Ramstedt, Drs M.
LMU,IVA Germany
[IN, ID, SG][Ant, Rel, CuS, PolS, Lit]

Randall, J.
47 Moreton Street
SW1V 2NY London
United Kingdom
[CuS, Rel, Ant, PolS, Lit]

Randeria, Dr S.
FUB,OS Germany
[IN][Soc, DevS, GenS, Ant, CuS]

Ranjeva, Prof. R.
Int.G Netherlands
[MG][Lin]

Rao, Dr A.
UK,IV Germany
[AF, IN,][Psy, DevS, Env, His, Ant, GenS]

Rappard-Boon, Drs Ch.E. van
F. van Mierisstraat 55
1071 RK Amsterdam
Netherlands
[JP][His, AHis]

Rappoport, Drs D.
CNRS,EM France
[ID][Ant]

Ras, Prof. dr J.J.
Prins Bernardlaan 19
2341 KH Oegstgeest
Netherlands
[ID, MY][Lit]

Raster, Prof. dr P.
UGE,LS Germany
[IN][Lin, Phi]

Rastorfer, Ir J.M.
CEDK Switzerland
[MM, TH][His, CuS]

Rastyannikov, Prof.dr V.G.
RASP,IOS Russia
[IN][Eco]

Raud, Prof. dr R.
UH,HT,AA Finland
rein.raud@helsinki.fi
[JP][His, Phi, Rel, Lit]

Rault-Leyrat, L.R.
CNRS,EM France
[BT, CN, HK, IN, ID, JP, KR, MO, TW, TH, TI][His, Rel, Ant, AHis, Ant, Lin, Arch, Phi, His]

Raunig, Prof. dr W.
SMVM Germany
[AF, PK][AHis, Ant, Arch, His]

Rauws, Drs A.J.
Komaba International Students House, Room 2-108, 4-5-29
Komaba, Meguro-ku
153 Tokyo
Japan
[JP][AHis, Ant, Arch, His]

Ravels-Smulders, Drs M.C. van
SIM Netherlands
c.vanravelssmulders@rgl.ruu.nl
[CN, HK][IR, PolS, Law]

Raven, Dr E.M.
RUL,KERN Netherlands
abiaraven@rulletleiden.univ.nl
[BD, IN, NP, PK, LK][His, Arch, AHis]

Rayevsky, Dr D.S.
RASP,IOS Russia
[ASIA][CuS]

Raymond, C.
EFEO,BIB France
[MM][His, Arch, Rel, AHis]

Raza, Dr R.
UIO,DSO Italy
[AF, IN, KZ, PK, TJ][His, Lit, IR]

Razanajatovo, L.C.
Ruiterskamp 45
6662 TE Elst
Netherlands
[MG][IR, Lit, His]

Reader, Dr I.J.
NIAS Denmark
reader@nias.ku.dk
[JP][Soc, Rel, Ant]

Rebergen, W.W.
Netherlands
wils@xs4all.nl

Reclus-Sun, M.
INALCO France
[CN][Lan]

Reede, Mr J.L. de
UvA,VS Netherlands
[IN][PolS, Law]

Reenen, Dr J.H. van
Begijnhof 23-B
1012 WT Amsterdam
Netherlands
[ID][GenS, Ant]

Reenen, Drs A.D. van
VU,FL Netherlands
sofie@let.vu.nl
[ID][His, Rel, Lit, His, AHis]

Reesink, Dr G.P.
RUL,TCZOAO,PD
Netherlands
reesink@rullet.leidenuniv.nl
[PG][Lin]

Reetz, Dr D.
CMOS Germany
[IN, PK][His, PolS, Rel, IR]

Régnier, Dr P.T.
UG,MARC Switzerland
regnier@uni2a.unige.ch
[DevS, IR]

Regnot, V.
UP8, France
[CN][Arch]

Reichel, H. J.
CG Germany
[CN, HK][AHis, CuS]

Reichenstein, B.
FUB,W,IW Germany
[CN, HK, SG, TW][IR, DevS, Eco]

Reichert, P.
8, Chemin de Bannscheid
67140 Barr
France
[AF, PK,][Lin]

Reijnders, Drs P.A.M.
FIA Netherlands
[IN][His, AHis]

Reijnders, Drs T.
Zuideinde 116
1121 DH Landsmeer
Netherlands
[HK, ID, KR, MO, PI][AHis]

Reimers, Drs C.
USTI,SCJS United Kingdom
[JP][His]

Rein, Dr A.
UL,IE Germany
[ID][Ant, CuS, GenS, Rel]

Reinecke, Drs G.
UHAM,IPS Germany
[TH][PolS]

Reiniche, Dr M.-L.
UL3,CREO France
[IN][Ant, His, Soc]

Reisner, Dr M.L.
MSU,IAAS,CIBS Russia
[Lin, Lit]

Remarchouk, Dr V.V.
MSU,IAAS,CIBS Russia
[VN][AHis, CuS, His, Lin]

Ren, C.
UTM,CUP France
[CN][His, Ant, Soc]

Renard-Clamagirand, Dr B.
CNRS,LASEMA France
[ID][Ant]

Renardet-Widjojo, Drs L.
20 Avenue d'Ivry
Tour Tokyo Appt. 222
75013 Paris
France
[ID][Lit, His, CuS]

Renaud, F.
CNRS,CRLAO France
[CN][Lin]

Rengkung, E.
KITLV Netherlands
rengkung@rullet.leidenuniv.nl
[ID][Lin, Lit]

Rennert, Drs H.
UB,ZA,TB Germany
[BT, CN, IN, MN, NP, TI][Lin, Lit, His, CuS, His, Phi, Rel, AHis]

Rentner, Prof. dr R.
HUB,AA,KI Germany
[KR][Lit]

Renwarin, Drs W.P.
KUN,IDS Netherlands
[KR][Ant]

Resche, N.
CF, BIHEC France
resche@ext.jussieu.fr
[CN, TW][Ant]

Reshetov, Dr.o A.M.
PGMAE,K Russia
[SG][Ant]

Reuland, Prof. dr E.J.
UU,OGC Netherlands

Revel, Prof.N.
CNRS,IRSEA France
[PH][Lin, Ant]

Revilla Diez, Drs J.
UHNV,EG Germany
[VN][Eco]

Rey, M.-C.
MNAAG France
[CN][Eco]

Reynders, Dr ir J.J.
Vijzelweg 16
9463 TM Eext
Netherlands
[ID, PG][Agr, Arch, DevS, Env]

Reznikov, Dr V.L.
RASP,IOS Russia
[PI][PolS]

Rezvan, Dr E.
RASP,IOS Russia
[Env, Arch, DevS, Agr]

Rheeden, Drs H.A. van
UvA,ATW Netherlands
h.a.van.rheeden@let.uva.nl
[ID][Lin]

Ria, A.R.
Plataanstraat 78 ZW
2023 SG Haarlem
Netherlands

Riaboff, I.
22 rue de la Pomme
31000 Toulouse
France
[TI][Lin]

Ribemont, F.
MBAB France
[CN, KR][His, AHis]

Richardson, C.
73 Hillbrook Road
SW17 8SF London
United Kingdom
[PH][AHis]

Richardson, Dr J.A.
73, Hillbrook Road
SW17 8SF London
United Kingdom
[PH][PolS, His]

Richter, ML
LMU,IOAK Germany
RICHTERAM@LRZ-MUENCHEN.DE
[CN, HK, JP, TW][Ant, Arch, AHis, His, Law, Lin, Lit, Phi, Rel]

Richter, Dr G.
HUB,AA,IS Germany
[CN, HK, MO, MY, SG, TW, TI][Lin]

Richter, Prof. S.
UL,OI Germany
richters@rz.uni-leipzig.de
[JP][Phi, CuS]

Ridder, Ir J.M.
CNV Netherlands
j.ridder@cnv.nl
[ID, NP, PG,][Eco, DevS, Ant, IR, Soc]

Riddington, P.
Parkland Drive \Wengerwooth
S42 600 Chesterfield
United Kingdom
[CN, HK, TW][Lin, Edu]

Rieger, Dr H.C.
RKU,SI Germany
[IN, ID, MY, NP, PK, PH, SG, TH][DevS, Env, Eco]

Riel, Drs P.H. van
SARI Netherlands
[ID][Ant]

Riel-Lamers, Drs G.M.P. van
KUN,UB Netherlands
4149031@mco1.azn.kun.nl
[ID][His, Ant, Rel]

Rieländer, Drs K.
GAUG,ISV Germany
[ID, PI, PG][Eco, Ant, CuS, Soc]

Riemann, Drs J.
PUM,SIN Germany
riemann@mailer.uni-marburg.de
[CN, HK, TW][AHis, Arch, CuS, His]

Rienks, Drs A.S.
UvA,ASC Netherlands
[ID][Ant, DevS]

Rigg, Dr J.D.
UDU,DG United Kingdom
j.d.rigg@durham.ac.uk
[ID, LA, TH][Geo, Env, Agr, DevS]

Rigter MA, J.E.
Hondecoeterstraat 20 hs
1071 LS Amsterdam
Netherlands

Rijn, Ir P.J. van
Frans Langeveldlaan 72
1251 XZ Laren
Netherlands
[BD, IN, ID, LA, MY, PH, LK, TH, VN][DevS, Agr, Env]

Rinsampessy, Dr E.P.

Kraayenberg 91-12
6601 PN Wychen
Netherlands
[CN, ID, JP, MY, PG, SG][Ant, Soc, Rel, IR, Edu]

Ripert, B.

CNRS,MSCH France
[NP, TI][Geo]

Rispoli, Dr F.

ISLAO Italy
[CN, IN, ID, LA, MM, PH, SG, LK, TH, VN][Ant, Arch]

Risseeuw, Prof. dr C.I.

RUL,CA/SNWS Netherlands
Risseeuw@rulfsw.leidenuniv.nl
[IN, LK][Ant, His, GenS, DevS, Rel, Law]

Ritter, J.A.

EKUT,SSK Germany
juergen.ritter@uni-tuebingen.de
[CN, HK, TW][CuS, His]

Rivkin, L.M.

BGCC United Kingdom
[AHis, Arch, Ant, CuS, His, DevS]

Robb, Prof. P.G.

SOAS,DH United Kingdom
pr4@soas.ac.uk
[BD, IN, PK][His]

Robenhagen, H.

Polarisvaenget 23
2620 Albertslund
Denmark
[His]

Robert, J.

INALCO France
[JP][His]

Robert, J.-N.

UP7,UAO France
[JP][Lit]

Robertie, P. de la

UA,SIN France
[CN][Lit]

Roberts, Dr C.R.

UBR,DAS United Kingdom
c.r.roberts@bradford.ac.uk
[IN][Ant, Arch]

Roberts, Drs D.C.

9 Eton Court
West Hallam
DE7 6NB Derbys
United Kingdom
[CN, HK, IN, ID, JP, KR, MY, SG, TW][DevS, Eco, IR]

Robinet, I.

UAM1,LSH France
[CN][His]

Robinne, Dr F.

CNRS,IRSEA France
[MM][AntAnt]

Robinson, Prof. F.C.R.

UL,RHBNC,DH United Kingdom
[BD, IN, PK][His, Rel]

Robotka, Dr B.

HUB,AA,SOA Germany
[IN, PK][His]

Robson-McKillop, Drs R.L.

KITLV Netherlands
Robson@rullet.LeidenUniv.nl
[ID, MY][Ant, Rel, Arch]

Roca, Drs A.

CEA Spain
[MG][Ant, Rel, Arch]

Rochat de la Vallee, E.R.

IR France
[CN, TW][Phi, Lin, Rel]

Rocher, Prof. dr A.

UMMB,DEEO,DU France
[JP][Lit, Rel, Phi]

Rodao, Prof. F.R.

UCM,ICA Spain
iasiao2@sis.ucm.es
[JP, PI, PH][His, IR]

Rodenburg, Dr J.

CDR Denmark
[ID, MY][Ant, GenS, Env, DevS]

Rodriguez, N.L.H. van

Balistraat 64-A
2585 XV The Hague
Netherlands

Rodríguez Ubeda, M.M.

Satvrnino Baquer, N°3- 6°B
22003 Huesca
Spain
[BD, ID, JP, MY, MM, PH, SG, TH, VN][Eco, IR, Soc]

Rodriguez-Eiras, J.A.

Pmaha 9, 1°A
28220 Majadahonda
Spain
[JP, KG, MG, MN, PI, PG, PH, TJ, TI, TM][Agr, Eco, Edu, Env, His, Soc]

Rodriquez Doctorate, N.

EFEO France
[CMBODIA, ID, LA, MM, TH, VN][AHis]

Roelofs, Drs J.D.

Lekstraat 162-II
1079 EZ Amsterdam
Netherlands
[IN, ID, LK][Soc, GenS, DevS]

Roesgaard, Dr M.

UC,FH,DAS Denmark
roesgd@coco.ihi.ku.dk
[JP][Ant, Soc, Edu]

Roesler, Drs U.

PUM,IND Germany
roesleru@mailer.uni-marburg.de
[IN, TI][Lin, Lit, Rel]

Roetz, Dr H.

JWGU,IOOP,SIN Germany
[CN][Phi, His]

Rogojine, Dr A.

IWEIR Russia
[BN, KH, ID, JP, LA, MY, MM, PH, SG, TH, VN][Env, Eco, IR, DevS]

Rohde, Prof. dr K.E.

UB,ED Germany
[CN, HK, ID, JP, KR, PH, SG, TW, TH][Soc, Eco, Env, DevS, CuS, IR]

Rohde, Drs M.R.

IFA Germany
[JP][Eco, IR, DevS, PolS]

Rohdewohld, R.

Raven, Str. 5
13347 Berlin
Germany
[ID][PolS, Eco, IR, DevS]

Roland, N.

INALCO France
[JP][Eco]

Román, Dr L.

SSE,DE Sweden
glr@hhs.se
[VN][DevS, Eco]

Roman Marugan, Dr P.

UCM,PS,DCPA Spain
[JP][PolS]

Romich, Dr M.F.

RWTH,CF Germany
romich@rwth-aachen.de
[CN, HK, SG, TH][DevS, Soc, PolS, Eco]

Romijn, Dr H.A.

OU,FE United Kingdom
[PK][DevS, Eco]

Ronge, V.

Kanterring 35
5330 Ittenbach
Germany
[TI][DevS, Eco]

Ronge, N.G.

Kanterring 35
5330 Ittenbach
Germany
[TI][Eco, DevS]

Rongen, O.B.

Eilert Sundsgaten 18
4000 Stavanger
Norway
[CN][Phi]

Ronnås, Dr P.

SSE,DE Sweden
gpr@hhs.se
[KH, CN, IN, LA, MM, PI, PG, TH, VN][DevS, Agr, Eco]

Roo, Dr A.J. de

EUR,R Netherlands
deroo@rrj.frg.eur.nl
[CN, HK, JP, MO, TH, VN][Law]

Roo, R.H.H. de
ING,GDC Netherlands
[CN, HK, JP, MO, TH, VN][Law, Eco]

Roodenburg, C.
Boerhaavestraat 124
3132 RJ Vlaardingen
Netherlands
[ID, MY, SG][Eco, IR, Lin, Soc]

Rookmaaker, T.D.
James Wattstraat 75/420
1097 DL Amsterdam
Netherlands
[His, Eco]

Rooney, Dr D.F.
7 Egerton Place
SW3 2EF London
United Kingdom
[KH, TH][His, AHis]

Roos, Drs S.
UTU,SSPH Finland
santuo@utu.fi
[ID][IR]

Roos, Drs M.E.
RUL,CNWS Netherlands
roosme@rullet.leidenuniv.nl
[Lin]

Roosmalen, Drs P.K.M. van
Gillis van Ledenberchstr. 27-II
1052 TX Amsterdam
Netherlands
[ID][His, AHis]

Roper, Dr G.J.
UC,IBU United Kingdom
gjr@ula.cam.ac.uk
[AF, BD, AF, BD, BN, IN, ID, KZ, MY, MV, PK,][CuS]

Roscchin, Dr M.Yu.
RASP,IOS Russia
[His, Soc]

Rosen, Prof. S.
SU,IOL,DKS Sweden
staffan.rosen@orient.su.se
[KR][Arch, Lin]

Rosenstein, Dr L.L.
SOAS,CSEAS United Kingdom
lr1@soas.ac.uk
[IN][Lit, Lin]

Roshchin, Dr S.K.
RASP,IOS Russia
[MN][Eco, His]

Roskam, R.E.
Burgsteeg 2
2312 JS Leiden
Netherlands
[ID][Lin, Lit]

Rosker, Dr J.
UL,FF,OAAS Slovenia
jana.rosker@uni-lj.si
[CN, TW, TI][Phi, Rel, GenS, Soc, PolS]

Rossi, Prof. A.V.
UIO,DAS Italy
[AF, BD, AF, BD, IN, PK, TJ, TM][Rel, PolS, Lin, Arch, Ant]

Rossi-Filibeck, E. de
URLS,DOS Italy
[TI][Lin, His, Lit]

Rosu, Dr A.
CF,IEO France
[IN][CuS]

Rotermund, Prof. H.O.
CNRS,EPHE,CJ France
[JP][Soc, Rel, CuS]

Roth, Drs D.
LW,DDE Netherlands
dik.roth@alg.ar.wau.nl
[ID][Soc, PolSAgr, DevS, Ant]

Roth, Dr R.B.
LMS Germany
[ID, MG, MY, PH][CuS, His]

Rothermund, Prof. dr D.
EASAS,RKU Germany
[IN][His]

Roudenko, Drs E.
Sumskoy Proezd 2,fl.4, App.47
113208 Moscow
Russia
[ID][Lin, CuS, Lit]

Rouhomäki, Drs O.
UH,VT,S Finland
[LA, TH][Ant]

Roukodelnicova, M.B.
RAS,IOS,AL Russia
[CN, TW][Lin]

Rousset, Dr H.A.
29, rue Brézin
75014 Paris
France
[CN, JP, KR, PI][CuS, His, Arch, AHis, Ant]

Rouw, L.P. de
Klimmenderstraat 109
6343 AA Klimmen
Netherlands

Roux, A.
UP8, France
[CN][IR, His]

Rovers, E.
RUG,BIG Netherlands
[IN][Eco]

Rovetta BA, Pablo
ITR Spain
[CN, HK, KR ,][Eco, His, IR, Lin, Lit, PolS, Soc]

Rovetta Dubinsky, Pablo
ITR Spain
[CN, TW][Eco, Env, IR, Lin, PolS]

Rowley, Dr G.G.
UW,CC,JSC United Kingdom
rowleygg@cardiff.ac.uk
[JP][Lit]

Rox, Drs L.
Jeremiestraat 25
3511 TW Utrecht
Netherlands
[ID][His, Lin]

Roy, O.
AU,CNRS France
[AF, IR, KZ, PK, TJ, TM, UZ][PolS]

Ruben, Drs R.
LW,DDE Netherlands
Ruerd.ruben@alg.oe.wau.nl
[IN, ID, PK][Agr, Eco, Env]

Rudie, Dr I.
DMA Norway
ingrid.rudie@ima.uio.no
[MY][Ant]

Rüdiger, Drs A.
RKU,SI Germany
[AF, BD, AF, BD, IN, PK, TJ][Soc, Rel, CuS, IR, PolS]

Rudoy, Dr V.I.
RASP,IOS,DSSEAS Russia
[Rel, CuS, Phi]

Rueb, Drs P.D.
Kerkstraat 38
2271 GT Voorburg
Netherlands
[IN, ID][His]

Rueland, Prof. dr J.
UR,WSF,IPV Germany
[IN, ID, MY, MM, PH, SG, TH][IR, PolS, DevS]

Ruenkaew, P.
UBI,FS Germany
pruenkaew@sozjur.uni-bielefeld.de
[TH][GenS, DevS, Soc]

Rühle, Mr K.H.
Stralsunder Strasse 45
04357 Leipzig
Germany
[CN, HK, JP, KR, TW, TI][His, Lit, Lin, CuS]

Ruigrok, Dr W.M.
RIIM,USG Switzerland
winfried.ruigrok@fim.unisg.ch
[DevS, PolS]

Ruijter, Prof. dr A. de
CERES Netherlands
[Phi, Ant]

Ruiter, Drs T.G.
Westerstraat 289
1015 MH Amsterdam
Netherlands
[ID][Agr, Soc, Eco, DevS, His, Ant]

Ruiter, Drs W.
TU,CICAT Netherlands
[DevS]

Ruiz, Dr José M.
UVD,JAP Spain
[JP][Lin, Rel]

Ruizendaal, Drs R.E.
RUL,CNWS Netherlands
[CN, HK, TW][Ant, Rel]

Rumiantsev, Prof.dr M.K.
MSU,IAAS,CIBS Russia
[CN][Lin]

Russell, Dr A.J.
UDU,DA United Kingdom
a.j.russell@durham.ac.uk
[IN, NP][DevS, Env, Ant, CuS]

Russo, Dr A.
UB,DES Italy
[CN][Edu, CuS, PolS, Soc, Lit, Phi, Ant]

Rüstau, Dr H.
HUB,AA,SOA,SL Germany
[Phi, Rel, CuS]

Rutt, C.R.
UDU,DEAS United Kingdom
[CN, KR][Lit]

Rutten, Dr M.A.F.
UvA,ASSR,CASA
Netherlands
[IN, ID, MY,][Ant, Soc]

Rutten, Dr R.A.
UvA,ASC,CASA Netherlands
[PH][DevS, Ant]

Rutz, Prof. dr W.
RUB,GI Germany
[ID][Env, CuS, Eco, His]

Ruud, Dr A.E.
UO,EACS Norway
a.e.ruud@hi.uio/no
[IN][Ant, His]

Ruygrok, Drs W.F.
Prinses Irenestraat 26
4231 AZ Meerkerk
Netherlands
[ID, JP, PG,][His, PolS, Soc]

Ruyven, Drs L.W. van
RUL,OWZ Netherlands
Ruyven@rullet.leidenuniv.nl
[ID, JP, PG,][Eco]

Ruyver, C. de
Keviestraat 19
9000 Gent
Belgium

Ryabinin, Dr A.L.
RASP,IOS Russia
[VN][His]

Ryabinina, Dr E.D.
RASP,IOS Russia
[Eco]

Ryan, Dr J.T.
16 Tindal Street
SW9 6UP London
United Kingdom
[CN, ID, JP, MY, PH, SG, VN][Eco]

Rygaloff, A.
CNRS,CRLAO France
[Lin]

Rykova, Dr S.L.
RAS,IOS,DC Russia
[CN][His]

Saane, Drs P.A. van
Postbus 16685
1001 RD Amsterdam
Netherlands
[ID, MY][Lin]

Säävälä, Drs M.S.
UvA,ASSR,CASA
Netherlands
saavala@pscw.uva.nl
[IN][Ant]

Sabattini, Drs M.
UV,DSIEO,C Italy
[CN, HK, LA, MO, SG, TW, TH][His, Lit, Lin]

Sabban, F.S.
CNRS,ARCHIPEL France
[CN, JP, MN, TW][Agr, Ant, CuS]

Sablina, E.
Groholsky pereulok 30-1-22
129010 Moscow
Russia
[JP][CuS, His, IR]

Sacareau, Dr I.
CNRS,MSCH France
[NP, TI][Geo]

Sachsenmaier, Dr D.
Sundgauallee 12-03314
79110 Freiburg
Germany
[CN, TW][Rel, IR, His, CuS]

Sadokova, Dr A.R.
RAS,IWL Russia
[JP][Lit]

Safronova, Dr A.L.
MSU,IAAS,CIBS Russia
[LK][Rel, His]

Sagant, Dr Ph.
UL3,CREO France
[NP, TI][Phi, Rel]

Sagart, Dr L.
CNRS,CRLAO France
sagart@ehess.fr
[CN, HK, TW][Lin]

Sagaster, Prof. dr K.
UB,ZA Germany
[CN, MN, PK, SM, TI][Rel, Phi, Lit, Lin, His, AHis, CuS, His]

Sagiyama, Prof. I.
UF,IGOLT Italy
[JP][Lit]

Sagli, Drs G.
UO,IGPCM,SM Norway
gry.sagli@samfunnsmed.uio.no
[CN][CuS]

Sahar, B.
INALCO France
[ID][CuS]

Saich, Prof. dr A.J.
FF, IC China P.R.
[CN, HK, TW][Ant, PolS, His, DevS]

Saith, Prof. dr A.
ISS Netherlands
[CN, IN,][Agr, Eco, DevS, His]

Saito, T.
INALCO France
[JP][Edu]

Saito, S.
UTM,CUP France
[JP][Edu]

Sakai, C.
UP7,UAO France
[JP][Lit]

Sakamoto, R.
7 Laurance Close
CO7 7EJ Elmstead Market, Colchester
United Kingdom
[JP][CuS, Ant, Soc]

Sakamoto, Dr K.
Vechtstraat 24
2515 SR The Hague
Netherlands
kum:@wirkub.nl
[JP][CuS, Lit]

Salazar, Drs W.M.W.T.
SOAS,DH United Kingdom
[ID, PH][His]

Saller, C.
Anschuetzgasse 29/9
1150 Vienna
Austria
[TI][PolS]

Salles, Dr J.F.
INALCO France
[BD, IN, MM, NP, PK, LK][His, AHis, Arch, His]

Salmon, Dr C.
CNRS,EHESS France
[CN, ID, SG, VN][Rel, Lit, CuS, His]

Saltford, J.F.
UHU,DSEAS United Kingdom
[ID, PG][IR]

Salvaert, A.
BAMEP France
[CN][Lit]

Salverda, Prof. R.
UCL United Kingdom
[ID][Lit, Law, Lin]

Salzmann, Dr B.
UHNV,BP Germany
[KR, MY, SG, TW][Soc]

Samad, Mr A.Y.
UBR,DSES United Kingdom
a.y.samad@bradford.ac.uk
[BD, IN, PK][His, PolS, Soc]

Samarani, G.
UV,DSIEO,J Italy
[CN, TW, VN][His]

Samarina, I. V.
RAS,IL Russia
@iling.msk.su
[, VN][Lin]

Samely, Dr U.
MMU,FH,DL United Kingdom
[ID][Lin]

Samossiuok, K.
SHM,OD Russia
[TI][Lin]

Samosuik, Dr K.F.
Russia
[AHis, CuS, Rel]

Samoyeov, Dr N.A.
SPU,FOS,DAS Russia
[CN, JP][IR, His]

Samoylov, Dr N.A.
[CN][His, IR]

Samozvantsev, Dr A.M.
RASP,IOS Russia
[IN][His]

Sampedro Fromont, X.
UCM, EEE,DEI Spain
[JP][Eco]

Samphel, T.
30, Ave Gambetta
78400 Chatou
France
[TI][His, IR]

Samuel, Dr G.B.
UL,DRS United Kingdom
g.samuel1@lancaster.ac.uk
[BD, IN, NP, TI][Rel, Ant]

Sanchez Gomez, Luis Angel
UCM,GH,DPE Spain
[PH][Ant, His]

Sandee, Drs H.M.
VU,VOAE Netherlands
hm.sandee@dienst.vu.nl
[ID][DevS, Eco]

Sanders, Drs M.
AH, TPNAF Netherlands
[CN, HK, IN, ID, JP, KR, MY, PH, TH][DevS, Eco]

Sandouk, Drs S.
124 Bis, Rue de la République
93230 Romainville
France
[AF, IN, PK][Phi, His, Lit, Rel]

Sandra, Prof. D.E.E.
UB,DES Italy
[KH ID, LA, TH, VN][Ant, CuS, Edu, GenS]

Sanna, G.
UIO,DSO Italy
[CN, TW][Ant, Lit]

Santa Maria, Prof. dr L.
UIO,DAS Italy
[BN, ID, MY, SG][Lit, Lin, IR, His]

Santangelo, Prof. P.
UIO,DAS Italy
[CN, HK, KR, TW][His]

Santos, A.
UC,FEI,DB Spain
santosa@buc.unicau.es
[JP,][AHis]

Santos Alves, Dr J.M.
Urbanizaçao Varandas de Monsanto
Lote 17-A, 9§ Esq.
Estrada do Zambujal
2720 Alfragide
Portugal
[ID, MO][His]

Santoso, Drs S.
UvA,VS Netherlands
[ID][AHis, IR, His, PolS, His]

Saptari, Dr R.
KUN,CPS Netherlands
r.saptari@maw.kun.nl
[ID][DevS, Ant, Soc]

Sarianidi, Dr V.I.
Russia
[Arch]

Sarkisov, Dr K.O.
RAS,IOS,CJS Russia
[JP][His, IR, PolS]

Sarmela, Prof. dr M.
UH,VT,S Finland
[His, PolS]

Sasse, Prof. dr W.
RUB,FOAW,KOR Germany
or5a007@rrz.uni-hamburg.de
[KR][Lin, CuS]

Sathyamurthy, Dr T.V.
UY,DP United Kingdom
tvs1@unix.york.ac.uk
[IN][PolS, IR, DevS, Soc, Rel]

Sato, Drs N.
IOCFT Hungary
[CN, JP, KR, TW][Edu, Eco]

Satterthwaite, D.
IIED United Kingdom
[PH][PolS, IR]

Sauarlia, Dr L
UTR,SAI Norway
lisbet.sauarlia@sv.ntnu.no
[CN, TW][Ant]

Sauerborn, Prof. J.
JLUG,ITR Germany
[CN, IN, ID, NP, PI, PH, VN][Agr, Env]

Saunders, Dr G.E.
AA, FH, DH Republic of Cyprus
[BN, MY, SG][His]

Sautter, Ch.
CNRS,CRJC France
[JP][Eco]

Savelieva, Dr T.K.
RASP,IOS Russia
[Eco]

Saville, Mr A.
NMS,DA United Kingdom
as@nms.ac.uk
[JP, KR,][Arch]

Savolainen, Hanna-Mari
UH,VT,S Finland
[ID,][Ant]

Sazanova, Dr N.M.
MSU,IAAS,CIBS Russia
[IN][CuS, Lit]

Scalabrino, Drs C.J.
UP7, GHSS France
[KH, IN, LA, VN][Rel, Arch, His, Phi, Psy, His, IR, AHis, PolS]

Scalise, Prof. M.
UP,CEUP Italy
[JP][Lin, Lit]

Scalliet, Dr M.O.
RUL,BIB Netherlands
[ID][His, AHis, Arch, CuS]

Scammel, Dr G.V.
CU,PC United Kingdom
[IN, MO,][His]

Scaramella, L.
Civ. 141
38022 Caldes
Italy

Scarduelli, P.
DSAAS Italy
[ID][Ant]

Schaab-Hanke, Dr D.
UHAM,SKC,TBI Germany
[CN, HK, TW][PolS, CuS, His]

Schaap, R.
VJK Netherlands
[JP][AHis]

Schach, Mr L.
1 rue Stendhal
77330 Ozoir
France
[AHis]

Schäfer, Drs E.S.
Smaragdstraat 78
1074 HJ Amsterdam
Netherlands
[ID, MY, PI, PG, PH, SG, TH, VN][His, Eco, IR, CuS]

Schalk, Prof. dr P.
GU,ARK Sweden
[KH, IN, LA, MM, LK, TH, VN][Phi, AHis, CuS, Arch, His, Rel]

Schalke, Dr H.J.W.G.
TNO, IAG Netherlands
schalke@iag.tno.nl
[KH, CN, HK, JP, KR, MY, PI, PK, PG, PH, SG,][Arch, Ant, Env]

Schaller, J.I.M.
Im Johannistal 23
42119 Wuppertal
Germany
[TH][Lin]

Schaller, Prof. dr E.
HUB,AA,SOA,SL Germany
[IN][PolS, Soc]

Schamoni, Prof. W.
RKU,OAW,JAP Germany
[JP][Lit]

Schampers, Drs A.J.J.
NOVIB Netherlands
[IN, NP, LK][DevS, Soc]

Scharping, Prof. dr Th.
UK,OAS,MCS Germany
t.scharping@uni-koeln.de
[CN, TW][PolS, Soc, Eco]

Scheepers, Dr A.R.
Wibautstraat 111-II
1091 GL Amsterdam
Netherlands
[CN, IN, JP,][Phi, His, Rel]

Schefold, Prof. dr R.
RUL,CA/SNWS Netherlands
[ID][Ant]

Scheltema, Prof. mr M.
RUG,VBB Netherlands
mscheltema@rechten.rug.nl
[ID, VN][Law]

Schendel, J.C.M. van
Bulaaq Uitg. Netherlands
[ID, VN][Ant, Lit, Phi, Lin, PolS, Rel]

Schendel, Prof. dr H.W. van
UvA,MAG Netherlands
vanschendel@mgs.fhk.eur.nl
[BD, IN, MM,][His, Ant]

Schenk, Dr H.
UvA,VPD Netherlands
schenk@ivip.frw.uva.nl
[CN, IN, ID, LK, TH, VN][DevS, Env]

Schenk-Sandbergen, Dr L.Ch.
UvA,ASC,CASA Netherlands
loes@nld.toolnet.org
[BD, CN, IN, LA, VN][GenS, DevS, Env, Ant]

Scherer, Dr S.
14 Rue Martel
95290 L'Isle Adam
France
[ID][His, CuS, IR, Lit, PolS]

Scherrer-Schaub, C.A.
UL,DOLC Switzerland
[IN, TI][Arch, His, Phi, Rel]

Scheuringer, Drs K.
US, IE Austria
karl.scheuringer@mh.sbg.ac.at
[ID][Edu, CuS, Psy]

Schied, Dr M.
RKU,SI Germany
[BD, IN, PK, LK][His, Phi, PolS, Rel]

Schiel, Dr T.
UBAY,KW,E Germany
[ID, MY, PG, SG][Soc, His, Ant, Agr, Env, DevS, PolS]

Schiermeier, Drs K.E.N.B.
RUL,VKA Netherlands
[JP][AHis, Lin]

Schilder, Prof. dr G.
UU,VSGO Netherlands
g.schilder@frw.ruu.nl
[His]

Schilder, Drs A.M.Th.
UMA Netherlands
[His, Edu]

Schillig, Dr D
LMU,IOAK,SIN Germany
Dennis.Schillng@liz-muenchen.de
[CN, JP, TW, TI][CuS, Phi, Rel]

Schilt, J.W.
Hoogte Kadijk 167-1
1018 BJ Amsterdam
Netherlands
[ID, PH][His, IR]

Schimmelpenninck, Drs A.M.
CHIME Netherlands
[CN][CuS, Lin, Ant, Lit, His, AHis]

Schimmelpfennig, Drs M.
RKU,OAW,SIN Germany
[CN][Arch, His]

Schipper, Prof. dr K.M.
RUL,SI Netherlands
kschipper@rullet.leidenuniv.nl
[KH, CN, TW][Rel, Ant, His]

Schipper, Prof. dr M.
RUL,VAILW Netherlands
[KH, CN, TW][Lit]

Schippers, Dr H.
TUE Netherlands
[ID][His]

Schlerath, Prof. dr B.
FUB,IGS Germany
[IN, IR][Lin, CuS, Rel]

Schlicher, Dr M.
RKU,SI,DPS Germany
[IN, ID, MM, PH][His, PolS, IR]

Schlingloff, Prof. dr D.
LMU,II Germany
[IN][AHis, CuS, Arch, Lit, Rel]

Schmid, Prof. dr W.A.
EPZ,IAE Switzerland
schmid@orl.arch.ethz.ch
[CN][Env, Edu, DevS]

Schmid, Dr A.
Bergheimerstrasse 82
69115 Heidelberg
Germany
[IN, PK][His, Ant]

Schmid-Schoenbein, C.
Hoehenweg 18
9000 St. Gallen
Switzerland
[HK, JP, KR, MO][Eco, IR, PolS]

Schmidt, Dr J.D.
AU, RCDIR Denmark
Jds@i4.auc.dk
[ID, KR, MY, PH, SG, TH, VN][Soc, IR, DevS]

Schmidt, Dr O.
UTT,DPS Italy
[PK][His, Ant]

Schmidt, H.C.
UHAM,SIS Germany
[ID, PI][Ant, Lin]

Schmidt, J.H.L.
Noûnebourren 25
9132 EJ Engwierum
Netherlands
[IN, TI][Arch, AHis]

Schmidt - Glintzer, Prof. dr H.R.H.
HAB Germany
schmidt-gl@hab.de
[CN][His, Rel, Lit, CuS]

Schmidt-Vogt, Dr D.
RKU,SI,AG Germany
[NP, TH][Env]

Schmit, Dr L.T.
RUL,TCZOAO,PD
Netherlands
schmit@rullet.leidenuniv.nl
[ID][Ant]

Schmitt, K.
UHAM,SKC,KTV Germany
or5.05@wz.uni-hamburg.de
[CN, TI][Soc, Phi, Lin, Ant, Rel]

Schmitt, Prof. dr R.
US,VIGSI Germany
[AF, IN, KZ, PK, TJ, TM, UZ][Lin, His]

Schmitz, Dr A.
LMU,IVA Germany
[KZ, MN, TJ, TM, UZ][Rel, Ant, Lit, PolS, CuS, Soc, His]

Schmutz, G.M.
UZ,AS,OS Switzerland
[CN, TW][Soc, Ant, Edu]

Schneider, Dr H.
HHU,GI Germany
schneide@uni.duesseldorf.de
[PH, TH][Geo, CuS, DevS]

Schneider, Dr J.
FUB,AW,IPKG Germany
[IN, TI][Rel, Lit, Lin]

Schneider, Dr J.
UBE,IE Switzerland
schneider@ethno.unibe.ch
[ID][Ant, Env, Agr]

Schneider-Sliwa, Prof. dr R.
UB,GI Switzerland
[HK, IN, LK][DevS]

Schnepp, Drs Th.
Kerpener Strasse 3
50937 Cologne
Germany
[ID][AntAnt, CuS]

Schoch, Drs G.W.
TNO,MP Netherlands
schoch@mp.tno.nl
[CN, HK, ID, JP, SG, TW][Eco]

Schoembucher, Dr E.
CMOS Germany
[IN][Rel, Ant, Lin, GenS, CuS]

Schoenhals, M.
SU,CPAS Sweden
michael.schoenhals@orient.su.se
[CN][His, PolS]

Schoepe, Dr R.
Sonnenweg 22
66119 Saarbrücken
Germany
[AF, CN, HK, IN, KR, MO, MN, TI][Lin, Phi]

Schokhin, V. K.
RAS,IP,DOP Russia
[IN,][Phi]

Schokker, Dr G.H.
RUL,KERN Netherlands
[IN][Lit, Rel, Lin]

Scholten, Drs J.
RUL,TCJK Netherlands
[JP][Lit]

Schömbucher, Dr E.
RKU,SI Germany
[IN][Ant, Lin, Rel, CuS, GenS]

Schooneveld, Dr J.E.
Pijlkruid 4
2635 KM Den Hoorn
Netherlands
[JP][His]

Schoor, Drs W.J. van der
EFEO,BIB France
geschiedenis@fys.ruu.nl
[ID][His]

Schoorl, Prof. dr J.W.
Groen van Prinstererlaan 37
1272 GB Huizen (N.H.)
Netherlands
[IN, ID, PK][DevS, Ant]

Schoot, Dr H.A. van der
Ds V.d. Boschlaan 30
2286 PM Rijswijk Z.H.
Netherlands
[KH, ID][DevS, Eco]

Schottenhammer, Dr A.
IIAS Netherlands
schottenham@rullet.leidenuniv.nl
[CN, HK, TW][Phi, His, Eco, PolS]

Schouten, Dr M.J.C.
UBI,DSCS Portugal
schouten@alpha2.ubi.pt
[ID][His, Ant]

Schouten, Drs P.H.
Lijnbaansgracht 297-I
1017 RN Amsterdam
Netherlands
[BN, ID, MY][Ant, Soc]

Schouten, Drs N.A.M.
Van der Vinnestraat 42 ZW
2023 AH Haarlem
Netherlands
[CN, HK][AHis, CuS, Arch, His]

Schouw, Drs M.H. van der
Standhazenstraat 40
3312 IR Dordrecht
Netherlands
[ID, MY][AHis, Arch, CuS, His]

Schrader, Dr H.
UBI,FS,SDRC Germany
heiko.schrader@post-uni-bielefeld.de
[IN, ID, MY, NP, SG,][Soc, Eco, Ant, CuS]

Schrammel, Drs U.S.
Delbrück Str. 2
28209 Bremen
Germany
[CN, HK, TW, TI][Eco, Env]

Schreiner, Prof. dr L.
KHW Germany
[KH, ID, LA, MY, MM, PH][Rel, Ant, His]

Schreiner, Dr K.H.
JWGU,IOOP,SOAW
Germany
pesch@indoger.unizh.ch
[ID][His, PolS, Rel]

Schreuel, Drs E.J.
Louvre 192
2907 WE Capelle a/d IJssel
Netherlands
[ID][DevS, Eco]

Schrijver, Dr P.C.H.
RUL,VTW Netherlands
[Lin]

Schrijvers, Prof. dr J.
UvA,INDRA Netherlands
[LK][GenS, DevS, Ant]

Schröder, K.
Rudolf Hahn Str. 39
5300 Bonn 3
Germany
[MM][Ant, GenS, DevS]

Schröter, Dr S.
JGU,IEAS Germany
[CN, IN, ID, , LK][Ant]

Schucher, Dr G.
DGAK Germany
[CN][Soc]

Schüller, Dr M.S.
IFA Germany
[CN][DevS, Agr, Eco]

Schult, Dr V.
UP,SEAS Germany
[PH][His]

Schulte Nordholt, Dr N.G.
UT,TDG Netherlands
n.g.schultenordholt@tdg.utwente.nl
[ID][DevS, PolS, Env]

Schulte Nordholt, Dr H.G.C.
UvA,ASC,CASA Netherlands
[ID][Soc, His, Ant]

Schultink, Prof. dr H.
Prins Bernhardlaan 26
3722 AG Bilthoven
Netherlands

Schulz Zinda, Drs Y.
LMU,IOAK,SIN Germany
ucc02ch@sunmail.lrz-muenchen.de
[CN, KR][CuS, Phi]

Schulze, Dr F.
UK,OS,MA Germany
[ID, MY][His, CuS, Rel, Lit]

Schulze, F.
Van Ostadestraat 236-I
1073 TV Amsterdam
Netherlands
[CN, JP][His, Rel]

Schumacher, Dr J.
UG,FL,DSA Switzerland
[CN][Lit, Phi]

Schumacher, Prof. R.
UK,MI Germany
ruediger.schumacher@uni-koeln.de
[ID][Part]

Schutte, Prof. dr G.J.
UvA,MAG Netherlands
[ID][His]

Schütte, H.
UB, DH Germany
[IR]

Schütte, Dr H.W.
Grindelberg 77
20144 Hamburg
Germany
[CN][His, CuS]

Schütte, Dr H.
UBR,GI Germany
[PI, VN][Soc, CuS, His]

Schuurman, Dr F.J.
KUN,IDS Netherlands
[LK][DevS]

Schweiger, Drs I.
RKU,OAW,SIN Germany
irmy@gw.sino.uni-heidelberg.de
[CN][Lit]

Schweinfurth, Prof. dr U.
RKU,SI,AG Germany
[AF, BT, IN, ID, LA, MG, MY, MM, NP, PI, PG,][Agr, DevS, Env, Arch, IR]

Schwerin, Dr K. von
FUB,IE Germany
[IN, PK][His]

Schwidder, Drs L.E.G.
IISG,IISH Netherlands
esc@iisg.nl
[ID][His]

Schwinghammer, Drs E.
UP,SEAS Germany
[ID, MY][DevS, Eco, CuS, His]

Schwörer, Dr G.
JGU,MI Germany
[MM, TH][CuS, Ant]

Scolari, V.
ISIAO Italy
[IN, JP, MY][CuS, His, AHis]

Seckel, Prof. dr D.
RKU,KI,AA Germany
[CN, JP, KR][His, AHis]

Secretary General, The
DFG Germany

Seddon, Prof. J.D.
UEA,ODG,SDS United Kingdom
J.d.seddon@uea.ac.uk
[NP][Ant, IR, Soc, PolS, DevS]

Sedlovskaya, Dr A.N.
RAS,IEA Russia
[Ant]

Sedov, Dr A. V.
RASP,IOS Russia
sedov@sed.msk.ru
[AF, BD, IN, MG, PK, LK, TJ, TM][Arch]

Seebass, Prof. dr T.
UI, IM Austria
tilman.seebass@uibk.ac.at
[ID][PolS, Soc, Ant, IR, DevS]

Seegers, L.A.
Van Haerlemlaan 38
1901 JP Castricum
Netherlands

Seeland, Dr K.
EHT Switzerland
seeland@waho.etzh/ch
[BT, IN, NP, PK,][Rel, Soc, Env, Ant]

Seele, C.
UB,ZA Germany
seele@pwyz.rhein.de
[TI][Soc, GenS]

Segers, Drs W.A.I.M.
EFEO,ID Indonesia
[ID][His]

Segjy, Marianne
UB2,SSP France
[ID,][Ant, Arch, Rel]

Seguy, C.
INALCO France
[CN][Lan]

Seguy, Ch.
USHS,LLCE France
[JP][CuS]

Seifert, Prof. dr W.
RKU,OAW,JAP Germany
[JP][Soc, PolS]

Seitz, Prof. dr S.
ALU,IVK Germany
seitz@ruf.uni-freiburg.de
[MY, PH][Ant]

Seizelet, E.A.F.
CNRS,IAO France
eseizele@mrash.fr
[JP, KR][Law, Edu, PolS]

Sekem, W.
INALCO France
[ID, MY][PolS, Law, Edu]

Sekiguchi, H.
UP7,UAO France
[JP][Lin]

Selier, Dr F.J.M.
VU, DCA Netherlands
[PK][Ant]

Sellato, B.
CNRS,IRSEA France
[ID, MY][Ant, His]

Sellmeijer-Fujita, M.
Rietkraag 55
3121 TC Schiedam
Netherlands
[JP][Psy]

Sellner, Dr M.B.
US, IS Austria
manfred.sellner@sbg.ac.at
[KHCN, HK, ID, JP, KR, LA, MN, MM, NP, PG, TW,][CuS, Lin]

Seltmann, Dr F.M.
Ahornstrasse 52
70597 Stuttgart
Germany
[IN, ID, TH][CuS]

Semah, F.
IPH France
[ID, PI][Arch]

Semanov, Dr V.I.
MSU,IAAS,CIBS Russia
[CN][Lit]

Semashko, Dr I.M.
RAS,IEA Russia
[IN][Ant]

Semenas, Dr A.L.
RASP,IOS Russia
[CN][Lin]

Semenenko, Dr I.I.
MSU,IAAS,CIBS Russia
[CN][Lit, Phi, Rel]

Semetko, Prof. dr H.A.
UvA,VCW Netherlands
semetko@pscw.uva.nl
[CN, HK, IN, JP, KR, MN, TW, TI][PolS, Soc, Psy]

Semionov, Dr G.L.
Russia
[CuS]

Senatorov, Dr A.I.
IWEIR Russia
[JP][PolS]

Senft, Dr G.
MPIP, CARG Netherlands
gunter (at)mpi.nl
[PI, PG][Ant, Lin]

Senger, Prof. dr H. von
ALU,OS Germany
[CN, JP, TW][Lit, PolS, Law, CuS]

Sens, Drs A.P.G.
UU,OGC Netherlands
angelie.sens@let.ruu.nl
[CN, JP, TW][His, CuS]

Seppänen, J.
HUT Finland
jouko.seppanen@hut.fi
[BT, BN, KHCN, HK, ID, JP, KR, LA, MY, MM, NP][IR, Eco, Ant, CuS, Lin, His, AHis, Phi, Arch, Rel, PolS]

Serebriakov, Dr E.A.
[CN][Lit]

Serebriany, Dr S.D.
RSUH,IASH Russia
[BD, IN, PK][Rel, CuS, Phi, Lin, Lit]

Serenko, Dr I. N.
9-2 Ramenky Str., Flat 236
117607 Moscow
Russia
[BD, IN, PK,][CuS, Edu, His, IR, Rel, Soc]

Seret, Mr A.
De Wolzaklaan 3
7211 AR Eefde
Netherlands
[CN, IN, ID, PI, LK][Phi, Lit, Lin, Rel, CuS]

Serova, Dr S.A.
RASP,IOS Russia
[CN][AHis]

Serrano Valentin, Carlos
Santiago Bernabeu, 12
28036 Madrid
Spain
[HK, JP, KR, TW][Eco, IR]

Servaes, Prof. dr J.E.J.G.
KUB, RCC Belgium
[BT, MY, PH, SG, TH][CuS, Ant, Soc, DevS]

Sethupathy, E.
INALCO France
[IN][Ant, DevS, CuS, Soc]

Setyawati,-Vayda, M.A.
United States of America
[ID][Ant, Agr, Env, DevS]

Sevela, M.
33, Rue R. Rolland
94250 Gentilly
France
[JP][His]

Sevenheck, Drs A.J.J.
Netherlands
teun.sevenheck@teleac.nl
[JP][Edu]

Severen, S. van
ULB Belgium
[JP][Lin]

Seyock, Drs B.
HHU,JAP Germany
[JP, KR][His, Arch]

Shabalina, Dr G.S.
RAS,IOS,AL Russia
[Eco, Edu]

Shabelnikova, Dr E.M.
SPU,FOS,DAS Russia
[CN][Lin]

Shaimpdanova, I.H.
RAS,IOS,DHO Russia
[TM][His]

Shalyapina, Dr Z.M.
RAS,IOS,AL Russia
[JP][Lin]

Sharipova, Dr R.M.
RASP,IOS Russia
[CuS, Rel]

Sharma, Dr Gh.
UV,DEAS Italy
sharmave@unive.it
[IN][Lin, Lit]

Sharma, Mr L.K.
TTI United Kingdom
[BD, IN, NP, PK, LK][PolS, Soc, Rel, DevS, CuS, IR, Phi, Lit]

Sharpe, Dr P.A.
UEX,DAL United Kingdom
pasharpe@exeter.ac.uk
[JP][Lin]

Shaumian, Dr T.
RAS,IOS,DHO Russia
[IN, PK, TI][His, PolS, IR]

Shaumyan, Dr T.L.
RASP,IOS Russia
[IN][His, PolS]

Shaw, Mr G.W.
NCOLR,OIO,CBL United Kingdom
graham.shaw@bl.uk
[BD, IN, NP, PK, LK][CuS]

Sheehan, Dr J.
KU,DSSA United Kingdom
[CN, JP, KR, VN][PolS, His]

Sheftelevich, Dr N.S.
MSU,IAAS,CIBS Russia
[JP][Lit]

Shen, D.
INALCO France
[CN][Lan]

Shepherd, Dr A.W.
UB,ILGS,D,AG United Kingdom
a.w.shepherd@bham.ac.uk
[BD, IN, NP,][DevS, Env]

Shepperdson, Mr M.J.
UW,UCS,CDS United Kingdom
m.j.shepperdson@swansea.ac.uk
[BD, CN, HK, IN, ID, JP, KZ, NP, PK, LK][DevS, Agr, Eco, PolS, Soc]

Sherkova, Dr T.A.
RASP,IOS Russia
[CuS]

Shevchenko, Dr N.Yu.Yu.
RASP,IOS Russia
[JP][Eco]

Shevelev, Dr K.V.
RAS,IFES,FEB Russia
[CN][His]

Shi-Tao, L.
UJML3,FL France
[CN][Lit]

Shih, Drs J.H.
OU,OI United Kingdom
[CN, IN,][Rel]

Shilovtsev, Dr S.I.
RASP,IOS Russia
[Eco, IR]

Shim, S.-J.
5, rue Lefevre
75015 Paris
France
[KR][CuS, Lit, GenS]

Shimamori, Dr R.
UJML3,FL France
[JP][Lin]

Shin, J.-C.
INALCO France
[KR][His, AHis]

Shioji, Prof. Etsuro
UPF, FEE,DE Spain
shioji@upf.es
[JP][Eco]

Shkarban, Dr L.I.
RAS,IOS,AL Russia
[PH, VN][Lin]

Shkoda, Dr V.G.
Russia
[CuS, Rel]

Shmeleva, Dr G.V.
RASP,IOS Russia
[VN][CuS]

Shokhin, Dr V.K.

[IN][Phi]

Shrestha, Drs B.G.
RUL,KERN Netherlands
[IN, NP][Lit, CuS, Rel, PolS, Ant]

ShukurovProf.Denissov, Dr Japan.
RASP,IOS Russia
[CuS]

Shun-Chiu Yau, .
CNRS,CRLAO France
[CN][Lit, Rel, PolS, Ant, CuS]

Shutova, Dr Ye.I.
RASP,IOS Russia
[CN][Lin]

Siary, Dr G.M.M.
UPV France
[JP][Lit]

Sibeth, Drs A.F.
MVF Germany
sibeth.achim@stadt-frankfurt.de
[ID][Ant]

Sichrovsky, Prof. H.
BICS Austria
[CN, IN, KR, MN, PH,][CuS, His, PolS, IR]

Siddivo, M.
UIO,DSO Italy
[CN][Eco]

Sidel, Dr J.T.
SOAS United Kingdom
jsl3@soas.ac.uk
[PH][PolS]

Sideri, Prof. dr S.
ISS Netherlands
sideri@ISS.NL
[CN][DevS, Eco]

Sidorov, Dr M.A.
RASP,IOS Russia
[IN, PK][IR]

Siemers, Drs G.
IFA Germany
[MN, MM, PG, PH][PolS, IR, Eco]

Sierpinska, Drs A.M.
Graspieper 5
3738 SB Maartensdijk
Netherlands
[PI][Geo]

Sigmond, Dr J.P.
RMA Netherlands
[CN, IN, ID, JP, MO, PI, LK, TW, VN][CuS, His, AHis, Arch]

Sigurdson, Prof. J.
SSE,ASTRA,EAST Sweden
japjs@hhs.se
[CN, HK, JP, KR, SG, TW, VN][IR, DevS, Eco, PolS]

Siika, M.
UTU,SSPH Finland
MARSIIKA@UTU.FI
[CN, JP, TW][IR, His]

Sijmonsbergen, Drs J.
Eerste Helmersstraat 144
1054 EJ Amsterdam
Netherlands
[ID][His]

Silberstein, Dr B.
UL3,CREO France
[BD, IN][His, Geo]

Silhe, N.
CNRS,MSCH France
[NP, TI][Ant]

Silva, Drs P.L. de
VU, DCA Netherlands
dasilva@educ.uva.nl
[LK][DevS, Ant]

Simmons, Dr C.
USA,DE United Kingdom
c.simmons@econ.salf.ac.uk
[CN, IN,][DevS]

Simon, Dr J.C.
CNRS,IREPD France
[JP, KR, MY, TW, TH][Soc, IR, His, Eco, DevS, PolS]

Simon, Prof. dr A.
MVB Germany
[ID][AntAnt]

Simonet, J.M.
KMKG,HCS Belgium
[CN][Arch, CuS, His, AHis]

Simoniya, Dr A.A.

[Eco]

Simoniya, Prof.dr N.A.
IWEIR Russia
[PolS, Soc]

Simonsen, J.
AU,FH,DESA Denmark
[KZ][Ant]

Sims, V.
LSI United Kingdom
[KZ][Edu, CuS, Lit, IR, Lin, Soc, GenS, Env, PolS, DevS, Eco]

Simson, Prof. dr G. von
UO,FA,EOS Norway
g.v.simson@easteur-orient.uio.no
[IN][Rel, Lit]

Singh, R.N.
VAM,ISEAD United Kingdom
[TI][Env, Soc, Agr, IR, DevS]

Singh, Dr G.
DMU,SH United Kingdom
gus@dmu.ac.uk
[IN, PK, LK][DevS, PolS]

Singh, Dr N.
Asterstraat 49
6708 DJ Wageningen
Netherlands
[BD, BT, CN, IN, ID, NP, PK, SM, LK, VN][Agr, Env, DevS, Soc, IR]

Singh, V. P.
UY,IAAS United Kingdom
ups100@york.ac.uk
[IN][Arch, DevS, Env]

Sinitsyn, Dr B.V.
PGMAE,K Russia
[KR][Eco]

Sinitsyn, Dr Ye.P.

[CN][His]

Sinitsyn, Dr A.Yu.

[MM][Ant]

Sinnema, Drs T.
Eikenlaan 61
9321 GC Peize
Netherlands
[BT, CN, ID, JP, KR, MO, NP, PI, PG, TW, TI][GenS, CuS, Soc, His, Edu]

Sirag, K.H.
Cyclaamstraat 52
2565 PG 's-Gravenhage
Netherlands

Siregar, Drs T.M.
SAS,OI Netherlands
[CN, ID][PolS, Eco, Agr]

Siripaphanh, Dr B
LPI France
[LA][His]

Siriprachai, S.
UL,NASEAS Sweden
somboon.siriprachai@ehk.lu.se
[TH][Eco, DevS]

Sirk, Dr S.
RAS,IOS,AL Russia
comm-pub@comlab.vega.msk.su
[ID, MY][Lin]

Sirk, Dr Kh.
RASP,IOS Russia
[Lin]

Sitohang-Nababan, Drs E.L.M.
UP,SEAS Germany
[ID][Lin]

Sitompoel, R.
Willemsparksweg 176
1071 HT Amsterdam
Netherlands

Sivam, J.P.A.
LU,FA,DEAL Sweden
[CN][His, Lit, Law, CuS]

Sivertseva, Dr T.F.
RAS,IOS,DNME Russia
[Ant, Soc, GenS, CuS]

Sivignon,
61 Rue Greneta
. Paris
France
[BD, CN, HK, IN, ID, JP, KR, MY, PI, PK, PH,][Eco, Geo]

Skar, Dr H.O.
NUPI Norway
skar@nias.ku.dk
[NP][PolS, Ant, Rel, DevS, CuS]

Sklair, Drs L.
LSEPS,DS United Kingdom
l.sklair@lse.ac.uk
[DevS, Soc]

Skliarov, Dr L.E.
RAS,IOS,AL Russia
[IR][IR, PolS, His]

Skov, T.S.
Absalonsgade 11st. th
1658 Copenhagen V.
Demark
[ID][Rel, CuS]

Skutsch, Dr M.M.
UT,TDG Netherlands
m.m.skutsch@tdg.utwente.nl
[IN, LK][GenS, DevS]

Skyhawk, H. von
RKU,SI,DHR Germany
[IN, MN, NP, PK, SM, TI, TM][Phi, Rel, Ant, Lit, CuS]

Slaats, Dr Mr H.M.C.
KUN,IV Netherlands
h.slaats@jur.kun.nl
[ID][DevS, Law]

Slaje, Prof. dr W.
MLU,KAW,II Germany
[IN, TI][Rel, Phi, Lit, CuS]

Slamet-Velsink, Dr I.E.
Wilde Wingerdlaan 161
2803 VX Gouda
Netherlands
[ID][Ant]

Slater, Dr R.P.
UB,SPP United Kingdom
[BD, IN, ID, MY, PK, PH, LK][PolS, Ant, DevS, Eco]

Slawinski, Prof. dr Hab.
PAN,CSNEC Poland
[CN, HK, TH][DevS, Ant, Eco, PolS]

Slesarchuk, Dr G.I.
RASP,IOS Russia
[MN][His]

Slikkerveer, Dr L.J.
RUL,CA/SNWS Netherlands
[ID][Ant, Agr, DevS]

Slob, Drs J.
RvZ Netherlands
[ID][Rel]

Slobodník, Drs M.
SAS,IOAS Slovak Republic
[CN, TI][His, IR]

Smadja, J.
CNRS,MSCH France
[NP][Env, Geo]

Small, B.
44 Upland Road
SE22 9EF London
United Kingdom

Smedal, Dr O.H.
UT,FSS,IA Norway
olafs@isv.vit.no
[ID,][Ant]

Smeets, Dr C.J.M.A.
IIAS Netherlands
cjmasmeets@rullet.leidenuniv.nl
[KZ, TM, UZ][Ant, Lin]

Smeets, Dr H.J.A.J.
RUL,VTW Netherlands
[Soc, Lin]

Smeets, Drs H.M.A.G.
MHMSM Netherlands
[ID][His]

Smets, Drs P.G.S.M.
VU, DCA Netherlands
pgsm.smets@scw.vu.nl
[IN][DevS]

Smid, J.W.

RUG,BIG Netherlands
efv@eco.rug.nl
[MY, SG][Eco]

Smidt, Prof. dr J.

Van der Dussenweg 8
2614 XE Delft
Netherlands
[ID, PK, PH, TH][Eco]

Smiers, Dr J.

HKU Netherlands
[ID, PK, PH, TH][Lit, CuS, PolS]

Smit, Drs H.C.

RUL, JIP Netherlands
[JP][Lin]

Smit, Prof. ir K.

TU,FLR Netherlands
[CN, ID][Lin]

Smit, Mr R.R.

Raamweg 40
2596 HN The Hague
Netherlands

Smit, Drs T.S.

Ds. L. Touwenlaan 9
8754 BP Makkum
Netherlands
[ID, PI, PG][Lin]

Smith, Dr N.S.H.

UvA,ATW Netherlands
nsmith@let.uva.nl
[CN][Lin]

Smith, Mr S.

BC,TUEU United Kingdom
[BD, IN, PK, LK][His, Edu]

Smith, Dr S.A.

UES,DH United Kingdom
smits@essex.ac.uk
[CN][His]

Smith, Dr D.

UL,DRS United Kingdom
d.smith@lancs.ac.uk
[IN][Rel, His, Lit, AHis]

Smith, D.B.

UU,DHPP United Kingdom
db.smith@ulst.ac.uk
[JP, KR][IR, PolS, Eco, His]

Smith, Dr D.A.

LJMU, DJ United Kingdom
[PH][Lin]

Smith, G.

CNRS,IRSEA France
[ID][Ant]

Smits, Dr I.B.

RUL,TCJK Netherlands
ibsmits@rullet.leidenuniv.nl
[CN, JP][His, Lit]

Smits, Drs L.

Godschalkstraat 100
3084 RG Rotterdam
Netherlands
[ID, PI][CuS, Ant, Rel, Lin, His]

Smitsendonk, Dr A.G.O.

44, Avenue Clodoald
92210 Saint Cloud
France
[CN, HK, IN, ID, JP, TH][Law, Eco, IR, Soc, Rel, PolS, DevS]

Smolarz, B.

INALCO,JK France
[JP][Geo, Agr]

Smolders, Drs A.P.

Zilverkarper 12
2318 NC Leiden
Netherlands
[JP][His]

Smourova, Dr N.M.

MSU,IAAS,CIBS Russia
[ID][Lit]

Smurowa, Dr N.M.

MSU,IAAS,DSEAP Russia
[ID, MY][Lit]

Smyth, Dr I.A.

ADO United Kingdom
ismyth@oxfam.or.uk
[ID][GenS, DevS]

Snelder, Dr D.J.

RUL,CESP Netherlands
snelder@rulsfb.univleiden.nl
[PH][Env, Agr]

Snell, Dr R.

SOAS,DSA United Kingdom
rs6@soas.ac.uk
[IN][Lin, Lit]

Snellgrove, Prof. D.

Via Matteo Gay 26/7
100 66 Torre Pellice
Italy
[KH, IN, ID, MY, TH][AHis, Rel, Arch, His]

Snoeck, J.

Emmastraat 15
2595 EG The Hague
Netherlands

Soar BA, MA, M.J.

SOAS United Kingdom
[IN,][AHis, His, Rel]

Sobisch, J.-U.

UHAM,KGIT Germany
[TI][Arch, His, Rel, AHis]

Soboleva, Dr E.S.

PGMAE,K Russia
[HK, IN, ID, PI, PG,][Rel, His, Ant, AHis]

Sodderland, Mr J.W.

ND,LF Netherlands
[CN, ID, JP, TW][Law]

Soenoto Rivai, S.F.

UIO,DAS Italy
[ID, MY][Lin, Lit, GenS]

Soffner, U.A.

Wagenstraat 166
2512 BB The Hague
Netherlands
[ID][His, Lin]

Sofronov, Prof. dr M.V.

MSU,IAAS,CIBS Russia
[CN, MN, TI][Ant, Arch, Lin, Lit]

Sok, P.

INALCO France
[KH][Lan]

Sokolov, Prof. dr A.A.

RAS,IOS,AL Russia
[VN][AHis, Lin, Phi, Lit, PolS, CuS, Soc, His]

Sollewijn Gelpke, Drs J.H.F.

La Bastide du Bois Biak
83460 Taradeau
France
[ID, PG][His]

Solntsev, Prof. dr V.M.

RAS,IL Russia
SOLNTSEV@ILING.MSK.SU
[MN, CN, VN,][Lin]

Solntseva, Dr N.V.

RASP,IOS Russia
[Lin]

Solomonik, Dr I.N.

Bolshoi Tishinski per. 37-56
123 557 Moscow
Russia
[BD, KH, CN, HK, IN, ID, JP, MY, MM, PK,][His, AHis]

Somerwil, J.

Reguliersgracht 40
1017 LS Amsterdam
Netherlands

Son, Drs T. van

Plataanweg 12
3053 LP Rotterdam
Netherlands
[ID][Law, Lit, Lin, Env]

Song, L.

USHS,LLCE France
[CN][Lan]

Soni, Dr J.

PUM,IND Germany
[IN][Lin, Phi, Rel]

Sonneveld, Dr J.F.M.

UvA,ASSR,CASA
Netherlands
a723a11@hasara11.bitnet
[IN][Edu]

Sopo, J.

UO,H Finland
[JP][Lin]

Sorensen, P.

Ny Strandvej 36 B
3060 Espergærde
Denmark
[KH, LA, MM, TH, VN][Arch]

Sorensen, Dr H.H.

UC,FH,DAS Denmark
[CN, KR, TI][His, AHis, Rel, CuS]

Sörensson, S.E.

Tietsgade 70
1704 Copenhagen
Denmark
[Ant]

Sorokin, Dr A.A.

[Eco]

Sorokin, Dr V.F.

RAS,IFES,FEB Russia
[CN, TW][Lit, CuS]

Sotelo Navalpotro, J.A.

UCM,GH,GF Spain
[IN, JP, PH][Env, Geo]

Souckova, Dr J.

NMP Czech Republic
[AHis, CuS, His, Arch]

Southwold-Llewellyn, Dr S.

LW,DS Netherlands
sarah.southwold@alg.asnw.wau.nl
[PK, LK][Ant, Agr, Env, GenS, Eco, DevS]

Souyri, P.-F.

EFEO,BIB France
[JP][His]

Souza, Prof. dr T.R. de

Avenida S. José 8,
s/c Esquerdo
2685 Sacavém
Portugal
[IN][Rel, PolS, His]

Spaan, Drs E.J.A.M.

KUN,SES Netherlands
[ID, LK][Ant]

Spacensky, D.

INALCO France
[CN][His, AHis]

Spadavecchia, Dr N.G.

ISIAO Italy
[JP][Lit]

Spakowski, N.

FUB,OS,SIN Germany
[CN][CuS, GenS, His]

Spangemacher, A.

CNRS,IRSEA France
[CN][Ant]

Spanjaard, Drs H.

Wethouder Frankeweg 39-I
1098 KX Amsterdam
Netherlands
[ID][His, AHis]

Sparkes, S.J.

UO,FSS,EM Norway
[TH][Ant]

Sparreboom, Dr M.

NWO, GW Netherlands
sparreboom@nwo.nl
[IN][Lit, Rel]

Speckmann, Prof. dr J.D.

NIAS Netherlands
[ID, LK][Ant, Soc]

Spee, Drs M.H.

VMGVL Netherlands
[ID, PI, PG][AHis, Ant]

Spencer, Dr J.R.

UE,DSA United Kingdom
jrs@uk.ac.ed.festival
[LK][Rel, CuS, Ant, Edu, Soc, His]

Spencer-Oatey, Dr H.

ULU,KLCC United Kingdom
helen.spencer-Oatey@luton.ac.uk
[CN, HK, MO, TW][Lin]

Spengen, Dr W. van

UvA,VPD Netherlands
spengen@isg.frw.uva.nl
[MN, NP, TI][Geo, Ant, His]

Speyer, B.

FUB,W,IW Germany
speyer@ccmailer.wiwiss.fu-berlin.de
[CN, HK][IR, Eco]

Spiekerman-Middelplaats, M.Y.M.

TU Netherlands
m.middelplaats@bu.tudelft.nl
[CN, HK, IN, ID, JP, PH, SG, TW, TH, VN][Env]

Spiertz, Mr H.L.J.

LW,DDE Netherlands
joepspiertz@alg@ar.wau.nl
[ID][DevS, Law]

Spindler, Prof. dr M.R.

RUL,FG Netherlands
[MG][CuS, Rel, His]

Spit, W.J.L.

Maertensplein 4
3738 Gj Maartensdijk
Netherlands
[ID][His, Rel, CuS]

Splinter, Drs H.A.M. van der

RUL,IBR Netherlands
[ID][His, IR]

Spooner, Prof. F.C.

31 Chatsworth Avenue
BR1 5DP Bromley, Kent
United Kingdom
[CN, IN, ID, JP][Eco, His]

Srinivasan, Dr P.

Hermann-Lönsstrasse 6
21465 Reinbek
Germany
[IN][Ant]

Srivastava-Johri, Dr I.

RSIA Netherlands
[IN][Phi]

Staal, Dr P.M. van der

TU,FWTMW Netherlands
vanderstaal@wtm.tudelft.nl
[JP, PH][PolS]

Staat, Drs D.W.

MB Netherlands
[ID][His, Ant]

Stachowski, Dr M.

UJ,IOP,CP Poland
marstach@vela.filg.uj.edu.pl
[KZ, KR, MN, TM][Lin]

Städe, B.

Denmark

Staden, Drs M. van

RUL,TCZOAO,PD
Netherlands
staden@rullet.leidenuniv.nl
[ID][Lin]

Staemmler, Drs B.

UT,FAP Germany
staeza01@urt-stud.uni-trier.de
[JP][Rel]

Stafutti, Dr S.

UT,IOS Italy
[CN][Lin, Lit]

Stahl, Dr H.

UW,IS Germany
helga.stahl@rzhub.uni-wuerzburg.de
[CN][Arch, His, CuS]

Stahlberg, Drs S.M.

UB,ZA Germany
[MN][CuS, DevS, His, Lin, Soc, PolS]

Staiger, Dr B.

IFA Germany
ifahh@rrz.uni-hamburg.de
[CN][Edu, His, CuS]

Stam, Prof. dr J.A.

EUR,DSVJ Netherlands
stam@jpk.few.eur.nl
[CN, HK, ID, JP, KR, MY, PH, SG, TW, TH][DevS, Eco, IR]

Standaert, Prof. dr N.

KUL,SIN Belgium
Nicolas.standeart@arts.kuleuven.ac.be
[Phi, IR, His, CuS, Rel]

Standen, Dr N.L.

OU,SJC,ICS United Kingdom
standen@fyfield.sjc.ox.ac.uk
[CN][His]

Standing, Dr H.

USUS,AFRAS United Kingdom
[BD, IN][GenS, DevS, Ant]

Stanyukovich, M.V.

IMAE Russia
org@ethn.mae.spb.su
[PH][GenS, DevS, Ant]

Stargardt, Prof. J.M.

CU,DG United Kingdom
[IN, MM, TH][Rel, ArchAgrAHis]

Stark, Dr U.B.

RKU,SI,MSALL Germany
[IN][Lit]

Starr, Drs R.M.

EJ United Kingdom
[JP][His, CuS, AHis, Edu, His, IR]

Starr, Mr D.F.
UDU,BAKS United Kingdom
d.f.starr@durham.ac.uk
[CN, JP, KR][Phi, Lin]

Stasik, Dr D.
UW,IOS,DI Poland
[IN][Lit]

Stearns, L.L.M.
Wessels Gate 13
0165 Olso
Norway
[CN][Law, GenS, DevS]

Stebleva, Dr I.V.
RASP,IOS Russia
[Lit]

Stebline-Kamensky, Prof. dr I.M.
SPU,FOS,DAS Russia
[AF, CN, IN, IR, KZ, PK, TJ, TM][Lin, Lit, Rel]

Stecinski, Drs J.
SACCP Poland
[KH, VN][AHis]

Steeds, Mr D.
'Glen Rosa', Brynymor Road
\Aberystwyth
SY23 2HX Ceredigian, Wales
United Kingdom
[AF, BN, CN, JP, MM, TW, TI, VN][IR, His]

Steenbeek, Dr O.W.
EUR,EW,F Netherlands
steenbeek@few.eur.nl
[JP, SG][Eco]

Steenbrink, Dr K.A.
UU,IIMO Netherlands
ksteenbrin@ggl.ruu.nl
[ID][Rel]

Steengaard, Prof. N.P.
UC,DH Denmark
[Rel]

Stefanchuk, Dr L.G.
RASP,IOS Russia
[PI,][Eco, His]

Steffensen, Drs K.N.
SOAS,DEPS United Kingdom
ks@soas.ac.uk
[JP, MY, SG][PolS, IR]

Steffensen, Dr S.K.
Japan
ss.tyo@isiscs.u-tokyo.ac.jp
[JP, KR][Soc, PolS, Eco, DevS]

Stegewerns, Drs D.
RUL,CNWS Netherlands
stegewerns@rullet.leidenuniv.n
l
[JP][His, IR]

Steijlen, Drs G.I.J.
UvA,ASC,CASA Netherlands
[ID][Ant]

Stein, Dr W.
SMVM Germany
[KH, IN, LA, MM, LK, TH, VN][Ant, CuS, AHis, Arch, His]

Steiner, Dr R.
PUM,IND Germany
steiner@mailer.uni-marburg.de
[IN, NP, TI][Lit, Phi]

Steinhauer, Dr H.
RUL,TCZOAO Netherlands
steinhauer@rullet.leidenuniv.nl
[BN, KH, ID, LA, MY, TH, VN][Lin, Ant]

Steinkellner, Prof. dr E.
UW,ITBS Austria
[IN, NP, TI][Rel, Phi]

Steinmann, B.
CNRS,IRSEA France
[BT, CN, IN, NP, SM, TI][His]

Stel, Dr J.H.
GOA Netherlands
Stel@nwo.nl
[BD, CN, IN, ID, JP, KR, MG, MY, PK, PH, LK,][Env, Eco]

Stellrecht, Prof. dr I.
EKUT,IE Germany
irmtraud.stellrecht@uni-tuebingen.de
[IN, KZ, PK, TJ, TM][His, Ant, Rel]

Stengs, Drs I.L.
UvA,ZZOAS,EN Netherlands
[TH][Rel, His, Ant]

Stepanov, Dr Ye.D.
RAS,IFES,FEB Russia
[CN][His]

Stepanyants, Prof.dr M.T.
[Phi, Rel]

Stephan, R.
BSBIB,AOA Germany
[CN][Rel, His, Ant]

Stephane, Dr S.D.
19 â Busseau
77570 Aufferville
France
[ID, PG,][DevS, His, PolS]

Stepuguina, Dr T.V.
RASP,IOS Russia
[CN][His]

Steringa, F.A.
UU,VG Netherlands
f.a.steringa@stud.let.ruu.nl
[KZ][His, CuS]

Sterk, Dr J.G.M.
SISWO Netherlands
siswo@sara.nl
[KZ][Soc]

Sterk, Drs R.A.
Leidseweg 71
3531 BE Utrecht
Netherlands
[ID][Soc, PolS, Psy]

Stern, Dr H.
UL3,CREO France
[IN][Soc]

Sternfeld, Drs E.
Fidicinstr. 35
10965 Berlin
Germany
[CN][GenS, Env]

Stickings, S.R.
UCL,FL United Kingdom
s.stickings@ucl.ac.uk
[JP][Law]

Stietencron, Prof. dr H. von
EKUT,SIVRW Germany
[IN][CuS, Phi, His, Rel]

Stigter, A.P. de
Netherlands
[IN][AHis]

Stiller, Dr D.F.R.
Robert-Bosch-weg 19
63165 Mühlheim am Main
Germany
[ID, JP, KR, MY, SG][Law]

Stöber, Dr G.
TUCW,DR Germany
gei@is.gaertner.de
[IN, PK,][Ant, DevS, Edu]

Stock, Dr J.P.J.
UDU,MS United Kingdom
j.p.j.stock@durham.ac.uk
[CN][Law]

Stockinger, B.
KFU,IS Austria
[TI][Law]

Stockinger, Drs J.
UW,IV Austria
A6241Gac@helios.eduz.univie
.ac.at
[PH][CuS, Ant]

Stockwell, Prof. A.J.
RHBNC,DH United Kingdom
[MY, SG][His]

Stoddard-Karmay, Dr H.
INALCO France
[TI][Lan]

Stoel, R.B.
Waardkerksteeg 33
2312 RS Leiden
Netherlands
[ID][Lin]

Stokhof, Prof. dr W.A.L.
IIAS Netherlands
[KH, ID, LA, TH, VN][Lit, Lin]

Stolk, M.D.
Braambesweg 43
5632 SB Eindhoven
Netherlands
[ID, JP][CuS, Psy, Soc, Rel]

Stone, Drs E.V.
ULEED,DEAS United Kingdom
[CN][DevS]

Stoop, Dr W.A.
KIT Netherlands
[CN][Agr, Env]

Storbacka, C.

Packaregatan 2 B 48
20100 Äbo
Finland
[Agr, Env]

Storck, Ir. P.W.A.

Andreashof 16
3511 VM Utrecht
Netherlands
[LK][DevS, Agr, Eco, Ant]

Storm, Dr S.T.H.

EUR,EW,TE Netherlands
storm@cvo.few.eur.nl
[IN][Agr, DevS, Eco]

Stoye, Drs M.

FUB,AW,IPKG Germany
[IN][His, AHis, Arch]

Strandberg, Drs G.S.

Farstavagen 37
12334 Stockholm-Farsta
Sweden

Strange, Dr R.N.

KCL,MC United Kingdom
roger.strange@kcl.ac.uk
[CN, HK,][Eco]

Strassner, Dr R.

LMU,GSI Germany
[ID, MY, PH][PolS, Psy, IR, CuS, Rel, Soc]

Straten, Mr H.M. van

DOEN Netherlands
hedda@doen.nl
[BD, IN, ID, KZ, MG, MM, TJ, TH][Env, Ant, Law]

Straten, Drs N.H. van

RUL,SI Netherlands
[CN][Law]

Streef, E.

NSMA Netherlands
[CN, HK, ID, JP, LK][Env, Law, Ant]

Streefland, Prof. dr P.H.

UvA,ASSR Netherlands
[BD, IN, NP, PK,][DevS]

Streumer, Drs P.

UU,CBM Netherlands
p.streumer@cbm.ruu.nl
[IN, LK][Edu, Ant, His, DevS, CuS]

Strickland, Dr S.S.

UCL,DA United Kingdom
[ID, MY, MN, NP, PH,][Ant]

Strijbosch, Prof. dr F.

KUN,VTER Netherlands
[ID, MY, MN, NP, PH,][Ant, Law]

Strik, Prof. B.

Blankenstraat 376-C
1018 SK Amsterdam
Netherlands
[BD, IN, JP, MN, TI][CuS]

Strnad, Dr J.

ASCR,OI,SC Czech Republic
strnad@orient.cas.cz
[IN][His, Lin]

Stroek, A.J.

Vrijheidslaan 858
2321 DX Leiden
Netherlands
[CN, LA, TH, TI][Rel, His, CuS]

Strom, A.K.

DMA Norway
axel.strom@ima.uio.no
[IN, TI][CuS, Ant, Rel]

Stroo, Drs M.

Kariboestraat 119
3523 PC Utrecht
Netherlands
[Ant, CuS, Rel]

Stroomer, Dr H.J.

RUL,VTCIMO Netherlands
[CuS, Lit, Lin]

Strube Dipl.Dec., J.T.

RUB,FOAW Germany
JENS.T.STRUBE@rz.ruhr-uni-bochum.de
[JP,][Eco]

Struben, Drs P.

Govert Flinckstraat 39-A
1072 EC Amsterdam
Netherlands
[IN][His]

Struve, D.

UP7,UAO France
[JP][His]

Stuijvenberg, P. van

EC,BMB Netherlands
[IN, TH][Eco, DevS]

Sturm, Drs Th.

Borselstrasse 2
22765 Hamburg
Germany
[CN][Lit]

Suárez Girard, A.-H.

Vinyes Velles 26
08170 Montornès Oel Vallès
(Barcelona)
Spain
[CN][Lin, Lit, Phi, Rel]

Subedi, Dr S.P.

ISS Netherlands
[NP, SM, TI][Env, IR, Law, PolS]

Subrahmanyam, Dr S.

UL3,CREO France
sanjay@ehess.fr
[AF, BD, AF, BD, IN, ID, MO, MM,][His, Eco]

Suchomel, Dr F.A.

NGP Czech Republic
[CN, HK, JP, KR][Arch, AHis]

Sudrajat, Drs A.

UvA,ASSR,CASA
Netherlands
sudrajat@pscw.una.nl
[ID][Soc, His]

Suero Tellitu, T.

ISJT Spain
[CN, HK, IN, NP, PK, LK, TH, TI][Ant, Phi, PolS, Rel, Soc]

Sukanda-Tessier, Dr V.

EFEO,UB,DCI France
[ID][Ant, Arch]

Sukanda-Tessier, B.

UB2,SSP France
[IN, ID,][Ant, Rel]

Sukharchuk, Dr G.D.

RASP,IOS Russia
[CN][His]

Sukhochev, Dr A.S.

RASP,IOS Russia
[IN, PK][Lit]

Sukhorukov, Dr V.T.

RASP,IOS Russia
[CN][Lit]

Sukrisno, Drs A.

Carmenlaan 25
1183 SC Amstelveen
Netherlands
[CN, ID, VN][Ant, His, PolS]

Sulitskaya, Dr T.I.

RASP,IOS Russia
[IR]

Summers, L.J.

UHU,DSEAS United Kingdom
ljsummers@seas.hull.ac.uk
[KH][PolS, GenS, DevS]

Sun, L.

ISS Netherlands
sun@iss.nl
[CN][Eco, DevS]

Sundermann, Dr W.

HUB, ZAGA Germany
[IR][His]

Supriyanto, Drs I.

RUL,TCZOAO Netherlands
Supriyanto@rullet.leidenuniv.n
l
[ID][CuS, Lin, Lit]

Supriyanto-Breur, Drs C.A.

RUL,CILC Netherlands
[ID][Law]

Suret-Canale, J.

UP7,UAO France
[KR][His, PolS]

Surie, Drs H.G.

Obrechtlaan 200
9402 TP Assen
Netherlands
[Soc]

Suringa, Mr P.

Klungsstraat 79
2565 VG 's Gravenhage
Netherlands
[AF, IN, ID, KZ, MY, MM, PI, PK, PH, SG,][Law, AHis, Lit, IR, His, Phi, His, Edu, CuS, DevS, Eco, PolS]

Suslina, Dr S.S.

RASP,IOS Russia
[KR][Eco]

Sutedja-Liem, Drs H.T.

RUL,CNWS Netherlands
[ID][Lit, Lin]

Sutherland, Prof. dr H.A.
VU, DCA Netherlands
[ID, MY, SG][CuS, His, Ant]

Suvorova, Prof. A.A.
RAS,IOS,ALD Russia
[IN, PK][AHis, CuS, Lit, His]

Suwondo, Drs K.
UvA,ASSR,CASA Netherlands
[ID][DevS, Agr, Ant]

Svantesson, J.O.
LU,DLP Sweden
jan-olof.svantesson@ling.lu.se
[CN, LA, MN][Lin]

Svarcov , Dr Z.
CU,FF,DEAS Czech Republic
zdenka.svarcova@ff.uni.cz
[JP][Lit, Lin]

Svarverud, Dr R.
NACS Norway
runesva@hedda.uio.no
[CN][His, Phi, PolS]

Svensson, Dr T. G.
UO,FSS,EM Norway
t.g.Svensson@ima.uiono
[JP][Ant]

Svensson, Prof. dr Th.
NIAS Denmark
ths@nias.ku.dk
[ID, MY][PolS, Eco, His]

Svistunova, Dr N.P.
RASP,IOS Russia
[CN][His]

Svitkova, Dr I.
EUSAV Slovak Republic
[CN][Rel, CuS]

Swaan, Prof. dr A. de
UvA,ASSR,CASA Netherlands
a723ads@hasara11
[Soc, PolS]

Swahn, Prof. J.Ö.
LU,PESEAS,IO Sweden
jos@eth.lu.se
[LA, VN][PolS, Soc]

Swain, Drs A
UU,DPCR Sweden
ashok.swain@pcr.uu.se
[BD, IN, NP, PK,][PolS, IR, Env]

Swallow, Dr D.A.
VAM,ISEAD United Kingdom
[IN, MM][His, Ant, CuS, AHis]

Swiercz, Drs J.
UW,IOS,DFES Poland
[KH, CN, VN][Lin]

Sy-A-Foek, I.D.S.
UNESCO,NC Netherlands
[CN, HK, TW][PolS, Law, DevS]

Sybesma, S.
NLN B.V. Netherlands
[CN, HK, JP, KR, MY, SG][Lin]

Sybesma, Dr R.P.E.
RUL,SI Netherlands
sybesma@rullet.leidenuniv.nl
[CN, HK, TW][Lin]

Sykora, Drs J.
CU,FF,DEAS Czech Republic
jan.sykora@ff.cuni.cz
[JP][Rel, IR, Phi, His, PolS, Eco, Soc]

Syomin, Dr A.V.
RAS,IOS,CJS Russia
[CN, JP, KR][His, IR, Eco, PolS]

Szentirmai, Mr J.
Szemlöhegy u. 16
1025 Budapest
Hungary
[JP][Env, His, AHis, Eco, Rel]

Szirimai, Dr A.
TUE,DTDS Netherlands
a.e.szirmai@tm.tue.nl
[DevS, Eco]

Szók cs, Dr A.
IOCFT Hungary
[JP][Lin, Edu]

Sztulman, Drs H.
UTM,CUP France
[Soc, Psy, His, AHis]

Ta, T.H.
UP7,UAO France
[VN][Lin]

Tacoli, C.
LSEPS,DG United Kingdom
[PH][Lin]

Tadié, J.
UP,G France
[ID][Geo]

Taeymans, M.J.M.
KMP Belgium
[PolS, Law, IR]

Taguchi, M.
UP7,UAO France
[JP][Lin]

Tahitu, Dr E.
LSEM Netherlands
[ID][Edu, Lin]

Tähkämaa, Drs J.P.
UTU,SSPH Finland
juhtah@utu.fi
[CN, TW][IR, PolS]

Taillard, Ch.
CNRS,LASEMA France
[LA, TH, VN][DevS, Eco, Geo]

Takagi, Prof. K.
UAM,CEAO Spain
[JP][His, Lin, Lit, AHis]

Takahashi, Prof. M.
HKA,DM Netherlands
[JP][Edu]

Takken, Dr W.
LW,VE Netherlands
willem.takken@medew.ento.wau.nl
[Env, DevS, Agr]

Taksami, Dr M.
PGMAE,K Russia
[Ant]

Tálas, Dr B.
IOCFT Hungary
[CN, HK, TW][Eco, IR, PolS]

Talbot, Dr I.
UWA,SISL United Kingdom
[IN, PK][PolS, IR, Eco]

Tamba, A.
INALCO France
[JP][Eco, PolS, IR]

Tamba, I.
CNRS,CRLAO France
tamba@chess.fr
[JP][Lin]

Tambovtsev, Prof. dr Y.A.
Aeroport Street 55-57
630021 Novosibirsk 21
Russia
[JP, KZ, MN, TJ, TM][Lin]

Tamburello, Drs G.
Ir. J. Mulderplein 130
1018 MZ Amsterdam
Netherlands
[CN][Lit]

Tamm, I.
UT,IE Estonia
ilmar@utlib.es
[CN][IR, Eco]

Tamogami, K.
INALCO France
[JP][IR, Eco]

Tan, I.H.
Rembrandtlaan 112
6717 NN Ede
Netherlands
[CN, HK, TW][AHis]

Tan, Ir Y.Y.
Jupiterstraat 149
9742 EW Groningen
Netherlands
[CN, HK][His, CuS]

Tan, H.-M.
UP7,UAO France
[CN][Lin]

Tanaka, H.M.
UES United Kingdom
[JP][Soc, CuS]

Tang, D.E.
Postbus 960
6200 AZ Maastricht
Netherlands

Tarab Tulku, .
TLI Denmark
[TI][CuS, Soc]

Tarabout, Dr G.
UL3,CREO France
[IN][Rel, Ant]

Tarnutzer, Dr A.
UZI,DG Switzerland
[IN, ID, NP, PK, PH, SM,][Ant, GenS, DevS]

Taselaar, Drs A.P.
RUL,CNWS Netherlands
taselaar@rullet.leidenuniv.nl
[ID][His]

Taubmann, Prof. dr W.H.
UBR,GI Germany
Taubmann@ggr.uni-bremen.de
[CN, HK][Eco, DevS]

Tauscher, Dr H.
UW,ITBS Austria
[TI][Eco, DevS]

Tauscher-Lamberg, M.
UW,ITBS Austria
[TI][Eco, DevS]

Tavim MA, J.A.
IICT,CEAA Portugal
[IN][His]

Tawa-Lama, S.
CNRS,MSCH France
[NP, TI][Soc]

Tayanin, D.
LU,DLP Sweden
damrong.tayanin@ling.lu.se
[KH, LA, MM, TH, VN][CuS, Env, Agr, Ant, Rel]

Taylor, Dr D.D.
SOAS,DEPS United Kingdom
dt1@soas.ac.uk
[IN, PK][His, PolS]

Taylor, Dr J.G.
SU,LPSS United Kingdom
TaylorJG@vax.sbu.ac.uk
[CN, ID][Soc, DevS]

Taylor, Prof. R.H.
SOAS,CSEAS United Kingdom
[MM][PolS]

Tching, K.
UP7,UAO France
[CN, TW][Soc]

Teensma, Dr B.N.
Zandzegge 21
2318 ZK Leiden
Netherlands
[IN, ID, MO, MY][His]

Teerink, Drs R.
EC, SC Belgium
[IN][DevS, Agr, Ant, Soc, GenS]

Teerlink, Ir J.
HIS Netherlands
[IN, ID][DevS]

Teeuw, Prof. dr A.
Thorbeckestraat 14
2313 HE Leiden
Netherlands
[BN, ID, MY][Lit, Lin, CuS]

Teeuwen, Dr M.J.
UW,CC,JSC United Kingdom
teeuwen@cardiff.ac.uk
[JP][Rel]

Tegbaru, Drs A.
SU,DSA Sweden
[BT, TH][CuS, DevS, Env, Ant]

Tehishev, Prof.dr E.R.
IL,DEAL Russia
[Lin]

Teichler, Prof. dr U.
KU,WZBHF Germany
teichler@hochschulforschung.uni.kassel.de
[JP][Soc]

Teillers, A.F.
Schaapsloopven 39
5646 HV Eindhoven
Netherlands
[IN, ID][CuS, Lin]

Teljeur, Dr D.
Brakenbrughstraat 17rd
2023 DS Haarlem
Netherlands
[ID, PI][Ant]

Teller, Drs W.
RUL, BB Netherlands

Telo, Prof. A.J.
UL,FF,DH Portugal
[MO][His]

Tenhaeff, Drs C.M.
UE,DAS United Kingdom
[IN][DevS]

Tenishev, Dr Prof. E. R.
RAS,IL Russia
sysop@iling.msc.su
[KZ, KG, CN, TM][Ant, Lin, Lit]

Terada, Dr A.
CNRS,CRLAO France
[JP][Lin]

Terhal, Dr P.H.J.J.
EUR,EW,TE Netherlands
terhal@few.eur.nl
[IN][Eco]

Termorshuizen, Dr G.P.A.
KITLV Netherlands
[ID][Lit, His]

Termorshuizen-Arts, Drs M.J.H.W.
RUL,CILC Netherlands
[ID][Law]

Terpstra, T.
Netherlands

Terrada, H.
UJML3,FL France
[JP][Law]

Tertitsky, Dr K.M.
RAS,IFES,FEB Russia
[CN][His]

Tertrais, Prof. H.T.
110 rue des Grands Champs
75020 Paris
France
[KH, LA, VN][His, IR]

Terwiel, Prof. dr B.J.
UHAM,SKC,TBI Germany
or4a011@rzz-cip-1.rrz.uni-hamburg.de
[LA, MM, TH][His, Ant]

Teschke, Drs R.
LMU,IOAK Germany
richard.teschke@ltz.uni-munchen.de
[CN, HK, TW][Lin, His]

Tesselkine, Dr A.S.
MT,OA Russia
[BN, ID, KZ, MY, PG, TJ, TM, UZ][Ant, AHis, Lin, His, CuS]

Teszler, Drs R.K.
UvA,FEWE Netherlands
[BN, ID, KZ, MY, PG, TJ, TM, UZ][DevS]

Teygeler, Drs R.
DNP Netherlands
[ID][Ant, CuS, Lit]

Thambiah, S.
UHU,DSEAS United Kingdom
[ID, MY, MM][Ant]

The, Drs S.G.
Schouwenhove 146
2332 DT Leiden
Netherlands

Thelle, Dr H.H.
UC, IH Denmark
natla@coco.ihi.kv.dk
[CN][Lit, PolS, Soc, His]

Thesen, Sara
Graeff Str. 26
50823 Köln
Germany
[ID,][Ant]

Theunissen, Drs A.R.
Vinkenstraat 102-I
1013 JV Amsterdam
Netherlands
[JP][His, Lin, Lit]

Theunissen, G.
Sturmbergweg 20
94034 Passau
Germany

Thiede, Dr U.
An der Ronne 184
50859 Cologne
Germany
[JP][Env, Ant, His, CuS, Eco]

Thierry, Dr S.T.
CNRS,EPHE,SR France
[KH, LA, TH][Lit, Lin, CuS, Rel]

Thieu, S.
INALCO France
[JP][Lit]

Thin, Dr N.
UE,DSA United Kingdom
n.thin@ed.ac.uk
[IN][Env, DevS, Soc, Ant, Rel]

Thion, Dr S.
CNRS,CASCIP France
lemoine@msh-paris.fr
[KH, LA, MM, TH, VN][Soc, Rel, PolS, His, Ant]

Thirkell, A.
LSEPS,DG United Kingdom
[PH][Ant, His, PolS, Soc, Rel]

Thoburn, Dr J.T.
UEA,ODG,SDS United Kingdom
j.t.thoburn@uea.ac.uk
[CN, HK, ID, MY][Eco]

Thogersen, Drs S.
UA,DPIR United Kingdom
OSTst@hum.aau.dk
[CN][Edu, Soc]

Thölen, Drs K.
UZ,AS,OS Switzerland
sbib@oas.unizh.ch
[CN, HK, JP, MY, MM, SG, TW, TH][Arch, His, AHis, Lit]

Thomas, Dr D.R.
CSIC,SOC United Kingdom
[CuS, His, AHis, Rel]

Thomas, Prof. dr H.
ISS Netherlands
thomas@iss.nl
[IN, PK][DevS]

Thomas, A.
Beeklaan 402
2562 BH The Hague
Netherlands

Thomas, Mr I.D.
UEA,ODG,SDS United Kingdom
[BD, PK,][DevS]

Thomaz, Prof. L.F.F.R.
UNL,CHAM Portugal
[DevS]

Thomès, Ch.
BNF,DEE France
[CN][Lit]

Thomi, Dr V.
Gellerstr. 45A
4052 Basel
Switzerland
[IN, TI][His, Phi, Psy, CuS, Rel, AHis]

Thomi, Dr P.
II Switzerland
[IN][Lin, Lit, Rel, Phi]

Thompson, Prof. M.R.
FAU,IPW Germany
[MM, PH][Ant, Env, Arch]

Thompson, Dr J.B.
UBR,DAS United Kingdom
j.b.thompson@bradford.ac.uk
[IN, KR, LK, TH][Ant, Env, Arch]

Thoonen, Drs A.A.M.
KUN,CPS Netherlands
l.thoonen@maw.kun.nl
[ID, PG][Rel, GenS, Ant]

Thorborg, Dr E.M.
UC,S Denmark
[CN, HK, MO, TW, TI][DevS, PolS, Eco, His, GenS]

Thorner, A.
UL3,CREO France
[IN][His]

Thote, Dr A.
CNRS,EC France
[CN][AHis, Arch]

Thoyer, C.
INALCO France
[JP][His, Arch, AHis]

Thrift, Dr N.J.
UBRI,DG United Kingdom
n.j.thrift@uk.ac.bristol
[VN][Geo]

Thung, Prof. dr P.J.
Prins Hendriklaan 5
2341 JA Oegstgeest
Netherlands
[ID][Phi]

Thunoe, Drs M.
NIAS Denmark
mette@coco.lhi.ku.dk
[CN, HK, SG, TW][Ant, Lit, Edu, Soc, DevS, CuS, His]

Tibrewala, V.
INSEAD,EAC,BIB France
[IN][Lit, His, AHis, Arch]

Tichelman, Dr F.
IISG,IISH Netherlands
[ID][His]

Tieman-van Ede, Drs Y.M.
UvA,ASSR,CASA Netherlands
[NP, TI][GenS, Ant, Rel]

Tiemersma, Dr D.
EUR,W Netherlands
d.tiemersma@fwb.eur.nl
[IN, ID][Phi, Rel]

Tikhotskaya, Dr I.S.
RASP,IOS Russia
[JP][Eco]

Tikhvinsky, Prof.dr S.L.
RAS,IFES,FEB Russia
[CN][His]

Tillemans, Prof. dr T.J.F.
UL,DOLC Switzerland
tim.tillemans@orient.unil.ch
[IN, TI][Phi, Rel]

Tilly, M.
Netherlands

Timmer, Drs J.
RUL,TCZOAO,PD Netherlands
isirtim@rullet.leidenuniv.nl
[ID, PG][Soc, Ant, DevS, CuS]

Timofeeva, Dr I.S.
MSU,IAAS,CIBS Russia
[MM][Lin]

Timonina, Dr I.L.
RASP,IOS Russia
[JP][Eco]

Tims, Prof. dr W.
VU,CWFS Netherlands
[BD, CN, IN, ID, PK, TH][Eco, Agr, DevS]

Titarenko, Prof. dr M.L.
RAS,IFES,FEB Russia
titarenk@ifes.msk.su
[CN][PolS, Phi, IR]

Titus, Dr M.J.
UU,DSG Netherlands
titus@frw.ruu.nl
[ID][Geo]

Tjin A Jung, O.E.
Postbus 347
1115 ZG Duivendrecht
Netherlands
[MO][Soc]

Tjiomas, D.S.
Freiherr Von Stein Str. 10
60323 Frankfurt
Germany
[MO][Soc, POLITICS, Phi]

Tjoa, Drs M.L.M.
RUL,TCJK Netherlands
tjoa@rullet.leidenuniv.nl
[JP, KR][His]

Tjon Pian Gi, W.L.
IACT Netherlands
[ID][His]

Tjwan, Dr G.G.
Sinjeur Semeynsstraat 4
1183 EM Amstelveen
Netherlands
[CN, ID][His]

Tkachenko, Dr G. A.
RSUH,IASH Russia
afn@rggu.msk.ru
[CN][CuS, His, Phi, Rel]

Tkacheva, Dr A.A.
RASP,IOS Russia
[IN][Rel]

Toda, Drs D.N.
UHAM,SIS Germany
[ID][CuS, Lit]

Todd, Mr H.A.
BL,OIOC United Kingdom
[JP][CuS, Lit, His]

Toffin, Prof. G.
CNRS,MSCH France
[IN, NP][Ant, Rel, CuS]

Togores Sanchez, L.E.
USPC, FCHDC,DH Spain
[KH CN, JP, LA, MO, PI, PH, TH, TW, VN][IR, His]

Toiviainen, Dr H.
UH,HT,RI Finland
[CN, JP, KR][His]

Tol, Dr R.G.
KITLV Netherlands
tol@rullet.leidenuniv.nl
[ID, MY][Lit, Lin]

Tollenaere, Dr H.A.O. de
Haagplein 23
2311 AC The Hague
Netherlands
[IN, ID, LK][His, PolS, Rel]

Tollini, Prof. A.
UV,DSIEO,J Italy
[JP][Lin]

Tolsma, Drs G.J.
RUL,VTW Netherlands
tolsma@rullet.leidenuniv.nl
[BD, BT, IN, NP, PK, SM, LK, TI][Lin]

Tomala, Dr K.
PAN,IES Poland
[CN, HK, SG, TW, TI][PolS, Soc, Phi, Edu]

Tomlinson, Dr B.R.
USTR,DH United Kingdom
[IN][Eco, His]

Tong, Y.
GU,DL,C Sweden
Youhua@ling.gu.se
[CN][Lin]

Tönnesson, Dr S.
NIAS Denmark
stein@nias.ku.dk
[KH, ID, LA, MY, SG, VN][IR, His]

Top, Ir G.M. van den
RUL,CESP Netherlands
vandentop@rulcml.leidenuniv.nl
[PH, LK][Agr, DevS, Env]

Torkunov, Prof. A.
MSIIR,DOS Russia
[KR][IR]

Tormo Sanz, Leandro
UV,FGH,DHM Spain
[PH][His]

Törnquist, Dr C.O.
UO, PS Norway
olle.tornquist@stv.uio.no
[IN, ID, PH][DevS, PolS]

Toroptsev, Dr S.A.
RAS,IFES,FEB Russia
[CN][CuS]

Toropygina, Dr M.
RASP,IOS Russia
[JP][Lit]

Torri, Prof. M.
UT,DPS Italy
[IN][PolS, His]

Toth, E
HAS Hungary
[BHUTARI, IN, MN, NP, TI][CuS, Edu, His, Lin, Lit, Phi, Psy, Rel, Soc]

Toullelan, P.-Y.
INALCO France
[PI][Geo]

Tournadre, N.
CNRS,LACITO France
[CN, TI][Lin]

Touwen, Drs L.J.
RUL,VG Netherlands
touwen@rullet.leidenuniv.nl
[ID][His, Eco]

Touwen-Bouwsma, Dr E.
RIOD Netherlands
[ID][His, Ant]

Tovstykh, I.A.
RASP,IOS Russia
[IN][Lit]

Tozzi, Dr D.T.
URLS,DOS Italy
[CN, JP, MO, MN, TI][Soc, His, Eco]

Tran, Dr N.B.
CNRS,IRSEA France
[VN][Eco]

Trân, Q.H.
CNRS,EM France
[KH, CN, HK, IN, ID, JP, KR, LA, MN, PH, TW][CuS, Ant]

Trankell, Dr I.B.
UU,DA Sweden
ing-britt.trankell@antro.uu.se
[KH, LA, TH][Ant]

Trappmann, Drs J.
EKUT,SSK Germany
[KR][CuS, Lin, Lit]

Treu-Dijkman, S.M.G.
Klompven 16-A
5062 AJ Oisterwijk
Netherlands
[ID][Lin, DevS, Edu]

Trier, Dr J.
FHM Denmark
[LA, MY, PH, TH, VN][Arch, Rel, Lin, Ant]

Trinh, Prof. V.T.
CNRS,IRSEA France
[CN, JP, TH, VN][Edu, Soc, His]

Trískov , Dr.H.
ASCR,OI Czech Republic
triskova@orient.cas.cz
[CN][Lin]

Trolliet, P.
INALCO France
[CN][Geo]

Trombert, Dr E.
CNRS,MIDIC France
[CN][Agr, His, Eco, Ant]

Trommsdorff, Prof. G.
UKON,SF,EP Germany
gisela.trommsdorff@uni-konstanz.de
[CN, JP][Soc, Psy, CuS]

Tropper, K.
UW,ITBS Austria
[TI][Soc, Psy, CuS]

Trouwborst, Prof. dr A.A.
Prof. Asselbergsstraat 3
6524 RR Nijmegen
Netherlands
[ID][Ant]

Truong, Dr D.H.D.
FIS Netherlands
[CN, LA, SG, VN][IR, Eco, Env]

Tschudin, Dr J.J.
UP7,UAO France
[JP][Lit]

Tsendina, Dr A.D.
Yeniseiskaya 25 KV, 173
129281 Moscow
Russia
[MN][Lit]

Tsu Kamara, M.
INALCO France
[JP][Lit]

Tsundue, Drs K.
RUB,GI Germany
kunchok.tsundue@rz.ruhr.uni.bochum.de
[TI][Agr]

Tsvetkov, Dr Yu.V.
RASP,IOS Russia
[IN][Lit]

Tsvetkova, Dr N.N.
RASP,IOS Russia
[Eco]

Tsvetova, Dr I.A.
RAS,IFES,FEB Russia
[PolS, IR]

Tsyganov, Dr Y.
Ramenki 25-3-674
117607 Moscow
Russia
[CN, KR][Eco, IR]

Tuck, P.J.N.
LUI,FA,DH United Kingdom
pj630@liv.ac.uk
[TH, VN][His]

Tulloch, Drs C.D.
UPF,FPCA,DPE Spain
tulloch-christopher@peri.upf.es
[JP][Ant]

Tumarkin, Prof. dr D.D.
RAS,IEA,SEAAO Russia
[ID, PI, PG, SG][CuS, DevS, Arch, Eco, His, Ant]

Turcq, Dr D.F.
INSEAD,EAC,BIB France
dturcg@innet.be
[CN, HK, IN, ID, JP, KR, TW][Eco]

Turin, Drs M.
Prinsengracht 907
1017 KD Amsterdam
Netherlands

Turpin, Dr D.V.
Verdeil 9
1005 Lausanne
Switzerland
[CN, JP, KR][Soc]

Tütüncü, Drs M.
SOTA Netherlands
[AF, KZ, MN, TM, UZ][CuS, DevS, Env, Lit, Lin, His]

Tuxsen, H.
Artillerivej 72, 4.tr
2300 Copenhagen S
Denmark
[CuS, DevS, Env, His, Lin, Lit]

Tyapkina, Dr N.I.
RASP,IOS Russia
[CN][His]

Tzen, M.L.
CNRS,EPHE,SHP France

U Tin Htway,
RKU,SI Germany
[MM][DevS, PolS]

Ubaghs, Drs J.M.M.
J. de Graeflaan 52
1181 DN Amstelveen
Netherlands
[KH, IN, ID, MY, MM, LK, VN][CuS, His]

Uebach, Dr H.
BAWS,KZAS Germany
[IN, TI][CuS, His]

Uhlenbeck, Drs Ch.
UeB Netherlands
[JP][His, Ant, AHis]

Uhlenbeck, Prof. dr E.M.
Dr Kuyperlaan 11
2215 NE Voorhout
Netherlands
[ID][Lin]

Uhlin, A.
LU,DPS Sweden
Anders.Uhlin@svet.lu.se
[ID][PolS]

Ukai, Drs K.
RUL,SI Netherlands
kukai@rullet.leidenuniv.nl
[CN][Lit]

Ullmann, S.
Leipziger Str. 117
10117 Berlin
Germany
[CN][Lin]

Ulrich, R.G.
Dalveen 83
2544 SC The Hague
Netherlands

Ulsnes, L.E.
Svoldergt 9
0271 Oslo 2
Norway

Ulyakhin, Dr V.N.
RASP,IOS Russia
[Eco]

Um, Dr H.K.
QUB,DSA United Kingdom
[KZ, KR, UZ][AntAnt]

Unterbeck, Dr B.
Heinrich von Kleist strasse 22
15711 Könings Wusterhausen
Germany
[CN, KR][Lin]

Urlyapov, Dr V.F.
RASP,IOS Russia
[IR]

Usov, Dr V.N.
RAS,IFES,FEB Russia
Titarenk@ifes.msk.su
[CN, TW][His]

Uspenski, Dr M.V.
SHM,OD Russia
[JP][AHis, CuS]

Ussov, Dr V.N.
RAS,IFES,FEB Russia
[CN][His]

Utas, Prof. B.
UU,DAAS Sweden
bo.utas@afro.uu.se
[AF, TJ][Rel, Lit, His, Lin, CuS]

UUsikylä, Drs H.A.
UH,VT,S Finland
Heli.Uusikyla@helsinki.fi
[BD][Ant]

Uyl, Dr M.H.G. den
VU, DCA Netherlands
[IN][GenS]

Vaage, T.
UO,FA,EOS Norway
[CN, HK, MO, MM, TW][PolS]

Vacek, Prof. dr J.
ASCR,OI,SC Czech Republic
Jaroslav.vacek@ruk.cuni.cz
[BD, BTIN, ID, JP, KR, MN, NP, PK, LK][Phi, Rel, Lit, Lin]

Vaczi, Drs M.T.
Elandstraat 84
1016 SG Amsterdam
Netherlands
[BD, CN, HK, IN, ID, MG, NP, SG, LK, TW, TI][Rel, AHis, GenS, CuS]

Vaerman, Drs B.
KUL,OAB Belgium
benedicte.vearman@bib.huleuven.ac.be
[CN, HK, JP, TW][GenSAHis, Rel, CuS, His]

Väisänen, S.E.V.
UO,NSG Finland
svaisane@phoenix.oulu.fi
[ID][Geo, DevS]

Valentin, J.C.P.
ADO United Kingdom
pvalentin@oxfam.orf.uk
[KH, CN, HK, ID, JP, KR, LA, MY, MN, MM, PI, PG][Env, Ant, CuS, Lin, His, Arch]

Valk, Dr š.
AS,EFA Estonia
valk@erak.tartu.ee
[IN][Rel]

Valle Alvarez Maestre, M. del
UC,FL,CHA Spain
[PH][His]

Vallette-Hómery, M.
UP7,UAO,EC France
[CN, TW][Lit]

Vallot, B.
1, Grande Rue
70160 La Villedieu en Fontenette, Faverney
France
[VN][Lit]

Valota, Prof. A.
UP,DMCH Italy
[JP][His]

Vandamme, Dr M.R.C.A.
UU,VOTC Netherlands
marc-vandamme@let.ruu.nl
[KZ, TM, UZ][Lin, Lit]

Vanhanen, Dr T.
UH,VT,Y Finland
[BD, BT, IN, NP, PK, LK][PolS]

Vanhonacker, W.
INSEAD,EAC,BIB France
[CN][PolS]

Vanin, Dr Yu.V.
RASP,IOS Russia
[KR][His]

Vanina, Dr E.Yu.
RAS,IOS,CIS Russia
[IN][His]

Vanthemsche, Dr G.
Hanssenlaan 38
3080 Tervuren
Belgium

Vanthielen, Prof. W.
Belgium
walter.vanthielen@rsftew.luc.ac.be
[IN][Eco]

Vanwalle, Drs I.A.M.A.
Kattenberg 73
Gent
Belgium
[CN, HK, TW, TI][AHis, Lin, Lit, Phi, Soc, His]

Vardul, Dr I.F.
RASP,IOS Russia
[JP][Lin]

Varela Regueira, Ma del Mar
Cañizares, 3 - 2° Ext-Dcha
28012 Madrid
Spain
[JP, KR][His, IR]

Varentsov, Dr K.M.

RASP,IOS Russia
[Eco]

Vargas Anguita, G.

UB,FBA,DE Spain
[IN, JP][]

Vashist, G.K.

ISIAO Italy
[IN, PK, LK][Lit, Rel]

Vasilyev, Dr D.

RAS,IOS,AL Russia
[CN, KZ, MN, TJ, TI, TM][Arch, Rel, Lin, AHis, Ant]

Vasilyev, Dr V.F.

RAS,IOS,AL Russia
[MM][PolS, IR, His]

Vasilyevitch, Prof. dr T.A.

MSIIR Russia
[KR][IR, His]

Vassilevskaya, Dr I.I.

RASP,IOS Russia
[IR]

Vassiliev, Prof. A.

11/13 Pravda Str., App. 103
125124 Moscow
Russia
[KZ, TM][Rel, PolS, IR, His]

Vassiliev, Dr A.M.

[His, IR]

Vassiliev, Prof.dr L.S.

RASP,IOS Russia
[CuS, Rel, His]

Vassilieva, Dr L.A.

RASP,IOS Russia
[IN][Lit]

Vearman, Drs B.

Franz Guillaumelaan 65 B7
1140 Brussel
Belgium
Benedicte.Vaerman@bib.kuleuven.ac.be
[HK, JP, TW][PolS]

Veaux, F.

UMMB,DEEO,DU France
[CN][Lan]

Veen, Dr K.W. van der

Ripperdapark 32
2011 KE Haarlem
Netherlands
[Ant]

Veen, Drs M.H.E. van der

KITLV,EUROSEAS
Netherlands
[IN, ID][His, DevS]

Veenhoven, Dr R.

EUR,VS Netherlands
veenhoven@soc.fsw.eur.nl
[JP][Psy, Soc]

Veenkamp, Drs C.B.W.

IIAS Netherlands
veenkamp@rullet.leidenuniv.nl
[ID][His, CuS]

Veer, Prof. dr P. van der

UvA,GM Netherlands
pvdveer@sara.nl
[IN, NP][Rel, Ant, Soc, PolS]

Veerdonk, Drs J.A.L.B. van den

RUL,TCZOAO Netherlands
jacb@rullet.leidenuniv.nl
[IN, ID, MY,][Lin, Arch, Lit]

Veere, Mr H. van der

RUL,TCJK Netherlands
[CN, IN, JP, TI][Rel, Phi]

Veering, Drs A.J.A.

VU, DCA Netherlands
aja.veering@scw.vu.nl
[ID][Eco, His]

Veggel, Drs C.J. van

Netherlands
[ID][His, Eco]

Veiga, M.

Rua de Gondarein 1068 R/C
4150 Porto
Portugal
[ID][Law]

Veit, Prof. dr W.F.

SMB,MFEA Germany
[His, Arch, AHis]

Velde, Drs P.G.E.I.J. van der

IIAS Netherlands
vdvelde@rullet.leidenuniv.nl
[IN, ID, JP, LK, TW][Lit, His]

Velden, Drs A.M. van der

PSO Netherlands
[IN][DevS]

Vellema, S.R.

TAO Netherlands
[PH][Soc]

Vellut, Prof. J.L.

Belgium
vellut@cont.ucl.ac.be

Velzen, Dr J.H. van

De Vriesstraat 2A
2613 CB Delft
Netherlands
[IN, ID][GenS, Ant, DevS]

Velzen, Drs P.F. van

RUL,CNWS Netherlands
[ID, PI][CuS, Lin]

Velzen, Dr A. van

De Vriesstraat 2A
2613 CB Delft
Netherlands
[IN, ID][Ant, DevS, GenS]

Ven, Drs J.W. van de

LW,DDE Netherlands
john.vandeven@alg.ar.wau.nl
[ID][Env, Agr, Ant, Law]

Ven, P.D. van der

Netherlands

Ven, Dr H.J. van de

CU,FOS United Kingdom
[CN][His]

Venbrux, Dr H.J.M.

KUN,CPS Netherlands
eric.venbrux@pjmi.knaw.nl
[PI][Rel, Ant]

Vepsä, M.

Lapinlahdenkatu 23 B 30
00180 Helsinki
Finland
[MM, TH][Art]

Vera-Sanso, Dr P.

UK,EC,DSSA United Kingdom
p.vera-sanso@ukc.ac.uk
[IN][Ant]

Verbeek, H.R.

Ameland 57
3524 AM Utrecht
Netherlands
[ID][CuS, GenS]

Verbeek, J.J.M.

Netherlands
[ID][Eco, IR, Agr, Law]

Verboom, Drs A.W.C.

RUL,KERN Netherlands
[CN, IN, LK, TH, TI][Phi, Lit, Rel, Lin]

Verbruggen, Prof. dr H.

VU,IM Netherlands
harmen.verbruggen@ivm.vu.nl
[BT, IN, ID][Env, Eco, IR]

Vercammen, A.L.

RUL,KERN Netherlands
[IN][His]

Vercammen, Dr D.K.J.

Ballaerstraat 114
(TASC)
2018 Antwerp
Belgium
[CN][Ant, Phi, His, Rel]

Verdilhac, de

UP7,UAO France
[CN, JP, KR, VN][Eco]

Verdoorn, Drs J.D.L.

Grote Steenweg 445
2600 Antwerp
Belgium
[CN][Eco, IR]

Vereeken, Drs B.

Min.BuZa Netherlands
[BD, BT, CN, IN, LA, PK, TI, VN][Ant, DevS]

Vereijken, Drs C.M.J.L.

PCD Netherlands
[JP][Psy, Ant]

Verellen, Dr C.F.

EFEO,BIB France
[CN][Rel, CuS, Lit, His]

Verhaar, Drs P.

Berkstraat 12
2565 MS The Hague
Netherlands
[ID][His, IR, Lit, Lin]

Verhaar, Dr J.W.M.
't Hoenstraat 30
2596 HZ The Hague
Netherlands
[ID, PI, PG][Lin, Phi]

Verhagen, Dr P.C.
RUL,KERN Netherlands
pverhagen@rullet.leidenuniv.nl
[BT, IN, MN, NP, TI][Rel, Lin, Lit, Phi]

Verhoef, Ing J.C.
Azaleastraat 17
5922 EC Venlo
Netherlands
[ID][His]

Verhoeven, Drs P.R.F.
Pagodedreef 53
3564 XR Utrecht
Netherlands
[VN][Lin]

Vérin, Prof. P.
INALCO France
ceroi@inalco.fr
[MG][Rel, GenS, His, Ant]

Verma, J.N.
TA United Kingdom
[IN][CuS]

Vermeer, Dr E.B.
RUL,SI Netherlands
[CN, TW][His, Env, DevS, Agr, Eco]

Vermeersch, Drs S.A.C.
SOAS,DH United Kingdom
sv1@soas.ac.uk
[CN, KR][His, Rel]

Vermeulen, Drs A.C.J.
Den Hoorn 1
2712 BB Zoetermeer
Netherlands
[IN, ID, JP, LK, TW][His]

Vermeulen, Drs H.F.
RUL,CNWS Netherlands
vermeulh@rullet.leidenuniv.nl
[TJ][Soc, CuS, Ant, His, Lin]

Vernieres, Prof. M.V.
UP1,LES France
[ID, MY, PH, TH, VN][Edu, Eco]

Verpoorten, Dr J.M.
ULG,HPO Belgium
[IN][Phi]

Verrips, Prof. J.
UvA,ASC,CASA Netherlands
[IN][Rel, Ant]

Verschoor, I.B.
ECIA Netherlands
[ID, JP, KR, NP, SG, TW][His, Phi, CuS, PolS, Eco]

Verschuur, Ir H.P.
Steenakker 5
1261 CR Blaricum
Netherlands
[CN, HK][IR]

Versteegh, Prof. dr C.M.M.
KUN, VTCMO Netherlands
[CN, HK][Lin, Lit]

Verstraeten, P.P.M.
Netherlands
[Soc]

Vertogradova, Dr V.V.
RASP,IOS Russia
[IN][CuS, Lin, Rel]

Vervliet, Drs J.B.
RUL,BIB Netherlands
vervliet@rulub.leidenuniv.nl
[BD, IN, ID, PK,][His, Eco]

Verzijlbergen, Drs H.E.
KUN,CPS Netherlands
e.verzijlbergen@maw.kun.nl
[ID][His, GenS, Ant]

Vesterinen, Dr I.
Finland
[JP, KR][Ant]

Vetter, Prof. dr T.E.
RUL,KERN Netherlands
[IN, TI][Phi, Rel]

Vial, E.
UAM1.SLH,DH France
[IN, TI][His]

Viallé, Drs C.R.M.K.L.
RUL,VG Netherlands
[CN, JP][His, AHis]

Viaro, Dr A.V.
IUED Switzerland
[CN, HK, IN, ID, MY, PK, SG, LK][Env, Ant, DevS]

Vidal, D.
UL3,CREO France
[IN][Ant]

Vidiassova, Dr M.F.
MSU,IAAS,DSEAP Russia
Maria@polit.iaas.msu.su
[KZ][Soc, PolS, His, Eco, DevS]

Vié, M.
INALCO France
[JP][His]

Viellard-Baron, M.
UMMB,DEEO,DU France
[JP][Lit]

Vielle, Dr CH.
KUL,DOS Belgium
VIELLE@LING.UCL.AC.BE
[AF, IN, PK, SRI LANGA, TJ,][Lin, Lit, Rel]

Vienne, Dr M.S. de
UR1,IGR France
[ID, VN][Eco]

Vieten, M.
Netherlands

Vigneau, Prof. R.
26, rue Jean-Pierre Timbaud
75011 Paris
France
[IN, JP, LK][Lit]

Vikír, Prof. L.S.
UO,FA,CS Norway
l.s.vikor@inl.uio.no
[ID, MY][Lin]

Vikor, K.S.
Norway
knut.vikor@smi.uib.no

Vilaro Giralt, R.
Pintor Fortuny 33-3° 1s
08001 Barcelona
Spain
[JP, KR, PH, TW, VN][Eco, IR, PolS]

Villalba Fernandez, Dr J.
Japan
cc79508@komaba.ecc.u-tokio.ac.jp
[JP][Rel, Phi, AHis, IR]

Villalba Fernández, J.
UCM, GH,HAC Spain
evasia@eucmvx.sim.vcm.es
[JP][AHis, IR, Phi, Rel]

Vinaik, R.
6 Oban House
E14 0JB London
United Kingdom
[IN, PK][His, DevS]

Vingerhoets, Dr J.W.A.
United Kingdom

Vink, Dr W.
RUL,OR/HB Netherlands
[PG][His]

Vinkovics, Dr J.
FHMEAA Hungary
[MN, TI][His, Lin, AHis]

Vinogradova, Dr N.M.
RASP,IOS Russia
[CuS]

Vinyamata Camp, E.
URL Spain
[CN, JP][IR, Soc, Psy]

Viola, Dr M.A.
IICT,CEU Portugal
[MN, TI][Ant, Law]

Virgin, Drs L.
NME,BIB Sweden
[JP][His, AHis]

Virtanen, Dr K.
JY,DL Finland
kvirtane@dodo.jyu.fi
[IN][Lit, His, AHis, Phi]

Vis, Mr B.C.
RUG,VBB Netherlands
b.s.vis@rechten.rug.nl
[VN][DevS, Law]

Vischer, Dr M.P.
Weesperzijde 96
1091 EL Amsterdam
Netherlands
[ID][Ant, His, Rel]

Vishnevskaya, Dr N.A.
RAS,IWL Russia
[IN][Lit]

Visscher, Drs S.
Republic of Singapore
A723sva@hasara11.bitnet
[ID, MY, SG][PolS, Soc, His]

Visser, Drs T.
Mus.V Netherlands
[AF, KZ, TJ, TM][CuS, Ant]

Visser, Dr L.E.
UvA,ASC,CASA Netherlands
[ID][DevS, Ant]

Visser-Elias, M.M.
Nijelantstraat 3
2597 TH The Hague
Netherlands
[JP][His]

Vitiello, Dr G.
IIAS Netherlands
vitiello@rullet.leidenuniv.nl
[CN][GenS, Lit]

Vittinghoff, Drs N.P.
RKU,OAW,SIN Germany
[CN, HK, JP][CuS, His]

Vittinghoff, Prof. dr H.
LMU,IOAK Germany
[CN, TW][CuS, Phi, His]

Vizcarra, H.
INALCO France
[CN][Lan]

Vliet, P. van de
Arkelse Onderweg 54
4206 AH Gorinchem
Netherlands
[CN][Phi, His, Ant, Arch, Lit, Rel, AHis]

Vochala, J.
Hrusick 2511 \Sporilov 2
41100 Prague
Czech Republic
[CN][Lin, Lit]

Vogel, Prof. dr H.U.
EKUT,SSK Germany
hans-ulrich.vogel@uni-tuebingen.de
[CN][His, CuS]

Vogel, Prof. dr C.
UB,SI Germany
[IN, TI][Lit]

Vogel, Drs K.K.
UT,CEAPS Germany
vogel@pcmail.uni-trier.de
[JP, KR][GenS, PolS]

Vogel, Dr J.
EUR,HK Netherlands
vogel@mgs@fhk.eur.nl
[ID][His]

Vogelsang, Dr W.J.
RUL,CNWS Netherlands
vogelsang@rullet.leidenuniv.nl
[AF, IN, KZ, PK, TJ, TM][Lin, His, Arch, Rel, AHis]

Vogelweith, G.
USHS,LLCE France
[CN][AHis, Rel, Lin, His, Arch, His]

Vohra, Dr R.
SBI Luxemburg
[TI][His, CuS, GeoAHis, DevS]

Voisin, F.
CNRS,LACITO France
[ID][AHis, Geo, His, CuS, DevS]

Volhonski, Dr B.M.
MSU,IAAS,CIBS Russia
[MALDIVES, SRI LANCA][Lin, Lit]

Volkov, Dr V.V.
[MN][Arch]

Volkova, Dr L.A.
RAS,IFES,FEB Russia
[CN][Eco]

Vollmer, Dr K.
UHAM,SKC,TBI Germany
k-vollmer@public.uni-hamburg.de
[JP][His, CuS, Rel, Lit]

Volodin, Dr A.G.
RASP,IOS Russia
[IN][PolS]

Volpi, G.
S24O Italy
[BN, KH, CN, HK, IN, ID, JP, KR, LA, MO, MY, MN][PolS, IR, Agr, Eco, Env]

Vombruck, Dr G.
LSEPS,DA United Kingdom
g.vom-bruck@lse.ac.uk
[BN, KH, CN, HK, IN, ID, JP, KR, LA, MO, MY, MN][Ant]

Vonck, Drs H.M.
UvA,VMW Netherlands
[ID][Part]

Voogd, Drs P. de
HR Netherlands
p.de.voogd.@cb.hro.nl
[KH, CN, MY, MN, PK, VN][DevS, GenS, Soc, Edu]

Voogt, Dr A.J. De
Da Costalaan 1
3743 HT Baarn
Netherlands
[MG, PI][Lin, CuS, Psy]

Voogt, Drs P.R.
KIT Netherlands
[ID, MY, PH, SG, TH, VN][Ant]

Voorhoeve, Dr C.L.
RUL,TCZOAO,PD
Netherlands
[ID, PG][DevS, Lin]

Voorst-Mulder, J.C.M. van
Netherlands

Voronin, Dr S.V.
RASP,IOS Russia
[IN, LK][Soc]

Vorontsov, Dr A.V.
RASP,IOS Russia
[IR]

Vos, Drs M.L.
UvA,VP Netherlands
vos@pscw.uva.nl
[ID][PolS]

Vos, Prof. dr F.
Hazenboslaan 5
2341 SE Oegstgeest
Netherlands
[JP, KR][Rel, Lit, His]

Vos, Dr R.P.
ISS Netherlands
[DevS, Eco]

Voskresenski, Dr D.N.
MSU,IAAS,CIBS Russia
[CN][Rel, CuS, Lit, Phi]

Voskresensky, Dr A.D.
RAS,IFES,FEB Russia
[CN][His, IR]

Voskressenski, Dr A.D.
RAS,IFES,CRC Russia
[CN][IR, DevS, PolS, His, CuS]

Voskuil, Dr J.E.
Netherlands
[ID, MY, PH][Lin]

Vreede-de Stuers, Dr S.C.L.
Van Heutszlaan 56
3743 JP Baarn
Netherlands
[IN, ID][Ant]

Vreeswijk, Drs L.
Waverstraat 62 II
1079 VN Amsterdam
Netherlands
[IN, NP, PH, LK][Ant, DevS]

Vriens, A.M.G.
189,rue du Dr. Canvin
13012 Marseille
France
[TI][Rel]

Vries, Drs I. de
APAF Netherlands
[ID, PI, PG][AHis, Rel, GenS, Ant]

Vries, Prof. dr L.J. de
RUL,TCZOAO,PD
Netherlands
ljdevries@rullet.leidenuniv.nl
[ID][Lin]

Vries, Prof. dr J.W. de
RUL,VN Netherlands
[ID][Lin]

Vries, K. de
Kaiserstraat 16 A
2311 GR Leiden
Netherlands
[IN, PK][Rel, His]

Vries, Drs J.H.A.
Govert Flinckstraat 249-I
1073 BX Amsterdam
Netherlands
[TH][His, AHis, Rel, Ant, His]

Vries Robbé, A. de
Milletstraat 43-I
1077 ZC Amsterdam
Netherlands
[ID, LK][Arch, His, Ant, AHis]

Vrieze, Drs J.
NF Netherlands
[AHis, Arch]

Vruggink, Drs H.D.
Davidstraat 52
9725 BT Groningen
Netherlands
[ID][Lin]

Vu, Drs H.
JGU,IP Germany
vuh000@goofy.zdv.uni-mainz.de
[VN][IR, PolS]

Vu Xuan Quang, Dr .
VUE,DIE Austria
h9451817@falbala.wu-wien.ac.at
[JP, KR, VN][Eco]

Vyatkin, Dr A.R.
RASP,IOS Russia
[Soc]

Vybornov, Dr V.Ya.
RASP,IOS Russia
[PI][Eco]

Waal, Drs H.C.J.M.
UU,DSG Netherlands
[MY][Geo, GenS]

Waals, Drs J.D. van der
Korte Keizersdwarsstraat 11 (huis)
1011 GJ Amsterdam
Netherlands
[ID, PI, PG][His, CuS, His, AHis]

Waardenburg, Prof. dr J.G.
EUR,EW,TE Netherlands
[CN, IN,][DevS]

Wad, P.
Gadevangsvej 127
3400 Hilleröd
Denmark
[DevS]

Wädow, Dr. G.
MS Germany
monumenta.serica@t-online.de
[CN, HK, TW][AHis, CuS, His, Rel]

Waelty, Dr S.
UZI,DG Switzerland
waelty@geo.unizh.ch
[IN, ID][Ant, Env, DevS]

Wagenaar, Dr L.J.
AHM,BIB Netherlands
[IN, ID, LK][His]

Wagner, Prof. dr R.
RKU,OAW,SIN Germany
wagner@gw.sino.uni-heidelberg.de
[CN][Phi, Lit, His, CuS]

Wagner, J.
Schleppbahn Str. 10
44225 Dortmund
Germany
[JP][His, AHis, CuS]

Wagner, Drs V.
Tengstr. 25
80798 Munich
Germany
[CN][PolS, Soc, CuS, His]

Wagner, Dr D.B.
Reverdilsgade 3, 1.th.
1701 Copenhagen V
Denmark
[CN][His, Arch]

Wagner-Van Leeuwen, Drs M.E.
Immergrünweg 6
89522 Heidenheim
Germany
[CN][Lin, Lit]

Wahab, Dr I.
UvA,FEWE Netherlands
wahab@butler.fee.uva.nl
[DevS, Eco]

Wahab Ali, Prof. dr A.
65 Jalan SS 1/23, Kampung Tunku
47300 Petaling Jaya
Malaysia
[BN, ID, MY, SG][Lit]

Waley MA, Dr P.T. Waley
ULEED,SG United Kingdom
p.waley@geog.leeds.ac.uk
[JP][Ant, Env]

Waligora, Dr M.
HUB,AA,SOA Germany
melitta=waligora@asa.hu-berlin.de
[IN][Phi, Soc, CuS, His]

Waliullah, A.-M.
UL3,CREO France
[IN][Lit]

Walker, V.M.K.
OBU,SAC United Kingdom
vmkwalker@brookes.ac.uk
[GenS, DevS]

Walker, L.
10 Rodway Road
SW15 5DS London
United Kingdom
[PH][Lit]

Wall, Mr D.G.
SOAS United Kingdom
dw10@soas.ac.uk
[CN][Eco]

Walle, Prof. dr W.F. van de
KUL,DAS Belgium
wille.vandewalle@arts.kuleuven.ac.be
[JP][AHis, Lin, His]

Wallensteiner, E.M.
Sternwartestrasse 420
1180 Vienna
Austria
[IN][CuS, Ant]

Walraven, Prof. dr B.C.A.
RUL,TCJK Netherlands
Walraven@Rullet.LeidenUniv.nl
[KR][His, Lit, Rel, Ant]

Walter, A.
UMMB,DEEO,DU France
[JP][Lit]

Wandelt, Dr I.
Matthiasstrasse 8
50354 Hürth
Germany
[ID][Edu, Lin]

Wang, Dr Q.
AU, DPS Denmark
[CN][PolS]

Wang, T.
SOAS,DAA United Kingdom
wt@soas.ac.uk
[CN][Arch, AHis]

Wang, B.
UAM1,LSH France
[CN][Lit]

Wang, Dr H.
China P.R.
[CN, IN,][Soc]

Wang, H.
BM,DCM United Kingdom
[CN, JP, KR, VN][His, AHis, Arch, His]

Wang, J.
AU,DEAS,OI Denmark
ostjw@hum.aau.dk
[CN, HK, JP, SG, TW][Lin, Lit, CuS, Edu, His, AHis]

Wang, Dr F.T.
CNRS,EPHE,SR,T France
[CN, TW, TI][Rel]

Wang, N.
UP8, France
[His]

Wang, Mr D.T.C.
UL,CDCE Switzerland
[CN, HK, JP, KR, MY, PH, SG, TH, VN][PolS, Law]

Wang-Tang, L.J.
EOIM,DJ Spain
[TW][Lin]

Waniek, Dr A.I.
UB,FL,OL Romania
[JP][CuS, Lit]

Waraeksiri, A.
INALCO France
[TH][CuS, Lit]

Warnk, Drs H.
JWGU,IOOP,SOAW
Germany
[ID, MY, TH][His, Ant]

Washbrook, Dr D.A.
OU,FOS,ICS United Kingdom
david.washbrook@st-antonys.ox.ac.uk
[IN, LK][His]

Wasia-Kuipers, Drs J.B.
Dordtsesteen 2
3961 XP Wijk bij Duurstede
Netherlands
[ID][Ant]

Wassmann, Prof. dr J.
RKU,IE Germany
[ID, MY][Ant]

Watanabe, Prof. T.
CCAD United Kingdom
[JP][AHis]

Watson, Prof. W.
Cefn Y Maes \Parc
LL23 7JS Bala Gwynedd,
Wales
United Kingdom
[CN, JP, TH][Arch, His, AHis]

Watson, Dr J.R.
UB,ILGS,DLGD United Kingdom
j.r.watson@birmingham.ac.uk
[IN, MY,][Eco, DevS]

Wawrzyniak, Dr A.
MAIP Poland
[AF, IN, ID, LA, MY, NP, LK, VN][CuS, Ant]

Weber, B.
HUB, ZSKJ Germany
[JP][CuS]

Weber, J.
UL3,CREO France
[IN][His]

Weber, Dr E.
RKU,SI,AG Germany
[IN][Soc, PolS, Env, Eco, DevS]

Wedell-Wedellsborg, A.
AU,DEAS,OI Denmark
Ostivy@hum.aau.dk
[CN][Lit, CuS]

Wee, Prof. H.F.A.van der
KUL, CES Belgium
[IN, ID, JP, MO,][Eco, His]

Weerd, Drs J. van der
Netherlands
j.c.van_der_weerd@cri.leidenuniv.nl
[ID, TH][Eco, His]

Weggel, Dr O.
IFA Germany
[CN, HK, LA, TW, TI, VN][Law, Rel, Soc, CuS, Phi, Lin, PolS, IR]

Weigeun-Schwiedrzik, Prof. S.
RKU,OAW,SIN Germany
sws@gw.sino.uni-heidelberg.de
[CN, HK][His, Lit, PolS, CuS]

Wein, Dr R.
KKF Germany
[KR][PolS, His]

Weinberger-Thomas, Prof. C.
INALCO,CRESCIC France
[IN][CuS, Lit, Rel, Soc]

Weinert, Ch.
UHAM,SKC,KTV Germany
weinert@rrz.uni-hamburg.de
[CN, HK, TW][Rel, Lit, Soc, CuS]

Weishaupt, M.
USHS,LLCE France
[JP][Lan]

Weitenberg, Drs F.S.J.J.
RUG,VA Netherlands
weitenberg@let.rug.nl
[KZ, TJ][Rel, Env, Arch, Soc]

Weitenberg, Prof. dr J.J.S.
RUL,VTW Netherlands
Weitenberg@rullet.univleiden.nl
[KZ, TJ][Lit, Lin]

Weiz, Drs B.
Lindwurmstrasse 159-A
80337 Munich
Germany
[Ant]

Wellens, K.
UO,EAI,BIB Norway
[CN, TW, TI][Ant, Rel, Lit]

Weller, Drs P.G.
UD,RRC,,SESS United Kingdom
p.g.weller@derby.ac.uk
[IN, ID, MY][Rel]

Welling, R.L.
Statenweg 158-A
3039 JP Rotterdam
Netherlands

Welling, W.
Statenweg 31
3039 HA Rotterdam
Netherlands
[CN, IN, ID, JP, KR, MN, TH, TI, VN][AHis]

Welling, Drs K.O.H.
Muz.Th. Netherlands
[CN, IN, ID, JP, KR, MN, TH, TI, VN][Art]

Welzen, Drs K.F.
Postweg 47
6523 KS Nijmegen
Netherlands
[ID][Psy]

Welzig, Prof. dr W.
OAW Austria

Wendt, Dr H.R.
ALU,HS Germany
[IN, PH,][His, Edu, CuS, Lin]

Wenner, D.
BPB Germany
[MM][Env, Edu, GenS, PolS, Rel, Eco, DevS, CuS, IR]

Werba, Dr Ch.H.
UW,IIA Austria
[IN][Lin, Lit, Rel, Psy]

Werff, Dr P.E. van der
VU,IM Netherlands
werff@ivm.vu.nl
[CN, IN, PI][Env, Ant, DevS]

Werger-Klein, K.E.
Nieuwe Gracht 145
3512 LL Utrecht
Netherlands
[JP][His]

Werker, K. de
Netherlands
[SG][His]

Werkman, Drs P.E.
CHW Netherlands
p.werkman@chw.nl
[ID][PolS, IR, His, Edu]

Werner, Dr W.L.
RKU,SI,AG Germany
[IN, PH, SC, LK, TH][Env, DevS]

Wersch, Dr H.W.M. van
Batenstein 76
2403 PJ Alphen a/d Rijn
Netherlands
[IN][Soc, Ant]

Werth, Dr L.
FUB,PSW,IE,A Germany
[IN, PK][Ant]

Wertheim, Prof. dr W.F.
Generaal Foulkesweg 225
6703 DJ Wageningen
Netherlands
[CN, ID][Soc, His]

Wery, Prof. mr P.L.
Nicolaas Maeslaan 11
2343 SB Oegstgeest
Netherlands
[ID][Law]

Wessel, Drs M.G.J. van
UvA,ASSR,CASA
Netherlands
vanwessel@pscw.uva.nl
[IN][Ant]

Wessel, Prof. I.W.
HUB,AA,SOA Germany
ingrid=wessel@rz.hu-berlin.de
[ID][His, PolS]

Wesseling, Prof. dr H.L.
KNAW,IRQA Netherlands
[His]

Wesselius, Drs J.
RHM,OT-V Netherlands
[ID, JP][Lin, His]

Wessing, Dr R.
Stephensonstraat 42
2561 XW The Hague
Netherlands
[ID][Ant]

Westad, Dr O.A.
NI Norway
[CN, TW][His, IR]

Westenburg, G.
Netherlands
[CN, TW][CuS, Law, IR, His, Eco, Agr, Env]

Westergaard, Dr K.
CDR Denmark
kwe@cdr.dk
[BD, IN][PolS, DevS]

Westerkamp, Drs W.
VMN Netherlands
[ID][Ant, Arch]

Westermann, Drs R.
HAGAA Netherlands
[CN, ID][AHis, CuS, Eco]

Westman, Drs B.W.
Jellerod Have 21
2980 Kokkedal
Denmark
[IN][Rel, AHis, Ant, His]

Weststeijn, Prof. dr W.G.
Voltaplein 40hs
1098 NS Amsterdam
Netherlands
[KZ, TJ, TM][Lit, CuS]

Weulersse, D.
UP7,UAO France
[CN][Lit, His]

Wezler, Prof. dr A.
UHAM,KGIT Germany
wezler@orientalistik.uni-hamburg.de
[IN, NP][CuS, Rel, Phi, Lit, Law, Lin]

Whalley, Dr J.
UWA,DE,DERC United Kingdom
[IN, KR, PG, PH, TW, VN][Eco]

White, Prof. dr B.N.F.
ISS Netherlands
ben.white@iss.nl
[ID][Soc, DevS, Ant, POPULATION]

Whitfield, Prof. R.
SOAS,DAA United Kingdom
rw5@soas.ac.uk
[CN, JP, KR, TW][His, AHis]

Whitfield, Dr S.
BL,OIOC United Kingdom
susan.whitfield@bl.uk
[CN][Rel, His, CuS]

Whitmore, Dr T.C.
CU,DG United Kingdom
[BN, KH, ID, LA, MY, MM, PI, PG, PH, SG, TH][Env]

Wichelen, Drs C.B.J. van
HIVOS Netherlands
[IN, ID, MY, PH, SG,][Soc, Phi, Ant, DevS, Rel]

Wichmann, Drs P.
WWUM,IP Germany
wichman@uni-muenster.de
[BN, CN, ID, JP, MY, PH, SG, TH, VN][IR, PolS]

Wickham-Smith, Drs S.J.S.
76 Bullingdon Road
OX4 1QL Oxford
United Kingdom
[MN, TI][Lin, Rel]

Wiechen, P.J. van
Mauritsstraat 32
4811 ER Breda
Netherlands
[IN, ID, JP, MO, MY, PI, LK][AHis, CuS, Ant, Arch, His]

Wiedenhof, Dr J.M.
RUL,SI Netherlands
jmwied@rullet.leidenuniv.nl
[CN, TW][Lin]

Wiegmans, Drs B.W.
Prins Bernhardplein 64
1037 BG Amsterdam
Netherlands
[ID, JP, KR, MY, MM, SG, TH][Eco]

Wiel, A.N. van der
VNHS Netherlands
[ID, JP. LK][His, AHis, Arch]

Wieringa, Dr E.P.
Van Swietenstraat 21
2334 EA Leiden
Netherlands
[BN, ID, MY, SG][Lit]

Wieringa, Dr S.E.
ISS Netherlands
wieringa@iss.nl
[IN, ID][GenS, DevS]

Wigboldus, Ir J.S.
LW,DRH Netherlands
[CN, ID][Agr, His]

Wignesan, Dr T.
CNRS,EHESS France
[ID, MY][His, Agr]

Wijsman, Drs P.L.
RUL,TCJK Netherlands
wijsman@rullet.leidenuniv.nl
[JP][Lit]

Wild, Y.
Baumgartenweg 57
4132 Muttenz
Switzerland
[JP][His]

Wilder, Dr W.D.
UDU,DA United Kingdom
w.d.wilder@durham.ac.uk
[BN, KH, ID, MY, PH, SG, TH, VN][GenS, DevS, Ant]

Wilhelm, Prof. dr F.
LMU,II Germany
[IN, TI][PolS, CuS, Lit, His]

Will, Prof. P.-E.
CF France
Will@ext.jussieu.fr
[CN, TW][His]

Willekens, Prof. dr F.J.
RUG,FRW Netherlands
f.j.willekens@frw.rug.nl
[CN, TW][DevS]

Willemse, Drs C.L.A.
Vrijheidslaan 640
2321 DV Leiden
Netherlands
[CN, TW][GenS, Ant, Rel]

Williamson, Dr P.J.
INSEAD,EAC,BIB France
williamson@insead.fr
[CN, HK, IN, ID, JP, MY, PH, SG, LK, TW, TH, VN][DevS, Eco]

Willis, Dr M.
SSAS United Kingdom
[IN][His, CuS, His, AHis]

Winarta, Drs E.
Gouden Leeuw 134
1103 KB Amsterdam
Netherlands
[ID][Ant, Lit]

Winid, Prof. dr B.
UW,FGRS,IDC Poland
[BD, BT, IN, KR, MY, NP, PK, PH, SG, TH][PolS, DevS, Env, Geo]

Wisseman Christie, Prof. dr J.
UHU,DSEAS United Kingdom
c.j.christie@hist.hull.ac.uk
[ID, MY,][Arch, His]

Wit, Dr J.W. de
ISS Netherlands
dewit@iss.nl
[IN][DevS, Ant]

Witkam, Dr J.J.
RUL,BIB Netherlands
witkam@rulub.leidenuniv.nl
[BD, ID, KZ, MY, PK, TJ, TM][His, Rel, Lit]

Wiuf, J.
Kongebrovej 43
4180 Soroe
Denmark
[KH, IN, TH][Phi, Rel, Lit]

Wlodarczyk, A.
CNRS,JAP France
[JP][Lin]

Woelders, Dr M.O.
Van Brouchovenlaan 7
2343 HC Oegstgeest
Netherlands
[ID][Lit]

Woerkom-Chong, Drs W.L. van
RUL,SI Netherlands
docchin@rullet.leidenuniv.nl
[CN][Phi]

Wolffers, Prof. dr I
VU,MFHC Netherlands
[BD, KH, ID, MY, LK, TH, VN][DevS]

Wolters, Dr W.G.
KUN,CPS Netherlands
[ID, PH][Ant, DevS]

Wolvekamp, Drs P.S.
BO Netherlands
[BD, BT, KH, CN, IN, ID, LA, MY, MM, NP][Agr, IR, DevS, Env, GenS]

Wondergem, P.S.
Westerzicht 364
4385 BM Vlissingen
Netherlands

Wongsomenggolo, Drs S.
Hasebroekstr. 102/2
1053 DA Amsterdam
Netherlands
[ID][Soc, His, Ant]

Wood, Drs F.
BL,OIOC United Kingdom
frances.wood@bl.uk
[CN][Arch, CuS, His, AHis]

Wood MA, MSC, M.A.C.

MWOOD@EUROPARL.EU.INT
[PolS]

Worm, Drs V.
DIEM Denmark
worm\int@merkur.cbs.dk
[CN, HK, TW][Soc, Eco, Ant]

Woronoff, Dr J.A.
H19 Route de Vésequin
01280 Prévessin
France
[HK, JP, KR, SG, TW][Eco, IR, DevS, PolS]

Wouden, Drs A.A. van der
UU,DSG Netherlands
a.wouden@frw.ruu.nl
[ID][DevS]

Wu, Y.
INALCO France
[CN][Lan]

Wu, J.Y.T.
RUL,SI Netherlands
WU@Rullet.Leiden.Univ.nl
[CN, HK, TW][Lit]

Wu, Dr W.-P.
UHU,IPAS United Kingdom
[CN, HK, SG, TW][Eco, CuS]

Wu, Prof. P.
EKUT,SSK Germany
pi.wu@uni-tuebingen.de
[CN][His, PolS]

Wu, Dr C.-Y.
9 Rue Robespierre
94200 Ivry sur Seine
France
[CN, IN, TI][Lit, Rel, Phi, Lin, His]

Wu, Dr K.
LUI,FSES,DG United Kingdom
Kegang.wu@liverpool.ac.uk
[CN, NP][Agr, Env]

Wu-Beyens, I.CH.
KUL, CES Belgium
[CN, HK, JP, SG, TW][PolS, IR, His, Agr, DevS, Env]

Wuisman, Dr J.J.J.M.
Bank B. Indonesia
[DevS]

Wurm, A.
UW,IIA Austria
[IN][His, Lit, Rel]

Xinzhong Yao, Dr
UWL,DTRIS United Kingdom
yao@lampeter.ac.uk
[CN, JP, KR, TW][Rel, Phi]

Xu, D.
CNRS,CRLAO France
[CN][Lin]

Ya.Elianov, ProfDr. A.
MSU,IAAS,CIBS Russia
[DevS, Eco, His]

Yagmur, Drs K.
KUB,VTW Netherlands
k.yagmur@kub.nl
[Lin, CuS]

Yakovlev, Dr A.I.

[PolS, Soc]

Yakovlev, Prof. A.G.
RAS,IFES,CRC Russia
[VN][His, Eco, IR]

Yakubovsky, Dr V.
RAS,IFES,FEB Russia
[HK, JP, KR, TW][Eco, PolS, IR]

Yaldiz, Prof. dr M.
MIKB Germany
[AF, BD, AF, BD, BT, IN, NP, PK, LK, TI][Arch, His, AHis, Rel]

Yamaguchi, K.
UJML3,FL France
[JP][Lan]

Yamasaki, Y.
INALCO France
[JP][]

Yang, J.-H.
INALCO France
[CN][Lan]

Yang, F.
UMMB,DEEO,DU France
[CN][Lan]

Yang, D.
UP8, France
[CN][Lan]

Yang, J.
EC United Kingdom
[CN][Edu]

Yang-de Witte, Drs C.H.
IIAS Netherlands
yang@rullet.leidenuniv.nl
[CN][IR, PolS]

Yashkin, Prof. Dr. V.A.
RASP,IOS Russia
[Eco, IR]

Yaskina, Dr G.S.
RASP,IOS Russia
[MN][]

Yatskovskaya, K.N.
RASP,IOS Russia
[MN][Lit]

Yegorova, M.N.
RASP,IOS Russia
[IN][PolS, Soc]

Yelizarenkova, Dr T.
RASP,IOS Russia
[IN][Lin]

Yeon, Dr J.H.
SOAS,CKS United Kingdom
[KR][Lin, Lit]

Yerassov, Dr B.S.
RASP,IOS Russia
[CuS]

Yeremin, V.N.
RASP,IOS Russia
[JP][Law]

Yermakova, Dr L.M.
RASP,IOS Russia
[JP][Lit]

Yin Yin, M.
INALCO France
[MM][Lan]

Yip, Dr P.C.
ULEED,DEAS United Kingdom
p.c.yip@leeds.ac.uk
[CN, HK][Lin, CuS]

Yoneda, Y.Y.
Gerard Doustraat 166
2526 NK The Hague
Netherlands
[JP][AHis]

York, Dr M.
BCHE,SRD United Kingdom
[IN, NP][Arch, IR, Rel, Soc, CuS]

Yoshida, N.
JEJ Belgium
naoto.yoshida@pophost.eunet.be
[JP][IR, Eco]

Yperen, Dr M.I.L.
KITLV Netherlands
yperen@rullet.leidenuniv.nl
[ID][Eco, IR]

Yurlov, Dr F.N.
RASP,IOS Russia
[IN][His, PolS]

Yurlova, Dr Ye.S.
RASP,IOS Russia
[IN][His]

Zaborowski, Dr H.J.
FUB,OS Germany
[CN, KR][CuS, His, LitAnt, Rel]

Zahariin, Dr B.A.
MSU,IAAS,CIBS Russia
[IN][Lin]

Zaini-Lajoubert, M.
CNRS,ARCHIPEL France
[ID, MY][Soc, GenS, His, Lit, Rel]

Zaitsev, Dr V.V.

[CN][Phi]

Zaitsev, Dr V.N.

[AF,][His, Lit]

Zakaznikova, Dr Ye.P.
RASP,IOS Russia
[His, PolS, Soc]

Zakaznikova, Dr Y.P.
RAS,IOS,AL Russia
[BN, ID, MY, PH, SG, TH][DevS, Soc, PolS, His]

Zakharyin, Dr B.A.
MSU,IAAS,DIP Russia
[IN][Lin]

Zalesskaya, Dr V.N.
SHM,OD Russia
[ASIA MINOR][Arch, AHis, CuS]

Zamperini, Dr S.
SOAS United Kingdom
[BD, IN, NP, PK, LK][His, IR]

Zanden, Drs T.A.M. van der
Jan de Hartogplein 43
2353 LL Leiderdorp
Netherlands
[IN, ID][His, CuS]

Zani-Lajoubert, M.
CNRS,EHESS France
[ID, MY][CuS, His]

Zanier, Prof. C.
UP,DMCH Italy
zanier@stm.unipl.it
[CN, IN, JP,][His]

Zanten, Dr E.A. van
RUL,CA/SNWS Netherlands
zanten@rulfsw.leidenuniv.nl
[ID][His]

Zanten, Dr W. van
RUL,CA/SNWS Netherlands
zanten@rulfsw.leidenuniv.nl
[ID][PArtAnt]

Zaremba, Dr P.A.
RCBP,KUI Poland
[CN, HK, JP, MO, MY, SG, TW, TH][DevS, Env, Eco]

Zarrabi, H.
43 Bd. de Verdun
92400 Courbevoie
France

Zavadskaya, Prof. dr V.
RASP,IOS Russia
[CN][AHis]

Zeeuw, D. de
Minervaplein 6hs
1077 TN Amsterdam
Netherlands
[BD, CN, IN, ID, MY, PK, LK, TW][Env, Agr]

Zeeventer, Drs L.T.M. van
Lijsterbesstraat 45
6523 JP Nijmegen
Netherlands
[CN, JP][PolS, DevS, IR]

Zeimal, Dr T.I.

[Arch, AHis, CuS]

Zeimal, Dr E.V.
Russia
[AHis, CuS]

Zejan, Dr M.C.
SSE,DE Sweden
gmz@hhs.se
[KH, CN, TH, VN][DevS, Eco]

Zeller, Dr G.
EKUT,BIB Germany
gabriele.zeller@ub.uni-tuebingen.de
[TI][Rel, Lit, CuS]

Zevalkink, Drs J.
KUN,VOP Netherlands
zevalkink@psych.kun.nl
[ID][Ant, Psy]

Zhang, Dr W.
UG,MARC Switzerland
[CN, TW][IR]

Zhang, Dr N.
99, Rue du Bac
75005 Paris
France
[CN, HK, TW][Lit, CuS, Soc, Phi]

Zhang, Y.
INALCO France
[CN][Lan]

Zhang, Dr W.
ISS Netherlands
weiguo@iss.nl
[CN][Soc, DevS]

Zhang, Dr Y.
IIAS Netherlands
zhang@rullet.leidenuniv.nl
[CN, JP][Law]

Zhang, Drs V.
LMU,IOAK,SIN Germany
violetta.zhang@lrz.uni-muenchen.de
[CN, MN][CuS, His]

Zhang, Prof. dr G.
UT,SIN Germany
[CN][His]

Zhao, Dr H.Y.H.
SOAS,DEA United Kingdom
yz@soas.ac.uk
[CN, HK, TW][CuS]

Zhao, Z.
UTM,CUP France
[CN][CuS]

Zharova, Dr O.V.
RASP,IOS Russia
[PolS]

Zheng, G.
UAM1,LSH France
[CN][Lit]

Zheng, Prof. dr Ch.
CNRS,IRSEA France
[CN, HK, MO, SG, TW][His, Ant]

Zheng, H.
UWE,SL,ECL United Kingdom
zhengh@westminster.ac.uk
[CN, HK][Arch, AHis, Lit]

Zhigalina, Dr O.I.
RAS,IOS,AL Russia
[IR][PolS, Rel, Soc, IR, His]

Zhmuida, Dr I.V.
RASP,IOS Russia
[, PK][Eco, IR]

Zhogolev, Dr D.A.
RAS,IFES,CRC Russia
Titarenk@ifes.msk.su
[CN, HK, MO, TW, TI][PolS, DevS, Soc, Law, Eco, His]

Zhukov, Dr A.Ye.
RASP,IOS Russia
[JP][His]

Zhukov, Prof. dr A.A.
SPU,FOS,DAS Russia
[MG][Rel, Lit, CuS, Lin]

Zhukovskaya, Dr N.L.
RAS,IEA Russia
[MN][Ant]

Zieck, Drs M.Y.A.
UvA,VVIB Netherlands
[KH, PK][Law]

Ziem, K.
SWP,FIPS,A Germany
[MM][Law]

Zieme, Dr P.
HUB, ZAGA Germany
[JP, MN][Rel]

Zijlmans, Dr G.C.
South Korea
[ID][Soc, His]

Zimmermann, Dr G.R.
TUCW,IGG Germany
[ID, MY, TH][Geo]

Zingel, Dr W.-P.
RKU,SI,IWE Germany
[BD, IN, PK, LK][Agr, Env, Eco]

Zins, Dr M.J.
UL3,CREO France
[IN][PolS]

Zipoli, Prof. R.
UV,DEAS Italy
zipoli@unive.it
[IR][Lit, Lin]

Zoller, Dr C.P.
RKU,SI,DI Germany
ce0@ix.urz.uni-heidelberg.de
[IN][Ant, Lin, Lit, Rel]

Zomer, Drs H.
Muiderslot 39
5037 HJ Tilburg
Netherlands
[ID, JP][IR, Eco, CuS]

Zondag, Drs H.A.
Hadidreef 3e
3563 HC Utrecht
Netherlands
[Ant]

Zoomers, Drs H.C.M.
VWS Netherlands
[MM, TH][His, IR, PolS]

Zoomers, Dr E.B.
Kruithuisstraat 120
1018 WW Amsterdam
Netherlands
[DevS]

Zorn, Dr B.
MVK Austria
[CN, HK, JP, KR, TW][Ant, Arch, Ant, His, AHis]

Zotov, O.V.
RAS,IOS,DC Russia
[CN][PolS, His]

Zotz, Dr V.
UW,IP Austria
[CN, IN, JP, TI][Phi, CuS, Rel, His]

Zubkova, Dr L.
Smient 27
3435 VJ Nieuwegein
Netherlands
[IN][Lit]

Zubov, Dr A.B.
RASP,IOS Russia
[TH][PolS]

Zuiderhoek, Dr B.
Fideliolaan 102
1183 PP Amstelveen
Netherlands
[ID, MM][His]

Zuiderweg, Drs A.
UvA,VHNTL Netherlands
[ID][His, AHis, CuS, GenS, His, Rel, Lit]

Zürcher, Prof. dr E.J.
IISG,IISH Netherlands
ezu@iisg.nl
[IR][His]

Zürcher, Prof. dr E.
RUL,SI Netherlands
[CN][Rel]

Zurndorfer, Dr H.T.
RUL,SI Netherlands
zurndorf@rullet.leidenuniv.nl
[CN][His]

Zutt, S.
Fokke Simonszstraat 30-h
1017 TH Amsterdam
Netherlands
[VN][Ant]

Zvelebil, Prof. dr K.V.
Rue de Moulin a Huile
11160 Cabrespine
France
[IN, LK][Rel, Lit, CuS, Lin]

Zviagelskaia, Dr I.D.
RCSRIS Russia
zviagel@glas.apc.org
[KZ, TJ, TM][IR, PolS]

Zwan, P.J. van der
AFM Netherlands
[MG][His, CuS, Rel, His, AHis, Ant]

Zwart, Dr F. de
IIAS Netherlands
iiasguest24@rullet.leidenuniv.n
l
[IN][PolS]

Zwijnenburg, Ph.A.
Fazantenweg 18
7451 HD Holten
Netherlands
[CN, ID, LA, MY, TH][His]

DIRECTORY B

ASIANISTS

BY REGION

AND COUNTRY

OF INTEREST

AND DISCIPLINE

Southeast Asia

BRUNEI DARUSSALAM

Belgium

Baetens-Beardsmore , Drs H.
Edu, Lin

Gonzalo Castellanos , Dr A.
IR

Finland

Seppänen , J.
IR, Eco, Ant, CuS, Lin, His, AHis, Phi, Arch, Rel, PolS

France

Barbiche , Prof. dr J.-P.
Law, IR, His, PolS, Eco, DevS, CuS, Edu, Soc

Camroux , Dr D.F.
His, IR, Soc, PolS

Feillard , Drs A.
IR, GenS, His, Soc, PolS, Rel, Eco

Gazano , A.
Law

Guen , H. le
AHis, CuS, Env, Ant, Arch, His, Soc, Rel, His

Jacq-Hergoualc'h , Dr M.
Rel, His, Arch, His, AHis

Lechervy , Chr.
IR, PolS

Népote , J.
Ant, Rel, PolS, Lit, Eco, His

Orberger , Dr B.
Lin, Lit, Geo

Ordonnadu , G.
IR, Eco

Raillon , Dr F.
Soc, Eco, IR, His, PolS, DevS, Rel

Germany

Carstens , Dr R.
His, Edu, CuS, AHis, Lin, Lit, DevS, PolS, Rel

Gröpper , Drs D.
CuS, AHis, Arch, His, Ant

Kraas , Dr F.
Ant, DevS, CuS, Geo

Krause , Prof. E.D.
Lin

Kummer , Dr M.E.F.
Psy, RelAgr, Phi, Soc, Lin, IR, Eco, His, Ant, PolS, Env, E

Lobo , Dr W.
AHis, Ant, Arch

Lummer , Drs E.
His, Ant, CuS, Lit

Moeller , Dr K.
IR, PolS

Nothofer , Prof. dr B.
Ant, Lit, Lin, CuS

Wichmann , Drs P.
IR, PolS

Italy

Conti , Dr G.
Lin, Rel, Law

Santa Maria , Prof. dr L.
Lit, Lin, IR, His

Volpi , G.
PolS, IR, Agr, Eco, Env

Malaysia

Wahab Ali , Prof. dr A.
Lit

Netherlands

Arens , Drs J.F.
Lit, His, CuS

Baas , Prof. dr P.
Env

Doderlein de Win , E.F.
Law, IR, Edu, Eco, Agr, DevS

Haringhuizen , Drs W.
PolS, Ant, IR

Heller , Y.J.
Rel, CuS, His, AHis

Mensink , Drs O.H.
AHis, Ant, CuS, His

Oosterwijk , A.J.
His, Ant, Arch

Peters , Drs F.H.
DevS, His

Pompe , Dr J.H.
PolS, DevS, Env, IR, Agr, Ant, Eco, Soc, CuS, Edu, Phi, Law,

Schouten , Drs P.H.
Ant, Soc

Steinhauer , Dr H.
Lin, Ant

Teeuw , Prof. dr A.
Lit, Lin, CuS

Wieringa , Dr E.P.
Lit

Poland

Lukaszuk , Dr L.B.
Law, Eco, IR, DevS

Republic of Cyprus

Saunders , Dr G.E.
His

Russia

Demin , L.M.
His, AHis

Nikulina , Dr L.V.
DevS, CuS, Ant, Env, Edu, His, Rel, Arch

Rogojine , Dr A.
Env, Eco, IR, DevS

Tesselkine , Dr A.S.
Ant, AHis, Lin, His, CuS

Zakaznikova , Dr Y.P.
DevS, Soc, PolS, His

Spain

Bustelo , Dr P.
DevS, Eco

Sweden

Amer , Dr R.
IR, PolS, His

United Kingdom

Braginsky , Prof. V.I.
Rel, Lit

Brown , Dr N.D.
Env

Carter , Dr L.J.
His

Chin , Dr J.
PolS, DevS, His

Crosbie , Dr A.J.
IR, Env, Eco, Geo, DevS

Ellen , Prof. R.F.
Env, Ant

Francis , Mr.S.
His, DevS, IR

Gallop , Drs A.T.
Lit, His, AHis

Heng , J.W.M.
His, Arch, AHis

Huxley , Dr T.J.
IR, PolS

King , Prof. V.T.
DevS, Soc, Ant, Env

Kratz , Dr E.U.
Lit, CuS

Roper , Dr G.J.
CuS

Steeds , Mr D.
IR, His

Whitmore , Dr T.C.
Env

Wilder , Dr W.D.
GenS, DevS, Ant

CAMBODIA

Austria

Balzar , Dr D.M.
CuS, His, AHis

Sellner , Dr M.B.
CuS, Lin

Belgium

Carpano , R.
Eco, IR

Gonzalo Castellanos , Dr A.
IR

Czech Republic

Pospisilova , Dr D.
Rel, AHis

Denmark

Magnussen , Drs T.
DevS, IR, PolS

Sorensen , P.
Arch

Tönnesson , Dr S.
IR, His

Denmark

Wiuf, J.
Phi, Rel, Lit

Finland

Jokinen, Drs J.J.
DevS, IR, PolS

Seppänen, J.
IR, Eco, Ant, CuS, Lin, His, AHis, Phi, Arch, Rel, PolS

France

Antypa, U.
His

Barbiche, Prof. dr J.-P.
Law, IR, His, PolS, Eco, DevS, CuS, Edu, Soc

Bertrand, Dr D.
Psy, Rel, Ant

Bezançon, P.
Edu, His

Blayac, A.A.
Lit, His, Phi, Edu, Psy, Soc

Blazy, S.
His

Botsch, A.A.
Eco, DevS, IR, Edu, Law

Boudarel, G.
IR, PolS, CuS, His, Ant, GenS

Bourdier, Dr F.
CuS, Ant, Env, DevS

Bruneau, Dr M.
PolS, DevS, CuS, Geo, Agr

Chagnaud, F.J.
Eco, Agr, Env, DevS

Clair, Dr S.A.
His

Daniel, A.D.
Lin, Lit

Durand, Dr F.B.
Env, Agr, Lit, DevS

Eisenbruch, M.
Psy, Ant

Ferlus, M.
Lin

Filliozat, J.
Rel, Lit

Forest, Dr A.
His, Rel

Francois, Dr I.M.
IR, PolS

Frederic, L.F.
AHis, CuS, Arch, Rel, His

Gaucher, J.
Art

Gerbault, D.P.
CuS, Lin

Gobalakchenane, Dr M.
CuS, His, Rel, Soc

Heide, Dr S. von der
Ant, DevSAHis, Env, CuS, Rel, PolS

Hemery, Dr D.
His

Hor, Mr N.H.
Law, His, IR, PolS, Soc, CuS

Jacq-Hergoualc'h, Dr M.
Rel, His, Arch, His, AHis

Jacques, C.
His

Jarrige, J.F.
His, CuS, Arch, AHis

Khing, Dr H.D.
Lin, Rel, His, Lit

Lamant, Prof. P.L.
SocAHis, CuS, Arch, Rel, His

Lange, Dr C.
His, Rel, Ant, His, AHis, Soc

Lechervy, Chr.
IR, PolS

Loch, P.
Lan

Mak Phoeun, Dr
His

Mantienne, F.
His, Eco

Moreau, P.
Art

Móriot, Prof. CH.
Ant

Mourer, R.
AHis, Ant

Munier MA, M.C.
Arch, AHis, CuS, Rel

Népote, J.
Ant, Rel, PolS, Lit, Eco, His

Nguyên, Prof. dr T.A.
IR, CuS, His, Rel, Lit

Orberger, Dr B.
Lin, Lit, Geo

Ordonnadu, G.
IR, Eco

Pitoun MA,
Arch, AHis, Lit

Po Dharma Quang, Dr
Lin, Lit, His

Pouvatchy, Dr J.R.
Rel, His, PolS, IR

Ramirez, Dr P.
Ant, His, PolS, Soc

Rodriquez Doctorate, N.
AHis

Scalabrino, Drs C.J.
Rel, Arch, His, Phi, Psy, His, IR, AHis, PolS

Sok, P.
Lan

Tertrais, Prof. H.T.
His, IR

Thierry, Dr S.T.
Lit, Lin, CuS, Rel

Thion, Dr S.
Soc, Rel, PolS, His, Ant

Trân, Q.H.
CuS, Ant

Germany

Bauer, Prof. dr C.H.R.
Lit, Rel, Ant, Lin, His, Arch

Beusch, Drs D.
PolS, IR

Chhim, K.
His

Engelbert, Dr J.T.
His, IR

Geisler, Drs G.H.S.
Geo, Env, DevS

Goetzfried, Dr F.X.
His, Phi, Ant, Rel

Klotz, Drs S.
PolS, IR

Kraas, Dr F.
Ant, DevS, CuS, Geo

Kuckertz, Prof. dr J.
His, Ant

Kulke, Prof. dr H.
His, Soc, Rel

Kummer, Dr M.E.F.
Psy, RelAgr, Phi, Soc, Lin, IR, Eco, His, Ant, PolS, Env, E

Lobo, Dr W.
AHis, Ant, Arch

Mischung, Prof. R.
Ant, Soc, Rel

Moeller, Dr K.
IR, PolS

Müller, K.
PolS, CuS, His

Müller, M.
His, AHis

Neuser, Drs J.
Lit, Lin, CuS, Rel

Nguyen, Dr T.-H.
AHis, Rel, CuS, His, Arch, Ant, Soc

Schreiner, Prof. dr L.
Rel, Ant, His

Stein, Dr W.
Ant, CuS, AHis, Arch, His

Italy

Albanese, M.
His, AHis, Rel, Phi

Collotti Pischel, Prof. E
His, PolS

Orioli, Dr H.
Ant, His, Arch, AHis

Sandra, Prof. D.E.E.
Ant, CuS, Edu, GenS

Snellgrove, Prof. D.
AHis, Rel, Arch, His

Volpi, G.
PolS, IR, Agr, Eco, Env

Netherlands

Burgler, Dr R.A.
Ant, PolS, His

Netherlands

Chutiwongs, Dr N.
Rel, His, Arch, AHis

Cowan, Drs F.M.
GenS, DevS, CuS, Ant, Env, LinAgr

Feddema, Drs R.
PolS, IR, His, Eco

Grant, Dr M.E.
Lit, IR, His, AHis, Rel

Guyt, Drs H.J.
His, IR, AHis, Lin, CuS, DevS

Hanssen, Drs L.M.
Ant, CuS

Haringhuizen, Drs W.
PolS, Ant, IR

Heemst, Drs J.J.P. van
Eco

Hoefnagels, Ir H.A.M.
Agr, Eco, Law

Kal, Drs W.H.
Env, Lin, DevS, Agr, CuS, Ant, CuS, GenS

Kamp, E.P. van der
His

Kessel-Hagesteijn, Dr R.R. van
His, Ant

Kleinen, Dr J.G.G.M.
Ant

Mensink, Drs O.H.
AHis, Ant, CuS, His

Montyn, J.
Phi, AHis, CuS, Lit

Patmo, Drs S.
Edu, Soc, Ant, DevS

Pluvier, Dr J.M.
His, DevS, IR

Schalke, Dr H.J.W.G.
Arch, Ant, Env

Schipper, Prof. dr K.M.
Rel, Ant, His

Schoot, Dr H.A. van der
DevS, Eco

Steinhauer, Dr H.
Lin, Ant

Stokhof, Prof. dr W.A.L.
Lit, Lin

Ubaghs, Drs J.M.M.
CuS, His

Voogd, Drs P. de
DevS, GenS, Soc, Edu

Wolffers, Prof. dr I
DevS

Wolvekamp, Drs P.S.
Agr, IR, DevS, Env, GenS

Zieck, Drs M.Y.A.
Law

Poland

Goralski, Prof. dr
PolS, His, IR

Krzyzanowski, Dr L.K.
AHis

Lukaszuk, Dr L.B.
Law, Eco, IR, DevS

Olbrys, Drs M.
Lin, Lit

Stecinski, Drs J.
AHis

Swiercz, Drs J.
Lin

Russia

Bektimirova, Prof.dr N.N.
Rel, His, PolS

Kobelev, Dr E.V.
PolS, His, IR

Mosyakov, Dr D.V.
Eco, PolS, His

Rogojine, Dr A.
Env, Eco, IR, DevS

Solomonik, Dr I.N.
His, AHis

Spain

Albarrán Serrano, Antonio
Lit

Bustelo, Dr P.
DevS, Eco

Castillo Rodriguez, S.
IR

Garcia-Ormaechea Quero, C.
AHis, Geo, His, Lit, Rel, Phi

Gouzalez Molina, A.
IR, Soc

Jimenez Valentin, J.M.
Eco, Env, IR

Navarro Celada, F.

Pajares Ruiz, J.M.
AHis, Eco, Geo, Soc

Togores Sanchez, L.E.
IR, His

Sweden

Amer, Dr R.
IR, PolS, His

Bratthall, Prof. D.
Eco

Hammargren, Drs H.A.
PolS, IR, DevS

Hansson, E.
PolS

Lindell, Drs K.
Lin, CuS, Env

Ronnås, Dr P.
DevS, Agr, Eco

Schalk, Prof. dr P.
Phi, AHis, CuS, Arch, His, Rel

Tayanin, D.
CuS, Env, Agr, Ant, Rel

Trankell, Dr I.B.
Ant

Zejan, Dr M.C.
DevS, Eco

Switzerland

Duc-Reynaert, M.J.
Edu, Ant

United Kingdom

Carey, Dr P.B.R.
His, IR, CuS, Lit, Rel

Carter, Dr L.J.
His

Chapman, G.
His, AHis, CuS

Clarence-Smith, Dr W.G.
His

Cook, M.
Eco

Dunn, Mr A.J-J.
IR, Edu, CuS, Ant

Gethin, Dr R.M.L.
Rel

Glover, Dr I.C.
Arch

Guy, Drs J.S.
His, AHis

Heng, J.W.M.
His, Arch, AHis

Lowe, Dr P.C.
IR, His

McGregor, Dr C.D.
IR

Moore, Dr E.H.
AHis, Arch

Mürer, O.H.A.
Arch, His, AHis

Park, S.S.
Psy, PolS, Phi, SocAHis, DevS, Env, Edu, IR, Law

Picken, Dr L.E.R.
CuS

Rooney, Dr D.F.
His, AHis

Summers, L.J.
PolS, GenS, DevS

Valentin, J.C.P.
Env, Ant, CuS, Lin, His, Arch

Whitmore, Dr T.C.
Env

Wilder, Dr W.D.
GenS, DevS, Ant

INDONESIA

Austria

Allinger, Dr E.
Rel, His, CuS, Arch, AHis

Balzar, Dr D.M.
CuS, His, AHis

Lee, Dr S.-K.
CuS, Lit

Min Tjoa, Prof. dr A.
Edu

Scheuringer, Drs K.
Edu, CuS, Psy

ASIANISTS BY REGION AND COUNTRY OF INTEREST

Austria

Seebass, Prof. dr T.

PolS, Soc, Ant, IR, DevS

Sellner, Dr M.B.

CuS, Lin

Belgium

Ballegeer, J.

PolS, Law

Bogart, K.J.

Edu, CuS

Carpano, R.

Eco, IR

Gonzalo Castellanos, Dr A.

IR

Jorgensen, F.V.

IR, DevS, Env, PolS, Law

Laskewicz, Drs Z.A.L.

CuS, Lin, Ant

Lesthaeghe, Prof. R.

DevS, Soc

Persoons, Dr M.A.

AHis, Edu, IR, Lin, Phi

Piquard, B.

Rel, PolS, Ant

Prins, B. de

His

Wee, Prof. H.F.A.van der

Eco, His

Czech Republic

Hubinger, Prof. dr V.

PolS, Ant, Soc

Hulec, Dr O.

His, AHis, CuS, Arch, IR, Eco, Phi, Lit, Lin

Pospisilova, Dr D.

Rel, AHis

Vacek, Prof. dr J.

Phi, Rel, Lit, Lin

Demark

Skov, T.S.

Rel, CuS

Denmark

Asmussen, Drs V.M.S.

Ant, Rel

Bakker, Dr P.J.

His, Lin, Ant

Bubandt, Dr N.

Ant

Cribb, Prof. R.B.

PolS, His, Env

Fleming, Prof. D.E.B.

Soc, DevS

Jacobsen, Dr M.

PolS, CuS, IR, Ant

Mahmoodi, A.

Soc, PolS, His, Eco, DevS, CuS

Rodenburg, Dr J.

Ant, GenS, Env, DevS

Schmidt, Dr J.D.

Soc, IR, DevS

Svensson, Prof. dr Th.

PolS, Eco, His

Tönnesson, Dr S.

IR, His

Finland

Antikainen-Kokko, Dr A.

IR

Kaartinen, Dr T.A.

Ant

Karunaratne, Dr J.A.

DevS, Eco

Kivimäki, Dr T.A.

PolS, IR, DevS

Kotilainen, Dr E.-M.E

Ant, GenS

Roos, Drs S.

IR

Savolainen, Hanna-Mari

Ant

Seppänen, J.

IR, Eco, Ant, CuS, Lin, His, AHis, Phi, Arch, Rel, PolS

France

Adriaensens, Drs G.M.J.E.

Soc

Arom, S.

Ant, CuS, Edu

Avé, J.

Lin

Baks, Dr Ch.

Agr, Ant, Law

Barbiche, Prof. dr J.-P.

Law, IR, His, PolS, Eco, DevS, CuS, Edu, Soc

Barraud, C.

Ant

Baye, Dr E.B.

DevS, Env, Eco

Beers, Dr G.G. van

DevS, Eco, Soc

Berra, A.B. Annette

Bertrand, R.

PolS

Blanchard, F.

PolS

Blazy, S.

His

Bompard, J.M

Agr, Env

Bonneff, Dr M.

CuS

Bonnithon, H.

Ant

Botsch, A.A.

Eco, DevS, IR, Edu, Law

Bouteiller, E.

DevS, Eco

Bouvier, Dr H.

AntAnt, PArt

Breton, Dr S.

Geo, Ant

Bry, M.-F.

Rel, Psy

Cayrac-Blanchard, F.

PolS, IR

Chaponniere, Dr J.R.

IR, Eco, PolS, DevS

Charras, M.

Geo, Env, DevS, Ant

Collin, H.

Law, Soc, PolS, Eco, IR

Couto, Dr D.

Arch, His, PolS

De Coppet, Prof. D

Ant, Soc

Dolk, Dr E.C.

Lit, His

Durand, Dr F.B.

Env, Agr, Lit, DevS

Dury, Drs S.

Agr, Eco

Fédensieu, Dr A.

Ant

Feillard, Drs A.

IR, GenS, His, Soc, PolS, Rel, Eco

Fouquin, M.F.

Eco

Franck, M.

Geo

Frederic, L.F.

AHis, CuS, Arch, Rel, His

Gamage, J.

Env

Gazano, A.

Law

Gobalakchenane, Dr M.

CuS, His, Rel, Soc

Grimaud-Hervé, D.

Arch

Guerreiro, Dr A.

Ant

Guillot, C.

Rel

Haas-Lambert, A.-M.

His

Headley, Dr S.C.

Ant, Rel

Henry, R.

Lin, GenS, Env, CuS, AHis, Arch, IR, Lit, Phi, Psy

Hurpré, Dr J.F.

AHis, Arch

Husson, Dr L.

Soc, His, Ant

Jacq-Hergoualc'h, Dr M.

Rel, His, Arch, His, AHis

Jarrige, J.F.

His, CuS, Arch, AHis

Jaussaud, Dr J.

Eco, IR

Kalpana Kartik MA,

Ant, AHis, CuS, Rel

France

Koubi, J.
Soc

Labrousse, Prof. dr P.
Agr

Labrousse-Soemargono, F.
Agr

Lamant, Prof. P.L.
SocAHis, CuS, Arch, Rel, His

Lancret, N.
Art

Leothaud, G.
His

Lombard, Prof. dr D.
His

Macdonald, Dr C.J.H.
CuS, Ant, Lin, Rel

Móriot, Prof. CH.
Ant

Nooy-Palm, Prof. dr C.H.M.
Arch, AHis, Env, Ant, Rel

Orberger, Dr B.
Lin, Lit, Geo

Ordonnadu, G.
IR, Eco

Pellard, S.
His, Arch, AHis

Perlas, Dr Ch.
Ant, CuS

Picard, Dr M.
Ant, Rel, Soc, CuS

Raillon, Dr F.
Soc, Eco, IR, His, PolS, DevS, Rel

Rakotofiringa, Prof. H.
Lin, Lit

Rappoport, Drs D.
Ant

Rault-Leyrat, L.R.
His, Rel, Ant, AHis, Ant, Lin, Arch, Phi, His

Renard-Clamagirand, Dr B.
Ant

Renardet-Widjojo, Drs L.
Lit, His, CuS

Rodriquez Doctorate, N.
AHis

Sahar, B.
CuS

Salmon, Dr C.
Rel, Lit, CuS, His

Scherer, Dr S.
His, CuS, IR, Lit, PolS

Segjy, Marianne
Ant, Arch, Rel

Sekem, W.
PolS, Law, Edu

Sellato, B.
Ant, His

Semah, F.
Arch

Sivignon,
Eco, Geo

Smith, G.
Ant

Smitsendonk, Dr A.G.O.
Law, Eco, IR, Soc, Rel, PolS, DevS

Sollewijn Gelpke, Drs J.H.F.
His

Stephane, Dr S.D.
DevS, His, PolS

Subrahmanyam, Dr S.
His, Eco

Sukanda-Tessier, B.
Ant, Rel

Sukanda-Tessier, Dr V.
Ant, Arch

Tadié, J.
Geo

Trân, Q.H.
CuS, Ant

Turcq, Dr D.F.
Eco

Vernieres, Prof. M.V.
Edu, Eco

Vienne, Dr M.S. de
Eco

Voisin, F.
AHis, Geo, His, CuS, DevS

Wignesan, Dr T.
His, Agr

Williamson, Dr P.J.
DevS, Eco

Zaini-Lajoubert, M.
Soc, GenS, His, Lit, Rel

Zani-Lajoubert, M.
CuS, His

Germany

Ackermann, Dr A.
Ant, CuS, Soc

Antweiler, Prof. dr C.
DevS, Ant

Baars, M.
Soc

Bauer, Prof. dr C.H.R.
Lit, Rel, Ant, Lin, His, Arch

Blazy, Dr H.
Lin, Psy, CuS, Phi, Lit

Brauns, Drs T.
DevS, Env, Agr

Buchholt, Dr H.
CuS, DevS, Geo, Soc, His

Burdman, M.M.
His, Eco, DevS

Cain, Dr H.
Rel, Lin, Ant

Carle, Dr R.
Lit

Carstens, Dr R.
His, Edu, CuS, AHis, Lin, Lit, DevS, PolS, Rel

Dahm, Prof. dr B.
Rel, His, CuS

Damshäuser, Drs B.
Lin, Lit, PolS, Phi

Daszenies, Drs J.
Rel, Ant

Dengel, Dr H.
Rel, AHis, Eco, Arch, DevS, His

Dietrich, Dr S.
Ant, Rel, His

Dosch, Drs J.
IR, PolS

Draguhn, Dr W.
PolS, IR, Eco, DevS

Dürr, Prof. dr H.B.
Ant, Env, DevS, Soc, PolS, CuS

Franke, Prof. dr W.
His, Rel

Gerke, Prof. dr S.
CuS, Soc, DevS

Gottowik, Dr
Ant

Graevenitz, Prof. dr A. von
Phi, AHis

Graf, Drs A.W.
Lit

Gropp, Dr G.C.A.
Phi, Lit, His, Rel, Arch, AHis, CuS, Ant, Lin

Gröpper, Drs D.
CuS, AHis, Arch, His, Ant

Haffner, Prof. dr W.N.
Env

Hager, D.
Eco, IR, PolS

Hanisch, Prof. dr R.
IR, DevS, PolS

Heeschen, Dr V.
Lin, CuS, Ant, Phi, Rel

Heinschke, Dr M.
Lit

Henze, Prof. J.
Edu

Hildebrandt Diplom, Sabine

Hoeppe MSc, G
Ant, Env

Hofmann, Drs Z.S.
Ant, Rel, Phi, CuS

Jebens, Drs H.J.
CuS, Rel, Phi

Kaden, Dr M.
Eco

Kannen, B.
CuS, Ant, Rel, Soc

Kevenhörster, Prof. dr P.K.
PolS

Klenner, Prof. Dr Wolfgang
DevS, Eco

Klotz, Drs S.
PolS, IR

Germany

Kohl , Prof. dr K.-H.
Rel, His, Ant

Kraus , Dr W.
AHis, Rel

Krause , Prof. E.D.
Lin

Krebs , Dr G.
Edu, His, PolS, IR

Krüger , Prof. dr H.
IR, Law, Rel, Soc, Eco

Kubitscheck , Prof. H.D.
His, Ant

Kuhnt-Saptodewo , Dr S.T.
AHis, Lin, Lit, Rel, CuS, GenS, Ant

Kulke , Prof. dr H.
His, Soc, Rel

Kummer , Dr M.E.F.
Psy, RelAgr, Phi, Soc, Lin, IR, Eco, His, Ant, PolS, Env, E

Laubscher , Prof. dr M.S.
Rel, Ant

Linder Sabine , Drs L.
Ant, Arch, Soc

Lobo , Dr W.
AHis, Ant, Arch

Lorenz , Prof. D.
Eco

Lummer , Drs E.
His, Ant, CuS, Lit

Machetzki , Dr R.
DevS, Eco, PolS

Mahdi , Ir W.
Lin

Martokusumo , Ir W.
Art

Menzel , Prof. U.
IR, PolS

Meyer-Tran , E.
DevS, Agr, His, Soc, Eco

Moeller , Dr K.
IR, PolS

Müller , K.
PolS, CuS, His

Müller , M.
His, AHis

Müller , Prof. J.
Soc, Rel, Phi, DevS, CuS, IR

Müller-Hofstede , Drs C.
PolS, Soc, His, IR, CuS, DevS

Nass , O.
Eco

Nothofer , Prof. dr B.
Ant, Lit, Lin, CuS

Pampusé Philé , Dr K.H.
CuS, Lin

Partecke , M.P.
Ant, Lin, Rel

Partenheimer-Bein , A.
His

Pink , Prof. P.
Rel, Phi, Lit

Platenkamp , Prof. dr J.D.M.
CuS, Soc, Ant, Rel

Probojo , Dr L.
Soc

Ramstedt , Drs M.
Ant, Rel, CuS, PolS, Lit

Rein , Dr A.
Ant, CuS, GenS, Rel

Rieger , Dr H.C.
DevS, Env, Eco

Rieländer , Drs K.
Eco, Ant, CuS, Soc

Rohde , Prof. dr K.E.
Soc, Eco, Env, DevS, CuS, IR

Rohdewohld , R.
PolS, Eco, IR, DevS

Roth , Dr R.B.
CuS, His

Rueland , Prof. dr J.
IR, PolS, DevS

Rutz , Prof. dr W.
Env, CuS, Eco, His

Sauerborn , Prof. J.
Agr, Env

Schiel , Dr T.
Soc, His, Ant, Agr, Env, DevS, PolS

Schlicher , Dr M.
His, PolS, IR

Schmidt , H.C.
Ant, Lin

Schnepp , Drs Th.
AntAnt, CuS

Schrader , Dr H.
Soc, Eco, Ant, CuS

Schreiner , Prof. dr L.
Rel, Ant, His

Schröter , Dr S.
Ant

Schulze , Dr F.
His, CuS, Rel, Lit

Schumacher , Prof. R.
Part

Schweinfurth , Prof. dr U.
Agr, DevS, Env, Arch, IR

Schwinghammer , Drs E.
DevS, Eco, CuS, His

Seltmann , Dr F.M.
CuS

Sibeth , Drs A.F.
Ant

Simon , Prof. dr A.
AntAnt

Sitohang-Nababan , Drs E.L.M.
Lin

Stiller , Dr D.F.R.
Law

Strassner , Dr R.
PolS, Psy, IR, CuS, Rel, Soc

Toda , Drs D.N.
CuS, Lit

Wandelt , Dr I.
Edu, Lin

Warnk , Drs H.
His, Ant

Wassmann , Prof. dr J.
Ant

Wessel , Prof. I.W.
His, PolS

Wichmann , Drs P.
IR, PolS

Zimmermann , Dr G.R.
Geo

Germay

Houben , Dr V.J.H.
His

Hungary

Ehrlich , Prof. E.
Eco, DevS

Indonesia

Hendrawan , Drs S.
DevS, PolS

Italy

Citro , M
CuS, Lit

Conti , Dr G.
Lin, Rel, Law

dell'Anglese , Dr E.
PolS, Env, Geo

Giambelli , Dr R.A.
Soc, Ant,

Gianto , Prof. A.
Lin, Rel

Marinelli , Dr M.M.
His, IR, PolS, DevS

Masala , F.
Edu

McVey , Dr R.T.
PolS, His

Nalesini MA, Oscar
Arch

Radicchi , Prof. dr A.
Lin, Lit, Rel

Rispoli , Dr F.
Ant, Arch

Sandra , Prof. D.E.E.
Ant, CuS, Edu, GenS

Santa Maria , Prof. dr L.
Lit, Lin, IR, His

Scarduelli , P.
Ant

Snellgrove , Prof. D.
AHis, Rel, Arch, His

Soenoto Rivai , S.F.
Lin, Lit, GenS

Volpi , G.
PolS, IR, Agr, Eco, Env

Malaysia

Wahab Ali, Prof. dr A.
Lit

Netherlands

Aelst, Drs A. van
His

Ammerlaan, Drs R.P.J.
Lit, Rel, Lin, Law, Psy

Angerler, Drs J.
His, Ant

Anrooy, Drs F. van
His

Arens, Drs J.F.
Lit, His, CuS

Arnoldus-Schröder, Drs V.
Edu, Ant, CuS

Arps, Prof. dr B.
Lit, Lin, CuS

Asselbergs, Drs G.
Agr, Eco, Edu

Atman, Dr R.E.
DevS

Attema, Drs Y.
AHis, CuS, His

Baak, Dr P.
PolS, His, Soc, Eco, Agr

Baardewijk, Drs F.G. van
Agr, Eco, His, Soc

Baas, Prof. dr P.
Env

Bakels, Drs J.
AHis, Ant

Bakker, Dr F.L.
Rel

Bakker, Drs M.E.
Lit

Barend-van Haeften, Dr M.L.
Lit

Barendregt, Drs B.A.
AntAnt

Barends, F.
Agr, Phi, His, AHis, Rel, Law, IR, His, Edu, Arch, Ant, CuS,

Bastiaansen, Drs A.C.G.M.
IR, Eco, Edu

Beck, Prof. dr H.L.
Rel

Bedner, Mr A.W.
Soc, Law

Beek, Drs J.E.F. ter
Lit, Lin

Beek, Mr T.J. van
PolS, IR

Beije, Drs C.F.
Lin

Bellen, Drs M.W.
His, AHis

Benda Beckmann, Mr dr K. von
Law, Env, Ant

Benda Beckmann, Prof. dr F. von
DevS, Law, Ant

Berge, Dr T. v.d.
PolS, Lit, His

Bergink, Drs D.
Rel, Psy, Lin, His, Edu, Ant, GenS, CuS

Beukers, Prof. dr H.
His

Bhattacharya, Dr B.
His

Biervliet, Drs W.E.
Edu

Bloembergen, M.
His

Blussé, Dr J.L.
IR, His

Boelaars, Dr H.J.W.M.
Soc, Rel

Boelaars, Dr J.H.M.C.
Rel, Ant

Boele van Hensbroek, P.
Law, Eco

Boelhouwer, R.H.
Eco, Lit, IR

Boender, Dr C.J.B.
Soc, Law, Env

Boer, E. de
Soc, Ant, CuS

Boeren, Drs A.J.J.M.
Edu, Ant

Bogaerts, Drs E.M.
Phi, IR, AHis, Rel, Lit, Lin, His, Ant

Boin, Drs M.M.O.
His

Boomgaard, Prof. dr P.
His, Env

Bootsma, Dr N.A.
His, IR

Borkent, Drs H.
Ant, Soc

Bosma, Drs U.T.
His

Brakel, Drs J.H. van
His, AHis, Arch, Ant

Brantas, Drs G.C.
Lit, His

Bras, Drs C.H.
Ant

Bree, D.M. de
CuS

Breman, Prof. dr J.C.
DevS, His, Eco, Ant, Soc

Brinke, Ir H.W. ten
Agr, Edu

Brinks, Drs H.
His

Brommer, A.B.
Eco, CuS, His

Brug, Ir dr P.J. van der
His

Bruggraaff, Drs W.
His

Bruijn, E.J. de
His

Bruijn, Drs I.D.R.
His

Bruijn, Prof. dr J.R.
His

Bruin, Ir D. de
DevS, Env

Bruinessen, Dr M.M. van
Rel, His, Ant

Buddingh, P.
Edu

Bunder, Drs M.A.
His

Burght, Prof. dr Gr.
Law

Buyze, Drs A.
AHis, Ant, Rel, Lit, CuS, IR

Campo, Dr J.N.F.M. A'
IR, PolS, His

Captain, Drs E.S.J.
IR, His, GenS

Casparis, Prof. dr J.G. de
AHis, Rel, His, Arch, His

Chan, Drs Y.W.F.
PolS, GenS, Ant, Lit, His

Chou, Dr C.
Ant

Christiaans, P.A.
His

Chutiwongs, Dr N.
Rel, His, Arch, AHis

Clason, Prof. dr A.T.
DevS

Claver, Drs A.
His

Colombijn, Dr F.
Soc, Env, Ant, His

Courtens, Drs I.A.M.
GenS, Ant

Cowan, Drs F.M.
GenS, DevS, CuS, Ant, Env, LinAgr

Crince le Roy, E.A.W.
DevS, AHis, Edu

Dahles, Dr H.
Ant, CuS

Dalen, Prof. J.Chr. van
DevS, Edu, Soc, Eco, IR, PolS, Env

Dam, Dr J.E. van

Darma Palguna, Drs I.B.M.
Lit

Deelstra, T.
Env

Delden, Drs M.C. van
Ant, His, Soc

Netherlands

Derks, Dr W.A.G.
Lit

Derveld, Dr F.E.R.
Eco

Dijk, Drs T. van
His, Rel, AHis, Ant

Dijk, Prof. dr C. van
His, Rel

Dijksterhuis, C.
GenS, Ant, CuS, Soc

Dijkstra, Drs G.H.
Soc, Rel, Phi, Eco, His, IR, Psy, PolS

Dirkzwager, Drs M.H.
Ant

Djajadiningrat-Nieuwenhuis, Drs M.
His, GenS, Ant, IR

Djajasoebrata, Drs A.M.L.R.
Ant, AHis

Djumaini, Dr M.
PolS, Law

Doderlein de Win, E.F.
Law, IR, Edu, Eco, Agr, DevS

Doel, Dr H.W. van den
His

Dol, Drs P.H.
Lin

Domenig, Ir G.
Rel

Dongen, Drs A.M. van
Ant

Donkers, J.K.J.
AHis, Ant, Arch

Doop, J.V.
Lin

Douwes, Dr D.
His, Rel

Drooglever, Prof. dr P.J.
PolS, IR, His

Dubbeldam, Prof. dr L.F.B.
Ant, Edu

Duermeijer, Ir A.J.
AHis, Arch, DevS

Dumas, Drs R.M.
PArt, Lit, CuS

Dusseldorp, D.B.W.M. van
Ant, Agr, DevS, PolS, Soc

Duuren, Drs D.A.P. van
Ant, CuS

Duyker, Drs M.
Arch

Eigenhuijsen, J.Th.N.
Eco

Eindhoven, Drs J.D.R.
IR

Eisma, Prof. dr D.
Env

Elands, Drs M.
IR, His

Elbers, Dr C.T.M.
Eco

Emmer, Prof. dr P.C.
His

Emst, Dr P. van
Ant, His

Engelenhoven, Dr A.Th.P.G. van
Lin

Enk, E.M.C. van
His

Ensering, Drs E.
Rel, His, Soc

Epskamp, Dr C.P.
AHis, Ant

Erpecum, I.L. van
Lit, Law, CuS, AHis

Erve, Dr H.J. van der
Ant, Soc

Es, Dr A.J.H. van
Agr

Eyck van Heslinga, Dr E.S. van
His

Fahner, Dr Chr.
Ant, Rel, Lin

Fasseur, Prof. dr C.
His

Fauzia, Drs A.
His

Feriyanto, F.
His, AHis

Frank, Drs E.
Eco, Soc

Gaastra, Dr F.S.
His

Gadiot, M.M.P.E.H.
Ant, AHis, GenS, Arch, His, IR, Psy, Soc, DevS

Galindo, Drs A.
Eco, GenS, DevS

Gall, Dr H.C.
His, Law

Gelder, Drs R. van
CuS, His, IR

Genugten, Drs Y.A. van
Lin, Lit

Giel, Mr P.
Env, DevS

Giesbers, Dr H.W.M.
Edu, Lin

Ginkel, Prof. dr J.A. van
Geo, DevS

Goderbauer, Drs J.P.L.
PolS

Goes, Drs B.A. van der
Ant

Gomperts, Drs A.T.
AHis

Gontscharoff, C.
IR, DevS

Goor, Dr J. van
His, IR

Gooszen, Dr A.J.
His, Geo

Graaf, T. de
His

Graaff, Drs B.G.J. de
His, IR

Grijns, Dr C.D.
Lin

Groen, Prof. P.M.H.
His

Groenen, Drs I.G.M.E.
CuS

Groenendael, Dr Clara van
Ant, Rel, Lin

Groot, W.T. de
Env, Ant, DevS

Groot, Drs H.U. de
Rel, Lin, Lit

Gunawan, Dr B.
His, Soc, DevS

Habiboe, Drs R.R.F.
His

Haitsma, T.J.
IR

Halsema, W.B. van
Rel

Hamelink, Prof. dr C.J.
IR, Law

Hanssen, Drs L.M.
Ant, CuS

Haringhuizen, Drs W.
PolS, Ant, IR

Harsono, S.
Agr, GenS, Eco, DevS

Harst, Dr J.F. van der
Lit, Phi

Harteveld, Ir K.
Agr, Eco, IR, Soc, DevS

Hartkamp-Jonxis, Drs E.
His, AHis

Hartog, Dr A.P. den
Ant, DevS

Hartveld, Drs ing A.J.
Agr, Eco, DevS, Soc

Hartveldt, Dr D.
Lin

Heemst, Drs J.J.P. van
Eco

Heering, Drs E.L.
GenS, DevS

Heersink, Dr C.G.
His

Heij, Dr C.J.
Edu, Env, DevS

Heinemeijer, Prof. dr W.F.
Env, Geo

Heins, Dr E.L.
Ant

Heins, Drs J.J.F.
Env, DevS

Netherlands

Heller, Y.J.
Rel, CuS, His, AHis

Hengel, Drs A. van
Eco, IR

Henley, Dr D.E.F.
Geo, His

Heringa, R.
Rel, His, Ant

Hermens, B.
Agr, Env, IR

Herst, Drs D.
His, GenSAHis

Heuvel, Ing T. van den
Agr

Heuven, Dr V.J.J.P. van
Lin

Hinzler, Dr H.I.R.
Lit, Arch, AHis, Ant

Hisyam, Drs M.
Soc, Rel, His

Hitipeuw-Palyama, E.J.
Ant, Lit, Edu

Hoebink, Dr P.R.J.
DevS, PolS, CuS

Hoefnagels, Ir H.A.M.
Agr, Eco, Law

Hoeij Schilthoven Pompe, Mr S.
Law

Hoek, Drs A. van der
Rel

Hoekema, Dr A.G.
Rel

Hoekstra, Drs H.F.M.F.
Ant

Hoffmanns, Drs P.R.
AHis, Arch

Holtrot, Prof. D.N.
CuS, Ant, His, Lit, Rel, Phi

Holzner, Dr B.M.
GenS, Psy, DevS

Hommes, Prof. dr E.W.
DevS, Ant

Hoogerbrugge, J.
AHis, CuS

Hoogland, Drs J.G.D.
Eco, DevS, Env

Horn, Drs N.A. van
His, Eco

Hospes, Dr ir O.
Soc

Hout, Drs I.C. van
Rel, CuS, CuS, Ant

Hudcovicova, A.
CuS

Hugenholtz, Drs W.R.
His

Huisman, Dr H.
Geo, DevS

Huizer, Prof. dr G.J.
Rel, IR, Env, DevS

Huizinga, Drs F.
His

Hulst, W.A.
Eco

Hüsken, Prof. dr F.A.M.
DevS, Ant, His

Huyser, Drs G.L.J.
IR

Hylkema, S.
Rel, Ant, Lin

IJiri, Drs Y.
Rel, AHis, Phi, CuS

Indro Nugroho-Heins, Drs M.
PArt, His, Ant

Iongh, Ir H.H. de
Env

Ishaja, Drs F.A.
His

Jaarsma, Dr S.R.
Ant

Jacobs, Drs E.M.
His

Jager, Drs Y.M. de
Lit

James, Dr J.
DevS, Eco

Jansen, Drs T.E.
DevS, GenS, His

Jaquet, Drs F.G.P.
His

Jehle, Dr E.
IR, DevS, Eco, Edu, Law

Jelsma, Drs J.
Arch

Jong, Dr C.G.F. de
Rel, His

Jong, Dr J. de
CuS, IR, His

Jong, Dr J.J.P. de
IR, His

Jong, Dr S.C.N. de
CuS, DevS

Jong, Drs A.H.
His, GenS

Jong Boers, Drs B.D. de
Ant, His

Jonge, Dr H.M.C. de
Ant, DevS

Jonge, Drs ing J.D. de
Soc, Agr

Jonge, Drs N.C. de
Soc, Rel, Ant, His, AHis

Jongeling, Dr M.C.
Rel, His, GenS, Ant

Jordaan, Dr R.E.
His, AHis, Ant, Arch

Josselin de Jong, Prof. dr P.E. de
Ant

Jung, Drs J.I.
Edu, His, Lin, CuS

Kal, Drs W.H.
Env, Lin, DevS, Agr, CuS, Ant, CuS, GenS

Kamp, E.P. van der
His

Kaptein, Dr N.J.G.
Rel

Kardinaal, Drs A.H.
His, PolS, IR

Karssen, Dr C.M.
DevS, Env, Agr, Eco, Edu, Soc, GenS

Kater, Dr A.
Ant, DevS

Kemner, Ir R.
CuS, His

Kempen, M. van
Ant, Rel, CuS

Keppy, Drs P.J.
His, Ant

Kessel-Hagesteijn, Dr R.R. van
His, Ant

Kester, Drs J.J. van
DevS, GenS, Ant, Rel, Soc

Keurs, Dr P.J. ter
Ant, CuS, His, AHis

Klamer, Dr M.A.F.
Lin

Klein, Prof. dr P.W.
His

Klokke, Dr A.H.
Lin, Rel

Klokke, Dr M.J.
Arch

Klooster, Dr H.A.J.
His

Klugkist, Drs C.W.
Edu, CuS, His

Knaap, Dr G.J.
His

Knapen, Drs J.J.
Ant, His, Env

Knorringa, Dr P.
Eco, DevS

Koesoebjono, R.H.S.I.
DevS, GenS, Eco

Koesoebjono-Sarwono, Dr S.
DevS, Psy, Soc, GenS, Ant

Kok, Drs J.T. van de
His, Ant, CuS

Kol, Prof. dr J.
DevS, Eco, Agr

Koning, Dr J.B.M.
GenS, Ant

Koolen, Dr G.M.J.M.
Edu, CuS, His, Rel

Koolhof, Drs S.
Lit, Lin

Kouwen, H.J.
His, IR, DevS, Ant

Kretzschmar, A.E.
His

Netherlands

Krijnen, Drs H.G.
Eco

Kroes, Drs G.C.
Ant, Rel

Kruijswijk, M.F.
AHis, CuS, His

Kruip, Drs D.
Ant

Kusin, Prof. dr J.A.
GenS

Kuypers, Drs S.A.M.
Soc, Ant

Kuyvenhoven, Prof. dr A.
DevS, Eco

Kwee, Ir H.G.
Art

Laar, Dr A.J.M. van de
Eco, DevS

Lammerts van Bueren, Dr E.M.
Eco, Env, Soc

Lancee, Mr L.E.
Law

Lange, Drs ir Ph.G. de
Env, Ant

Laseur, Dr W.J.J.
DevS

Lautenbach, Drs H.
His

Lawson, Drs Y.B.
Soc, Ant, IR

Lieshout, Ir M. van
Agr

Ligthart, Drs M.J.H.M.
Env, PolS, DevS

Linck, Drs F.C.
Ant

Lindblad, Dr J.T.
His, Eco

Lindhoud, Drs P.C.
His

Lingen, Ing J.
His

Linn, Drs R.E.
His, PolS, DevS, Soc

Linschooten, Drs R.
IR, PolS, Lin, CuS, Eco, His

Litamahuputty, Drs B.H.J.
Lin

Locher-Scholten, Dr E.B.
IR, GenS, His

Loop, Dr T.H.M. van der
Env, DevS, Eco

Lopez, Drs S.
CuS, His, AHis

Loven, Drs K.
Lit

Lucardie, Drs G.R.E.
Ant, DevS

Lunsingh Scheurleer, Drs P.
AHis, Arch

Luttik, Drs J.
His

Maan, Drs E.E.
Soc, DevS

Mackay, Drs C.H.
Ant, His, IR

Maier, Prof. dr H.M.J.
Lit

Maing-van der Werff, Drs H.I.
GenS, Ant

Malcontent, Drs P.A.M.
His

Manschot, Drs E.B.
PolS, Eco

Manuhutu, Drs W. Chr.
His

Manurung-Boekhoudt, C.M.A.
Ant

Marey, A.J.F.
Rel, Law

Massier, Drs A.W.H.
DevS, Lin, Law, His

Maters, Drs M.J.
His

Meer, N.J. van der
His

Meer, Dr ir C.L.J. van der
DevS, Agr

Meij, Drs Th. C. van der
Lit, His, AHis, Lin

Meij, Prof. J.M. de
His, Law

Meijer, Dr H.
IR, His

Meijs, Drs M.A.G.
IR, Rel, Ant, CuS

Meiracker, Drs C.H. van den
Ant

Menick, Drs R.H.
Lin

Mensink, Drs O.H.
AHis, Ant, CuS, His

Messing, Mr A.J.
Law

Meuldijk, Drs I.M.
Soc, Agr, GenS, Env, Ant, DevS

Meulenbeld, Drs B.C.
CuS, His, Ant, AHis, Rel, Arch

Miedema, Dr J.
CuS, Rel, His, Ant, DevS, Soc

Miedema, Drs B.J.
DevS, Eco, Agr

Miert, Dr H. van
His

Mijn, Ir F.E. van der
DevS, Env

Minde, Dr D. van
Lin

Minnee, Drs P.
CuS, IR, Eco, Edu

Minnigh, Ir P.E.
DevS, Env

Molen, Dr W. van der
Lit

Moll, Dr Ir. H.A.J.
Eco, Agr

Moltzer, Drs R.
Ant

Montyn, J.
Phi, AHis, CuS, Lit

Moor, Drs J.A. de
His

Muijzenberg, Prof. dr O.D. van den
Soc, DevS, Ant, His

Mulder, Dr N.
Soc, Ant

Müller, Drs B.
Ant, GenS

Muller, Drs H
His, Rel

Nadal Uceda, F. de
Ant, Arch, Lin, Phi, Psy, Rel

Nagtegaal, Dr L.W.
His, Env

Nas, Dr P.J.M.
Ant, DevS, Soc

Neve, Drs R.G. de
His

Niehof, Prof. dr A.
Ant, Soc

Niemeijer, Drs H.E.
Rel, His

Niemöller, Dr B.
Rel, His

Niessen, Mr N.J.A.P.B.
Law, DevS

Nieuwenhuijze, Prof. dr C.A.O. van
Rel, Soc, DevS, CuS

Nijs, Drs C.F. de
Lin, Lit

Nolten, Drs H.M.
GenS, Geo

Nooy, Drs C.I.
PolS, Env, IR, DevS

Odé, Dr C.
Lin

Olden, Drs J.F. van
Ant, Law

Ommen, Drs A.F. van
IR, PolS

Oosterhout, Drs D.W.J.H. van
Ant

Oosterwijk, A.J.
His, Ant, Arch

Opgenort, Drs J.R.M.L.
Lin

Otto, Dr J.M.
DevS, Law, Env

Netherlands

Ouden, Dr J.H.B. den
DevS, Ant, Agr, GenS

Oudheusden, Drs O.M.
His

Overweel, Drs J.A.
DevS, His

Paasman, Dr A.N.
Lit

Pasch, Drs J.P.M. van der
Lin, Lit

Pasveer, Drs J.M.
Arch

Patmo, Drs S.
Edu, Soc, Ant, DevS

Pattiruhu, M.
Lan

Peeters, Dr J.C.M.
His

Persoon, Dr G.A.
DevS, Ant, Env

Peters, Drs F.H.
DevS, His

Plantema, Drs E.P.
Lin, CuS

Ploeg, Dr A.
Ant

Plomp, Drs M.
Lit

Pluvier, Dr J.M.
His, DevS, IR

Poeze, Dr H.A.
His, PolS, IR

Politon, S.
AHis, Arch, Phi, Lin, CuS, His, Rel

Pollmann-Schlichting, Drs M.T.
Ant, His, Lit

Pompe, Dr J.H.
PolS, DevS, Env, IR, Agr, Ant, Eco, Soc, CuS, Edu, Phi, Law,

Pompe, Mr S.
Law

Poortinga, Dr F.H.
Psy

Portier, Dr M.K.
Ant, Law

Post, Dr P
IR, Ant, His

Postel-Coster, Prof. dr E.
DevS, Ant, GenS

Pouwer, Prof. dr J.
Ant

Prchal, Drs M.
PolS, His, Rel

Prince, Drs G.H.A.
His

Prins, Prof. dr H.H.T.
Env

Promés, Drs H.J.A.
His, Lin, Rel, LitAnt

Put, Drs M.
Agr, Env, Soc, DevS

Putten, Drs F.P. van der
His, IR, PolS, Eco

Putten, Drs J. van der
Lin, His

Raben, Dr R.
His, Ant

Rahman, Drs S.
CuS

Ras, Prof. dr J.J.
Lit

Reenen, Dr J.H. van
GenS, Ant

Reijnders, Drs T.
AHis

Rengkung, E.
Lin, Lit

Reynders, Dr ir J.J.
Agr, Arch, DevS, Env

Rheeden, Drs H.A. van
Lin

Ridder, Ir J.M.
Eco, DevS, Ant, IR, Soc

Riel, Drs P.H. van
Ant

Riel-Lamers, Drs G.M.P. van
His, Ant, Rel

Rienks, Drs A.S.
Ant, DevS

Rinsampessy, Dr E.P.
Ant, Soc, Rel, IR, Edu

Robson-McKillop, Drs R.L.
Ant, Rel, Arch

Roelofs, Drs J.D.
Soc, GenS, DevS

Roodenburg, C.
Eco, IR, Lin, Soc

Roosmalen, Drs P.K.M. van
His, AHis

Roskam, R.E.
Lin, Lit

Roth, Drs D.
Soc, PolSAgr, DevS, Ant

Rox, Drs L.
His, Lin

Ruben, Drs R.
Agr, Eco, Env

Rueb, Drs P.D.
His

Ruiter, Drs T.G.
Agr, Soc, Eco, DevS, His, Ant

Rutten, Dr M.A.F.
Ant, Soc

Ruygrok, Drs W.F.
His, PolS, Soc

Saane, Drs P.A. van
Lin

Sandee, Drs H.M.
DevS, Eco

Sanders, Drs M.
DevS, Eco

Santoso, Drs S.
AHis, IR, His, PolS, His

Saptari, Dr R.
DevS, Ant, Soc

Scalliet, Dr M.O.
His, AHis, Arch, CuS

Schäfer, Drs E.S.
His, Eco, IR, CuS

Schefold, Prof. dr R.
Ant

Scheltema, Prof. mr M.
Law

Schenk, Dr H.
DevS, Env

Schilt, J.W.
His, IR

Schippers, Dr H.
His

Schmit, Dr L.T.
Ant

Schoch, Drs G.W.
Eco

Schoor, Drs W.J. van der
His

Schoorl, Prof. dr J.W.
DevS, Ant

Schoot, Dr H.A. van der
DevS, Eco

Schouten, Drs P.H.
Ant, Soc

Schouw, Drs M.H. van der
AHis, Arch, CuS, His

Schreuel, Drs E.J.
DevS, Eco

Schulte Nordholt, Dr H.G.C.
Soc, His, Ant

Schulte Nordholt, Dr N.G.
DevS, PolS, Env

Schutte, Prof. dr G.J.
His

Schwidder, Drs L.E.G.
His

Segers, Drs W.A.I.M.
His

Seret, Mr A.
Phi, Lit, Lin, Rel, CuS

Sigmond, Dr J.P.
CuS, His, AHis, Arch

Sijmonsbergen, Drs J.
His

Singh, Dr N.
Agr, Env, DevS, Soc, IR

Sinnema, Drs T.
GenS, CuS, Soc, His, Edu

Siregar, Drs T.M.
PolS, Eco, Agr

Slaats, Dr Mr H.M.C.
DevS, Law

Slamet-Velsink, Dr I.E.
Ant

ASIANISTS BY REGION AND COUNTRY OF INTEREST

Netherlands

Slikkerveer, Dr L.J.
Ant, Agr, DevS

Slob, Drs J.
Rel

Smeets, Drs H.M.A.G.
His

Smidt, Prof. dr J.
Eco

Smit, Drs T.S.
Lin

Smit, Prof. ir K.
Lin

Smits, Drs L.
CuS, Ant, Rel, Lin, His

Sodderland, Mr J.W.
Law

Soffner, U.A.
His, Lin

Son, Drs T. van
Law, Lit, Lin, Env

Spaan, Drs E.J.A.M.
Ant

Spanjaard, Drs H.
His, AHis

Speckmann, Prof. dr J.D.
Ant, Soc

Spee, Drs M.H.
AHis, Ant

Spiekerman-Middelplaats, M.Y.M.
Env

Spiertz, Mr H.L.J.
DevS, Law

Spit, W.J.L.
His, Rel, CuS

Staat, Drs D.W.
His, Ant

Staden, Drs M. van
Lin

Stam, Prof. dr J.A.
DevS, Eco, IR

Steenbrink, Dr K.A.
Rel

Steijlen, Drs G.I.J.
Ant

Steinhauer, Dr H.
Lin, Ant

Stel, Dr J.H.
Env, Eco

Sterk, Drs R.A.
Soc, PolS, Psy

Stoel, R.B.
Lin

Stokhof, Prof. dr W.A.L.
Lit, Lin

Stolk, M.D.
CuS, Psy, Soc, Rel

Straten, Mr H.M. van
Env, Ant, Law

Streef, E.
Env, Law, Ant

Sudrajat, Drs A.
Soc, His

Sukrisno, Drs A.
Ant, His, PolS

Supriyanto, Drs I.
CuS, Lin, Lit

Supriyanto-Breur, Drs C.A.
Law

Suringa, Mr P.
Law, AHis, Lit, IR, His, Phi, His, Edu, CuS, DevS, Eco, PolS

Sutedja-Liem, Drs H.T.
Lit, Lin

Sutherland, Prof. dr H.A.
CuS, His, Ant

Suwondo, Drs K.
DevS, Agr, Ant

Tahitu, Dr E.
Edu, Lin

Taselaar, Drs A.P.
His

Teensma, Dr B.N.
His

Teerlink, Ir J.
DevS

Teeuw, Prof. dr A.
Lit, Lin, CuS

Teillers, A.F.
CuS, Lin

Teljeur, Dr D.
Ant

Termorshuizen, Dr G.P.A.
Lit, His

Termorshuizen-Arts, Drs M.J.H.W.
Law

Teygeler, Drs R.
Ant, CuS, Lit

Thoonen, Drs A.A.M.
Rel, GenS, Ant

Thung, Prof. dr P.J.
Phi

Tichelman, Dr F.
His

Tiemersma, Dr D.
Phi, Rel

Timmer, Drs J.
Soc, Ant, DevS, CuS

Tims, Prof. dr W.
Eco, Agr, DevS

Titus, Dr M.J.
Geo

Tjon Pian Gi, W.L.
His

Tjwan, Dr G.G.
His

Tol, Dr R.G.
Lit, Lin

Tollenaere, Dr H.A.O. de
His, PolS, Rel

Touwen, Drs L.J.
His, Eco

Touwen-Bouwsma, Dr E.
His, Ant

Treu-Dijkman, S.M.G.
Lin, DevS, Edu

Trouwborst, Prof. dr A.A.
Ant

Ubaghs, Drs J.M.M.
CuS, His

Uhlenbeck, Prof. dr E.M.
Lin

Vaczi, Drs M.T.
Rel, AHis, GenS, CuS

Veen, Drs M.H.E. van der
His, DevS

Veenkamp, Drs C.B.W.
His, CuS

Veerdonk, Drs J.A.L.B. van den
Lin, Arch, Lit

Veering, Drs A.J.A.
Eco, His

Veggel, Drs C.J. van
His, Eco

Velde, Drs P.G.E.I.J. van der
Lit, His

Velzen, Dr A. van
Ant, DevS, GenS

Velzen, Dr J.H. van
GenS, Ant, DevS

Velzen, Drs P.F. van
CuS, Lin

Ven, Drs J.W. van de
Env, Agr, Ant, Law

Verbeek, H.R.
CuS, GenS

Verbruggen, Prof. dr H.
Env, Eco, IR

Verhaar, Dr J.W.M.
Lin, Phi

Verhaar, Drs P.
His, IR, Lit, Lin

Verhoef, Ing J.C.
His

Vermeulen, Drs A.C.J.
His

Verschoor, I.B.
His, Phi, CuS, PolS, Eco

Vervliet, Drs J.B.
His, Eco

Verzijlbergen, Drs H.E.
His, GenS, Ant

Vischer, Dr M.P.
Ant, His, Rel

Visscher, Drs S.
PolS, Soc, His

Visser, Dr L.E.
DevS, Ant

Vogel, Dr J.
His

ASIANISTS BY REGION AND COUNTRY OF INTEREST

Netherlands

Vonck , Drs H.M.
Part

Voogt , Drs P.R.
Ant

Voorhoeve , Dr C.L.
DevS, Lin

Vos , Drs M.L.
PolS

Voskuil , Dr J.E.
Lin

Vreede-de Stuers , Dr S.C.L.
Ant

Vries , Drs I. de
AHis, Rel, GenS, Ant

Vries , Prof. dr J.W. de
Lin

Vries , Prof. dr L.J. de
Lin

Vries Robbé , A. de
Arch, His, Ant, AHis

Vruggink , Drs H.D.
Lin

Waals , Drs J.D. van der
His, CuS, His, AHis

Wagenaar , Dr L.J.
His

Wasia-Kuipers , Drs J.B.
Ant

Welling , Drs K.O.H.
Art

Welzen , Drs K.F.
Psy

Werkman , Drs P.E.
PolS, IR, His, Edu

Wertheim , Prof. dr W.F.
Soc, His

Wery , Prof. mr P.L.
Law

Wesselius , Drs J.
Lin, His

Wessing , Dr R.
Ant

Westerkamp , Drs W.
Ant, Arch

Westermann , Drs R.
AHis, CuS, Eco

White , Prof. dr B.N.F.
Soc, DevS, Ant, POPULATION

Wichelen , Drs C.B.J. van
Soc, Phi, Ant, DevS, Rel

Wiechen , P.J. van
AHis, CuS, Ant, Arch, His

Wiegmans , Drs B.W.
Eco

Wiel , A.N. van der
His, AHis, Arch

Wieringa , Dr E.P.
Lit

Wieringa , Dr S.E.
GenS, DevS

Wigboldus , Ir J.S.
Agr, His

Winarta , Drs E.
Ant, Lit

Witkam , Dr J.J.
His, Rel, Lit

Woelders , Dr M.O.
Lit

Wolffers , Prof. dr I
DevS

Wolters , Dr W.G.
Ant, DevS

Wolvekamp , Drs P.S.
Agr, IR, DevS, Env, GenS

Wongsomenggolo , Drs S.
Soc, His, Ant

Wouden , Drs A.A. van der
DevS

Yperen , Dr M.I.L.
Eco, IR

Zanden , Drs T.A.M. van der
His, CuS

Zanten , Dr E.A. van
His

Zanten , Dr W. van
PArtAnt

Zeeuw , D. de
Env, Agr

Zevalkink , Drs J.
Ant, Psy

Zijlmans , Dr G.C.
Soc, His

Zomer , Drs H.
IR, Eco, CuS

Zuiderhoek , Dr B.
His

Zuiderweg , Drs A.
His, AHis, CuS, GenS, His, Rel, Lit

Zwijnenburg , Ph.A.
His

Norway

Barth , Dr F.
DevS, Ant

Bergersen , A.
GenS

Br†ten , E.
Ant, CuS

Broch , Dr H.B.B.
Psy, CuS, Ant

Grotterud MA, Kari
Ant, Rel

Hiorth , Dr F.
Soc, Rel, Phi

Holm , S.
GenS, Ant, CuS

Johansen , Prof. dr O.K.
Arch

Lie , Prof. R.K.
Phi, DevS

Munthe , Prof. L.
CuS, His, Rel

Smedal , Dr O.H.
Ant

Vikír , Prof. L.S.
Lin

Philippines

Berg , Dr E. van den
Edu

Poland

Goralski , Prof. dr
PolS, His, IR

Kulig , Prof. J.
Eco, IR

Lukaszuk , Dr L.B.
Law, Eco, IR, DevS

Wawrzyniak , Dr A.
CuS, Ant

Portugal

Lobato , Dr M.L.M.
His

Mira Borges , M.C.
His

Pinto de Sousa , P.J.C.
His

Santos Alves , Dr J.M.
His

Schouten , Dr M.J.C.
His, Ant

Veiga , M.
Law

Russia

Alleva , Dr N.F.
Lin, Lit

Bandilenko , Dr G.G.
AHis, CuS, Ant, His

Boitsov , Dr V.V.
DevS, Eco, Geo, IR

Cherepnyova , Dr E.A.
His, PolS

Chufrin , Dr G.I.
IR, Eco

Demidioek , Dr L.N.
Lin

Demidiuk , Dr L.N.
Lin

Demin , L.M.
His, AHis

Deopik , D.V.
Arch, CuS, Rel, Ant, His

Dorofeeva , Dr T.V.
Edu, Lin

Drugov , Dr A.Y.
PolS, IR

Efimova , Prof. L.
His, Rel, PolS

Golubeva , Dr H.
PolS

Ilyushenkó , V.I.
His

Kondrashkina , Dr E.A.
Lin

Russia

Kozlov, Dr A.A.
His, Eco

Kullanda, Dr S.V.
His, Lin

Lostragine, Mr V.N.
Lin, His

Makarenko, Prof. dr V.A.
Lin, Lit, His, Ant, Edu, CuS, Rel

Nikulina, Dr L.V.
DevS, CuS, Ant, Env, Edu, His, Rel, Arch

Ogloblin, Prof. A.K.
Lin

Parnickel, Prof. dr B.B.
Lit

Parnikel, Dr B.B.
Lit

Pogadaev, Dr V.
His, CuS

Rogojine, Dr A.
Env, Eco, IR, DevS

Roudenko, Drs E.
Lin, CuS, Lit

Sirk, Dr S.
Lin

Smourova, Dr N.M.
Lit

Smurowa, Dr N.M.
Lit

Soboleva, Dr E.S.
Rel, His, Ant, AHis

Solomonik, Dr I.N.
His, AHis

Tesselkine, Dr A.S.
Ant, AHis, Lin, His, CuS

Tumarkin, Prof. dr D.D.
CuS, DevS, Arch, Eco, His, Ant

Zakaznikova, Dr Y.P.
DevS, Soc, PolS, His

Spain

Bustelo, Dr P.
DevS, Eco

Canto, Dr P.
DevS, IR, Eco

Elías de Tejada Lozano, Diplomat F.
Eco, Lit, PolS

Fernández-Shaw Baldasano, C.M.

Garcia-Ormaechea Quero, C.
AHis, Geo, His, Lit, Rel, Phi

Gonzales de Orduña Criado, Silvia
DevS

Gouzalez Molina, A.
IR, Soc

Jimenez Valentin, J.M.
Eco, Env, IR

Mas Murcia, A.
Eco

Mellen Blanco, F.
Ant, Arch, AHis, His

Navarro Celada, F.

Olalla Cuervo, MA I.
AHis

Picornell Marti, P.
Eco, Env, His

Rodríguez Ubeda, M.M.
Eco, IR, Soc

Sweden

Amer, Dr R.
IR, PolS, His

Aspengren, E.
Edu, His

Bratthall, Prof. D.
Eco

Cardholm, M.
IR

Hansson, E.
PolS

Hasselgren, J.H.
His, Rel

Hellmann, J.
Ant

Hoadley, Prof. dr M. C.
His

Huldt, Prof. B.
IR, His

Lundström-Burghoorn, Dr W.S.Y.M.C.
Ant, DevS, GenS

Myrman, Y.
PolS

Nelson, Drs E.N.
Ant

Törnquist, Dr C.O.
DevS, PolS

Uhlin, A.
PolS

Switzerland

Eeuwijk, Drs P. van
Ant

Ehrensperger, A.
Ant, Env

Galizia, Dr M.
Soc, PolS, Law, His, DevS, CuS

Hottinger, Prof. dr L.C.
IR, DevS, PolS

Jong, Dr W. de
Ant, GenS

Keck, Dr V.
Ant

Klausing, Andreas
IR, PolS, Soc

Leemann, Prof. dr A.
Agr, DevS, CuS

Lüem, B.
Ant, CuS

Lutz, P.
Eco, GenS, Env, Edu

Marschall, Prof. dr W.
Arch, Agr, Ant

Prodolliet, Dr S.
GenS, His, Ant

Schneider, Dr J.
Ant, Env, Agr

Schreiner, Dr K.H.
His, PolS, Rel

Tarnutzer, Dr A.
Ant, GenS, DevS

Viaro, Dr A.V.
Env, Ant, DevS

Waelty, Dr S.
Ant, Env, DevS

United Kingdom

Auty, Dr R.M.
DevS, Env, Eco

Barnes, Dr R.H.
Ant

Beatty, Dr A.W.
Ant

Berg, R. van den
Lin

Birkin, I.
Ant

Booth, Prof. A.E.
Agr, Eco, Edu, GenS, His, DevS

Braginsky, Prof. V.I.
Rel, Lit

Brown, Dr I.G.
His

Brown, Dr N.D.
Env

Bryant, Dr R.L.
Geo, PolS, DevS, Env

Carey, Dr P.B.R.
His, IR, CuS, Lit, Rel

Carter, Dr L.J.
His

Cedercreutz, S.J.T.
Ant

Chalmers, Dr M.
IR

Chapman, G.
His, AHis, CuS

Chin, Dr J.
PolS, DevS, His

Choi, D.-J.
PolS

Clarence-Smith, Dr W.G.
His

Cockburn, Mr R.C.
DevS, CuS

Coleman, Drs P.H.
Edu

Conway, Dr B.M.
Edu

Crosbie, Dr A.J.
IR, Env, Eco, Geo, DevS

United Kingdom
Davis, Drs C.E.
DevS, GenS, Ant
Ellen, Prof. R.F.
Env, Ant
Elliott, D.
AHis
Ferdinand, Drs C.I.P.
PolS, DevS, His, Eco, IR
Ford, Dr N.J.
Geo, GenS, DevS, CuS
Gallop, Drs A.T.
Lit, His, AHis
Gavin, Dr T.
Ant
Harding, Dr A.J.
Law, Env
Harris, Drs N.
DevS, Eco
Harriss, Dr J.C.
DevS, Ant
Hawthorn, Mr G.P.
IR, DevS, PolS
Hayward, Dr K.
Lin
Heng, J.W.M.
His, Arch, AHis
Herry-Priyono, B.
DevS, His, Phi, PolS
Hitchcock, Dr M.J.
Soc, Ant, DevS
Hobart, Dr P.M.
CuS, Ant
Howe, Dr L.E.A.
Ant
Hughes, Dr D.W.
Ant
Hughes-Freeland, Dr F.A.
Ant
Huxley, Dr T.J.
IR, PolS
Iyer, Dr A.
AHis, Arch
Jones, Dr R.
Lin, Lit, Rel
Jones, Mr S.C.
Eco, DevS
Kerloque, Drs F.G.
CuS
King, Prof. V.T.
DevS, Soc, Ant, Env
Kirkpatrick, Prof. C.H.
Env, Eco
Koktvedgaard Zeitzen, M.
Ant, Arch, GenS
Kratz, Dr E.U.
Lit, CuS
Lambourn, Dr E.A.
AHis, Arch
Lenman, Prof. B.P.
His
Maloney, Dr B.K.
Env
Marett, Dr P.
Rel, Law
Marr, Dr J.R.
Lin, His, CuS, Arch, His, Phi, Rel, AHis, Lit
Milton, Dr A.
Rel, PolS
Mürer, O.H.A.
Arch, His, AHis
Parikh, Prof. A.
Eco, DevS, Agr
Park, S.S.
Psy, PolS, Phi, SocAHis, DevS, Env, Edu, IR, Law
Parnwell, Dr M.J.G.
DevS, Env, Geo
Patty-Noach, Dr
Ant, GenS
Phillips, Dr N.G.
Lit, Lin
Picken, Dr L.E.R.
CuS
Plumbe, A.J.
DevS
Preston, Dr D.A.
Geo, Agr, DevS, Env
Pusey, Dr J.G.
Lin
Putzel, Drs J.J.
DevS, Env, PolS
Rigg, Dr J.D.
Geo, Env, Agr, DevS
Roberts, Drs D.C.
DevS, Eco, IR
Roper, Dr G.J.
CuS
Ryan, Dr J.T.
Eco
Salazar, Drs W.M.W.T.
His
Saltford, J.F.
IR
Salverda, Prof. R.
Lit, Law, Lin
Samely, Dr U.
Lin
Shepperdson, Mr M.J.
DevS, Agr, Eco, PolS, Soc
Slater, Dr R.P.
PolS, Ant, DevS, Eco
Smyth, Dr I.A.
GenS, DevS
Spooner, Prof. F.C.
Eco, His
Strickland, Dr S.S.
Ant
Taylor, Dr J.G.
Soc, DevS
Thambiah, S.
Ant
Thoburn, Dr J.T.
Eco
Valentin, J.C.P.
Env, Ant, CuS, Lin, His, Arch
Weller, Drs P.G.
Rel
Whitmore, Dr T.C.
Env
Wilder, Dr W.D.
GenS, DevS, Ant
Wisseman Christie, Prof. dr J.
Arch, His

United States of America
Setyawati,-Vayda, M.A.
Ant, Agr, Env, DevS

Yugoslavia
Furundzic, V.
Psy, Rel, Lit, Lin, Edu, His, Phi, AHis
Imamovic, E.
His, CuS, AHis

LAOS

Austria
Balzar, Dr D.M.
CuS, His, AHis
Sellner, Dr M.B.
CuS, Lin

Belgium
Adams, N.
GenS, His, DevS
Gonzalo Castellanos, Dr A.
IR

Denmark
Ewers, K.
Ant, Env, DevS
Ivarsson, Dr S.
His
Magnussen, Drs T.
DevS, IR, PolS
Sorensen, P.
Arch
Tönnesson, Dr S.
IR, His
Trier, Dr J.
Arch, Rel, Lin, Ant

Finland
Jokinen, Drs J.J.
DevS, IR, PolS
Rouhomäki, Drs O.
Ant
Seppänen, J.
IR, Eco, Ant, CuS, Lin, His, AHis, Phi, Arch, Rel, PolS

France
Barbiche, Prof. dr J.-P.
Law, IR, His, PolS, Eco, DevS, CuS, Edu, Soc

ASIANISTS BY REGION AND COUNTRY OF INTEREST

France

Bertrand, Dr D.
Psy, Rel, Ant

Bezançon, P.
Edu, His

Blayac, A.A.
Lit, His, Phi, Edu, Psy, Soc

Bompard, J.M
Agr, Env

Boudarel, G.
IR, PolS, CuS, His, Ant, GenS

Chagnaud, F.J.
Eco, Agr, Env, DevS

Choron-Baix, Dr C.
Ant, Rel

Clotte, M.
Lin

Crunelle, G.
Ant, Lit, Lin, Law, IR, Psy, Rel, Soc, Edu, PolS, Arch, His,

Dessaint, Prof. W.L.
Ant

Deuve, J.
His

Dore, A.
DevS, CuS, Ant

Dung, Drs T.T.
Rel, Lin, Edu, Ant, CuS

Ferlus, M.
Lin

Filliozat, J.
Rel, Lit

Fóray, Dr J.-C.
Lin, His

Formoso, Dr B.
Rel, Soc, Ant

Gay, B.
His

Gerbault, D.P.
CuS, Lin

Goscha, Chr.
His

Greck, F.
His

Hemery, Dr D.
His

Hemmet, Ch.
Ant

Henry, R.
Lin, GenS, Env, CuS, AHis, Arch, IR, Lit, Phi, Psy

Inthamone, L.
Lan

Jacq-Hergoualc'h, Dr M.
Rel, His, Arch, His, AHis

Lafont, Prof. dr P.B.
His, Rel

Lamant, Prof. P.L.
SocAHis, CuS, Arch, Rel, His

Lange, Dr C.
His, Rel, Ant, His, AHis, Soc

Lemoine, Dr J.
CuS, Ant, GenS, His, Psy, Rel

Levy-Ward, Dr A.
Ant, Lin

Moreau, P.
Art

Móriot, Prof. CH.
Ant

Munier MA, M.C.
Arch, AHis, CuS, Rel

Népote, J.
Ant, Rel, PolS, Lit, Eco, His

Nguyen, Dr D.N.
Soc, Ant, DevS, Edu

Nguyên, Prof. dr T.A.
IR, CuS, His, Rel, Lit

Orberger, Dr B.
Lin, Lit, Geo

Ordonnadu, G.
IR, Eco

Papeté, Drs J.F.
Ant, Lin, Rel

Rodriquez Doctorate, N.
AHis

Scalabrino, Drs C.J.
Rel, Arch, His, Phi, Psy, His, IR, AHis, PolS

Siripaphanh, Dr B
His

Taillard, Ch.
DevS, Eco, Geo

Tertrais, Prof. H.T.
His, IR

Thierry, Dr S.T.
Lit, Lin, CuS, Rel

Thion, Dr S.
Soc, Rel, PolS, His, Ant

Trân, Q.H.
CuS, Ant

Germany

Bauer, Prof. dr C.H.R.
Lit, Rel, Ant, Lin, His, Arch

Beusch, Drs D.
PolS, IR

Cheutching, L.C.
Phi, His

Geisler, Drs G.H.S.
Geo, Env, DevS

Goetzfried, Dr F.X.
His, Phi, Ant, Rel

Heberer, Prof. dr Th.
Ant, Rel, DevS, GenS, Eco, PolS, Soc

Hinüber, Prof. dr O. von
His, CuS, Arch, His, Law, Lit, AHis, Phi, Rel, Lin

Hundius, Prof. H.
Lit, Lin

Janz, K.E.
Ant, Agr, GenS, DevS

Klotz, Drs S.
PolS, IR

Kraas, Dr F.
Ant, DevS, CuS, Geo

Kuckertz, Prof. dr J.
His, Ant

Kummer, Dr M.E.F.
Psy, RelAgr, Phi, Soc, Lin, IR, Eco, His, Ant, PolS, Env, E

Lobo, Dr W.
AHis, Ant, Arch

Lorenz, Prof. D.
Eco

Mischung, Prof. R.
Ant, Soc, Rel

Moeller, Dr K.
IR, PolS

Müller, K.
PolS, CuS, His

Neuser, Drs J.
Lit, Lin, CuS, Rel

Nguyen, Dr T.-H.
AHis, Rel, CuS, His, Arch, Ant, Soc

Platenkamp, Prof. dr J.D.M.
CuS, Soc, Ant, Rel

Raendchen, Drs O.
CuS, Ant, Lin, Lit

Schreiner, Prof. dr L.
Rel, Ant, His

Schweinfurth, Prof. dr U.
Agr, DevS, Env, Arch, IR

Stein, Dr W.
Ant, CuS, AHis, Arch, His

Terwiel, Prof. dr B.J.
His, Ant

Weggel, Dr O.
Law, Rel, Soc, CuS, Phi, Lin, PolS, IR

Italy

Ciarla, Dr R.
His, AHis, CuS, Arch, Ant

Orioli, Dr H.
Ant, His, Arch, AHis

Rispoli, Dr F.
Ant, Arch

Sabattini, Drs M.
His, Lit, Lin

Sandra, Prof. D.E.E.
Ant, CuS, Edu, GenS

Volpi, G.
PolS, IR, Agr, Eco, Env

Netherlands

Bruin, Ir D. de
DevS, Env

Burgler, Dr R.A.
Ant, PolS, His

Chutiwongs, Dr N.
Rel, His, Arch, AHis

Cowan, Drs F.M.
GenS, DevS, CuS, Ant, Env, LinAgr

Guyt, Drs H.J.
His, IR, AHis, Lin, CuS, DevS

Netherlands

Haringhuizen, Drs W.
PolS, Ant, IR

Hoefnagels, Ir H.A.M.
Agr, Eco, Law

Jehle, Dr E.
IR, DevS, Eco, Edu, Law

Kal, Drs W.H.
Env, Lin, DevS, Agr, CuS, Ant, CuS, GenS

Kamp, E.P. van der
His

Kessel-Hagesteijn, Dr R.R. van
His, Ant

Koesoebjono, R.H.S.I.
DevS, GenS, Eco

Linden, F.J.W.T. van der
IR, PolS

Mensink, Drs O.H.
AHis, Ant, CuS, His

Montyn, J.
Phi, AHis, CuS, Lit

Oosterwijk, A.J.
His, Ant, Arch

Patmo, Drs S.
Edu, Soc, Ant, DevS

Pluvier, Dr J.M.
His, DevS, IR

Schenk-Sandbergen, Dr L.Ch.
GenS, DevS, Env, Ant

Steinhauer, Dr H.
Lin, Ant

Stokhof, Prof. dr W.A.L.
Lit, Lin

Stroek, A.J.
Rel, His, CuS

Truong, Dr D.H.D.
IR, Eco, Env

Vereeken, Drs B.
Ant, DevS

Wolvekamp, Drs P.S.
Agr, IR, DevS, Env, GenS

Zwijnenburg, Ph.A.
His

Norway

Bleie, T.
Env, Ant, GenS, DevS, CuS

Poland

Goralski, Prof. dr
PolS, His, IR

Lukaszuk, Dr L.B.
Law, Eco, IR, DevS

Olbrys, Drs M.
Lin, Lit

Wawrzyniak, Dr A.
CuS, Ant

Russia

Ioanesian, Dr S.J.
Edu, DevS, IR, Agr, Eco

Ioanesyan, Dr S.I.
Eco

Kobelev, Dr E.V.
PolS, His, IR

Morev, Dr L.N.
CuS, Lin

Osipov, Prof. dr Y.M.
Lit, Rel

Rogojine, Dr A.
Env, Eco, IR, DevS

Spain

Albarrán Serrano, Antonio
Lit

Bustelo, Dr P.
DevS, Eco

Castillo Rodriguez, S.
IR

Garcia-Ormaechea Quero, C.
AHis, Geo, His, Lit, Rel, Phi

Navarro Celada, F.

Pajares Ruiz, J.M.
AHis, Eco, Geo, Soc

Togores Sanchez, L.E.
IR, His

Sweden

Aijmer, Dr L.G.
Ant

Amer, Dr R.
IR, PolS, His

Bratthall, Prof. D.
Eco

Bryder, Dr H.P.
Ant, Rel

Corlin, Dr C.G.
DevS, Ant

Djurfeldt, Dr G.
Soc, Agr, DevS

Eriksson, Drs I.E.
DevS

Hammargren, Drs H.A.
PolS, IR, DevS

Hansson, E.
PolS

Hovemyr, Dr A.P.
Rel, His, CuS

Jerndal, Drs R.
Geo, DevS

Kullberg, Dr A.I.
Edu, Env

Lindell, Drs K.
Lin, CuS, Env

Lundström, S.H.I.
Geo, GenS, DevS

Ronnås, Dr P.
DevS, Agr, Eco

Schalk, Prof. dr P.
Phi, AHis, CuS, Arch, His, Rel

Svantesson, J.O.
Lin

Swahn, Prof. J.Ö.
PolS, Soc

Tayanin, D.
CuS, Env, Agr, Ant, Rel

Trankell, Dr I.B.
Ant

Switzerland

Ehrensperger, A.
Ant, Env

United Kingdom

Carter, Dr L.J.
His

Crosbie, Dr A.J.
IR, Env, Eco, Geo, DevS

Dixon, Dr C.J.
Geo

Drakakis-Smith, Prof. D.
DevS

Gethin, Dr R.M.L.
Rel

Huxley, Mr A.D.
Law, His

Lowe, Dr P.C.
IR, His

Park, S.S.
Psy, PolS, Phi, SocAHis, DevS, Env, Edu, IR, Law

Picken, Dr L.E.R.
CuS

Rigg, Dr J.D.
Geo, Env, Agr, DevS

Valentin, J.C.P.
Env, Ant, CuS, Lin, His, Arch

Whitmore, Dr T.C.
Env

MALAYSIA

Austria

Min Tjoa, Prof. dr A.
Edu

Belgium

Bogart, K.J.
Edu, CuS

Carpano, R.
Eco, IR

Hacourt, B.J.H.
DevS, Ant

Lim, Dr P.
DevS, Soc, PolS

Pelkmans, Prof. dr J.
IR, Eco

Piquard, B.
Rel, PolS, Ant

Servaes, Prof. dr J.E.J.G.
CuS, Ant, Soc, DevS

Czech Republic

Hulec, Dr O.
His, AHis, CuS, Arch, IR, Eco, Phi, Lit, Lin

Denmark

Fleming, Prof. D.E.B.
Soc, DevS

Denmark

Fold, N.F.
DevS
Grathwohl, J.U.
Ant, Law
Mahmoodi, A.
Soc, PolS, His, Eco, DevS, CuS
Martinussen, Prof. dr J.
Eco, DevS, PolS
Padolecchia Polo, Prof. S.P.
DevS, PolS, Rel, Edu, Eco, Soc, Env, IR, CuS
Rodenburg, Dr J.
Ant, GenS, Env, DevS
Schmidt, Dr J.D.
Soc, IR, DevS
Svensson, Prof. dr Th.
PolS, Eco, His
Tönnesson, Dr S.
IR, His
Trier, Dr J.
Arch, Rel, Lin, Ant

Finland

Antikainen-Kokko, Dr A.
IR
Haikonen, Dr J.
DevS, Eco, PolS
Karunaratne, Dr J.A.
DevS, Eco
Kortteinen, Dr T.
Agr, Soc, DevS
Seppänen, J.
IR, Eco, Ant, CuS, Lin, His, AHis, Phi, Arch, Rel, PolS

France

Barbiche, Prof. dr J.-P.
Law, IR, His, PolS, Eco, DevS, CuS, Edu, Soc
Blanchard, F.
PolS
Bompard, J.M
Agr, Env
Botsch, A.A.
Eco, DevS, IR, Edu, Law
Bouteiller, E.
DevS, Eco
Brun, Dr C. le
Eco, IR, PolS
Bry, M.-F.
Rel, Psy
Camroux, Dr D.F.
His, IR, Soc, PolS
Cheng, S.H.
AHis, CuS, Rel
Daillie, F.-R.
Lit, CuS
Delaune, Dr F.
Eco, DevS
Dolk, Dr E.C.
Lit, His
Durand, Dr F.B.
Env, Agr, Lit, DevS
Feillard, Drs A.
IR, GenS, His, Soc, PolS, Rel, Eco
Ferlus, M.
Lin
Fouquin, M.F.
Eco
Gazano, A.
Law
Gobalakchenane, Dr M.
CuS, His, Rel, Soc
Guillot, C.
Rel
Jacq-Hergoualc'h, Dr M.
Rel, His, Arch, His, AHis
Jaussaud, Dr J.
Eco, IR
Kalpana Kartik MA,
Ant, AHis, CuS, Rel
Lamant, Prof. P.L.
SocAHis, CuS, Arch, Rel, His
Lechervy, Chr.
IR, PolS
Massard-Vincent, Dr J.
Ant
Moussay, G.
Lit
Munier MA, M.C.
Arch, AHis, CuS, Rel
Orberger, Dr B.
Lin, Lit, Geo
Ordonnadu, G.
IR, Eco
Perlas, Dr Ch.
Ant, CuS
Po Dharma Quang, Dr
Lin, Lit, His
Pouvatchy, Dr J.R.
Rel, His, PolS, IR
Raillon, Dr F.
Soc, Eco, IR, His, PolS, DevS, Rel
Rakotofiringa, Prof. H.
Lin, Lit
Sekem, W.
PolS, Law, Edu
Sellato, B.
Ant, His
Simon, Dr J.C.
Soc, IR, His, Eco, DevS, PolS
Sivignon,
Eco, Geo
Vernieres, Prof. M.V.
Edu, Eco
Wignesan, Dr T.
His, Agr
Williamson, Dr P.J.
DevS, Eco
Zaini-Lajoubert, M.
Soc, GenS, His, Lit, Rel
Zani-Lajoubert, M.
CuS, His

Germany

Ackermann, Dr A.
Ant, CuS, Soc
Antweiler, Prof. dr C.
DevS, Ant
Baloch, Dr I.
PolS, CuS, His
Bauer, Prof. dr C.H.R.
Lit, Rel, Ant, Lin, His, Arch
Blazy, Dr H.
Lin, Psy, CuS, Phi, Lit
Brauns, Drs T.
DevS, Env, Agr
Carle, Dr R.
Lit
Carstens, Dr R.
His, Edu, CuS, AHis, Lin, Lit, DevS, PolS, Rel
Dahm, Prof. dr B.
Rel, His, CuS
Dengel, Dr H.
Rel, AHis, Eco, Arch, DevS, His
Dosch, Drs J.
IR, PolS
Draguhn, Dr W.
PolS, IR, Eco, DevS
Franke, Prof. dr W.
His, Rel
Gerke, Prof. dr S.
CuS, Soc, DevS
Gröpper, Drs D.
CuS, AHis, Arch, His, Ant
Hanisch, Prof. dr R.
IR, DevS, PolS
Heberer, Prof. dr Th.
Ant, Rel, DevS, GenS, Eco, PolS, Soc
Heidt, Dr E.U.
CuS, Edu
Henze, Prof. J.
Edu
Hohnholz, Prof. J.
DevS, Agr, Geo
Kannen, B.
CuS, Ant, Rel, Soc
Kevenhörster, Prof. dr P.K.
PolS
Klotz, Drs S.
PolS, IR
Knall, Prof. B.R.
IR, Edu, PolS, Eco, DevS
Kraas, Dr F.
Ant, DevS, CuS, Geo
Kraus, Dr W.
AHis, Rel
Krause, Prof. E.D.
Lin
Krüger, Prof. dr H.
IR, Law, Rel, Soc, Eco

Germany

Kubitscheck, Prof. H.D.
His, Ant

Kummer, Dr M.E.F.
Psy, RelAgr, Phi, Soc, Lin, IR, Eco, His, Ant, PolS, Env, E

Liew-Herres, Dr F.M.
His

Lobo, Dr W.
AHis, Ant, Arch

Lorenz, Prof. D.
Eco

Lummer, Drs E.
His, Ant, CuS, Lit

Machetzki, Dr R.
DevS, Eco, PolS

Moeller, Dr K.
IR, PolS

Müller, K.
PolS, CuS, His

Nass, O.
Eco

Nothofer, Prof. dr B.
Ant, Lit, Lin, CuS

Pink, Prof. P.
Rel, Phi, Lit

Pretzell, Dr K.A.
Rel, CuS, PolS, Ant

Richter, Dr G.
Lin

Rieger, Dr H.C.
DevS, Env, Eco

Roth, Dr R.B.
CuS, His

Rueland, Prof. dr J.
IR, PolS, DevS

Salzmann, Dr B.
Soc

Schiel, Dr T.
Soc, His, Ant, Agr, Env, DevS, PolS

Schrader, Dr H.
Soc, Eco, Ant, CuS

Schreiner, Prof. dr L.
Rel, Ant, His

Schulze, Dr F.
His, CuS, Rel, Lit

Schweinfurth, Prof. dr U.
Agr, DevS, Env, Arch, IR

Schwinghammer, Drs E.
DevS, Eco, CuS, His

Seitz, Prof. dr S.
Ant

Stiller, Dr D.F.R.
Law

Strassner, Dr R.
PolS, Psy, IR, CuS, Rel, Soc

Warnk, Drs H.
His, Ant

Wassmann, Prof. dr J.
Ant

Wichmann, Drs P.
IR, PolS

Zimmermann, Dr G.R.
Geo

Hungary

Ehrlich, Prof. E.
Eco, DevS

Nyiri, Drs P.D.
Ant, PolS

Italy

Citro, M
CuS, Lit

Conti, Dr G.
Lin, Rel, Law

Diglio, Prof. S.
IR, Eco, DevS, CuS

Giambelli, Dr R.A.
Soc, Ant,

Marinelli, Dr M.M.
His, IR, PolS, DevS

Masala, F.
Edu

Nalesini MA, Oscar
Arch

Orioli, Dr H.
Ant, His, Arch, AHis

Santa Maria, Prof. dr L.
Lit, Lin, IR, His

Scolari, V.
CuS, His, AHis

Snellgrove, Prof. D.
AHis, Rel, Arch, His

Soenoto Rivai, S.F.
Lin, Lit, GenS

Volpi, G.
PolS, IR, Agr, Eco, Env

Malaysia

Wahab Ali, Prof. dr A.
Lit

Netherlands

Arens, Drs J.F.
Lit, His, CuS

Asselbergs, Drs G.
Agr, Eco, Edu

Attema, Drs Y.
AHis, CuS, His

Baas, Prof. dr P.
Env

Bastiaansen, Drs A.C.G.M.
IR, Eco, Edu

Bertsch, Drs H.B.
Soc, Eco

Boelhouwer, R.H.
Eco, Lit, IR

Boer, E. de
Soc, Ant, CuS

Bogaerts, Drs E.M.
Phi, IR, AHis, Rel, Lit, Lin, His, Ant

Boomgaard, Prof. dr P.
His, Env

Bruijn, E.J. de
His

Bruin, Ir D. de
DevS, Env

Bruinessen, Dr M.M. van
Rel, His, Ant

Casparis, Prof. dr J.G. de
AHis, Rel, His, Arch, His

Chai, Drs M.
CuS

Choenni, Dr C.E.S.
His, IR, Phi, PolS, Rel, Lit, DevS, Soc

Chutiwongs, Dr N.
Rel, His, Arch, AHis

Daane, Dr ir J.R.V.
Soc

Dam, Dr J.E. van

Derks, Dr W.A.G.
Lit

Dijk, Prof. dr C. van
His, Rel

Doderlein de Win, E.F.
Law, IR, Edu, Eco, Agr, DevS

Duermeijer, Ir A.J.
AHis, Arch, DevS

Dumas, Drs R.M.
PArt, Lit, CuS

Gajentaan, Mr H.
PolS, IR, DevS

Gertsch, Drs L.J.
CuS, DevS

Giel, Mr P.
Env, DevS

Ginkel, Prof. dr J.A. van
Geo, DevS

Grijns, Dr C.D.
Lin

Grunsven, Dr L.M.J. van
DevS, Eco, Geo, IR

Gunawan, Dr B.
His, Soc, DevS

Haitsma, T.J.
IR

Hamelink, Prof. dr C.J.
IR, Law

Haringhuizen, Drs W.
PolS, Ant, IR

Harteveld, Ir K.
Agr, Eco, IR, Soc, DevS

Hartog, Dr A.P. den
Ant, DevS

Heersink, Dr C.G.
His

Heuvel, Ing T. van den
Agr

Hoefnagels, Ir H.A.M.
Agr, Eco, Law

Hoeij Schilthoven Pompe, Mr S.
Law

Netherlands

Hulst, W.A.
Eco

Huyser, Drs G.L.J.
IR

Jacobs, Drs E.M.
His

Jager, Drs Y.M. de
Lit

Jansen, Drs T.E.
DevS, GenS, His

Jehle, Dr E.
IR, DevS, Eco, Edu, Law

Josselin de Jong, Prof. dr P.E. de
Ant

Jung, Drs J.I.
Edu, His, Lin, CuS

Junne, Prof. G.C.A.
IR, DevS, PolS, Env

Karssen, Dr C.M.
DevS, Env, Agr, Eco, Edu, Soc, GenS

Keppy, Drs P.J.
His, Ant

Keurs, Dr P.J. ter
Ant, CuS, His, AHis

Klugkist, Drs C.W.
Edu, CuS, His

Knaap, Dr G.J.
His

Kroes, Drs G.C.
Ant, Rel

Kurian, Dr R.
Eco, DevS

Ligthart, Drs M.J.H.M.
Env, PolS, DevS

Lingen, Ing J.
His

Lopez, Drs S.
CuS, His, AHis

Lucardie, Drs G.R.E.
Ant, DevS

Maier, Prof. dr H.M.J.
Lit

Minde, Dr D. van
Lin

Minnee, Drs P.
CuS, IR, Eco, Edu

Moltzer, Drs R.
Ant

Muijzenberg, Prof. dr O.D. van den
Soc, DevS, Ant, His

Naerssen, Dr A.L. van
DevS, Geo

Nolten, Drs H.M.
GenS, Geo

Ommen, Drs A.F. van
IR, PolS

Ouden, Dr J.H.B. den
DevS, Ant, Agr, GenS

Patmo, Drs S.
Edu, Soc, Ant, DevS

Peters, Drs F.H.
DevS, His

Pinkers, Ir M.J.H.P.
IR, DevS, EduAgr

Plomp, Drs M.
Lit

Pluvier, Dr J.M.
His, DevS, IR

Pompe, Dr J.H.
PolS, DevS, Env, IR, Agr, Ant, Eco, Soc, CuS, Edu, Phi, Law,

Prchal, Drs M.
PolS, His, Rel

Putten, Drs J. van der
Lin, His

Ras, Prof. dr J.J.
Lit

Rinsampessy, Dr E.P.
Ant, Soc, Rel, IR, Edu

Robson-McKillop, Drs R.L.
Ant, Rel, Arch

Roodenburg, C.
Eco, IR, Lin, Soc

Rutten, Dr M.A.F.
Ant, Soc

Saane, Drs P.A. van
Lin

Sanders, Drs M.
DevS, Eco

Schäfer, Drs E.S.
His, Eco, IR, CuS

Schalke, Dr H.J.W.G.
Arch, Ant, Env

Schouten, Drs P.H.
Ant, Soc

Schouw, Drs M.H. van der
AHis, Arch, CuS, His

Smid, J.W.
Eco

Stam, Prof. dr J.A.
DevS, Eco, IR

Steinhauer, Dr H.
Lin, Ant

Stel, Dr J.H.
Env, Eco

Suringa, Mr P.
Law, AHis, Lit, IR, His, Phi, His, Edu, CuS, DevS, Eco, PolS

Sutherland, Prof. dr H.A.
CuS, His, Ant

Sybesma, S.
Lin

Teensma, Dr B.N.
His

Teeuw, Prof. dr A.
Lit, Lin, CuS

Tol, Dr R.G.
Lit, Lin

Ubaghs, Drs J.M.M.
CuS, His

Veerdonk, Drs J.A.L.B. van den
Lin, Arch, Lit

Visscher, Drs S.
PolS, Soc, His

Voogd, Drs P. de
DevS, GenS, Soc, Edu

Voogt, Drs P.R.
Ant

Voskuil, Dr J.E.
Lin

Waal, Drs H.C.J.M.
Geo, GenS

Wichelen, Drs C.B.J. van
Soc, Phi, Ant, DevS, Rel

Wiechen, P.J. van
AHis, CuS, Ant, Arch, His

Wiegmans, Drs B.W.
Eco

Wieringa, Dr E.P.
Lit

Witkam, Dr J.J.
His, Rel, Lit

Wolffers, Prof. dr I
DevS

Wolvekamp, Drs P.S.
Agr, IR, DevS, Env, GenS

Zeeuw, D. de
Env, Agr

Zwijnenburg, Ph.A.
His

Norway

Harbsmeier, Prof. dr C.
His, Phi, Lit, Lin, CuS, AHis

Larsen, Dr A.K.
Ant

Lund, Prof. R.
GenS, Geo, DevS

Rudie, Dr I.
Ant

Vikir, Prof. L.S.
Lin

Poland

Goralski, Prof. dr
PolS, His, IR

Gudowski, J.
Eco, Agr, DevS

Kulig, Prof. J.
Eco, IR

Lukaszuk, Dr L.B.
Law, Eco, IR, DevS

Wawrzyniak, Dr A.
CuS, Ant

Winid, Prof. dr B.
PolS, DevS, Env, Geo

Zaremba, Dr P.A.
DevS, Env, Eco

Portugal

Lobato, Dr M.L.M.
His

Portugal
Pinto de Sousa, P.J.C.
His

Republic of Cyprus
Saunders, Dr G.E.
His

Russia
Alieva, Dr N.F.
Lin, Lit

Chufrin, Dr G.I.
IR, Eco

Demidioek, Dr L.N.
Lin

Dorofeeva, Dr T.V.
Edu, Lin

Efimova, Prof. L.
His, Rel, PolS

Goryayeva, Dr L.V.
Lit

Gurevich, Dr E.M.
His, PolS, Phi

Gusev, Dr M.N.
Eco, IR

Kondrashkina, Dr E.A.
Lin

Kullanda, Dr S.V.
His, Lin

Lostragine, Mr V.N.
Lin, His

Makarenko, Prof. dr V.A.
Lin, Lit, His, Ant, Edu, CuS, Rel

Nikulina, Dr L.V.
DevS, CuS, Ant, Env, Edu, His, Rel, Arch

Ogloblin, Prof. A.K.
Lin

Parnickel, Prof. dr B.B.
Lit

Parnikel, Dr B.B.
Lit

Pogadaev, Dr V.
His, CuS

Rogojine, Dr A.
Env, Eco, IR, DevS

Sirk, Dr S.
Lin

Smurowa, Dr N.M.
Lit

Solomonik, Dr I.N.
His, AHis

Tesselkine, Dr A.S.
Ant, AHis, Lin, His, CuS

Zakaznikova, Dr Y.P.
DevS, Soc, PolS, His

Spain
Bustelo, Dr P.
DevS, Eco

Canto, Dr P.
DevS, IR, Eco

Castillo Rodriguez, S.
IR

Elías de Tejada Lozano, Diplomat F.
Eco, Lit, PolS

Escurriola Sans, Jordi
His, Lin, Lit, Phi, Soc

Fernández Miguélez, J.
IR

Gonzales de Orduña Criado, Silvia
DevS

Jimenez Valentin, J.M.
Eco, Env, IR

Martinell Gifre, E.
Lin

Mas Murcia, A.
Eco

Monclés, Dr A.
Env, Edu

Navarro Celada, F.

Pajares Ruiz, J.M.
AHis, Eco, Geo, Soc

Perez Miguel, A.
Ant, GenS, His, IR

Rodríguez Ubeda, M.M.
Eco, IR, Soc

Sweden
Abdulsomad, K.
DevS, Eco

Allwood, Prof. J.
Lin, Phi

Amer, Dr R.
IR, PolS, His

Jirström, Dr M.
Agr, DevS

Lundström-Burghoorn, Dr W.S.Y.M.C.
Ant, DevS, GenS

Ooi, Drs K.B.
PolS, His, Phi

Palmgren, I.
DevS

Switzerland
Galizia, Dr M.
Soc, PolS, Law, His, DevS, CuS

Klausing, Andreas
IR, PolS, Soc

Thölen, Drs K.
Arch, His, AHis, Lit

Viaro, Dr A.V.
Env, Ant, DevS

Wang, Mr D.T.C.
PolS, Law

United Kingdom
Auty, Dr R.M.
DevS, Env, Eco

Balasubramanyam, Prof. V.N.
DevS, Eco

Belshaw, Prof. D.G.R.
DevS, Env, Agr, Eco,

Booth, Prof. A.E.
Agr, Eco, Edu, GenS, His, DevS

Bowman, Drs M.I.
Rel

Braginsky, Prof. V.I.
Rel, Lit

Brown, Dr I.G.
His

Brown, Dr N.D.
Env

Bunt, Dr G.
CuS, Ant, Law, Rel

Carswell, Prof. J.W.
AHis, CuS, His

Carter, Dr L.J.
His

Chalmers, Dr M.
IR

Chin, Dr J.
PolS, DevS, His

Choi, D.-J.
PolS

Chong, Mr G.
Env

Clarence-Smith, Dr W.G.
His

Cockburn, Mr R.C.
DevS, CuS

Conway, Dr B.M.
Edu

Crosbie, Dr A.J.
IR, Env, Eco, Geo, DevS

Dixon, Dr C.J.
Geo

Drakakis-Smith, Prof. D.
DevS

Dunn, Mr A.J-J.
IR, Edu, CuS, Ant

Dwyer, Prof. D.J.
DevS

Eyre, Dr A.
Rel, Soc

Ferdinand, Drs C.I.P.
PolS, DevS, His, Eco, IR

Ford, Dr N.J.
Geo, GenS, DevS, CuS

Gallop, Drs A.T.
Lit, His, AHis

Garforth, Prof. dr C.J.
Agr, Edu

Gavin, Dr T.
Ant

Ghosh, Dr D.
DevS, Eco

Godman, Dr A.
Lin, Edu

Harding, Dr A.J.
Law, Env

Harris, Drs F.M.
Ant

United Kingdom

Harris, Drs N.
DevS, Eco

Heng, J.W.M.
His, Arch, AHis

Henry, Dr J.C.K.
His

Hitchcock, Dr M.J.
Soc, Ant, DevS

Huxley, Dr T.J.
IR, PolS

Jones, Dr R.
Lin, Lit, Rel

Kidd, Mr J.B.
CuS, Edu

King, Prof. V.T.
DevS, Soc, Ant, Env

Kirkpatrick, Prof. C.H.
Env, Eco

Koktvedgaard Zeitzen, M.
Ant, Arch, GenS

Kratz, Dr E.U.
Lit, CuS

Lambourn, Dr E.A.
AHis, Arch

Ling, Prof. T.O.
Rel

Lowe, Dr P.C.
IR, His

Marr, Dr J.R.
Lin, His, CuS, Arch, His, Phi, Rel, AHis, Lit

Mirza, Prof. H.R.
DevS, Eco

Nossiter, Prof. T.J.
Soc, PolS, IR, DevS, His

Ooi, Drs K.G.
His

Parikh, Prof. A.
Eco, DevS, Agr

Park, S.S.
Psy, PolS, Phi, SocAHis, DevS, Env, Edu, IR, Law

Parnwell, Dr M.J.G.
DevS, Env, Geo

Phillips, Dr N.G.
Lit, Lin

Picken, Dr L.E.R.
CuS

Plumbe, A.J.
DevS

Prasad, Drs S.
Soc, Ant, Eco, DevS

Preston, Dr D.A.
Geo, Agr, DevS, Env

Putzel, Drs J.J.
DevS, Env, PolS

Roberts, Drs D.C.
DevS, Eco, IR

Roper, Dr G.J.
CuS

Ryan, Dr J.T.
Eco

Slater, Dr R.P.
PolS, Ant, DevS, Eco

Steffensen, Drs K.N.
PolS, IR

Stockwell, Prof. A.J.
His

Strickland, Dr S.S.
Ant

Thambiah, S.
Ant

Thoburn, Dr J.T.
Eco

Valentin, J.C.P.
Env, Ant, CuS, Lin, His, Arch

Watson, Dr J.R.
Eco, DevS

Weller, Drs P.G.
Rel

Whitmore, Dr T.C.
Env

Wilder, Dr W.D.
GenS, DevS, Ant

Wisseman Christie, Prof. dr J.
Arch, His

MYANMAR

Austria

Allinger, Dr E.
Rel, His, CuS, Arch, AHis

Kapp, M.
CuS, Ant, Soc, Rel

Sellner, Dr M.B.
CuS, Lin

Belgium

Carpano, R.
Eco, IR

Gonzalo Castellanos, Dr A.
IR

Czech Republic

Becka, Dr J.
Rel

Hulec, Dr O.
His, AHis, CuS, Arch, IR, Eco, Phi, Lit, Lin

Denmark

Ewers, K.
Ant, Env, DevS

Gravers, Dr M.
Env, His, Rel, PolS, Soc, CuS, Ant

Magnussen, Drs T.
DevS, IR, PolS

Morch, M.J.V.
Ant

Sorensen, P.
Arch

Finland

Jokinen, Drs J.J.
DevS, IR, PolS

Moilanen, Dr I.A.
Ant, His, AHis, Rel

Seppänen, J.
IR, Eco, Ant, CuS, Lin, His, AHis, Phi, Arch, Rel, PolS

Vepsä, M.
Art

France

Bernot, D
Lin

Bernot, D.
Lin

Brac de la Perriere, Dr B.
Ant

Bruneau, Dr M.
PolS, DevS, CuS, Geo, Agr

Cao, Dr T.L.
Lin

Cardinaud, M.-H.
Lan

Chagnaud, F.J.
Eco, Agr, Env, DevS

Couderc, P.
AntAnt

Coyaud, Dr M.
Ant, Lin

Dessaint, Prof. W.L.
Ant

Even, M.-D.
His, GenS

Ferlus, M.
Lin

Filliozat, J.
Rel, Lit

Frederic, L.F.
AHis, CuS, Arch, Rel, His

Gerbault, D.P.
CuS, Lin

Gobalakchenane, Dr M.
CuS, His, Rel, Soc

Guillon, Dr E.
Ant, AHis, Arch, Rel, His

Lafont, Prof. dr P.B.
His, Rel

Lamant, Prof. P.L.
SocAHis, CuS, Arch, Rel, His

Lechervy, Chr.
IR, PolS

Lubeigt, G.
His, AHis, Agr, DevS, Ant, PolS, Env, Arch, Eco, CuS, Geo, H

Mantienne, F.
His, Eco

Mazaudon, M.
Lin

Munier MA, M.C.
Arch, AHis, CuS, Rel

Orberger, Dr B.
Lin, Lit, Geo

France

Ordonnadu , G.
IR, Eco

Pichard , Ir L.
Lit, Soc

Raymond , C.
His, Arch, Rel, AHis

Robinne , Dr F.
AntAnt

Rodriquez Doctorate, N.
AHis

Salles , Dr J.F.
His, AHis, Arch, His

Subrahmanyam , Dr S.
His, Eco

Thion , Dr S.
Soc, Rel, PolS, His, Ant

Yin Yin , M.
Lan

Germany

Bass , Dr H.H.
DevS, Eco, IR

Bauer , Prof. dr C.H.R.
Lit, Rel, Ant, Lin, His, Arch

Bauer , Prof. dr C.H.R.
Lit, Rel, Ant, Lin, His, Arch

Bechert , Prof. H.H.
His, Lit, Rel, CuS

Borchers , Drs D.
CuS, Lin

Braun , Dr H.
His, Lit, Rel

Bruns , A.
Rel

Esche , Dr A.
Lin, Lit

Feistel , Dr H.O.
CuS, Lit, Rel, Lin

Frasch , Drs T.
His

Frasch , Drs T.
His

Goettingen , Drs D.
PolS, IR

Gröpper , Drs D.
CuS, AHis, Arch, His, Ant

Heberer , Prof. dr Th.
Ant, Rel, DevS, GenS, Eco, PolS, Soc

Hinüber , Prof. dr O. von
His, CuS, Arch, His, Law, Lit, AHis, Phi, Rel, Lin

Hoffmann , J.
Eco, His, PolS

Jakobi , Drs S.
GenS, PolS

Khin , M.S.
His

Klovth , Th.
IR, PolS

Korff , Dr R.
CuS, DevS, Soc

Kott , D.
CuS, His, Law

Kraas , Dr F.
Ant, DevS, CuS, Geo

Kubitscheck , Prof. H.D.
His, Ant

Kummer , Dr M.E.F.
Psy, RelAgr, Phi, Soc, Lin, IR, Eco, His, Ant, PolS, Env, E

Linder Sabine , Drs L.
Ant, Arch, Soc

Lobo , Dr W.
AHis, Ant, Arch

Lorenz , J.
AHis, CuS, His

Lorenz , Prof. D.
Eco

Lulei , Prof. W.
DevS, IR, Law, Eco

Mischung , Prof. R.
Ant, Soc, Rel

Moeller , Dr K.
IR, PolS

Müller , K.
PolS, CuS, His

Neuser , Drs J.
Lit, Lin, CuS, Rel

Prager , Drs S.
Rel, PolS, His, CuS

Prunner , Dr G.
Ant, Rel, CuS

Rueland , Prof. dr J.
IR, PolS, DevS

Schlicher , Dr M.
His, PolS, IR

Schreiner , Prof. dr L.
Rel, Ant, His

Schröder , K.
Ant, GenS, DevS

Schweinfurth , Prof. dr U.
Agr, DevS, Env, Arch, IR

Schwörer , Dr G.
CuS, Ant

Siemers , Drs G.
PolS, IR, Eco

Stein , Dr W.
Ant, CuS, AHis, Arch, His

Terwiel , Prof. dr B.J.
His, Ant

Thompson , Prof. M.R.
Ant, Env, Arch

U Tin Htway ,
DevS, PolS

Wenner , D.
Env, Edu, GenS, PolS, Rel, Eco, DevS, CuS, IR

Ziem , K.
Law

Hungary

Nyiri , Drs P.D.
Ant, PolS

Italy

Albanese , M.
His, AHis, Rel, Phi

Bordone , Prof. S.
His

Ciarla , Dr R.
His, AHis, CuS, Arch, Ant

Orioli , Dr H.
Ant, His, Arch, AHis

Rispoli , Dr F.
Ant, Arch

Volpi , G.
PolS, IR, Agr, Eco, Env

Luxemburg

Leider , J.P.
His

Netherlands

Deelstra , T.
Env

Dijk , Drs W.O.
Rel, CuS, His, Lin

Gautam , Dr M.K.
Rel, Soc, Lit, Lin, His, Ant, CuS, PolS, Env

Ginkel , Drs W.T. van
His, Geo, IR

Guyt , Drs H.J.
His, IR, AHis, Lin, CuS, DevS

Haringhuizen , Drs W.
PolS, Ant, IR

Hoefnagels , Ir H.A.M.
Agr, Eco, Law

Jansen , Drs M.H.M.
Ant

Jehle , Dr E.
IR, DevS, Eco, Edu, Law

Kessel-Hagesteijn , Dr R.R. van
His, Ant

Koesoebjono , R.H.S.I.
DevS, GenS, Eco

Kortlandt , Prof. dr F.H.H.
Lin

Montyn , J.
Phi, AHis, CuS, Lit

Oosterwijk , A.J.
His, Ant, Arch

Pluvier , Dr J.M.
His, DevS, IR

Schendel , Prof. dr H.W. van
His, Ant

Schendel , Prof. dr H.W. van
His, Ant

Straten , Mr H.M. van
Env, Ant, Law

Suringa , Mr P.
Law, AHis, Lit, IR, His, Phi, His, Edu, CuS, DevS, Eco, PolS

Ubaghs , Drs J.M.M.
CuS, His

Netherlands

Wiegmans, Drs B.W.
Eco

Wolvekamp, Drs P.S.
Agr, IR, DevS, Env, GenS

Zoomers, Drs H.C.M.
His, IR, PolS

Zuiderhoek, Dr B.
His

Norway

Bleie, T.
Env, Ant, GenS, DevS, CuS

Melby, E.
DevS, CuS

Vaage, T.
PolS

Poland

Goralski, Prof. dr
PolS, His, IR

Lukaszuk, Dr L.B.
Law, Eco, IR, DevS

Portugal

Guedes, Drs M.A.M.
His

Russia

Azovsky, Dr I.P.
Eco

Boitsov, Dr V.V.
DevS, Eco, Geo, IR

Burman, Dr A.D.
His, CuS, Lit, AHis

Gavrilova, Dr A.G.
His, Ant

Ilyushenko, V.I.
His

Osipov, Prof. dr Y.M.
Lit, Rel

Rogojine, Dr A.
Env, Eco, IR, DevS

Solomonik, Dr I.N.
His, AHis

Timofeeva, Dr I.S.
Lin

Vasilyev, Dr V.F.
PolS, IR, His

Spain

Bustelo, Dr P.
DevS, Eco

Castillo Rodriguez, S.
IR

Garcia-Ormaechea Quero, C.
AHis, Geo, His, Lit, Rel, Phi

Navarro Celada, F.

Pajares Ruiz, J.M.
AHis, Eco, Geo, Soc

Rodríguez Ubeda, M.M.
Eco, IR, Soc

Sweden

Amer, Dr R.
IR, PolS, His

Gren-Eklund, Prof. G.
Lit, Lin, Phi, Rel, CuS

Hammargren, Drs H.A.
PolS, IR, DevS

Hovemyr, Dr A.P.
Rel, His, CuS

Karlsson, Drs K.
Rel

Ronnås, Dr P.
DevS, Agr, Eco

Schalk, Prof. dr P.
Phi, AHis, CuS, Arch, His, Rel

Tayanin, D.
CuS, Env, Agr, Ant, Rel

Switzerland

Rastorfer, Ir J.M.
His, CuS

Thölen, Drs K.
Arch, His, AHis, Lit

United Kingdom

Allott, Drs A. J.
PolS, Lit, Lin, His, Rel, Edu

Bray, Drs J.N.
His, IR, PolS

Brown, Dr I.G.
His

Bryant, Dr R.L.
Geo, PolS, DevS, Env

Cameron, Mr J.
Edu, Env, Phi, Eco, CuS, DevS

Carey, Dr P.B.R.
His, IR, CuS, Lit, Rel

Carter, Dr L.J.
His

Chapman, G.
His, AHis, CuS

Coleman, Drs G.
DevS

Cook, M.
Eco

Cook, Dr A.S.
His

French, Mr P.R.
His, Lit

Gethin, Dr R.M.L.
Rel

Green MA, A.R.
AHis

Guy, Drs J.S.
His, AHis

Hall, Dr A.R.
Ant, IR, PolS

Harris, Drs N.
DevS, Eco

Heng, J.W.M.
His, Arch, AHis

Herbert, Drs P.M.
AHis

Herbert, Drs P.M.
AHis

Houtman, Dr G.
Ant, Lit, Rel

Huxley, Dr T.J.
IR, PolS

Huxley, Mr A.D.
Law, His

Kawanami, Dr H.
Ant, Rel

Lenman, Prof. B.P.
His

Lowe, Dr P.C.
IR, His

Marr, Dr J.R.
Lin, His, CuS, Arch, His, Phi, Rel, AHis, Lit

Moore, Dr E.H.
AHis, Arch

Okell, Mr J.W.A.
Lit, Lin

Park, S.S.
Psy, PolS, Phi, SocAHis, DevS, Env, Edu, IR, Law

Stargardt, Prof. J.M.
Rel, ArchAgrAHis

Steeds, Mr D.
IR, His

Swallow, Dr D.A.
His, Ant, CuS, AHis

Taylor, Prof. R.H.
PolS

Thambiah, S.
Ant

Valentin, J.C.P.
Env, Ant, CuS, Lin, His, Arch

Whitmore, Dr T.C.
Env

PACIFIC ISLANDS

Austria

Mückler, Drs H.N.
PolS, His, Ant

Denmark

Bakker, Dr P.J.
His, Lin, Ant

Gullestrup, Prof. H.
His, Soc, IR, Eco, Ant, DevS, CuS, PolS

Padolecchia Polo, Prof. S.P.
DevS, PolS, Rel, Edu, Eco, Soc, Env, IR, CuS

Finland

Karunaratne, Dr J.A.
DevS, Eco

Nordman MA, G.M.
CuS, Lit

Seppänen, J.
IR, Eco, Ant, CuS, Lin, His, AHis, Phi, Arch, Rel, PolS

France

Bompard, J.M
Agr, Env

France

Camroux, Dr D.F.
His, IR, Soc, PolS

Charpentier, Dr J.M.
Ant, Lin, Edu, CuS

Crowe, Dr P.R.
Rel, His, Ant, AHis, Ant, Psy, Arch, Soc

De Coppet, Prof. D
Ant, Soc

Dung, Drs T.T.
Rel, Lin, Edu, Ant, CuS

Kalpana Kartik MA,
Ant, AHis, CuS, Rel

Lemarechal, Dr A.
Lin

Móriot, Prof. CH.
Ant

Nooy-Palm, Prof. dr C.H.M.
Arch, AHis, Env, Ant, Rel

Ordonnadu, G.
IR, Eco

Plessis, Drs F.
Lin, Ant

Raison, Prof. F.
Rel, AHis, Ant, CuS

Rousset, Dr H.A.
CuS, His, Arch, AHis, Ant

Semah, F.
Arch

Sivignon,
Eco, Geo

Toullelan, P.-Y.
Geo

Germany

Ahrens, Prof. Dr T
Rel

Blazy, Dr H.
Lin, Psy, CuS, Phi, Lit

Cain, Dr H.
Rel, Lin, Ant

Carstens, Dr R.
His, Edu, CuS, AHis, Lin, Lit, DevS, PolS, Rel

Eliasson, Prof. S.S.E.
Lin

Faust, Dr H.
DevS, CuS

Heeschen, Dr V.
Lin, CuS, Ant, Phi, Rel

Hoeppe MSc, G
Ant, Env

Jebens, Drs H.J.
CuS, Rel, Phi

Klotz, Drs S.
PolS, IR

Lommel, Dr A.
His, AHis, CuS

Moeller, Dr K.
IR, PolS

Rieländer, Drs K.
Eco, Ant, CuS, Soc

Sauerborn, Prof. J.
Agr, Env

Schmidt, H.C.
Ant, Lin

Schütte, Dr H.
Soc, CuS, His

Schweinfurth, Prof. dr U.
Agr, DevS, Env, Arch, IR

Italy

Volpi, G.
PolS, IR, Agr, Eco, Env

Netherlands

Arnoldus-Schröder, Drs V.
Edu, Ant, CuS

Boon, Drs G.J.
Ant, His

Borsboom, Dr A.P.
Rel, Ant

Claessen, Prof. dr H.J.M.
Ant, His

Dijkstra, Drs G.H.
Soc, Rel, Phi, Eco, His, IR, Psy, PolS

Doornbos, Prof. dr M.R.
DevS, PolS, Soc

Emmer, Prof. dr P.C.
His

Grijp, Dr P. van der
DevS, Eco, Agr, His, Ant

Heuvel, Ing T. van den
Agr

Hoekstra, Drs H.F.M.F.
Ant

Hoetjes, Dr B.J.S.
PolS, IR, Agr, DevS

Jaarsma, Dr S.R.
Ant

Koesoebjono, R.H.S.I.
DevS, GenS, Eco

Kommers, Dr J.H.M.
Ant

Kooyman, Dr S.
AHis

Lucardie, Drs G.R.E.
Ant, DevS

Marey, A.J.F.
Rel, Law

Meijl, Dr A.H.M. van
His, DevS, Ant

Meiracker, Drs C.H. van den
Ant

Mey, Dr L.M. van der
IR, PolS

Nieuwenhuijsen, Drs J.W. van
Ant

Nieuwenhuijsen-Riedeman, Dr C.H. van
Ant

Oosterwijk, A.J.
His, Ant, Arch

Ploeg, Dr A.
Ant

Reijnders, Drs T.
AHis

Schäfer, Drs E.S.
His, Eco, IR, CuS

Schalke, Dr H.J.W.G.
Arch, Ant, Env

Senft, Dr G.
Ant, Lin

Seret, Mr A.
Phi, Lit, Lin, Rel, CuS

Sierpinska, Drs A.M.
Geo

Sigmond, Dr J.P.
CuS, His, AHis, Arch

Sinnema, Drs T.
GenS, CuS, Soc, His, Edu

Smit, Drs T.S.
Lin

Smits, Drs L.
CuS, Ant, Rel, Lin, His

Spee, Drs M.H.
AHis, Ant

Suringa, Mr P.
Law, AHis, Lit, IR, His, Phi, His, Edu, CuS, DevS, Eco, PolS

Teljeur, Dr D.
Ant

Velzen, Drs P.F. van
CuS, Lin

Venbrux, Dr H.J.M.
Rel, Ant

Verhaar, Dr J.W.M.
Lin, Phi

Voogt, Dr A.J. De
Lin, CuS, Psy

Vries, Drs I. de
AHis, Rel, GenS, Ant

Waals, Drs J.D. van der
His, CuS, His, AHis

Werff, Dr P.E. van der
Env, Ant, DevS

Wiechen, P.J. van
AHis, CuS, Ant, Arch, His

Wolvekamp, Drs P.S.
Agr, IR, DevS, Env, GenS

Poland

Majewicz, Prof. dr A.F.
Lin, Ant

Russia

Aliyeva, Dr N.F.
Lin

Belkov, Dr P.L.
Ant

Bem, Dr K.Yu.
His

Chelintseva, Dr N.P.
His, IR

Russia
Lebedeva, Dr N.B.
IR
Lipovsky, Dr K.Yu.
Eco
Malakhovsky, Prof.dr K.V.
His, PolS
Meshkov, Dr K.Yu.
Ant
Nikolayev, Dr V.P.
IR, PolS
Petrikovskaya, A.S.
CuS, Lit
Putilov, Dr B.N.
Ant
Reznikov, Dr V.L.
PolS
Soboleva, Dr E.S.
Rel, His, Ant, AHis
Stefanchuk, Dr L.G.
Eco, His
Tumarkin, Prof. dr D.D.
CuS, DevS, Arch, Eco, His, Ant
Vybornov, Dr V.Ya.
Eco

Spain
Amorés Gonell, F.
Ant, Arch, Lin
Casado-Fresnillo, Dr C.
Lin
Castillo Rodriguez, S.
IR
Elizalde Perez-Grueso, Dr D.
His, IR
Escurriola Sans, Jordi
His, Lin, Lit, Phi, Soc
Fernández-Shaw Baldasano, C.M.
Gallego Fresnillo, C.
His
Garci -Ab solo, Dr A.
His, Ant, CuS
Gil, Prof. J.
His, Lit
Jimenez Valentin, J.M.
Eco, Env, IR
Martinell Gifre, E.
Lin
Mellen Blanco, F.
Ant, Arch, AHis, His
Navarro Celada, F.
Nieto Piñeroba, Dr. J.A.
Ant
Quilis, Antonio
Lin
Rodao, Prof. F.R.
His, IR
Rodriguez-Eiras, J.A.
Agr, Eco, Edu, Env, His, Soc
Togores Sanchez, L.E.
IR, His

Sweden
Lambert, Prof. B.H.
PolS
Ronnås, Dr P.
DevS, Agr, Eco

Switzerland
Eichenberger, C.A.
CuS, Ant, Soc
Keck, Dr V.
Ant

United Kingdom
Cameron, Mr J.
Edu, Env, Phi, Eco, CuS, DevS
Chapman, G.
His, AHis, CuS
Chin, Dr J.
PolS, DevS, His
Crosbie, Dr A.J.
IR, Env, Eco, Geo, DevS
Jones, Mr S.C.
Eco, DevS
O'Connor, Drs K.
CuS, Ant, Soc
Prasad, Drs S.
Soc, Ant, Eco, DevS
Valentin, J.C.P.
Env, Ant, CuS, Lin, His, Arch
Whitmore, Dr T.C.
Env

PAPUA NEW GUINEA

Austria
Sellner, Dr M.B.
CuS, Lin

Denmark
Jacobsen, Dr M.
PolS, CuS, IR, Ant
Otto, Prof. dr T.H.A.H.
Ant

Finland
Nordman MA, G.M.
CuS, Lit
Seppänen, J.
IR, Eco, Ant, CuS, Lin, His, AHis, Phi, Arch, Rel, PolS

France
Breton, Dr S.
Geo, Ant
Chaponniere, Dr J.R.
IR, Eco, PolS, DevS
Charpentier, Dr J.M.
Ant, Lin, Edu, CuS
Crowe, Dr P.R.
Rel, His, Ant, AHis, Ant, Psy, Arch, Soc
De Coppet, Prof. D
Ant, Soc
Gamage, J.
Env
Jeudy-Ballini, Dr M.
Ant, CuS
Kalpana Kartik MA,
Ant, AHis, CuS, Rel
Ordonnadu, G.
IR, Eco
Pellard, S.
His, Arch, AHis
Sollewijn Gelpke, Drs J.H.F.
His
Stephane, Dr S.D.
DevS, His, PolS

Germany
Ahrens, Prof. Dr T
Rel
Beer, Dr B.
Ant
Gröpper, Drs D.
CuS, AHis, Arch, His, Ant
Heeschen, Dr V.
Lin, CuS, Ant, Phi, Rel
Hoeppe MSc, G
Ant, Env
Jebens, Drs H.J.
CuS, Rel, Phi
Klotz, Drs S.
PolS, IR
Kohl, Prof. dr K.-H.
Rel, His, Ant
Moeller, Dr K.
IR, PolS
Platenkamp, Prof. dr J.D.M.
CuS, Soc, Ant, Rel
Rieländer, Drs K.
Eco, Ant, CuS, Soc
Schiel, Dr T.
Soc, His, Ant, Agr, Env, DevS, PolS
Schweinfurth, Prof. dr U.
Agr, DevS, Env, Arch, IR
Siemers, Drs G.
PolS, IR, Eco

Italy
Conti, Dr G.
Lin, Rel, Law
Volpi, G.
PolS, IR, Agr, Eco, Env

Netherlands
Arnoldus-Schröder, Drs V.
Edu, Ant, CuS
Baas, Prof. dr P.
Env
Beek, Dr A.G. van
Ant
Borsboom, Dr A.P.
Rel, Ant
Bree, D.M. de
CuS
Bruggraaff, Drs W.
His

Netherlands
Duuren, Drs D.A.P. van
Ant, CuS
Haringhuizen, Drs W.
PolS, Ant, IR
Heuvel, Ing T. van den
Agr
Hitipeuw-Palyama, E.J.
Ant, Lit, Edu
Hoekstra, Drs H.F.M.F.
Ant
Hoogerbrugge, J.
AHis, CuS
Jaarsma, Dr S.R.
Ant
Kaa, Prof. dr D.J. van de
His
Keurs, Dr P.J. ter
Ant, CuS, His, AHis
Kooyman, Dr S.
AHis
Lange, Drs ir Ph.G. de
Env, Ant
Levinson, Prof. S.C.
Psy, Lin, Ant
Lucardie, Drs G.R.E.
Ant, DevS
Mackenzie, Prof. dr J.L.
Lin
Marey, A.J.F.
Rel, Law
Meiracker, Drs C.H. van den
Ant
Miedema, Dr J.
CuS, Rel, His, Ant, DevS, Soc
Nieuwenhuijsen, Drs J.W. van
Ant
Nieuwenhuijsen-Riedeman, Dr C.H. van
Ant
Oosterwijk, A.J.
His, Ant, Arch
Peters, Drs F.H.
DevS, His
Ploeg, Dr A.
Ant
Pouwer, Prof. dr J.
Ant
Reesink, Dr G.P.
Lin
Reynders, Dr ir J.J.
Agr, Arch, DevS, Env
Ridder, Ir J.M.
Eco, DevS, Ant, IR, Soc
Rinsampessy, Dr E.P.
Ant, Soc, Rel, IR, Edu
Ruygrok, Drs W.F.
His, PolS, Soc
Schäfer, Drs E.S.
His, Eco, IR, CuS
Schalke, Dr H.J.W.G.
Arch, Ant, Env
Seufl, Dr G.
Ant, Lin
Sinnema, Drs T.
GenS, CuS, Soc, His, Edu
Smit, Drs T.S.
Lin
Spee, Drs M.H.
AHis, Ant
Thoonen, Drs A.A.M.
Rel, GenS, Ant
Timmer, Drs J.
Soc, Ant, DevS, CuS
Verhaar, Dr J.W.M.
Lin, Phi
Vink, Dr W.
His
Voorhoeve, Dr C.L.
DevS, Lin
Vries, Drs I. de
AHis, Rel, GenS, Ant
Waals, Drs J.D. van der
His, CuS, His, AHis
Wolvekamp, Drs P.S.
Agr, IR, DevS, Env, GenS

Norway
Barth, Dr F.
DevS, Ant

Poland
Majewicz, Prof. dr A.F.
Lin, Ant

Russia
Soboleva, Dr E.S.
Rel, His, Ant, AHis
Tesselkine, Dr A.S.
Ant, AHis, Lin, His, CuS
Tumarkin, Prof. dr D.D.
CuS, DevS, Arch, Eco, His, Ant

Spain
Fernández-Shaw Baldasano, C.M.
Jimenez Valentin, J.M.
Eco, Env, IR
Mellen Blanco, F.
Ant, Arch, AHis, His
Navarro Celada, F.
Rodriguez-Eiras, J.A.
Agr, Eco, Edu, Env, His, Soc

Sweden
Aijmer, Dr L.G.
Ant
Ronnås, Dr P.
DevS, Agr, Eco

Switzerland
Eeuwijk, Drs P. van
Ant
Hottinger, Prof. dr L.C.
IR, DevS, PolS
Keck, Dr V.
Ant

United Kingdom
Auty, Dr R.M.
DevS, Env, Eco
Belshaw, Prof. D.G.R.
DevS, Env, Agr, Eco,
Booth, Prof. A.E.
Agr, Eco, Edu, GenS, His, DevS
Carswell, Prof. J.W.
AHis, CuS, His
Ellen, Prof. R.F.
Env, Ant
Maloney, Dr B.K.
Env
Saltford, J.F.
IR
Valentin, J.C.P.
Env, Ant, CuS, Lin, His, Arch
Whalley, Dr J.
Eco
Whitmore, Dr T.C.
Env

PHILIPPINES

Austria
Sichrovsky, Prof. H.
CuS, His, PolS, IR
Stockinger, Drs J.
CuS, Ant

Belgium
Ballegeer, J.
PolS, Law
Carpano, R.
Eco, IR
Gonzalo Castellanos, Dr A.
IR
Pelkmans, Prof. dr J.
IR, Eco
Servaes, Prof. dr J.E.J.G.
CuS, Ant, Soc, DevS

Denmark
Norlund, Dr I.M.
His, GenS, DevS
Schmidt, Dr J.D.
Soc, IR, DevS
Trier, Dr J.
Arch, Rel, Lin, Ant

Finland
Antikainen-Kokko, Dr A.
IR
Karunaratne, Dr J.A.
DevS, Eco
Kivimäki, Dr T.A.
PolS, IR, DevS
Seppänen, J.
IR, Eco, Ant, CuS, Lin, His, AHis, Phi, Arch, Rel, PolS

France
Barbiche, Prof. dr J.-P.
Law, IR, His, PolS, Eco, DevS, CuS, Edu, Soc
Baye, Dr E.B.
DevS, Env, Eco
Botsch, A.A.
Eco, DevS, IR, Edu, Law

France

Brun, Dr C. le
Eco, IR, PolS
Chaponniere, Dr J.R.
IR, Eco, PolS, DevS
Coyaud, Dr M.
Ant, Lin
De Coppet, Prof. D
Ant, Soc
Francisco, E.
IR, DevS, His
Gazano, A.
Law
Guen, H. le
AHis, CuS, Env, Ant, Arch, His, Soc, Rel, His
Jacq-Hergoualc'h, Dr M.
Rel, His, Arch, His, AHis
Lamant, Prof. P.L.
SocAHis, CuS, Arch, Rel, His
Lechervy, Chr.
IR, PolS
Lemarechal, Dr A.
Lin
Loyré, Dr G.
His, Rel, PolS, Ant
Macdonald, Dr C.J.H.
CuS, Ant, Lin, Rel
Magannon, E.
Ant
Orberger, Dr B.
Lin, Lit, Geo
Ordonnadu, G.
IR, Eco
Ortiz, E.
Lit
Plessis, Drs F.
Lin, Ant
Potet, Dr J.P.G.
Lin
Pottier, M.
Raillon, Dr F.
Soc, Eco, IR, His, PolS, DevS, Rel
Revel, Prof.N.
Lin, Ant
Sivignon,
Eco, Geo
Trân, Q.H.
CuS, Ant
Vernieres, Prof. M.V.
Edu, Eco
Williamson, Dr P.J.
DevS, Eco

Germany

Beer, Dr B.
Ant
Berner, Dr E.
Soc, Ant
Blazy, Dr H.
Lin, Psy, CuS, Phi, Lit
Braeunlein, Dr P.J.
Rel, Ant, CuS
Brauns, Drs T.
DevS, Env, Agr
Bronger, Prof. D.
DevS
Buchholt, Dr H.
CuS, DevS, Geo, Soc, His
Cain, Dr H.
Rel, Lin, Ant
Carle, Dr R.
Lit
Carstens, Dr R.
His, Edu, CuS, AHis, Lin, Lit, DevS, PolS, Rel
Dahm, Prof. dr B.
Rel, His, CuS
Dosch, Drs J.
IR, PolS
Hager, D.
Eco, IR, PolS
Hanisch, Prof. dr R.
IR, DevS, PolS
Heberer, Prof. dr Th.
Ant, Rel, DevS, GenS, Eco, PolS, Soc
Henze, Prof. J.
Edu
Hohnholz, Prof. J.
DevS, Agr, Geo
Kevenhörster, Prof. dr P.K.
PolS
Klotz, Drs S.
PolS, IR
Krische, S.
DevS, Env, Geo
Lummer, Drs E.
His, Ant, CuS, Lit
Moeller, Dr K.
IR, PolS
Müller, Prof. J.
Soc, Rel, Phi, DevS, CuS, IR
Pfennig, Dr W.
His, PolS, DevS, IR
Rieger, Dr H.C.
DevS, Env, Eco
Rohde, Prof. dr K.E.
Soc, Eco, Env, DevS, CuS, IR
Roth, Dr R.B.
CuS, His
Rueland, Prof. dr J.
IR, PolS, DevS
Sauerborn, Prof. J.
Agr, Env
Schlicher, Dr M.
His, PolS, IR
Schneider, Dr H.
Geo, CuS, DevS
Schreiner, Prof. dr L.
Rel, Ant, His
Schult, Dr V.
His
Schweinfurth, Prof. dr U.
Agr, DevS, Env, Arch, IR
Seitz, Prof. dr S.
Ant
Siemers, Drs G.
PolS, IR, Eco
Strassner, Dr R.
PolS, Psy, IR, CuS, Rel, Soc
Thompson, Prof. M.R.
Ant, Env, Arch
Wendt, Dr H.R.
His, Edu, CuS, Lin
Werner, Dr W.L.
Env, DevS
Wichmann, Drs P.
IR, PolS

Hungary

Birks, L.
Eco, DevS, Env, Agr, IR
Illyefalvi-Vitez, Prof. Z.
Edu

Italy

Ciarla, Dr R.
His, AHis, CuS, Arch, Ant
Marinelli, Dr M.M.
His, IR, PolS, DevS
Masala, F.
Edu
Rispoli, Dr F.
Ant, Arch
Volpi, G.
PolS, IR, Agr, Eco, Env

Netherlands

Baas, Prof. dr P.
Env
Bakker, Dr W.A.
Soc, Ant
Bastiaansen, Drs A.C.G.M.
IR, Eco, Edu
Baud, Dr I.S.A.
DevS, GenS, Eco, Soc
Beers, Mr H.A.J.J. van
Law, DevS, GenS
Beukering, P.J.H. van
IR, Eco, Env, DevS
Biervliet, Drs W.E.
Edu
Boer, E. de
Soc, Ant, CuS
Boeren, Drs A.J.J.M.
Edu, Ant
Bootsma, Dr N.A.
His, IR
Brinke, Ir H.W. ten
Agr, Edu
Brunt, Prof. dr L.
Ant, Soc
Byster, Drs E.D.
IR, CuS, His, Lit, Phi, AHis

Netherlands

Casparis, Prof. dr J.G. de
AHis, Rel, His, Arch, His

Cowan, Drs F.M.
GenS, DevS, CuS, Ant, Env, LinAgr

Dijkstra, Drs G.H.
Soc, Rel, Phi, Eco, His, IR, Psy, PolS

Doderlein de Win, E.F.
Law, IR, Edu, Eco, Agr, DevS

Druijven, Dr P.C.J.
Geo, Env, Agr, DevS

Dubbeldam, Prof. dr L.F.B.
Ant, Edu

Duermeijer, Ir A.J.
AHis, Arch, DevS

Dusseldorp, D.B.W.M. van
Ant, Agr, DevS, PolS, Soc

Galindo, Drs A.
Eco, GenS, DevS

Giel, Mr P.
Env, DevS

Groot, W.T. de
Env, Ant, DevS

Hamelink, Prof. dr C.J.
IR, Law

Hardon, Dr A.P.
Ant, GenS

Haringhuizen, Drs W.
PolS, Ant, IR

Hendriks, M.
Ant

Hendriks, Drs M.B.
Ant

Hoefnagels, Ir H.A.M.
Agr, Eco, Law

Huizer, Prof. dr G.J.
Rel, IR, Env, DevS

Jehle, Dr E.
IR, DevS, Eco, Edu, Law

Junne, Prof. G.C.A.
IR, DevS, PolS, Env

Kal, Drs W.H.
Env, Lin, DevS, Agr, CuS, Ant, CuS, GenS

Karssen, Dr C.M.
DevS, Env, Agr, Eco, Edu, Soc, GenS

Keurs, Dr P.J. ter
Ant, CuS, His, AHis

Keysers, Drs L.
GenS, DevS

Kleinen, Dr J.G.G.M.
Ant

Kolko, Dr G.
Eco, PolS

Kurian, Dr R.
Eco, DevS

Kusin, Prof. dr J.A.
GenS

Ligthart, Drs M.J.H.M.
Env, PolS, DevS

Maaren, F. van
IR, Eco, DevS

Mensink, Drs O.H.
AHis, Ant, CuS, His

Moharir, Dr V.V.
PolS, DevS, Edu

Montyn, J.
Phi, AHis, CuS, Lit

Moonen, Drs E.M.B.
Env, Agr

Muijzenberg, Prof. dr O.D. van den
Soc, DevS, Ant, His

Mulder, Dr N.
Soc, Ant

Nadal Uceda, F. de
Ant, Arch, Lin, Phi, Psy, Rel

Naerssen, Dr A.L. van
DevS, Geo

Nguyen, Dr N.L.
CuS, DevS

Niehof, Prof. dr A.
Ant, Soc

Ommen, Drs A.F. van
IR, PolS

Oorthuizen, Ir H.J.M.
Agr, DevS

Patmo, Drs S.
Edu, Soc, Ant, DevS

Persoon, Dr G.A.
DevS, Ant, Env

Pluvier, Dr J.M.
His, DevS, IR

Pompe, Dr J.H.
PolS, DevS, Env, IR, Agr, Ant, Eco, Soc, CuS, Edu, Phi, Law,

Prchal, Drs M.
PolS, His, Rel

Rutten, Dr R.A.
DevS, Ant

Sanders, Drs M.
DevS, Eco

Schäfer, Drs E.S.
His, Eco, IR, CuS

Schalke, Dr H.J.W.G.
Arch, Ant, Env

Schilt, J.W.
His, IR

Smidt, Prof. dr J.
Eco

Snelder, Dr D.J.
Env, Agr

Spiekerman-Middelplaats, M.Y.M.
Env

Staal, Dr P.M. van der
PolS

Stam, Prof. dr J.A.
DevS, Eco, IR

Stel, Dr J.H.
Env, Eco

Suringa, Mr P.
Law, AHis, Lit, IR, His, Phi, His, Edu, CuS, DevS, Eco, PolS

Top, Ir G.M. van den
Agr, DevS, Env

Vellema, S.R.
Soc

Voogt, Drs P.R.
Ant

Voskuil, Dr J.E.
Lin

Vreeswijk, Drs L.
Ant, DevS

Wichelen, Drs C.B.J. van
Soc, Phi, Ant, DevS, Rel

Wolters, Dr W.G.
Ant, DevS

Wolvekamp, Drs P.S.
Agr, IR, DevS, Env, GenS

Norway

Lamvik, G.M.
Ant

Philippines

Berg, Dr E. van den
Edu

Poland

Goralski, Prof. dr
PolS, His, IR

Lukaszuk, Dr L.B.
Law, Eco, IR, DevS

Winid, Prof. dr B.
PolS, DevS, Env, Geo

Portugal

Marques Gvedes, Prof. dr A.
Ant

Oliveira e Costa, Dr J.P.
His, Rel

Russia

Alieva, Dr N.F.
Lin, Lit

Boitsov, Dr V.V.
DevS, Eco, Geo, IR

Kozlov, Dr A.A.
His, Eco

Levtonova, Dr Y.O.
His, PolS, IR

Levtonova, Dr Yu.O.
PolS

Makarenko, Prof. dr V.A.
Lin, Lit, His, Ant, Edu, CuS, Rel

Meshkov, Dr K.Yu.
Ant

Rogojine, Dr A.
Env, Eco, IR, DevS

Shkarban, Dr L.I.
Lin

Solomonik, Dr I.N.
His, AHis

Russia

Stanyukovich, M.V.
GenS, DevS, Ant

Zakaznikova, Dr Y.P.
DevS, Soc, PolS, His

Spain

Beltran Antolin, Dr J.
Soc, Ant

Bustelo, Dr P.
DevS, Eco

Canto, Dr P.
DevS, IR, Eco

Casado-Fresnillo, Dr C.
Lin

Castillo Rodriguez, S.
IR

Cuesta Garcia, Antonio
His

Elías de Tejada Lozano, Diplomat F.
Eco, Lit, PolS

Elizalde Perez-Grueso, Dr D.
His, IR

Fernández Miguélez, J.
IR

Fernández-Shaw Baldasano, C.M.

Fradera, Dr J.M.
His

Fradera Barceló, J.N.
His

Gallego Fresnillo, C.
His

Garci -Ab solo, Dr A.
His, Ant, CuS

Gil, Prof. J.
His, Lit

Gomez Pradas, Muriel
AHis, Ant

Jimenez Valentin, J.M.
Eco, Env, IR

Maestro Yarza, Irene
ECOMICS, DEVELOPMENT STUDIES

Mas Murcia, A.
Eco

Molina Memije, A.
His, Lit

Navarro Celada, F.

Navasquillo Sarrjon, C.
His

Olle Rodriguez, M.M.
His

Ortiz Armengol, P.
Geo, His, IR, Lit

Picornell Marti, P.
Eco, Env, His

Quilis, Antonio
Lin

Rodao, Prof. F.R.
His, IR

Rodríguez Ubeda, M.M.
Eco, IR, Soc

Rodriguez-Eiras, J.A.
Agr, Eco, Edu, Env, His, Soc

Sanchez Gomez, Luis Angel
Ant, His

Sotelo Navalpotro, J.A.
Env, Geo

Togores Sanchez, L.E.
IR, His

Tormo Sanz, Leandro
His

Valle Alvarez Maestre, M. del
His

Vilaro Giralt, R.
Eco, IR, PolS

Sweden

Amer, Dr R.
IR, PolS, His

Annerstedt, Prof. J.O.E.
His, Eco, IR, PolS

Törnquist, Dr C.O.
DevS, PolS

Switzerland

Ahmed, Dr I.
Env, Agr, Eco

Künzi, A.
PolS, Eco, DevS

Lutz, P.
Eco, GenS, Env, Edu

Tarnutzer, Dr A.
Ant, GenS, DevS

Wang, Mr D.T.C.
PolS, Law

United Kingdom

Alejo, Prof. A.E.
Ant

Auty, Dr R.M.
DevS, Env, Eco

Barker, Dr N.H.
Ant, Rel

Belshaw, Prof. D.G.R.
DevS, Env, Agr, Eco,

Bevis, G.G.
His, Lit, AHis

Booth, Prof. A.E.
Agr, Eco, Edu, GenS, His, DevS

Brown, Dr I.G.
His

Bryant, Dr R.L.
Geo, PolS, DevS, Env

Burns, M.
Arch, His, AHis, CuS, Ant

Cannell, F.
His, IR, PolS, Soc

Carey, Dr P.B.R.
His, IR, CuS, Lit, Rel

Carino, J.
CuS, Rel, Lit, His, IR

Carswell, Prof. J.W.
AHis, CuS, His

Carter, Dr L.J.
His

Cedercreutz, S.J.T.
Ant

Chant, Dr S.
DevS, GenS

Clarence-Smith, Dr W.G.
His

Clarke, G.
His, AHis

Clarke, Dr G.
PolS, DevS

Cook, M.
Eco

Crosbie, Dr A.J.
IR, Env, Eco, Geo, DevS

Cummings, I.
Eco, CuS, PolS, Env

Dixon, Dr C.J.
Geo

Ford, Dr N.J.
Geo, GenS, DevS, CuS

Heng, J.W.M.
His, Arch, AHis

Henry, Dr J.C.K.
His

Hodgkinson, E.
Eco

Huxley, Dr T.J.
IR, PolS

Johnson, M.
Ant

Kazer, K.
Rel, Ant

King, Prof. U.
Phi, His, Edu, Ant, GenS, CuS, Rel, Soc

Kirkpatrick, Prof. C.H.
Env, Eco

Mikamo, S.
Env, DevS

Nettleton, G.
Lin, CuS, His, Lit

Park, S.S.
Psy, PolS, Phi, SocAHis, DevS, Env, Edu, IR, Law

Picken, Dr L.E.R.
CuS

Prall, J.
PolS, DevS

Preston, Dr D.A.
Geo, Agr, DevS, Env

Putzel, Drs J.J.
DevS, Env, PolS

Richardson, C.
AHis

Richardson, Dr J.A.
PolS, His

Ryan, Dr J.T.
Eco

United Kingdom

Salazar, Drs W.M.W.T.
His

Satterthwaite, D.
PolS, IR

Sidel, Dr J.T.
PolS

Slater, Dr R.P.
PolS, Ant, DevS, Eco

Smith, Dr D.A.
Lin

Strickland, Dr S.S.
Ant

Tacoli, C.
Lin

Thirkell, A.
Ant, His, PolS, Soc, Rel

Valentin, J.C.P.
Env, Ant, CuS, Lin, His, Arch

Walker, L.
Lit

Whalley, Dr J.
Eco

Whitmore, Dr T.C.
Env

Wilder, Dr W.D.
GenS, DevS, Ant

SINGAPORE

Austria

Mosch, Dr N.
CuS, Phi

Belgium

Baetens-Beardsmore, Drs H.
Edu, Lin

Bogart, K.J.
Edu, CuS

Carpano, R.
Eco, IR

Della Pietra, B.
IR, His, CuS

Fang, Dr S.-S.
CuS, Edu

Gonzalo Castellanos, Dr A.
IR

Jorgensen, F.V.
IR, DevS, Env, PolS, Law

Lim, Dr P.
DevS, Soc, PolS

Pelkmans, Prof. dr J.
IR, Eco

Servaes, Prof. dr J.E.J.G.
CuS, Ant, Soc, DevS

Wu-Beyens, I.CH.
PolS, IR, His, Agr, DevS, Env

Denmark

Fleming, Prof. D.E.B.
Soc, DevS

Grathwohl, J.U.
Ant, Law

Ostergaard, Dr C.S.
Agr, Soc, PolS, IR, DevS

Padolecchia Polo, Prof. S.P.
DevS, PolS, Rel, Edu, Eco, Soc, Env, IR, CuS

Schmidt, Dr J.D.
Soc, IR, DevS

Thunoe, Drs M.
Ant, Lit, Edu, Soc, DevS, CuS, His

Tönnesson, Dr S.
IR, His

Wang, J.
Lin, Lit, CuS, Edu, His, AHis

Finland

Antikainen-Kokko, Dr A.
IR

Haikonen, Dr J.
DevS, Eco, PolS

Karunaratne, Dr J.A.
DevS, Eco

Seppänen, J.
IR, Eco, Ant, CuS, Lin, His, AHis, Phi, Arch, Rel, PolS

France

Baille, B.
Ant

Barbiche, Prof. dr J.-P.
Law, IR, His, PolS, Eco, DevS, CuS, Edu, Soc

Baye, Dr E.B.
DevS, Env, Eco

Botsch, A.A.
Eco, DevS, IR, Edu, Law

Bouteiller, E.
DevS, Eco

Brun, Dr C. le
Eco, IR, PolS

Chaponniere, Dr J.R.
IR, Eco, PolS, DevS

Cheng, S.H.
AHis, CuS, Rel

Collin, H.
Law, Soc, PolS, Eco, IR

Delaune, Dr F.
Eco, DevS

Foucher, Dr M.
IR, PolS, Eco

Fouquin, M.F.
Eco

Gazano, A.
Law

Godement, Prof. dr F.L.
His, IR

Henry, R.
Lin, GenS, Env, CuS, AHis, Arch, IR, Lit, Phi, Psy

Jacq-Hergoualc'h, Dr M.
Rel, His, Arch, His, AHis

Jarrige, J.F.
His, CuS, Arch, AHis

Jaussaud, Dr J.
Eco, IR

Lagaune, E.
Ant

Lamant, Prof. P.L.
SocAHis, CuS, Arch, Rel, His

Margolin, J.L.
IR, Eco, His, PolS

Orberger, Dr B.
Lin, Lit, Geo

Ordonnadu, G.
IR, Eco

Perlas, Dr Ch.
Ant, CuS

Raillon, Dr F.
Soc, Eco, IR, His, PolS, DevS, Rel

Salmon, Dr C.
Rel, Lit, CuS, His

Sivignon,
Eco, Geo

Williamson, Dr P.J.
DevS, Eco

Woronoff, Dr J.A.
Eco, IR, DevS, PolS

Zheng, Prof. dr Ch.
His, Ant

Germany

Ackermann, Dr A.
Ant, CuS, Soc

Albrecht, E.W.
Eco

Carstens, Dr R.
His, Edu, CuS, AHis, Lin, Lit, DevS, PolS, Rel

Dengel, Dr H.
Rel, AHis, Eco, Arch, DevS, His

Dosch, Drs J.
IR, PolS

Draguhn, Dr W.
PolS, IR, Eco, DevS

Flüchter, Prof. dr W.
Geo, Env

Franke, Prof. dr W.
His, Rel

Friebel, M.
Eco

Gerke, Prof. dr S.
CuS, Soc, DevS

Gröpper, Drs D.
CuS, AHis, Arch, His, Ant

Hanisch, Prof. dr R.
IR, DevS, PolS

Heberer, Prof. dr Th.
Ant, Rel, DevS, GenS, Eco, PolS, Soc

Heidt, Dr E.U.
CuS, Edu

Heilmann, Dr S.
Soc, PolS, IR, His

Henze, Prof. J.
Edu

ASIANISTS BY REGION AND COUNTRY OF INTEREST

Germany

Hohnholz, Prof. J.
DevS, Agr, Geo

Jahnke, M.
Law, Eco, CuS

Knall, Prof. B.R.
IR, Edu, PolS, Eco, DevS

Kraas, Dr F.
Ant, DevS, CuS, Geo

Krause, Prof. E.D.
Lin

Krüger, Prof. dr H.
IR, Law, Rel, Soc, Eco

Kummer, Dr M.E.F.
Psy, RelAgr, Phi, Soc, Lin, IR, Eco, His, Ant, PolS, Env, E

Lorenz, Prof. D.
Eco

Lummer, Drs E.
His, Ant, CuS, Lit

Machetzki, Dr R.
DevS, Eco, PolS

Moeller, Dr K.
IR, PolS

Müller, K.
PolS, CuS, His

Müller-Hofstede, Drs C.
PolS, Soc, His, IR, CuS, DevS

Nass, O.
Eco

Opitz, Prof. P.J.
Phi, His, IR

Pohl, Prof. dr M.
PolS, His

Ramstedt, Drs M.
Ant, Rel, CuS, PolS, Lit

Reichenstein, B.
IR, DevS, Eco

Richter, Dr G.
Lin

Rieger, Dr H.C.
DevS, Env, Eco

Rohde, Prof. dr K.E.
Soc, Eco, Env, DevS, CuS, IR

Romich, Dr M.F.
DevS, Soc, PolS, Eco

Rueland, Prof. dr J.
IR, PolS, DevS

Salzmann, Dr B.
Soc

Schiel, Dr T.
Soc, His, Ant, Agr, Env, DevS, PolS

Schrader, Dr H.
Soc, Eco, Ant, CuS

Stiller, Dr D.F.R.
Law

Wichmann, Drs P.
IR, PolS

Hungary

Birks, L.
Eco, DevS, Env, Agr, IR

Ehrlich, Prof. E.
Eco, DevS

Lukàs, É
AHis, IR, His, CuS

Nyiri, Drs P.D.
Ant, PolS

Italy

Campana, Dr A.
His, IR, PolS

Giambelli, Dr R.A.
Soc, Ant,

Marinelli, Dr M.M.
His, IR, PolS, DevS

Orioli, Dr H.
Ant, His, Arch, AHis

Rispoli, Dr F.
Ant, Arch

Sabattini, Drs M.
His, Lit, Lin

Santa Maria, Prof. dr L.
Lit, Lin, IR, His

Volpi, G.
PolS, IR, Agr, Eco, Env

Malaysia

Wahab Ali, Prof. dr A.
Lit

Netherlands

Arens, Drs J.F.
Lit, His, CuS

Asselbergs, Drs G.
Agr, Eco, Edu

Attema, Drs Y.
AHis, CuS, His

Baas, Prof. dr P.
Env

Bastiaansen, Drs A.C.G.M.
IR, Eco, Edu

Bertsch, Drs H.B.
Soc, Eco

Boelhouwer, R.H.
Eco, Lit, IR

Bruijn, E.J. de
His

Bruijninckx, Drs W.P.M.
Eco, IR

Brunt, Prof. dr L.
Ant, Soc

Choenni, Dr C.E.S.
His, IR, Phi, PolS, Rel, Lit, DevS, Soc

Chou, Dr C.
Ant

Dam, Dr J.E. van
Derveld, Dr F.E.R.
Eco

Dijkstra, Drs G.H.
Soc, Rel, Phi, Eco, His, IR, Psy, PolS

Dishoeck, Drs E.R. van
Eco, Edu, Phi, CuS

Doderlein de Win, E.F.
Law, IR, Edu, Eco, Agr, DevS

Dongen, Drs P.L.F. van
His, Ant, AHis

Duermeijer, Ir A.J.
AHis, Arch, DevS

Dumas, Drs R.M.
PArt, Lit, CuS

Gertsch, Drs L.J.
CuS, DevS

Giel, Mr P.
Env, DevS

Grijns, Dr C.D.
Lin

Grunsven, Dr L.M.J. van
DevS, Eco, Geo, IR

Haitsma, T.J.
IR

Hamelink, Prof. dr C.J.
IR, Law

Haringhuizen, Drs W.
PolS, Ant, IR

Hartog, Dr A.P. den
Ant, DevS

Heersink, Dr C.G.
His

Hoefnagels, Ir H.A.M.
Agr, Eco, Law

Hulst, W.A.
Eco

Jansen, Drs T.E.
DevS, GenS, His

Jehle, Dr E.
IR, DevS, Eco, Edu, Law

Jongsma-Blanche Koelensmid, Drs H.T.
AHis, Arch, CuS, His

Josselin de Jong, Prof. dr P.E. de
Ant

Junne, Prof. G.C.A.
IR, DevS, PolS, Env

Keppy, Drs P.J.
His, Ant

Kol, Prof. dr J.
DevS, Eco, Agr

Lau, W.Y.
SocAHis, CuS

Lie, Drs H.
Eco, Ant

Lopez, Drs S.
CuS, His, AHis

Muijzenberg, Prof. dr O.D. van den
Soc, DevS, Ant, His

Nolten, Drs H.M.
GenS, Geo

Ommen, Drs A.F. van
IR, PolS

Patmo, Drs S.
Edu, Soc, Ant, DevS

Netherlands

Peters, Drs F.H.
DevS, His

Pluvier, Dr J.M.
His, DevS, IR

Pompe, Dr J.H.
PolS, DevS, Env, IR, Agr, Ant, Eco, Soc, CuS, Edu, Phi, Law,

Post, Dr P
IR, Ant, His

Prchal, Drs M.
PolS, His, Rel

Putten, Drs F.P. van der
His, IR, PolS, Eco

Putten, Drs J. van der
Lin, His

Rinsampessy, Dr E.P.
Ant, Soc, Rel, IR, Edu

Roodenburg, C.
Eco, IR, Lin, Soc

Schäfer, Drs E.S.
His, Eco, IR, CuS

Schalke, Dr H.J.W.G.
Arch, Ant, Env

Schoch, Drs G.W.
Eco

Smid, J.W.
Eco

Spiekerman-Middelplaats, M.Y.M.
Env

Stam, Prof. dr J.A.
DevS, Eco, IR

Steenbeek, Dr O.W.
Eco

Suringa, Mr P.
Law, AHis, Lit, IR, His, Phi, His, Edu, CuS, DevS, Eco, PolS

Sutherland, Prof. dr H.A.
CuS, His, Ant

Sybesma, S.
Lin

Truong, Dr D.H.D.
IR, Eco, Env

Vaczi, Drs M.T.
Rel, AHis, GenS, CuS

Verschoor, I.B.
His, Phi, CuS, PolS, Eco

Visscher, Drs S.
PolS, Soc, His

Voogt, Drs P.R.
Ant

Wichelen, Drs C.B.J. van
Soc, Phi, Ant, DevS, Rel

Wiegmans, Drs B.W.
Eco

Wieringa, Dr E.P.
Lit

Norway

Harbsmeier, Prof. dr C.
His, Phi, Lit, Lin, CuS, AHis

Poland

Lukaszuk, Dr L.D.
Law, Eco, IR, DevS

Tomala, Dr K.
PolS, Soc, Phi, Edu

Winid, Prof. dr B.
PolS, DevS, Env, Geo

Zaremba, Dr P.A.
DevS, Env, Eco

Republic of Cyprus

Saunders, Dr G.E.
His

Russia

Alexakhina, Prof. dr A.
Edu, Lin

Chufrin, Dr G.I.
IR, Eco

Gurevich, Dr E.M.
His, PolS, Phi

Kozlov, Dr A.A.
His, Eco

Makarenko, Prof. dr V.A.
Lin, Lit, His, Ant, Edu, CuS, Rel

Parnickel, Prof. dr B.B.
Lit

Reshetov, Dr.o A.M.
Ant

Rogojine, Dr A.
Env, Eco. IR, DevS

Solomonik, Dr I.N.
His, AHis

Tumarkin, Prof. dr D.D.
CuS, DevS, Arch, Eco, His, Ant

Zakaznikova, Dr Y.P.
DevS, Soc, PolS, His

Spain

Bustelo, Dr P.
DevS, Eco

Canto, Dr P.
DevS, IR, Eco

Casares Vidal, D.
Eco

Castillo Rodriguez, S.
IR

Elías de Tejada Lozano, Diplomat F.
Eco, Lit, PolS

Fernández Miguélez, J.
IR

Garcia-Ormaechea Quero, C.
AHis, Geo, His, Lit, Rel, Phi

Mas Murcia, A.
Eco

Navarro Celada, F.

Rodríguez Ubeda, M.M.
Eco, IR, Soc

Sweden

Bratthall, Prof. D.
Eco

Sigurdson, Prof. J.
IR, DevS, Eco, PolS

Switzerland

Jing Li, A.
IR, PolS

Thölen, Drs K.
Arch, His, AHis, Lit

Viaro, Dr A.V.
Env, Ant, DevS

Wang, Mr D.T.C.
PolS, Law

United Kingdom

Auty, Dr R.M.
DevS, Env, Eco

Booth, Prof. A.E.
Agr, Eco, Edu, GenS, His, DevS

Braginsky, Prof. V.I.
Rel, Lit

Bunt, Dr G.
CuS, Ant, Law, Rel

Cameron, Mr J.
Edu, Env, Phi, Eco, CuS, DevS

Carswell, Prof. J.W.
AHis, CuS, His

Carter, Dr L.J.
His

Chalmers, Dr M.
IR

Chin, Dr J.
PolS, DevS, His

Choi, D.-J.
PolS

Conway, Dr B.M.
Edu

Crosbie, Dr A.J.
IR, Env, Eco, Geo, DevS

Dixon, Dr C.J.
Geo

Drakakis-Smith, Prof. D.
DevS

Gallop, Drs A.T.
Lit, His, AHis

Harding, Dr A.J.
Law, Env

Harris, Drs N.
DevS, Eco

Hawthorn, Mr G.P.
IR, DevS, PolS

Heng, J.W.M.
His, Arch, AHis

Hook, Dr B.G.
IR, DevS

Huxley, Dr T.J.
IR, PolS

Jones, Dr R.
Lin, Lit, Rel

Kirkpatrick, Prof. C.H.
Env, Eco

Koktvedgaard Zeitzen, M.
Ant, Arch, GenS

Li, Dr W.
Lin, Edu, Psy

United Kingdom

Ling, Prof. T.O.
Rel

Marett, Dr P.
Rel, Law

Marr, Dr J.R.
Lin, His, CuS, Arch, His, Phi, Rel, AHis, Lit

Mirza, Prof. H.R.
DevS, Eco

Nossiter, Prof. T.J.
Soc, PolS, IR, DevS, His

Parikh, Prof. A.
Eco, DevS, Agr

Park, S.S.
Psy, PolS, Phi, SocAHis, DevS, Env, Edu, IR, Law

Plumbe, A.J.
DevS

Preston, Dr P.W.
PolS, DevS

Roberts, Drs D.C.
DevS, Eco, IR

Ryan, Dr J.T.
Eco

Steffensen, Drs K.N.
PolS, IR

Stockwell, Prof. A.J.
His

Valentin, J.C.P.
Env, Ant, CuS, Lin, His, Arch

Whitmore, Dr T.C.
Env

Wilder, Dr W.D.
GenS, DevS, Ant

Wu, Dr W.-P.
Eco, CuS

THAILAND

Austria

Balzar, Dr D.M.
CuS, His, AHis

Min Tjoa, Prof. dr A.
Edu

Sellner, Dr M.B.
CuS, Lin

Belgium

Ballegeer, J.
PolS, Law

Bogart, K.J.
Edu, CuS

Carpano, R.
Eco, IR

Gonzalo Castellanos, Dr A.
IR

Pelkmans, Prof. dr J.
IR, Eco

Servaes, Prof. dr J.E.J.G.
CuS, Ant, Soc, DevS

Czech Republic

Pospisilova, Dr D.
Rel, AHis

Denmark

Brun, Prof. V.
Lin, Lit, Rel

Bugge, Dr H.
Rel, His

Eggers-Lura, A.M.A.E.
His

Ewers, K.
Ant, Env, DevS

Gravers, Dr M.
Env, His, Rel, PolS, Soc, CuS, Ant

Henriksen, Drs M.A.
Arch, CuS

Ivarsson, Dr S.
His

Lauridsen, Prof. L.S.
DevS

Martinussen, Prof. dr J.
Eco, DevS, PolS

Morch, M.J.V.
Ant

Schmidt, Dr J.D.
Soc, IR, DevS

Sorensen, P.
Arch

Trier, Dr J.
Arch, Rel, Lin, Ant

Wiuf, J.
Phi, Rel, Lit

Finland

Antikainen-Kokko, Dr A.
IR

Jokinen, Drs J.J.
DevS, IR, PolS

Karunaratne, Dr J.A.
DevS, Eco

Rouhomäki, Drs O.
Ant

Seppänen, J.
IR, Eco, Ant, CuS, Lin, His, AHis, Phi, Arch, Rel, PolS

Vepsä, M.
Art

France

Baffie, Dr J.
His, Soc, PolS, CuS

Barbiche, Prof. dr J.-P.
Law, IR, His, PolS, Eco, DevS, CuS, Edu, Soc

Blazy, S.
His

Bogdan, E.
Art

Botsch, A.A.
Eco, DevS, IR, Edu, Law

Bouteiller, E.
DevS, Eco

Bruneau, Dr M.
PolS, DevS, CuS, Geo, Agr

Chagnaud, F.J.
Eco, Agr, Env, DevS

Chaponniere, Dr J.R.
IR, Eco, PolS, DevS

Choron-Baix, Dr C.
Ant, Rel

Collin, H.
Law, Soc, PolS, Eco, IR

Coyaud, Dr M.
Ant, Lin

Debono, F.
Lit, Soc

Delouche, Prof. G.
Lit, Lin

Dessaint, Prof. W.L.
Ant

Dore, A.
DevS, CuS, Ant

Ferlus, M.
Lin

Filliozat, J.
Rel, Lit

Fóray, Dr J.-C.
Lin, His

Forest, Dr A.
His, Rel

Fouquin, M.F.
Eco

Gerbault, D.P.
CuS, Lin

Gobalakchenane, Dr M.
CuS, His, Rel, Soc

Guillon, Dr E.
Ant, AHis, Arch, Rel, His

Hemmet, Ch.
Ant

Inthamone, L.
Lan

Ivanoff, Dr I.J.
Soc, Arch, Ant

Jacq-Hergoualc'h, Dr M.
Rel, His, Arch, His, AHis

Jacques, C.
His

Kalpana Kartik MA,
Ant, AHis, CuS, Rel

Khing, Dr H.D.
Lin, Rel, His, Lit

Lafont, Prof. dr P.B.
His, Rel

Lamant, Prof. P.L.
SocAHis, CuS, Arch, Rel, His

Lange, Dr C.
His, Rel, Ant, His, AHis, Soc

Lechervy, Chr.
IR, PolS

Lemoine, Dr J.
CuS, Ant, GenS, His, Psy, Rel

Levy-Ward, Dr A.
Ant, Lin

Lowira, C.
Ant

ASIANISTS BY REGION AND COUNTRY OF INTEREST

France

Lubeigt, G.

His, AHis, Agr, DevS, Ant, PolS, Env, Arch, Eco, CuS, Geo, H

Mantienne, F.

His, Eco

Mourer, R.

AHis, Ant

Munier MA, M.C.

Arch, AHis, CuS, Rel

Népote, J.

Ant, Rel, PolS, Lit, Eco, His

Orberger, Dr B.

Lin, Lit, Geo

Ordonnadu, G.

IR, Eco

Papeté, Drs J.F.

Ant, Lin, Rel

Pellard, S.

His, Arch, AHis

Pichard, Ir L.

Lit, Soc

Pooput, W.

His, Arch, AHis

Rault-Leyrat, L.R.

His, Rel, Ant, AHis, Ant, Lin, Arch, Phi, His

Rodriquez Doctorate, N.

AHis

Simon, Dr J.C.

Soc, IR, His, Eco, DevS, PolS

Sivignon,

Eco, Geo

Smitsendonk, Dr A.G.O.

Law, Eco, IR, Soc, Rel, PolS, DevS

Taillard, Ch.

DevS, Eco, Geo

Thierry, Dr S.T.

Lit, Lin, CuS, Rel

Thion, Dr S.

Soc, Rel, PolS, His, Ant

Trân, Q.H.

CuS, Ant

Trinh, Prof. V.T.

Edu, Soc, His

Vernieres, Prof. M.V.

Edu, Eco

Waraeksiri, A.

CuS, Lit

Williamson, Dr P.J.

DevS, Eco

Germany

Axel, Dr M.

Psy, Ant, PSYCHIATRY

Bauer, Prof. dr C.H.R.

Lit, Rel, Ant, Lin, His, Arch

Beusch, Drs D.

PolS, IR

Brauns, Drs T.

DevS, Env, Agr

Bronger, Prof. D.

DevS

Dahm, Prof. dr B.

Rel, His, CuS

Dannecker, Drs P.

PolS, GenS, DevS, Soc, Eco

Domes, Prof. dr J.

Soc, PolS, DevS

Dosch, Drs J.

IR, PolS

Draguhn, Dr W.

PolS, IR, Eco, DevS

Franke, Prof. dr W.

His, Rel

Goettingen, Drs D.

PolS, IR

Goetzfried, Dr F.X.

His, Phi, Ant, Rel

Gröpper, Drs D.

CuS, AHis, Arch, His, Ant

Haffner, Prof. dr W.N.

Env

Hager, D.

Eco, IR, PolS

Hanisch, Prof. dr R.

IR, DevS, PolS

Heberer, Prof. dr Th.

Ant, Rel, DevS, GenS, Eco, PolS, Soc

Hell, S.

His, IR

Henze, Prof. J.

Edu

Hinüber, Prof. dr O. von

His, CuS, Arch, His, Law, Lit, AHis, Phi, Rel, Lin

Hohnholz, Prof. J.

DevS, Agr, Geo

Hundius, Prof. H.

Lit, Lin

Kannen, B.

CuS, Ant, Rel, Soc

Kevenhörster, Prof. dr P.K.

PolS

Knall, Prof. B.R.

IR, Edu, PolS, Eco, DevS

Korff, Dr H.R.

DevS, CuS, Soc

Kraas, Dr F.

Ant, DevS, CuS, Geo

Kuckertz, Prof. dr J.

His, Ant

Kummer, Dr M.E.F.

Psy, RelAgr, Phi, Soc, Lin, IR, Eco, His, Ant, PolS, Env, E

Linder Sabine, Drs L.

Ant, Arch, Soc

Lobo, Dr W.

AHis, Ant, Arch

Lorenz, Prof. D.

Eco

Machetzki, Dr R.

DevS, Eco, PolS

Michaelsen, Dr H.

CuS, His, AHis

Mischung, Prof. R.

Ant, Soc, Rel

Moeller, Dr K.

IR, PolS

Müller, M.

His, AHis

Nass, O.

Eco

Neuser, Drs J.

Lit, Lin, CuS, Rel

Pfennig, Dr W.

His, PolS, DevS, IR

Pretzell, Dr K.A.

Rel, CuS, PolS, Ant

Raendchen, Drs O.

CuS, Ant, Lin, Lit

Reinecke, Drs G.

PolS

Rieger, Dr H.C.

DevS, Env, Eco

Rohde, Prof. dr K.E.

Soc, Eco, Env, DevS, CuS, IR

Romich, Dr M.F.

DevS, Soc, PolS, Eco

Rueland, Prof. dr J.

IR, PolS, DevS

Ruenkaew, P.

GenS, DevS, Soc

Schaller, J.I.M.

Lin

Schmidt-Vogt, Dr D.

Env

Schneider, Dr H.

Geo, CuS, DevS

Schweinfurth, Prof. dr U.

Agr, DevS, Env, Arch, IR

Schwörer, Dr G.

CuS, Ant

Seltmann, Dr F.M.

CuS

Stein, Dr W.

Ant, CuS, AHis, Arch, His

Terwiel, Prof. dr B.J.

His, Ant

Warnk, Drs H.

His, Ant

Werner, Dr W.L.

Env, DevS

Wichmann, Drs P.

IR, PolS

Zimmermann, Dr G.R.

Geo

Hungary

Birks, L.

Eco, DevS, Env, Agr, IR

Ehrlich, Prof. E.

Eco, DevS

Hungary

Illyefalvi-Vitez, Prof. Z.
Edu

Italy

Ciarla, Dr R.
His, AHis, CuS, Arch, Ant

Marinelli, Dr M.M.
His, IR, PolS, DevS

McVey, Dr R.T.
PolS, His

Orioli, Dr H.
Ant, His, Arch, AHis

Rispoli, Dr F.
Ant, Arch

Sabattini, Drs M.
His, Lit, Lin

Sandra, Prof. D.E.E.
Ant, CuS, Edu, GenS

Snellgrove, Prof. D.
AHis, Rel, Arch, His

Volpi, G.
PolS, IR, Agr, Eco, Env

Netherlands

Ariyasajsiskul, Drs S.
IR, His

Atman, Dr R.E.
DevS

Bastiaansen, Drs A.C.G.M.
IR, Eco, Edu

Beek, Mr T.J. van
PolS, IR

Beers, Mr H.A.J.J. van
Law, DevS, GenS

Bergink, Drs D.
Rel, Psy, Lin, His, Edu, Ant, GenS, CuS

Boeren, Drs A.J.J.M.
Edu, Ant

Bogaerts, Drs E.M.
Phi, IR, AHis, Rel, Lit, Lin, His, Ant

Borstlap, Drs A.V.
His, AHis

Brinke, Ir H.W. ten
Agr, Edu

Bruijn, E.J. de
His

Bruin, Ir D. de
DevS, Env

Brummelhuis, Dr H.C.F. ten
Ant

Burght, Prof. dr Gr.
Law

Burgler, Dr R.A.
Ant, PolS, His

Busser, Drs R.B.P.M.
IR, Eco

Chemparathy, Prof. dr G.
Rel, Phi

Chutiwongs, Dr N.
Rel, His, Arch, AHis

Cowan, Drs F.M.
GenS, DevS, CuS, Ant, Env, LinAgr

Deelstra, T.
Env

Doderlein de Win, E.F.
Law, IR, Edu, Eco, Agr, DevS

Dubbeldam, Prof. dr L.F.B.
Ant, Edu

Duermeijer, Ir A.J.
AHis, Arch, DevS

Dumas, Drs R.M.
PArt, Lit, CuS

Epskamp, Dr C.P.
AHis, Ant

Gertsch, Drs L.J.
CuS, DevS

Ginkel, Prof. dr J.A. van
Geo, DevS

Goor, Dr J. van
His, IR

Grunsven, Dr L.M.J. van
DevS, Eco, Geo, IR

Hamelink, Prof. dr C.J.
IR, Law

Haringhuizen, Drs W.
PolS, Ant, IR

Harteveld, Ir K.
Agr, Eco, IR, Soc, DevS

Haude, Dr D.K.H.
DevS, Eco

Hengel, Drs A. van
Eco, IR

Hermens, B.
Agr, Env, IR

Heuvel, Ing T. van den
Agr

Hoefnagels, Ir H.A.M.
Agr, Eco, Law

Hudcovicova, A.
CuS

Huizer, Prof. dr G.J.
Rel, IR, Env, DevS

Jagtenberg, Dr R.W.
Law

Jansen, Dr K.
Eco, DevS

Jansen, Drs M.H.M.
Ant

Jehle, Dr E.
IR, DevS, Eco, Edu, Law

Junne, Prof. G.C.A.
IR, DevS, PolS, Env

Kal, Drs W.H.
Env, Lin, DevS, Agr, CuS, Ant, CuS, GenS

Kater, Dr A.
Ant, DevS

Kessel-Hagesteijn, Dr R.R. van
His, Ant

Kloppenborg, Prof. dr M.A.G.T.
His, Lin, Lit, Rel

Knippenberg, Drs L.W.J.
His, DevS, Env, PolS

Koesoebjono, R.H.S.I.
DevS, GenS, Eco

Kortlandt, Prof. dr F.H.H.
Lin

Kusin, Prof. dr J.A.
GenS

Lopez, Drs S.
CuS, His, AHis

Maan, Drs E.E.
Soc, DevS

Meer, N.J. van der
His

Meer, Dr ir C.L.J. van der
DevS, Agr

Mensink, Drs O.H.
AHis, Ant, CuS, His

Montyn, J.
Phi, AHis, CuS, Lit

Mulder, Dr N.
Soc, Ant

Nguyen, Dr N.L.
CuS, DevS

Nielen, Dr J.E.
DevS

Ommen, Drs A.F. van
IR, PolS

Patmo, Drs S.
Edu, Soc, Ant, DevS

Peltenburg, Drs M.E.
DevS

Pluvier, Dr J.M.
His, DevS, IR

Prchal, Drs M.
PolS, His, Rel

Roo, Dr A.J. de
Law

Sanders, Drs M.
DevS, Eco

Schäfer, Drs E.S.
His, Eco, IR, CuS

Schalke, Dr H.J.W.G.
Arch, Ant, Env

Schenk, Dr H.
DevS, Env

Smidt, Prof. dr J.
Eco

Spiekerman-Middelplaats, M.Y.M.
Env

Stam, Prof. dr J.A.
DevS, Eco, IR

Steinhauer, Dr H.
Lin, Ant

Stel, Dr J.H.
Env, Eco

Netherlands

Stengs, Drs I.L.
Rel, His, Ant

Stokhof, Prof. dr W.A.L.
Lit, Lin

Straten, Mr H.M. van
Env, Ant, Law

Stroek, A.J.
Rel, His, CuS

Stuijvenberg, P. van
Eco, DevS

Tims, Prof. dr W.
Eco, Agr, DevS

Verboom, Drs A.W.C.
Phi, Lit, Rel, Lin

Voogt, Drs P.R.
Ant

Vries, Drs J.H.A.
His, AHis, Rel, Ant, His

Welling, Drs K.O.H.
Art

Wiegmans, Drs B.W.
Eco

Wolffers, Prof. dr I
DevS

Wolvekamp, Drs P.S.
Agr, IR, DevS, Env, GenS

Zoomers, Drs H.C.M.
His, IR, PolS

Zwijnenburg, Ph.A.
His

Norway

Lund, Prof. R.
GenS, Geo, DevS

Sparkes, S.J.
Ant

Poland

Lukaszuk, Dr L.B.
Law, Eco, IR, DevS

Majewicz, Prof. dr A.F.
Lin, Ant

Slawinski, Prof. dr Hab.
DevS, Ant, Eco, PolS

Winid, Prof. dr B.
PolS, DevS, Env, Geo

Zaremba, Dr P.A.
DevS, Env, Eco

Russia

Dolnikova, Dr V.A.
His

Fomicheva, Dr Y.A.
PolS, IR

Grikurov, Dr S.S.
Eco, IR

Ivanova, Dr E.V.
Ant

Kozlov, Dr A.A.
His, Eco

Morev, Dr L.N.
CuS, Lin

Osipov, Prof. dr Y.M.
Lit, Rel

Rogojine, Dr A.
Env, Eco, IR, DevS

Solomonik, Dr I.N.
His, AHis

Zakaznikova, Dr Y.P.
DevS, Soc, PolS, His

Zubov, Dr A.B.
PolS

Spain

Albarrán Serrano, Antonio
Lit

Bustelo, Dr P.
DevS, Eco

Canto, Dr P.
DevS, IR, Eco

Castillo Rodriguez, S.
IR

Elías de Tejada Lozano, Diplomat F.
Eco, Lit, PolS

Fernández Miguélez, J.
IR

Gonzales de Orduña Criado, Silvia
DevS

Gouzalez Molina, A.
IR, Soc

Jimenez Valentin, J.M.
Eco, Env, IR

Kim, Drs S.-H.
Arch, Rel, Phi, Lit, His, AHis

Navarro Celada, F.

Pajares Ruiz, J.M.
AHis, Eco, Geo, Soc

Rodríguez Ubeda, M.M.
Eco, IR, Soc

Suero Tellitu, T.
Ant, Phi, PolS, Rel, Soc

Togores Sanchez, L.E.
IR, His

Sweden

Abdulsomad, K.
DevS, Eco

Amer, Dr R.
IR, PolS, His

Bratthall, Prof. D.
Eco

Corlin, Dr C.G.
DevS, Ant

Hammargren, Drs H.A.
PolS, IR, DevS

Hansson, Prof. I.L
Lin, Rel

Hovemyr, Dr A.P.
Rel, His, CuS

Karlsson, Drs K.
Rel

Lindberg Falk, M.L.F.
CuS, Rel, Ant, GenS, Soc

Lindell, Drs K.
Lin, CuS, Env

Ronnås, Dr P.
DevS, Agr, Eco

Schalk, Prof. dr P.
Phi, AHis, CuS, Arch, His, Rel

Siriprachai, S.
Eco, DevS

Tayanin, D.
CuS, Env, Agr, Ant, Rel

Trankell, Dr I.B.
Ant

Zejan, Dr M.C.
DevS, Eco

Switzerland

Ahmed, Dr I.
Env, Agr, Eco

Leemann, Prof. dr A.
Agr, DevS, CuS

Rastorfer, Ir J.M.
His, CuS

Thölen, Drs K.
Arch, His, AHis, Lit

Wang, Mr D.T.C.
PolS, Law

United Kingdom

Arghiros, Dr D.
Ant, DevS

Auty, Dr R.M.
DevS, Env, Eco

Belshaw, Prof. D.G.R.
DevS, Env, Agr, Eco,

Booth, Prof. A.E.
Agr, Eco, Edu, GenS, His, DevS

Brailey, Dr N.J.
His

Brown, Dr I.G.
His

Bryant, Dr R.L.
Geo, PolS, DevS, Env

Carswell, Prof. J.W.
AHis, CuS, His

Carter, Dr L.J.
His

Chalmers, Dr M.
IR

Chapman, G.
His, AHis, CuS

Cockburn, Mr R.C.
DevS, CuS

Conway, Dr B.M.
Edu

Cook, M.
Eco

Cousins, Drs L.S.
His, Rel, Lit

Crosbie, Dr A.J.
IR, Env, Eco, Geo, DevS

Dixon, Dr C.J.
Geo

United Kingdom

Dunn, Mr A.J-J.
IR, Edu, CuS, Ant

Elliott, D.
AHis

Ferdinand, Drs C.I.P.
PolS, DevS, His, Eco, IR

Ford, Dr N.J.
Geo, GenS, DevS, CuS

Garforth, Prof. dr C.J.
Agr, Edu

Gethin, Dr R.M.L.
Rel

Glover, Dr I.C.
Arch

Guy, Drs J.S.
His, AHis

Harris, Drs N.
DevS, Eco

Harrison, Dr R.V.
Lit, CuS, GenS

Heng, J.W.M.
His, Arch, AHis

Heron, Dr C.P.
Arch

Houtman, Dr G.
Ant, Lit, Rel

Howard, Dr K.D.
Ant, Rel

Huxley, Dr T.J.
IR, PolS

Huxley, Mr A.D.
Law, His

Kemp, Prof. J.H.
Ant, CuS, Rel

King, Prof. U.
Phi, His, Edu, Ant, GenS, CuS, Rel, Soc

Lenman, Prof. B.P.
His

Ling, Prof. T.O.
Rel

Lowe, Dr P.C.
IR, His

Maloney, Dr B.K.
Env

Marr, Dr J.R.
Lin, His, CuS, Arch, His, Phi, Rel, AHis, Lit

McCargo, Dr D.J.
PolS

McDonnel, Dr J.G.
Arch

McGregor, Dr J.A.
DevS, Ant, His

Moore, Dr E.H.
AHis, Arch

Park, S.S.
Psy, PolS, Phi, SocAHis, DevS, Env, Edu, IR, Law

Parnwell, Dr M.J.G.
DevS, Env, Geo

Picken, Dr L.E.R.
CuS

Plumbe, A.J.
DevS

Putzel, Drs J.J.
DevS, Env, PolS

Rigg, Dr J.D.
Geo, Env, Agr, DevS

Rooney, Dr D.F.
His, AHis

Stargardt, Prof. J.M.
Rel, ArchAgrAHis

Thompson, Dr J.B.
Ant, Env, Arch

Tuck, P.J.N.
His

Valentin, J.C.P.
Env, Ant, CuS, Lin, His, Arch

Watson, Prof. W.
Arch, His, AHis

Whitmore, Dr T.C.
Env

Wilder, Dr W.D.
GenS, DevS, Ant

Yugoslavia

Imamovic, E.
His, CuS, AHis

VIETNAM

Austria

Sellner, Dr M.B.
CuS, Lin

Vu Xuan Quang, Dr .
Eco

Belgium

Adams, N.
GenS, His, DevS

Ballegeer, J.
PolS, Law

Carpano, R.
Eco, IR

Gonzalo Castellanos, Dr A.
IR

Lambrecht, M.
AHis

Czech Republic

Hubinger, Prof. dr V.
PolS, Ant, Soc

Denmark

Baark, Dr E.
His, DevS, Env, CuS

Ewers, K.
Ant, Env, DevS

Gammeltoft, Drs T.
GenS, Ant

Gravers, Dr M.
Env, His, Rel, PolS, Soc, CuS, Ant

Hansen, J.Chr.K.
His

Herno, Drs R.
IR, PolS

Magnussen, Drs T.
DevS, IR, PolS

Masina, P.P.
DevS, His, IR

Nielsen, Drs H.A.
PolS, DevS

Norlund, Dr I.M.
His, GenS, DevS

Ostergaard, Dr C.S.
Agr, Soc, PolS, IR, DevS

Padolecchia Polo, Prof. S.P.
DevS, PolS, Rel, Edu, Eco, Soc, Env, IR, CuS

Prag, J.
DevS

Schmidt, Dr J.D.
Soc, IR, DevS

Sorensen, P.
Arch

Tönnesson, Dr S.
IR, His

Trier, Dr J.
Arch, Rel, Lin, Ant

Finland

Jokinen, Drs J.J.
DevS, IR, PolS

Närhi, Drs P.
His, CuS, Rel, Ant

Palmujoki, E.A.
PolS, IR

Seppänen, J.
IR, Eco, Ant, CuS, Lin, His, AHis, Phi, Arch, Rel, PolS

France

Albis, R.
Eco

André-Pallois, Dr N.
His, AHis

Balaize, C.
Ant, Agr, CuS, Rel

Barbiche, Prof. dr J.-P.
Law, IR, His, PolS, Eco, DevS, CuS, Edu, Soc

Bertrand, Dr D.
Psy, Rel, Ant

Bezançon, P.
Edu, His

Blanc, Dr M.E.
Soc, GenS

Blayac, A.A.
Lit, His, Phi, Edu, Psy, Soc

Botsch, A.A.
Eco, DevS, IR, Edu, Law

Boudarel, G.
IR, PolS, CuS, His, Ant, GenS

Brocheux, Prof. P.B.
His

Cao, Dr T.L.
Lin

France

Chagnaud, F.J.
Eco, Agr, Env, DevS

Charpentier, Dr J.M.
Ant, Lin, Edu, CuS

Collin, H.
Law, Soc, PolS, Eco, IR

Coyaud, Dr M.
Ant, Lin

Cunin, P.
Ant, Soc, Eco

Dang, T.
Lit

Daniel, V.
Soc

Dauphin, A.
Lit

Dessaint, Prof. W.L.
Ant

Dinh, T.H.
Soc

Dumont, Prof. R.
Agr, Env, DevS

Dung, Drs T.T.
Rel, Lin, Edu, Ant, CuS

Durand, Dr F.B.
Env, Agr, Lit, DevS

Ferlus, M.
Lin

Fóray, Dr J.-C.
Lin, His

Forest, Dr A.
His, Rel

Fourniau, Prof. Ch.
His

Gantès, G. de
His

Gerbault, D.P.
CuS, Lin

Guénel, A.
CuS, His

Guillaume, X.
His, ArchAgr, Env

Guillemin, A.
Soc

Guillon, Dr E.
Ant, AHis, Arch, Rel, His

Heide, Dr S. von der
Ant, DevSAHis, Env, CuS, Rel, PolS

Hemery, Dr D.
His

Hemmet, Ch.
Ant

Jacq-Hergoualc'h, Dr M.
Rel, His, Arch, His, AHis

Jarrige, J.F.
His, CuS, Arch, AHis

Jaussaud, Dr J.
Eco, IR

Kiss, A.
Ant, Phi, Psy

Korwenski, N.
Soc

Krowolski, N.
Ant

Lamant, Prof. P.L.
SocAHis, CuS, Arch, Rel, His

Lange, Dr C.
His, Rel, Ant, His, AHis, Soc

Langlet, Dr P.
His

Larcher, A.
His

Le Failler, Dr Ph.
His

Le Och-Mach, T.-C.
Lan

Lê Thành Khôi, Prof. dr
His, CuS, Edu

Lechervy, Chr.
IR, PolS

Lemoine, Dr J.
CuS, Ant, GenS, His, Psy, Rel

Macdonald, Dr C.J.H.
CuS, Ant, Lin, Rel

Mancini, J.-M.
His

Mantienne, F.
His, Eco

Maurice, A.-M.
Rel, Ant

Moreau, P.
Art

Móriot, Prof. CH.
Ant

Népote, J.
Ant, Rel, PolS, Lit, Eco, His

Nguyen, M.H.
Lan

Nguyen, Q.
Lan

Nguyen, T.
Soc

Nguyen, Dr D.N.
Soc, Ant, DevS, Edu

Nguyen, Dr P.P.
Edu, Lin, Lit

Nguyen, Dr V.K.
His

Nguyen, Dr X.L.
Rel, Ant

Nguyên, Prof. dr T.A.
IR, CuS, His, Rel, Lit

Niederer, B.
Lin, His, Ant

Orberger, Dr B.
Lin, Lit, Geo

Ordonnadu, G.
IR, Eco

Pasquel Rageau, Dr Ch.
CuS, His

Pham Dan Binh,
Lin

Pham Dinh Tieu, N.-A.
Lan

Phan Thanh Thuy, Dr
Lin

Po Dharma Quang, Dr
Lin, Lit, His

Pouvatchy, Dr J.R.
Rel, His, PolS, IR

Pozner, P.
His

Prévot, M.
Lin

Raffi, G.
His

Rault-Leyrat, L.R.
His, Rel, Ant, AHis, Ant, Lin, Arch, Phi, His

Rodriquez Doctorate, N.
AHis

Salmon, Dr C.
Rel, Lit, CuS, His

Scalabrino, Drs C.J.
Rel, Arch, His, Phi, Psy, His, IR, AHis, PolS

Sivignon,
Eco, Geo

Ta, T.H.
Lin

Taillard, Ch.
DevS, Eco, Geo

Tertrais, Prof. H.T.
His, IR

Thion, Dr S.
Soc, Rel, PolS, His, Ant

Trân, Q.H.
CuS, Ant

Tran, Dr N.B.
Eco

Trinh, Prof. V.T.
Edu, Soc, His

Vallot, B.
Lit

Verdilhac, de
Eco

Vernieres, Prof. M.V.
Edu, Eco

Vienne, Dr M.S. de
Eco

Williamson, Dr P.J.
DevS, Eco

Germany

Bass, Dr H.H.
DevS, Eco, IR

Bauer, Prof. dr C.H.R.
Lit, Rel, Ant, Lin, His, Arch

Dahm, H.
IR, Eco

Germany

Dahm, Prof. dr B.
Rel, His, CuS

Dewall, Dr M.V. von
His, CuS, Arch, Ant, AHis

Draguhn, Dr W.
PolS, IR, Eco, DevS

Duy-Tu, Prof. dr V.
Lit, Lin, His

Engelbert, Dr J.T.
His, IR

Geisler, Drs G.H.S.
Geo, Env, DevS

Gerke, Prof. dr S.
CuS, Soc, DevS

Goettingen, Drs D.
PolS, IR

Goetzfried, Dr F.X.
His, Phi, Ant, Rel

Grossheim, Dr M.
His

Hager, D.
Eco, IR, PolS

Heberer, Prof. dr Th.
Ant, Rel, DevS, GenS, Eco, PolS, Soc

Henze, Prof. J.
Edu

Klotz, Drs S.
PolS, IR

Knall, Prof. B.R.
IR, Edu, PolS, Eco, DevS

Kohl MA, Arko
His, PolS, Soc

Kraas, Dr F.
Ant, DevS, CuS, Geo

Kummer, Dr M.E.F.
Psy, RelAgr, Phi, Soc, Lin, IR, Eco, His, Ant, PolS, Env, E

Linder Sabine, Drs L.
Ant, Arch, Soc

Lobo, Dr W.
AHis, Ant, Arch

Lommel, Dr A.
His, AHis, CuS

Lorenz, Prof. D.
Eco

Meyer-Tran, E.
DevS, Agr, His, Soc, Eco

Mischung, Prof. R.
Ant, Soc, Rel

Moeller, Dr K.
IR, PolS

Müller, K.
PolS, CuS, His

Müller-Hofstede, Drs C.
PolS, Soc, His, IR, CuS, DevS

Nass, O.
Eco

Nguyen, Dr M.H.
Lin

Nguyen, Dr T.-H.
AHis, Rel, CuS, His, Arch, Ant, Soc

Nguyen, Drs U.
Edu

Pews, Dr H.U.
Eco, DevS, Geo

Raendchen, Drs O.
CuS, Ant, Lin, Lit

Raitza, Dr K.
Lin

Revilla Diez, Drs J.
Eco

Sauerborn, Prof. J.
Agr, Env

Schütte, Dr H.
Soc, CuS, His

Schweinfurth, Prof. dr U.
Agr, DevS, Env, Arch, IR

Stein, Dr W.
Ant, CuS, AHis, Arch, His

Vu, Drs H.
IR, PolS

Weggel, Dr O.
Law, Rel, Soc, CuS, Phi, Lin, PolS, IR

Wichmann, Drs P.
IR, PolS

Hungary

Bassa, Dr Z.
Eco

Ehrlich, Prof. E.
Eco, DevS

Ivnyi, Dr Z.
IR, PolS

Italy

Ciarla, Dr R.
His, AHis, CuS, Arch, Ant

Collotti Pischel, Prof. E
His, PolS

Marinelli, Dr M.M.
His, IR, PolS, DevS

Montessoro, F.
His

Orioli, Dr H.
Ant, His, Arch, AHis

Rispoli, Dr F.
Ant, Arch

Samarani, G.
His

Sandra, Prof. D.E.E.
Ant, CuS, Edu, GenS

Volpi, G.
PolS, IR, Agr, Eco, Env

Netherlands

Aelst, Drs A. van
His

Arnoldus-Schröder, Drs V.
Edu, Ant, CuS

Bastiaansen, Drs A.C.G.M.
IR, Eco, Edu

Beek, Mr T.J. van
PolS, IR

Boele van Hensbroek, P.
Law, Eco

Boelhouwer, R.H.
Eco, Lit, IR

Borstlap, Drs A.V.
His, AHis

Boselie, Drs D.
Ant

Brinke, Ir H.W. ten
Agr, Edu

Brouwer, A.A.
CuS, Eco, His, IR, PolS, Psy, Rel, Phi

Bruijninckx, Drs W.P.M.
Eco, IR

Bruin, Ir D. de
DevS, Env

Bui, V.Q.
His, Eco, Lin, Soc, EduAgr

Burgler, Dr R.A.
Ant, PolS, His

Chutiwongs, Dr N.
Rel, His, Arch, AHis

Cowan, Drs F.M.
GenS, DevS, CuS, Ant, Env, LinAgr

Dalen, Prof. J.Chr. van
DevS, Edu, Soc, Eco, IR, PolS, Env

Dang, Dr D.B.
CuS

Doderlein de Win, E.F.
Law, IR, Edu, Eco, Agr, DevS

Dongen, Drs P.L.F. van
His, Ant, AHis

Ellman, Prof. dr M.J.
Eco, DevS

Feddema, Drs R.
PolS, IR, His, Eco

Giel, Mr P.
Env, DevS

Gontscharoff, C.
IR, DevS

Grant, Dr M.E.
Lit, IR, His, AHis, Rel

Hanssen, Drs L.M.
Ant, CuS

Haringhuizen, Drs W.
PolS, Ant, IR

Heins, Drs J.J.F.
Env, DevS

Hermens, B.
Agr, Env, IR

Heuvel, Ing T. van den
Agr

Netherlands

Hoefnagels, Ir H.A.M.
Agr, Eco, Law

Hommes, Prof. dr E.W.
DevS, Ant

Hoogland, Drs J.G.D.
Eco, DevS, Env

Ishaja, Drs F.A.
His

Jagtenberg, Dr R.W.
Law

Jehle, Dr E.
IR, DevS, Eco, Edu, Law

Kal, Drs W.H.
Env, Lin, DevS, Agr, CuS, Ant, CuS, GenS

Kamp, E.P. van der
His

Karssen, Dr C.M.
DevS, Env, Agr, Eco, Edu, Soc, GenS

Kater, Dr A.
Ant, DevS

Kessel-Hagesteijn, Dr R.R. van
His, Ant

Kleinen, Dr J.G.G.M.
Ant

Koesoebjono, R.H.S.I.
DevS, GenS, Eco

Kolko, Dr G.
Eco, PolS

Kortlandt, Prof. dr F.H.H.
Lin

Lanjouw, Dr G.J.
Eco, Edu

Malcontent, Drs P.A.M.
His

Meuldijk, Drs I.M.
Soc, Agr, GenS, Env, Ant, DevS

Mierlo, Drs H.W.R. van
Lin, CuS, AHis

Minnigh, Ir P.E.
DevS, Env

Montyn, J.
Phi, AHis, CuS, Lit

Muijzenberg, Prof. dr O.D. van den
Soc, DevS, Ant, His

Ngo, T.T.L.
Lin

Nguyen, Dr N.L.
CuS, DevS

Nguyen, Prof. X.H.
CuS, Agr, Arch, Lit

Nielen, Dr J.E.
DevS

Ommen, Drs A.F. van
IR, PolS

Oosterwijk, A.J.
His, Ant, Arch

Opdam, Drs J.H.M.
DevS

Ouden, Dr J.H.B. den
DevS, Ant, Agr, GenS

Patmo, Drs S.
Edu, Soc, Ant, DevS

Pinkers, Ir M.J.H.P.
IR, DevS, EduAgr

Pluvier, Dr J.M.
His, DevS, IR

Prchal, Drs M.
PolS, His, Rel

Roo, Dr A.J. de
Law

Schäfer, Drs E.S.
His, Eco, IR, CuS

Schalke, Dr H.J.W.G.
Arch, Ant, Env

Scheltema, Prof. mr M.
Law

Schenk, Dr H.
DevS, Env

Schenk-Sandbergen, Dr L.Ch.
GenS, DevS, Env, Ant

Sigmond, Dr J.P.
CuS, His, AHis, Arch

Singh, Dr N.
Agr, Env, DevS, Soc, IR

Spiekerman-Middelplaats, M.Y.M.
Env

Steinhauer, Dr H.
Lin, Ant

Stokhof, Prof. dr W.A.L.
Lit, Lin

Sukrisno, Drs A.
Ant, His, PolS

Truong, Dr D.H.D.
IR, Eco, Env

Ubaghs, Drs J.M.M.
CuS, His

Vereeken, Drs B.
Ant, DevS

Verhoeven, Drs P.R.F.
Lin

Vis, Mr B.C.
DevS, Law

Voogd, Drs P. de
DevS, GenS, Soc, Edu

Voogt, Drs P.R.
Ant

Welling, Drs K.O.H.
Art

Wolffers, Prof. dr I
DevS

Wolvekamp, Drs P.S.
Agr, IR, DevS, Env, GenS

Zutt, S.
Ant

Norway

Bleie, T.
Env, Ant, GenS, DevS, CuS

Poland

Goralski, Prof. dr
PolS, His, IR

Gudowski, J.
Eco, Agr, DevS

Krzyzanowski, Dr L.K.
AHis

Kulig, Prof. J.
Eco, IR

Lukaszuk, Dr L.B.
Law, Eco, IR, DevS

Majewicz, Prof. dr A.F.
Lin, Ant

Olbrys, Drs M.
Lin, Lit

Stecinski, Drs J.
AHis

Swiercz, Drs J.
Lin

Wawrzyniak, Dr A.
CuS, Ant

Rumania

Liushnea, Dr D.S.
DevS, Eco, IR, PolS

Russia

Alexakhina, Prof. dr A.
Edu, Lin

Alieva, Dr N.F.
Lin, Lit

Andreeva, V. A.
Lin

Deopik, D.V.
Arch, CuS, Rel, Ant, His

Filimonova, T.N.
Lin, Lit

Grigorieva, N.V.
Ant, Rel

Kobelev, Dr E.V.
PolS, His, IR

Lethiaghin, Dr D. V.

Murasheva, Dr G.F.
His, IR

Nikitin, Dr A.V.
Phi

Nikulin, Prof. N.I.
Lit

Novakova, Dr O.V.
Geo, His, Soc, Edu

Pozner, Dr P.V.
CuS, His

Remarchouk, Dr V.V.
AHis, CuS, His, Lin

Rogojine, Dr A.
Env, Eco, IR, DevS

Ryabinin, Dr A.L.
His

Samarina, I. V.
Lin

Shkarban, Dr L.I.
Lin

Russia

Shmeleva, Dr G.V.

CuS

Sokolov, Prof. dr A.A.

AHis, Lin, Phi, Lit, PolS, CuS, Soc, His

Solntsev, Prof. dr V.M.

Lin

Solomonik, Dr I.N.

His, AHis

Yakovlev, Prof. A.G.

His, Eco, IR

Spain

Albarrán Serrano, Antonio

Lit

Bustelo, Dr P.

DevS, Eco

Castillo Rodriguez, S.

IR

Elías de Tejada Lozano, Diplomat F.

Eco, Lit, PolS

Esparrago Rodilla MA, Luis

Agr, PolS

Fernández Miguélez, J.

IR

Gouzalez Molina, A.

IR, Soc

Illionnet, D.

Lin

Jimenez Valentin, J.M.

Eco, Env, IR

Manso, L.

Agr, Edu, Env, His, IR

Mas Murcia, A.

Eco

Navarro Celada, F.

Pajares Ruiz, J.M.

AHis, Eco, Geo, Soc

Rodríguez Ubeda, M.M.

Eco, IR, Soc

Togores Sanchez, L.E.

IR, His

Vilaro Giralt, R.

Eco, IR, PolS

Sweden

Amer, Dr R.

IR, PolS, His

Andersen, H.

Eco

Annerstedt, Prof. J.O.E.

His, Eco, IR, PolS

Bratthall, Prof. D.

Eco

Corlin, Dr C.G.

DevS, Ant

Hammargren, Drs H.A.

PolS, IR, DevS

Hansson, E.

PolS

Jerneck, Dr A.

DevS, Eco

Kokko, Dr A.O.

Eco, DevS

Lindell, Drs K.

Lin, CuS, Env

Lindskog, E.I.M.

Soc, DevS, GenS, Ant, CuS

Lundström-Burghoorn, Dr W.S.Y.M.C.

Ant, DevS, GenS

Román, Dr L.

DevS, Eco

Ronnås, Dr P.

DevS, Agr, Eco

Schalk, Prof. dr P.

Phi, AHis, CuS, Arch, His, Rel

Sigurdson, Prof. J.

IR, DevS, Eco, PolS

Swahn, Prof. J.Ö.

PolS, Soc

Tayanin, D.

CuS, Env, Agr, Ant, Rel

Zejan, Dr M.C.

DevS, Eco

Switzerland

Jing Li, A.

IR, PolS

Lutz, P.

Eco, GenS, Env, Edu

Wang, Mr D.T.C.

PolS, Law

United Kingdom

Aldis, L.

Eco

Auty, Dr R.M.

DevS, Env, Eco

Booth, Prof. A.E.

Agr, Eco, Edu, GenS, His, DevS

Brown, Dr I.G.

His

Carswell, Prof. J.W.

AHis, CuS, His

Carter, Dr L.J.

His

Chalmers, Dr M.

IR

Chapman, G.

His, AHis, CuS

Choi, D.-J.

PolS

Clarence-Smith, Dr W.G.

His

Crosbie, Dr A.J.

IR, Env, Eco, Geo, DevS

Dixon, Dr C.J.

Geo

Drakakis-Smith, Prof. D.

DevS

Dunn, Mr A.J-J.

IR, Edu, CuS, Ant

Ferdinand, Drs C.I.P.

PolS, DevS, His, Eco, IR

Glanville, Drs J.J.M.

Ant, GenS, His

Glover, Dr I.C.

Arch

Harris, Drs N.

DevS, Eco

Healy, Dr D.

Lit, Lin

Heng, J.W.M.

His, Arch, AHis

Henry, Dr J.C.K.

His

Heron, Dr C.P.

Arch

Huxley, Dr T.J.

IR, PolS

Lowe, Dr P.C.

IR, His

McGregor, Dr C.D.

IR

Nossiter, Prof. T.J.

Soc, PolS, IR, DevS, His

Park, S.S.

Psy, PolS, Phi, SocAHis, DevS, Env, Edu, IR, Law

Provine, Prof. dr R.C.

Lin

Putzel, Drs J.J.

DevS, Env, PolS

Ryan, Dr J.T.

Eco

Sheehan, Dr J.

PolS, His

Steeds, Mr D.

IR, His

Thrift, Dr N.J.

Geo

Tuck, P.J.N.

His

Valentin, J.C.P.

Env, Ant, CuS, Lin, His, Arch

Wang, H.

His, AHis, Arch, His

Whalley, Dr J.

Eco

Wilder, Dr W.D.

GenS, DevS, Ant

South Asia

BANGLADESH

Austria

Allinger, Dr E.

Rel, His, CuS, Arch, AHis

Loseries, Dr A.S.

His, Rel, CuS, Phi, His, AHis, DevS, Ant

Belgium

Carpano, R.
Eco, IR

Gonzalo Castellanos, Dr A.
IR

Hacourt, B.J.H.
DevS, Ant

Piquard, B.
Rel, PolS, Ant

Czech Republic

Kostic, Dr S.
Rel, Lin, Phi

Pospisilova, Dr D.
Rel, AHis

Vacek, Prof. dr J.
Phi, Rel, Lit, Lin

Denmark

Ewers, K.
Ant, Env, DevS

Madsen, Dr S.T.
Soc, PolS, DevS, Env, Rel, Ant, IR, Law, His

Martinussen, Prof. dr J.
Eco, DevS, PolS

Nielsen, Drs H.A.
PolS, DevS

Westergaard, Dr K.
PolS, DevS

Finland

Hossain, M.
DevS, IR, PolS

Karunaratne, Dr J.A.
DevS, Eco

UUsikylä, Drs H.A.
Ant

Vanhanen, Dr T.
PolS

France

Adamo, S.A.
AHis, CuS, His, Rel, Soc

Bernard, J.A.
IR, His, Eco, PolS

Bhattacharja, S.
Rel, Lit, His

Bhattacharya, Prof. F.
CuS, Ant, Lit, Rel

Casevitz, Prof. M.H.
Arch, Lin, Rel

Dumont, Prof. R.
Agr, Env, DevS

Heide, Dr S. von der
Ant, DevSAHis, Env, CuS, Rel, PolS

Kasi-Henkus, C.
Eco, DevS

Mohammad, A.T.
His, Soc, Rel

Mukhherjee, Dr P.
His, Lit, Phi, Rel, AHis, Soc, His

Pitoun MA,
Arch, AHis, Lit

Salles, Dr J.F.
His, AHis, Arch, His

Silberstein, Dr B.
His, Geo

Sivignon,
Eco, Geo

Subrahmanyam, Dr S.
His, Eco

Germany

Baumann, Dr G.
Lit, Rel, Lin

Brustinow, Dr A.
DevS

Buddruss, Prof. G.A.
His, Rel, Lin, Ant, CuS, Lit

Dannecker, Drs P.
PolS, GenS, DevS, Soc, Eco

Das, Prof. dr R.P.
CuS, Lin, Rel

Elsenhans, Prof. dr H.
DevS

Gatzlaff, Dr M.
Lit, CuS, Lin

Gippert, Prof. J.
His, Lit, Phi, Lin, CuS, Rel

Goettingen, Drs D.
PolS, IR

Herbers, H.
GenS, Agr, CuS

Lengerke, Dr H.J. von
Env, Agr, Geo

Lobo, Dr W.
AHis, Ant, Arch

Loke-Schwalbe, Dr P.M.L.
CuS, Ant

Mahn, Dr S.
His, AHis, CuS, Arch

Malik, Dr J.
His, Rel, CuS, Edu, His, Lit

Mallick, Drs S.
Rel, Lit, Law, His

Nespital, Prof. dr H.
Lit, CuS, His, Lin

Oesterheld, Dr J.
Soc, His, PolS

Plaeschke, Dr H.
AHis, Arch

Plaeschke, Dr I.
His, Arch, AHis

Rüdiger, Drs A.
Soc, Rel, CuS, IR, PolS

Schied, Dr M.
His, Phi, PolS, Rel

Yaldiz, Prof. dr M.
Arch, His, AHis, Rel

Zingel, Dr W.-P.
Agr, Env, Eco

Italy

Rossi, Prof. A.V.
Rel, PolS, Lin, Arch, Ant

Netherlands

Bal, Drs E.W.
His

Biervliet, Drs W.E.
Edu

Bijlert, Dr V.A. van
Phi, Rel, Lin, CuS, His

Björkman, Prof. dr J.W.
PolS, DevS

Bruin, Ir D. de
DevS, Env

Byster, Drs E.D.
IR, CuS, His, Lit, Phi, AHis

Chhachhi, Drs A.
GenS, Soc

Chutiwongs, Dr N.
Rel, His, Arch, AHis

Cowan, Drs F.M.
GenS, DevS, CuS, Ant, Env, LinAgr

Custers, Dr P.J.J.M.
Eco, GenS, PolSAgr

Evers, Drs B.H.
DevS, Env, Eco, Agr

Gaay Fortman, Prof. B. de
Eco, Law

Gajentaan, Mr H.
PolS, IR, DevS

Gautam, Dr M.K.
Rel, Soc, Lit, Lin, His, Ant, CuS, PolS, Env

Gemeren, Drs A.J.G. van
His

Guimaraes, Ir J.P.C.
Eco, Env, DevS

Hamelink, Prof. dr C.J.
IR, Law

Harteveld, Ir K.
Agr, Eco, IR, Soc, DevS

Heins, Drs J.J.F.
Env, DevS

Hoefnagels, Ir H.A.M.
Agr, Eco, Law

Hoetjes, Dr B.J.S.
PolS, IR, Agr, DevS

Hommes, Prof. dr E.W.
DevS, Ant

Kabir, Dr M.R.
Eco

Kal, Drs W.H.
Env, Lin, DevS, Agr, CuS, Ant, CuS, GenS

Keysers, Drs L.
GenS, DevS

Kusin, Prof. dr J.A.
GenS

Meijs, Drs M.A.G.
IR, Rel, Ant, CuS

Meuldijk, Drs I.M.
Soc, Agr, GenS, Env, Ant, DevS

Miedema, Drs B.J.
DevS, Eco, Agr

ASIANISTS BY REGION AND COUNTRY OF INTEREST

Netherlands
Moharir, Dr V.V.
PolS, DevS, Edu
Mohkamsing, Drs N.
Rel, AHis, Lit, Phi
Oorthuizen, Ir H.J.M.
Agr, DevS
Oosterwijk, A.J.
His, Ant, Arch
Opdam, Drs J.H.M.
DevS
Ouden, Dr J.H.B. den
DevS, Ant, Agr, GenS
Patel, Drs B.
Law, PolS, IR
Pinkers, Ir M.J.H.P.
IR, DevS, EduAgr
Raven, Dr E.M.
His, Arch, AHis
Schendel, Prof. dr H.W. van
His, Ant
Schenk-Sandbergen, Dr L.Ch.
GenS, DevS, Env, Ant
Singh, Dr N.
Agr, Env, DevS, Soc, IR
Stel, Dr J.H.
Env, Eco
Straten, Mr H.M. van
Env, Ant, Law
Streefland, Prof. dr P.H.
DevS
Strik, Prof. B.
CuS
Tims, Prof. dr W.
Eco, Agr, DevS
Tolsma, Drs G.J.
Lin
Vaczi, Drs M.T.
Rel, AHis, GenS, CuS
Vereeken, Drs B.
Ant, DevS
Vervliet, Drs J.B.
His, Eco
Witkam, Dr J.J.
His, Rel, Lit
Wolffers, Prof. dr I
DevS
Wolvekamp, Drs P.S.
Agr, IR, DevS, Env, GenS
Zeeuw, D. de
Env, Agr

Norway
Bleie, T.
Env, Ant, GenS, DevS, CuS
Kristiansen, Prof. K.
Rel, CuS, Lin, Lit
Melby, E.
DevS, CuS
Miranda, Dr A.
DevS

Poland
Jamsheer, Prof. H.
IR, His, PolS, Rel
Winid, Prof. dr B.
PolS, DevS, Env, Geo

Russia
Komarov, Dr E.N.
Soc, His, PolS
Moskalenko, Prof. V.N.
His, IR
Niyazi, Dr A.
Env, Rel, PolS
Polonskaya, Dr L.R.
Rel, His
Sedov, Dr A. V.
Arch
Serebriany, Dr S.D.
Rel, CuS, Phi, Lin, Lit
Serenko, Dr I. N.
CuS, Edu, His, IR, Rel, Soc
Solomonik, Dr I.N.
His, AHis

Spain
Garcia-Ormaechea Quero, C.
AHis, Geo, His, Lit, Rel, Phi
Pechaczek, Drs M.J.A.
GenS, Soc, Edu, DevS, CuS
Rodríguez Ubeda, M.M.
Eco, IR, Soc

Sweden
Eden, Dr N.A.S.W.
His, IR, Rel, His, DevS, Agr, Ant
Johansson, Drs J.H.
Ant
Lundström-Burghoorn, Dr W.S.Y.M.C.
Ant, DevS, GenS
Swain, Drs A
PolS, IR, Env

Switzerland
Ahmed, Dr I.
Env, Agr, Eco
Bigger, A.
CuS, His, Lit, Rel
Etienne, Prof. G.
His, Agr, Eco, PolS, DevS
Hussain, W.
CuS, Eco, His, IR, PolS, Rel

United Kingdom
Ali, Dr K.A.
CuS, Ant
Andrews, Dr A.Y.
Soc, CuS, Rel
Auty, Dr R.M.
DevS, Env, Eco
Bradnock, Dr R.W.
Env, Agr, IR, Geo, DevS
Brammer, H.
Lit, PArt, Rel, Ant
Cameron, Mr J.
Edu, Env, Phi, Eco, CuS, DevS
Carter, Dr L.J.
His
Chandramohan, Dr B.
Lit, DevS, Edu, IR, Lin, CuS
Chapman, Prof. G.P.
Geo, Agr, Env, DevS
Coningham, Dr R.A.E.
Arch, Ant, CuS, His, AHis
Cook, Dr A.S.
His
Crosbie, Dr A.J.
IR, Env, Eco, Geo, DevS
Desai, Prof. M.J.
DevS, Eco
Dudrah, R.K.
CuS, Soc
Evans, Dr K.K.
AHis, Rel, GenS, His
French, Mr P.R.
His, Lit
Garforth, Prof. dr C.J.
Agr, Edu
Ghosh, Dr D.
DevS, Eco
Gombrich-Gupta, Dr S.
Rel, GenS, CuS, Phi, Lit
Good, Dr A.
DevS, Rel, His, GenS, Ant
Haan, Dr A. de
Soc, DevS, His
Hall, Dr A.R.
Ant, IR, PolS
Harriss, Dr J.C.
DevS, Ant
Harriss-White, Dr B.
Eco, DevS, Agr, GenS
James, Drs D.
PolS, His
Jeffery, Dr P.M.
DevS, GenS, Ant, Soc
Jeffery, Dr R.
DevS, Soc, Ant, GenS, Env
Johnson, Dr G.
His
Jones, Mr S.C.
Eco, DevS
Kothari, Dr U.
CuS, GenS, Agr, DevS
Kundu, Dr A.
DevS, IR, PolS, His
Lenman, Prof. B.P.
His
Lipton, Dr M.
DevS, Agr, Eco
Manor, Prof. J.G.
PolS
McGrail, Prof.dr S.F.
Ant, Arch
McGregor, Dr J.A.
DevS, Ant, His

ASIANISTS BY REGION AND COUNTRY OF INTEREST

United Kingdom

Menski, Dr W.

CuS, Rel, Law, Edu

Morris-Jones, Prof. W.H.

PolS

Newman, Dr R.K.

His

Nossiter, Prof. T.J.

Soc, PolS, IR, DevS, His

Parikh, Prof. A.

Eco, DevS, Agr

Peach, Dr C.

Geo, Soc

Robb, Prof. P.G.

His

Robinson, Prof. F.C.R.

His, Rel

Roper, Dr G.J.

CuS

Samad, Mr A.Y.

His, PolS, Soc

Samuel, Dr G.B.

Rel, Ant

Sharma, Mr L.K.

PolS, Soc, Rel, DevS, CuS, IR, Phi, Lit

Shaw, Mr G.W.

CuS

Shepherd, Dr A.W.

DevS, Env

Shepperdson, Mr M.J.

DevS, Agr, Eco, PolS, Soc

Slater, Dr R.P.

PolS, Ant, DevS, Eco

Smith, Mr S.

His, Edu

Standing, Dr H.

GenS, DevS, Ant

Thomas, Mr I.D.

DevS

Zamperini, Dr S.

His, IR

BHUTAN

Austria

Allinger, Dr E.

Rel, His, CuS, Arch, AHis

Loseries, Dr A.S.

His, Rel, CuS, Phi, His, AHis, DevS, Ant

Much, Dr M.T.W.

Phi, Rel

Belgium

Alphen, J. van

AHis, Ant, Lin, His

Servaes, Prof. dr J.E.J.G.

CuS, Ant, Soc, DevS

Bulgaria

Fedotoff, Prof. dr A.

Rel, Lit, CuS

Czech Republic

Krása, Dr M.

His

Pospisilova, Dr D.

Rel, AHis

Vacek, Prof. dr J.

Phi, Rel, Lit, Lin

Denmark

Pedersen, Prof. dr P.

His, CuS, Ant, Phi, Psy, Rel, Env

Estonia

Kark, M.

CuS, Lin, Phi, AHis, Rel, Edu

Finland

Hossain, M.

DevS, IR, PolS

Seppänen, J.

IR, Eco, Ant, CuS, Lin, His, AHis, Phi, Arch, Rel, PolS

Vanhanen, Dr T.

PolS

France

Dessaint, Prof. W.L.

Ant

Frederic, L.F.

AHis, CuS, Arch, Rel, His

Heide, Dr S. von der

Ant, DevSAHis, Env, CuS, Rel, PolS

Jarrige, J.F.

His, CuS, Arch, AHis

Jest, C.

DevS

Kasi-Henkus, C.

Eco, DevS

Kaushik, S.Ch.

His

Massonnet, P.

His, IR, Soc, Rel, PolS, AHis, DevS, Law, Env, CuS, Lin, His

Meyer, F.

Ant, Rel, His, CuS

Michailovsky, B.

Lin

Pommaret, Dr F.

Rel, His, CuS, His, Ant, AHis

Rault-Leyrat, L.R.

His, Rel, Ant, AHis, Ant, Lin, Arch, Phi, His

Steinmann, B.

His

Germany

Baumann, Dr G.

Lit, Rel, Lin

Dodin, T.

Phi, Lit, Rel, Soc, Lin, IR, His, Ant, DevS, CuS, PolS

Goettingen, Drs D.

PolS, IR

Grönbold, Dr G.C.

CuS, Rel, Lit

Kahlen, Prof. W.

Rel, Ant, AHis

Kreutzmann, Prof. dr H.J.

Agr, DevS, Ant

Lobo, Dr W.

AHis, Ant, Arch

Loke-Schwalbe, Dr P.M.L.

CuS, Ant

Mahn, Dr S.

His, AHis, CuS, Arch

Oesterheld, Dr J.

Soc, His, PolS

Plaeschke, Dr H.

AHis, Arch

Plaeschke, Dr I.

His, Arch, AHis

Rennert, Drs H.

Lin, Lit, His, CuS, His, Phi, Rel, AHis

Schweinfurth, Prof. dr U.

Agr, DevS, Env, Arch, IR

Yaldiz, Prof. dr M.

Arch, His, AHis, Rel

Italy

Mortarivergaracaffarelli, Prof. P.

Arch, AHis

Netherlands

Björkman, Prof. dr J.W.

PolS, DevS

Chemparathy, Prof. dr G.

Rel, Phi

Chutiwongs, Dr N.

Rel, His, Arch, AHis

Cowan, Drs F.M.

GenS, DevS, CuS, Ant, Env, LinAgr

Deelstra, T.

Env

Driem, Dr G.L. van

DevS, Lin, Ant, His

Gautam, Dr M.K.

Rel, Soc, Lit, Lin, His, Ant, CuS, PolS, Env

Grent, P.C.M.

CuS, Lin, Lit, Rel, Phi

Guyt, Drs H.J.

His, IR, AHis, Lin, CuS, DevS

Hagendoorn, Prof. dr A.J.M.W.

His

Hoefnagels, Ir H.A.M.

Agr, Eco, Law

Hoetjes, Dr B.J.S.

PolS, IR, Agr, DevS

Jepma, Prof. C.J.

Env, DevS, Eco

Kal, Drs W.H.

Env, Lin, DevS, Agr, CuS, Ant, CuS, GenS

Linden, F.J.W.T. van der

IR, PolS

Meulenbeld, Drs B.C.

CuS, His, Ant, AHis, Rel, Arch

Netherlands
Mohkamsing, Drs N.
Rel, AHis, Lit, Phi
Oonk, Drs G.
DevS, His, Ant
Patel, Drs B.
Law, PolS, IR
Plaisier, Drs H.
Lin
Prchal, Drs M.
PolS, His, Rel
Singh, Dr N.
Agr, Env, DevS, Soc, IR
Sinnema, Drs T.
GenS, CuS, Soc, His, Edu
Tolsma, Drs G.J.
Lin
Verbruggen, Prof. dr H.
Env, Eco, IR
Vereeken, Drs B.
Ant, DevS
Verhagen, Dr P.C.
Rel, Lin, Lit, Phi
Wolvekamp, Drs P.S.
Agr, IR, DevS, Env, GenS

Norway
Barth, Dr F.
DevS, Ant
Bleie, T.
Env, Ant, GenS, DevS, CuS
Kvaerne, P.
Rel

Poland
Winid, Prof. dr B.
PolS, DevS, Env, Geo

Russia
Ivanov, Dr B.A.
CuS, Ant, His, Rel
Prazauskas, Dr A.A.
Rel, His, PolS

Switzerland
Kloetzli, Prof. dr F.A.
Agr
Noesberger, Prof. J.
Agr
Seeland, Dr K.
Rel, Soc, Env, Ant

United Kingdom
Bray, Drs J.N.
His, IR, PolS
Carter, Dr L.J.
His
Chapman, G.
His, AHis, CuS
Desai, Prof. M.J.
DevS, Eco
French, Mr P.R.
His, Lit
Hall, Dr A.R.
Ant, IR, PolS
Hutt, Dr M.J.
AHis, CuS, Lit
Kundu, Dr A.
DevS, IR, PolS, His
Menski, Dr W.
CuS, Rel, Law, Edu
Picken, Dr L.E.R.
CuS

United States of America
Khoo, Drs M.J.
Rel, Arch, Ant
Pagel, Prof. U.
Lin, Rel

INDIA

Munshi, Dr S.
His, CuS, GenS

Austria
Allinger, Dr E.
Rel, His, CuS, Arch, AHis
Joshi, Drs R.R.
Lit, Lin
Lee, Dr S.-K.
CuS, Lit
Loseries, Dr A.S.
His, Rel, CuS, Phi, His, AHis, DevS, Ant
Luczanits, Dr Ch.
His, AHis, Rel, Arch
Mesquita, Dr R.A.C.
Rel, His, Phi
Much, Dr M.T.W.
Phi, Rel
Oberhammer, Prof. dr G.
Rel, Phi
Podzeit, Dr U.
Rel
Sichrovsky, Prof. H.
CuS, His, PolS, IR
Steinkellner, Prof. dr E.
Rel, Phi
Wallensteiner, E.M.
CuS, Ant
Werba, Dr Ch.H.
Lin, Lit, Rel, Psy
Wurm, A.
His, Lit, Rel
Zotz, Dr V.
Phi, CuS, Rel, His

Belgium
Alphen, J. van
AHis, Ant, Lin, His
Ballegeer, J.
PolS, Law
Callewaert, Dr W.M
Lit, CuS, Rel
Carpano, R.
Eco, IR
Coulie, Prof. dr B.R.R.
AHis, Soc, Lin, Phi, DevS, Ant, Eco, His, Lit
Degryse, Dr K.M.
His
Deliege, Dr R.
Ant
Gonzalo Castellanos, Dr A.
IR
Hacourt, B.J.H.
DevS, Ant
Jacquemin, A.R.A
Soc, DevS, PolS
Lesthaeghe, Prof. R.
DevS, Soc
Mawet, Prof. F.
Lin
Persoons, Dr M.A.
AHis, Edu, IR, Lin, Phi
Piquard, B.
Rel, PolS, Ant
Prins, B. de
His
Teerink, Drs R.
DevS, Agr, Ant, Soc, GenS
Verpoorten, Dr J.M.
Phi
Vielle, Dr CH.
Lin, Lit, Rel
Wee, Prof. H.F.A.van der
Eco, His

Bulgaria
Fedotoff, Prof. dr A.
Rel, Lit, CuS

China P.R.
Wang, Dr H.
Soc

Czech Republic
Dvorak, Drs J.
Lit, Lin
Filipsky, Dr I.
Rel, Lin, His
Hulec, Dr O.
His, AHis, CuS, Arch, IR, Eco, Phi, Lit, Lin
Kalvodov, Prof. dr D.
Eco, Phi, Law, His, Lin
Kostic, Dr S.
Rel, Lin, Phi
Krása, Dr M.
His
Marek, Dr J.
CuS, Lit
Markov, Dr D.
Soc, Lit, Rel, GenS, CuS
Pospisilova, Dr D.
Rel, AHis
Strnad, Dr J.
His, Lin
Vacek, Prof. dr J.
Phi, Rel, Lit, Lin

Denmark
Aktor, M.
Ant, Lin, Rel, Lit, His

Denmark

Andersen, Dr P.B.
Ant, Lit, Soc, Rel

Baark, Dr E.
His, DevS, Env, CuS

Bakker, Dr P.J.
His, Lin, Ant

Beek, Dr M. van
DevS, Soc, PolS, Ant

Bugge, Dr H.
Rel, His

Bundgaard, Dr H.
Ant

Ewers, K.
Ant, Env, DevS

Goebel, Prof. E.
His

Hojgaard, Mr F.C.
His

Javed, M.A.
CuS, Rel, IR, Soc

Karpen, Dr A.P.
CuS

Lehrmann Rasmussen, Dr J.
Eco, Phi, DevS

Madsen, Dr S.T.
Soc, PolS, DevS, Env, Rel, Ant, IR, Law, His

Mahmoodi, A.
Soc, PolS, His, Eco, DevS, CuS

Martinussen, Prof. dr J.
Eco, DevS, PolS

Padolecchia Polo, Prof. S.P.
DevS, PolS, Rel, Edu, Eco, Soc, Env, IR, CuS

Pedersen, Prof. dr P.
His, CuS, Ant, Phi, Psy, Rel, Env

Westergaard, Dr K.
PolS, DevS

Westman, Drs B.W.
Rel, AHis, Ant, His

Wiuf, J.
Phi, Rel, Lit

Estonia

Kark, M.
CuS, Lin, Phi, AHis, Rel, Edu

Valk, Dr š.
Rel

Finland

Aalto, Prof. dr P.
His, DevS

Hossain, M.
DevS, IR, PolS

Karttunen, Dr K.J.
CuS

Karunaratne, Dr J.A.
DevS, Eco

Parpola, Prof. A.
Lit, Arch, Rel, CuS, Lin

Vanhanen, Dr T.
PolS

Virtanen, Dr K.
Lit, His, AHis, Phi

France

Adamo, S.A.
AHis, CuS, His, Rel, Soc

Akkitham, N.
His, Eco, IR

Alwis Perera, D.R. De
Lin, IR, Eco

Andrès, Dr E.
Ant, Phi, Rel

Angot, M.
Lit

Arnaud, M.A.
Ant, Rel, Eco, Edu, Soc

Bakaya, A.
Edu, CuS, GenS, Env, Lit, DevS, Soc, Lin

Baks, Dr Ch.
Agr, Ant, Law

Balbir, Prof. N.
Lit, Rel, Lin

Bansat-Boudon, Dr.L.
Lit, Phi, Lin, Rel

Barbiche, Prof. dr J.-P.
Law, IR, His, PolS, Eco, DevS, CuS, Edu, Soc

Barbier-Kontler, Dr C.
Phi, Rel

Berinstain, Dr Vallerie
AHis, His

Bernard, J.A.
IR, His, Eco, PolS

Bhattacharja, S.
Rel, Lit, His

Bhattacharya, Prof. F.
CuS, Ant, Lit, Rel

Biardeau, M.
Phi, Ant

Blamont, Dr D.
Agr, DevS

Bossé, Dr.
GenS, Soc, Rel, Lin, Ant

Botsch, A.A.
Eco, DevS, IR, Edu, Law

Bourdier, Dr F.
CuS, Ant, Env, DevS

Brocquet, S.
Lin

Broquet, J.
Rel, Phi, Lit

Bruguière, Dr Ph.
Soc, His, AHis, Ant

Cadene, Prof. Ph.
DevS, Geo

Casevitz, Prof. M.H.
Arch, Lin, Rel

Chambard, Prof. J.-L.
Ant

Champion, C.
Lit

Clementin-Ojha, C.
Ant, Rel

Clotte, M.
Lin

Colas Doctorate, G
CuS, His, Lit, Phi, Rel

Cornillet, M.
His

Couto, Dr D.
Arch, His, PolS

Crombe, V.
His, CuS, AHis, Rel, His, Arch

Dagens, Prof. B.
Rel, His

Daluwa Thumul, G.J.
Lan

Dournon, Dr G.
AntAnt

Dumont, Prof. L.
His

Dumont, Prof. R.
Agr, Env, DevS

Durand-Daste, Mr F.
Geo

Dutta, S.
Lit

Edouard, N.
Lin, Rel

Filliozat, J.
Rel, Lit

Flacelière, M.-H.
Lin

Foucher, Dr M.
IR, PolS, Eco

Fourcade, Dr M.
His, GenS

Frederic, L.F.
AHis, CuS, Arch, Rel, His

Gaborieau, Dr M.
His, Ant

Gaillard, Dr C.
Arch

Galey, Dr J.C.
Soc, Rel, CuS, Ant

Gamage, J.
Env

Gaucher, J.
Art

Gauthier, A.
Rel

Gobalakchenane, Dr M.
CuS, His, Rel, Soc

Graff, Dr V.
PolS

Gricourt, Drs M.R.
Lit

Gros, Prof. F.E.
CuS, Lit, Rel

Guillon, Dr E.
Ant, AHis, Arch, Rel, His

Haas-Lambert, A.-M.
His

ASIANISTS BY REGION AND COUNTRY OF INTEREST

France

Heide, Dr S. von der
Ant, DevSAHis, Env, CuS, Rel, PolS

Heuze-Brigant, Dr G.L.D.
DevS, Env, Soc, Ant, Eco

Hulin, M.
Phi

Hurpré, Dr J.F.
AHis, Arch

Hurtig, Ch.
PolS

Jacq-Hergoualc'h, Dr M.
Rel, His, Arch, His, AHis

Jaffrelot, Dr Ch.
PolS

Jarrige, J.F.
His, CuS, Arch, AHis

Jayasinghe, M.A.
Lan

Joshi, S.
Lan

Kalpana Kartik MA,
Ant, AHis, CuS, Rel

Kasi-Henkus, C.
Eco, DevS

Kennedy, Dr L.A.
Eco, PolS, DevS

Kroell, Dr A.
His

Landy, Dr F.
Agr, DevS, Geo, Eco

Larcher, A.
His

Lardinois, R.
Soc, His

Lévy, A.-M.
Lan

Liyanaratne, J.
IR, Eco, DevS, PolS

Macdonald, Prof. A.W.
Ant, Rel

Mahias, Dr M.-C.
Ant

Malamoud, Mr Ch.
Lin

Mallison, Dr F.
Rel, Lin, Lit, His, CuS

Markovits, Prof. C.
His

Massonnet, P.
His, IR, Soc, Rel, PolS, AHis, DevS, Law, Env, CuS, Lin, His

Matringe, Dr D.
Lin, Lit, Soc, Ant, CuS, Rel

Meyer, Dr E.P.
His

Mézin, L.
His, AHis

Michailovsky, B.
Lin

Mohammad, A.T.
His, Soc, Rel

Montaut, A.
Lit

Montoya, M.
IR

Moutal, P.
Ant

Mukhherjee, Dr P.
His, Lit, Phi, Rel, AHis, Soc, His

Murr, Dr S.
Phi

Naudou, E.
Lan

Oguibenine, Prof. B.
Lit, CuS, Lin, Rel

Okada, A.
His, AHis

Padoux, Dr A.
CuS, Rel, Phi, Lin, Ant

Parliter-Renault, A.
His, AHis

Pellard, S.
His, Arch, AHis

Pilot-Raichoor, Dr C.
Lin

Pinault, G.-J.
Rel

Pitoëff, P.
Ant

Pitoun MA,
Arch, AHis, Lit

Porcher, M.-C.
Lit, Lin

Pouchepadass, Dr J.
His

Racine, Drs J.-L.
DevS, PolS, IR

Raj, Dr K.
Geo, His

Rault-Leyrat, L.R.
His, Rel, Ant, AHis, Ant, Lin, Arch, Phi, His

Reiniche, Dr M.-L.
Ant, His, Soc

Rosu, Dr A.
CuS

Salles, Dr J.F.
His, AHis, Arch, His

Sandouk, Drs S.
Phi, His, Lit, Rel

Scalabrino, Drs C.J.
Rel, Arch, His, Phi, Psy, His, IR, AHis, PolS

Sethupathy, E.
Ant, DevS, CuS, Soc

Silberstein, Dr B.
His, Geo

Sivignon,
Eco, Geo

Smitsendonk, Dr A.G.O.
Law, Eco, IR, Soc, Rel, PolS, DevS

Steinmann, B.
His

Stern, Dr H.
Soc

Subrahmanyam, Dr S.
His, Eco

Sukanda-Tessier, B.
Ant, Rel

Tarabout, Dr G.
Rel, Ant

Thorner, A.
His

Tibrewala, V.
Lit, His, AHis, Arch

Toffin, Prof. G.
Ant, Rel, CuS

Trân, Q.H.
CuS, Ant

Turcq, Dr D.F.
Eco

Vidal, D.
Ant

Vigneau, Prof. R.
Lit

Waliullah, A.-M.
Lit

Weber, J.
His

Weinberger-Thomas, Prof. C.
CuS, Lit, Rel, Soc

Williamson, Dr P.J.
DevS, Eco

Wu, Dr C.-Y.
Lit, Rel, Phi, Lin, His

Zins, Dr M.J.
PolS

Zvelebil, Prof. dr K.V.
Rel, Lit, CuS, Lin

Germany

Ahrens, Prof. Dr T
Rel

Ahuja, R.
His

Aithal, Dr P.
Lit, Lin, CuS, Rel

Albino, M.
Lin

Albrecht, E.W.
Eco

Alt, Drs B.
Rel, Lin, Phi

Aschoff, Prof. dr J.C.
CuS

Babing, Dr F.
Rel, His

Baloch, Dr I.
PolS, CuS, His

Germany

Basu, Dr H.
Ant, Rel
Bauer, Prof. dr C.H.R.
Lit, Rel, Ant, Lin, His, Arch
Baumann, Dr G.
Lit, Rel, Lin
Bechert, Prof. H.H.
His, Lit, Rel, CuS
Beltz, J
Ant, Rel
Berkemer, Dr G.
His, CuS, Ant, Rel
Bhatt, Prof. dr B.
Rel, Lit, His
Bock-Raming, Dr A.
His, CuS, Lit, Rel, AHis
Bohle, Prof. H.G.
CuS, GenS, Agr, Env, DevS
Bollée, Prof. W. B.
Rel, Lit, Lin
Borchers, Drs D.
CuS, Lin
Brandtner, Drs M.
Arch, His
Braun, Dr H.
His, Lit, Rel
Brentjes, Dr S.
Phi
Brinkhaus, Prof. dr H.
CuS, Lit, Rel
Bronger, Prof. D.
DevS
Brückner, Prof. dr H.
Phi, Lit, Rel
Bruhn, Prof. dr K.
AHis
Buddruss, Prof. G.A.
His, Rel, Lin, Ant, CuS, Lit
Burdman, M.M.
His, Eco, DevS
Casimir, Prof. dr M.J.
Psy, Arch, Ant, His, GenS, Agr
Conzelmann, Dr E.
Ant, Rel, Soc
Dalmia, Dr V.
CuS, Rel, His, Lit
Dannecker, Drs P.
PolS, GenS, DevS, Soc, Eco
Das, Prof. dr R.P.
CuS, Lin, Rel
Degener, Dr A.C.
Rel, Lin
Dharampal-Frick, Dr G.
Rel, His, Ant
Domroes, Prof. dr M.R.J.
Agr, Geo, Env
Draguhn, Dr W.
PolS, IR, Eco, DevS
Ebbatson, Dr P.
Lin, Rel, Phi, Lit
Eimer, Dr H.
Lit, His
Elsenhans, Prof. dr H.
DevS
Enskat, Drs M.
DevS, PolS
Falk, Prof. dr H.
CuS, Lit, Rel
Faust, Dr H.
DevS, CuS
Feistel, Dr H.O.
CuS, Lit, Rel, Lin
Forssman, Prof. dr B.
Lin
Frasch, Drs T.
His
Freitag, Dr G.J.
Eco
Fuchs, Dr M.
Rel, Ant, Soc, CuS
Gaenszle, Dr M.
Rel, Lin, Ant, CuS
Gail, Prof. dr A.
His, AHis
Gatzlaff, Dr M.
Lit, CuS, Lin
Gengnagel, Dr J.P.
Rel, CuS, Phi
Gippert, Prof. J.
His, Lit, Phi, Lin, CuS, Rel
Goettingen, Drs D.
PolS, IR
Gorter, Dr P.L.H.M.
Eco, Agr, DevS, Ant, Soc, PolS
Grönbold, Dr G.C.
CuS, Rel, Lit
Gropp, Dr G.C.A.
Phi, Lit, His, Rel, Arch, AHis, CuS, Ant, Lin
Grötzbach, Prof. dr E.
Rel, Geo, CuS
Grünendahl, Drs R.
Rel, Lin
Haar, Prof. dr B.J. ter
Lit, Rel
Haffner, Prof. dr W.N.
Env
Hager, D.
Eco, IR, PolS
Hanneder, Drs J.
Phi, Rel, Lin, Lit
Hartmann, Prof. J.-U.
Rel, Lit
Hauser, B.
Rel, Ant, DevS, CuS
Heidrich, Dr P.
Soc, Agr, His
Heidrich, Prof. dr J.
His, IR
Heitkoetter, Drs M.
PolS, DevS, GenS, Geo
Herbers, H.
GenS, Agr, CuS
Hinüber, Dr H. von
Law, His, Rel, Lin, Phi, Lit
Hinüber, Prof. dr O. von
His, CuS, Arch, His, Law, Lit, AHis, Phi, Rel, Lin
Hoeppe MSc, G
Ant, Env
Hofmann, Drs Z.S.
Ant, Rel, Phi, CuS
Hohnholz, Prof. J.
DevS, Agr, Geo
Knall, Prof. B.R.
IR, Edu, PolS, Eco, DevS
Kraatz, Dr M.
Rel
Krebs, C.
Ant, Env
Krengel, Dr M.
Soc, Edu, Ant, DevS
Kuckertz, Prof. dr J.
His, Ant
Kuhl, Drs M.
Lin, Phi, CuS, His, AHis, Lit, Rel
Kulke, Prof. dr H.
His, Soc, Rel
Laping, Dr J.
PolS, CuS, DevS, Env, Ant, IR, Rel, Soc, His
Laubscher, Prof. dr M.S.
Rel, Ant
Lehmann, Dr T.
Lin
Lengerke, Dr H.J. von
Env, Agr, Geo
Linkenbach, Dr A.
Soc, Ant, Env
Lobo, Dr W.
AHis, Ant, Arch
Loke-Schwalbe, Dr P.M.L.
CuS, Ant
Lorenz, Prof. D.
Eco
Lütt, Dr J.K.
His, Rel
Mahn, Dr S.
His, AHis, CuS, Arch
Malik, Dr J.
His, Rel, CuS, Edu, His, Lit
Malinar, Dr A.
Rel, Phi, Lit, GenS, CuS
Mallick, Drs S.
Rel, Lit, Law, His
Mann, Dr M.
His, Env
Maue, Dr D.
Rel, Lin, Lit, Phi
Maxwell, Prof. dr T.S.
His, AHis

Germany

Mayer, Dr A.L.
Rel, Phi

Mayer, Drs M.
Soc, Env, DevS

Mayer-König, Dr B.H.
Phi, Rel, Lit

Merz, Drs R.M.
His, Agr, Soc, Eco, DevS, PolS

Mevissen, Drs G.J.R.
His, AHis

Mischung, Prof. R.
Ant, Soc, Rel

Müller, K.
PolS, CuS, His

Müller, M.
His, AHis

Müller, Dr T.J.
His, Rel

Muller-Boker, Dr U.
GenS, Agr, CuS, DevS, Env

Müller-Hofstede, Drs C.
PolS, Soc, His, IR, CuS, DevS

Mylius, Prof. K.
CuS, Lin, Lit, Rel

Narten, Prof. dr J.
Lin

Nespital, Prof. dr H.
Lit, CuS, His, Lin

Neuss, J.
Rel, His, Lin, His, AHis

Njammasch, Prof. dr M.
His

Oesterheld, Dr J.
Soc, His, PolS

Panglung, Dr J.L.
CuS, Phi, Rel

Partenheimer-Bein, A.
His

Pfeiffer, Dr M.
Lin, Rel, Lit, CuS

Plaeschke, Dr H.
AHis, Arch

Plaeschke, Dr I.
His, Arch, AHis

Poley, Drs U.M.
Rel, His, CuS, Arch, Phi, AHis, Lin

Pope, Dr A.D.
His

Prunner, Dr G.
Ant, Rel, CuS

Rai, Dr S.S.
PolS, IR

Ramstedt, Drs M.
Ant, Rel, CuS, PolS, Lit

Randeria, Dr S.
Soc, DevS, GenS, Ant, CuS

Rao, Dr A.
Psy, DevS, Env, His, Ant, GenS

Raster, Prof. dr P.
Lin, Phi

Reetz, Dr D.
His, PolS, Rel, IR

Rennert, Drs H.
Lin, Lit, His, CuS, His, Phi, Rel, AHis

Rieger, Dr H.C.
DevS, Env, Eco

Robotka, Dr B.
His

Roesler, Drs U.
Lin, Lit, Rel

Rothermund, Prof. dr D.
His

Rüdiger, Drs A.
Soc, Rel, CuS, IR, PolS

Rueland, Prof. dr J.
IR, PolS, DevS

Sauerborn, Prof. J.
Agr, Env

Schaller, Prof. dr E.
PolS, Soc

Schied, Dr M.
His, Phi, PolS, Rel

Schlerath, Prof. dr B.
Lin, CuS, Rel

Schlicher, Dr M.
His, PolS, IR

Schlingloff, Prof. dr D.
AHis, CuS, Arch, Lit, Rel

Schmid, Dr A.
His, Ant

Schmitt, Prof. dr R.
Lin, His

Schneider, Dr J.
Rel, Lit, Lin

Schoembucher, Dr E.
Rel, Ant, Lin, GenS, CuS

Schoepe, Dr R.
Lin, Phi

Schömbucher, Dr E.
Ant, Lin, Rel, CuS, GenS

Schrader, Dr H.
Soc, Eco, Ant, CuS

Schröter, Dr S.
Ant

Schweinfurth, Prof. dr U.
Agr, DevS, Env, Arch, IR

Schwerin, Dr K. von
His

Seltmann, Dr F.M.
CuS

Skyhawk, H. von
Phi, Rel, Ant, Lit, CuS

Slaje, Prof. dr W.
Rel, Phi, Lit, CuS

Soni, Dr J.
Lin, Phi, Rel

Srinivasan, Dr P.
Ant

Stark, Dr U.B.
Lit

Stein, Dr W.
Ant, CuS, AHis, Arch, His

Steiner, Dr R.
Lit, Phi

Stellrecht, Prof. dr I.
His, Ant, Rel

Stietencron, Prof. dr H. von
CuS, Phi, His, Rel

Stöber, Dr G.
Ant, DevS, Edu

Stoye, Drs M.
His, AHis, Arch

Uebach, Dr H.
CuS, His

Vogel, Prof. dr C.
Lit

Waligora, Dr M.
Phi, Soc, CuS, His

Weber, Dr E.
Soc, PolS, Env, Eco, DevS

Wendt, Dr H.R.
His, Edu, CuS, Lin

Werner, Dr W.L.
Env, DevS

Werth, Dr L.
Ant

Wezler, Prof. dr A.
CuS, Rel, Phi, Lit, Law, Lin

Wilhelm, Prof. dr F.
PolS, CuS, Lit, His

Yaldiz, Prof. dr M.
Arch, His, AHis, Rel

Zingel, Dr W.-P.
Agr, Env, Eco

Zoller, Dr C.P.
Ant, Lin, Lit, Rel

Hungary

Birtalan, Dr A.
AHis, Rel, Phi, Lit, Lin, His, Arch, GenS

Porció, Drs T.
Lit, Rel, CuS

Toth, E
CuS, Edu, His, Lin, Lit, Phi, Psy, Rel, Soc

Italy

Albanese, M.
His, AHis, Rel, Phi

Caracchi, Dr P.
Lin, Lit, Rel

Cossio, Dr C.
Lit

Crespi Reghizzi, Prof. G.
PolS, DevS, IR, Law

Dolcini, Dr D.M.
His, Lin, Lit, Rel, CuS

Eichinger Ferro-Luzzi, Dr G.
CuS, Ant, Lit, Rel

Offredi, Prof. M.
His, Lit, AHis

Italy

Panattoni , E.A.
Lin, CuS, Lit, Rel

Piano , Prof. S
CuS, Lin, Lit, Rel

Pistilli , Drs G.M.
Lit, His

Radicchi , Prof. dr A.
Lin, Lit, Rel

Raza , Dr R.
His, Lit, IR

Rispoli , Dr F.
Ant, Arch

Rossi , Prof. A.V.
Rel, PolS, Lin, Arch, Ant

Scolari , V.
CuS, His, AHis

Sharma , Dr Gh.
Lin, Lit

Snellgrove , Prof. D.
AHis, Rel, Arch, His

Torri , Prof. M.
PolS, His

Vashist , G.K.
Lit, Rel

Volpi , G.
PolS, IR, Agr, Eco, Env

Zanier , Prof. C.
His

Nepal

Shrestha , Drs B.G.
Lit, CuS, Rel, PolS, Ant

Netherlands

Alibux , R.F.
IR, His

Arnoldus-Schröder , Drs V.
Edu, Ant, CuS

Attema , Drs Y.
AHis, CuS, His

Baak , Dr P.
PolS, His, Soc, Eco, Agr

Bakker , Prof. dr H.T.
Arch, Rel, Phi, His, CuS, AHis, Lit

Bal , Drs E.W.
His

Bangoer , N.
Lit

Barendse , Dr R.J.
His, Eco

Barkhuis , Dr R.
Rel, CuS

Bastiaansen , Drs A.C.G.M.
IR, Eco, Edu

Battum-v.d.Horst , M. van
His

Baud , Dr I.S.A.
DevS, GenS, Eco, Soc

Bavinck , Drs J.M.
DevS, Ant

Beek , Mr T.J. van
PolS, IR

Beekes , Prof. dr R.S.P.
Lin

Beers , Mr H.A.J.J. van
Law, DevS, GenS

Benda Beckmann , Prof. dr F. von
DevS, Law, Ant

Bentinck , Drs J.V.
Geo, Env

Berkel , Ir C.W.M. van
Env

Beukering , P.J.H. van
IR, Eco, Env, DevS

Beumer , Drs W.G.M.
AHis

Bhattacharya , Dr B.
His

Bhola , R.
Rel, LitAnt, CuS

Biervliet , Drs W.E.
Edu

Bijlert , Dr V.A. van
Phi, Rel, Lin, CuS, His

Björkman , Prof. dr J.W.
PolS, DevS

Bodewitz , Prof. dr H.W.
Lin, Lit, Rel

Bogaerts , Drs E.M.
Phi, IR, AHis, Rel, Lit, Lin, His, Ant

Bonouvrié , Drs N.C.
Rel

Boon , D.
AHis, Rel, CuS, Phi, His

Boon , Drs H.
Geo

Bor , Dr J.
IR

Brakel , Drs J.H. van
His, AHis, Arch, Ant

Breet , Drs J.A. de
Rel, Lin, His

Breman , Prof. dr J.C.
DevS, His, Eco, Ant, Soc

Brinke , Ir H.W. ten
Agr, Edu

Brouwer , A.A.
CuS, Eco, His, IR, PolS, Psy, Rel, Phi

Bruijn , Dr T. de
Rel, His, Lit

Bruijn , Drs B. de
DevS, Soc, Psy, Ant

Bruijn , Prof. dr J.T.P. de
Lit, Rel

Bruijn , P.J.J. de
His, AHis

Bruijne , Prof. dr G.A. de
Geo

Bruijninckx , Drs W.P.M.
Eco, IR

Bruin , Ir D. de
DevS, Env

Brunt , Prof. dr L.
Ant, Soc

Burg , Drs C.J.G. van der
Ant, Lit, Rel, Soc

Buuren , Drs B.L.M. van
Ant, DevS

Byster , Drs E.D.
IR, CuS, His, Lit, Phi, AHis

Casparis , Prof. dr J.G. de
AHis, Rel, His, Arch, His

Chemparathy , Prof. dr G.
Rel, Phi

Chhachhi , Drs A.
GenS, Soc

Choenni , Dr C.E.S.
His, IR, Phi, PolS, Rel, Lit, DevS, Soc

Chutiwongs , Dr N.
Rel, His, Arch, AHis

Clancy , Dr J.S.
Env

Clason , Prof. dr A.T.
DevS

Coelen , Drs M.
His, Rel

Cowan , Drs F.M.
GenS, DevS, CuS, Ant, Env, LinAgr

Crince le Roy , E.A.W.
DevS, AHis, Edu

Damsteegt , Dr Th.
Lit, Lin

Deelstra , T.
Env

Dietz , Dr A.J.
Agr

Dijk , Drs W.O.
Rel, CuS, His, Lin

Dijkstra , Drs G.H.
Soc, Rel, Phi, Eco, His, IR, Psy, PolS

Doornbos , Prof. dr M.R.
DevS, PolS, Soc

Driem , Dr G.L. van
DevS, Lin, Ant, His

Driessen , Drs J.M.C.
Psy, Lit, Lin

Druijven , Dr P.C.J.
Geo, Env, Agr, DevS

Dunham , Dr D.M.
CuS, DevS, Agr

Emmer , Prof. dr P.C.
His

Erpecum , I.L. van
Lit, Law, CuS, AHis

Es , Dr A.J.H. van
Agr

Netherlands

Fijneman, Drs Y.
Psy, DevS

Foekema, Drs G.M.M.
Arch, His, AHis

Frank, Drs E.
Eco, Soc

Gaastra, Dr F.S.
His

Gaay Fortman, Prof. B. de
Eco, Law

Gajentaan, Mr H.
PolS, IR, DevS

Gangaram Panday, A.J.
Art

Gasper, Dr D.R.
Eco, Phi, PolS, DevS

Gautam, Dr M.K.
Rel, Soc, Lit, Lin, His, Ant, CuS, PolS, Env

Geer, Drs A.A.E. van der
Lin

Gelder, Drs R. van
CuS, His, IR

George, Drs S.
Ant, Agr, Soc

Gerrits, Drs A.C.M.
AHis

Gertsch, Drs L.J.
CuS, DevS

Giel, Mr P.
Env, DevS

Gijsbers, Drs D.J.
Env, Eco

Gijsen, Drs R.P.E.M.
His

Gommans, Dr J.J.L.
His

Gontscharoff, C.
IR, DevS

Goor, Dr J. van
His, IR

Grent, P.C.M.
CuS, Lin, Lit, Rel, Phi

Groenendael, Dr Clara van
Ant, Rel, Lin

Groot, Drs G.A. de
Eco

Groot, Drs I. de
Ant, GenS

Guyt, Drs H.J.
His, IR, AHis, Lin, CuS, DevS

Haar, Dr J.G.J. ter
Rel, Lit

Hagendoorn, Prof. dr A.J.M.W.
His

Haitsma, T.J.
IR

Haldar, Mr A.
PolS

Hamelink, Prof. dr C.J.
IR, Law

Hande, B.E.
Phi, AHis, Arch, Lit

Hanssen, Drs L.M.
Ant, CuS

Hartkamp-Jonxis, Drs E.
His, AHis

Heesterman, Prof. dr J.C.
His, Rel

Heijn, Drs A.
IR, Eco

Heins, Drs J.J.F.
Env, DevS

Henke, Drs R.F.W.
Psy, Ant, DevS, Soc

Hermens, B.
Agr, Env, IR

Hermse, Drs M.A.A.
CuS, Phi, His, Rel, GenS, Lit, Lin, AHis, Psy

Hoefnagels, Ir H.A.M.
Agr, Eco, Law

Hoek, Drs A.W. van den
Rel, Ant, Lin, CuS

Hoetjes, Dr B.J.S.
PolS, IR, Agr, DevS

Hofland, J.C.
Rel

Holdstock, Prof. T.L.
Psy

Hommes, Prof. dr E.W.
DevS, Ant

Hospes, Dr ir O.
Soc

Houben, Dr J.E.M.
Rel, His, Lin, Lit, Phi

Hudcovicova, A.
CuS

Huizer, Prof. dr G.J.
Rel, IR, Env, DevS

Hulst, W.A.
Eco

Hutter, Dr I.
Ant

IJiri, Drs Y.
Rel, AHis, Phi, CuS

Immig, Drs O.I.
Soc, His, IR, Rel, Eco, PolS

Jacobs, Dr H.K.
His

Jacobs, Drs E.M.
His

Janssen, Drs F.H.P.M.
His, AHis, Arch

Jehle, Dr E.
IR, DevS, Eco, Edu, Law

Jepma, Prof. C.J.
Env, DevS, Eco

Jong, Drs A.H.
His, GenS

Jong, Prof. dr F. de
CuS, Rel

Junne, Prof. G.C.A.
IR, DevS, PolS, Env

Kal, Drs W.H.
Env, Lin, DevS, Agr, CuS, Ant, CuS, GenS

Kamphorst, Drs J.
His, GenS

Kersenboom, Dr S.C.
Rel, Lin, Ant

Keysers, Drs L.
GenS, DevS

Khosla, Dr A.
DevS, Eco

Kloppenborg, Prof. dr M.A.G.T.
His, Lin, Lit, Rel

Knorringa, Dr P.
Eco, DevS

Kolff, Prof. dr D.H.A.
His, Ant, Law

Koningh, R.T.M. de
His, IR, AHis

Kooij, Prof. dr K.R. van
Arch

Kortlandt, Prof. dr F.H.H.
Lin

Kulikov, Dr L.J.
Lin

Kurian, Dr R.
Eco, DevS

Kusin, Prof. dr J.A.
GenS

Laar, Dr A.J.M. van de
Eco, DevS

Lamsweerde, F. van
Ant

Lannoy, Drs M. de
His

Letsch, Drs M.
Ant

Levinson, Prof. S.C.
Psy, Lin, Ant

Lieten, Dr G.K.
Soc, DevS, Agr

Linck, Drs F.C.
Ant

Linden, B. van der
CuS, His, Rel

Linden, Dr J.J. van der
DevS

Lingen, Ing J.
His

Loop, Dr T.H.M. van der
Env, DevS, Eco

Lopez, Drs S.
CuS, His, AHis

Lubotsky, Dr A.
Lin

Lunsingh Scheurleer, Drs P.
AHis, Arch

Netherlands

Maaker, Drs E. de
Ant

Maas, Dr A.J.J.
His, AHis

Malcontent, Drs P.A.M.
His

McKay, Dr A.C.
His, Rel

Menon, Dr A.G.
Rel, Lit, Lin

Meulenbeld, Dr G.J.
Lin, Lit

Meulenbeld, Drs B.C.
CuS, His, Ant, AHis, Rel, Arch

Miedema, Drs B.J.
DevS, Eco, Agr

Moharir, Dr V.V.
PolS, DevS, Edu

Mohkamsing, Drs N.
Rel, AHis, Lit, Phi

Molinga, Dr P.P.
Agr, DevS

Moll, Dr Ir. H.A.J.
Eco, Agr

Mooij, Dr ir J.E.
DevS, PolS

Muijzenberg, Prof. dr O.D. van den
Soc, DevS, Ant, His

Naastepad, Drs C.W.M.
Eco

Nadal Uceda, F. de
Ant, Arch, Lin, Phi, Psy, Rel

Nagel, Dr B.M.J.
Rel, Phi

Nederveen Pieterse, Dr J.P.
Ant, Soc, Rel, PolS, Phi, DevS

Newalsing, R.N.
PolS

Nielen, Dr J.E.
DevS

Nieuwenhuys, Dr O.
Ant, DevS, GenS

Nijenhuis, Dr E. te
Part

Nugteren, Dr A.
Phi, Rel

Ommen, Drs A.F. van
IR, PolS

Oonk, G.J.B.
DevS, IR

Oonk, Drs G.
DevS, His, Ant

Oort, Drs M.S.
Lit, Rel, Lin, Phi

Oosterwijk, A.J.
His, Ant, Arch

Opdam, Drs J.H.M.
DevS

Ouden, Dr J.H.B. den
DevS, Ant, Agr, GenS

Oudheusden, Drs O.M.
His

Parthasarathi, Dr P.
Eco, His

Patel, Drs B.
Law, PolS, IR

Pederson, Drs E.W.
Lin

Pels, Dr P.J.
Ant, His

Peltenburg, Drs M.E.
DevS

Pesch, L.
Edu, CuS

Pinkers, Ir M.J.H.P.
IR, DevS, EduAgr

Plukker, Dr D.F.
Lin, Lit

Poortinga, Dr F.H.
Psy

Prins, Dr W.J.M.
DevS

Put, Drs M.
Agr, Env, Soc, DevS

Rammandanlall, Drs J.
Ant

Raven, Dr E.M.
His, Arch, AHis

Reede, Mr J.L. de
PolS, Law

Reijnders, Drs P.A.M.
His, AHis

Risseeuw, Prof. dr C.I.
Ant, His, GenS, DevS, Rel, Law

Roelofs, Drs J.D.
Soc, GenS, DevS

Rovers, E.
Eco

Ruben, Drs R.
Agr, Eco, Env

Rueb, Drs P.D.
His

Rutten, Dr M.A.F.
Ant, Soc

Säävälä, Drs M.S.
Ant

Saith, Prof. dr A.
Agr, Eco, DevS, His

Sanders, Drs M.
DevS, Eco

Schampers, Drs A.J.J.
DevS, Soc

Scheepers, Dr A.R.
Phi, His, Rel

Schendel, Prof. dr H.W. van
His, Ant

Schenk, Dr H.
DevS, Env

Schenk-Sandbergen, Dr L.Ch.
GenS, DevS, Env, Ant

Schmidt, J.H.L.
Arch, AHis

Schokker, Dr G.H.
Lit, Rel, Lin

Schoorl, Prof. dr J.W.
DevS, Ant

Semetko, Prof. dr H.A.
PolS, Soc, Psy

Seret, Mr A.
Phi, Lit, Lin, Rel, CuS

Sigmond, Dr J.P.
CuS, His, AHis, Arch

Singh, Dr N.
Agr, Env, DevS, Soc, IR

Skutsch, Dr M.M.
GenS, DevS

Smets, Drs P.G.S.M.
DevS

Sparreboom, Dr M.
Lit, Rel

Spiekerman-Middelplaats, M.Y.M.
Env

Srivastava-Johri, Dr I.
Phi

Stel, Dr J.H.
Env, Eco

Storm, Dr S.T.H.
Agr, DevS, Eco

Straten, Mr H.M. van
Env, Ant, Law

Streefland, Prof. dr P.H.
DevS

Streumer, Drs P.
Edu, Ant, His, DevS, CuS

Strik, Prof. B.
CuS

Struben, Drs P.
His

Stuijvenberg, P. van
Eco, DevS

Suringa, Mr P.
Law, AHis, Lit, IR, His, Phi, His, Edu, CuS, DevS, Eco, PolS

Teensma, Dr B.N.
His

Teerlink, Ir J.
DevS

Teillers, A.F.
CuS, Lin

Tenhaeff, Drs C.M.
DevS

Terhal, Dr P.H.J.J.
Eco

Thomas, Prof. dr H.
DevS

Tiemersma, Dr D.
Phi, Rel

Tims, Prof. dr W.
Eco, Agr, DevS

Tollenaere, Dr H.A.O. de
His, PolS, Rel

Netherlands

Tolsma, Drs G.J.
Lin
Ubaghs, Drs J.M.M.
CuS, His
Uyl, Dr M.H.G. den
GenS
Vaczi, Drs M.T.
Rel, AHis, GenS, CuS
Veen, Drs M.H.E. van der
His, DevS
Veer, Prof. dr P. van der
Rel, Ant, Soc, PolS
Veerdonk, Drs J.A.L.B. van den
Lin, Arch, Lit
Veere, Mr H. van der
Rel, Phi
Velde, Drs P.G.E.I.J. van der
Lit, His
Velden, Drs A.M. van der
DevS
Velzen, Dr A. van
Ant, DevS, GenS
Velzen, Dr J.H. van
GenS, Ant, DevS
Verboom, Drs A.W.C.
Phi, Lit, Rel, Lin
Verbruggen, Prof. dr H.
Env, Eco, IR
Vercammen, A.L.
His
Vereeken, Drs B.
Ant, DevS
Verhagen, Dr P.C.
Rel, Lin, Lit, Phi
Vermeulen, Drs A.C.J.
His
Vervliet, Drs J.B.
His, Eco
Vetter, Prof. dr T.E.
Phi, Rel
Vogelsang, Dr W.J.
Lin, His, Arch, Rel, AHis
Vreede-de Stuers, Dr S.C.L.
Ant
Vreeswijk, Drs L.
Ant, DevS
Vries, K. de
Rel, His
Waardenburg, Prof. dr J.G.
DevS
Wagenaar, Dr L.J.
His
Welling, Drs K.O.H.
Art
Werff, Dr P.E. van der
Env, Ant, DevS
Wersch, Dr H.W.M. van
Soc, Ant
Wessel, Drs M.G.J. van
Ant
Wichelen, Drs C.B.J. van
Soc, Phi, Ant, DevS, Rel
Wiechen, P.J. van
AHis, CuS, Ant, Arch, His
Wieringa, Dr S.E.
GenS, DevS
Wit, Dr J.W. de
DevS, Ant
Wolvekamp, Drs P.S.
Agr, IR, DevS, Env, GenS
Zanden, Drs T.A.M. van der
His, CuS
Zeeuw, D. de
Env, Agr
Zubkova, Dr L.
Lit
Zwart, Dr F. de
PolS

Norway

Aase, Prof. dr T.H.
DevS, Geo, Ant
Barth, Dr F.
DevS, Ant
Bleie, T.
Env, Ant, GenS, DevS, CuS
Braarvig, Prof. dr J.
Lit, Rel, Phi, DevS, His, CuS, Lin
Egden, S.E.
Ant
Fosse, Drs L.M.
Lin, Lit
Jacobsen, Prof. dr K.A.
Rel
Knutsen, Drs H.M.
DevS, Env
Kristiansen, Prof. K.
Rel, CuS, Lin, Lit
Mikkelsen, Prof. dr E.
Rel, Arch
Miranda, Dr A.
DevS
Odegaard, S.E.
Ant
Price, Dr P.G.
His
Ruud, Dr A.E.
Ant, His
Simson, Prof. dr G. von
Rel, Lit
Strom, A.K.
CuS, Ant, Rel

Poland

Debnicki, Dr K.
PolS, IR, His
Gudowski, J.
Eco, Agr, DevS
Jamsheer, Prof. H.
IR, His, PolS, Rel
Kieniewicz, Prof. J.
His
Leszczynski, Prof. L.
Soc, PolS, Law, Eco
Milewska, I.
Edu, Lin, Lit, CuS
Olbrys, Drs M.
Lin, Lit
Stasik, Dr D.
Lit
Wawrzyniak, Dr A.
CuS, Ant
Winid, Prof. dr B.
PolS, DevS, Env, Geo

Portugal

Almeida Teles e Cunha, Drs J.M. de
His
Antunes Dias, L.F.
His
Beitis Hanso, M.
His
Macaista Malheiros, Drs J.
Geo
Mascarenhas, J. A. S.
His
Oliveira e Costa, Dr J.P.
His, Rel
Souza, Prof. dr T.R. de
Rel, PolS, His
Tavim MA, J.A.
His

Rumania

Bercea, R.
Rel, Phi

Russia

Alayev, Prof. dr L.B.
His
Alekseeva, Dr E.A.
Lin
Alikhanova, Dr Yu.M.
CuS, Lit
Andronov, Dr M.S.
Lin
Androssov, Dr V.P.
Rel, Phi
Ashrafyan, Dr K.Z.
His
Bongard-Levin, Prof.dr G.M.
CuS, His
Chernyshev, Dr V.A.
Lin
Chicherov, Dr A.I.
Eco, His
Chufrin, Dr G.I.
IR, Eco
Datshenko, Dr G.M.
Lin
Dubianski, Prof. A.M.
Ant, Lit, Rel

Russia

Elkanidze , Dr M.M.
Arch, His, Phi, Psy, Ant, His, Rel, Soc, AHis, CuS

Farizov , Prof.dr I.O.
Ant, DevS, His, IR, Lin

Fets , K.A.
His, PolS

Gafurova , Dr N.B.
Lit

Gavryushina , Dr N.D.
Lit

Glebov , N.V.
Lin, Lit

Goryacheva , Dr A.M.
Eco

Grintser , Dr P.A.
Lit

Hohlova , Dr L.V.
Lin, Soc

Issayeva , Dr N.V.
Rel, Phi

Ivanov , Dr B.A.
CuS, Ant, His, Rel

Kalinnikova , Dr Ya.
Lit

Kashin , Dr V.P.
His

Khokhlova , Dr L.V.
Lin

Khoros , Dr V.G.
His, PolS, DevS, CuS

Klimova , Dr T.N.
Eco

Klyuyev , Dr B.I.
His, Lin, PolS

Knyazhinskaya , Dr L.A.
Eco

Komarov , Dr E.N.
Soc, His, PolS

Krasnodembskaya , Dr N.G.
Ant, Lit

Kutsenkov , Dr A.A.
His, PolS

Lamshukov , Dr V.K.
Lit

Lelyukhin , Dr D.N.
His

Lidova , Dr N.
AHis, CuS, His, Lit, Phi, Rel

Liperovsky , Dr V.P.
Lin

Lunyov , Dr S.I.
IR

Lysenko , Dr V.G.
Phi

Makarenko , Prof. dr V.A.
Lin, Lit, His, Ant, Edu, CuS, Rel

Malyarov , Dr O.V.
Eco

Maretina , Dr S.A.
Ant

Martyshin , Dr O.V.
PolS

Mezentseva , O. V.
CuS, Phi, Rel

Mitrokhin , Dr L.V.
CuS, His

Moskalenko , Prof. V.N.
His, IR

Mukhamedova , Dr D.M.
His

Niyazi , Dr A.
Env, Rel, PolS

Pleshova , Dr M.A.
His, PolS

Polonskaya , Dr L.R.
Rel, His

Potabenko , Dr S.I.
CuS, His

Prazauskas , Dr A.A.
Rel, His, PolS

Prigarina , Dr N.I.
Lit

Rastyannikov , Prof.dr V.G.
Eco

Samozvantsev , Dr A.M.
His

Sazanova , Dr N.M.
CuS, Lit

Schokhin , V. K.
Phi

Sedov , Dr A. V.
Arch

Semashko , Dr I.M.
Ant

Serebriany , Dr S.D.
Rel, CuS, Phi, Lin, Lit

Serenko , Dr I. N.
CuS, Edu, His, IR, Rel, Soc

Shaumian , Dr T.
His, PolS, IR

Shaumyan , Dr T.L.
His, PolS

Shokhin , Dr V.K.
Phi

Sidorov , Dr M.A.
IR

Soboleva , Dr E.S.
Rel, His, Ant, AHis

Solomonik , Dr I.N.
His, AHis

Stebline-Kamensky , Prof. dr I.M.
Lin, Lit, Rel

Sukhochev , Dr A.S.
Lit

Suvorova , Prof. A.A.
AHis, CuS, Lit, His

Tkacheva , Dr A.A.
Rel

Tovstykh , I.A.
Lit

Tsvetkov , Dr Yu.V.
Lit

Vanina , Dr E.Yu.
His

Vassilieva , Dr L.A.
Lit

Vertogradova , Dr V.V.
CuS, Lin, Rel

Vishnevskaya , Dr N.A.
Lit

Volodin , Dr A.G.
PolS

Voronin , Dr S.V.
Soc

Yegorova , M.N.
PolS, Soc

Yelizarenkova , Dr T.
Lin

Yurlov , Dr F.N.
His, PolS

Yurlova , Dr Ye.S.
His

Zahariin , Dr B.A.
Lin

Zakharyin , Dr B.A.
Lin

Spain

Albarrán Serrano , Antonio
Lit

Avilla Gomez , S.
Lit, Phi, His, Ant, His, AHis, Rel

Borreguero Sancho , E.
Soc, Rel, PolS, His, AHis

Cairó I Céspedes , G.
Eco

Ceruera Fernández , I.
AHis, His

Coll Compte , X.
Psy, Phi, Rel

Comas Montoya , Dr R.
AHis, His

Díez Galán , Dr J.
AHis, Lit

Elías de Tejada Lozano , Diplomat F.
Eco, Lit, PolS

Esparrago Rodilla MA, Luis
Agr, PolS

Fernández Miguélez , J.
IR

Fernandez-Del-Campo Barbadillo , E.
AHis

Ferro Payero , M.J.
AHis, His

Garcia-Ormaechea Quero , C.
AHis, Geo, His, Lit, Rel, Phi

Gonzales de Orduña Criado , Silvia
DevS

Merinero Martin , M.J.
His, PolS

Spain

Monclés, Dr A.
Env, Edu

Nieto-Sandoval Millan, V.
His

Olalla Cuervo, MA I.
AHis

Pajares Ruiz, J.M.
AHis, Eco, Geo, Soc

Perez Miguel, A.
Ant, GenS, His, IR

Picornell Marti, P.
Eco, Env, His

Sotelo Navalpotro, J.A.
Env, Geo

Suero Tellitu, T.
Ant, Phi, PolS, Rel, Soc

Vargas Anguita, G.

Sweden

Amer, Dr R.
IR, PolS, His

Benz, Drs M.
Lit, Lin, CuS

Djurfeldt, Dr G.
Soc, Agr, DevS

Eden, Dr N.A.S.W.
His, IR, Rel, His, DevS, Agr, Ant

Ekstrand, Prof. L.H.
Psy, DevS, CuS

Gren-Eklund, Prof. G.
Lit, Lin, Phi, Rel, CuS

Hatti, Prof. N.
Agr, DevS, Ant, His

Huldt, Prof. B.
IR, His

Jorgensen, B.D.
IR

Lambert, Prof. B.H.
PolS

Magnusson, J.A.
PolS, Soc

Meynert, Drs M.J.
GenS, Edu

Myrman, Y.
PolS

Oetke, Prof. dr C.
Lin, Phi

Ronnås, Dr P.
DevS, Agr, Eco

Schalk, Prof. dr P.
Phi, AHis, CuS, Arch, His, Rel

Swain, Drs A
PolS, IR, Env

Törnquist, Dr C.O.
DevS, PolS

Switzerland

Ahmed, Dr I.
Env, Agr, Eco

Bigger, A.
CuS, His, Lit, Rel

Brunner, Dr H.
Rel

Diaconscu, Drs B.
CuS, Lin, Lit, Phi, Psy, Rel

Ducor, Dr J.
Rel, Ant, GenS

Egenter, Ir N.
Rel, Ant, CuS, His, AHis

Etienne, Prof. G.
His, Agr, Eco, PolS, DevS

Geiser, Dr U.
DevS, Geo, Env

Hottinger, Prof. dr L.C.
IR, DevS, PolS

Hussain, W.
CuS, Eco, His, IR, PolS, Rel

Kloetzli, Prof. dr F.A.
Agr

Lee, H.
Env, Eco, Edu, CuS

Leukart, Dr A.P.
Lin

Milbert, Dr I.M.
PolS, Law, GenS, Soc, Env

Moser, Dr R.
Ant

Pfister, Drs B.
DevS, His, PolS, IR

Scherrer-Schaub, C.A.
Arch, His, Phi, Rel

Schneider-Sliwa, Prof. dr R.
DevS

Seeland, Dr K.
Rel, Soc, Env, Ant

Tarnutzer, Dr A.
Ant, GenS, DevS

Thomi, Dr P.
Lin, Lit, Rel, Phi

Thomi, Dr V.
His, Phi, Psy, CuS, Rel, AHis

Tillemans, Prof. dr T.J.F.
Phi, Rel

Viaro, Dr A.V.
Env, Ant, DevS

Waelty, Dr S.
Ant, Env, DevS

Turkey

Girdner, Dr E.J.
IR

United Kingdom

Ali, Dr K.A.
CuS, Ant

Anderson, Drs M.
Env, Law, DevS

Andrews, Dr A.Y.
Soc, CuS, Rel

Ansorge, Drs C.A.
His, Arch, CuS, Rel, Lit, Phi

Ardley, Drs J.C.
PolS

Arnold, Prof. D.J.
His

Asher, Prof. R.E.
Lit, Lin

Auty, Dr R.M.
DevS, Env, Eco

Bakewell, Mr A.D.

Balasubramanyam, Prof. V.N.
DevS, Eco

Banks, Dr M.J.
Ant

Bates, Dr C.N.
His

Bayly, Prof. dr C.A.
His

Belshaw, Prof. D.G.R.
DevS, Env, Agr, Eco,

Bevir, Dr M.
His, Phi

Birkin, I.
Ant

Bradnock, Dr R.W.
Env, Agr, IR, Geo, DevS

Bray, Drs J.N.
His, IR, PolS

Brockington, Dr J.L.
Lin, Rel, Lit

Brown, Prof. J. M.
Rel, GenS, His

Burlet, S.D.
His, PolS, Ant

Burton, Drs J.A.
His, IR

Cameron, Mr J.
Edu, Env, Phi, Eco, CuS, DevS

Caplan, Prof. dr L.
Ant

Carrithers, Prof. dr M.
CuS, His, Rel, Soc, Ant

Carswell, Prof. J.W.
AHis, CuS, His

Carter, Dr L.J.
His

Carter, Dr M.D.
His

Cassen, Prof. R.H.
Env, DevS, Eco, Edu, POPULATION

Chandramohan, Dr B.
Lit, DevS, Edu, IR, Lin, CuS

Chapman, G.
His, AHis, CuS

Chapman, Prof. G.P.
Geo, Agr, Env, DevS

Charsley, Dr S.R.
Ant

Cockburn, Mr R.C.
DevS, CuS

Coleman, Drs G.
DevS

United Kingdom

Collins , Dr P.S.
His

Coningham , Dr R.A.E.
Arch, Ant, CuS, His, AHis

Cook , Dr A.S.
His

Copley , Mr A.R.H.
Rel, His

Cousins , Drs L.S.
His, Rel, Lit

Crosbie , Dr A.J.
IR, Env, Eco, Geo, DevS

Deol , Mr J.S.
AHis, His, Lit

Desai , Prof. M.J.
DevS, Eco

Dewey , Dr C.J.
His

Didier B.A. , Drs B.J.
Edu, Ant, Phi

Dudrah , R.K.
CuS, Soc

Dundas , Drs P.
Lit, His, Lin

Dwyer , Dr R.M.J.
Lit, Lin, CuS

Dyson , Prof. T.P.G.
DevS, Agr

Elliott , D.
AHis

Evans , Dr K.K.
AHis, Rel, GenS, His

Flood , Dr G.D.
CuS, Rel

Fraser , Prof. T.G.
His

French , Mr P.R.
His, Lit

Fuller , Prof. C.J.
Ant

Fynes , Dr R.C.C.
His, Rel, Lit, CuS

Garforth , Prof. dr C.J.
Agr, Edu

Gethin , Dr R.M.L.
Rel

Ghosh , Dr D.
DevS, Eco

Glover , Dr I.C.
Arch

Gombrich , Prof. R.F.
Rel, Lin, Ant

Gombrich-Gupta , Dr S.
Rel, GenS, CuS, Phi, Lit

Good , Dr A.
DevS, Rel, His, GenS, Ant

Gooptu , Dr N.
PolS, DevS, His

Guy , Drs J.S.
His, AHis

Haan , Dr A. de
Soc, DevS, His

Hall , Dr A.R.
Ant, IR, PolS

Harris , Drs N.
DevS, Eco

Harriss , Dr J.C.
DevS, Ant

Harriss-White , Dr B.
Eco, DevS, Agr, GenS

Henry , Dr J.C.K.
His

Holmström , Dr M.
DevS, Ant

Howell , Dr J.A.
DevS, PolS, GenS

Hutt , Dr M.J.
AHis, CuS, Lit

Jackson , Dr E.M.
Rel

Jaffer , Dr A.K.H.
CuS, His, AHis

James , Drs D.
PolS, His

Jeffery , Dr P.M.
DevS, GenS, Ant, Soc

Jeffery , Dr R.
DevS, Soc, Ant, GenS, Env

Johnson , Dr G.
His

Jones , Dr R.M.
Ant

Jones , Mr S.C.
Eco, DevS

Kaul , C.
His

Killingley , Dr D.H.
Lin, Rel

King , Prof. U.
Phi, His, Edu, Ant, GenS, CuS, Rel, Soc

Kirkpatrick , Prof. C.H.
Env, Eco

Kothari , Dr U.
CuS, GenS, Agr, DevS

Kundu , Dr A.
DevS, IR, PolS, His

Lamba , Drs J.K.
AHis, CuS, His

Lambourn , Dr E.A.
AHis, Arch

Lenman , Prof. B.P.
His

Lipton , Dr M.
DevS, Agr, Eco

Mac Dowal , Prof. dr D.W.
Arch, AHis

Manning , Dr C.M.
His

Manor , Prof. J.G.
PolS

Marett , Dr P.
Rel, Law

Marr , Dr J.R.
Lin, His, CuS, Arch, His, Phi, Rel, AHis, Lit

Mayer , Dr R.D.S.
Rel

Mayer , Prof. A.C.
Ant

Mayoux , Dr L.C.
DevS, Ant, GenS

McDonaugh D.Phil, C.E.
Ant

McDonnel , Dr J.G.
Arch

McGrail , Prof.dr S.F.
Ant, Arch

McGregor , Dr R.S.
Rel, Lit, Lin, His

Menski , Dr W.
CuS, Rel, Law, Edu

Miles , M.
DevS, Edu

Mitter , Dr P.
His, AHis, CuS

Moodley , Mr D.
His

Morris-Jones , Prof. W.H.
PolS

Mürer , O.H.A.
Arch, His, AHis

Newman , Dr R.K.
His

Nossiter , Prof. T.J.
Soc, PolS, IR, DevS, His

O'Hanlon , Dr R.
His, GenS

Parikh , Prof. A.
Eco, DevS, Agr

Park , S.S.
Psy, PolS, Phi, SocAHis, DevS, Env, Edu, IR, Law

Parru , Dr J.P.
Ant

Peach , Dr C.
Geo, Soc

Pettigrew , Dr J.M.
Ant

Pinney , Dr C.
His, AHis, Ant, CuS

Plumbe , A.J.
DevS

Prakash , Drs A.
DevS, PolS

Robb , Prof. P.G.
His

Roberts , Dr C.R.
Ant, Arch

Roberts , Drs D.C.
DevS, Eco, IR

United Kingdom

Robinson, Prof. F.C.R.
His, Rel

Roper, Dr G.J.
CuS

Rosenstein, Dr L.L.
Lit, Lin

Russell, Dr A.J.
DevS, Env, Ant, CuS

Samad, Mr A.Y.
His, PolS, Soc

Samuel, Dr G.B.
Rel, Ant

Sathyamurthy, Dr T.V.
PolS, IR, DevS, Soc, Rel

Scammel, Dr G.V.
His

Sharma, Mr L.K.
PolS, Soc, Rel, DevS, CuS, IR, Phi, Lit

Shaw, Mr G.W.
CuS

Shepherd, Dr A.W.
DevS, Env

Shepperdson, Mr M.J.
DevS, Agr, Eco, PolS, Soc

Shih, Drs J.H.
Rel

Simmons, Dr C.
DevS

Singh, V. P.
Arch, DevS, Env

Singh, Dr G.
DevS, PolS

Slater, Dr R.P.
PolS, Ant, DevS, Eco

Smith, Dr D.
Rel, His, Lit, AHis

Smith, Mr S.
His, Edu

Snell, Dr R.
Lin, Lit

Soar BA, MA, M.J.
AHis, His, Rel

Spooner, Prof. F.C.
Eco, His

Standing, Dr H.
GenS, DevS, Ant

Stargardt, Prof. J.M.
Rel, ArchAgrAHis

Swallow, Dr D.A.
His, Ant, CuS, AHis

Talbot, Dr I.
PolS, IR, Eco

Taylor, Dr D.D.
His, PolS

Thin, Dr N.
Env, DevS, Soc, Ant, Rel

Thompson, Dr J.B.
Ant, Env, Arch

Tomlinson, Dr B.R.
Eco, His

Vera-Sanso, Dr P.
Ant

Verma, J.N.
CuS

Vinaik, R.
His, DevS

Washbrook, Dr D.A.
His

Watson, Dr J.R.
Eco, DevS

Weller, Drs P.G.
Rel

Whalley, Dr J.
Eco

Willis, Dr M.
His, CuS, His, AHis

York, Dr M.
Arch, IR, Rel, Soc, CuS

Zamperini, Dr S.
His, IR

United States of America

Pagel, Prof. U.
Lin, Rel

Yugoslavia

Jevremovic, Dr P.
IR, Law, PolS

LADAKH

Spain

Comas Montoya, Dr R.
AHis, His

Garcia-Ormaechea Quero, C.
AHis, Geo, His, Lit, Rel, Phi

NEPAL

Austria

Allinger, Dr E.
Rel, His, CuS, Arch, AHis

Loseries, Dr A.S.
His, Rel, CuS, Phi, His, AHis, DevS, Ant

Much, Dr M.T.W.
Phi, Rel

Sellner, Dr M.B.
CuS, Lin

Steinkellner, Prof. dr E.
Rel, Phi

Belgium

Alphen, J. van
AHis, Ant, Lin, His

Carpano, R.
Eco, IR

Gonzalo Castellanos, Dr A.
IR

Bulgaria

Fedotoff, Prof. dr A.
Rel, Lit, CuS

Czech Republic

Hulec, Dr O.
His, AHis, CuS, Arch, IR, Eco, Phi, Lit, Lin

Kostic, Dr S.
Rel, Lin, Phi

Krása, Dr M.
His

Pospisilova, Dr D.
Rel, AHis

Vacek, Prof. dr J.
Phi, Rel, Lit, Lin

Denmark

Beek, Dr M. van
DevS, Soc, PolS, Ant

Duus, K.D.
His, DevS, PolS, Soc, CuS

Ewers, K.
Ant, Env, DevS

Lehrmann Rasmussen, Dr J.
Eco, Phi, DevS

Madsen, Dr S.T.
Soc, PolS, DevS, Env, Rel, Ant, IR, Law, His

Martinussen, Prof. dr J.
Eco, DevS, PolS

Nielsen, Drs H.A.
PolS, DevS

Pedersen, Prof. dr P.
His, CuS, Ant, Phi, Psy, Rel, Env

Estonia

Kark, M.
CuS, Lin, Phi, AHis, Rel, Edu

Finland

Hossain, M.
DevS, IR, PolS

Karttunen, Dr K.J.
CuS

Karunaratne, Dr J.A.
DevS, Eco

Seppänen, J.
IR, Eco, Ant, CuS, Lin, His, AHis, Phi, Arch, Rel, PolS

Vanhanen, Dr T.
PolS

France

Adamo, S.A.
AHis, CuS, His, Rel, Soc

Aubriot, Dr O.
Ant

Bazin, N.
AHis

Béguin, G.
GenS, Law, DevS

Bernede, F.
PolS, IR, His, Eco

Bernier, X.
Geo

Blamont, Dr D.
Agr, DevS

Bouillier, Dr V.B.
Ant, Rel, Ant

France

Boulnois, Dr L.
His, Geo

Collin, H.
Law, Soc, PolS, Eco, IR

Delsol, Ch.
Ant

Dessaint, Prof. W.L.
Ant

Dollfus, P.
Ant

Gaborieau, Dr M.
His, Ant

Heide, Dr S. von der
Ant, DevSAHis, Env, CuS, Rel, PolS

Helffer, M.
Ant

Holle, A.
Geo

Jarrige, J.F.
His, CuS, Arch, AHis

Jest, C.
DevS

Karmay, S.
His, Lit, Phi, Ant, Rel

Kasi-Henkus, C.
Eco, DevS

Kaushik, S.Ch.
His

Krauskopff, Dr G.
Ant

Labbal, V.
Agr

Laurent-Perrey, I.
AHis

Lebreton, A.-S.
Art

Lecomte-Tilouine, Dr M.
Ant

Macdonald, Prof. A.W.
Ant, Rel

Massonnet, P.
His, IR, Soc, Rel, PolS, AHis, DevS, Law, Env, CuS, Lin, His

Mathou, Th.
His

Mazaudon, M.
Lin

Mercier, N.
Soc

Meyer, F.
Ant, Rel, His, CuS

Michailovsky, B.
Lin

Padoux, Dr A.
CuS, Rel, Phi, Lin, Ant

Pant, M.R.
His

Perrey, Ch.
Lin

Ramirez, Dr P.
Ant, His, PolS, Soc

Ripert, B.
Geo

Sacareau, Dr I.
Geo

Sagant, Dr Ph.
Phi, Rel

Salles, Dr J.F.
His, AHis, Arch, His

Silhe, N.
Ant

Smadja, J.
Env, Geo

Steinmann, B.
His

Tawa-Lama, S.
Soc

Toffin, Prof. G.
Ant, Rel, CuS

Germany

Aschoff, Prof. dr J.C.
CuS

Baumann, Dr G.
Lit, Rel, Lin

Bock-Raming, Dr A.
His, CuS, Lit, Rel, AHis

Bohle, Prof. H.G.
CuS, GenS, Agr, Env, DevS

Brinkhaus, Prof. dr H.
CuS, Lit, Rel

Buddruss, Prof. G.A.
His, Rel, Lin, Ant, CuS, Lit

Dodin, T.
Phi, Lit, Rel, Soc, Lin, IR, His, Ant, DevS, CuS, PolS

Ebbatson, Dr P.
Lin, Rel, Phi, Lit

Ehrhard, Drs F.K.
Rel, Phi, Lit, CuS

Eimer, Dr H.
Lit, His

Gaenszle, Dr M.
Rel, Lin, Ant, CuS

Gail, Prof. dr A.
His, AHis

Gatzlaff, Dr M.
Lit, CuS, Lin

Georg, Dr S.
Lin

Gippert, Prof. J.
His, Lit, Phi, Lin, CuS, Rel

Grönbold, Dr G.C.
CuS, Rel, Lit

Gropp, Dr G.C.A.
Phi, Lit, His, Rel, Arch, AHis, CuS, Ant, Lin

Grünendahl, Drs R.
Rel, Lin

Haffner, Prof. dr W.N.
Env

Hinüber, Dr H. von
Law, His, Rel, Lin, Phi, Lit

Hinüber, Prof. dr O. von
His, CuS, Arch, His, Law, Lit, AHis, Phi, Rel, Lin

Klotz, Drs S.
PolS, IR

Knall, Prof. B.R.
IR, Edu, PolS, Eco, DevS

Krebs, C.
Ant, Env

Krengel, Dr M.
Soc, Edu, Ant, DevS

Kreutzmann, Prof. dr H.J.
Agr, DevS, Ant

Linder Sabine, Drs L.
Ant, Arch, Soc

Lobo, Dr W.
AHis, Ant, Arch

Mahn, Dr S.
His, AHis, CuS, Arch

Mayer-König, Dr B.H.
Phi, Rel, Lit

Mevissen, Drs G.J.R.
His, AHis

Müller, K.
PolS, CuS, His

Müller, M.
His, AHis

Muller-Boker, Dr U.
GenS, Agr, CuS, DevS, Env

Nespital, Prof. dr H.
Lit, CuS, His, Lin

Oesterheld, Dr J.
Soc, His, PolS

Pews, Dr H.U.
Eco, DevS, Geo

Plaeschke, Dr H.
AHis, Arch

Plaeschke, Dr I.
His, Arch, AHis

Rennert, Drs H.
Lin, Lit, His, CuS, His, Phi, Rel, AHis

Rieger, Dr H.C.
DevS, Env, Eco

Sauerborn, Prof. J.
Agr, Env

Schmidt-Vogt, Dr D.
Env

Schrader, Dr H.
Soc, Eco, Ant, CuS

Schweinfurth, Prof. dr U.
Agr, DevS, Env, Arch, IR

Skyhawk, H. von
Phi, Rel, Ant, Lit, CuS

Steiner, Dr R.
Lit, Phi

Germany

Wezler, Prof. dr A.
CuS, Rel, Phi, Lit, Law, Lin

Yaldiz, Prof. dr M.
Arch, His, AHis, Rel

Hungary

Birtalan, Dr A.
AHis, Rel, Phi, Lit, Lin, His, Arch, GenS

Toth, E
CuS, Edu, His, Lin, Lit, Phi, Psy, Rel, Soc

Italy

Crespi Reghizzi, Prof. G.
PolS, DevS, IR, Law

Giambelli, Dr R.A.
Soc, Ant,

Nepal

Shrestha, Drs B.G.
Lit, CuS, Rel, PolS, Ant

Netherlands

Asselbergs, Drs G.
Agr, Eco, Edu

Benda Beckmann, Mr dr K. von
Law, Env, Ant

Beukering, P.J.H. van
IR, Eco, Env, DevS

Björkman, Prof. dr J.W.
PolS, DevS

Boon, D.
AHis, Rel, CuS, Phi, His

Bruin, Ir D. de
DevS, Env

Chemparathy, Prof. dr G.
Rel, Phi

Chutiwongs, Dr N.
Rel, His, Arch, AHis

Cowan, Drs F.M.
GenS, DevS, CuS, Ant, Env, LinAgr

Deelstra, T.
Env

Driem, Dr G.L. van
DevS, Lin, Ant, His

Duermeijer, Ir A.J.
AHis, Arch, DevS

Dusseldorp, D.B.W.M. van
Ant, Agr, DevS, PolS, Soc

Elbers, Dr C.T.M.
Eco

Gautam, Dr M.K.
Rel, Soc, Lit, Lin, His, Ant, CuS, PolS, Env

Germeraad, Dr ir P.W.
Env, Ant, CuS

Gijsen, Drs R.P.E.M.
His

Grent, P.C.M.
CuS, Lin, Lit, Rel, Phi

Guyt, Drs H.J.
His, IR, AHis, Lin, CuS, DevS

Hamelink, Prof. dr C.J.
IR, Law

Henke, Drs R.F.W.
Psy, Ant, DevS, Soc

Hoefnagels, Ir H.A.M.
Agr, Eco, Law

Hoek, Drs A.W. van den
Rel, Ant, Lin, CuS

Hoetjes, Dr B.J.S.
PolS, IR, Agr, DevS

Hudcovicova, A.
CuS

Jansen, Drs M.H.M.
Ant

Kal, Drs W.H.
Env, Lin, DevS, Agr, CuS, Ant, CuS, GenS

Karssen, Dr C.M.
DevS, Env, Agr, Eco, Edu, Soc, GenS

Keysers, Drs L.
GenS, DevS

Kloppenborg, Prof. dr M.A.G.T.
His, Lin, Lit, Rel

Kooij, Prof. dr K.R. van
Arch

Kortlandt, Prof. dr F.H.H.
Lin

Lieten, Dr G.K.
Soc, DevS, Agr

Meulenbeld, Drs B.C.
CuS, His, Ant, AHis, Rel, Arch

Mirage, M.
CuS

Moharir, Dr V.V.
PolS, DevS, Edu

Mohkamsing, Drs N.
Rel, AHis, Lit, Phi

Oonk, Drs G.
DevS, His, Ant

Opdam, Drs J.H.M.
DevS

Patel, Drs B.
Law, PolS, IR

Plaisier, Drs H.
Lin

Put, Drs M.
Agr, Env, Soc, DevS

Raven, Dr E.M.
His, Arch, AHis

Ridder, Ir J.M.
Eco, DevS, Ant, IR, Soc

Schampers, Drs A.J.J.
DevS, Soc

Singh, Dr N.
Agr, Env, DevS, Soc, IR

Sinnema, Drs T.
GenS, CuS, Soc, His, Edu

Spengen, Dr W. van
Geo, Ant, His

Streefland, Prof. dr P.H.
DevS

Tieman-van Ede, Drs Y.M.
GenS, Ant, Rel

Tolsma, Drs G.J.
Lin

Vaczi, Drs M.T.
Rel, AHis, GenS, CuS

Veer, Prof. dr P. van der
Rel, Ant, Soc, PolS

Verhagen, Dr P.C.
Rel, Lin, Lit, Phi

Verschoor, I.B.
His, Phi, CuS, PolS, Eco

Vreeswijk, Drs L.
Ant, DevS

Wolvekamp, Drs P.S.
Agr, IR, DevS, Env, GenS

Norway

Aase, Prof. dr T.H.
DevS, Geo, Ant

Bleie, T.
Env, Ant, GenS, DevS, CuS

Braarvig, Prof. dr J.
Lit, Rel, Phi, DevS, His, CuS, Lin

Kristiansen, Prof. K.
Rel, CuS, Lin, Lit

Kvaerne, P.
Rel

Odegaard, S.E.
Ant

Skar, Dr H.O.
PolS, Ant, Rel, DevS, CuS

Poland

Debnicki, Dr K.
PolS, IR, His

Gudowski, J.
Eco, Agr, DevS

Wawrzyniak, Dr A.
CuS, Ant

Winid, Prof. dr B.
PolS, DevS, Env, Geo

Russia

Aganina, Dr L.A.
Lit

Ivanov, Dr B.A.
CuS, Ant, His, Rel

Prazauskas, Dr A.A.
Rel, His, PolS

Spain

Albarrán Serrano, Antonio
Lit

Borreguero Sancho, E.
Soc, Rel, PolS, His, AHis

Coll Compte, X.
Psy, Phi, Rel

Comas Montoya, Dr R.
AHis, His

Garcia-Ormaechea Quero, C.
AHis, Geo, His, Lit, Rel, Phi

Kim, Drs S.-H.
Arch, Rel, Phi, Lit, His, AHis

Spain

Suero Tellitu, T.

Ant, Phi, PolS, Rel, Soc

Sweden

Magnusson, J.A.

PolS, Soc

Swain, Drs A

PolS, IR, Env

Switzerland

Ahmed, Dr I.

Env, Agr, Eco

Bigger, A.

CuS, His, Lit, Rel

Ducor, Dr J.

Rel, Ant, GenS

Heller, Dr A.

CuS, AHis, Rel, His

Kloetzli, Prof. dr F.A.

Agr

Lutz, P.

Eco, GenS, Env, Edu

Milbert, Dr I.M.

PolS, Law, GenS, Soc, Env

Moser, Dr R.

Ant

Oppitz, Prof. M.

Rel, Ant

Seeland, Dr K.

Rel, Soc, Env, Ant

Tarnutzer, Dr A.

Ant, GenS, DevS

United Kingdom

Allen, Dr N.J.

Ant

Belshaw, Prof. D.G.R.

DevS, Env, Agr, Eco,

Bradnock, Dr R.W.

Env, Agr, IR, Geo, DevS

Cameron, Mr J.

Edu, Env, Phi, Eco, CuS, DevS

Caplan, Prof. dr L.

Ant

Carter, Dr L.J.

His

Coleman, Drs G.

DevS

Desai, Prof. M.J.

DevS, Eco

Garforth, Prof. dr C.J.

Agr, Edu

Hall, Dr A.R.

Ant, IR, PolS

Harris, Drs N.

DevS, Eco

Harriss, Dr J.C.

DevS, Ant

Humphrey, Dr C.

Ant, Env, Rel, Soc

Hutt, Dr M.J.

AHis, CuS, Lit

James, Drs D.

PolS, His

King, Prof. U.

Phi, His, Edu, Ant, GenS, CuS, Rel, Soc

Kundu, Dr A.

DevS, IR, PolS, His

Marr, Dr J.R.

Lin, His, CuS, Arch, His, Phi, Rel, AHis, Lit

McDonaugh D.Phil, C.E.

Ant

Menski, Dr W.

CuS, Rel, Law, Edu

Park, S.S.

Psy, PolS, Phi, SocAHis, DevS, Env, Edu, IR, Law

Russell, Dr A.J.

DevS, Env, Ant, CuS

Samuel, Dr G.B.

Rel, Ant

Seddon, Prof. J.D.

Ant, IR, Soc, PolS, DevS

Sharma, Mr L.K.

PolS, Soc, Rel, DevS, CuS, IR, Phi, Lit

Shaw, Mr G.W.

CuS

Shepherd, Dr A.W.

DevS, Env

Shepperdson, Mr M.J.

DevS, Agr, Eco, PolS, Soc

Strickland, Dr S.S.

Ant

Subedi, Dr S.P.

Env, IR, Law, PolS

Wu, Dr K.

Agr, Env

York, Dr M.

Arch, IR, Rel, Soc, CuS

Zamperini, Dr S.

His, IR

United States of America

Khoo, Drs M.J.

Rel, Arch, Ant

PAKISTAN

Austria

Allinger, Dr E.

Rel, His, CuS, Arch, AHis

Luczanits, Dr Ch.

His, AHis, Rel, Arch

Belgium

Ballegeer, J.

PolS, Law

Coulie, Prof. dr B.R.R.

AHis, Soc, Lin, Phi, DevS, Ant, Eco, His, Lit

Hacourt, B.J.H.

DevS, Ant

Lesthaeghe, Prof. R.

DevS, Soc

Piquard, B.

Rel, PolS, Ant

Vielle, Dr CH.

Lin, Lit, Rel

Czech Republic

Hulec, Dr O.

His, AHis, CuS, Arch, IR, Eco, Phi, Lit, Lin

Kostic, Dr S.

Rel, Lin, Phi

Marek, Dr J.

CuS, Lit

Pospisilova, Dr D.

Rel, AHis

Vacek, Prof. dr J.

Phi, Rel, Lit, Lin

Denmark

Ferdinand, K.

DevS, Ant, CuS

Hojgaard, Mr F.C.

His

Javed, M.A.

CuS, Rel, IR, Soc

Madsen, Dr S.T.

Soc, PolS, DevS, Env, Rel, Ant, IR, Law, His

Martinussen, Prof. dr J.

Eco, DevS, PolS

Mozaffari-Mehdi, Prof. M.M.

PolS, Rel, IR

Pedersen, Prof. dr P.

His, CuS, Ant, Phi, Psy, Rel, Env

Finland

Hossain, M.

DevS, IR, PolS

Karttunen, Dr K.J.

CuS

Parpola, Prof. A.

Lit, Arch, Rel, CuS, Lin

Vanhanen, Dr T.

PolS

France

Abou-Zahab, M.-P.

Lit

Adamo, S.A.

AHis, CuS, His, Rel, Soc

Berinstain, Dr Vallerie

AHis, His

Bernard, J.A.

IR, His, Eco, PolS

Besenval, R.

Arch

Botsch, A.A.

Eco, DevS, IR, Edu, Law

Foucher, Dr M.

IR, PolS, Eco

Gaborieau, Dr M.

His, Ant

Gaillard, Dr C.

Arch

France

Heide, Dr S. von der
Ant, DevSAHis, Env, CuS, Rel, PolS
Heuze-Brigant, Dr G.L.D.
DevS, Env, Soc, Ant, Eco
Jarrige, J.F.
His, CuS, Arch, AHis
Kasi-Henkus, C.
Eco, DevS
Kroell, Dr A.
His
Lyonnet, B.
Arch
Matringe, Dr D.
Lin, Lit, Soc, Ant, CuS, Rel
Mohammad, A.T.
His, Soc, Rel
Moreau, P.
Art
Mukhherjee, Dr P.
His, Lit, Phi, Rel, AHis, Soc, His
Pitoun MA,
Arch, AHis, Lit
Racine, Drs J.-L.
DevS, PolS, IR
Raj, Dr K.
Geo, His
Reichert, P.
Lin
Roy, O.
PolS
Salles, Dr J.F.
His, AHis, Arch, His
Sandouk, Drs S.
Phi, His, Lit, Rel
Sivignon,
Eco, Geo

Germany

Baloch, Dr I.
PolS, CuS, His
Basu, Dr H.
Ant, Rel
Baumann, Dr G.
Lit, Rel, Lin
Bohle, Prof. H.G.
CuS, GenS, Agr, Env, DevS
Brentjes, Dr S.
Phi
Buddruss, Prof. G.A.
His, Rel, Lin, Ant, CuS, Lit
Casimir, Prof. dr M.J.
Psy, Arch, Ant, His, GenS, Agr
Degener, Dr A.C.
Rel, Lin
Gatzlaff, Dr M.
Lit, CuS, Lin
Glatzer, Dr B.
GenS, DevS, CuS, Soc, Ant
Gropp, Dr G.C.A.
Phi, Lit, His, Rel, Arch, AHis, CuS, Ant, Lin
Grötzbach, Prof. dr E.
Rel, Geo, CuS
Haar, Prof. dr B.J. ter
Lit, Rel
Herbers, H.
GenS, Agr, CuS
Hinüber, Dr H. von
Law, His, Rel, Lin, Phi, Lit
Hinüber, Prof. dr O. von
His, CuS, Arch, His, Law, Lit, AHis, Phi, Rel, Lin
Hohnholz, Prof. J.
DevS, Agr, Geo
Knall, Prof. B.R.
IR, Edu, PolS, Eco, DevS
Kreutzmann, Prof. dr H.J.
Agr, DevS, Ant
Krüger, Prof. dr H.
IR, Law, Rel, Soc, Eco
Mahn, Dr S.
His, AHis, CuS, Arch
Malik, Dr J.
His, Rel, CuS, Edu, His, Lit
Mallick, Drs S.
Rel, Lit, Law, His
Mann, Dr M.
His, Env
Mayer-König, Dr B.H.
Phi, Rel, Lit
Merz, Drs R.M.
His, Agr, Soc, Eco, DevS, PolS
Müller, M.
His, AHis
Muller-Boker, Dr U.
GenS, Agr, CuS, DevS, Env
Nespital, Prof. dr H.
Lit, CuS, His, Lin
Oesterheld, Dr J.
Soc, His, PolS
Plaeschke, Dr H.
AHis, Arch
Plaeschke, Dr I.
His, Arch, AHis
Prunner, Dr G.
Ant, Rel, CuS
Raunig, Prof. dr W.
AHis, Ant, Arch, His
Reetz, Dr D.
His, PolS, Rel, IR
Rieger, Dr H.C.
DevS, Env, Eco
Robotka, Dr B.
His
Rüdiger, Drs A.
Soc, Rel, CuS, IR, PolS
Sagaster, Prof. dr K.
Rel, Phi, Lit, Lin, His, AHis, CuS, His
Schied, Dr M.
His, Phi, PolS, Rel
Schmid, Dr A.
His, Ant
Schmitt, Prof. dr R.
Lin, His
Schwerin, Dr K. von
His
Skyhawk, H. von
Phi, Rel, Ant, Lit, CuS
Stellrecht, Prof. dr I.
His, Ant, Rel
Stöber, Dr G.
Ant, DevS, Edu
Werth, Dr L.
Ant
Yaldiz, Prof. dr M.
Arch, His, AHis, Rel
Zingel, Dr W.-P.
Agr, Env, Eco

Italy

Ferraro, Dr F.
Lin, Ant
Nicolini, Dr B
His, PolS
Raza, Dr R.
His, Lit, IR
Rossi, Prof. A.V.
Rel, PolS, Lin, Arch, Ant
Schmidt, Dr O.
His, Ant
Vashist, G.K.
Lit, Rel

Netherlands

Alibux, R.F.
IR, His
Asselbergs, Drs G.
Agr, Eco, Edu
Beekes, Prof. dr R.S.P.
Lin
Beers, Mr H.A.J.J. van
Law, DevS, GenS
Björkman, Prof. dr J.W.
PolS, DevS
Brouwer, A.A.
CuS, Eco, His, IR, PolS, Psy, Rel, Phi
Bruijn, Dr T. de
Rel, His, Lit
Bruijn, Prof. dr J.T.P. de
Lit, Rel
Chhachhi, Drs A.
GenS, Soc
Choenni, Dr C.E.S.
His, IR, Phi, PolS, Rel, Lit, DevS, Soc
Cowan, Drs F.M.
GenS, DevS, CuS, Ant, Env, LinAgr
Dijksterhuis, C.
GenS, Ant, CuS, Soc
Duermeijer, Ir A.J.
AHis, Arch, DevS

Netherlands

Evers , Drs B.H.

DevS, Env, Eco, Agr

Farooqi , Drs K.H.

Rel, CuS, Soc, His, GenS, Env, DevS

Gautam , Dr M.K.

Rel, Soc, Lit, Lin, His, Ant, CuS, PolS, Env

Giel , Mr P.

Env, DevS

Gommans , Dr J.J.L.

His

Guyt , Drs H.J.

His, IR, AHis, Lin, CuS, DevS

Haar , Dr J.G.J. ter

Rel, Lit

Hanssen , Drs L.M.

Ant, CuS

Heemst , Drs J.J.P. van

Eco

Hoefnagels , Ir H.A.M.

Agr, Eco, Law

Hoetjes , Dr B.J.S.

PolS, IR, Agr, DevS

Hoogland , Drs J.G.D.

Eco, DevS, Env

Houben , Dr J.E.M.

Rel, His, Lin, Lit, Phi

Hulst , W.A.

Eco

Immig , Drs O.I.

Soc, His, IR, Rel, Eco, PolS

Jager , Drs L.M.H. de

His

Jehle , Dr E.

IR, DevS, Eco, Edu, Law

Jong , Prof. dr F. de

CuS, Rel

Kal , Drs W.H.

Env, Lin, DevS, Agr, CuS, Ant, CuS, GenS

Keysers , Drs L.

GenS, DevS

Kolff , Prof. dr D.H.A.

His, Ant, Law

Kooij , Prof. dr K.R. van

Arch

Kruijk , Drs J.L. de

DevS, Eco

Lautenbach , Drs H.

His

Lieten , Dr G.K.

Soc, DevS, Agr

Linden , B. van der

CuS, His, Rel

Linden , Dr J.J. van der

DevS

Lingen , Ing J.

His

Maas , C.H.J.M.

His, AHis

Meijs , Drs M.A.G.

IR, Rel, Ant, CuS

Meuldijk , Drs I.M.

Soc, Agr, GenS, Env, Ant, DevS

Meulenbeld , Drs B.C.

CuS, His, Ant, AHis, Rel, Arch

Mohkamsing , Drs N.

Rel, AHis, Lit, Phi

Oonk , Drs G.

DevS, His, Ant

Ouden , Dr J.H.B. den

DevS, Ant, Agr, GenS

Patel , Drs B.

Law, PolS, IR

Picavet , Drs R.T.C.M.

Eco, DevS

Pinkers , Ir M.J.H.P.

IR, DevS, EduAgr

Rammandanlall , Drs J.

Ant

Raven , Dr E.M.

His, Arch, AHis

Ruben , Drs R.

Agr, Eco, Env

Schalke , Dr H.J.W.G.

Arch, Ant, Env

Schoorl , Prof. dr J.W.

DevS, Ant

Selier , Dr F.J.M.

Ant

Singh , Dr N.

Agr, Env, DevS, Soc, IR

Smidt , Prof. dr J.

Eco

Southwold-Llewellyn , Dr S.

Ant, Agr, Env, GenS, Eco, DevS

Stel , Dr J.H.

Env, Eco

Streefland , Prof. dr P.H.

DevS

Suringa , Mr P.

Law, AHis, Lit, IR, His, Phi, His, Edu, CuS, DevS, Eco, PolS

Thomas , Prof. dr H.

DevS

Tims , Prof. dr W.

Eco, Agr, DevS

Tolsma , Drs G.J.

Lin

Vereeken , Drs B.

Ant, DevS

Vervliet , Drs J.B.

His, Eco

Vogelsang , Dr W.J.

Lin, His, Arch, Rel, AHis

Voogd , Drs P. de

DevS, GenS, Soc, Edu

Vries , K. de

Rel, His

Witkam , Dr J.J.

His, Rel, Lit

Wolvekamp , Drs P.S.

Agr, IR, DevS, Env, GenS

Zeeuw , D. de

Env, Agr

Zieck , Drs M.Y.A.

Law

Norway

Aase , Prof. dr T.H.

DevS, Geo, Ant

Barth , Dr F.

DevS, Ant

Kristiansen , Prof. K.

Rel, CuS, Lin, Lit

Pakistan

Iqbal , Dr Z.

DevS, Eco

Poland

Debnicki , Dr K.

PolS, IR, His

Jamsheer , Prof. H.

IR, His, PolS, Rel

Winid , Prof. dr B.

PolS, DevS, Env, Geo

Portugal

Almeida Teles e Cunha , Drs J.M. de

His

Macaista Malheiros , Drs J.

Geo

Russia

Alayev , Prof. dr L.B.

His

Aristova , Dr L.B.

Eco, Edu

Belokrenitsky , Dr V.Y.

Soc, PolS, His, IR

Datshenko , Dr G.M.

Lin

Glebov , N.V.

Lin, Lit

Komarov , Dr E.N.

Soc, His, PolS

Morozova , Dr M. Yu

GenS, Agr, Eco, Env

Moskalenko , Prof. V.N.

His, IR

Nikolaeva , M.L.

PolS, Soc

Niyazi , Dr A.

Env, Rel, PolS

Pelevin , Dr M.S.

Lin, Lit

Pleshov , Dr O.V.

His

Polonskaya , Dr L.R.

Rel, His

Sedov , Dr A. V.

Arch

Russia

Serebriany, Dr S.D.
Rel, CuS, Phi, Lin, Lit

Serenko, Dr I. N.
CuS, Edu, His, IR, Rel, Soc

Shaumian, Dr T.
His, PolS, IR

Sidorov, Dr M.A.
IR

Solomonik, Dr I.N.
His, AHis

Stebline-Kamensky, Prof. dr I.M.
Lin, Lit, Rel

Sukhochev, Dr A.S.
Lit

Suvorova, Prof. A.A.
AHis, CuS, Lit, His

Zhmuida, Dr I.V.
Eco, IR

Spain

Borreguero Sancho, E.
Soc, Rel, PolS, His, AHis

Elías de Tejada Lozano, Diplomat F.
Eco, Lit, PolS

Fernandez-Del-Campo Barbadillo, E.
AHis

Garcia-Ormaechea Quero, C.
AHis, Geo, His, Lit, Rel, Phi

Gonzales de Orduña Criado, Silvia
DevS

Suero Tellitu, T.
Ant, Phi, PolS, Rel, Soc

Sweden

Eden, Dr N.A.S.W.
His, IR, Rel, His, DevS, Agr, Ant

Huldt, Prof. B.
IR, His

Magnusson, J.A.
PolS, Soc

Swain, Drs A
PolS, IR, Env

Switzerland

Ahmed, Dr I.
Env, Agr, Eco

Bigger, A.
CuS, His, Lit, Rel

Centlivres, Prof. P.
CuS, Ant

Etienne, Prof. G.
His, Agr, Eco, PolS, DevS

Geiser, Dr U.
DevS, Geo, Env

Hottinger, Prof. dr L.C.
IR, DevS, PolS

Hussain, W.
CuS, Eco, His, IR, PolS, Rel

Kloetzli, Prof. dr F.A.
Agr

Lutz, P.
Eco, GenS, Env, Edu

Milbert, Dr I.M.
PolS, Law, GenS, Soc, Env

Seeland, Dr K.
Rel, Soc, Env, Ant

Tarnutzer, Dr A.
Ant, GenS, DevS

Viaro, Dr A.V.
Env, Ant, DevS

Turkey

Girdner, Dr E.J.
IR

United Kingdom

Ali, Dr K.A.
CuS, Ant

Andrews, Dr A.Y.
Soc, CuS, Rel

Ansorge, Drs C.A.
His, Arch, CuS, Rel, Lit, Phi

Auty, Dr R.M.
DevS, Env, Eco

Bakewell, Mr A.D.

Belshaw, Prof. D.G.R.
DevS, Env, Agr, Eco,

Bradnock, Dr R.W.
Env, Agr, IR, Geo, DevS

Bray, Drs J.N.
His, IR, PolS

Bunt, Dr G.
CuS, Ant, Law, Rel

Cameron, Mr J.
Edu, Env, Phi, Eco, CuS, DevS

Carter, Dr L.J.
His

Chandramohan, Dr B.
Lit, DevS, Edu, IR, Lin, CuS

Coleman, Drs G.
DevS

Coningham, Dr R.A.E.
Arch, Ant, CuS, His, AHis

Cook, Dr A.S.
His

Crosbie, Dr A.J.
IR, Env, Eco, Geo, DevS

Deol, Mr J.S.
AHis, His, Lit

Desai, Prof. M.J.
DevS, Eco

Dewey, Dr C.J.
His

Dudrah, R.K.
CuS, Soc

Evans, Dr K.K.
AHis, Rel, GenS, His

French, Mr P.R.
His, Lit

Garforth, Prof. dr C.J.
Agr, Edu

Gooptu, Dr N.
PolS, DevS, His

Haidrani, Dr S.
CuS, His, Lit

Harris, Drs N.
DevS, Eco

Harriss, Dr J.C.
DevS, Ant

Hussein, Dr A.
PolS, CuS, Edu, DevS, Rel, Soc

Jackson, Dr E.M.
Rel

Jaffer, Dr A.K.H.
CuS, His, AHis

James, Drs D.
PolS, His

Jeffery, Dr P.M.
DevS, GenS, Ant, Soc

Jeffery, Dr R.
DevS, Soc, Ant, GenS, Env

Johnson, Dr G.
His

Jones, Dr R.M.
Ant

Jones, Mr S.C.
Eco, DevS

King, Prof. U.
Phi, His, Edu, Ant, GenS, CuS, Rel, Soc

Kundu, Dr A.
DevS, IR, PolS, His

Lenman, Prof. B.P.
His

Lipton, Dr M.
DevS, Agr, Eco

Mac Dowal, Prof. dr D.W.
Arch, AHis

Malik, Dr I.H.
His

Marr, Dr J.R.
Lin, His, CuS, Arch, His, Phi, Rel, AHis, Lit

Mayer, Prof. A.C.
Ant

McGrail, Prof.dr S.F.
Ant, Arch

Menski, Dr W.
CuS, Rel, Law, Edu

Miles, M.
DevS, Edu

Morris-Jones, Prof. W.H.
PolS

Newman, Dr R.K.
His

Nossiter, Prof. T.J.
Soc, PolS, IR, DevS, His

Parikh, Prof. A.
Eco, DevS, Agr

Park, S.S.
Psy, PolS, Phi, SocAHis, DevS, Env, Edu, IR, Law

Peach, Dr C.
Geo, Soc

United Kingdom
Rahim, Dr E.
DevS, Eco
Robb, Prof. P.G.
His
Robinson, Prof. F.C.R.
His, Rel
Romijn, Dr H.A.
DevS, Eco
Roper, Dr G.J.
CuS
Samad, Mr A.Y.
His, PolS, Soc
Sharma, Mr L.K.
PolS, Soc, Rel, DevS, CuS, IR, Phi, Lit
Shaw, Mr G.W.
CuS
Shepperdson, Mr M.J.
DevS, Agr, Eco, PolS, Soc
Singh, Dr G.
DevS, PolS
Slater, Dr R.P.
PolS, Ant, DevS, Eco
Smith, Mr S.
His, Edu
Talbot, Dr I.
PolS, IR, Eco
Taylor, Dr D.D.
His, PolS
Thomas, Mr I.D.
DevS
Vinaik, R.
His, DevS
Zamperini, Dr S.
His, IR

United States of America
Khoo, Drs M.J.
Rel, Arch, Ant

Yugoslavia
Furundzic, V.
Psy, Rel, Lit, Lin, Edu, His, Phi, AHis
Jevremovic, Dr P.
IR, Law, PolS

SIKKIM

Austria
Much, Dr M.T.W.
Phi, Rel

Bulgaria
Fedotoff, Prof. dr A.
Rel, Lit, CuS

France
Heide, Dr S. von der
Ant, DevSAHis, Env, CuS, Rel, PolS
Steinmann, B.
His

Germany
Mahn, Dr S.
His, AHis, CuS, Arch
Sagaster, Prof. dr K.
Rel, Phi, Lit, Lin, His, AHis, CuS, His
Skyhawk, H. von
Phi, Rel, Ant, Lit, CuS

Netherlands
Chemparathy, Prof. dr G.
Rel, Phi
Chutiwongs, Dr N.
Rel, His, Arch, AHis
Driem, Dr G.L. van
DevS, Lin, Ant, His
Gautam, Dr M.K.
Rel, Soc, Lit, Lin, His, Ant, CuS, PolS, Env
Guyt, Drs H.J.
His, IR, AHis, Lin, CuS, DevS
Hoetjes, Dr B.J.S.
PolS, IR, Agr, DevS
Plaisier, Drs H.
Lin
Singh, Dr N.
Agr, Env, DevS, Soc, IR
Tolsma, Drs G.J.
Lin
Wolvekamp, Drs P.S.
Agr, IR, DevS, Env, GenS

Switzerland
Tarnutzer, Dr A.
Ant, GenS, DevS

United Kingdom
Belshaw, Prof. D.G.R.
DevS, Env, Agr, Eco,
Marr, Dr J.R.
Lin, His, CuS, Arch, His, Phi, Rel, AHis, Lit
Subedi, Dr S.P.
Env, IR, Law, PolS

United States of America
Pagel, Prof. U.
Lin, Rel

SRI LANKA

Austria
Allinger, Dr E.
Rel, His, CuS, Arch, AHis
Much, Dr M.T.W.
Phi, Rel

Belgium
Carpano, R.
Eco, IR
Gonzalo Castellanos, Dr A.
IR
Lesthaeghe, Prof. R.
DevS, Soc
Vielle, Dr CH.
Lin, Lit, Rel

Czech Republic
Dvorak, Drs J.
Lit, Lin
Filipsky, Dr I.
Rel, Lin, His
Hulec, Dr O.
His, AHis, CuS, Arch, IR, Eco, Phi, Lit, Lin
Kostic, Dr S.
Rel, Lin, Phi
Pospisilova, Dr D.
Rel, AHis
Vacek, Prof. dr J.
Phi, Rel, Lit, Lin

Denmark
Bakker, Dr P.J.
His, Lin, Ant
Bugge, Dr H.
Rel, His
Lehrmann Rasmussen, Dr J.
Eco, Phi, DevS
Madsen, Dr S.T.
Soc, PolS, DevS, Env, Rel, Ant, IR, Law, His
Martinussen, Prof. dr J.
Eco, DevS, PolS
Pedersen, Prof. dr P.
His, CuS, Ant, Phi, Psy, Rel, Env

Finland
Hossain, M.
DevS, IR, PolS
Karttunen, Dr K.J.
CuS
Karunaratne, Dr J.A.
DevS, Eco
Vanhanen, Dr T.
PolS

France
Adamo, S.A.
AHis, CuS, His, Rel, Soc
Alwis Perera, D.R. De
Lin, IR, Eco
Daluwa Thumul, G.J.
Lan
Filliozat, J.
Rel, Lit
Gamage, J.
Env
Gobalakchenane, Dr M.
CuS, His, Rel, Soc
Gros, Prof. F.E.
CuS, Lit, Rel
Guillon, Dr E.
Ant, AHis, Arch, Rel, His
Heide, Dr S. von der
Ant, DevSAHis, Env, CuS, Rel, PolS
Henry, R.
Lin, GenS, Env, CuS, AHis, Arch, IR, Lit, Phi, Psy
Jacq-Hergoualc'h, Dr M.
Rel, His, Arch, His, AHis
Jayasinghe, M.A.
Lan
Kasi-Henkus, C.
Eco, DevS

France

Liyanaratne, J.
IR, Eco, DevS, PolS

Meyer, Dr E.P.
His

Salles, Dr J.F.
His, AHis, Arch, His

Sivignon,
Eco, Geo

Vigneau, Prof. R.
Lit

Williamson, Dr P.J.
DevS, Eco

Zvelebil, Prof. dr K.V.
Rel, Lit, CuS, Lin

Germany

Albrecht, E.W.
Eco

Bauer, Prof. dr C.H.R.
Lit, Rel, Ant, Lin, His, Arch

Baumann, Dr G.
Lit, Rel, Lin

Bechert, Prof. H.H.
His, Lit, Rel, CuS

Bohle, Prof. H.G.
CuS, GenS, Agr, Env, DevS

Braun, Dr H.
His, Lit, Rel

Buddruss, Prof. G.A.
His, Rel, Lin, Ant, CuS, Lit

Domroes, Prof. dr M.R.J.
Agr, Geo, Env

Ebbatson, Dr P.
Lin, Rel, Phi, Lit

Eimer, Dr H.
Lit, His

Frasch, Drs T.
His

Gail, Prof. dr A.
His, AHis

Gippert, Prof. J.
His, Lit, Phi, Lin, CuS, Rel

Grönbold, Dr G.C.
CuS, Rel, Lit

Haffner, Prof. dr W.N.
Env

Hannibal, Dr A.S.
Arch

Hinüber, Dr H. von
Law, His, Rel, Lin, Phi, Lit

Hinüber, Prof. dr O. von
His, CuS, Arch, His, Law, Lit, AHis, Phi, Rel, Lin

Janz, K.E.
Ant, Agr, GenS, DevS

Klotz, Drs S.
PolS, IR

Knall, Prof. B.R.
IR, Edu, PolS, Eco, DevS

Krebs, C.
Ant, Env

Krische, S.
DevS, Env, Geo

Kulke, Prof. dr H.
His, Soc, Rel

Lengerke, Dr H.J. von
Env, Agr, Geo

Lobo, Dr W.
AHis, Ant, Arch

Loke-Schwalbe, Dr P.M.L.
CuS, Ant

Mahn, Dr S.
His, AHis, CuS, Arch

Mann, Dr M.
His, Env

Mayer, Drs M.
Soc, Env, DevS

Merz, Drs R.M.
His, Agr, Soc, Eco, DevS, PolS

Nespital, Prof. dr H.
Lit, CuS, His, Lin

Oesterheld, Dr J.
Soc, His, PolS

Plaeschke, Dr H.
AHis, Arch

Plaeschke, Dr I.
His, Arch, AHis

Schied, Dr M.
His, Phi, PolS, Rel

Schröter, Dr S.
Ant

Schweinfurth, Prof. dr U.
Agr, DevS, Env, Arch, IR

Stein, Dr W.
Ant, CuS, AHis, Arch, His

Werner, Dr W.L.
Env, DevS

Yaldiz, Prof. dr M.
Arch, His, AHis, Rel

Zingel, Dr W.-P.
Agr, Env, Eco

Hungary

Illyefalvi-Vitez, Prof. Z.
Edu

Italy

Albanese, M.
His, AHis, Rel, Phi

Pistilli, Drs G.M.
Lit, His

Rispoli, Dr F.
Ant, Arch

Vashist, G.K.
Lit, Rel

Netherlands

Atman, Dr R.E.
DevS

Attema, Drs Y.
AHis, CuS, His

Bavinck, Drs J.M.
DevS, Ant

Beumer, Drs W.G.M.
AHis

Björkman, Prof. dr J.W.
PolS, DevS

Bogaerts, Drs E.M.
Phi, IR, AHis, Rel, Lit, Lin, His, Ant

Bruijn, E.J. de
His

Bruijn, Drs B. de
DevS, Soc, Psy, Ant

Bruijn, P.J.J. de
His, AHis

Buuren, Drs B.L.M. van
Ant, DevS

Byster, Drs E.D.
IR, CuS, His, Lit, Phi, AHis

Casparis, Prof. dr J.G. de
AHis, Rel, His, Arch, His

Chemparathy, Prof. dr G.
Rel, Phi

Chhachhi, Drs A.
GenS, Soc

Choenni, Dr C.E.S.
His, IR, Phi, PolS, Rel, Lit, DevS, Soc

Christiaans, P.A.
His

Chutiwongs, Dr N.
Rel, His, Arch, AHis

Cowan, Drs F.M.
GenS, DevS, CuS, Ant, Env, LinAgr

Dechering, Dr W.H.J.C.
DevS, Soc, Ant

Dijkstra, Drs G.H.
Soc, Rel, Phi, Eco, His, IR, Psy, PolS

Dishoeck, Drs E.R. van
Eco, Edu, Phi, CuS

Duermeijer, Ir A.J.
AHis, Arch, DevS

Dunham, Dr D.M.
CuS, DevS, Agr

Dusseldorp, D.B.W.M. van
Ant, Agr, DevS, PolS, Soc

Gaay Fortman, Prof. B. de
Eco, Law

Gajentaan, Mr H.
PolS, IR, DevS

Gall, Dr H.C.
His, Law

Gautam, Dr M.K.
Rel, Soc, Lit, Lin, His, Ant, CuS, PolS, Env

Gelder, Drs R. van
CuS, His, IR

Goor, Dr J. van
His, IR

Guimaraes, Ir J.P.C.
Eco, Env, DevS

Hamelink, Prof. dr C.J.
IR, Law

Netherlands

Haude, Dr D.K.H.
DevS, Eco

Heemst, Drs J.J.P. van
Eco

Heins, Drs J.J.F.
Env, DevS

Hoebink, Dr P.R.J.
DevS, PolS, CuS

Hoefnagels, Ir H.A.M.
Agr, Eco, Law

Hoetjes, Dr B.J.S.
PolS, IR, Agr, DevS

Hoffmanns, Drs P.R.
AHis, Arch

Hommes, Prof. dr E.W.
DevS, Ant

Horst, Dr J. van der
PolS, Rel

Houben, Dr J.E.M.
Rel, His, Lin, Lit, Phi

Huizer, Prof. dr G.J.
Rel, IR, Env, DevS

Jacobs, Drs E.M.
His

Jehle, Dr E.
IR, DevS, Eco, Edu, Law

Jepma, Prof. C.J.
Env, DevS, Eco

Kal, Drs W.H.
Env, Lin, DevS, Agr, CuS, Ant, CuS, GenS

Karssen, Dr C.M.
DevS, Env, Agr, Eco, Edu, Soc, GenS

Kloos, Prof. dr P.
Ant, DevS

Kloppenborg, Prof. dr M.A.G.T.
His, Lin, Lit, Rel

Knaap, Dr G.J.
His

Koesoebjono, R.H.S.I.
DevS, GenS, Eco

Kolff, Prof. dr D.H.A.
His, Ant, Law

Kooij, Prof. dr K.R. van
Arch

Kuethe, Mr F.Ph.
PolS, Phi, Lit, His

Kurian, Dr R.
Eco, DevS

Kusin, Prof. dr J.A.
GenS

Lautenbach, Drs H.
His

Lingen, Ing J.
His

Menon, Dr A.G.
Rel, Lit, Lin

Mohkamsing, Drs N.
Rel, AHis, Lit, Phi

Onderdenwijngaard, Drs T.A.
Ant

Oosterwijk, A.J.
His, Ant, Arch

Opdam, Drs J.H.M.
DevS

Ouden, Dr J.H.B. den
DevS, Ant, Agr, GenS

Patel, Drs B.
Law, PolS, IR

Quist, Drs C.
GenS, DevS

Raben, Dr R.
His, Ant

Raven, Dr E.M.
His, Arch, AHis

Risseeuw, Prof. dr C.I.
Ant, His, GenS, DevS, Rel, Law

Roelofs, Drs J.D.
Soc, GenS, DevS

Schampers, Drs A.J.J.
DevS, Soc

Schenk, Dr H.
DevS, Env

Schrijvers, Prof. dr J.
GenS, DevS, Ant

Schuurman, Dr F.J.
DevS

Seret, Mr A.
Phi, Lit, Lin, Rel, CuS

Sigmond, Dr J.P.
CuS, His, AHis, Arch

Silva, Drs P.L. de
DevS, Ant

Singh, Dr N.
Agr, Env, DevS, Soc, IR

Skutsch, Dr M.M.
GenS, DevS

Southwold-Llewellyn, Dr S.
Ant, Agr, Env, GenS, Eco, DevS

Spaan, Drs E.J.A.M.
Ant

Speckmann, Prof. dr J.D.
Ant, Soc

Stel, Dr J.H.
Env, Eco

Storck, Ir. P.W.A.
DevS, Agr, Eco, Ant

Streef, E.
Env, Law, Ant

Streumer, Drs P.
Edu, Ant, His, DevS, CuS

Suringa, Mr P.
Law, AHis, Lit, IR, His, Phi, His, Edu, CuS, DevS, Eco, PolS

Tollenaere, Dr H.A.O. de
His, PolS, Rel

Tolsma, Drs G.J.
Lin

Top, Ir G.M. van den
Agr, DevS, Env

Ubaghs, Drs J.M.M.
CuS, His

Vaczi, Drs M.T.
Rel, AHis, GenS, CuS

Velde, Drs P.G.E.I.J. van der
Lit, His

Verboom, Drs A.W.C.
Phi, Lit, Rel, Lin

Vermeulen, Drs A.C.J.
His

Vreeswijk, Drs L.
Ant, DevS

Vries Robbé, A. de
Arch, His, Ant, AHis

Wagenaar, Dr L.J.
His

Wiechen, P.J. van
AHis, CuS, Ant, Arch, His

Wiel, A.N. van der
His, AHis, Arch

Wolffers, Prof. dr I
DevS

Wolvekamp, Drs P.S.
Agr, IR, DevS, Env, GenS

Zeeuw, D. de
Env, Agr

Norway

Knutsen, Drs H.M.
DevS, Env

Kristiansen, Prof. K.
Rel, CuS, Lin, Lit

Lie, Prof. R.K.
Phi, DevS

Lund, Prof. R.
GenS, Geo, DevS

Mikkelsen, Prof. dr E.
Rel, Arch

Miranda, Dr A.
DevS

Poland

Wawrzyniak, Dr A.
CuS, Ant

Portugal

Flores, Dr J.
His, IR

Russia

Alayev, Prof. dr L.B.
His

Bongard-Levin, Prof.dr G.M.
CuS, His

Elkanidze, Dr M.M.
Arch, His, Phi, Psy, Ant, His, Rel, Soc, AHis, CuS

Komarov, Dr E.N.
Soc, His, PolS

Krasnodembskaya, Dr N.G.
Ant, Lit

Lidova, Dr N.
AHis, CuS, His, Lit, Phi, Rel

Russia
Makarenko, Prof. dr V.A.
Lin, Lit, His, Ant, Edu, CuS, Rel
Maslov, Dr Yu.N.
Eco
Moskalenko, Prof. V.N.
His, IR
Safronova, Dr A.L.
Rel, His
Sedov, Dr A. V.
Arch
Solomonik, Dr I.N.
His, AHis
Volhonski, Dr B.M.
Lin, Lit
Voronin, Dr S.V.
Soc

Spain
Albarrán Serrano, Antonio
Lit
Borreguero Sancho, E.
Soc, Rel, PolS, His, AHis
Coll Compte, X.
Psy, Phi, Rel
Olalla Cuervo, MA I.
AHis
Suero Tellitu, T.
Ant, Phi, PolS, Rel, Soc

Sri Lanka
Hollup, Dr O.
DevS, Ant

Sweden
Bratthall, Prof. D.
Eco
Gren-Eklund, Prof. G.
Lit, Lin, Phi, Rel, CuS
Schalk, Prof. dr P.
Phi, AHis, CuS, Arch, His, Rel

Switzerland
Ahmed, Dr I.
Env, Agr, Eco
Geiser, Dr U.
DevS, Geo, Env
Lutz, P.
Eco, GenS, Env, Edu
Schneider-Sliwa, Prof. dr R.
DevS
Viaro, Dr A.V.
Env, Ant, DevS

United Kingdom
Auty, Dr R.M.
DevS, Env, Eco
Bakewell, Mr A.D.
Barron, Dr T.J.
His
Belshaw, Prof. D.G.R.
DevS, Env, Agr, Eco,
Bradnock, Dr R.W.
Env, Agr, IR, Geo, DevS
Brown, Dr N.D.
Env
Carrithers, Prof. dr M.
CuS, His, Rel, Soc, Ant
Carswell, Prof. J.W.
AHis, CuS, His
Carter, Dr L.J.
His
Carter, Dr M.D.
His
Chandramohan, Dr B.
Lit, DevS, Edu, IR, Lin, CuS
Chapman, Prof. G.P.
Geo, Agr, Env, DevS
Coningham, Dr R.A.E.
Arch, Ant, CuS, His, AHis
Cousins, Drs L.S.
His, Rel, Lit
Crosbie, Dr A.J.
IR, Env, Eco, Geo, DevS
Desai, Prof. M.J.
DevS, Eco
Dudrah, R.K.
CuS, Soc
Evans, Dr K.K.
AHis, Rel, GenS, His
French, Mr P.R.
His, Lit
Gethin, Dr R.M.L.
Rel
Gombrich, Prof. R.F.
Rel, Lin, Ant
Good, Dr A.
DevS, Rel, His, GenS, Ant
Gooptu, Dr N.
PolS, DevS, His
Hall, Dr A.R.
Ant, IR, PolS
Harriss, Dr J.C.
DevS, Ant
Henry, Dr J.C.K.
His
Jackson, Dr E.M.
Rel
Jaffer, Dr A.K.H.
CuS, His, AHis
James, Drs D.
PolS, His
Jeffery, Dr R.
DevS, Soc, Ant, GenS, Env
Johnson, Dr G.
His
Jones, Dr R.M.
Ant
King, Prof. U.
Phi, His, Edu, Ant, GenS, CuS, Rel, Soc
Kundu, Dr A.
DevS, IR, PolS, His
Lenman, Prof. B.P.
His
Lipton, Dr M.
DevS, Agr, Eco
Mac Dowal, Prof. dr D.W.
Arch, AHis
Manor, Prof. J.G.
PolS
Marr, Dr J.R.
Lin, His, CuS, Arch, His, Phi, Rel, AHis, Lit
McGrail, Prof.dr S.F.
Ant, Arch
Menski, Dr W.
CuS, Rel, Law, Edu
Nossiter, Prof. T.J.
Soc, PolS, IR, DevS, His
Park, S.S.
Psy, PolS, Phi, SocAHis, DevS, Env, Edu, IR, Law
Plumbe, A.J.
DevS
Rajapakse, Drs D.A.
Agr, DevS, Eco, GenS, Ant
Sharma, Mr L.K.
PolS, Soc, Rel, DevS, CuS, IR, Phi, Lit
Shaw, Mr G.W.
CuS
Shepperdson, Mr M.J.
DevS, Agr, Eco, PolS, Soc
Singh, Dr G.
DevS, PolS
Slater, Dr R.P.
PolS, Ant, DevS, Eco
Smith, Mr S.
His, Edu
Spencer, Dr J.R.
Rel, CuS, Ant, Edu, Soc, His
Thompson, Dr J.B.
Ant, Env, Arch
Washbrook, Dr D.A.
His
Zamperini, Dr S.
His, IR

Yugoslavia
Jevremovic, Dr P.
IR, Law, PolS

East Asia

CHINA

Austria
Galinski, C.
Edu, Lin
Lecher, Drs H.E.
His, Soc
Lee, Dr S.-K.
CuS, Lit
Min Tjoa, Prof. dr A.
Edu
Mosch, Dr N.
CuS, Phi

Austria

Natschläger , H.
Arch, AHis, GenS, His

Pilz , Prof. dr E.
His

Sellner , Dr M.B.
CuS, Lin

Sichrovsky , Prof. H.
CuS, His, PolS, IR

Zorn , Dr B.
Ant, Arch, Ant, His, AHis

Zotz , Dr V.
Phi, CuS, Rel, His

Belgium

Arrault ., Dr A.
Rel, Soc, PolS, CuS, His

Ballegeer , J.
PolS, Law

Boden , J.
Lin, AHis, Lit, His

Chan , M.Y.
CuS

Coulie , Prof. dr B.R.R.
AHis, Soc, Lin, Phi, DevS, Ant, Eco, His, Lit

Defoort , Dr C.M.G.
Phi

Degryse , Dr K.M.
His

Delanghe , H.
IR, His, PolS

Della Pietra , B.
IR, His, CuS

Dessein , Dr B.
Phi

Dudink , Dr A.C.
Rel, His

Fang , Dr S.-S.
CuS, Edu

Halsberghe , Dr N.M.
His

Heyndrickx , J.J.
Rel

Konings , P.
His

Lesthaeghe , Prof. R.
DevS, Soc

Meyer , Dr J.A.M. de
Lit, Rel, His, Phi

Pairoux , Prof. S.
His, IR, CuS, Soc

Pape , Mr W.
IR, Law, Eco, PolS

Persoons , Dr M.A.
AHis, Edu, IR, Lin, Phi

Simonet , J.M.
Arch, CuS, His, AHis

Vaerman , Drs B.
GenSAHis, Rel, CuS, His

Vanwalle , Drs I.A.M.A.
AHis, Lin, Lit, Phi, Soc, His

Vercammen , Dr D.K.J.
Ant, Phi, His, Rel

Verdoorn , Drs J.D.L.
Eco, IR

Wu-Beyens , I.CH.
PolS, IR, His, Agr, DevS, Env

Bulgaria

Cherrington , Dr R.L.
Soc, CuS, PolS

Devedjieva , Dr E.
IR, His, CuS

Fedotoff , Prof. dr A.
Rel, Lit, CuS

Gerganova , Drs K.M.G.
Ant, Rel, Phi, His

China P.R.

Lamouroux , Ch.
His

Wang , Dr H.
Soc

Czech Republic

Ando , V.
Law, Env, DevS

Borotov , Drs L.
Lit, His, AHis

Dr¡nek , Dr V.
IR

Hermanov , Dr Z.
Lit, Lin

Heroldov , Mgr. H.
His, Edu

Hor kov , Drs D.
Lit, Rel

Hulec , Dr O.
His, AHis, CuS, Arch, IR, Eco, Phi, Lit, Lin

Kalvodov , Prof. dr D.
Eco, Phi, Law, His, Lin

Kolmas , Prof. dr J.
Phi, CuS, Ant, His, Lit, Rel

Liscák , Dr V.
Rel, His, Phi, Lin, CuS

Lomov , Dr O.
Lit

Suchomel , Dr F.A.
Arch, AHis

Trískov , Dr.H.
Lin

Vochala , J.
Lin, Lit

Denmark

Andersen , A.H.
DevS, Ant

Aronstein , M.
PolS

Baark , Dr E.
His, DevS, Env, CuS

Bakken , Dr B.
Soc

Bruun , Drs O.
Ant

Clausen , Drs S.C.
Soc, PolS, His

Dong , C.
Soc

Goebel , Prof. E.
His

Gullestrup , Prof. H.
His, Soc, IR, Eco, Ant, DevS, CuS, PolS

Henriksen , Drs M.A.
Arch, CuS

Hornby , J.E.
CuS, AHis

Javed , M.A.
CuS, Rel, IR, Soc

Jutil , Drs S.
Arch, His

Konge Nielsen , Drs M.
Lin

Li , X.
DevS, PolS, IR

Littrup , Dr L.
His, Edu

Masina , P.P.
DevS, His, IR

Mikkelsen , G.B.
His, Phi, Rel, CuS

Nielsen , Prof. B.
Phi, Rel

Ostergaard , Dr C.S.
Agr, Soc, PolS, IR, DevS

Padolecchia Polo , Prof. S.P.
DevS, PolS, Rel, Edu, Eco, Soc, Env, IR, CuS

Petersen , J.O.
His

Sorensen , Dr H.H.
His, AHis, Rel, CuS

Thelle , Dr H.H.
Lit, PolS, Soc, His

Thogersen , Drs S.
Edu, Soc

Thorborg , Dr E.M.
DevS, PolS, Eco, His, GenS

Thunoe , Drs M.
Ant, Lit, Edu, Soc, DevS, CuS, His

Wang , J.
Lin, Lit, CuS, Edu, His, AHis

Wang , Dr Q.
PolS

Wedell-Wedellsborg , A.
Lit, CuS

Worm , Drs V.
Soc, Eco, Ant

Finland

Heikkinen , V.
Soc, Ant

Finland

Huang, Dr P.Z.Z.
Rel, His, Arch, Ant, CuS, Phi
Janhunen, Prof. dr J.A.
AHis, CuS, Ant, Arch, Lin
Jokinen, Drs J.J.
DevS, IR, PolS
Kivimäki, Dr T.A.
PolS, IR, DevS
Luova, Drs O.E.
IR, PolS
Mattila BA, M.M.
AHis, Lit
Seppänen, J.
IR, Eco, Ant, CuS, Lin, His, AHis, Phi, Arch, Rel, PolS
Siika, M.
IR, His
Tähkämaa, Drs J.P.
IR, PolS
Toiviainen, Dr H.
His

France

Abud, M.
Lit
Abud, Drs M.
Phi, Lin, His, Lit, CuS, His, AHis
Albis, R.
Eco
Aletton, V.
Ant
Alleton, Dr V.A.
Lit, Lin
André, Y.
Lit
Ang, Dr I.
Rel, His, Ant
Aubert, Dr C.
DevS, Agr, Ant, Eco, Soc
Aubin, F.
Soc, Law, His
Bady, Prof. P
Lit
Baille, B.
Ant
Balaize, C.
Ant, Agr, CuS, Rel
Barbiche, Prof. dr J.-P.
Law, IR, His, PolS, Eco, DevS, CuS, Edu, Soc
Barbier-Kontler, Dr C.
Phi, Rel
Bastid-Bruguière, M.
His
Baud Berthier, Dr G
Eco, His
Baye, Dr E.B.
DevS, Env, Eco
Béguin, G.
GenS, Law, DevS
Bellassen, Dr J.B.
Lin
Billion, R.
His, Phi, Lit, Lin, IR, Edu
Bissat, V.
Lit
Blanchon, Dr F.
His, Arch, His, AHis
Blayac, A.A.
Lit, His, Phi, Edu, Psy, Soc
Blazy, S.
His
Boisguerin, R.
Lit
Botsch, A.A.
Eco, DevS, IR, Edu, Law
Bottero, F.
Lin
Boully, J.L.
Lit
Bouteiller, E.
DevS, Eco
Brenier, J.
His
Bussotti, M.
AHis, CuS
Busuttil, J.
Lin
Cadart, Drs C.E.A.
PolS, IR, His
Cauquelin, Drs C.J.
Rel, Ant
Chagnaud, F.J.
Eco, Agr, Env, DevS
Chang, I.
Edu, IR, Lin, DevS, CuS, Lit
Chao, J.
GenS, DevS
Charbonnier, Dr J.
CuS, Rel, Phi, His
Chen, C.
Lit
Chen, L.
Soc, His
Cheng, S.H.
AHis, CuS, Rel
Cheng, Dr A.L.
CuS, His, Phi
Cheng-Cadart, Dr Y.X.
PolS, CuS, His, IR
Cheng-Wang, A.
Lin
Chevrier, Y.
His
Cohen, M.
His, Rel
Collin, H.
Law, Soc, PolS, Eco, IR
Cornet, C.
His
Coyaud, Dr M.
Ant, Lin
Crombe, V.
His, CuS, AHis, Rel, His, Arch
Curien, Dr A.
Lit
Dallidet, M.
Lin
Damon, Dr F.Y.
DevS, His
Debaine-Francfort, Dr C.
Arch
Delacour, C.
His
Delahaye, Dr H.
His, CuS, AHis
Delemarle-Charton, M.
Ant, His, Soc
Desirat, M.
Lin
Despeux-Fays-Long, Prof. C.
CuS
Desroches, J.-P.
CuS
Dienstag, C.
Arch
Diény, J. P.
His, Lit
Dinety, J.-C.
Geo
Djamouri, Dr R.
Lin
Dolinski, M.
Lan
Domenach, Dr J.L.
IR, PolS
Dore, A.
DevS, CuS, Ant
Drège, Prof. J.-P.
CuS, His, Edu
Drocourt, Z.T.
Lin
Dumont, Prof. R.
Agr, Env, DevS
Dumoulin-Genest, M.-P.
His
Durand-Dastès, V.
Lit
Dutrait, N.
Lit
Elisséeff, Dr D.
Arch, His, AHis
Fabre, Prof. G.F.
CuS, Env, Eco, DevS, Soc
Fan, F.
Lit
Fava, P.
Psy, Lit, CuS, Ant, His, Arch, AHis, Soc, Rel, Phi
Ferlus, M.
Lin

France

Formoso, Dr B.
Rel, Soc, Ant

Frederic, L.F.
AHis, CuS, Arch, Rel, His

Fresnais, J.
Eco

Gai, J.
Lan

Galy, L.
His, Lit, AHis

Ged, F.
CuS, DevS

Gentelle, Dr P.P.
Env, Arch, Geo

Gernet, Prof. J.
Rel, Phi, Law

Giès, J.
His, Arch

Gipoulon, C.
Lin

Gipouloux, Dr F.
Eco, Soc

Godement, Prof. dr F.L.
His, IR

Goossaert, V.
His, Rel

Gournay, A.
Arch, His, AHis

Guiheux, Dr G.
Eco, Soc, His

Gyss-Vermande, C.G.V.
Rel, His, AHis

Hamon, C.
Eco

Han, M.
AHis

Heide, Dr S. von der
Ant, DevSAHis, Env, CuS, Rel, PolS

Henriot, Chr.
His

Ho, K.-C.
Lit

Hoa, M.
Lin

Holzman, D.
Lit

Hómery, M.
Lit

Horuichi, A.
His

Hu-Sterk, F.
Lit

Huang, M.
Lit

Huang, R.
Lan

Iljic, R.
Lin

Jami, C.
CuS, His

Jaussaud, Dr J.
Eco, IR

Jest, C.
DevS

Jousse, C.
Lan

Jullien, F.
Lit

Kalinowski, M.
Lit, His

Kamenarovic, Dr I.P.
Phi

Karmay, S.
His, Lit, Phi, Ant, Rel

Kiss, A.
Ant, Phi, Psy

Kneib, A.
AHis

Kuo, Dr L.
Rel

Labat, A.
Lin

Lagaune, E.
Ant

Laureillard, Dr M.
His, AHis

Lavoix, V.
His, Lin, Lit

Le Nouëne, P.L.N.
AHis, Arch

Lemoine, Dr J.
CuS, Ant, GenS, His, Psy, Rel

Lesseur, C.
AHis

Lévy, Dr A.
Lit

Lew, Dr R.
Soc, PolS

Li, D.C.S.
Lit

Liu, R.
Lan

Liu-Sun, H.
Lan

Lo, X.-X.
Lan

Lochen, C.
Lan

Lombard, Prof. dr D.
His

Lu, S.
Lan

Lu, Dr L.
Ant

Lu, Drs H.
Ant

Lucas, A.
Lin

Lyssenko, N.
Lin

MacMorran, I.
His

Macouin, F.
His, AHis

Maitre, E.
His

Mantienne, F.
His, Eco

Maucuer, M.
AHis, Phi

Maury, F.
Lin

Métailié, M.-H.
Lit

Mézin, L.
His, AHis

Micollier, Dr E.
Ant

Mong, A.
Lan

Monnet, N.
Lit

Moreau, P.
Art

Moucuer, M.
Law, GenS, His

Naour,
His

Nguyen-Tri, Ch.
Ant, DevS

Niederer, B.
Lin, His, Ant

Nivard, J.
GenS, Soc

Nodot, E.
Arch, His, AHis

Noirbusson-Soubra, S.S.
AHis

Obringer, Dr F.O.
Ant, His, CuS

Orberger, Dr B.
Lin, Lit, Geo

Ordonnadu, G.
IR, Eco

Pairault, Prof. dr Th.
Eco, Soc, Ant

Papeté, Drs J.F.
Ant, Lin, Rel

Paris, Dr M.C.
Lin

Pastor, J.C.
Phi

Paul, Dr W.
Lin

Peh, G.-K.
Lit

Pellard, S.
His, Arch, AHis

Penent, J.
His

Peyraube, A.
Lit

France

Picard, Dr F.
Rel
Pimpaneau, Dr J.
Lit
Pirazzoli-t'Serstevens, Dr M.
Arch, AHis
Plantier, F.
CuS, Lin
Primel, Drs A.-G.
His
Puyraimond, G.
PolS, DevS, Env
Quiquemelle, M.-C.
His, CuS
Rabusseau, M.
Eco
Rabut, I.
Lin, Lit
Raibaud, M.
His
Rault-Leyrat, L.R.
His, Rel, Ant, AHis, Ant, Lin, Arch, Phi, His
Reclus-Sun, M.
Lan
Regnot, V.
Arch
Ren, C.
His, Ant, Soc
Renaud, F.
Lin
Resche, N.
Ant
Rey, M.-C.
Eco
Ribemont, F.
His, AHis
Robertie, P. de la
Lit
Robinet, I.
His
Rochat de la Vallee, E.R.
Phi, Lin, Rel
Rousset, Dr H.A.
CuS, His, Arch, AHis, Ant
Roux, A.
IR, His
Sabban, F.S.
Agr, Ant, CuS
Sagart, Dr L.
Lin
Salmon, Dr C.
Rel, Lit, CuS, His
Salvaert, A.
Lit
Seguy, C.
Lan
Shen, D.
Lan
Shi-Tao, L.
Lit
Shun-Chiu Yau,
Lit, Rel, PolS, Ant, CuS
Sivignon,
Eco, Geo
Smitsendonk, Dr A.G.O.
Law, Eco, IR, Soc, Rel, PolS, DevS
Song, L.
Lan
Spacensky, D.
His, AHis
Spangemacher, A.
Ant
Steinmann, B.
His
Tan, H.-M.
Lin
Tching, K.
Soc
Thomès, Ch.
Lit
Thote, Dr A.
AHis, Arch
Tournadre, N.
Lin
Trân, Q.H.
CuS, Ant
Trinh, Prof. V.T.
Edu, Soc, His
Trolliet, P.
Geo
Trombert, Dr E.
Agr, His, Eco, Ant
Turcq, Dr D.F.
Eco
Vallette-Hómery, M.
Lit
Vanhonacker, W.
PolS
Veaux, F.
Lan
Verdilhac, de
Eco
Verellen, Dr C.F.
Rel, CuS, Lit, His
Vizcarra, H.
Lan
Vogelweith, G.
AHis, Rel, Lin, His, Arch, His
Wang, B.
Lit
Wang, Dr F.T.
Rel
Weulersse, D.
Lit, His
Will, Prof. P.-E.
His
Williamson, Dr P.J.
DevS, Eco
Wu, Y.
Lan
Wu, Dr C.-Y.
Lit, Rel, Phi, Lin, His
Xu, D.
Lin
Yang, D.
Lan
Yang, F.
Lan
Yang, J.-H.
Lan
Zhang, Y.
Lan
Zhang, Dr N.
Lit, CuS, Soc, Phi
Zhao, Z.
CuS
Zheng, G.
Lit
Zheng, Prof. dr Ch.
His, Ant

Germany

Ahrens, Prof. Dr T
Rel
Albrecht, E.W.
Eco
Arnold, M.
Arch, His, AHis
Asim, Dr I.A.
Arch, CuS, His
Bass, Dr H.H.
DevS, Eco, IR
Bauer, Prof. dr C.H.R.
Lit, Rel, Ant, Lin, His, Arch
Bellers, Prof. dr J.
Eco
Braun, W.H.
Ant
Bronger, Prof. D.
DevS
Budde, Drs A.
CuS, Soc, DevS, Geo, His
Burdman, M.M.
His, Eco, DevS
Chen, Dr F.
Soc, His
Chiao, Prof. dr W.C.
Phi, Lin, His, Eco
Daberkow, R.
CuS, Lit
Dege, Prof. dr E.
Eco, Agr
Dewall, Dr M.V. von
His, CuS, Arch, Ant, AHis
Doering, Drs O.
Phi
Domes, Prof. dr J.
Soc, PolS, DevS
Dorofeeva-Lichtmann, Dr V.V.
Geo, CuS, His

ASIANISTS BY REGION AND COUNTRY OF INTEREST

Germany

Draguhn, Dr W.
PolS, IR, Eco, DevS
Drexler, Christian
His, Lit
Eberspaecher, Drs C.
PolS, His
Eberstein, Prof. dr B.
Lit, Eco
Ebner von Eschenbach, Dr S.
His, Ant, Rel
Eggert, Dr M.
Lit, CuS
Federlein, Drs D.
His, Lin, Rel
Felber, Prof. R.
PolS, CuS, IR, His
Fessen-Henjes, Dr I.
Lit, CuS
Fischer, D.
PolS, Eco
Fischer, Dr P.
His, Rel
Flessel, Prof. dr K.
Soc, Lin, His, CuS
Flitsch, Dr M.
Agr, CuS, Ant, Rel
Flüchter, Prof. dr W.
Geo, Env
Franke, Prof. dr H.
His
Franke, Prof. dr W.
His, Rel
Frankenhauser, Dr U.
Phi, CuS, His, Rel
Frenzel, R.F.
Eco
Friebel, M.
Eco
Friedrich, Dr M.K.A.
Phi, CuS
Gaenszbauer, Dr M.
Lit, GenS, CuS, Rel
Geisler, Drs G.H.S.
Geo, Env, DevS
Giele, Drs E.
His, Arch
Gimm, Prof. M.
His, AHis, Lit, Rel
Gimpel, D.
Lit, CuS
Goettingen, Drs D.
PolS, IR
Goetzfried, Dr F.X.
His, Phi, Ant, Rel
Graevenitz, Prof. dr A. von
Phi, AHis
Gransow, Dr B.
Eco, Soc, GenS, PolS, DevS
Gruner, Prof. dr
Lit
Grünfelder, Mr A.
Lit
Gütinger, E.
His, PolS
Hager, D.
Eco, IR, PolS
Halbeisen, Dr H.
PolS
Hana, Dr K.
PolS, His, DevS
Heberer, Prof. dr Th.
Ant, Rel, DevS, GenS, Eco, PolS, Soc
Heiduk, Dr G.
Eco
Heilmann, Dr S.
Soc, PolS, IR, His
Heinzig, Dr D.
His, PolS, IR
Hemmann, M.
Law, His, Eco, Env
Henze, Prof. J.
Edu
Herbers-Lee, S.
PolS
Heuser, Prof. R.
Law
Hildebrandt Diplom, Sabine
Hinüber, Dr H. von
Law, His, Rel, Lin, Phi, Lit
Hohnholz, Prof. J.
DevS, Agr, Geo
Hong, Dr E.P.
His, IR
Jaeger, Drs H.
CuS, Rel, Phi
Jahnke, M.
Law, Eco, CuS
Jakobi, Drs S.
GenS, PolS
Janz, K.E.
Ant, Agr, GenS, DevS
Jungmann, Prof. dr B.
AHis
Jüttner, Prof. Dr G.
AHis, CuS, His
Kaden, Prof. dr K.
Lin
Kames, Drs P.
Lit, AHis, CuS, His
Kampen, T.
PolS, IR, His
Karl, Dr I.
Lin
Kautz, Dr U.
His, Lin, AHis, Lit
Kevenhörster, Prof. dr P.K.
PolS
Kittlaus, Drs M.
PolS, GenS
Klaschka, Dr S.J.
Lit, Soc, PolS
Klenner, Prof. Dr Wolfgang
DevS, Eco
Klöpsch, Dr V.
Lit, Lin
Knödel, Dr S.
CuS, GenS
Koerbs, C.
His, Edu, Phi
Koester, Drs K.
Eco
Kott, D.
CuS, His, Law
Kraas, Dr F.
Ant, DevS, CuS, Geo
Krebs, Dr G.
Edu, His, PolS, IR
Kreutzmann, Prof. dr H.J.
Agr, DevS, Ant
Krieg, Dr R.E.
GenS, DevS
Kriegeskorte, Dr M.
His, CuS
Kruessmann, Dr I.K.
IR, CuS, Edu, Lit
Kubin, Prof. dr W.
Lit, Phi, Rel
Kuckertz, Prof. dr J.
His, Ant
Kuehner, Dr H.
Lit, Phi, His, PolS
Kuhl, Drs M.
Lin, Phi, CuS, His, AHis, Lit, Rel
Kuhn, Prof. D.
CuS, His, Arch
Kupfer, Dr P.
Lin, CuS
Kurz, Dr J.L.
His
Lackner, Prof. dr M.
Phi, His
Lauer, Drs U.
AHis
Leibold, M.
Rel, Phi, His
Leutner, Prof. dr M.
GenS, CuS, His
Liew-Herres, Dr F.M.
His
Linder Sabine, Drs L.
Ant, Arch, Soc
Link, Drs U.A.
Lit, His, Phi
Linz, Drs J.
CuS, His
Lipinsky, Drs A.
GenS, Law, DevS
Lippe-Fan, Dr Y.Q. von der
CuS, Lin
Lippert, Prof. W.L.
Lin, His

Germany

Liu, Dr J.-K.
PolS, Law, IR

Lorenz, Prof. D.
Eco

Machetzki, Dr R.
DevS, Eco, PolS

Magone, R.P.
Lit, Edu

Martin, Prof. dr B.
His

Martin, Prof. H.
CuS, Lit

Maue, Dr D.
Rel, Lin, Lit, Phi

Mayer, Dr A.L.
Rel, Phi

Menzel, Prof. U.
IR, PolS

Messner, Drs A.
His, Soc, Ant, CuS, Law

Meyer, Drs S.
CuS, Eco

Mischung, Prof. R.
Ant, Soc, Rel

Mittag, Dr J.H.
His, CuS, Rel

Moeller, Dr K.
IR, PolS

Müller, M.
His, AHis

Müller, S.
AHis, Ant, CuS, His, Arch

Müller, Dr R.
His, DevS, PolS, Env

Müller, Prof. dr E.
Lit, GenS, CuS

Müller-Hofstede, Drs C.
PolS, Soc, His, IR, CuS, DevS

Müller-Saini, Dr G.
His, CuS, Ant, Phi, Rel

Nagel-Angermann, Drs M.
His, Phi, AHis, Lit, Lin, Arch, Rel

Nickel, Drs L.R.
His, AHis, Arch

Nieh, Dr Y.H.
PolS, Law, IR, Eco, His

Obi, Drs L.
Rel, CuS, Ant

Opitz, Prof. P.J.
Phi, His, IR

Osterhammel, Dr J.K.
IR, His

Paulus, A-G.
CuS, DevS, Eco, IR, Lin

Pennarz, Dr J.P.
Ant, DevS

Pfennig, Dr W.
His, PolS, DevS, IR

Pigulla, Dr A.
His, PolS, IR

Ping, Q.
His, CuS, AHis

Piontek-Ma, Drs E.
His, CuS, Soc, GenS

Plempe, Drs D.
Rel

Pohl, Prof. dr K.H.
His, CuS, AHis, Phi, Lit, Rel

Prüch, Dr M.M.
Arch, His, AHis

Prunner, Dr G.
Ant, Rel, CuS

Quirin, Dr M. Th.
His, PolS, Phi, CuS

Rackwitz-Ziegler, Drs N.
Lit, CuS, His

Rai, Dr S.S.
PolS, IR

Reichel, H. J.
AHis, CuS

Reichenstein, B.
IR, DevS, Eco

Rennert, Drs H.
Lin, Lit, His, CuS, His, Phi, Rel, AHis

Richter, ML
Ant, Arch, AHis, His, Law, Lin, Lit, Phi, Rel

Richter, Dr G.
Lin

Riemann, Drs J.
AHis, Arch, CuS, His

Ritter, J.A.
CuS, His

Roetz, Dr H.
Phi, His

Rohde, Prof. dr K.E.
Soc, Eco, Env, DevS, CuS, IR

Romich, Dr M.F.
DevS, Soc, PolS, Eco

Rühle, Mr K.H.
His, Lit, Lin, CuS

Sachsenmaier, Dr D.
Rel, IR, His, CuS

Sagaster, Prof. dr K.
Rel, Phi, Lit, Lin, His, AHis, CuS, His

Sauerborn, Prof. J.
Agr, Env

Schaab-Hanke, Dr D.
PolS, CuS, His

Scharping, Prof. dr Th.
PolS, Soc, Eco

Schillig, Dr D
CuS, Phi, Rel

Schimmelpfennig, Drs M.
Arch, His

Schmidt - Glintzer, Prof. dr H.R.H.
His, Rel, Lit, CuS

Schmitt, K.
Soc, Phi, Lin, Ant, Rel

Schoepe, Dr R.
Lin, Phi

Schrammel, Drs U.S.
Eco, Env

Schröter, Dr S.
Ant

Schucher, Dr G.
Soc

Schüller, Dr M.S.
DevS, Agr, Eco

Schulz Zinda, Drs Y.
CuS, Phi

Schütte, Dr H.W.
His, CuS

Schweiger, Drs I.
Lit

Seckel, Prof. dr D.
His, AHis

Senger, Prof. dr H. von
Lit, PolS, Law, CuS

Spakowski, N.
CuS, GenS, His

Speyer, B.
IR, Eco

Stahl, Dr H.
Arch, His, CuS

Staiger, Dr B.
Edu, His, CuS

Stephan, R.
Rel, His, Ant

Sternfeld, Drs E.
GenS, Env

Sturm, Drs Th.
Lit

Taubmann, Prof. dr W.H.
Eco, DevS

Teschke, Drs R.
Lin, His

Trommsdorff, Prof. G.
Soc, Psy, CuS

Ullmann, S.
Lin

Unterbeck, Dr B.
Lin

Vittinghoff, Drs N.P.
CuS, His

Vittinghoff, Prof. dr H.
CuS, Phi, His

Vogel, Prof. dr H.U.
His, CuS

Wädow, Dr. G.
AHis, CuS, His, Rel

Wagner, Drs V.
PolS, Soc, CuS, His

Wagner, Prof. dr R.
Phi, Lit, His, CuS

Wagner-Van Leeuwen, Drs M.E.
Lin, Lit

ASIANISTS BY REGION AND COUNTRY OF INTEREST

Germany

Weggel, Dr O.
Law, Rel, Soc, CuS, Phi, Lin, PolS, IR

Weigeun-Schwiedrzik, Prof. S.
His, Lit, PolS, CuS

Weinert, Ch.
Rel, Lit, Soc, CuS

Wichmann, Drs P.
IR, PolS

Wu, Prof. P.
His, PolS

Zaborowski, Dr H.J.
CuS, His, LitAnt, Rel

Zhang, Drs V.
CuS, His

Zhang, Prof. dr G.
His

Hungary

Birtalan, Dr A.
AHis, Rel, Phi, Lit, Lin, His, Arch, GenS

Ehrlich, Prof. E.
Eco, DevS

Hajnal MA, L
Ant, AHis, CuS, Edu, His, Lin, Lit, Rel

Hidasi, Prof. J.
Lin, IR, Edu, Soc, CuS

Illyefalvi-Vitez, Prof. Z.
Edu

Ivnyi, Dr Z.
IR, PolS

Lukàs, É
AHis, IR, His, CuS

Nyiri, Drs P.D.
Ant, PolS

Sato, Drs N.
Edu, Eco

Tálas, Dr B.
Eco, IR, PolS

Italy

Abbiati, Prof. M.
Lin

Banti Pereira, Dr J.
His, CuS, His, AHis

Bertuccioli, Dr G.
Lit, His

Bordone, Prof. S.
His

Bressan, Dr L.
Lin, Edu

Bulfoni, C.
Eco, Lin

Caboara, Drs M.
His, Agr, Ant

Campana, Dr A.
His, IR, PolS

Carioti, Dr P.
His

Cavalieri, Dr R.C.
Law, IR, PolS

Ceresa, Dr M.
Ant, Lit, CuS

Ciarla, Dr R.
His, AHis, CuS, Arch, Ant

Collotti Pischel, Prof. E
His, PolS

Corradini, Prof. P.
Law, IR, His

Crespi Reghizzi, Prof. G.
PolS, DevS, IR, Law

Esposito, Dr M.
Rel

Fanin, C.
IR, Lin, His, Lit

Fossati, Prof. G.
His, AHis

Gallio, Dr R.
Law, His

Iannaccone, Prof. I.
His

Lanciotti, Prof. L.
Rel, Lit

Lippiello, Drs T.
Rel

Marinelli, Dr M.M.
His, IR, PolS, DevS

Masi, Dr E.M.
His, Lit

Masini, Dr F.
Lit, Lin

Miranda, E.M.
Eco, His

Mortarivergaracaffarelli, Prof. P.
Arch, AHis

Orioli, Dr H.
Ant, His, Arch, AHis

Paderni, Dr P.
GenS, His

Patella, Drs P.E.
AHis, Phi, His

Piacentini, Dr P.M.
Eco, DevS

Podest, Dr M.
Lin, Rel

Pozzana, Dr C.
Phi, Lit, CuS, Lin, His

Pregadio, Dr F.
Rel

Rispoli, Dr F.
Ant, Arch

Russo, Dr A.
Edu, CuS, PolS, Soc, Lit, Phi, Ant

Sabattini, Drs M.
His, Lit, Lin

Samarani, G.
His

Sanna, G.
Ant, Lit

Santangelo, Prof. P.
His

Siddivo, M.
Eco

Stafutti, Dr S.
Lin, Lit

Tozzi, Dr D.T.
Soc, His, Eco

Volpi, G.
PolS, IR, Agr, Eco, Env

Zanier, Prof. C.
His

Netherlands

Aelst, Drs A. van
His

Ashkenazy, Drs I.
Ant, His

Asselbergs, Drs G.
Agr, Eco, Edu

Bastiaansen, Drs A.C.G.M.
IR, Eco, Edu

Beek, Mr T.J. van
PolS, IR

Beekes, Prof. dr R.S.P.
Lin

Belt, Drs J.H.J.
Ant, AHis, CuS, His, Rel, His

Berg, Dr M.E. van den
Lin

Berkel, Ir C.W.M. van
Env

Beukering, P.J.H. van
IR, Eco, Env, DevS

Biervliet, Drs W.E.
Edu

Blom, H.W.
His

Blussé, Dr J.L.
IR, His

Boin, Drs M.M.O.
His

Boon, D.
AHis, Rel, CuS, Phi, His

Borstlap, Drs A.V.
His, AHis

Bouwers, Drs A.
Soc, PolS, Eco

Bragdon, J.
AHis, Phi, AHis

Brinke, Ir H.W. ten
Agr, Edu

Brouwer, A.A.
CuS, Eco, His, IR, PolS, Psy, Rel, Phi

Bruijn, E.J. de
His

Bruijninckx, Drs W.P.M.
Eco, IR

Bruin, Ir D. de
DevS, Env

Bruschke-Johnson, Drs L.
AHis

Netherlands

Burght, Prof. dr Gr.
Law

Cheng, Dr S.
His

Cowan, Drs F.M.
GenS, DevS, CuS, Ant, Env, LinAgr

Daan, K.
Env, CuS

Dalen, Prof. J.Chr. van
DevS, Edu, Soc, Eco, IR, PolS, Env

Dam, Dr J.E. van

Deelstra, T.
Env

Deng, T.
PolS, Soc, DevS, CuS

Derveld, Dr F.E.R.
Eco

Diana, Dr I.P.F. de
Psy, Edu

Dijk, Drs W.O.
Rel, CuS, His, Lin

Dijkstra, Drs G.H.
Soc, Rel, Phi, Eco, His, IR, Psy, PolS

Dishoeck, Drs E.R. van
Eco, Edu, Phi, CuS

Dongen, Drs A.M. van
Ant

Dongen, Drs P.L.F. van
His, Ant, AHis

Donker Duyvis, Drs P.
AHis, Arch, Ant, His

Douw, Dr L.M.
CuS, IR, Soc, Ant, His, DevS

Driem, Dr G.L. van
DevS, Lin, Ant, His

Driessen, Drs B.
Edu, CuS

Druijven, Dr P.C.J.
Geo, Env, Agr, DevS

Dubbeldam, Prof. dr L.F.B.
Ant, Edu

Eigenhuijsen, J.Th.N.
Eco

Eisma, Prof. dr D.
Env

Eliëns, Prof. dr T.M.
AHis

Engelfriet, Drs P.M.
His

Es, Dr A.J.H. van
Agr

Etty, Drs B.
IR

Evers, Drs B.H.
DevS, Env, Eco, Agr

Eykhoff, P.
His

Franse-Hagenbeek, A.A.
Lin

Gaastra, Dr F.S.
His

Geense, Drs P.H.A.M.
Edu, Soc

Georgieva, Drs V.
His, Rel

Giel, Mr P.
Env, DevS

Gijsbers, Drs D.J.
Env, Eco

Go, M.A.
Soc, Ant, CuS

Gonsalves, Drs C.M.
Law

Grant, Dr M.E.
Lit, IR, His, AHis, Rel

Grent, P.C.M.
CuS, Lin, Lit, Rel, Phi

Groot, J.J.R.
Agr, Env

Haft, Dr L.L.
Lit

Hagenaar, Dr E.P.G.
Lit

Hagendoorn, Prof. dr A.J.M.W.
His

Haringhuizen, Drs W.
PolS, Ant, IR

Harteveld, Ir K.
Agr, Eco, IR, Soc, DevS

Heerink, Dr N.B.M.
Env, Agr, DevS, Eco

Hendriks, Drs A.P.C.
PolS, IR, Eco, CuS, His

Hermens, B.
Agr, Env, IR

Hintzen, Drs G.H.
IR, Law, Phi, PolS, His

Hoefnagels, Ir H.A.M.
Agr, Eco, Law

Hoekema, Dr A.G.
Rel

Hoogenhout, Drs S.
AHis

Hooghe, Drs I.M.A.
IR

Hoogland, Drs J.G.D.
Eco, DevS, Env

Huang, Dr W.
DevS, IR, Eco

Huizer, Prof. dr G.J.
Rel, IR, Env, DevS

Idema, Prof. dr W.L.
Lit

IJiri, Drs Y.
Rel, AHis, Phi, CuS

Ishaja, Drs F.A.
His

Jacobs, Drs E.M.
His

Jagtenberg, Dr R.W.
Law

Janssen, M.
Phi, His

Jehle, Dr E.
IR, DevS, Eco, Edu, Law

Jongsma-Blanche Koelensmid, Drs H.T.
AHis, Arch, CuS, His

Junne, Prof. G.C.A.
IR, DevS, PolS, Env

Kal, Drs W.H.
Env, Lin, DevS, Agr, CuS, Ant, CuS, GenS

Karssen, Dr C.M.
DevS, Env, Agr, Eco, Edu, Soc, GenS

Keijser, Drs A.S.
Lit

Kloet, Drs ir B.J.
CuS, Ant, PolS, Soc

Kortlandt, Prof. dr F.H.H.
Lin

Korzec, Dr M.
PolS

Kouwenhoven, F.
Ant, CuS

Kramers, Prof. dr R.P.
Phi, Rel

Kruidenier, Drs J.H.
His

Kuiper, Drs P.N.
Lit

Kwee, Ir H.G.
Art

Landsberger, Dr S.R.
PolS, IR

Lange, Dr L.H. de
His

Lau, W.Y.
SocAHis, CuS

Leenhouts, Drs M.A.
Lit

Leeuw, Dr K.L. v.d.
Phi

Leung, Drs A.
Lin

Li, Dr Y.
Law

Li, Drs X.F.
AHis

Liang, Prof. dr J.C.P.
Lin

Lie, Drs H.
Eco, Ant

Linden, F.J.W.T. van der
IR, PolS

Lindhoud, Drs P.C.
His

Netherlands

Mallee , Drs H.P.
Ant, DevS, Agr, Soc

Meer , Drs M.G. van der
Lit

Meerman , J.M.M.
His

Meijs , Drs M.A.G.
IR, Rel, Ant, CuS

Meredith , Mr P.I.
Art

Messing , Mr A.J.
Law

Mierlo , Drs H.W.R. van
Lin, CuS, AHis

Minnee , Drs P.
CuS, IR, Eco, Edu

Minnema , Mr H.E.
Law

Nadal Uceda , F. de
Ant, Arch, Lin, Phi, Psy, Rel

Ngo , Drs T.-W.
PolS, DevS

Nguyen , Dr N.L.
CuS, DevS

Nuijten , Drs I.G.
Phi, Rel

Ommen , Drs A.F. van
IR, PolS

Otto , Dr J.M.
DevS, Law, Env

Patmo , Drs S.
Edu, Soc, Ant, DevS

Peverelli , Dr P.J.
Eco

Piek , Drs J.G.
IR, DevS, PolS

Pijl-Ketel , Ch. van der
AHis

Pinxteren , Drs M.H.M. van
CuS

Plaisier , Drs H.
Lin

Politon , S.
AHis, Arch, Phi, Lin, CuS, His, Rel

Prchal , Drs M.
PolS, His, Rel

Putten , Drs F.P. van der
His, IR, PolS, Eco

Radtke , Prof. dr K.W.
PolS, Lit, IR, His

Ravels-Smulders , Drs M.C. van
IR, PolS, Law

Rinsampessy , Dr E.P.
Ant, Soc, Rel, IR, Edu

Roo , Dr A.J. de
Law

Ruizendaal , Drs R.E.
Ant, Rel

Saith , Prof. dr A.
Agr, Eco, DevS, His

Sanders , Drs M.
DevS, Eco

Schalke , Dr H.J.W.G.
Arch, Ant, Env

Scheepers , Dr A.R.
Phi, His, Rel

Schenk , Dr H.
DevS, Env

Schenk-Sandbergen , Dr L.Ch.
GenS, DevS, Env, Ant

Schimmelpenninck , Drs A.M.
CuS, Lin, Ant, Lit, His, AHis

Schipper , Prof. dr K.M.
Rel, Ant, His

Schoch , Drs G.W.
Eco

Schottenhammer , Dr A.
Phi, His, Eco, PolS

Schouten , Drs N.A.M.
AHis, CuS, Arch, His

Schulze , F.
His, Rel

Semetko , Prof. dr H.A.
PolS, Soc, Psy

Seret , Mr A.
Phi, Lit, Lin, Rel, CuS

Sideri , Prof. dr S.
DevS, Eco

Sigmond , Dr J.P.
CuS, His, AHis, Arch

Singh , Dr N.
Agr, Env, DevS, Soc, IR

Sinnema , Drs T.
GenS, CuS, Soc, His, Edu

Siregar , Drs T.M.
PolS, Eco, Agr

Smit , Prof. ir K.
Lin

Smith , Dr N.S.H.
Lin

Smits , Dr I.B.
His, Lit

Sodderland , Mr J.W.
Law

Spiekerman-Middelplaats , M.Y.M.
Env

Stam , Prof. dr J.A.
DevS, Eco, IR

Stel , Dr J.H.
Env, Eco

Stoop , Dr W.A.
Agr, Env

Straten , Drs N.H. van
Law

Streef , E.
Env, Law, Ant

Stroek , A.J.
Rel, His, CuS

Sukrisno , Drs A.
Ant, His, PolS

Sun , L.
Eco, DevS

Sy-A-Foek , I.D.S.
PolS, Law, DevS

Sybesma , S.
Lin

Sybesma , Dr R.P.E.
Lin

Tamburello , Drs G.
Lit

Tan , I.H.
AHis

Tan , Ir Y.Y.
His, CuS

Tims , Prof. dr W.
Eco, Agr, DevS

Tjwan , Dr G.G.
His

Truong , Dr D.H.D.
IR, Eco, Env

Ukai , Drs K.
Lit

Vaczi , Drs M.T.
Rel, AHis, GenS, CuS

Veere , Mr H. van der
Rel, Phi

Verboom , Drs A.W.C.
Phi, Lit, Rel, Lin

Vereeken , Drs B.
Ant, DevS

Vermeer , Dr E.B.
His, Env, DevS, Agr, Eco

Verschuur , Ir H.P.
IR

Viallé , Drs C.R.M.K.L.
His, AHis

Vitiello , Dr G.
GenS, Lit

Voogd , Drs P. de
DevS, GenS, Soc, Edu

Waardenburg , Prof. dr J.G.
DevS

Welling , Drs K.O.H.
Art

Werff , Dr P.E. van der
Env, Ant, DevS

Wertheim , Prof. dr W.F.
Soc, His

Westermann , Drs R.
AHis, CuS, Eco

Wiedenhof , Dr J.M.
Lin

Wigboldus , Ir J.S.
Agr, His

Woerkom-Chong , Drs W.L. van
Phi

Wolvekamp , Drs P.S.
Agr, IR, DevS, Env, GenS

Wu , J.Y.T.
Lit

Netherlands
Yang-de Witte, Drs C.H.
IR, PolS
Zeeuw, D. de
Env, Agr
Zeeventer, Drs L.T.M. van
PolS, DevS, IR
Zhang, Dr W.
Soc, DevS
Zhang, Dr Y.
Law
Zürcher, Prof. dr E.
Rel
Zurndorfer, Dr H.T.
His
Zwijnenburg, Ph.A.
His

Norway
Barth, Dr F.
DevS, Ant
Berge, H.
His, PolS, Lit
Bordahl, Dr V.
Lin, Lit
Braarvig, Prof. dr J.
Lit, Rel, Phi, DevS, His, CuS, Lin
Buen, J.
PolS
Eifring, Prof. H.
Lit, Lin, CuS
Hansen, Dr M.H.
Ant, Edu
Harbsmeier, Prof. dr C.
His, Phi, Lit, Lin, CuS, AHis
Hjellum, T.
DevS, PolS, His
Liao, R.
IR, DevS, PolS, AHis
Liu, Drs B.S.
IR, PolS, Law
Rongen, O.B.
Phi
Sagli, Drs G.
CuS
Sauarlia, Dr L
Ant

Stearns, L.L.M.
Law, GenS, DevS
Svarverud, Dr R.
His, Phi, PolS
Vaage, T.
PolS
Wellens, K.
Ant, Rel, Lit
Westad, Dr O.A.
His, IR

Poland
Cyrzyk, Drs L.M.
His, IR
Kulig, Prof. J.
Eco, IR
Leszczynski, Prof. L.
Soc, PolS, Law, Eco
Li, Y.
Soc, Ant, CuS
Majewicz, Prof. dr A.F.
Lin, Ant
Slawinski, Prof. dr Hab.
DevS, Ant, Eco, PolS
Swiercz, Drs J.
Lin
Tomala, Dr K.
PolS, Soc, Phi, Edu
Zaremba, Dr P.A.
DevS, Env, Eco

Portugal
Guimaraes, Prof. dr A.L.
His
Loureiro, Prof. dr R.M.
His, CuS
Oliveira e Costa, Dr J.P.
His, Rel

Rumania
Balan, L.
CuS, Soc. Lin
Liushnea, Dr D.S.
DevS, Eco, IR, PolS

Russia
Ajimamudova, Dr V.S.
Lit
Alexakhina, Dr S.N.
Eco, Agr

Alexakhina, Prof. dr A.
Edu, Lin
Alimov, I.A.
CuS, Lit, Rel
Antonian, Dr K. V.
Lin
Balyuk, Dr I.A.
Eco
Bazhenova, E.S.
Eco, Env, Soc, Agr, GenS
Belov, Dr Ye.A
His
Berezny, Prof. dr L.A.
His
Blumkhen, S.I.
CuS, His, Phi, Rel, Arch
Boikova, Dr E.V.
IR, His, CuS
Bokshchanin, Dr A.A.
His
Borevskaya, Dr N.Ye.Ye.
CuS
Borokh, Dr L.N.
His
Borokh, Dr O.
Eco
Borovkova, Dr L.A.
His
Bubentsov, Dr Ye.V.
Eco
Choudodeyev, Dr J.V.
His
Dikarev, Dr A.D.
His
Dybo, Dr Prof. A. V.
Ant, Lin
Fadeeva, Dr E.Y.
Phi, Soc, CuS, Rel, Lit
Fedorenko, Dr N.T.
Lit
Feoktistov, Dr V.F.
Phi
Fomina, Dr N.I.
His
Galenovitch, Dr Y.M.
His

Ganshin, Dr G.A.
Eco
Garushyants, Dr Yu.M.
His
Gelbras, Dr V.G.
PolS, Eco, Soc
Girich, L.M.
Eco
Glunin, Dr V.I.
His
Golyghina, Dr K.I.
Lit
Gorbunova, Dr S.A.
Rel, His
Gorelova, Dr L.M.
Edu, His, Lin
Gudoshnikov, Prof. dr L.M.
PolS, Law
Guelbras, Prof.dr V.G.
Eco, His, PolS, Soc
Guirich, Dr L.M.
Eco
Ipatova, Dr A.S.
His
Jarylgassinova, Dr R.Sh.
Ant
Kalyuzhnaya, Dr N.M.
His
Karapetiants, Prof.dr A.M.
Ant, Lin, Lit, Phi, Rel
Karlussov, Dr V.V.
Eco
Katkova, Dr Z.D.
His
Khokhlov, Dr A.N.
His
Kobzev, Dr A.I.
Phi
Kondrashkina, Dr E.A.
Lin
Korimushin, Prof. dr I. V.
Ant, Arch, Lin
Kostyayeva, Dr A.S.
His, PolS
Kotova, Dr A.F.
Lin

Russia

Kozhin, Dr P.M.
His
Kozlov, Dr A.A.
His, Eco
Kroll, Y.L.
Phi, His, CuS
Krushinsky, Dr A.A.
Soc
Kryukov, Dr V.M.
His
Kuczera, Dr S.R.
His
Kulik, Dr B.T.
His
Kulpin, Dr E.S.
His
Kurbatov, Dr V.P.
Eco, His
Kuzes, Dr V.S.
His
Kuznetsov, Dr V.S.
His
Kychanov, Dr E.I.
Ant, His, Law, Lin, Rel
Lapina, Prof. Dr. Z.M.
CuS, Ant, His, Law, PolS
Larin, Dr A G
His, IR
Ledovsky, Dr A.M.
His
Lisiakova, L.
Eco, Soc, Agr
Lissevich, Dr I.S.
CuS, Rel
Lissevitc, I.S.
Phi, Rel, Lit
Lomanov, Dr A.V.
Phi
Malyavin, Dr V.V.
His
Mamayeva, Dr N.L.
His
Menshikov, Lev.
His, Rel, Lit
Menshikov, Dr L.N.
Arch, His, Lit
Moskalyov, Dr A.A.
Soc
Mugruzin, Dr A.S.
His
Myasnikov, Prof.dr V.S.
His, IR
Naumov, Dr I.N.
Eco
Nepomnin, Dr O.Ye.
His
Novgorodskaya, Dr N.Y.
His, PolS, IR
Novoselova, Dr L.V.
DevS, Eco, IR
Novossyolova, Dr L.V.
Eco
Onikienko, Dr A.
Eco, DevS
Ostrovski, Dr A.V.
Soc, Agr, PolS, Eco
Ostrovsky, Dr A.V.
Eco
Perelomov, Dr L.S.
His
Petrov, Dr A.I.
His
Pissarev, Prof.dr A.N.
His, PolS
Pivovarova, Prof. dr E.P.
Edu
Pomerantseva, Dr L.E.
His, Lit, Phi
Portyakov, Dr V.Ya.
Eco
Postrelova, Drs T.A.
His, AHis
Roukodelnicova, M.B.
Lin
Rumiantsev, Prof.dr M.K.
Lin
Rykova, Dr S.L.
His
Samoyeov, Dr N.A.
IR, His
Samoylov, Dr N.A.
His, IR
Semanov, Dr V.I.
Lit
Semenas, Dr A.L.
Lin
Semenenko, Dr I.I.
Lit, Phi, Rel
Serebriakov, Dr E.A.
Lit
Serova, Dr S.A.
AHis
Shabelnikova, Dr E.M.
Lin
Shevelev, Dr K.V.
His
Shutova, Dr Ye.I.
Lin
Sofronov, Prof. dr M.V.
Ant, Arch, Lin, Lit
Solntsev, Prof. dr V.M.
Lin
Solomonik, Dr I.N.
His, AHis
Sorokin, Dr V.F.
Lit, CuS
Stebline-Kamensky, Prof. dr I.M.
Lin, Lit, Rel
Stepanov, Dr Ye.D.
His
Stepuguina, Dr T.V.
His
Sukharchuk, Dr G.D.
His
Sukhorukov, Dr V.T.
Lit
Svistunova, Dr N.P.
His
Syomin, Dr A.V.
His, IR, Eco, PolS
Tenishev, Dr Prof. E. R.
Ant, Lin, Lit
Tertitsky, Dr K.M.
His
Tikhvinsky, Prof.dr S.L.
His
Titarenko, Prof. dr M.L.
PolS, Phi, IR
Tkachenko, Dr G. A.
CuS, His, Phi, Rel
Toroptsev, Dr S.A.
CuS
Tsyganov, Dr Y.
Eco, IR
Tyapkina, Dr N.I.
His
Usov, Dr V.N.
His
Ussov, Dr V.N.
His
Vasilyev, Dr D.
Arch, Rel, Lin, AHis, Ant
Volkova, Dr L.A.
Eco
Voskresenski, Dr D.N.
Rel, CuS, Lit, Phi
Voskresensky, Dr A.D.
His, IR
Voskressenski, Dr A.D.
IR, DevS, PolS, His, CuS
Zaitsev, Dr V.V.
Phi
Zavadskaya, Prof. dr V.
AHis
Zhogolev, Dr D.A.
PolS, DevS, Soc, Law, Eco, His
Zotov, O.V.
PolS, His

Slovenia

Carnogurska, Dr M.
Rel, Phi
Ceplak-Mencin, Dr R.
CuS, Ant
Hatalov, Dr H.
PolS, His
Mézerov, I.
GenS, Lit
Milcinski, Prof. dr M.
Phi, Rel
Rosker, Dr J.
Phi, Rel, GenS, Soc, PolS

Slovenia

Slobodník, Drs M.
His, IR

Svitkova, Dr I.
Rel, CuS

Spain

Anton Burgos, Dr F.J.
Geo

Beltran Antolin, Dr J.
Soc, Ant

Bustelo, Dr P.
DevS, Eco

Canto, Dr P.
DevS, IR, Eco

Castillo Rodriguez, S.
IR

Ceruera Fernández, I.
AHis, His

Comas Montoya, Dr R.
AHis, His

De Llanos Isidoro, P.
His, Lin, Lit, Phi

Delage, F.
IR, PolS

Díez Galán, Dr J.
AHis, Lit

Elías de Tejada Lozano, Diplomat F.
Eco, Lit, PolS

Esparrago Rodilla MA, Luis
Agr, PolS

Fanjul, Dr E.
Eco

Fanjuz Martin, E.
Eco

Fernandez Lommen, Dr Y.
Eco

Fernández Miguélez, J.
IR

Fisac Badell, Dr T.
Lit, GenS

Folch Fornes, Dr D.
His

Garcia, Fernando
AHis, Geo, His, IR, PolS

Garcia Erviti, J.
ECONOMIA

Garcia-Borron Martínez, M.-D.
Lin, Lit

Garmendia Herrero, E.
His

Gastllo Martinez, J.V.
Eco, Geo, Lin

Gil, Prof. J.
His, Lit

Golden, Prof. S.
CuS, Phi, Lit

Gonzales de Orduña Criado, Silvia
DevS

Gouzalez Molina, A.
IR, Soc

Gurbindo Lambán, N.
Ant

Hu Sun, P.-S.
Lit

Jimenez Valentin, J.M.
Eco, Env, IR

Kim, Drs S.-H.
Arch, Rel, Phi, Lit, His, AHis

Lopez Sastre, G.
Phi

Marco Mart¡nez, Dr C.
Lin

Marco Martínez, Consuelo
Lin

Mas Murcia, A.
Eco

Masachs Castell, J.
Eco, Geo, His, IR, Soc, PolS

Merinero Martin, M.J.
His, PolS

Molto Garcia, T.
Eco

Monclés, Dr A.
Env, Edu

Montero Moreno, J.
His, Lit, Rel

Moreno Garcia, J.
His, IR, PolS

Moreno Garcia, Dr J.
His, IR, PolS

Olle Rodriguez, M.M.
His

Pastrano, Dr F.
His, IR, Rel, Soc

Perez Miguel, A.
Ant, GenS, His, IR

Prevosti Monclus, Dr A.
Phi

Rovetta BA, Pablo
Eco, His, IR, Lin, Lit, PolS, Soc

Rovetta Dubinsky, Pablo
Eco, Env, IR, Lin, PolS

Suárez Girard, A.-H.
Lin, Lit, Phi, Rel

Suero Tellitu, T.
Ant, Phi, PolS, Rel, Soc

Togores Sanchez, L.E.
IR, His

Vinyamata Camp, E.
IR, Soc, Psy

Sweden

Aijmer, Dr L.G.
Ant

Allwood, Prof. J.
Lin, Phi

Amer, Dr R.
IR, PolS, His

Bratthall, Prof. D.
Eco

Bryder, Dr H.P.
Ant, Rel

Cardholm, M.
IR

Gao, J.
AHis, Phi, Lit, CuS, His

Greatrex, R.G.
Law, His

Gustafsson, Drs J.E.
Env

Hansson, Prof. I.L
Lin, Rel

Hart, Prof. T.G.
IR, His, PolS

Huldt, Prof. B.
IR, His

Jerneck, Dr A.
DevS, Eco

Johansson, Drs P.J.
CuS, His

Kaikkonen, Dr M.
Lit

Kjellgren, Drs B.
CuS, Soc, Psy, Rel

Malmqvist, Prof. N.G.D.
Lin, CuS, Lit

Nimerius, P.
PolS

Nordenhake, S.C.M.
Lin

Ooi, Drs K.B.
PolS, His, Phi

Park, Dr S.-C.
Eco, PolS

Pei, X.
Eco, Agr, PolS, His, DevS

Ragvald, Prof. L.R.
Lin, Lit, Rel

Ronnås, Dr P.
DevS, Agr, Eco

Schoenhals, M.
His, PolS

Sigurdson, Prof. J.
IR, DevS, Eco, PolS

Sivam, J.P.A.
His, Lit, Law, CuS

Svantesson, J.O.
Lin

Tong, Y.
Lin

Zejan, Dr M.C.
DevS, Eco

Switzerland

Altenburger, R.T.
CuS, Lin, Lit

Bichler, Mr
Ant, Phi

Billeter, Prof. J.F.
Lit, His, Phi, Rel

Switzerland

Ducor, Dr J.
Rel, Ant, GenS

Dunand, F.
His, AHis

Etienne, Prof. G.
His, Agr, Eco, PolS, DevS

Findeisen, Dr R.D.
Phi, GenS, Lit

Gassmann, Prof. dr R.H.
Phi, Lit, Lin

Girgis, Dr M.
CuS, His

Heller, Dr A.
CuS, AHis, Rel, His

Jing Li, A.
IR, PolS

Kinzelbach, Prof. dr W.K.H.
Env

Kloetzli, Prof. dr F.A.
Agr

Kühne, Drs C.
Lit

Lin, C.-W.
CuS, Psy, Ant

Oppitz, Prof. M.
Rel, Ant

Pfister, R.
His, CuS, AHis, Ant

Schmid, Prof. dr W.A.
Env, Edu, DevS

Schmutz, G.M.
Soc, Ant, Edu

Schumacher, Dr J.
Lit, Phi

Thölen, Drs K.
Arch, His, AHis, Lit

Turpin, Dr D.V.
Soc

Viaro, Dr A.V.
Env, Ant, DevS

Wang, Mr D.T.C.
PolS, Law

Zhang, Dr W.
IR

United Kingdom

Andrews, Dr B.J.
His

Ansorge, Drs C.A.
His, Arch, CuS, Rel, Lit, Phi

Ardley, Drs J.C.
PolS

Auty, Dr R.M.
DevS, Env, Eco

Aylmer, C.A.
Rel, Phi, Lin, Arch, His, IR, Lit

Baker, Dr P.W.
Law

Baker, Prof. dr H.D.R.
Law, Lin, Ant, His, CuS, Lit, Rel

Bakewell, Mr A.D.

Barnes, Prof. G.L.
Arch

Barrett, Prof. T.
Rel, His

Belshaw, Prof. D.G.R.
DevS, Env, Agr, Eco,

Berg, Dr D.D.
Lit, His, GenS

Birkin, I.
Ant

Birrell, Prof. A.M.
CuS, Lit, GenS

Bowring, Prof. R.J.
Rel, Lit

Breslin, Dr S.G.
Eco, PolS

Bruijn, Drs J.E. de
His, AHis, CuS

Bunnin, Dr N.F.
Phi

Burg, B. & C. von der
His, AHis

Cannon, Dr T.G.
DevS, Env

Cantlie, Dr J.
CuS, AHis

Carswell, Prof. J.W.
AHis, CuS, His

Cayley, J.
Lit, CuS

Chapman, G.
His, AHis, CuS

Chard, Dr R.
His, Rel

Christiansen, Dr F.
PolS, Env, DevS

Chung, Dr H.J.
Lit, GenS

Clayton, Dr D.W.
His, IR, DevS, Eco

Clegg, Dr J.R.
DevS

Clunas, Dr C.
His, Arch, His, AHis, CuS

Cockburn, Mr R.C.
DevS, CuS

Cook, M.
Eco

Crosbie, Dr A.J.
IR, Env, Eco, Geo, DevS

Dawson, R.
Lin, Phi, His

Deacon, Mr A.G.
His, Phi

Deckers, Drs W.
IR, DevS, PolS

Dikötter, Dr F.
His, CuS

Donald, S.
PolS, GenS, CuS, His, AHis

Dryburgh, Dr M.E.
His

Dudbridge, Prof. G.
Rel, Ant, GenS

Duxbury, Drs K.E.
PolS

Dwyer, Prof. D.J.
DevS

Edmonds, Dr R.L.
Env, Geo

Elliott, D.
AHis

Evans, Dr H.
GenS, His

Evans, Dr K.K.
AHis, Rel, GenS, His

Faure, Dr D.W.
His

Ferdinand, Drs C.I.P.
PolS, DevS, His, Eco, IR

Feuchtwang, Dr S.
Ant, Soc, Rel, His, DevS, CuS, PolS

Foot, Dr R.J.
IR

Forfar, D.J.
Ant, Soc, CuS, Rel

Fuehrer, Dr B.
Phi, Lin, CuS, Lit

Fukasawa, Dr Y.
CuS, Soc, Ant, Arch, His, Lin

Green MA, A.R.
AHis

Hansson, Dr A.
His

Harris, Drs N.
DevS, Eco

Hart, R.F.
His, PolS, IR

Helliwell, Drs D.J.
AHis, CuS, Rel

Hilton, Drs I.
IR

Hitchcock, Dr M.J.
Soc, Ant, DevS

Hoare, Dr J.E.
IR, His, PolS, CuS

Hockx, Dr M.L.L.G.
Lit

Hook, Dr B.G.
IR, DevS

Howell, Dr J.A.
DevS, PolS, GenS

Hoy, Dr C.S.
GenS

Hsu, E.
Ant

Humphrey, Dr C.
Ant, Env, Rel, Soc

United Kingdom

Huxley, Dr T.J.
IR, PolS
Jameson, Drs A.L.
CuS, His
Jones, Dr R.
Lin, Lit, Rel
Kan, Dr Q.
CuS, Lin
Kidd, Mr J.B.
CuS, Edu
King, Prof. U.
Phi, His, Edu, Ant, GenS, CuS, Rel, Soc
Kirkby, Dr R.J.R.
Eco, DevS, Env
Kornicki, Dr P.F.
CuS, His
Kranenburg, Drs L.G.
IR, Eco
Lancashire, Prof. R.D.
Lit, Rel
Lee, Drs J.T.
His
Lewis, Dr M.E.
Arch, His, Lin, Ant
Li, R.
PolS, IR
Li, Dr W.
Lin, Edu, Psy
Lightfoot, Drs S.
AHis
Liu, Drs T.T.
Lit
Lo, Dr A.H.B.
Lit
Loewe, Prof. dr M.A.N.
His
Loon, Prof. dr P. van der
His, Lin
Lowe, Dr P.C.
IR, His
MacFadyean, Dr N.J.
Eco, His
Marett, Dr P.
Rel, Law
Martin, A.E.
Lin
McClellan, Dr T.M.
Lit
McDougall, Prof. dr B.S.
Lit, GenS
McGregor, Dr C.D.
IR
McKillop, Drs E.D.
AHis, CuS, Rel, Lit, His
McMullen, Prof. D.L.
His
Merrett, Drs N.M.
Lin, Law, Eco, DevS
Mez, Dr H.
Law
Milwertz, Dr C.N.
CuS, GenS
Mirza, Prof. H.R.
DevS, Eco
Moffett, J.P.C.
His, Rel, Lit
Moore, Dr O.J.
Arch, His, AHis
Muir, J.C.
His
Mürer, O.H.A.
Arch, His, AHis
Norbury, P.
AHis, Rel, Env, Ant, Arch, His
Pak, Dr Y.S.
Arch, His, AHis
Paludan, A.
Arch
Park, S.S.
Psy, PolS, Phi, SocAHis, DevS, Env, Edu, IR, Law
Picken, Dr L.E.R.
CuS
Pieke, Dr F.N.
Ant
Porter, Dr R.
Rel, Lit, CuS
Provine, Prof. dr R.C.
Lin
Riddington, P.
Lin, Edu
Roberts, Drs D.C.
DevS, Eco, IR
Rutt, C.R.
Lit
Ryan, Dr J.T.
Eco
Sheehan, Dr J.
PolS, His
Shepperdson, Mr M.J.
DevS, Agr, Eco, PolS, Soc
Shih, Drs J.H.
Rel
Simmons, Dr C.
DevS
Smith, Dr S.A.
His
Spencer-Oatey, Dr H.
Lin
Spooner, Prof. F.C.
Eco, His
Standen, Dr N.L.
His
Starr, Mr D.F.
Phi, Lin
Steeds, Mr D.
IR, His
Stock, Dr J.P.J.
Law
Stone, Drs E.V.
DevS
Strange, Dr R.N.
Eco
Taylor, Dr J.G.
Soc, DevS
Thoburn, Dr J.T.
Eco
Valentin, J.C.P.
Env, Ant, CuS, Lin, His, Arch
Ven, Dr H.J. van de
His
Vermeersch, Drs S.A.C.
His, Rel
Wagner, Dr D.B.
His, Arch
Wall, Mr D.G.
Eco
Wang, H.
His, AHis, Arch, His
Wang, T.
Arch, AHis
Watson, Prof. W.
Arch, His, AHis
Whitfield, Dr S.
Rel, His, CuS
Whitfield, Prof. R.
His, AHis
Wood, Drs F.
Arch, CuS, His, AHis
Wu, Dr K.
Agr, Env
Wu, Dr W.-P.
Eco, CuS
Xinzhong Yao, Dr
Rel, Phi
Yip, Dr P.C.
Lin, CuS
Zhao, Dr H.Y.H.
CuS
Zheng, H.
Arch, AHis, Lit

Yugoslavia

Babic, Prof. B.
DevS, Eco
Furundzic, V.
Psy, Rel, Lit, Lin, Edu, His, Phi, AHis

HONG KONG

Austria

Mosch, Dr N.
CuS, Phi
Sellner, Dr M.B.
CuS, Lin
Zorn, Dr B.
Ant, Arch, Ant, His, AHis

Belgium

Baetens-Beardsmore, Drs H.
Edu, Lin
Boden, J.
Lin, AHis, Lit, His

Belgium

Bogart, K.J.
Edu, CuS

Coulie, Prof. dr B.R.R.
AHis, Soc, Lin, Phi, DevS, Ant, Eco, His, Lit

Della Pietra, B.
IR, His, CuS

Fang, Dr S.-S.
CuS, Edu

Heyndrickx, J.J.
Rel

Pairoux, Prof. S.
His, IR, CuS, Soc

Pelkmans, Prof. dr J.
IR, Eco

Vaerman, Drs B.
GenSAHis, Rel, CuS, His

Vanwalle, Drs I.A.M.A.
AHis, Lin, Lit, Phi, Soc, His

Vearman, Drs B.
PolS

Wu-Beyens, I.CH.
PolS, IR, His, Agr, DevS, Env

Bulgaria

Cherrington, Dr R.L.
Soc, CuS, PolS

Czech Republic

Drjnek, Dr V.
IR

Hulec, Dr O.
His, AHis, CuS, Arch, IR, Eco, Phi, Lit, Lin

Suchomel, Dr F.A.
Arch, AHis

Denmark

Baark, Dr E.
His, DevS, Env, CuS

Li, X.
DevS, PolS, IR

Littrup, Dr L.
His, Edu

Ostergaard, Dr C.S.
Agr, Soc, PolS, IR, DevS

Padolecchia Polo, Prof. S.P.
DevS, PolS, Rel, Edu, Eco, Soc, Env, IR, CuS

Thorborg, Dr E.M.
DevS, PolS, Eco, His, GenS

Thunoe, Drs M.
Ant, Lit, Edu, Soc, DevS, CuS, His

Wang, J.
Lin, Lit, CuS, Edu, His, AHis

Worm, Drs V.
Soc, Eco, Ant

Finland

Karunaratne, Dr J.A.
DevS, Eco

Kivimäki, Dr T.A.
PolS, IR, DevS

Nikkilä, Drs P.S.
Rel, Phi

Seppänen, J.
IR, Eco, Ant, CuS, Lin, His, AHis, Phi, Arch, Rel, PolS

France

Alleton, Dr V.A.
Lit, Lin

Baille, B.
Ant

Balaize, C.
Ant, Agr, CuS, Rel

Barbiche, Prof. dr J.-P.
Law, IR, His, PolS, Eco, DevS, CuS, Edu, Soc

Billion, R.
His, Phi, Lit, Lin, IR, Edu

Botsch, A.A.
Eco, DevS, IR, Edu, Law

Boully, J.L.
Lit

Bouteiller, E.
DevS, Eco

Brun, Dr C. le
Eco, IR, PolS

Chaponniere, Dr J.R.
IR, Eco, PolS, DevS

Cheng, Dr A.L.
CuS, His, Phi

Collin, H.
Law, Soc, PolS, Eco, IR

Couto, Dr D.
Arch, His, PolS

Dutrait, N.
Lit

Fouquin, M.F.
Eco

Gipouloux, Dr F.
Eco, Soc

Godement, Prof. dr F.L.
His, IR

Henry, R.
Lin, GenS, Env, CuS, AHis, Arch, IR, Lit, Phi, Psy

Ho, K.-C.
Lit

Jaussaud, Dr J.
Eco, IR

Lagaune, E.
Ant

Orberger, Dr B.
Lin, Lit, Geo

Ordonnadu, G.
IR, Eco

Paris, Dr M.C.
Lin

Quiquemelle, M.-C.
His, CuS

Rault-Leyrat, L.R.
His, Rel, Ant, AHis, Ant, Lin, Arch, Phi, His

Sagart, Dr L.
Lin

Sivignon,
Eco, Geo

Smitsendonk, Dr A.G.O.
Law, Eco, IR, Soc, Rel, PolS, DevS

Trân, Q.H.
CuS, Ant

Turcq, Dr D.F.
Eco

Williamson, Dr P.J.
DevS, Eco

Woronoff, Dr J.A.
Eco, IR, DevS, PolS

Zhang, Dr N.
Lit, CuS, Soc, Phi

Zheng, Prof. dr Ch.
His, Ant

Germany

Albrecht, E.W.
Eco

Arnold, M.
Arch, His, AHis

Braun, W.H.
Ant

Daberkow, R.
CuS, Lit

Dewall, Dr M.V. von
His, CuS, Arch, Ant, AHis

Doering, Drs O.
Phi

Domes, Prof. dr J.
Soc, PolS, DevS

Drexler, Christian
His, Lit

Eberstein, Prof. dr B.
Lit, Eco

Federlein, Drs D.
His, Lin, Rel

Fischer, D.
PolS, Eco

Flüchter, Prof. dr W.
Geo, Env

Friebel, M.
Eco

Gaenszbauer, Dr M.
Lit, GenS, CuS, Rel

Geisler, Drs G.H.S.
Geo, Env, DevS

Goettingen, Drs D.
PolS, IR

Graevenitz, Prof. dr A. von
Phi, AHis

Gransow, Dr B.
Eco, Soc, GenS, PolS, DevS

Grünfelder, Mr A.
Lit

Gütinger, E.
His, PolS

Hana, Dr K.
PolS, His, DevS

Germany

Heberer, Prof. dr Th.
Ant, Rel, DevS, GenS, Eco, PolS, Soc

Heilmann, Dr S.
Soc, PolS, IR, His

Heinzig, Dr D.
His, PolS, IR

Hemmann, M.
Law, His, Eco, Env

Henze, Prof. J.
Edu

Heuser, Prof. R.
Law

Hohnholz, Prof. J.
DevS, Agr, Geo

Jahnke, M.
Law, Eco, CuS

Jüttner, Prof. Dr G.
AHis, CuS, His

Kames, Drs P.
Lit, AHis, CuS, His

Kittlaus, Drs M.
PolS, GenS

Koester, Drs K.
Eco

Kraas, Dr F.
Ant, DevS, CuS, Geo

Kruessmann, Dr I.K.
IR, CuS, Edu, Lit

Lackner, Prof. dr M.
Phi, His

Lipinsky, Drs A.
GenS, Law, DevS

Lippe-Fan, Dr Y.Q. von der
CuS, Lin

Lorenz, Prof. D.
Eco

Machetzki, Dr R.
DevS, Eco, PolS

Martin, Prof. H.
CuS, Lit

Menzel, Prof. U.
IR, PolS

Mittler, Dr B.
His, Lit, CuS

Moeller, Dr K.
IR, PolS

Müller, K.
PolS, CuS, His

Müller, Dr R.
His, DevS, PolS, Env

Müller-Hofstede, Drs C.
PolS, Soc, His, IR, CuS, DevS

Müller-Saini, Dr G.
His, CuS, Ant, Phi, Rel

Nieh, Dr Y.H.
PolS, Law, IR, Eco, His

Opitz, Prof. P.J.
Phi, His, IR

Paulus, A-G.
CuS, DevS, Eco, IR, Lin

Pigulla, Dr A.
His, PolS, IR

Piontek-Ma, Drs E.
His, CuS, Soc, GenS

Rackwitz-Ziegler, Drs N.
Lit, CuS, His

Reichel, H. J.
AHis, CuS

Reichenstein, B.
IR, DevS, Eco

Richter, ML
Ant, Arch, AHis, His, Law, Lin, Lit, Phi, Rel

Richter, Dr G.
Lin

Riemann, Drs J.
AHis, Arch, CuS, His

Ritter, J.A.
CuS, His

Rohde, Prof. dr K.E.
Soc, Eco, Env, DevS, CuS, IR

Romich, Dr M.F.
DevS, Soc, PolS, Eco

Rühle, Mr K.H.
His, Lit, Lin, CuS

Schaab-Hanke, Dr D.
PolS, CuS, His

Schoepe, Dr R.
Lin, Phi

Schrammel, Drs U.S.
Eco, Env

Speyer, B.
IR, Eco

Taubmann, Prof. dr W.H.
Eco, DevS

Teschke, Drs R.
Lin, His

Vittinghoff, Drs N.P.
CuS, His

Wädow, Dr. G.
AHis, CuS, His, Rel

Weggel, Dr O.
Law, Rel, Soc, CuS, Phi, Lin, PolS, IR

Weigeun-Schwiedrzik, Prof. S.
His, Lit, PolS, CuS

Weinert, Ch.
Rel, Lit, Soc, CuS

Hungary

Ehrlich, Prof. E.
Eco, DevS

Lukàs, É
AHis, IR, His, CuS

Tálas, Dr B.
Eco, IR, PolS

Italy

Campana, Dr A.
His, IR, PolS

Cavalieri, Dr R.C.
Law, IR, PolS

Ciarla, Dr R.
His, AHis, CuS, Arch, Ant

Gallio, Dr R.
Law, His

Marinelli, Dr M.M.
His, IR, PolS, DevS

Orioli, Dr H.
Ant, His, Arch, AHis

Sabattini, Drs M.
His, Lit, Lin

Santangelo, Prof. P.
His

Volpi, G.
PolS, IR, Agr, Eco, Env

Netherlands

Bastiaansen, Drs A.C.G.M.
IR, Eco, Edu

Berg, Dr M.E. van den
Lin

Blom, H.W.
His

Bragdon, J.
AHis, Phi, AHis

Brouwer, A.A.
CuS, Eco, His, IR, PolS, Psy, Rel, Phi

Bruijn, E.J. de
His

Bruijninckx, Drs W.P.M.
Eco, IR

Brunt, Prof. dr L.
Ant, Soc

Burght, Prof. dr Gr.
Law

Deelstra, T.
Env

Deng, T.
PolS, Soc, DevS, CuS

Derveld, Dr F.E.R.
Eco

Dijkstra, Drs G.H.
Soc, Rel, Phi, Eco, His, IR, Psy, PolS

Dongen, Drs P.L.F. van
His, Ant, AHis

Donker Duyvis, Drs P.
AHis, Arch, Ant, His

Driessen, Drs B.
Edu, CuS

Eigenhuijsen, J.Th.N.
Eco

Emmer, Prof. dr P.C.
His

Es, Dr A.J.H. van
Agr

Franse-Hagenbeek, A.A.
Lin

Geense, Drs P.H.A.M.
Edu, Soc

Netherlands

Gontscharoff, C.
IR, DevS
Haitsma, T.J.
IR
Haringhuizen, Drs W.
PolS, Ant, IR
Hendriks, Drs A.P.C.
PolS, IR, Eco, CuS, His
Hintzen, Drs G.H.
IR, Law, Phi, PolS, His
Hoefnagels, Ir H.A.M.
Agr, Eco, Law
Hoekema, Dr A.G.
Rel
Hoogenhout, Drs S.
AHis
Idema, Prof. dr W.L.
Lit
Jagtenberg, Dr R.W.
Law
Jongsma-Blanche Koelensmid, Drs H.T.
AHis, Arch, CuS, His
Junne, Prof. G.C.A.
IR, DevS, PolS, Env
Keijser, Drs A.S.
Lit
Kloet, Drs ir B.J.
CuS, Ant, PolS, Soc
Kol, Prof. dr J.
DevS, Eco, Agr
Kramers, Prof. dr R.P.
Phi, Rel
Kuiken, Drs C.J.
Rel, Law, CuS
Landsberger, Dr S.R.
PolS, IR
Lau, W.Y.
SocAHis, CuS
Leung, Drs A.
Lin
Li, Dr Y.
Law
Lie, Drs H.
Eco, Ant
Linden, F.J.W.T. van der
IR, PolS
Mierlo, Drs H.W.R. van
Lin, CuS, AHis
Ngo, Drs T.-W.
PolS, DevS
Nuijten, Drs I.G.
Phi, Rel
Ommen, Drs A.F. van
IR, PolS
Oosterwijk, A.J.
His, Ant, Arch
Patmo, Drs S.
Edu, Soc, Ant, DevS
Prchal, Drs M.
PolS, His, Rel
Quispel, Drs C.I.
PolS, Phi, CuS, His
Ravels-Smulders, Drs M.C. van
IR, PolS, Law
Reijnders, Drs T.
AHis
Roo, Dr A.J. de
Law
Ruizendaal, Drs R.E.
Ant, Rel
Sanders, Drs M.
DevS, Eco
Schalke, Dr H.J.W.G.
Arch, Ant, Env
Schoch, Drs G.W.
Eco
Schottenhammer, Dr A.
Phi, His, Eco, PolS
Schouten, Drs N.A.M.
AHis, CuS, Arch, His
Semetko, Prof. dr H.A.
PolS, Soc, Psy
Spiekerman-Middelplaats, M.Y.M.
Env
Stam, Prof. dr J.A.
DevS, Eco, IR
Streef, E.
Env, Law, Ant
Sy-A-Foek, I.D.S.
PolS, Law, DevS
Sybesma, S.
Lin
Sybesma, Dr R.P.E.
Lin
Tan, I.H.
AHis
Tan, Ir Y.Y.
His, CuS
Vaczi, Drs M.T.
Rel, AHis, GenS, CuS
Verschuur, Ir H.P.
IR
Wu, J.Y.T.
Lit

Norway

Buen, J.
PolS
Liao, R.
IR, DevS, PolS, AHis
Vaage, T.
PolS

Poland

Cyrzyk, Drs L.M.
His, IR
Kulig, Prof. J.
Eco, IR
Slawinski, Prof. dr Hab.
DevS, Ant, Eco, PolS
Tomala, Dr K.
PolS, Soc, Phi, Edu
Zaremba, Dr P.A.
DevS, Env, Eco

Portugal

Flores, Dr J.
His, IR

Rumania

Liushnea, Dr D.S.
DevS, Eco, IR, PolS

Russia

Alexakhina, Prof. dr A.
Edu, Lin
Fadeeva, Dr E.Y.
Phi, Soc, CuS, Rel, Lit
Gelbras, Dr V.G.
PolS, Eco, Soc
Gudoshnikov, Prof. dr L.M.
PolS, Law
Gurevich, Dr E.M.
His, PolS, Phi
Kozlov, Dr A.A.
His, Eco
Soboleva, Dr E.S.
Rel, His, Ant, AHis
Solomonik, Dr I.N.
His, AHis
Yakubovsky, Dr V.
Eco, PolS, IR
Zhogolev, Dr D.A.
PolS, DevS, Soc, Law, Eco, His

Spain

Albarrán Serrano, Antonio
Lit
Beltran Antolin, Dr J.
Soc, Ant
Bustelo, Dr P.
DevS, Eco
Canto, Dr P.
DevS, IR, Eco
Casares Vidal, D.
Eco
Castillo Rodriguez, S.
IR
Ceruera Fernández, I.
AHis, His
Elías de Tejada Lozano, Diplomat F.
Eco, Lit, PolS
Esparrago Rodilla MA, Luis
Agr, PolS
Fernández Miguélez, J.
IR
Garcia, Fernando
AHis, Geo, His, IR, PolS
Garcia-Ormaechea Quero, C.
AHis, Geo, His, Lit, Rel, Phi
Gastllo Martinez, J.V.
Eco, Geo, Lin
Golden, Prof. S.
CuS, Phi, Lit

Spain

Lopez Sastre, G.
Phi

Mas Murcia, A.
Eco

Navarro Celada, F.

Ojeda Marin, Prof. Dr A.
IR, Law

Pastrano, Dr F.
His, IR, Rel, Soc

Rovetta BA, Pablo
Eco, His, IR, Lin, Lit, PolS, Soc

Serrano Valentin, Carlos
Eco, IR

Suero Tellitu, T.
Ant, Phi, PolS, Rel, Soc

Sweden

Aijmer, Dr L.G.
Ant

Bryder, Dr H.P.
Ant, Rel

Jerneck, Dr A.
DevS, Eco

Johansson, Drs P.J.
CuS, His

Kaikkonen, Dr M.
Lit

Kjellgren, Drs B.
CuS, Soc, Psy, Rel

Malmqvist, Prof. N.G.D.
Lin, CuS, Lit

Sigurdson, Prof. J.
IR, DevS, Eco, PolS

Switzerland

Billeter, Prof. J.F.
Lit, His, Phi, Rel

Findeisen, Dr R.D.
Phi, GenS, Lit

Jing Li, A.
IR, PolS

Lin, C.-W.
CuS, Psy, Ant

Schmid-Schoenbein, C.
Eco, IR, PolS

Schneider-Sliwa, Prof. dr R.
DevS

Thölen, Drs K.
Arch, His, AHis, Lit

Viaro, Dr A.V.
Env, Ant, DevS

Wang, Mr D.T.C.
PolS, Law

United Kingdom

Auty, Dr R.M.
DevS, Env, Eco

Baker, Prof. dr H.D.R.
Law, Lin, Ant, His, CuS, Lit, Rel

Barnes, Prof. G.L.
Arch

Berg, Dr D.D.
Lit, His, GenS

Bowman, Drs M.I.
Rel

Carter, Dr L.J.
His

Chapman, G.
His, AHis, CuS

Clayton, Dr D.W.
His, IR, DevS, Eco

Clunas, Dr C.
His, Arch, His, AHis, CuS

Cook, M.
Eco

Crosbie, Dr A.J.
IR, Env, Eco, Geo, DevS

Donald, S.
PolS, GenS, CuS, His, AHis

Drakakis-Smith, Prof. D.
DevS

Dwyer, Prof. D.J.
DevS

Edmonds, Dr R.L.
Env, Geo

Ferdinand, Drs C.I.P.
PolS, DevS, His, Eco, IR

Godman, Dr A.
Lin, Edu

Harris, Drs N.
DevS, Eco

Hart, R.F.
His, PolS, IR

Helliwell, Drs D.J.
AHis, CuS, Rel

Hoare, Dr J.E.
IR, His, PolS, CuS

Hook, Dr B.G.
IR, DevS

Howell, Dr J.A.
DevS, PolS, GenS

Kirkby, Dr R.J.R.
Eco, DevS, Env

Lancashire, Prof. R.D.
Lit, Rel

Li, R.
PolS, IR

Li, Dr W.
Lin, Edu, Psy

Lowe, Dr P.C.
IR, His

MacFadyean, Dr N.J.
Eco, His

McDougall, Prof. dr B.S.
Lit, GenS

Menski, Dr W.
CuS, Rel, Law, Edu

Merrett, Drs N.M.
Lin, Law, Eco, DevS

Nossiter, Prof. T.J.
Soc, PolS, IR, DevS, His

Park, S.S.
Psy, PolS, Phi, SocAHis, DevS, Env, Edu, IR, Law

Pieke, Dr F.N.
Ant

Riddington, P.
Lin, Edu

Roberts, Drs D.C.
DevS, Eco, IR

Shepperdson, Mr M.J.
DevS, Agr, Eco, PolS, Soc

Spencer-Oatey, Dr H.
Lin

Strange, Dr R.N.
Eco

Thoburn, Dr J.T.
Eco

Valentin, J.C.P.
Env, Ant, CuS, Lin, His, Arch

Wu, Dr W.-P.
Eco, CuS

Yip, Dr P.C.
Lin, CuS

Zhao, Dr H.Y.H.
CuS

Zheng, H.
Arch, AHis, Lit

Yugoslavia

Furundzic, V.
Psy, Rel, Lit, Lin, Edu, His, Phi, AHis

JAPAN

Villalba Fernandez, Dr J.
Rel, Phi, AHis, IR

Austria

Formanek, S.
Rel, CuS, His, Lit

Frühstück, Drs S.
Soc, GenS, His, Ant, CuS

Galinski, C.
Edu, Lin

Getreuer-Kargl, Dr I.
Ant, CuS, GenS

Lee, Dr S.-K.
CuS, Lit

Linhart, Prof. dr S.
His, Soc

Maderdonner, Dr M.
Soc

Manzenreiter, Drs W.
Ant, Soc

Min Tjoa, Prof. dr A.
Edu

Mosch, Dr N.
CuS, Phi

Sellner, Dr M.B.
CuS, Lin

Vu Xuan Quang, Dr .
Eco

Austria

Zorn, Dr B.
Ant, Arch, Ant, His, AHis

Zotz, Dr V.
Phi, CuS, Rel, His

Belgium

Ballegeer, J.
PolS, Law

Bogart, K.J.
Edu, CuS

Chan, M.Y.
CuS

Coulie, Prof. dr B.R.R.
AHis, Soc, Lin, Phi, DevS, Ant, Eco, His, Lit

Delanghe, H.
IR, His, PolS

Haute, Dr L. Van
CuS, Lit, Soc

Pape, Mr W.
IR, Law, Eco, PolS

Put, I.H.A. van
CuS

Vaerman, Drs B.
GenSAHis, Rel, CuS, His

Vearman, Drs B.
PolS

Walle, Prof. dr W.F. van de
AHis, Lin, His

Wee, Prof. H.F.A.van der
Eco, His

Wu-Beyens, I.CH.
PolS, IR, His, Agr, DevS, Env

Yoshida, N.
IR, Eco

Bulgaria

Gerganova, Drs K.M.G.
Ant, Rel, Phi, His

Holodovich, Dr L.A.
Rel, Lit

Czech Republic

Hor kov , Drs D.
Lit, Rel

Hulec, Dr O.
His, AHis, CuS, Arch, IR, Eco, Phi, Lit, Lin

Kalvodov , Prof. dr D.
Eco, Phi, Law, His, Lin

Liscák, Dr V.
Rel, His, Phi, Lin, CuS

Suchomel, Dr F.A.
Arch, AHis

Svarcov , Dr Z.
Lit, Lin

Sykora, Drs J.
Rel, IR, Phi, His, PolS, Eco, Soc

Vacek, Prof. dr J.
Phi, Rel, Lit, Lin

Denmark

Aronstein, M.
PolS

Ebsen, Drs L.
Edu

Gullestrup, Prof. H.
His, Soc, IR, Eco, Ant, DevS, CuS, PolS

Hornby, J.E.
CuS, AHis

Jeppesen, L.
Soc, Ant

Keld, L.
CuS, His

Lidin, Prof. O.G.
Phi, CuS

Nagashima, Prof. dr Y.
Lit, IR, His, CuS

Ostergaard, Dr C.S.
Agr, Soc, PolS, IR, DevS

Reader, Dr I.J.
Soc, Rel, Ant

Roesgaard, Dr M.
Ant, Soc, Edu

Wang, J.
Lin, Lit, CuS, Edu, His, AHis

Finland

Antikainen-Kokko, Dr A.
IR

Jalagin, Drs S.
His

Janhunen, Prof. dr J.A.
AHis, CuS, Ant, Arch, Lin

Keskinen, Dr E.O.
Psy

Konttinen, Dr A.
Env, Soc, GenS

Konttinen, Drs T.P.
PolS, His

Mattila BA, M.M.
AHis, Lit

Oinas-Kukkonen, Drs H.T.
IR, His

Rajala, Drs T.M.
Lit, CuS

Raud, Prof. dr R.
His, Phi, Rel, Lit

Seppänen, J.
IR, Eco, Ant, CuS, Lin, His, AHis, Phi, Arch, Rel, PolS

Siika, M.
IR, His

Sopo, J.
Lin

Toiviainen, Dr H.
His

Vesterinen, Dr I.
Ant

France

Abe, Dr J.
Lit

Abud, Drs M.
Phi, Lin, His, Lit, CuS, His, AHis

Akamatsu, P.
Eco, PolS

Akkitham, N.
His, Eco, IR

Albis, R.
Eco

Allioux, Y.-M.
Lit

Amemiya-Lombard, H.
Lit

Asari, M.
Phi, Lit

Aussedat Maitrise, AV
IR

Balaize, C.
Ant, Agr, CuS, Rel

Barbiche, Prof. dr J.-P.
Law, IR, His, PolS, Eco, DevS, CuS, Edu, Soc

Baud Berthier, Dr G
Eco, His

Bayard-Sakai, A.
Lit

Baye, Dr E.B.
DevS, Env, Eco

Bayou, H.
AHis, Arch, Lit

Becque, .
Rel

Béguin, G.
GenS, Law, DevS

Beillevaire, Dr P.
His, Rel, Ant

Bensaou, B.
Rel

Bergerot, H.
Ant

Berlinguez-Kono, N.
Soc

Berque, Prof. A.
Phi

Billion, T.
Lit, Phi, Lin, IR, His, Edu

Blayac, A.A.
Lit, His, Phi, Edu, Psy, Soc

Botsch, A.A.
Eco, DevS, IR, Edu, Law

Boubault, D.
Lin

Bouchy, A.-M.
Rel

Bouissou, J.-M.
Soc, IR, PolS, His

Bourdier, Dr ir M.J.F.
CuS

Briend, M.
AHis

Brun, Dr C. le
Eco, IR, PolS

Brunet, Y.
Lit

ASIANISTS BY REGION AND COUNTRY OF INTEREST

France

Cheng, S.H.
AHis, CuS, Rel

Cholley, J.
Lin

Cobbi, J.
Ant

Collin, H.
Law, Soc, PolS, Eco, IR

Condominas, G.
Lan

Cornilleau, K.
His

Coyaud, Dr M.
Ant, Lin

Crombe, V.
His, CuS, AHis, Rel, His, Arch

Delahaye, Dr H.
His, CuS, AHis

Delteil, Dr A.F.
Lit

Domenach, Dr J.L.
IR, PolS

Durey, Ms.
His, AHis

Elisséeff, Dr D.
Arch, His, AHis

Esmein, Dr J.C.
Eco

Fabre, Prof. A.J.J.
Lin, Lit

Faure, Dr G.L.
PolS, Eco

Fava, P.
Psy, Lit, CuS, Ant, His, Arch, AHis, Soc, Rel, Phi

Fiévé, Dr N.B.
Ant, His, Rel, Soc, CuS, DevS, PolS

Figuière, C.
Eco

Fouquin, M.F.
Eco

Frank, B.
Lit

Frederic, L.F.
AHis, CuS, Arch, Rel, His

Fujimori, B.
Phi, Lin, CuS, Lit

Fujimoto, E.
Lit

Fukuda, K.
CuS, Ant, Arch, Lin, Soc, His

Gaanier, C.
Lin

Galan, Ch.
Edu

Gile, D.
Lit, His

Gipouloux, Dr F.
Eco, Soc

Girard, F.
Rel

Giroux, M.S.
Lit

Godement, Prof. dr F.L.
His, IR

Gossot, A.
His, AHis

Gossot, Dr Anne
Arch, AHis

Goto, T.
AHis

Griolet, P.
Lin

Guelle, F.
IR, Eco

Guerreiro, Dr A.
Ant

Guiheux, Dr G.
Eco, Soc, His

Hamon, C.
Eco

Hatano, Y.
His, PolS

Hayashi, O.
DevS, IR, PolS

Hórail, Dr F.
His

Horuichi, A.
His

Ishizuki, H.
His

Ito, Y.
Edu, GenS

Jarrige, J.F.
His, CuS, Arch, AHis

Jaussaud, Dr J.
Eco, IR

Jeanne, S.
Eco

Kano, M.
Ant, Rel, Soc, CuS

Kitayama, S.
Psy, Ant, Phi

Kuo, Dr L.
Rel

Labrune, L.
Lin

Le Nestour, P.
Lin, Lit

Le Nouëne, P.L.N.
AHis, Arch

Lechervy, Chr.
IR, PolS

Lemoine, Dr J.
CuS, Ant, GenS, His, Psy, Rel

Lesseur, C.
AHis

Lévy, Ch.
His

Lozerand, E.
Lit

Lucas, Dr N.
Lin

Macé, F.
Rel

Macé, M.
His

Marquet, Ch.
His, Lit

Martzel, G.
AHis, Phi

Maucuer, M.
AHis, Phi

Mertz, M.
AHis

Meunier, P.
His, Rel, Arch, Ant, AHis, CuS

Meyer, A. de
PolS, IR

Mishio, S.
Ant, Soc, Rel

Móriot, Prof. CH.
Ant

Moucuer, M.
Law, GenS, His

Nakamura, N.
Lin

Noda, S.
His

Noël, H.
AHis, Arch

Ogura, M.
Lan

Orberger, Dr B.
Lin, Lit, Geo

Ordonnadu, G.
IR, Eco

Origas, J.-J.
Lit

Oshima, H.
Lin

Oshima, Hi.
Lin

Pellard, S.
His, Arch, AHis

Penent, J.
His

Petitmengin, S.
Lit

Picone, Drs M.J.
Ant, Rel

Pigeot, Prof. dr J.
Lit

Portier-Lehmans, Dr A.P.L.
His, CuS

Rault-Leyrat, L.R.
His, Rel, Ant, AHis, Ant, Lin, Arch, Phi, His

Robert, J.
His

France

Robert, J.-N.
Lit
Rocher, Prof. dr A.
Lit, Rel, Phi
Roland, N.
Eco
Rotermund, Prof. H.O.
Soc, Rel, CuS
Rousset, Dr H.A.
CuS, His, Arch, AHis, Ant
Sabban, F.S.
Agr, Ant, CuS
Saïto, S.
Edu
Saito, T.
Edu
Sakai, C.
Lit
Sautter, Ch.
Eco
Seguy, Ch.
CuS
Seizelet, E.A.F.
Law, Edu, PolS
Sekiguchi, H.
Lin
Sevela, M.
His
Shimamori, Dr R.
Lin
Siary, Dr G.M.M.
Lit
Simon, Dr J.C.
Soc, IR, His, Eco, DevS, PolS
Sivignon,
Eco, Geo
Smitsendonk, Dr A.G.O.
Law, Eco, IR, Soc, Rel, PolS, DevS
Smolarz, B.
Geo, Agr
Souyri, P.-F.
His
Struve, D.
His
Taguchi, M.
Lin
Tamba, A.
Eco, PolS, IR
Tamba, I.
Lin
Tamogami, K.
IR, Eco
Terada, Dr A.
Lin
Terrada, H.
Law
Thieu, S.
Lit
Thoyer, C.
His, Arch, AHis
Trần, Q.H.
CuS, Ant
Trinh, Prof. V.T.
Edu, Soc, His
Tschudin, Dr J.J.
Lit
Tsu Kamara, M.
Lit
Turcq, Dr D.F.
Eco
Verdilhac, de
Eco
Vié, M.
His
Viellard-Baron, M.
Lit
Vigneau, Prof. R.
Lit
Walter, A.
Lit
Weishaupt, M.
Lan
Williamson, Dr P.J.
DevS, Eco
Wlodarczyk, A.
Lin
Woronoff, Dr J.A.
Eco, IR, DevS, PolS
Yamaguchi, K.
Lan
Yamasaki, Y.

Germany

Antoni, Prof. dr K.
Ant, Phi, Rel, His
Arnold, M.
Arch, His, AHis
Axel, Dr M.
Psy, Ant, PSYCHIATRY
Banaschak, Drs P.
Ant, His, CuS
Bass, Dr H.H.
DevS, Eco, IR
Beermann, Drs R.E.
Lin
Bosse, F.
GenS, Eco, Soc, Agr
Brochlos, Dr A.
His
Brumann, Drs Chr.
Ant
Cseh, É.E.
AHis, Rel
Cuhls, Drs K.E.
Env, Eco, PolS, CuS
Dahlhausen, Drs S.
His
Derichs, Dr C.
IR, PolS
Draguhn, Dr W.
PolS, IR, Eco, DevS
Duppel-Takayama, Drs M.
Lit
Eberspaecher, Drs C.
PolS, His
Ehmcke, Prof. dr F.
Rel, Soc, His, CuS, Phi, Lit
Eschbach-Szabo, Prof. V.A.
Lin, His, CuS, Phi, Ant
Federlein, Drs D.
His, Lin, Rel
Fischer, Dr P.
His, Rel
Flüchter, Prof. dr W.
Geo, Env
Foljanty-Jost, Prof. dr G.
PolS, Env
Geisler, Drs G.H.S.
Geo, Env, DevS
Giele, Drs E.
His, Arch
Goettingen, Drs D.
PolS, IR
Graevenitz, Prof. dr A. von
Phi, AHis
Grimm, Drs C.
Rel, His, Soc, Phi, CuS, Lit
Haberland, Dr D.
CuS, Lit
Hana, Dr K.
PolS, His, DevS
Hasunuma, R.
His, Rel
Heiduk, Dr G.
Eco
Heinzig, Dr D.
His, PolS, IR
Hennig, A.
CuS
Herrmann, Dr W.
Lin
Heuser, Prof. R.
Law
Hijiya-Kirschnereit, Prof. I.
CuS, Lit, Lin
Hinüber, Dr H. von
Law, His, Rel, Lin, Phi, Lit
Hong, Dr E.P.
His, IR
Hummel, Dr H.
PolS, IR
Jaeger, Drs H.
CuS, Rel, Phi
Jungmann, Prof. dr B.
AHis
Jüttner, Prof. Dr G.
AHis, CuS, His
Kaden, Prof. dr K.
Lin
Kerde, Drs O.
PolS

ASIANISTS BY REGION AND COUNTRY OF INTEREST

Germany

Kevenhörster, Prof. dr P.K.
PolS

Klenner, Prof. Dr Wolfgang
DevS, Eco

Kobayashi, Dr M.B.
Psy, Edu, CuS

Koerbs, C.
His, Edu, Phi

Koester, Drs K.
Eco

Kraatz, Dr M.
Rel

Kracht, Prof. dr K.
Ant, His, Phi, Rel, CuS

Krebs, Dr G.
Edu, His, PolS, IR

Kreiner, Prof. dr J.
His, Ant, CuS

Kriegeskorte, Dr M.
His, CuS

Kuckertz, Prof. dr J.
His, Ant

Kuhl, Drs M.
Lin, Phi, CuS, His, AHis, Lit, Rel

Laube, Prof. J.
CuS, Edu, Phi, Rel

Lauer, Drs U.
AHis

Leinss, Dr G.L.
CuS, His

Linz, Drs J.
CuS, His

Loke-Schwalbe, Dr P.M.L.
CuS, Ant

Lorenz, Prof. D.
Eco

Manthey, B.
Lin

Martin, Prof. dr B.
His

Marx, C.
Lin

Maull, Prof. H.W.
IR

Mayer, Dr A.L.
Rel, Phi

Menzel, Prof. U.
IR, PolS

Meyer, E.-M.
His

Müller, K.
PolS, CuS, His

Müller, M.
His, AHis

Müller, Prof. K.
His

Müller-Hofstede, Drs C.
PolS, Soc, His, IR, CuS, DevS

Müller-Saini, Dr G.
His, CuS, Ant, Phi, Rel

Nabers, D.
PolS

Nahser, Dr S.
AHis

Nass, O.
Eco

Otto, Drs S.S.
Eco

Partenheimer-Bein, A.
His

Pascha, Prof. dr W.
Eco

Pauer, Prof. dr E.
His

Philipp MA, H.M.
Env, Law

Pigulla, Dr A.
His, PolS, IR

Plate, Drs P.A.
Env, Edu

Pohl, Prof. dr M.
PolS, His

Prunner, Dr G.
Ant, Rel, CuS

Putz, Drs O.P.
Lit

Pye, Prof. E.M.
Rel

Reimers, Drs C.
His

Richter, ML
Ant, Arch, AHis, His, Law, Lin, Lit, Phi, Rel

Richter, Prof. S.
Phi, CuS

Rohde, Drs M.R.
Eco, IR, DevS, PolS

Rohde, Prof. dr K.E.
Soc, Eco, Env, DevS, CuS, IR

Rühle, Mr K.H.
His, Lit, Lin, CuS

Schamoni, Prof. W.
Lit

Schillig, Dr D
CuS, Phi, Rel

Seckel, Prof. dr D.
His, AHis

Seifert, Prof. dr W.
Soc, PolS

Senger, Prof. dr H. von
Lit, PolS, Law, CuS

Seyock, Drs B.
His, Arch

Staemmler, Drs B.
Rel

Stiller, Dr D.F.R.
Law

Strube Dipl.Dec., J.T.
Eco

Teichler, Prof. dr U.
Soc

Thiede, Dr U.
Env, Ant, His, CuS, Eco

Trommsdorff, Prof. G.
Soc, Psy, CuS

Vittinghoff, Drs N.P.
CuS, His

Vogel, Drs K.K.
GenS, PolS

Vollmer, Dr K.
His, CuS, Rel, Lit

Wagner, J.
His, AHis, CuS

Weber, B.
CuS

Wichmann, Drs P.
IR, PolS

Zieme, Dr P.
Rel

Hungary

Bassa, Dr Z.
Eco

Birks, L.
Eco, DevS, Env, Agr, IR

Birtalan, Dr A.
AHis, Rel, Phi, Lit, Lin, His, Arch, GenS

Ehrlich, Prof. E.
Eco, DevS

Hajnal MA, L
Ant, AHis, CuS, Edu, His, Lin, Lit, Rel

Harangi, Dr L.
Soc, Edu

Hernádi, Dr A.
DevS, IR, Eco, Env

Hidasi, Prof. J.
Lin, IR, Edu, Soc, CuS

Kállay, Dr I.
His, Lin, Phi, Law, Eco

Lukàs, É
AHis, IR, His, CuS

Mojzes, Prof. I.
PolS, Edu

Sato, Drs N.
Edu, Eco

Szentirmai, Mr J.
Env, His, AHis, Eco, Rel

Szók cs, Dr A.
Lin, Edu

Italy

Banti Pereira, Dr J.
His, CuS, His, AHis

Boscaro, Prof. A.
Lit

Calvetti, Prof. P.
Lin

Campana, Dr A.
His, IR, PolS

Canova, Dr G.
Lit

Italy

Carioti, Dr P.
His

Ciapparoni La Rocca, Dr T.
Lit

Corradini, Prof. P.
Law, IR, His

Dalla Chiesa, Drs S.
Lin, Rel, Ant

De Prado Yepes, C.
Eco, IR

Faccaro, F.
Lit

Fanin, C.
IR, Lin, His, Lit

Filippini, Prof. C.M.
Eco

Fossati, Prof. G.
His, AHis

Kondo, Dr.E.
CuS, His, AHis

Marinelli, Dr M.M.
His, IR, PolS, DevS

Molteni Corrado, Dr C.M.
Eco

Nishimoto, Dr K.
Lit, Edu

Orsi, Prof. M.T.
Lit

Piacentini, Dr P.M.
Eco, DevS

Sagiyama, Prof. I.
Lit

Scalise, Prof. M.
Lin, Lit

Scolari, V.
CuS, His, AHis

Spadavecchia, Dr N.G.
Lit

Tollini, Prof. A.
Lin

Tozzi, Dr D.T.
Soc, His, Eco

Valota, Prof. A.
His

Volpi, G.
PolS, IR, Agr, Eco, Env

Zanier, Prof. C.
His

Japan

Hunter, Drs H.J.
AHis, Rel, His

Steffensen, Dr S.K.
Soc, PolS, Eco, DevS

Netherlands

Aelst, Drs A. van
His

Akkermans, Dr H.A.
Eco, His, IR

Anbeek, Dr C.W.
Phi, Rel

Bastiaansen, Drs A.C.G.M.
IR, Eco, Edu

Berge, Dr T. v.d.
PolS, Lit, His

Bertsch, Drs H.B.
Soc, Eco

Beukers, Prof. dr H.
His

Blussé, Dr J.L.
IR, His

Boin, Drs M.M.O.
His

Boon, D.
AHis, Rel, CuS, Phi, His

Boot, Prof. dr W.J.
His, Phi, Lit

Borstlap, Drs A.V.
His, AHis

Boyd, Dr R.A.
PolS

Bremen, Dr J.G. van
Ant, His

Brouwer, A.A.
CuS, Eco, His, IR, PolS, Psy, Rel, Phi

Brunt, Prof. dr L.
Ant, Soc

Bruschke-Johnson, Drs L.
AHis

Burgers, Dr A.B.
Lin, Eco

Busser, Drs R.B.P.M.
IR, Eco

Crump, Dr S.T.
Ant

Cwiertka, Dr K.J.
Soc, His, Ant

Daan, K.
Env, CuS

Deelstra, T.
Env

Derveld, Dr F.E.R.
Eco

Dijk, Drs W.O.
Rel, CuS, His, Lin

Dijkstra, Drs G.H.
Soc, Rel, Phi, Eco, His, IR, Psy, PolS

Dishoeck, Drs E.R. van
Eco, Edu, Phi, CuS

Dolce, Dr L.D.M.
CuS, Rel, Phi

Domenig, Ir G.
Rel

Donker Duyvis, Drs P.
AHis, Arch, Ant, His

Eijnsbergen, E. van
AHis, Lin

Eliëns, Prof. dr T.M.
AHis

Forrer, Dr M.
AHis

Gaastra, Dr F.S.
His

Gelder, Drs R. van
CuS, His, IR

Ginkel, Prof. dr J.A. van
Geo, DevS

Gonsalves, Drs C.M.
Law

Gontscharoff, C.
IR, DevS

Graaf, Dr T. de
Lin

Graaff, Drs B.G.J. de
His, IR

Grant, Dr M.E.
Lit, IR, His, AHis, Rel

Groen, Prof. P.M.H.
His

Groot, Drs G.P. de
PolS, Eco, Ant

Hagers, Drs S.J.
Lin

Hamelink, Prof. dr C.J.
IR, Law

Haringhuizen, Drs W.
PolS, Ant, IR

Heller, Y.J.
Rel, CuS, His, AHis

Hermens, B.
Agr, Env, IR

Hintzen, Drs G.H.
IR, Law, Phi, PolS, His

Hoefnagels, Ir H.A.M.
Agr, Eco, Law

Holdstock, Prof. T.L.
Psy

Hudcovicova, A.
CuS

Hulsbergen, T.
IR, AHis, Edu, CuS, His, Soc

Ing, E. van den
His, CuS, Lit, AHis

Inoue, F.
AHis, CuS, Lit, His

Jacobs, Drs E.M.
His

Jagtenberg, Dr R.W.
Law

Janssen, M.
Phi, His

Janssens, Dr R.V.A.
His, IR

Jehle, Dr E.
IR, DevS, Eco, Edu, Law

Jong, Dr J. de
CuS, IR, His

Netherlands

Jongsma-Blanche Koelensmid, Drs H.T.
AHis, Arch, CuS, His

Junne, Prof. G.C.A.
IR, DevS, PolS, Env

Kamstra, Prof. dr J.H.
Rel

Khosla, Dr A.
DevS, Eco

Klein, Prof. dr P.W.
His

Knight, Dr J.P.
Ant

Koesoebjono, R.H.S.I.
DevS, GenS, Eco

Kol, Prof. dr J.
DevS, Eco, Agr

Kortlandt, Prof. dr F.H.H.
Lin

Korzec, Dr M.
PolS

Lamers, Drs J.P.
His

Lasschuijt, Drs I.D.
IR, PolS

Lau, W.Y.
SocAHis, CuS

Lichtveld, A.
AHis

Lindhoud, Drs P.C.
His

Lunsing, W.M.
Ant, CuS, GenS, PolS

Meer, Dr ir C.L.J. van der
DevS, Agr

Meerman, J.M.M.
His

Meij, Prof. J.M. de
His, Law

Meijeraan, Drs H.
Geo, Env

Mensink, Drs O.H.
AHis, Ant, CuS, His

Meredith, Mr P.I.
Art

Messing, Mr A.J.
Law

Mierlo, Drs H.W.R. van
Lin, CuS, AHis

Mirage, M.
CuS

Moeshart, Drs H.J.
His, IR

Montyn, J.
Phi, AHis, CuS, Lit

Nadal Uceda, F. de
Ant, Arch, Lin, Phi, Psy, Rel

Nagel, Dr B.M.J.
Rel, Phi

Nishide, M.N.
IR, PolS, His

Ommen, Drs A.F. van
IR, PolS

Ondracek, Drs W.F.J.
Lit, Soc

Pijl-Ketel, Ch. van der
AHis

Pols, Dr A.
Lit, Lin

Poncini, G.
His, AHis, Arch

Poorter, Dr E.G. de
Lit

Post, Dr P
IR, Ant, His

Posthumus Meyjes, Drs H.C.
Ant, DevS, GenS

Prchal, Drs M.
PolS, His, Rel

Quispel, Drs C.I.
PolS, Phi, CuS, His

Rappard-Boon, Drs Ch.E. van
His, AHis

Rauws, Drs A.J.
AHis, Ant, Arch, His

Rinsampessy, Dr E.P.
Ant, Soc, Rel, IR, Edu

Roo, Dr A.J. de
Law

Ruygrok, Drs W.F.
His, PolS, Soc

Sakamoto, Dr K.
CuS, Lit

Sanders, Drs M.
DevS, Eco

Schaap, R.
AHis

Schalke, Dr H.J.W.G.
Arch, Ant, Env

Scheepers, Dr A.R.
Phi, His, Rel

Schiermeier, Drs K.E.N.B.
AHis, Lin

Schoch, Drs G.W.
Eco

Scholten, Drs J.
Lit

Schulze, F.
His, Rel

Sellmeijer-Fujita, M.
Psy

Semetko, Prof. dr H.A.
PolS, Soc, Psy

Sigmond, Dr J.P.
CuS, His, AHis, Arch

Sinnema, Drs T.
GenS, CuS, Soc, His, Edu

Smit, Drs H.C.
Lin

Smits, Dr I.B.
His, Lit

Sodderland, Mr J.W.
Law

Spiekerman-Middelplaats, M.Y.M.
Env

Staal, Dr P.M. van der
PolS

Stam, Prof. dr J.A.
DevS, Eco, IR

Steenbeek, Dr O.W.
Eco

Stegewerns, Drs D.
His, IR

Stel, Dr J.H.
Env, Eco

Stolk, M.D.
CuS, Psy, Soc, Rel

Streef, E.
Env, Law, Ant

Strik, Prof. B.
CuS

Sybesma, S.
Lin

Takahashi, Prof. M.
Edu

Theunissen, Drs A.R.
His, Lin, Lit

Tjoa, Drs M.L.M.
His

Uhlenbeck, Drs Ch.
His, Ant, AHis

Veenhoven, Dr R.
Psy, Soc

Veere, Mr H. van der
Rel, Phi

Velde, Drs P.G.E.I.J. van der
Lit, His

Vereijken, Drs C.M.J.L.
Psy, Ant

Vermeulen, Drs A.C.J.
His

Verschoor, I.B.
His, Phi, CuS, PolS, Eco

Viallé, Drs C.R.M.K.L.
His, AHis

Visser-Elias, M.M.
His

Vos, Prof. dr F.
Rel, Lit, His

Welling, Drs K.O.H.
Art

Werger-Klein, K.E.
His

Wesselius, Drs J.
Lin, His

Wiechen, P.J. van
AHis, CuS, Ant, Arch, His

Wiegmans, Drs B.W.
Eco

Wiel, A.N. van der
His, AHis, Arch

Netherlands

Wijsman, Drs P.L.
Lit

Yoneda, Y.Y.
AHis

Zeeventer, Drs L.T.M. van
PolS, DevS, IR

Zhang, Dr Y.
Law

Zomer, Drs H.
IR, Eco, CuS

Norway

Grönning, Dr T.
Soc

Liao, R.
IR, DevS, PolS, AHis

Svensson, Dr T. G.
Ant

Poland

Goralski, Prof. dr
PolS, His, IR

Kotanski, Prof. dr W.
Lin, CuS

Kulig, Prof. J.
Eco, IR

Leszczynski, Prof. L.
Soc, PolS, Law, Eco

Majewicz, Prof. dr A.F.
Lin, Ant

Melanowicz, Prof. M.
Lit

Mydel, Prof. R.
Eco

Pazasz-Rutkowska, Dr E.
His

Zaremba, Dr P.A.
DevS, Env, Eco

Portugal

Coutinho, Dr V.
His

Loureiro, Prof. dr R.M.
His, CuS

Oliveira e Costa, Dr J.P.
His, Rel

Rumania

Waniek, Dr A.I.
CuS, Lit

Russia

Alpatov, Dr V.M.
Lin

Arskaya, Dr L.P.
Eco

Berezina, Dr Yu.I.
Soc

Boronina, Dr I.A.
Lit

Bunin, Dr V.N.
PolS, IR

Bykova, Dr S.A.
Lin

Chegodar, Dr N.I.
CuS, Lit

Cherevko, Dr Yu.M.
Eco, IR

Denissov, Dr
Eco

Dinkevich, Dr A.I.
Eco

Dolin, Dr A.A.
Lit

Dybo, Dr Prof. A. V.
Ant, Lin

Golovnin, Prof.dr I.V.
Lin

Goregliad, Prof. dr V.N.
Lit, Rel

Grigorieva, Dr T.P.
Rel

Grishina, Dr V.A.
Lit, Phi

Grivnin, Prof.dr V.S.
Lin, Lit, PolS

Ignatovich, Dr A.N.
Rel, His

Ionova, Dr Yu.V.
Ant

Jarylgassinova, Dr R.Sh.
Ant

Joukov, Dr A.
His, PolS, Soc

Karelova, Dr L.B.
His, Phi, Rel

Katassonova, Dr Y.L.
CuS

Khlynov, Dr V.N.
PolS, Eco

Kirillova, O.B.
Edu, Lin

Kistanov, Dr V.O.
Eco

Koniahin, Dr V.A.
His, Lin

Korchaguina, Dr T.I.
Lin

Kovrizhkin, Dr S.V.
Eco

Kozlov, Dr A.A.
His, Eco

Kravtsevich, Dr A.I.
Eco

Krupyanko, Dr M.I.
IR

Ksenofontova, Dr G.A.
Ant

Kulikova, Dr L. V.
Edu, His

Latyshov, Dr I.A.
IR, PolS

Leschenko, Dr N.
Lin

Leshchenko, Dr N.F.
His

Markariants, Dr S.B.
Eco

Markov, Dr A.P.
His

Matrussova, Dr T.N.
Eco

Mayevski, Dr E.V.
Lin

Mazourik, Dr V.P.
Rel, Lit

Meshcheryakov, Dr A.N.
CuS, His

Molodyakova, Dr E.V.
His

Navlitskaya, Prof.dr G.B.
CuS, His

Netshaewa, Dr L.
Lin

Pavlyatenko, Dr V.N.
IR, PolS, Eco

Pirogov, Dr G.G.
Eco

Podlesskaya, Dr V.I.
Lin

Rogojine, Dr A.
Env, Eco, IR, DevS

Sablina, E.
CuS, His, IR

Sadokova, Dr A.R.
Lit

Samoyeov, Dr N.A.
IR, His

Sarkisov, Dr K.O.
His, IR, PolS

Senatorov, Dr A.I.
PolS

Shalyapina, Dr Z.M.
Lin

Sheftelevich, Dr N.S.
Lit

Shevchenko, Dr N.Yu.Yu.
Eco

Solomonik, Dr I.N.
His, AHis

Syomin, Dr A.V.
His, IR, Eco, PolS

Tambovtsev, Prof. dr Y.A.
Lin

Tikhotskaya, Dr I.S.
Eco

Timonina, Dr I.L.
Eco

Toropygina, Dr M.
Lit

Uspenski, Dr M.V.
AHis, CuS

Vardul, Dr I.F.
Lin

Yakubovsky, Dr V.
Eco, PolS, IR

ASIANISTS BY REGION AND COUNTRY OF INTEREST

Russia

Yeremin, V.N.
Law

Yermakova, Dr L.M.
Lit

Zhukov, Dr A.Ye.
His

Slovenia

Milcinski, Prof. dr M.
Phi, Rel

Spain

Albarrán Serrano, Antonio
Lit

Alejano Monge, M.
Eco, Lin

Anton Burgos, Dr F.J.
Geo

Bustelo, Dr P.
DevS, Eco

Cabañas, P.
AHis

Canto, Dr P.
DevS, IR, Eco

Casares Vidal, D.
Eco

Casero Fernandez, E.J.

Castillo Rodriguez, S.
IR

Catalan Aguila, J.
Env

Ceruera Fernández, I.
AHis, His

Cruz Alcaide, J.M.
Edu, Phi, Rel

De Llanos Isidoro, P.
His, Lin, Lit, Phi

Delage, F.
IR, PolS

Diaz Fernandez, Dr B.A.
Eco

Díez Faixat, V.

Díez Galán, Dr J.
AHis, Lit

Elías de Tejada Lozano, Diplomat F.
Eco, Lit, PolS

Elizalde Perez-Grueso, Dr D.
His, IR

Escurriola Sans, Jordi
His, Lin, Lit, Phi, Soc

Fenés Folch, E.
DevS

Fernández Miguélez, J.
IR

Fernández Salido, J.M.

Garceran Piqueras Roas Maria, Rosa

Garcia, Fernando
AHis, Geo, His, IR, PolS

Garcia Erviti, J.
ECONOMIA

García Gutiérrez Lic.Fil., F.
AHis, Rel

Garcia Weda, R.
Lin

Garcia-Ormaechea Quero, C.
AHis, Geo, His, Lit, Rel, Phi

Garmendia Herrero, E.
His

Garrigues Areiczo, M.
Eco

Gil, Prof. J.
His, Lit

Gomez Candela, Monica
AHis, Rel

Gomez Pradas, Muriel
AHis, Ant

González Valles, J.
Phi, Rel

Gouzalez Molina, A.
IR, Soc

Gurbindo Lambán, N.
Ant

Jimenez Blanco, I.
Eco

Jimenez Valentin, J.M.
Eco, Env, IR

Kim, Drs S.-H.
Arch, Rel, Phi, Lit, His, AHis

Kiuchi, Prof. Miyako

Lanzaco Salafranca, Drs F.
Eco, Lin, Phi, Psy, Rel, Soc

Lopez Navalon, J. A.
Eco, Lin, IR

Martinell Gifre, E.
Lin

Masachs Castell, J.
Eco, Geo, His, IR, Soc, PolS

Medina Bermejo, R.
AHis, His, IR, Lin

Mellen Blanco, F.
Ant, Arch, AHis, His

Merinero Martin, M.J.
His, PolS

Montero Moreno, J.
His, Lit, Rel

Morena Martin, T. de la
Edu

Moreno Garcia, J.
His, IR, PolS

Moreno Garcia, Dr J.
His, IR, PolS

Moreno Marcos, A.
Eco, IR

Navarro Celada, F.

Orduna Diez, L.
Eco, Law, PolS

Pajares Ruiz, J.M.
AHis, Eco, Geo, Soc

Palazuelos Manso, A.
Eco, Soc

Pastrano, Dr F.
His, IR, Rel, Soc

Planas, Prof. R.
Lin, CuS

Pont Ferrer, Beatriz
Eco, Edu, IR, PolS

Rodao, Prof. F.R.
His, IR

Rodríguez Ubeda, M.M.
Eco, IR, Soc

Rodriguez-Eiras, J.A.
Agr, Eco, Edu, Env, His, Soc

Roman Marugan, Dr P.
PolS

Ruiz, Dr José M.
Lin, Rel

Sampedro Fromont, X.
Eco

Santos, A.
AHis

Serrano Valentin, Carlos
Eco, IR

Shioji, Prof. Etsuro
Eco

Sotelo Navalpotro, J.A.
Env, Geo

Takagi, Prof. K.
His, Lin, Lit, AHis

Togores Sanchez, L.E.
IR, His

Tulloch, Drs C.D.
Ant

Varela Regueira, Ma del Mar
His, IR

Vargas Anguita, G.

Vilaro Giralt, R.
Eco, IR, PolS

Villalba Fernández, J.
AHis, IR, Phi, Rel

Vinyamata Camp, E.
IR, Soc, Psy

Sweden

Allwood, Prof. J.
Lin, Phi

Amer, Dr R.
IR, PolS, His

Anbäcken, E.M.
Rel, Phi

Bratthall, Prof. D.
Eco

Bryder, Dr H.P.
Ant, Rel

Dahlgren, Drs T.
His

Edström, Dr B.
IR

Fleetwood, J.E.V.
Eco, Edu

Sweden

Huldt, Prof. B.
IR, His

Iwanaga, Dr K.I.
PolS, IR

Lambert, Prof. B.H.
PolS

Lindberg-Wada, Prof. K.G.
Lit

Lundström, S.H.I.
Geo, GenS, DevS

Moberg, P.
CuS, Lit, His

Park, Dr S.-C.
Eco, PolS

Sigurdson, Prof. J.
IR, DevS, Eco, PolS

Virgin, Drs L.
His, AHis

Switzerland

Borner-Mouer, Dr E.J.
GenS, Soc

Ducor, Dr J.
Rel, Ant, GenS

Dunand, F.
His, AHis

Egenter, Ir N.
Rel, Ant, CuS, His, AHis

Findeisen, Dr R.D.
Phi, GenS, Lit

Jing Li, A.
IR, PolS

Klopfenstein, Prof. E
Lit

Lee, H.
Env, Eco, Edu, CuS

Loosli, Dr U.
Lin, CuS, PolS

Nibbio, N.
Ant, DevS

Ninomiya, Prof. M.
Phi, Lit

Schmid-Schoenbein, C.
Eco, IR, PolS

Thölen, Drs K.
Arch, His, AHis, Lit

Turpin, Dr D.V.
Soc

Wang, Mr D.T.C.
PolS, Law

Wild, Y.
His

United Kingdom

Ansorge, Drs C.A.
His, Arch, CuS, Rel, Lit, Phi

Barnes, Prof. G.L.
Arch

Barrett, Prof. T.
Rel, His

Birkin, I.
Ant

Bocking, Prof. B.
Rel

Bowring, Prof. R.J.
Rel, Lit

Brailey, Dr N.J.
His

Bruijn, Drs J.E. de
His, AHis, CuS

Burg, B. & C. von der
His, AHis

Cockburn, Mr R.C.
DevS, CuS

Cook, M.
Eco

Crosbie, Dr A.J.
IR, Env, Eco, Geo, DevS

Crump, Drs T.M.
CuS, Lit

Crump, Prof. J.D.
PolS, His

Deckers, Drs W.
IR, DevS, PolS

Drifte, Prof. R.
PolS, IR

Dryburgh, Dr M.E.
His

Ducaru, S.
GenS, Ant, Rel

Dunn, Mr A.J-J.
IR, Edu, CuS, Ant

Edmonds, Dr R.L.
Env, Geo

Elliott, D.
AHis

Ferdinand, Drs C.I.P.
PolS, DevS, His, Eco, IR

Forfar, D.J.
Ant, Soc, CuS, Rel

Fukasawa, Dr Y.
CuS, Soc, Ant, Arch, His, Lin

Glover, Dr I.C.
Arch

Hallett, Mr D.J.
Eco

Hardiman, Dr T.P.
IR, Eco

Harries, Dr P.T.
Lit

Hart, R.F.
His, PolS, IR

Hawthorn, Mr G.P.
IR, DevS, PolS

Hendry, Prof. R.J.
Ant

Hesselink, N.D.
Ant

Hoare, Dr J.E.
IR, His, PolS, CuS

Hook, Prof. G.D.
PolS, IR

Hughes, Dr D.W.
Ant

Hunter, Dr J.E.
His, Eco

Irisa, J.I.
DevS, Eco

Jameson, Drs A.L.
CuS, His

Kawanami, Dr H.
Ant, Rel

Kidd, Mr J.B.
CuS, Edu

Kikuchi, Y.
His, AHis, CuS

King, Prof. U.
Phi, His, Edu, Ant, GenS, CuS, Rel, Soc

Kornicki, Dr P.F.
CuS, His

Large, Dr S.S.
His

Lewis, Dr D.C.
Rel, Ant, CuS

Lewis, Dr J.B.
His

Li, R.
PolS, IR

Lingen, Drs B.M. van der
CuS, GenS

Lowe, Dr P.C.
IR, His

McCargo, Dr D.J.
PolS

Metzger-Court, Dr S.F.
Eco, His

Mirza, Prof. H.R.
DevS, Eco

Mürer, O.H.A.
Arch, His, AHis

Neary, Prof. I.J.
PolS

Nish, Prof. I.H.
PolS, His, IR

Norbury, P.
AHis, Rel, Env, Ant, Arch, His

O'Connor, Drs K.
CuS, Ant, Soc

Oda, Prof. H.
Law

Pak, Dr Y.S.
Arch, His, AHis

Park, S.S.
Psy, PolS, Phi, SocAHis, DevS, Env, Edu, IR, Law

Parker, H.S.E.
GenS, CuS, His

Peach, Dr C.
Geo, Soc

Picken, Dr L.E.R.
CuS

United Kingdom

Piper, Dr N.
Soc, GenS
Powell, Dr B.W.F.
Ant
Prasad, Drs S.
Soc, Ant, Eco, DevS
Provine, Prof. dr R.C.
Lin
Roberts, Drs D.C.
DevS, Eco, IR
Rowley, Dr G.G.
Lit
Ryan, Dr J.T.
Eco
Sakamoto, R.
CuS, Ant, Soc
Saville, Mr A.
Arch
Sharpe, Dr P.A.
Lin
Sheehan, Dr J.
PolS, His
Shepperdson, Mr M.J.
DevS, Agr, Eco, PolS, Soc
Smith, D.B.
IR, PolS, Eco, His
Spooner, Prof. F.C.
Eco, His
Starr, Drs R.M.
His, CuS, AHis, Edu, His, IR
Starr, Mr D.F.
Phi, Lin
Steeds, Mr D.
IR, His
Steffensen, Drs K.N.
PolS, IR
Stickings, S.R.
Law
Tanaka, H.M.
Soc, CuS
Teeuwen, Dr M.J.
Rel
Todd, Mr H.A.
CuS, Lit, His
Valentin, J.C.P.
Env, Ant, CuS, Lin, His, Arch
Waley MA, Dr P.T. Waley
Ant, Env
Wang, H.
His, AHis, Arch, His
Watanabe, Prof. T.
AHis
Watson, Prof. W.
Arch, His, AHis
Whitfield, Prof. R.
His, AHis
Xinzhong Yao, Dr
Rel, Phi

Yugoslavia

Imamovic, E.
His, CuS, AHis
Majstorac, Drs A.
CuS, His, Lit, Rel, AHis

KOREA

Austria

Lee, Dr S.-K.
CuS, Lit
Mosch, Dr N.
CuS, Phi
Sellner, Dr M.B.
CuS, Lin
Sichrovsky, Prof. H.
CuS, His, PolS, IR
Vu Xuan Quang, Dr.
Eco
Zorn, Dr B.
Ant, Arch, Ant, His, AHis

Belgium

Ballegeer, J.
PolS, Law

Bulgaria

Fedotoff, Prof. dr A.
Rel, Lit, CuS
Gerganova, Drs K.M.G.
Ant, Rel, Phi, His

Czech Republic

Gruberova, Drs I.M.
Lit, Rel
Hulec, Dr O.
His, AHis, CuS, Arch, IR, Eco, Phi, Lit, Lin
Klöslov, Zd.
His, Lit
Suchomel, Dr F.A.
Arch, AHis
Vacek, Prof. dr J.
Phi, Rel, Lit, Lin

Denmark

Aronstein, M.
PolS
Gullestrup, Prof. H.
His, Soc, IR, Eco, Ant, DevS, CuS, PolS
Helgesen, Dr G.H.
PolS, Soc, CuS
Hornby, J.E.
CuS, AHis
Magnussen, Drs T.
DevS, IR, PolS
Ostergaard, Dr C.S.
Agr, Soc, PolS, IR, DevS
Schmidt, Dr J.D.
Soc, IR, DevS
Sorensen, Dr H.H.
His, AHis, Rel, CuS

Finland

Forest, Drs M.H.
Lin
Janhunen, Prof. dr J.A.
AHis, CuS, Ant, Arch, Lin
Luova, Drs O.E.
IR, PolS
Seppänen, J.
IR, Eco, Ant, CuS, Lin, His, AHis, Phi, Arch, Rel, PolS
Toiviainen, Dr H.
His
Vesterinen, Dr I.
Ant

France

Albis, R.
Eco
Balaize, C.
Ant, Agr, CuS, Rel
Barbiche, Prof. dr J.-P.
Law, IR, His, PolS, Eco, DevS, CuS, Edu, Soc
Baud Berthier, Dr G
Eco, His
Botsch, A.A.
Eco, DevS, IR, Edu, Law
Bouchez, Dr D.
His, Lit
Bouissou, J.-M.
Soc, IR, PolS, His
Briend, M.
AHis
Brun, Dr C. le
Eco, IR, PolS
Cambon, P.
His
Chang, I.-B.
Lin
Chaponniere, Dr J.R.
IR, Eco, PolS, DevS
Cheng, S.H.
AHis, CuS, Rel
Choi, S.-U.
His
Choi-Chaballe, E.-S.
Lin
Coyaud, Dr M.
Ant, Lin
Delissen, Dr A.R.
His
Durey, Ms.
His, AHis
Fabre, Prof. A.J.J.
Lin, Lit
Fouquin, M.F.
Eco
Frederic, L.F.
AHis, CuS, Arch, Rel, His
Gipouloux, Dr F.
Eco, Soc
Godement, Prof. dr F.L.
His, IR
Guillemoz, Dr A.L.
GenS, CuS, Ant, Rel

France

Han, S.-I.
AHis
Jarrige, J.F.
His, CuS, Arch, AHis
Jaussaud, Dr J.
Eco, IR
Kim, H.-M.
Lin
Kim-Lee, B.
Lan
Lechervy, Chr.
IR, PolS
Lee, B.-J.
Ant
Li, Dr O.
His, Rel
Macouin, F.
His, AHis
Margolin, J.L.
IR, Eco, His, PolS
Móriot, Prof. CH.
Ant
Orange, Dr M.
Lit, His, IR, Law
Ordonnadu, G.
IR, Eco
Park, H.S.
Eco, PolS
Prost, M.
Lin
Rault-Leyrat, L.R.
His, Rel, Ant, AHis, Ant, Lin, Arch, Phi, His
Ribemont, F.
His, AHis
Rousset, Dr H.A.
CuS, His, Arch, AHis, Ant
Seizelet, E.A.F.
Law, Edu, PolS
Shim, S.-J.
CuS, Lit, GenS
Shin, J.-C.
His, AHis
Simon, Dr J.C.
Soc, IR, His, Eco, DevS, PolS
Sivignon,
Eco, Geo
Suret-Canale, J.
His, PolS
Trân, Q.H.
CuS, Ant
Turcq, Dr D.F.
Eco
Verdilhac, de
Eco
Woronoff, Dr J.A.
Eco, IR, DevS, PolS

Germany

Arnold, M.
Arch, His, AHis
Banaschak, Drs P.
Ant, His, CuS
Brochlos, Dr H.
Lit, Lin
Bronger, Prof. D.
DevS
Cho, Dr M.Y.
PolS
Chung, Dr Y.-S.
His
Dege, Prof. dr E.
Eco, Agr
Eikemeier, Prof. dr D.
His, Rel, Ant, CuS, Lit
Flüchter, Prof. dr W.
Geo, Env
Geisler, Drs G.H.S.
Geo, Env, DevS
Giele, Drs E.
His, Arch
Glatzer, Dr B.
GenS, DevS, CuS, Soc, Ant
Goettingen, Drs D.
PolS, IR
Graevenitz, Prof. dr A. von
Phi, AHis
Haftmann, Drs A.K.
CuS, Lin, Lit
Hager, D.
Eco, IR, PolS
Heberer, Prof. dr Th.
Ant, Rel, DevS, GenS, Eco, PolS, Soc
Heinzig, Dr D.
His, PolS, IR
Herbers-Lee, S.
PolS
Herrmann, Dr W.
Lin
Heuser, Prof. R.
Law
Hofmann, Drs Z.S.
Ant, Rel, Phi, CuS
Hong, Dr E.P.
His, IR
Jakobi, Drs S.
GenS, PolS
Jungmann, Prof. dr B.
AHis
Klenner, Prof. Dr Wolfgang
DevS, Eco
Krebs, Dr G.
Edu, His, PolS, IR
Kuhl, Drs M.
Lin, Phi, CuS, His, AHis, Lit, Rel
Lee, Drs W.-S.
Phi
Lein, Dr A.
DevS, PolS, IR, Eco
Liegl, Dr M.
His, PolS
Lorenz, Prof. D.
Eco
Machetzki, Dr R.
DevS, Eco, PolS
Maull, Prof. H.W.
IR
Menzel, Prof. U.
IR, PolS
Moeller, Dr K.
IR, PolS
Müller, M.
His, AHis
Müller-Hofstede, Drs C.
PolS, Soc, His, IR, CuS, DevS
Nabers, D.
PolS
Paik, Dr S.
Rel, Lit, His, CuS
Pascha, Prof. dr W.
Eco
Pews, Dr H.U.
Eco, DevS, Geo
Pfennig, Dr W.
His, PolS, DevS, IR
Pigulla, Dr A.
His, PolS, IR
Pohl, Prof. dr M.
PolS, His
Prunner, Dr G.
Ant, Rel, CuS
Rentner, Prof. dr R.
Lit
Rohde, Prof. dr K.E.
Soc, Eco, Env, DevS, CuS, IR
Rühle, Mr K.H.
His, Lit, Lin, CuS
Salzmann, Dr B.
Soc
Sasse, Prof. dr W.
Lin, CuS
Schoepe, Dr R.
Lin, Phi
Schulz Zinda, Drs Y.
CuS, Phi
Seckel, Prof. dr D.
His, AHis
Seyock, Drs B.
His, Arch
Stiller, Dr D.F.R.
Law
Trappmann, Drs J.
CuS, Lin, Lit
Unterbeck, Dr B.
Lin
Vogel, Drs K.K.
GenS, PolS
Wein, Dr R.
PolS, His
Zaborowski, Dr H.J.
CuS, His, LitAnt, Rel

Hungary

Bassa, Dr Z.
Eco

Birks, L.
Eco, DevS, Env, Agr, IR

Birtalan, Dr A.
AHis, Rel, Phi, Lit, Lin, His, Arch, GenS

Ehrlich, Prof. E.
Eco, DevS

Fendler, Dr K.
His, PolS, IR, Eco

Hajnal MA, L
Ant, AHis, CuS, Edu, His, Lin, Lit, Rel

Hidasi, Prof. J.
Lin, IR, Edu, Soc, CuS

Illyefalvi-Vitez, Prof. Z.
Edu

Osvath, G.
Rel, CuS, Lin, Lit, Soc

Sato, Drs N.
Edu, Eco

Italy

Campana, Dr A.
His, IR, PolS

Ciarla, Dr R.
His, AHis, CuS, Arch, Ant

Piacentini, Dr P.M.
Eco, DevS

Santangelo, Prof. P.
His

Volpi, G.
PolS, IR, Agr, Eco, Env

Japan

Steffensen, Dr S.K.
Soc, PolS, Eco, DevS

Netherlands

Bastiaansen, Drs A.C.G.M.
IR, Eco, Edu

Borstlap, Drs A.V.
His, AHis

Brinke, Ir H.W. ten
Agr, Edu

Brouwer, A.A.
CuS, Eco, His, IR, PolS, Psy, Rel, Phi

Bruschke-Johnson, Drs L.
AHis

Derveld, Dr F.E.R.
Eco

Dijk, Drs W.O.
Rel, CuS, His, Lin

Dijkstra, Drs G.H.
Soc, Rel, Phi, Eco, His, IR, Psy, PolS

Donker Duyvis, Drs P.
AHis, Arch, Ant, His

Eigenhuijsen, J.Th.N.
Eco

Es, Dr A.J.H. van
Agr

Feddema, Drs R.
PolS, IR, His, Eco

Hamelink, Prof. dr C.J.
IR, Law

Hanssen, Drs L.M.
Ant, CuS

Haringhuizen, Drs W.
PolS, Ant, IR

Hermens, B.
Agr, Env, IR

Hoesel, Drs R. van
Eco

Jehle, Dr E.
IR, DevS, Eco, Edu, Law

Junne, Prof. G.C.A.
IR, DevS, PolS, Env

Kortlandt, Prof. dr F.H.H.
Lin

Lau, W.Y.
SocAHis, CuS

Mensink, Drs O.H.
AHis, Ant, CuS, His

Meredith, Mr P.I.
Art

Meuldijk, Drs I.M.
Soc, Agr, GenS, Env, Ant, DevS

Mierlo, Drs H.W.R. van
Lin, CuS, AHis

Minnee, Drs P.
CuS, IR, Eco, Edu

Olof, Drs A.M.
Rel, Lit

Ommen, Drs A.F. van
IR, PolS

Ondracek, Drs W.F.J.
Lit, Soc

Oosterwijk, A.J.
His, Ant, Arch

Pijl-Ketel, Ch. van der
AHis

Prchal, Drs M.
PolS, His, Rel

Reijnders, Drs T.
AHis

Sanders, Drs M.
DevS, Eco

Schalke, Dr H.J.W.G.
Arch, Ant, Env

Semetko, Prof. dr H.A.
PolS; Soc, Psy

Sinnema, Drs T.
GenS, CuS, Soc, His, Edu

Stam, Prof. dr J.A.
DevS, Eco, IR

Stel, Dr J.H.
Env, Eco

Sybesma, S.
Lin

Tjoa, Drs M.L.M.
His

Verschoor, I.B.
His, Phi, CuS, PolS, Eco

Vos, Prof. dr F.
Rel, Lit, His

Walraven, Prof. dr B.C.A.
His, Lit, Rel, Ant

Welling, Drs K.O.H.
Art

Wiegmans, Drs B.W.
Eco

Poland

Cyrzyk, Drs L.M.
His, IR

Kulig, Prof. J.
Eco, IR

Leszczynski, Prof. L.
Soc, PolS, Law, Eco

Ogarek-Czoj, Dr H.
Rel, Lit

Stachowski, Dr M.
Lin

Winid, Prof. dr B.
PolS, DevS, Env, Geo

Russia

Atknine, V.D.
Lin

Bazhanova, Dr N.Ye.
Eco, His

Chufrin, Dr G.I.
IR, Eco

Gorely, Dr I.O.
His

Gryaznov, Dr G.V.
Eco

Gurevich, Dr E.M.
His, PolS, Phi

Ionova, Dr Yu.V.
Ant

Jarylgassinova, Dr R.Sh.
Ant

Kontsevich, Dr L.R.
Lin, Lit

Kourbanov, Dr S.O.
Soc, CuS, Edu, His, Rel, PhiAgr

Ksenofontova, Dr G.A.
Ant

Kulikova, Dr L. V.
Edu, His

Mazur, Dr Yu.N.
Lin

Mazurov, Dr V.M.
His

Nam, Dr S.G.
CuS

Petrov, Dr A.I.
His

Sinitsyn, Dr B.V.
Eco

Suslina, Dr S.S.
Eco

ASIANISTS BY REGION AND COUNTRY OF INTEREST

Russia

Syomin, Dr A.V.
His, IR, Eco, PolS

Torkunov, Prof. A.
IR

Tsyganov, Dr Y.
Eco, IR

Vanin, Dr Yu.V.
His

Vasilyevitch, Prof. dr T.A.
IR, His

Yakubovsky, Dr V.
Eco, PolS, IR

Spain

Bustelo, Dr P.
DevS, Eco

Canto, Dr P.
DevS, IR, Eco

Castillo Rodriguez, S.
IR

De Llanos Isidoro, P.
His, Lin, Lit, Phi

Garcia, Fernando
AHis, Geo, His, IR, PolS

Garcia-Ormaechea Quero, C.
AHis, Geo, His, Lit, Rel, Phi

Jimenez Valentin, J.M.
Eco, Env, IR

Kim, Drs S.-H.
Arch, Rel, Phi, Lit, His, AHis

Mas Murcia, A.
Eco

Navarro Celada, F.

Ojeda, Dr A.
Law, PolS

Ojeda Marin, Prof. Dr A.
IR, Law

Palazuelos Manso, A.
Eco, Soc

Pastrano, Dr F.
His, IR, Rel, Soc

Rovetta BA, Pablo
Eco, His, IR, Lin, Lit, PolS, Soc

Serrano Valentin, Carlos
Eco, IR

Varela Regueira, Ma del Mar
His, IR

Vilaro Giralt, R.
Eco, IR, PolS

Sweden

Amer, Dr R.
IR, PolS, His

Bryder, Dr H.P.
Ant, Rel

Hammargren, Drs H.A.
PolS, IR, DevS

Huldt, Prof. B.
IR, His

Park, Dr S.-C.
Eco, PolS

Rosen, Prof. S.
Arch, Lin

Sigurdson, Prof. J.
IR, DevS, Eco, PolS

Switzerland

Dunand, F.
His, AHis

Lee, H.
Env, Eco. Edu, CuS

Schmid-Schoenbein, C.
Eco, IR, PolS

Turpin, Dr D.V.
Soc

Wang, Mr D.T.C.
PolS, Law

United Kingdom

Auty, Dr R.M.
DevS, Env, Eco

Barnes, Prof. G.L.
Arch

Bowie, Mr N.J.G.
His, Phi

Bruijn, Drs J.E. de
His, AHis, CuS

Cherry, J.A.
Eco

Choi, D.-J.
PolS

Cockburn, Mr R.C.
DevS, CuS

Cook, M.
Eco

Crosbie, Dr A.J.
IR, Env, Eco, Geo, DevS

Deuchler, Prof. M.
His

Ferdinand, Drs C.I.P.
PolS, DevS, His, Eco, IR

Foot, Dr R.J.
IR

Forfar, D.J.
Ant, Soc, CuS, Rel

Fukasawa, Dr Y.
CuS, Soc, Ant, Arch, His, Lin

Grayson, Dr J.H.
Rel, Ant

Harris, Drs N.
DevS, Eco

Hawthorn, Mr G.P.
IR, DevS, PolS

Hesselink, N.D.
Ant

Hoare, Dr J.E.
IR, His, PolS, CuS

Howard, Dr K.D.
Ant, Rel

Kikuchi, Y.
His, AHis, CuS

King, Prof. U.
Phi, His, Edu, Ant, GenS, CuS, Rel, Soc

Kornicki, Dr P.F.
CuS, His

Lewis, Dr J.B.
His

Li, R.
PolS, IR

Lowe, Dr P.C.
IR, His

McKillop, Drs E.D.
AHis, CuS, Rel, Lit, His

Mirza, Prof. H.R.
DevS, Eco

Mürer, O.H.A.
Arch, His, AHis

Neary, Prof. I.J.
PolS

Nish, Prof. I.H.
PolS, His, IR

Norbury, P.
AHis, Rel, Env, Ant, Arch, His

Pak, Dr Y.S.
Arch, His, AHis

Park, S.S.
Psy, PolS, Phi, SocAHis, DevS, Env, Edu, IR, Law

Picken, Dr L.E.R.
CuS

Provine, Prof. dr R.C.
Lin

Roberts, Drs D.C.
DevS, Eco, IR

Rutt, C.R.
Lit

Saville, Mr A.
Arch

Sheehan, Dr J.
PolS, His

Smith, D.B.
IR, PolS, Eco, His

Starr, Mr D.F.
Phi, Lin

Thompson, Dr J.B.
Ant, Env, Arch

Um, Dr H.K.
AntAnt

Valentin, J.C.P.
Env, Ant, CuS, Lin, His, Arch

Vermeersch, Drs S.A.C.
His, Rel

Wang, H.
His, AHis, Arch, His

Whalley, Dr J.
Eco

Whitfield, Prof. R.
His, AHis

Xinzhong Yao, Dr
Rel, Phi

Yeon, Dr J.H.
Lin, Lit

Yugoslavia
Furundzic , V.
Psy, Rel, Lit, Lin, Edu, His, Phi, AHis

MACAU

Austria
Balzar , Dr D.M.
CuS, His, AHis

Belgium
Della Pietra , B.
IR, His, CuS
Wee , Prof. H.F.A.van der
Eco, His

Czech Republic
Drjnek , Dr V.
IR

Denmark
Ostergaard , Dr C.S.
Agr, Soc, PolS, IR, DevS
Padolecchia Polo , Prof. S.P.
DevS, PolS, Rel, Edu, Eco, Soc, Env, IR, CuS
Thorborg , Dr E.M.
DevS, PolS, Eco, His, GenS

France
Baille , B.
Ant
Bouteiller , E.
DevS, Eco
Briend , M.
AHis
Cheng , S.H.
AHis, CuS, Rel
Collin , H.
Law, Soc, PolS, Eco, IR
Couto , Dr D.
Arch, His, PolS
Henry , R.
Lin, GenS, Env, CuS, AHis, Arch, IR, Lit, Phi, Psy
Lagaune , E.
Ant
Lange , Dr C.
His, Rel, Ant, His, AHis, Soc
Orberger , Dr B.
Lin, Lit, Geo
Ordonnadu , G.
IR, Eco
Rault-Leyrat , L.R.
His, Rel, Ant, AHis, Ant, Lin, Arch, Phi, His
Subrahmanyam , Dr S.
His, Eco
Zheng , Prof. dr Ch.
His, Ant

Germany
Albrecht , E.W.
Eco
Domes , Prof. dr J.
Soc, PolS, DevS
Federlein , Drs D.
His, Lin, Rel
Flüchter , Prof. dr W.
Geo, Env
Heuser , Prof. R.
Law
Jahnke , M.
Law, Eco, CuS
Kraas , Dr F.
Ant, DevS, CuS, Geo
Moeller , Dr K.
IR, PolS
Nieh , Dr Y.H.
PolS, Law, IR, Eco, His
Richter , Dr G.
Lin
Schoepe , Dr R.
Lin, Phi

Hungary
Lukàs , É
AHis, IR, His, CuS

Italy
Sabattini , Drs M.
His, Lit, Lin
Tozzi , Dr D.T.
Soc, His, Eco
Volpi , G.
PolS, IR, Agr, Eco, Env

Netherlands
Abbink , Dr J.
Lin
Bastiaansen , Drs A.C.G.M.
IR, Eco, Edu
Brouwer , A.A.
CuS, Eco, His, IR, PolS, Psy, Rel, Phi
Burght , Prof. dr Gr.
Law
Dishoeck , Drs E.R. van
Eco, Edu, Phi, CuS
Hoetjes , Dr B.J.S.
PolS, IR, Agr, DevS
Jagtenberg , Dr R.W.
Law
Kuiken , Drs C.J.
Rel, Law, CuS
Linden , F.J.W.T. van der
IR, PolS
Ngo , Drs T.-W.
PolS, DevS
Nuijten , Drs I.G.
Phi, Rel
Ommen , Drs A.F. van
IR, PolS
Oosterwijk , A.J.
His, Ant, Arch
Reijnders , Drs T.
AHis
Roo , Dr A.J. de
Law
Sigmond , Dr J.P.
CuS, His, AHis, Arch
Sinnema , Drs T.
GenS, CuS, Soc, His, Edu
Teensma , Dr B.N.
His
Wiechen , P.J. van
AHis, CuS, Ant, Arch, His

Norway
Vaage , T.
PolS

Poland
Zaremba , Dr P.A.
DevS, Env, Eco

Portugal
Flores , Dr J.
His, IR
Guimaraes , Prof. dr A.L.
His
Loureiro , Prof. dr R.M.
His, CuS
Oliveira e Costa , Dr J.P.
His, Rel
Santos Alves , Dr J.M.
His
Telo , Prof. A.J.
His

Russia
Zhogolev , Dr D.A.
PolS, DevS, Soc, Law, Eco, His

Spain
Beltran Antolin , Dr J.
Soc, Ant
Bustelo , Dr P.
DevS, Eco
Castillo Rodriguez , S.
IR
Ceruera Fernández , I.
AHis, His
Esparrago Rodilla MA, Luis
Agr, PolS
Garcia-Ormaechea Quero , C.
AHis, Geo, His, Lit, Rel, Phi
Jimenez Valentin , J.M.
Eco, Env, IR
Martinell Gifre , E.
Lin
Mas Murcia , A.
Eco
Moncé Rebollo , Dr B.
Ant
Pastrano , Dr F.
His, IR, Rel, Soc
Togores Sanchez , L.E.
IR, His

Sweden
Aijmer , Dr L.G.
Ant

Switzerland
Jing Li , A.
IR, PolS
Schmid-Schoenbein , C.
Eco, IR, PolS

United Kingdom

Chapman, G.
His, AHis, CuS

Clarence-Smith, Dr W.G.
His

Edmonds, Dr R.L.
Env, Geo

Hoare, Dr J.E.
IR, His, PolS, CuS

Hook, Dr B.G.
IR, DevS

Jaffer, Dr A.K.H.
CuS, His, AHis

Merrett, Drs N.M.
Lin, Law, Eco, DevS

Park, S.S.
Psy, PolS, Phi, SoaAHis, DevS, Env, Edu, IR, Law

Scammel, Dr G.V.
His

Spencer-Oatey, Dr H.
Lin

TAIWAN

Austria

Lecher, Drs H.E.
His, Soc

Mosch, Dr N.
CuS, Phi

Pilz, Prof. dr E.
His

Sellner, Dr M.B.
CuS, Lin

Zorn, Dr B.
Ant, Arch, Ant, His, AHis

Belgium

Boden, J.
Lin, AHis, Lit, His

Coulie, Prof. dr B.R.R.
AHis, Soc, Lin, Phi, DevS, Ant, Eco, His, Lit

Della Pietra, B.
IR, His, CuS

Fang, Dr S.-S.
CuS, Edu

Heyndrickx, J.J.
Rel

Pape, Mr W.
IR, Law, Eco, PolS

Persoons, Dr M.A.
AHis, Edu, IR, Lin, Phi

Vaerman, Drs B.
GenSAHis, Rel, CuS, His

Vanwalle, Drs I.A.M.A.
AHis, Lin, Lit, Phi, Soc, His

Vearman, Drs B.
PolS

Wu-Beyens, I.CH.
PolS, IR, His, Agr, DevS, Env

Czech Republic

Borotov , Drs L.
Lit, His, AHis

Drịnek, Dr V.
IR

Hulec, Dr O.
His, AHis, CuS, Arch, IR, Eco, Phi, Lit, Lin

Denmark

Baark, Dr E.
His, DevS, Env, CuS

Hornby, J.E.
CuS, AHis

Lauridsen, Prof. L.S.
DevS

Li, X.
DevS, PolS, IR

Littrup, Dr L.
His, Edu

Ostergaard, Dr C.S.
Agr, Soc, PolS, IR, DevS

Thorborg, Dr E.M.
DevS, PolS, Eco, His, GenS

Thunoe, Drs M.
Ant, Lit, Edu, Soc, DevS, CuS, His

Wang, J.
Lin, Lit, CuS, Edu, His, AHis

Worm, Drs V.
Soc, Eco, Ant

Finland

Karunaratne, Dr J.A.
DevS, Eco

Kivimäki, Dr T.A.
PolS, IR, DevS

Seppänen, J.
IR, Eco, Ant, CuS, Lin, His, AHis, Phi, Arch, Rel, PolS

Siika, M.
IR, His

Tähkämaa, Drs J.P.
IR, PolS

France

Alleton, Dr V.A.
Lit, Lin

Aubert, Dr C.
DevS, Agr, Ant, Eco, Soc

Baille, B.
Ant

Balaize, C.
Ant, Agr, CuS, Rel

Barbiche, Prof. dr J.-P.
Law, IR, His, PolS, Eco, DevS, CuS, Edu, Soc

Bastid-Bruguière, M.
His

Billion, R.
His, Phi, Lit, Lin, IR, Edu

Blanchon, Dr F.
His, Arch, His, AHis

Botsch, A.A.
Eco, DevS, IR, Edu, Law

Boully, J.L.
Lit

Bouteiller, E.
DevS, Eco

Brun, Dr C. le
Eco, IR, PolS

Cauquelin, Drs C.J.
Rel, Ant

Chaponniere, Dr J.R.
IR, Eco, PolS, DevS

Cheng, S.H.
AHis, CuS, Rel

Cheng, Dr A.L.
CuS, His, Phi

Cheng, Dr Y.
Soc, Ant

Collin, H.
Law, Soc, PolS, Eco, IR

Coyaud, Dr M.
Ant, Lin

Domenach, Dr J.L.
IR, PolS

Dutrait, N.
Lit

Fouquin, M.F.
Eco

Gipouloux, Dr F.
Eco, Soc

Godement, Prof. dr F.L.
His, IR

Guiheux, Dr G.
Eco, Soc, His

Henry, R.
Lin, GenS, Env, CuS, AHis, Arch, IR, Lit, Phi, Psy

Ho, K.-C.
Lit

Jaussaud, Dr J.
Eco, IR

Kiss, A.
Ant, Phi, Psy

Lagaune, E.
Ant

Lévy, Dr A.
Lit

Margolin, J.L.
IR, Eco, His, PolS

Micollier, Dr E.
Ant

Obringer, Dr F.O.
Ant, His, CuS

Orberger, Dr B.
Lin, Lit, Geo

Ordonnadu, G.
IR, Eco

Pairault, Prof. dr Th.
Eco, Soc, Ant

Papeté, Drs J.F.
Ant, Lin, Rel

Paris, Dr M.C.
Lin

France

Plessis, Drs F.
Lin, Ant

Quiquemelle, M.-C.
His, CuS

Rabusseau, M.
Eco

Rault-Leyrat, L.R.
His, Rel, Ant, AHis, Ant, Lin, Arch, Phi, His

Resche, N.
Ant

Rochat de la Vallee, E.R.
Phi, Lin, Rel

Sabban, F.S.
Agr, Ant, CuS

Sagart, Dr L.
Lin

Simon, Dr J.C.
Soc, IR, His, Eco, DevS, PolS

Sivignon,
Eco, Geo

Tching, K.
Soc

Trân, Q.H.
CuS, Ant

Turcq, Dr D.F.
Eco

Vallette-Hómery, M.
Lit

Wang, Dr F.T.
Rel

Will, Prof. P.-E.
His

Williamson, Dr P.J.
DevS, Eco

Woronoff, Dr J.A.
Eco, IR, DevS, PolS

Zhang, Dr N.
Lit, CuS, Soc, Phi

Zheng, Prof. dr Ch.
His, Ant

Germany

Albrecht, E.W.
Eco

Arnold, M.
Arch, His, AHis

Chiao, Prof. dr W.C.
Phi, Lin, His, Eco

Daberkow, R.
CuS, Lit

Dewall, Dr M.V. von
His, CuS, Arch, Ant, AHis

Doering, Drs O.
Phi

Domes, Prof. dr J.
Soc, PolS, DevS

Draguhn, Dr W.
PolS, IR, Eco, DevS

Eberstein, Prof. dr B.
Lit, Eco

Federlein, Drs D.
His, Lin, Rel

Fischer, D.
PolS, Eco

Flessel, Prof. dr K.
Soc, Lin, His, CuS

Flüchter, Prof. dr W.
Geo, Env

Frankenhauser, Dr U.
Phi, CuS, His, Rel

Friebel, M.
Eco

Gaenszbauer, Dr M.
Lit, GenS, CuS, Rel

Geisler, Drs G.H.S.
Geo, Env, DevS

Giele, Drs E.
His, Arch

Goettingen, Drs D.
PolS, IR

Gransow, Dr B.
Eco, Soc, GenS, PolS, DevS

Güttinger, E.
His, PolS

Halbeisen, Dr H.
PolS

Hana, Dr K.
PolS, His, DevS

Heberer, Prof. dr Th.
Ant, Rel, DevS, GenS, Eco, PolS, Soc

Heilmann, Dr S.
Soc, PolS, IR, His

Henze, Prof. J.
Edu

Herbers-Lee, S.
PolS

Heuser, Prof. R.
Law

Jahnke, M.
Law, Eco, CuS

Jungmann, Prof. dr B.
AHis

Kames, Drs P.
Lit, AHis, CuS, His

Kittlaus, Drs M.
PolS, GenS

Klenner, Prof. Dr Wolfgang
DevS, Eco

Knödel, Dr S.
CuS, GenS

Koerbs, C.
His, Edu, Phi

Koester, Drs K.
Eco

Kott, D.
CuS, His, Law

Kruessmann, Dr I.K.
IR, CuS, Edu, Lit

Lackner, Prof. dr M.
Phi, His

Leutner, Prof. dr M.
GenS, CuS, His

Link, Drs U.A.
Lit, His, Phi

Lipinsky, Drs A.
GenS, Law, DevS

Lippe-Fan, Dr Y.Q. von der
CuS, Lin

Lorenz, Prof. D.
Eco

Machetzki, Dr R.
DevS, Eco, PolS

Martin, Prof. H.
CuS, Lit

Menzel, Prof. U.
IR, PolS

Meyer, Drs S.
CuS, Eco

Meyer-Tran, E.
DevS, Agr, His, Soc, Eco

Mittler, Dr B.
His, Lit, CuS

Moeller, Dr K.
IR, PolS

Müller, M.
His, AHis

Müller, S.
AHis, Ant, CuS, His, Arch

Müller, Dr R.
His, DevS, PolS, Env

Müller-Hofstede, Drs C.
PolS, Soc, His, IR, CuS, DevS

Müller-Saini, Dr G.
His, CuS, Ant, Phi, Rel

Nieh, Dr Y.H.
PolS, Law, IR, Eco, His

Obi, Drs L.
Rel, CuS, Ant

Paulus, A-G.
CuS, DevS, Eco, IR, Lin

Pennarz, Dr J.P.
Ant, DevS

Pigulla, Dr A.
His, PolS, IR

Piontek-Ma, Drs E.
His, CuS, Soc, GenS

Pohl, Prof. dr K.H.
His, CuS, AHis, Phi, Lit, Rel

Prunner, Dr G.
Ant, Rel, CuS

Rackwitz-Ziegler, Drs N.
Lit, CuS, His

Reichenstein, B.
IR, DevS, Eco

Richter, ML
Ant, Arch, AHis, His, Law, Lin, Lit, Phi, Rel

ASIANISTS BY REGION AND COUNTRY OF INTEREST

Germany

Richter, Dr G.
Lin

Riemann, Drs J.
AHis, Arch, CuS, His

Ritter, J.A.
CuS, His

Rohde, Prof. dr K.E.
Soc, Eco, Env, DevS, CuS, IR

Rühle, Mr K.H.
His, Lit, Lin, CuS

Sachsenmaier, Dr D.
Rel, IR, His, CuS

Salzmann, Dr B.
Soc

Schaab-Hanke, Dr D.
PolS, CuS, His

Scharping, Prof. dr Th.
PolS, Soc, Eco

Schillig, Dr D
CuS, Phi, Rel

Schrammel, Drs U.S.
Eco, Env

Senger, Prof. dr H. von
Lit, PolS, Law, CuS

Tesehke, Drs R.
Lin, His

Vittinghoff, Prof. dr H.
CuS, Phi, His

Wädow, Dr. G.
AHis, CuS, His, Rel

Weggel, Dr O.
Law, Rel, Soc, CuS, Phi, Lin, PolS, IR

Weinert, Ch.
Rel, Lit, Soc, CuS

Hungary

Birks, L.
Eco, DevS, Env, Agr, IR

Birtalan, Dr A.
AHis, Rel, Phi, Lit, Lin, His, Arch, GenS

Ehrlich, Prof. E.
Eco, DevS

Hajnal MA, L
Ant, AHis, CuS, Edu, His, Lin, Lit, Rel

Illyefalvi-Vitez, Prof. Z.
Edu

Lukàs, É
AHis, IR, His, CuS

Nyiri, Drs P.D.
Ant, PolS

Sato, Drs N.
Edu, Eco

Tálas, Dr B.
Eco, IR, PolS

Italy

Bertuccioli, Dr G.
Lit, His

Campana, Dr A.
His, IR, PolS

Cavalieri, Dr R.C.
Law, IR, PolS

Ciarla, Dr R.
His, AHis, CuS, Arch, Ant

Corradini, Prof. P.
Law, IR, His

Crespi Reghizzi, Prof. G.
PolS, DevS, IR, Law

Gallio, Dr R.
Law, His

Lanciotti, Prof. L.
Rel, Lit

Marinelli, Dr M.M.
His, IR, PolS, DevS

Orioli, Dr H.
Ant, His, Arch, AHis

Podest, Dr M.
Lin, Rel

Sabattini, Drs M.
His, Lit, Lin

Samarani, G.
His

Sanna, G.
Ant, Lit

Santangelo, Prof. P.
His

Volpi, G.
PolS, IR, Agr, Eco, Env

Netherlands

Bastiaansen, Drs A.C.G.M.
IR, Eco, Edu

Berg, Dr M.E. van den
Lin

Bertsch, Drs H.B.
Soc, Eco

Blom, H.W.
His

Blussé, Dr J.L.
IR, His

Boer, E. de
Soc, Ant, CuS

Boin, Drs M.M.O.
His

Brinke, Ir H.W. ten
Agr, Edu

Brouwer, A.A.
CuS, Eco, His, IR, PolS, Psy, Rel, Phi

Bruijn, E.J. de
His

Bruijninckx, Drs W.P.M.
Eco, IR

Brunt, Prof. dr L.
Ant, Soc

Cheng, Dr S.
His

Cowan, Drs F.M.
GenS, DevS, CuS, Ant, Env, LinAgr

Deng, T.
PolS, Soc, DevS, CuS

Derveld, Dr F.E.R.
Eco

Dijkstra, Drs G.H.
Soc, Rel, Phi, Eco, His, IR, Psy, PolS

Dishoeck, Drs E.R. van
Eco, Edu, Phi, CuS

Dongen, Drs P.L.F. van
His, Ant, AHis

Donker Duyvis, Drs P.
AHis, Arch, Ant, His

Engelfriet, Drs P.M.
His

Es, : r A.J.H. van
Agr

Everts, Drs N.
His

Franse-Hagenbeek, A.A.
Lin

Geense, Drs P.H.A.M.
Edu, Soc

Grant, Dr M.E.
Lit, IR, His, AHis, Rel

Haringhuizen, Drs W.
PolS, Ant, IR

Hendriks, Drs A.P.C.
PolS, IR, Eco, CuS, His

Hintzen, Drs G.H.
IR, Law, Phi, PolS, His

Hoefnagels, Ir H.A.M.
Agr, Eco, Law

Hoesel, Drs R. van
Eco

Hoogenhout, Drs S.
AHis

Huyser, Drs G.L.J.
IR

Idema, Prof. dr W.L.
Lit

Jehle, Dr E.
IR, DevS, Eco, Edu, Law

Kal, Drs W.H.
Env, Lin, DevS, Agr, CuS, Ant, CuS, GenS

Keijser, Drs A.S.
Lit

Kloet, Drs ir B.J.
CuS, Ant, PolS, Soc

Klugkist, Drs C.W.
Edu, CuS, His

Kol, Prof. dr J.
DevS, Eco, Agr

Koolen, Dr G.M.J.M.
Edu, CuS, His, Rel

Kramers, Prof. dr R.P.
Phi, Rel

Lau, W.Y.
SocAHis, CuS

Li, Dr Y.
Law

ASIANISTS BY REGION AND COUNTRY OF INTEREST

Netherlands

Lie, Drs H.
Eco, Ant

Linden, F.J.W.T. van der
IR, PolS

Mierlo, Drs H.W.R. van
Lin, CuS, AHis

Minnee, Drs P.
CuS, IR, Eco, Edu

Ngo, Drs T.-W.
PolS, DevS

Nuijten, Drs I.G.
Phi, Rel

Ommen, Drs A.F. van
IR, PolS

Oosterwijk, A.J.
His, Ant, Arch

Prchal, Drs M.
PolS, His, Rel

Ruizendaal, Drs R.E.
Ant, Rel

Schalke, Dr H.J.W.G.
Arch, Ant, Env

Schipper, Prof. dr K.M.
Rel, Ant, His

Schoch, Drs G.W.
Eco

Schottenhammer, Dr A.
Phi, His, Eco, PolS

Semetko, Prof. dr H.A.
PolS, Soc, Psy

Sigmond, Dr J.P.
CuS, His, AHis, Arch

Sinnema, Drs T.
GenS, CuS, Soc, His, Edu

Sodderland, Mr J.W.
Law

Spiekerman-Middelplaats, M.Y.M.
Env

Stam, Prof. dr J.A.
DevS, Eco, IR

Sy-A-Foek, I.D.S.
PolS, Law, DevS

Sybesma, Dr R.P.E.
Lin

Tan, I.H.
AHis

Vaczi, Drs M.T.
Rel, AHis, GenS, CuS

Velde, Drs P.G.E.I.J. van der
Lit, His

Vermeer, Dr E.B.
His, Env, DevS, Agr, Eco

Vermeulen, Drs A.C.J.
His

Verschoor, I.B.
His, Phi, CuS, PolS, Eco

Wiedenhof, Dr J.M.
Lin

Wu, J.Y.T.
Lit

Zeeuw, D. de
Env, Agr

Norway

Buen, J.
PolS

Eifring, Prof. H.
Lit, Lin, CuS

Liao, R.
IR, DevS, PolS, AHis

Sauarlia, Dr L
Ant

Vaage, T.
PolS

Wellens, K.
Ant, Rel, Lit

Westad, Dr O.A.
His, IR

Poland

Cyrzyk, Drs L.M.
His, IR

Kulig, Prof. J.
Eco, IR

Tomala, Dr K.
PolS, Soc, Phi, Edu

Zaremba, Dr P.A.
DevS, Env, Eco

Portugal

Oliveira e Costa, Dr J.P.
His, Rel

Rumania

Liushnea, Dr D.S.
DevS, Eco, IR, PolS

Russia

Alexakhina, Dr S.N.
Eco, Agr

Alexakhina, Prof. dr A.
Edu, Lin

Borokh, Dr O.
Eco

Choudodeyev, Dr J.V.
His

Fadeeva, Dr E.Y.
Phi, Soc, CuS, Rel, Lit

Gelbras, Dr V.G.
PolS, Eco, Soc

Gudoshnikov, Prof. dr L.M.
PolS, Law

Gurevich, Dr E.M.
His, PolS, Phi

Kozlov, Dr A.A.
His, Eco

Larin, Dr A G
His, IR

Lomanov, Dr A.V.
Phi

Menshikov, Lev.
His, Rel, Lit

Onikienko, Dr A.
Eco, DevS

Petrov, Dr A.I.
His

Roukodelnicova, M.B.
Lin

Solomonik, Dr I.N.
His, AHis

Sorokin, Dr V.F.
Lit, CuS

Usov, Dr V.N.
His

Yakubovsky, Dr V.
Eco, PolS, IR

Zhogolev, Dr D.A.
PolS, DevS, Soc, Law, Eco, His

Slovenia

Carnogurska, Dr M.
Rel, Phi

Hatalov, Dr H.
PolS, His

Rosker, Dr J.
Phi, Rel, GenS, Soc, PolS

Spain

Albarrán Serrano, Antonio
Lit

Anton Burgos, Dr F.J.
Geo

Beltran Antolin, Dr J.
Soc, Ant

Bustelo, Dr P.
DevS, Eco

Canto, Dr P.
DevS, IR, Eco

Casares Vidal, D.
Eco

Castillo Rodriguez, S.
IR

De Llanos Isidoro, P.
His, Lin, Lit, Phi

Delage, F.
IR, PolS

Esparrago Rodilla MA, Luis
Agr, PolS

Fernández Miguélez, J.
IR

Fisac Badell, Dr T.
Lit, GenS

Garcia, Fernando
AHis, Geo, His, IR, PolS

Garcia Erviti, J.
ECONOMIA

Garmendia Herrero, E.
His

Gastllo Martinez, J.V.
Eco, Geo, Lin

Golden, Prof. S.
CuS, Phi, Lit

Hu Sun, P.-S.
Lit

Jimenez Valentin, J.M.
Eco, Env, IR

Spain
Kim, Drs S.-H.
Arch, Rel, Phi, Lit, His, AHis
Lee Jen, W.-T.
Lin
Lopez Sastre, G.
Phi
Marco Mart¡nez, Dr C.
Lin
Marco Martínez, Consuelo
Lin
Mas Murcia, A.
Eco
Montero Moreno, J.
His, Lit, Rel
Navarro Celada, F.
Ojeda Marin, Prof. Dr A.
IR, Law
Olle Rodriguez, M.M.
His
Palazuelos Manso, A.
Eco, Soc
Pastrano, Dr F.
His, IR, Rel, Soc
Rovetta Dubinsky, Pablo
Eco, Env, IR, Lin, PolS
Serrano Valentin, Carlos
Eco, IR
Togores Sanchez, L.E.
IR, His
Vilaro Giralt, R.
Eco, IR, PolS
Wang-Tang, L.J.
Lin

Sweden
Aijmer, Dr L.G.
Ant
Amer, Dr R.
IR, PolS, His
Bryder, Dr H.P.
Ant, Rel
Gao, J.
AHis, Phi, Lit, CuS, His
Johansson, Drs P.J.
CuS, His
Kaikkonen, Dr M.
Lit
Malmqvist, Prof. N.G.D.
Lin, CuS, Lit
Park, Dr S.-C.
Eco, PolS
Sigurdson, Prof. J.
IR, DevS, Eco, PolS

Switzerland
Billeter, Prof. J.F.
Lit, His, Phi, Rel
Findeisen, Dr R.D.
Phi, GenS, Lit
Jing Li, A.
IR, PolS
Kinzelbach, Prof. dr W.K.H.
Env
Lin, C.-W.
CuS, Psy, Ant
Schmutz, G.M.
Soc, Ant, Edu
Thölen, Drs K.
Arch, His, AHis, Lit
Zhang, Dr W.
IR

United Kingdom
Ansorge, Drs C.A.
His, Arch, CuS, Rel, Lit, Phi
Auty, Dr R.M.
DevS, Env, Eco
Baker, Prof. dr H.D.R.
Law, Lin, Ant, His, CuS, Lit, Rel
Barnes, Prof. G.L.
Arch
Berg, Dr D.D.
Lit, His, GenS
Carswell, Prof. J.W.
AHis, CuS, His
Chapman, G.
His, AHis, CuS
Chard, Dr R.
His, Rel
Clunas, Dr C.
His, Arch, His, AHis, CuS
Crosbie, Dr A.J.
IR, Env, Eco, Geo, DevS
Deacon, Mr A.G.
His, Phi
Deckers, Drs W.
IR, DevS, PolS
Donald, S.
PolS, GenS, CuS, His, AHis
Edmonds, Dr R.L.
Env, Geo
Elliott, D.
AHis
Ferdinand, Drs C.I.P.
PolS, DevS, His, Eco, IR
Feuchtwang, Dr S.
Ant, Soc, Rel, His, DevS, CuS, PolS
Foot, Dr R.J.
IR
Harris, Drs N.
DevS, Eco
Helliwell, Drs D.J.
AHis, CuS, Rel
Hoare, Dr J.E.
IR, His, PolS, CuS
Hook, Dr B.G.
IR, DevS
King, Prof. U.
Phi, His, Edu, Ant, GenS, CuS, Rel, Soc
Kirkby, Dr R.J.R.
Eco, DevS, Env
Lancashire, Prof. R.D.
Lit, Rel
Lewis, Dr M.E.
Arch, His, Lin, Ant
Li, R.
PolS, IR
Li, Dr W.
Lin, Edu, Psy
Lightfoot, Drs S.
AHis
Liu, Drs T.T.
Lit
Lowe, Dr P.C.
IR, His
MacFadyean, Dr N.J.
Eco, His
Merrett, Drs N.M.
Lin, Law, Eco, DevS
Neary, Prof. I.J.
PolS
Nossiter, Prof. T.J.
Soc, PolS, IR, DevS, His
Park, S.S.
Psy, PolS, Phi, SocAHis, DevS, Env, Edu, IR, Law
Picken, Dr L.E.R.
CuS
Pieke, Dr F.N.
Ant
Riddington, P.
Lin, Edu
Roberts, Drs D.C.
DevS, Eco, IR
Spencer-Oatey, Dr H.
Lin
Steeds, Mr D.
IR, His
Valentin, J.C.P.
Env, Ant, CuS, Lin, His, Arch
Whalley, Dr J.
Eco
Whitfield, Prof. R.
His, AHis
Wu, Dr W.-P.
Eco, CuS
Xinzhong Yao, Dr
Rel, Phi
Zhao, Dr H.Y.H.
CuS

Yugoslavia
Furundzic, V.
Psy, Rel, Lit, Lin, Edu, His, Phi, AHis

Central Asia

AFGHANISTAN

Austria
Allinger, Dr E.
Rel, His, CuS, Arch, AHis

Belgium
Alphen, J. van
AHis, Ant, Lin, His
Cordier, Mr B. de
IR, His, PolS
Gonzalo Castellanos, Dr A.
IR
Vielle, Dr CH.
Lin, Lit, Rel

Czech Republic
Hruska, Prof. dr B.
Agr, His, Lit, Rel, Arch

Denmark
Ferdinand, K.
DevS, Ant, CuS
Javed, M.A.
CuS, Rel, IR, Soc
Morch, M.J.V.
Ant

France
Athari, Drs D.
Ant, Soc, DevS
Balland, Dr D.
Agr, Ant, Geo
Berinstain, Dr Vallerie
AHis, His
Berthier, A.
His, Rel, Phi, CuS, Lit, His, AHis, Lin
Bertille, Drs.
Arch
Besenval, R.
Arch
Cambon, P.
His
Francfort, H.P.
Arch
Gentelle, Dr P.P.
Env, Arch, Geo
Heide, Dr S. von der
Ant, DevSAHis, Env, CuS, Rel, PolS
Jarrige, J.F.
His, CuS, Arch, AHis
Kroell, Dr A.
His
Raczka, Prof. W.
DevS, Eco, His, PolS, IR
Reichert, P.
Lin
Roy, O.
PolS
Sandouk, Drs S.
Phi, His, Lit, Rel
Subrahmanyam, Dr S.
His, Eco

Germany
Baloch, Dr I.
PolS, CuS, His
Buddruss, Prof. G.A.
His, Rel, Lin, Ant, CuS, Lit
Casimir, Prof. dr M.J.
Psy, Arch, Ant, His, GenS, Agr
Degener, Dr A.C.
Rel, Lin
Fragner, Prof. B.G.
Lin, Lit, His, CuS
Glatzer, Dr B.
GenS, DevS, CuS, Soc, Ant
Gropp, Dr G.C.A.
Phi, Lit, His, Rel, Arch, AHis, CuS, Ant, Lin
Grötzbach, Prof. dr E.
Rel, Geo, CuS
Kaiser, Drs M.
DevS, Ant, Soc, PolS
Kohl MA, Arko
His, PolS, Soc
Kreutzmann, Prof. dr H.J.
Agr, DevS, Ant
Krüger, Prof. dr H.
IR, Law, Rel, Soc, Eco
Kügelgen, Dr A. von
Rel, Lit, His, Edu, CuS, Phi
Plaeschke, Dr H.
AHis, Arch
Plaeschke, Dr I.
His, Arch, AHis
Rao, Dr A.
Psy, DevS, Env, His, Ant, GenS
Raunig, Prof. dr W.
AHis, Ant, Arch, His
Rüdiger, Drs A.
Soc, Rel, CuS, IR, PolS
Schmitt, Prof. dr R.
Lin, His
Schoepe, Dr R.
Lin, Phi
Schweinfurth, Prof. dr U.
Agr, DevS, Env, Arch, IR
Yaldiz, Prof. dr M.
Arch, His, AHis, Rel

Hungary
Dobrovits, Drs M.A.
Rel, Lit, CuS, His, Ant

Italy
Ferraro, Dr F.
Lin, Ant
Nicolini, Dr B
His, PolS
Podest, Dr M.
Lin, Rel
Raza, Dr R.
His, Lit, IR
Rossi, Prof. A.V.
Rel, PolS, Lin, Arch, Ant

Netherlands
Bekius, Drs R.A.
Agr, Ant, Env, DevS, Eco
Bruinessen, Dr M.M. van
Rel, His, Ant
Buskens, Dr L.P.H.M.
Ant, His, Law, AHis, Rel
Farooqi, Drs K.H.
Rel, CuS, Soc, His, GenS, Env, DevS
Gommans, Dr J.J.L.
His
Guyt, Drs H.J.
His, IR, AHis, Lin, CuS, DevS
Hanssen, Drs L.M.
Ant, CuS
Hulst, W.A.
Eco
Immig, Drs O.I.
Soc, His, IR, Rel, Eco, PolS
Koesoebjono, R.H.S.I.
DevS, GenS, Eco
Lingen, Ing J.
His
Meijs, Drs M.A.G.
IR, Rel, Ant, CuS
Meulenbeld, Drs B.C.
CuS, His, Ant, AHis, Rel, Arch
Mohkamsing, Drs N.
Rel, AHis, Lit, Phi
Suringa, Mr P.
Law, AHis, Lit, IR, His, Phi, His, Edu, CuS, DevS, Eco, PolS
Tütüncü, Drs M.
CuS, DevS, Env, Lit, Lin, His
Visser, Drs T.
CuS, Ant
Vogelsang, Dr W.J.
Lin, His, Arch, Rel, AHis

Norway
Barth, Dr F.
DevS, Ant
Kristiansen, Prof. K.
Rel, CuS, Lin, Lit

Poland
Debnicki, Dr K.
PolS, IR, His
Jamsheer, Prof. H.
IR, His, PolS, Rel
Wawrzyniak, Dr A.
CuS, Ant

Russia
Aliev, Prof. S.M.
His, CuS, Rel
Aristova, Dr L.B.
Eco, Edu
Arunova, Dr M.R.
His
Belokrenitsky, Dr V.Y.
Soc, PolS, His, IR
Davydov, Dr A.D.
Eco
Grigoriev, Dr S.E.
CuS, IR, PolS
Guerassimova, Dr A.S.
Lit
Kharatischoily, G.S.
His

Russia
Khashimbekov, Dr Kh.
His
Korgun, Dr V.G.
His
Lagashova, Dr B.-R.
Ant
Mahkamov, Dr M.
His
Moskalenko, Prof. V.N.
His, IR
Pelevin, Dr M.S.
Lin, Lit
Plastun, Dr V.N.
His
Polonskaya, Dr L.R.
Rel, His
Sedov, Dr A. V.
Arch
Stebline-Kamensky, Prof. dr I.M.
Lin, Lit, Rel
Zaitsev, Dr V.N.
His, Lit

Spain
Elías de Tejada Lozano, Diplomat F.
Eco, Lit, PolS
Garcia-Ormaechea Quero, C.
AHis, Geo, His, Lit, Rel, Phi

Sweden
Hammargren, Drs H.A.
PolS, IR, DevS
Utas, Prof. B.
Rel, Lit, His, Lin, CuS

Switzerland
Bucherer-Dietschi, P.
His, CuS, IR
Centlivres, Prof. P.
CuS, Ant
Djalili, Dr M.R.
CuS, Soc, His, IR, DevS, PolS
Etienne, Prof. G.
His, Agr, Eco, PolS, DevS
Hussain, W.
CuS, Eco, His, IR, PolS, Rel

United Kingdom
Burton, Drs J.A.
His, IR
Coningham, Dr R.A.E.
Arch, Ant, CuS, His, AHis
Giustozzi, A.
PolS, IR, His
Harriss, Dr J.C.
DevS, Ant
Johnson, Dr G.
His
Jones, Dr R.M.
Ant
Jones, Dr S.
Ant
Mac Dowal, Prof. dr D.W.
Arch, AHis
Marr, Dr J.R.
Lin, His, CuS, Arch, His, Phi, Rel, AHis, Lit
Miles, M.
DevS, Edu
Picken, Dr L.E.R.
CuS
Roper, Dr G.J.
CuS
Steeds, Mr D.
IR, His

KAZACHSTAN

Belgium
Alphen, J. van
AHis, Ant, Lin, His
Cordier, Mr B. de
IR, His, PolS

Denmark
Mozaffari-Mehdi, Prof. M.M.
PolS, Rel, IR
Odgaard, Drs K.
Ant
Padolecchia Polo, Prof. S.P.
DevS, PolS, Rel, Edu, Eco, Soc, Env, IR, CuS
Pedersen, Prof. dr P.
His, CuS, Ant, Phi, Psy, Rel, Env
Simonsen, J.
Ant

France
Barbiche, Prof. dr J.-P.
Law, IR, His, PolS, Eco, DevS, CuS, Edu, Soc
Berthier, A.
His, Rel, Phi, CuS, Lit, His, AHis, Lin
Debaine-Francfort, Dr C.
Arch
Francfort, H.P.
Arch
Raczka, Prof. W.
DevS, Eco, His, PolS, IR
Radvanyi, Prof. dr J.
Eco, Geo
Roy, O.
PolS

Germany
Baloch, Dr I.
PolS, CuS, His
Brentjes, Prof. dr B.
AHis, Arch, Env
Fragner, Prof. B.G.
Lin, Lit, His, CuS
Gropp, Dr G.C.A.
Phi, Lit, His, Rel, Arch, AHis, CuS, Ant, Lin
Heinzig, Dr D.
His, PolS, IR
Kaiser, Drs M.
DevS, Ant, Soc, PolS
Kraas, Dr F.
Ant, DevS, CuS, Geo
Kreiser, Prof. Dr Klaus
AHis, CuS, His
Krüger, Prof. dr H.
IR, Law, Rel, Soc, Eco
Kügelgen, Dr A. von
Rel, Lit, His, Edu, CuS, Phi
Malik, Dr J.
His, Rel, CuS, Edu, His, Lit
Schmitt, Prof. dr R.
Lin, His
Schmitz, Dr A.
Rel, Ant, Lit, PolS, CuS, Soc, His
Stellrecht, Prof. dr I.
His, Ant, Rel

Hungary
Birtalan, Dr A.
AHis, Rel, Phi, Lit, Lin, His, Arch, GenS
Dobrovits, Drs M.A.
Rel, Lit, CuS, His, Ant

Italy
Campana, Dr A.
His, IR, PolS
Crespi Reghizzi, Prof. G.
PolS, DevS, IR, Law
Nicolini, Dr B
His, PolS
Podest, Dr M.
Lin, Rel
Raza, Dr R.
His, Lit, IR

Netherlands
Atabaki, Dr T.
PolS, His
Barendse, Dr R.J.
His, Eco
Bekius, Drs R.A.
Agr, Ant, Env, DevS, Eco
Bläsing, Dr U.
Lit, Lin
Es, Dr A.J.H. van
Agr
Gautam, Dr M.K.
Rel, Soc, Lit, Lin, His, Ant, CuS, PolS, Env
Ginkel, Drs W.T. van
His, Geo, IR
Groot, Dr A.H. de
Lit, IR, Rel, His
Guyt, Drs H.J.
His, IR, AHis, Lin, CuS, DevS
Hulst, W.A.
Eco
Jehle, Dr E.
IR, DevS, Eco, Edu, Law
Kouwen, H.J.
His, IR, DevS, Ant
Meijs, Drs M.A.G.
IR, Rel, Ant, CuS

Netherlands

Minnema, Mr H.E.

Law

Pinkers, Ir M.J.H.P.

IR, DevS, EduAgr

Steringa, F.A.

His, CuS

Straten, Mr H.M. van

Env, Ant, Law

Suringa, Mr P.

Law, AHis, Lit, IR, His, Phi, His, Edu, CuS, DevS, Eco, PolS

Tütüncü, Drs M.

CuS, DevS, Env, Lit, Lin, His

Vandamme, Dr M.R.C.A.

Lin, Lit

Visser, Drs T.

CuS, Ant

Vogelsang, Dr W.J.

Lin, His, Arch, Rel, AHis

Weitenberg, Drs F.S.J.J.

Rel, Env, Arch, Soc

Weststeijn, Prof. dr W.G.

Lit, CuS

Witkam, Dr J.J.

His, Rel, Lit

Poland

Jamsheer, Prof. H.

IR, His, PolS, Rel

Jankowski, Prof. H.

Lin

Stachowski, Dr M.

Lin

Rumania

Liushnea, Dr D.S.

DevS, Eco, IR, PolS

Russia

Aristova, Dr L.B.

Eco, Edu

Belokrenitsky, Dr V.Y.

Soc, PolS, His, IR

Dobronravin, Dr N.A.

Lin, Rel, Lit, His, Ant

Dybo, Dr Prof. A. V.

Ant, Lin

Kirabaev, Dr N.S.

Phi

Korimushin, Prof. dr I. V.

Ant, Arch, Lin

Kurylev, Dr V.P.

CuS, Ant

Landa, Dr L.Y.

His, Soc, PolS

Malashenko, Prof. A.V.

Rel, PolS

Morozova, Dr M. Yu

GenS, Agr, Eco, Env

Musayev, Prof. dr K. M.

Lin

Naumkin, Dr V.

Rel, PolS, IR, His, Ant

Niyazi, Dr A.

Env, Rel, PolS

Prazauskas, Dr A.A.

Rel, His, PolS

Stebline-Kamensky, Prof. dr I.M.

Lin, Lit, Rel

Tambovtsev, Prof. dr Y.A.

Lin

Tenishev, Dr Prof. E. R.

Ant, Lin, Lit

Tesselkine, Dr A.S.

Ant, AHis, Lin, His, CuS

Vasilyev, Dr D.

Arch, Rel, Lin, AHis, Ant

Vassiliev, Prof. A.

Rel, PolS, IR, His

Vidiassova, Dr M.F.

Soc, PolS, His, Eco, DevS

Zviagelskaia, Dr I.D.

IR, PolS

Spain

Berceló Mezquita, Dr J.L.

Env, His, PolS, Soc

Comas Montoya, Dr R.

AHis, His

Fernández Miguélez, J.

IR

Sweden

Hammargren, Drs H.A.

PolS, IR, DevS

Switzerland

Djalili, Dr M.R.

CuS, Soc, His, IR, DevS, PolS

Turkey

Bolukbasi, Dr S.

IR, PolS

United Kingdom

Burton, Drs J.A.

His, IR

Carswell, Prof. J.W.

AHis, CuS, His

Ferdinand, Drs C.I.P.

PolS, DevS, His, Eco, IR

Hull, Mr S.J.

Law

KöK, Dr H.

IR

Lewis, Dr D.C.

Rel, Ant, CuS

Marr, Dr J.R.

Lin, His, CuS, Arch, His, Phi, Rel, AHis, Lit

Park, S.S.

Psy, PolS, Phi, SocAHis, DevS, Env, Edu, IR, Law

Picken, Dr L.E.R.

CuS

Roper, Dr G.J.

CuS

Shepperdson, Mr M.J.

DevS, Agr, Eco, PolS, Soc

Um, Dr H.K.

AntAnt

KIRGIZISTAN

Germany

Kreiser, Prof. Dr Klaus

AHis, CuS, His

Italy

Nicolini, Dr B

His, PolS

Russia

Dybo, Dr Prof. A. V.

Ant, Lin

Korimushin, Prof. dr I. V.

Ant, Arch, Lin

Musayev, Prof. dr K. M.

Lin

Tenishev, Dr Prof. E. R.

Ant, Lin, Lit

Spain

Berceló Mezquita, Dr J.L.

Env, His, PolS, Soc

Comas Montoya, Dr R.

AHis, His

Fernández Miguélez, J.

IR

Rodriguez-Eiras, J.A.

Agr, Eco, Edu, Env, His, Soc

Turkey

Bolukbasi, Dr S.

IR, PolS

United Kingdom

Bakewell, Mr A.D.

KöK, Dr H.

IR

MONGOLIA

Austria

Allinger, Dr E.

Rel, His, CuS, Arch, AHis

Loseries, Dr A.S.

His, Rel, CuS, Phi, His, AHis, DevS, Ant

Much, Dr M.T.W.

Phi, Rel

Sellner, Dr M.B.

CuS, Lin

Sichrovsky, Prof. H.

CuS, His, PolS, IR

Belgium

Cordier, Mr B. de

IR, His, PolS

Hanibal, Mr J.

IR, PolS

Bulgaria

Fedotoff, Prof. dr A.

Rel, Lit, CuS

Czech Republic

Hulec, Dr O.

His, AHis, CuS, Arch, IR, Eco, Phi, Lit, Lin

Czech Republic

Liscák, Dr V.
Rel, His, Phi, Lin, CuS

Vacek, Prof. dr J.
Phi, Rel, Lit, Lin

Denmark

Baark, Dr E.
His, DevS, Env, CuS

Bruun, Drs O.
Ant

Ferdinand, K.
DevS, Ant, CuS

Magnussen, Drs T.
DevS, IR, PolS

Mozaffari-Mehdi, Prof. M.M.
PolS, Rel, IR

Ostergaard, Dr C.S.
Agr, Soc, PolS, IR, DevS

Padolecchia Polo, Prof. S.P.
DevS, PolS, Rel, Edu, Eco, Soc, Env, IR, CuS

Pedersen, Prof. dr P.
His, CuS, Ant, Phi, Psy, Rel, Env

Estonia

Kark, M.
CuS, Lin, Phi, AHis, Rel, Edu

Finland

Aalto, Prof. dr P.
His, DevS

Janhunen, Prof. dr J.A.
AHis, CuS, Ant, Arch, Lin

France

Aubin, F.
Soc, Law, His

Berthier, A.
His, Rel, Phi, CuS, Lit, His, AHis, Lin

Cheng, S.H.
AHis, CuS, Rel

Collin, H.
Law, Soc, PolS, Eco, IR

Coyaud, Dr M.
Ant, Lin

Hamayon, Dr R.N.
Rel, Lin, Ant

Legrand, Prof. J.
Lin, His

Ordonnadu, G.
IR, Eco

Raczka, Prof. W.
DevS, Eco, His, PolS, IR

Sabban, F.S.
Agr, Ant, CuS

Trân, Q.H.
CuS, Ant

Germany

Alt, Drs B.
Rel, Lin, Phi

Federlein, Drs D.
His, Lin, Rel

Frankenhauser, Dr U.
Phi, CuS, His, Rel

Georg, Dr S.
Lin

Goettingen, Drs D.
PolS, IR

Gropp, Dr G.C.A.
Phi, Lit, His, Rel, Arch, AHis, CuS, Ant, Lin

Heberer, Prof. dr Th.
Ant, Rel, DevS, GenS, Eco, PolS, Soc

Heinzig, Dr D.
His, PolS, IR

Heissig, Prof. dr W.
Lit, Rel, His

Henze, Prof. J.
Edu

Kahlen, Prof. W.
Rel, Ant, AHis

Kollmar-Paulenz, K.
His, Ant, Lit, Rel, CuS

Kraas, Dr F.
Ant, DevS, CuS, Geo

Lauer, Drs U.
AHis

Linder Sabine, Drs L.
Ant, Arch, Soc

Moeller, Dr K.
IR, PolS

Müller, M.
His, AHis

Müller, S.
AHis, Ant, CuS, His, Arch

Pews, Dr H.U.
Eco, DevS, Geo

Rennert, Drs H.
Lin, Lit, His, CuS, His, Phi, Rel, AHis

Sagaster, Prof. dr K.
Rel, Phi, Lit, Lin, His, AHis, CuS, His

Schmitz, Dr A.
Rel, Ant, Lit, PolS, CuS, Soc, His

Schoepe, Dr R.
Lin, Phi

Siemers, Drs G.
PolS, IR, Eco

Skyhawk, H. von
Phi, Rel, Ant, Lit, CuS

Stahlberg, Drs S.M.
CuS, DevS, His, Lin, Soc, PolS

Zhang, Drs V.
CuS, His

Zieme, Dr P.
Rel

Hungary

Birtalan, Dr A.
AHis, Rel, Phi, Lit, Lin, His, Arch, GenS

Dobrovits, Drs M.A.
Rel, Lit, CuS, His, Ant

Hajnal MA, L
Ant, AHis, CuS, Edu, His, Lin, Lit, Rel

Porció, Drs T.
Lit, Rel, CuS

Toth, E
CuS, Edu, His, Lin, Lit, Phi, Psy, Rel, Soc

Vinkovics, Dr J.
His, Lin, AHis

Italy

Campana, Dr A.
His, IR, PolS

Ciarla, Dr R.
His, AHis, CuS, Arch, Ant

Crespi Reghizzi, Prof. G.
PolS, DevS, IR, Law

Mortarivergaracaffarelli, Prof. P.
Arch, AHis

Tozzi, Dr D.T.
Soc, His, Eco

Volpi, G.
PolS, IR, Agr, Eco, Env

Netherlands

Asselbergs, Drs G.
Agr, Eco, Edu

Bläsing, Dr U.
Lit, Lin

Germeraad, Dr ir P.W.
Env, Ant, CuS

Ginkel, Drs W.T. van
His, Geo, IR

Grent, P.C.M.
CuS, Lin, Lit, Rel, Phi

Guyt, Drs H.J.
His, IR, AHis, Lin, CuS, DevS

Kortlandt, Prof. dr F.H.H.
Lin

Kouwen, H.J.
His, IR, DevS, Ant

Mierlo, Drs H.W.R. van
Lin, CuS, AHis

Minnema, Mr H.E.
Law

Nooijens, Drs A.I.
IR, PolS, His

Semetko, Prof. dr H.A.
PolS, Soc, Psy

Spengen, Dr W. van
Geo, Ant, His

Strik, Prof. B.
CuS

Tütüncü, Drs M.
CuS, DevS, Env, Lit, Lin, His

Verhagen, Dr P.C.
Rel, Lin, Lit, Phi

Voogd, Drs P. de
DevS, GenS, Soc, Edu

Welling, Drs K.O.H.
Art

Poland

Bareja-Starzynska, Drs A.
Rel, Lin, His, Lit

Jankowski, Prof. H.
Lin

Olbrys, Drs M.
Lin, Lit

Stachowski, Dr M.
Lin

Rumania

Liushnea, Dr D.S.
DevS, Eco, IR, PolS

Russia

Boikova, Dr E.V.
IR, His, CuS

Boikova, Dr Ye.V.
His, CuS

Dybo, Dr Prof. A. V.
Ant, Lin

Gerasimovich, Prof. dr L.K.
His, Rel

Golman, Dr M.I.
His

Graivoronsky, Dr V.V.
His

Korimushin, Prof. dr I. V.
Ant, Arch, Lin

Nadirov, Dr Sh.G.
IR, PolS

Narmaev, Dr B.M.
Rel, Lit

Orlovskaya, Dr M.N.
Lin

Ostrovskaya, E.A.
Rel, Phi, Soc

Piurbeer, Prof. G. T.
Lin

Roshchin, Dr S.K.
Eco, His

Slesarchuk, Dr G.I.
His

Sofronov, Prof. dr M.V.
Ant, Arch, Lin, Lit

Solntsev, Prof. dr V.M.
Lin

Tambovtsev, Prof. dr Y.A.
Lin

Tsendina, Dr A.D.
Lit

Vasilyev, Dr D.
Arch, Rel, Lin, AHis, Ant

Yaskina, Dr G.S.

Yatskovskaya, K.N.
Lit

Zhukovskaya, Dr N.L.
Ant

Slovenia

Ceplak-Mencin, Dr R.
CuS, Ant

Spain

Albarrán Serrano, Antonio
Lit

Berceló Mezquita, Dr J.L.
Env, His, PolS, Soc

Castillo Rodriguez, S.
IR

Comas Montoya, Dr R.
AHis, His

Fernandez Lommen, Dr Y.
Eco

Garcia-Ormaechea Quero, C.
AHis, Geo, His, Lit, Rel, Phi

Gil, Prof. J.
His, Lit

Kim, Drs S.-H.
Arch, Rel, Phi, Lit, His, AHis

Rodriguez-Eiras, J.A.
Agr, Eco, Edu, Env, His, Soc

Sweden

Bryder, Dr H.P.
Ant, Rel

Hammargren, Drs H.A.
PolS, IR, DevS

Svantesson, J.O.
Lin

Switzerland

Ducor, Dr J.
Rel, Ant, GenS

Heller, Dr A.
CuS, AHis, Rel, His

Oppitz, Prof. M.
Rel, Ant

United Kingdom

Ansorge, Drs C.A.
His, Arch, CuS, Rel, Lit, Phi

Carswell, Prof. J.W.
AHis, CuS, His

Chapman, G.
His, AHis, CuS

Coleman, Drs G.
DevS

Fukasawa, Dr Y.
CuS, Soc, Ant, Arch, His, Lin

Hoare, Dr J.E.
IR, His, PolS, CuS

Humphrey, Dr C.
Ant, Env, Rel, Soc

King, Prof. U.
Phi, His, Edu, Ant, GenS, CuS, Rel, Soc

KöK, Dr H.
IR

Lewis, Dr D.C.
Rel, Ant, CuS

Lowe, Dr P.C.
IR, His

Park, S.S.
Psy, PolS, Phi, SocAHis, DevS, Env, Edu, IR, Law

Picken, Dr L.E.R.
CuS

Strickland, Dr S.S.
Ant

Valentin, J.C.P.
Env, Ant, CuS, Lin, His, Arch

Wickham-Smith, Drs S.J.S.
Lin, Rel

United States of America

Khoo, Drs M.J.
Rel, Arch, Ant

TADZHIKISTAN

Belgium

Alphen, J. van
AHis, Ant, Lin, His

Cordier, Mr B. de
IR, His, PolS

Vielle, Dr CH.
Lin, Lit, Rel

Denmark

Mahmoodi, A.
Soc, PolS, His, Eco, DevS, CuS

Pedersen, Prof. dr P.
His, CuS, Ant, Phi, Psy, Rel, Env

France

Athari, Drs D.
Ant, Soc, DevS

Barbiche, Prof. dr J.-P.
Law, IR, His, PolS, Eco, DevS, CuS, Edu, Soc

Berthier, A.
His, Rel, Phi, CuS, Lit, His, AHis, Lin

Bertille, Drs .
Arch

Besenval, R.
Arch

Collin, H.
Law, Soc, PolS, Eco, IR

Francfort, H.P.
Arch

Kroell, Dr A.
His

Lyonnet, B.
Arch

Raczka, Prof. W.
DevS, Eco, His, PolS, IR

Roy, O.
PolS

Germany

Baloch, Dr I.
PolS, CuS, His

Brentjes, Dr S.
Phi

Brentjes, Prof. dr B.
AHis, Arch, Env

Buddruss, Prof. G.A.
His, Rel, Lin, Ant, CuS, Lit

Fragner, Prof. B.G.
Lin, Lit, His, CuS

ASIANISTS BY REGION AND COUNTRY OF INTEREST

Germany

Fragner , Prof. B.G.
Lin, Lit, His, CuS

Gippert , Prof. J.
His, Lit, Phi, Lin, CuS, Rel

Glatzer , Dr B.
GenS, DevS, CuS, Soc, Ant

Gropp , Dr G.C.A.
Phi, Lit, His, Rel, Arch, AHis, CuS, Ant, Lin

Heberer , Prof. dr Th.
Ant, Rel, DevS, GenS, Eco, PolS, Soc

Kaiser , Drs M.
DevS, Ant, Soc, PolS

Kraas , Dr F.
Ant, DevS, CuS, Geo

Kreiser , Prof. Dr Klaus
AHis, CuS, His

Kreutzmann , Prof. dr H.J.
Agr, DevS, Ant

Krüger , Prof. dr H.
IR, Law, Rel, Soc, Eco

Kügelgen , Dr A. von
Rel, Lit, His, Edu, CuS, Phi

Malik , Dr J.
His, Rel, CuS, Edu, His, Lit

Rüdiger , Drs A.
Soc, Rel, CuS, IR, PolS

Schmitt , Prof. dr R.
Lin, His

Schmitz , Dr A.
Rel, Ant, Lit, PolS, CuS, Soc, His

Stellrecht , Prof. dr I.
His, Ant, Rel

Hungary

Dobrovits , Drs M.A.
Rel, Lit, CuS, His, Ant

Italy

Campana , Dr A.
His, IR, PolS

Crespi Reghizzi , Prof. G.
PolS, DevS, IR, Law

Ferraro , Dr F.
Lin, Ant

Nicolini , Dr B
His, PolS

Podest , Dr M.
Lin, Rel

Raza , Dr R.
His, Lit, IR

Rossi , Prof. A.V.
Rel, PolS, Lin, Arch, Ant

Netherlands

Atabaki , Dr T.
PolS, His

Barendse , Dr R.J.
His, Eco

Bekius , Drs R.A.
Agr, Ant, Env, DevS, Eco

Berg , Drs G.R. van den
Lin, Rel, Lit

Bläsing , Dr U.
Lit, Lin

Bruijn , Prof. dr J.T.P. de
Lit, Rel

Evers , Drs B.H.
DevS, Env, Eco, Agr

Gautam , Dr M.K.
Rel, Soc, Lit, Lin, His, Ant, CuS, PolS, Env

Ginkel , Drs W.T. van
His, Geo, IR

Guyt , Drs H.J.
His, IR, AHis, Lin, CuS, DevS

Hanssen , Drs L.M.
Ant, CuS

Hulst , W.A.
Eco

Immig , Drs O.I.
Soc, His, IR, Rel, Eco, PolS

Kouwen , H.J.
His, IR, DevS, Ant

Mazgani , M.
Lin, Soc, His, Rel, CuS

Meijs , Drs M.A.G.
IR, Rel, Ant, CuS

Minnema , Mr H.E.
Law

Pinkers , Ir M.J.H.P.
IR, DevS, EduAgr

Straten , Mr H.M. van
Env, Ant, Law

Suringa , Mr P.
Law, AHis, Lit, IR, His, Phi, His, Edu, CuS, DevS, Eco, PolS

Vermeulen , Drs H.F.
Soc, CuS, Ant, His, Lin

Visser , Drs T.
CuS, Ant

Vogelsang , Dr W.J.
Lin, His, Arch, Rel, AHis

Weitenberg , Drs F.S.J.J.
Rel, Env, Arch, Soc

Weststeijn , Prof. dr W.G.
Lit, CuS

Witkam , Dr J.J.
His, Rel, Lit

Poland

Jamsheer , Prof. H.
IR, His, PolS, Rel

Rumania

Liushnea , Dr D.S.
DevS, Eco, IR, PolS

Russia

Aliev , Prof. S.M.
His, CuS, Rel

Aristova , Dr L.B.
Eco, Edu

Belokrenitsky , Dr V.Y.
Soc, PolS, His, IR

Braguinskaya , Dr L.I.
Lit

Dobronravin , Dr N.A.
Lin, Rel, Lit, His, Ant

Dybo , Dr Prof. A. V.
Ant, Lin

Edelman , Dr J.I.
Lin

Geurtsenberg , Prof. dr L.G.
His, Lin

Landa , Dr L.Y.
His, Soc, PolS

Malashenko , Prof. A.V.
Rel, PolS

Morozova , Dr M. Yu
GenS, Agr, Eco, Env

Moskalenko , Prof. V.N
His, IR

Naumkin , Dr V.
Rel, PolS, IR, His, Ant

Niyazi , Dr A.
Env, Rel, PolS

Sedov , Dr A. V.
Arch

Stebline-Kamensky , Pr
Lin, Lit, Rel

Tambovtsev , Prof. dr Y
Lin

Tesselkine , Dr A.S.
Ant, AHis, Lin, His, Cu

Vasilyev , Dr D.
Arch, Rel, Lin, AHis, A

Zviagelskaia , Dr I.D.
IR, PolS

Spain

Berceló Mezquita , Dr J
Env, His, PolS, Soc

Comas Montoya , Dr R
AHis, His

Fernández Miguélez , J
IR

Rodriguez-Eiras , J.A.
Agr, Eco, Edu, Env, Hi

Sweden

Hammargren , Drs H.A
PolS, IR, DevS

Utas , Prof. B.
Rel, Lit, His, Lin, CuS

Switzerland

Bucherer-Dietschi , P.
His, CuS, IR

Centlivres , Prof. P.
CuS, Ant

Djalili , Dr M.R.
CuS, Soc, His, IR, Dev

Hussain , W.
CuS, Eco, His, IR, PolS

United Kingdom

Burton , Drs J.A.
His, IR

Ferdinand , Drs C.I.P.
PolS, DevS, His, Eco, I

United Kingdom

Harriss, Dr J.C.
DevS, Ant

Hull, Mr S.J.
Law

KõK, Dr H.
IR

Marr, Dr J.R.
Lin, His, CuS, Arch, His, Phi, Rel, AHis, Lit

Park, S.S.
Psy, PolS, Phi, SocAHis, DevS, Env, Edu, IR, Law

Picken, Dr L.E.R.
CuS

Roper, Dr G.J.
CuS

TIBET

Austria

Allinger, Dr E.
Rel, His, CuS, Arch, AHis

Bischoff, F.
His, Lin, GenS, Phi, Rel, Arch, AHis, Lit

Geisler, T. Ch.
Geo, DevS, Env

Gmoser, K.
Arch

Harrer, H.
Ant, PolS, IR

Hazod, Dr G.
Ant, Rel

Kellner, B.
CuS, His

Klimburg-Salter, Dr D.
CuS, Lit, Edu, Soc, Rel, PolS

Krasser, Dr H.
His

Kronsteiner, K.
CuS, His, Phi

Lasic, H.
DevS

Loseries, Dr A.S.
His, Rel, CuS, Phi, His, AHis, DevS, Ant

Luczanits, Dr Ch.
His, AHis, Rel, Arch

Min Tjoa, Prof. dr A.
Edu

Much, Dr M.T.W.
Phi, Rel

Müller, W.
AHis, Ant, CuS, His, Arch

Nihom, Dr M.
DevS, Ant, GenS

Pemwieser, M.
Lit

Prets, Dr E.
DevS, PolS

Sellner, Dr M.B.
CuS, Lin

Steinkellner, Prof. dr E.
Rel, Phi

Stockinger, B.
Law

Tauscher, Dr H.
Eco, DevS

Tauscher-Lamberg, M.
Eco, DevS

Tropper, K.
Soc, Psy, CuS

Zotz, Dr V.
Phi, CuS, Rel, His

Belgium

Alphen, J. van
AHis, Ant, Lin, His

Boden, J.
Lin, AHis, Lit, His

Dungkar Lobzang, T.
Lin, Rel, Edu, Ant, CuS

Meyer, Dr J.A.M. de
Lit, Rel, His, Phi

Vanwalle, Drs I.A.M.A.
AHis, Lin, Lit, Phi, Soc, His

Bulgaria

Fedotoff, Prof. dr A.
Rel, Lit, CuS

Czech Republic

Hulec, Dr O.
His, AHis, CuS, Arch, IR, Eco, Phi, Lit, Lin

Kolmas, Prof. dr J.
Phi, CuS, Ant, His, Lit, Rel

Liscák, Dr V.
Rel, His, Phi, Lin, CuS

Vacek, Prof. dr J.
Phi, Rel, Lit, Lin

Denmark

Andersen, A.H.
DevS, Ant

Beek, Dr M. van
DevS, Soc, PolS, Ant

Javed, M.A.
CuS, Rel, IR, Soc

Mozaffari-Mehdi, Prof. M.M.
PolS, Rel, IR

Ostergaard, Dr C.S.
Agr, Soc, PolS, IR, DevS

Padolecchia Polo, Prof. S.P.
DevS, PolS, Rel, Edu, Eco, Soc, Env, IR, CuS

Pedersen, Prof. dr P.
His, CuS, Ant, Phi, Psy, Rel, Env

Sorensen, Dr H.H.
His, AHis, Rel, CuS

Tarab Tulku,
CuS, Soc

Thorborg, Dr E.M.
DevS, PolS, Eco, His, GenS

Estonia

Kark, M.
CuS, Lin, Phi, AHis, Rel, Edu

Finland

Seppänen, J.
IR, Eco, Ant, CuS, Lin, His, AHis, Phi, Arch, Rel, PolS

France

Aubin, F.
Soc, Law, His

Aubriot, Dr O.
Ant

Bazin, N.
AHis

Béguin, G.
GenS, Law, DevS

Bernede, F.
PolS, IR, His, Eco

Bernier, X.
Geo

Boulnois, Dr L.
His, Geo

Boussemart, M.-S.
CuS

Chayet, A.
Ant

Cheng, S.H.
AHis, CuS, Rel

Collin, H.
Law, Soc, PolS, Eco, IR

Coyaud, Dr M.
Ant, Lin

Dakpa, N.
Lan

Delsol, Ch.
Ant

Dessaint, Prof. W.L.
Ant

Dhogon, S.D.
Lan

Dollfus, P.
Ant

Even, M.-D.
His, GenS

Fava, P.
Psy, Lit, CuS, Ant, His, AHis, Soc, Rel, Phi

Frederic, L.F.
AHis, CuS, Arch, Rel, H

Friedlander, D.
Eco

Haas-Lambert, A.-M.
His

Hartwell, S.
Lin

Heide, Dr S. von der
Ant, DevSAHis, Env, C PolS

Helffer, M.
Ant

Holle, A.
Geo

Imaeda, Y.
Edu

France

Jarrige, J.F.
His, CuS, Arch, AHis
Jest, C.
DevS
Karmay, S.
His, Lit, Phi, Ant, Rel
Labbal, V.
Agr
Laurent-Perrey, I.
AHis
Lebreton, A.-S.
Art
Lecomte-Tilouine, Dr M.
Ant
Macdonald, Prof. A.W.
Ant, Rel
Massonnet, P.
His, IR, Soc, Rel, PolS, AHis, DevS, Law, Env, CuS, Lin, His
Mathou, Th.
His
Mazaudon, M.
Lin
Mercier, N.
Soc
Meyer, F.
Ant, Rel, His, CuS
Michailovsky, B.
Lin
Moreau, P.
Art
Oguibenine, Prof. B.
Lit, CuS, Lin, Rel
Pant, M.R.
His
Perrey, Ch.
Lin
Pommaret, Dr F.
Rel, His, CuS, His, Ant, AHis
Raj, Dr K.
Geo, His
Rault-Leyrat, L.R.
His, Rel, Ant, AHis, Ant, Lin, Arch, Phi, His
Riaboff, I.
Lin
Ripert, B.
Geo
Sacareau, Dr I.
Geo
Sagant, Dr Ph.
Phi, Rel
Samphel, T.
His, IR
Silhe, N.
Ant
Steinmann, B.
His
Stoddard-Karmay, Dr H.
Lan
Tawa-Lama, S.
Soc
Tournadre, N.
Lin
Trân, Q.H.
CuS, Ant
Vriens, A.M.G.
Rel
Wang, Dr F.T.
Rel
Wu, Dr C.-Y.
Lit, Rel, Phi, Lin, His

Germany

Alexander, A.
Lin, Edu
Alt, Drs B.
Rel, Lin, Phi
Aschoff, Prof. dr J.C.
CuS
Baloch, Dr I.
PolS, CuS, His
Bronger, Prof. D.
DevS
Buddruss, Prof. G.A.
His, Rel, Lin, Ant, CuS, Lit
Burdman, M.M.
His, Eco, DevS
Degener, Dr A.C.
Rel, Lin
Dietz, Dr S.
Agr
Dodin, T.
Phi, Lit, Rel, Soc, Lin, IR, His, Ant, DevS, CuS, PolS
Ebbatson, Dr P.
Lin, Rel, Phi, Lit
Ehrhard, Drs F.K.
Rel, Phi, Lit, CuS
Eimer, Dr H.
Lit, His
Engelhardt, Dr I.
His
Everding, K.-H.
GenS, His
Federlein, Drs D.
His, Lin, Rel
Fessen-Henjes, Dr I.
Lit, CuS
Flüchter, Prof. dr W.
Geo, Env
Friebel, M.
Eco
Gaenszbauer, Dr M.
Lit, GenS, CuS, Rel
Goettingen, Drs D.
PolS, IR
Graevenitz, Prof. dr A. von
Phi, AHis
Grönbold, Dr G.C.
CuS, Rel, Lit
Grünfelder, Mr A.
Lit
Haffner, Prof. dr W.N.
Env
Hartmann, Prof. J.-U.
Rel, Lit
Heberer, Prof. dr Th.
Ant, Rel, DevS, GenS, Eco, PolS, Soc
Heilmann, Dr S.
Soc, PolS, IR, His
Herdick, R.
AHis
Hessel, E.
GenS, His, AHis
Heuser, Prof. R.
Law
Hinüber, Dr H. von
Law, His, Rel, Lin, Phi,
Horlemann, B.
Lit, Rel
Jackson, Prof. D.P.
Rel, Lit
Kahlen, Prof. W.
Rel, Ant, AHis
Kollmar-Paulenz, K.
His, Ant, Lit, Rel, CuS
Kott, D.
CuS, His, Law
Kuckertz, Prof. dr J.
His, Ant
Linder Sabine, Drs L.
Ant, Arch, Soc
Loke-Schwalbe, Dr P.M
CuS, Ant
Mevissen, Drs G.J.R.
His, AHis
Moeller, Dr K.
IR, PolS
Müller, M.
His, AHis
Panglung, Dr J.L.
CuS, Phi, Rel
Pennarz, Dr J.P.
Ant, DevS
Pews, Dr H.U.
Eco, DevS, Geo
Poley, Drs U.M.
Rel, His, CuS, Arch, Ph Lin
Preisendanz, K.
Rel
Prunner, Dr G.
Ant, Rel, CuS
Rennert, Drs H.
Lin, Lit, His, CuS, His, AHis
Richter, Dr G.
Lin
Roesler, Drs U.
Lin, Lit, Rel

Germany

Ronge, N.G.
Eco, DevS

Ronge, V.
DevS, Eco

Rühle, Mr K.H.
His, Lit, Lin, CuS

Sagaster, Prof. dr K.
Rel, Phi, Lit, Lin, His, AHis, CuS, His

Schillig, Dr D
CuS, Phi, Rel

Schmitt, K.
Soc, Phi, Lin, Ant, Rel

Schneider, Dr J.
Rel, Lit, Lin

Schoepe, Dr R.
Lin, Phi

Schrammel, Drs U.S.
Eco, Env

Schweinfurth, Prof. dr U.
Agr, DevS, Env, Arch, IR

Seele, C.
Soc, GenS

Skyhawk, H. von
Phi, Rel, Ant, Lit, CuS

Slaje, Prof. dr W.
Rel, Phi, Lit, CuS

Sobisch, J.-U.
Arch, His, Rel, AHis

Steiner, Dr R.
Lit, Phi

Tsundue, Drs K.
Agr

Uebach, Dr H.
CuS, His

Vogel, Prof. dr C.
Lit

Weggel, Dr O.
Law, Rel, Soc, CuS, Phi, Lin, PolS, IR

Wilhelm, Prof. dr F.
PolS, CuS, Lit, His

Yaldiz, Prof. dr M.
Arch, His, AHis, Rel

Zeller, Dr G.
Rel, Lit, CuS

Hungary

Birtalan, Dr A.
AHis, Rel, Phi, Lit, Lin, His, Arch, GenS

Dobrovits, Drs M.A.
Rel, Lit, CuS, His, Ant

Hajnal MA, L
Ant, AHis, CuS, Edu, His, Lin, Lit, Rel

Porciò, Drs T.
Lit, Rel, CuS

Toth, E
CuS, Edu, His, Lin, Lit, Phi, Psy, Rel, Soc

Vinkovics, Dr J.
His, Lin, AHis

Italy

Diemberger, H.
Ant, Phi, Edu

Orioli, Dr H.
Ant, His, Arch, AHis

Podest, Dr M.
Lin, Rel

Rossi-Filibeck, E. de
Lin, His, Lit

Tozzi, Dr D.T.
Soc, His, Eco

Volpi, G.
PolS, IR, Agr, Eco, Env

Luxemburg

Vohra, Dr R.
His, CuS, GeoAHis, DevS

Netherlands

Ashkenazy, Drs I.
Ant, His

Belt, Drs J.H.J.
Ant, AHis, CuS, His, Rel, His

Boon, D.
AHis, Rel, CuS, Phi, His

Bragdon, J.
AHis, Phi, AHis

Breet, Drs J.A. de
Rel, Lin, His

Bruyn, E.
Psy, Rel

Chemparathy, Prof. dr G.
Rel, Phi

Chutiwongs, Dr N.
Rel, His, Arch, AHis

Deelstra, T.
Env

Driem, Dr G.L. van
DevS, Lin, Ant, His

Es, Dr A.J.H. van
Agr

Gautam, Dr M.K.
Rel, Soc, Lit, Lin, His, Ant, CuS, PolS, Env

Ginkel, Drs W.T. van
His, Geo, IR

Grent, P.C.M.
CuS, Lin, Lit, Rel, Phi

Guyt, Drs H.J.
His, IR, AHis, Lin, CuS, DevS

Hoetjes, Dr B.J.S.
PolS, IR, Agr, DevS

Hudcovicova, A.
CuS

Kloppenborg, Prof. dr M.A.G.T.
His, Lin, Lit, Rel

Kortlandt, Prof. dr F.H.H.
Lin

Linden, F.J.W.T. van der
IR, PolS

McKay, Dr A.C.
His, Rel

Meulenbeld, Drs B.C.
CuS, His, Ant, AHis, Rel, Arch

Mierlo, Drs H.W.R. van
Lin, CuS, AHis

Mirage, M.
CuS

Mohkamsing, Drs N.
Rel, AHis, Lit, Phi

Oonk, Drs G.
DevS, His, Ant

Plaisier, Drs H.
Lin

Politon, S.
AHis, Arch, Phi, Lin, CuS, His, Rel

Schmidt, J.H.L.
Arch, AHis

Semetko, Prof. dr H.A.
PolS, Soc, Psy

Sinnema, Drs T.
GenS, CuS, Soc, His, E

Spengen, Dr W. van
Geo, Ant, His

Strik, Prof. B.
CuS

Stroek, A.J.
Rel, His, CuS

Tieman-van Ede, Drs Y
GenS, Ant, Rel

Tolsma, Drs G.J.
Lin

Vaczi, Drs M.T.
Rel, AHis, GenS, CuS

Veere, Mr H. van der
Rel, Phi

Verboom, Drs A.W.C.
Phi, Lit, Rel, Lin

Vereeken, Drs B.
Ant, DevS

Verhagen, Dr P.C.
Rel, Lin, Lit, Phi

Vetter, Prof. dr T.E.
Phi, Rel

Welling, Drs K.O.H.
Art

Wolvekamp, Drs P.S.
Agr, IR, DevS, Env, Ge

Norway

Braarvig, Prof. dr J.
Lit, Rel, Phi, DevS, His

Buen, J.
PolS

Havnevik, Mr H.
Rel

Kvaerne, P.
Rel

Liao, R.
IR, DevS, PolS, AHis

Strom, A.K.
CuS, Ant, Rel

Norway
Wellens, K.
Ant, Rel, Lit

Poland
Bareja-Starzynska, Drs A.
Rel, Lin, His, Lit
Tomala, Dr K.
PolS, Soc, Phi, Edu

Rumania
Bercea, R.
Rel, Phi

Russia
Andreyev, A.I.
CuS, Rel, Soc
Beletskaja, Dr A. A.
His, Lin
Dylykova, Dr V.S.
Lit
Ermakova, Dr T.V.
CuS, Rel
Gelbras, Dr V.G.
PolS, Eco, Soc
Gorbunova, Dr S.A.
Rel, His
Lidova, Dr N.
AHis, CuS, His, Lit, Phi, Rel
Narmaev, Dr B.M.
Rel, Lit
Ostrovskaya, E.A.
Rel, Phi, Soc
Samossiuok, K.
Lin
Shaumian, Dr T.
His, PolS, IR
Sofronov, Prof. dr M.V.
Ant, Arch, Lin, Lit
Solomonik, Dr I.N.
His, AHis
Vasilyev, Dr D.
Arch, Rel, Lin, AHis, Ant
Zhogolev, Dr D.A.
PolS, DevS, Soc, Law, Eco, His

Slovenia
Ceplak-Mencin, Dr R.
CuS, Ant
Rosker, Dr J.
Phi, Rel, GenS, Soc, PolS
Slobodník, Drs M.
His, IR

Spain
Albarrán Serrano, Antonio
Lit
Berceló Mezquita, Dr J.L.
Env, His, PolS, Soc
Comas Montoya, Dr R.
AHis, His
Garcia, Fernando
AHis, Geo, His, IR, PolS
Gastllo Martinez, J.V.
Eco, Geo, Lin
Kim, Drs S.-H.
Arch, Rel, Phi, Lit, His, AHis
Pastrano, Dr F.
His, IR, Rel, Soc
Rodriguez-Eiras, J.A.
Agr, Eco, Edu, Env, His, Soc
Suero Tellitu, T.
Ant, Phi, PolS, Rel, Soc

Sweden
Corlin, Dr C.G.
DevS, Ant
Gustafsson, Drs J.E.
Env
Hammar, U.
AHis, Ant
Hammargren, Drs H.A.
PolS, IR, DevS
Hart, Prof. T.G.
IR, His, PolS
Kockum, K.
PolS, IR, His
Magnusson, J.A.
PolS, Soc
Oetke, Prof. dr C.
Lin, Phi
Olsson, I.
Ant, Rel

Switzerland
Brauen, Dr M.
Eco
Ducor, Dr J.
Rel, Ant, GenS
Haller, Dr F.
Lin
Heller, Dr A.
CuS, AHis, Rel, His
Henns, M.
CuS
Jing Li, A.
IR, PolS
Oppitz, Prof. M.
Rel, Ant
Scherrer-Schaub, C.A.
Arch, His, Phi, Rel
Thomi, Dr V.
His, Phi, Psy, CuS, Rel, AHis
Tillemans, Prof. dr T.J.F.
Phi, Rel

United Kingdom
Ardley, Drs J.C.
PolS
Bakewell, Mr A.D.
Barnett, Drs R.
Arch
Bray, Drs J.N.
His, IR, PolS
Cantwell, Dr C.
Ant, Rel
Carter, Dr L.J.
His
Chapman, G.
His, AHis, CuS
Clarke, Dr J.W.
His, AHis
Daniels, Ch.
Soc
Evans, Dr K.K.
AHis, Rel, GenS, His
French, Mr P.R.
His, Lit
Grist, N.
Lin
Harris, Drs N.
DevS, Eco
Hilton, Drs I.
IR
Hoare, Dr J.E.
IR, His, PolS, CuS
Humphrey, Dr C.
Ant, Env, Rel, Soc
Jones, Dr S.
Ant
King, Prof. U.
Phi, His, Edu, Ant, Gen Rel, Soc
Lowe, Dr P.C.
IR, His
Mayer, Dr R.D.S.
Rel
Park, S.S.
Psy, PolS, Phi, SocAHi Env, Edu, IR, Law
Picken, Dr L.E.R.
CuS
Samuel, Dr G.B.
Rel, Ant
Singh, R.N.
Env, Soc, Agr, IR, Dev
Steeds, Mr D.
IR, His
Subedi, Dr S.P.
Env, IR, Law, PolS
Wickham-Smith, Drs S
Lin, Rel

United States of America
Khoo, Drs M.J.
Rel, Arch, Ant
Pagel, Prof. U.
Lin, Rel

Yugoslavia
Furundzic, V.
Psy, Rel, Lit, Lin, Edu, AHis

TURKMENIA

Belgium
Cordier, Mr B. de
IR, His, PolS

Denmark

Chylinski, Dr E.A.C.
Soc, DevS, Eco, Rel, PolS

Mozaffari-Mehdi, Prof. M.M.
PolS, Rel, IR

Pedersen, Prof. dr P.
His, CuS, Ant, Phi, Psy, Rel, Env

France

Barbiche, Prof. dr J.-P.
Law, IR, His, PolS, Eco, DevS, CuS, Edu, Soc

Berthier, A.
His, Rel, Phi, CuS, Lit, His, AHis, Lin

Francfort, H.P.
Arch

Gentelle, Dr P.P.
Env, Arch, Geo

Kroell, Dr A.
His

Raczka, Prof. W.
DevS, Eco, His, PolS, IR

Roy, O.
PolS

Germany

Baloch, Dr I.
PolS, CuS, His

Brentjes, Prof. dr B.
AHis, Arch, Env

Fragner, Prof. B.G.
Lin, Lit, His, CuS

Glatzer, Dr B.
GenS, DevS, CuS, Soc, Ant

Gropp, Dr G.C.A.
Phi, Lit, His, Rel, Arch, AHis, CuS, Ant, Lin

Heberer, Prof. dr Th.
Ant, Rel, DevS, GenS, Eco, PolS, Soc

Kreiser, Prof. Dr Klaus
AHis, CuS, His

Krüger, Prof. dr H.
IR, Law, Rel, Soc, Eco

Schmitt, Prof. dr R.
Lin, His

Schmitz, Dr A.
Rel, Ant, Lit, PolS, CuS, Soc, His

Skyhawk, H. von
Phi, Rel, Ant, Lit, CuS

Stellrecht, Prof. dr I.
His, Ant, Rel

Hungary

Dobrovits, Drs M.A.
Rel, Lit, CuS, His, Ant

Italy

Crespi Reghizzi, Prof. G.
PolS, DevS, IR, Law

Nicolini, Dr B
His, PolS

Rossi, Prof. A.V.
Rel, PolS, Lin, Arch, Ant

Netherlands

Atabaki, Dr T.
PolS, His

Bekius, Drs R.A.
Agr, Ant, Env, DevS, Eco

Bläsing, Dr U.
Lit, Lin

Gautam, Dr M.K.
Rel, Soc, Lit, Lin, His, Ant, CuS, PolS, Env

Ginkel, Drs W.T. van
His, Geo, IR

Groot, Dr A.H. de
Lit, IR, Rel, His

Guyt, Drs H.J.
His, IR, AHis, Lin, CuS, DevS

Hanssen, Drs L.M.
Ant, CuS

Hulst, W.A.
Eco

Immig, Drs O.I.
Soc, His, IR, Rel, Eco, PolS

Kouwen, H.J.
His, IR, DevS, Ant

Meijs, Drs M.A.G.
IR, Rel, Ant, CuS

Minnema, Mr H.E.
Law

Tütüncü, Drs M.
CuS, DevS, Env, Lit, Lin, His

Vandamme, Dr M.R.C.A.
Lin, Lit

Visser, Drs T.
CuS, Ant

Vogelsang, Dr W.J.
Lin, His, Arch, Rel, AHis

Weststeijn, Prof. dr W.G.
Lit, CuS

Witkam, Dr J.J.
His, Rel, Lit

Poland

Jamsheer, Prof. H.
IR, His, PolS, Rel

Jankowski, Prof. H.
Lin

Stachowski, Dr M.
Lin

Rumania

Liushnea, Dr D.S.
DevS, Eco, IR, PolS

Russia

Dobronravin, Dr N.A.
Lin, Rel, Lit, His, Ant

Dybo, Dr Prof. A. V.
Ant, Lin

Korimushin, Prof. dr I. V.
Ant, Arch, Lin

Malashenko, Prof. A.V.
Rel, PolS

Morozova, Dr M. Yu
GenS, Agr, Eco, Env

Moskalenko, Prof. V.N.
His, IR

Musayev, Prof. dr K. M.
Lin

Naumkin, Dr V.
Rel, PolS, IR, His, Ant

Niyazi, Dr A.
Env, Rel, PolS

Prazauskas, Dr A.A.
Rel, His, PolS

Sedov, Dr A. V.
Arch

Shaimpdanova, I.H.
His

Stebline-Kamensky, Prof. dr I.M.
Lin, Lit, Rel

Tambovtsev, Prof. dr Y
Lin

Tenishev, Dr Prof. E. R
Ant, Lin, Lit

Tesselkine, Dr A.S.
Ant, AHis, Lin, His, Cu

Vasilyev, Dr D.
Arch, Rel, Lin, AHis, A

Vassiliev, Prof. A.
Rel, PolS, IR, His

Zviagelskaia, Dr I.D.
IR, PolS

Spain

Berceló Mezquita, Dr J
Env, His, PolS, Soc

Comas Montoya, Dr R
AHis, His

Fernández Miguélez, J
IR

Rodriguez-Eiras, J.A.
Agr, Eco, Edu, Env, Hi

Sweden

Hammargren, Drs H.A
PolS, IR, DevS

Switzerland

Bucherer-Dietschi, P.
His, CuS, IR

Centlivres, Prof. P.
CuS, Ant

Djalili, Dr M.R.
CuS, Soc, His, IR, Dev

Hussain, W.
CuS, Eco, His, IR, PolS

Turkey

Bolukbasi, Dr S.
IR, PolS

United Kingdom

Burton, Drs J.A.
His, IR

Carswell, Prof. J.W.
AHis, CuS, His

Ferdinand, Drs C.I.P.
PolS, DevS, His, Eco, I

Hull, Mr S.J.
Law

United Kingdom
KöK , Dr H.
IR
Lewis , Dr D.C.
Rel, Ant, CuS
Marr , Dr J.R.
Lin, His, CuS, Arch, His, Phi, Rel, AHis, Lit
Picken , Dr L.E.R.
CuS
Roper , Dr G.J.
CuS

UZBEKISTAN

Belgium
Alphen , J. van
AHis, Ant, Lin, His
Cordier , Mr B. de
IR, His, PolS

Denmark
Chylinski , Dr E.A.C.
Soc, DevS, Eco, Rel, PolS

France
Bacqué-Grammont , Dr J.
Rel, His
Bertille , Drs .
Arch
Francfort , H.P.
Arch
Gentelle , Dr P.P.
Env, Arch, Geo
Raczka , Prof. W.
DevS, Eco, His, PolS, IR
Radvanyi , Prof. dr J.
Eco, Geo
Roy , O.
PolS

Germany
Fragner , Prof. B.G.
Lin, Lit, His, CuS
Kaiser , Drs M.
DevS, Ant, Soc, PolS
Krengel , Dr M.
Soc, Edu, Ant, DevS
Kreutzmann , Prof. dr H.J.
Agr, DevS, Ant
Kügelgen , Dr A. von
Rel, Lit, His, Edu, CuS, Phi
Schmitt , Prof. dr R.
Lin, His
Schmitz , Dr A.
Rel, Ant, Lit, PolS, CuS, Soc, His

Hungary
Dobrovits , Drs M.A.
Rel, Lit, CuS, His, Ant

Netherlands
Atabaki , Dr T.
PolS, His
Bläsing , Dr U.
Lit, Lin
Bruinessen , Dr M.M. van
Rel, His, Ant
Gautam , Dr M.K.
Rel, Soc, Lit, Lin, His, Ant, CuS, PolS, Env
Ginkel , Drs W.T. van
His, Geo, IR
Groot , Dr A.H. de
Lit, IR, Rel, His
Guyt , Drs H.J.
His, IR, AHis, Lin, CuS, DevS
Kouwen , H.J.
His, IR, DevS, Ant
Tütüncü , Drs M.
CuS, DevS, Env, Lit, Lin, His
Vandamme , Dr M.R.C.A.
Lin, Lit

Russia
Belokrenitsky , Dr V.Y.
Soc, PolS, His, IR
Grounina , Prof.dr E.A.
Lin
Malashenko , Prof. A.V.
Rel, PolS
Tesselkine , Dr A.S.
Ant, AHis, Lin, His, CuS

Switzerland
Bucherer-Dietschi , P.
His, CuS, IR
Djalili , Dr M.R.
CuS, Soc, His, IR, DevS, PolS
Eichenberger , C.A.
CuS, Ant, Soc

United Kingdom
Burton , Drs J.A.
His, IR
Carswell , Prof. J.W.
AHis, CuS, His
Roper , Dr G.J.
CuS
Um , Dr H.K.
AntAnt

Insular Southwest Asia

MADAGASCAR

Belgium
Gonzalo Castellanos , Dr A.
IR

Czech Republic
Hulec , Dr O.
His, AHis, CuS, Arch, IR, Eco, Phi, Lit, Lin

France
Allibert , Dr C.
Ant, His, Arch
Beaujard , Dr P.
Ant
Blanc-Pamard , Chantal
Agr, DevS, Env
Henry , R.
Lin, GenS, Env, CuS, AHis, Arch, IR, Lit, Phi, Psy
Hübsch , Prof. B.
His, Rel
Mòriot , Prof. CH.
Ant
Raìson , Prof. F.
Rel, AHis, Ant, CuS
Rajaonarimanana , Prof.
CuS, Lit
Rakotofiringa , Prof. H.
Lin, Lit
Vérin , Prof. P.
Rel, GenS, His, Ant

Germany
Cain , Dr H.
Rel, Lin, Ant
Mahdi , Ir W.
Lin
Roth , Dr R.B.
CuS, His
Schweinfurth , Prof. dr
Agr, DevS, Env, Arch,

Italy
Mosca , Prof. L.
His, PolS

Netherlands
Barendse , Dr R.J.
His, Eco
Berger , Drs C.I.
Ant
Burmann , P.E.M.
Arch, Ant, His, CuS, AH
Ellis , Dr S.D.K.
His
Evers , Drs S.J.Th.M.
Ant
Gautam , Dr M.K.
Rel, Soc, Lit, Lin, His, A PolS, Env
Giel , Mr P.
Env, DevS
Hudcovicova , A.
CuS
Kouwenhoven , Drs A.P
Ant
Oosterwijk , A.J.
His, Ant, Arch
Ranjeva , Prof. R.
Lin
Razanajatovo , L.C.
IR, Lit, His
Spindler , Prof. dr M.R.
CuS, Rel, His
Stel , Dr J.H.
Env, Eco
Straten , Mr H.M. van
Env, Ant, Law

Netherlands
Vaczi, Drs M.T.
Rel, AHis, GenS, CuS
Voogt, Dr A.J. De
Lin, CuS, Psy
Zwan, P.J. van der
His, CuS, Rel, His, AHis, Ant

Norway
Dahl, Dr O.
Ant
Munthe, Prof. L.
CuS, His, Rel

Portugal
Pinto Da Costa, Mr R.M.
His

Russia
Dobronravin, Dr N.A.
Lin, Rel, Lit, His, Ant
Sedov, Dr A. V.
Arch
Zhukov, Prof. dr A.A.
Rel, Lit, CuS, Lin

Spain
Roca, Drs A.
Ant, Rel, Arch
Rodriguez-Eiras, J.A.
Agr, Eco, Edu, Env, His, Soc

Switzerland
Kloetzli, Prof. dr F.A.
Agr
Lutz, P.
Eco, GenS, Env, Edu
Marschall, Prof. dr W.
Arch, Agr, Ant

United Kingdom
Astuti, Dr R.
Ant, GenS
Bakewell, Mr A.D.
Belshaw, Prof. D.G.R.
DevS, Env, Agr, Eco,
Bloch, Prof. M.
Ant, DevS, GenS, CuS, Env
Carswell, Prof. J.W.
AHis, CuS, His
Middleton, Dr K.
Ant

MALDIVES

Netherlands
Kulikov, Dr L.J.
Lin

Norway
Mikkelsen, Prof. dr E.
Rel, Arch

Russia
Volhonski, Dr B.M.
Lin, Lit

United Kingdom
Carswell, Prof. J.W.
AHis, CuS, His
Roper, Dr G.J.
CuS

SEYCHELLES

Germany
Werner, Dr W.L.
Env, DevS

Russia
Dobronravin, Dr N.A.
Lin, Rel, Lit, His, Ant

Directory C

Universities, Institutes, Organisations, and Museums

Austria

BICS

Boltzmann-Institut für China- und Südostasien-Forschung
Department of History, Foreign Policy, International Politics
Wickenburgg. 4
1080 Vienna

HHM

Heinrich-Harrer-Museum
Bahnhof Straße 12
9375 Hüttenberg

IATS

International Association for Tibetan Studies
Postgasse 7/4/3
1010 Vienna

INFOTERM

International Information Centre for Terminology
Simmeringer Hauptstraße 24
1110 Vienna
T 43-1-74040441
F 43-1-74040740

KFU,IPB

Karl-Franzens-Universität
Institut für Medizinische Physik und Biophysik
(Institute of Medical Physics and Biophysics)
Harrachgasse 21
A-8010 Graz
T 43-316-3804135

KFU,IS

Karl-Franzens-Universität
Institut für Sportwissenschaften
(Institute of Sports Sciences)
Mozartgasse 14/i
A 8010 Graz
T 43-316-3802325

MVK

Museum für Völkerkunde
(Museum of Ethnography)
Neue Hofburg Heldenplatz
A-1014 Vienna
T 43-1-53430
F 43-1-5355320
voelkerkundemuseum@magnet.at

OAW

Österreichische Akademie der Wissenschaften
(Austrian Academy of Sciences)
Dr Ignaz Seipel-platz 2
1011 Vienna
T 43-1-515810
F 43-1-5139541

OAW,IKGA

Österreichische Akademie der Wissenschaften
Institut für Kultur- und Geistesgeschichte Asiens
(Institute for the Cultural and Intellectual History of Asia)
Postgasse 7/4/3
1010 Vienna
Visiting Address:
4. Stiege, 3. Stock
Dr Ignaz Seipel-platz 2
Eingang: Bäcker Str. 13
T 43-1-51581428
F 43-1-51581427
ias@oeaw.ac.at

OJG

Österreichische-Japanische Gesellschaft
(Austrian-Japanese Society)
Mattiellistraße 2-4
1040 Vienna
T 43-1-5138569

TUW, IST

Technical University of Wien Institute of Software Technology
Reselgasse 3/188
1040 Vienna
T 43-1-588014131
F 43-1-5040532

UI, IM

Universität Innsbruck
Institut für Musikwissenschaft
(Institute of Musicology)
Karl-Schoener-Straße 3
6020 Innsbruck
T 43-512-5074311
F 43-512-5072992

US, IE

Universität Salzburg
Institut für Erziehungswissenschaften
Muhlbacherhofweg 6
5020 Salzburg

US, IS

Universität Salzburg
Institut für Sprachwissenschaften
(Institute of Linguistics)
Mühlbacherhofweg 6
5020 Salzburg
T 43-662-80444250

UW,IIA

Universität Wien
Institut für Indologie und Altiranistik
(Institute of Indology and Early Iranian Studies)
Universitätsstraße 7
1010 Vienna
T 43-1-401032569
F 43-1-401032560
indologie@univie.ac.at

UW,IJS

Universität Wien
Institut für Japanologie
(Institute of Japanology)
Universitätsstraße 7
1010 Vienna
T 43-1-401032556
japanologie@univie.ac.at

UW,IP

Universität Wien
Institut für Philosophie
(Institute of Philosophy)
Universitätsstraße 7
1010 Vienna
T 43-1-401032402
F 43-1-4071677
philosophie@univie.ac.at

UW,IS

Universität Wien
Institut für Sinologie
(Institute of Sinology)
Rathausstraße 19/9
1010 Vienna
T 43-1-401032799
F 43-1-4020533
sinologie@univie.ac.at

UW,ITBS

Universität Wien
Institut für Tibetologie und Buddhismuskunde
(Institute of Tibetan and Buddhist Studies)
Maria Theresienstraße 3/11
1090 Vienna
T 43-1-3174493
F 43-1-3191857
itb@univie.ac.at

Austria

UW,IV

Universität Wien
Institut für Völkerkunde
(Institute of Ethnography)
Universitätsstraße 7/4
1010 Vienna
T 43-1-401032547
F 43-1-4009666
voelkerkunde@univie.ac.at

UW,SIU,AI

Universität Wien
Sprachwissenschaftliches Institut
Abteilung für Indogermanistik
(Institute of Linguistics, Department of Indo-Germanic Linguistics)
Dr Karl-Lueger-Ring 1
1010 Vienna
T 43-1-401032318
sprachwissenschaft@univie.ac.at

VUE,DIE

Vienna University of Economics
Department of Industrial Economics
Lorenz Muller Gasse 1A/323
1200 Vienna

Belgium

CCBC

Centre Culturel Belgique-Chine
Rue Edith Cavell 88
1480 Brussel
T 32-2-3431199
F 32-2-3431199

DSC,EB,LV

Dong Son Centre
Ecole de Bonsai
Livres Vietnamiens
1360 Chee de Wavre
1160 Brussel
T 32-2-6737549

EC, CDP

European Commission
Cellule de Prospective (CDP)
Arch. 25-8-11
Wetstraat 200
1049 Brussel
Visiting Address:
Rue Archimède 25 1040 Brussel
T 32-2-2952524
F 32-2-2952223

EC, DG I-J

European Commission DG I-J, SC 14-3/10 - External Economic Relations
Wetstraat 200
1049 Brussel
F 32-2-2990872

EC, SC

European Commission
SC 14 2/51
Wetstraat 200
1040 Brussel
T 32-2-2990971
F 32-2-2991062

EK

Embassy of Kyrgystan
133 Rue de Tenbosch
1050 Brussel
T 32-2-5346399
F 32-2-5342325
tchinguiz.aitmatov@inforboard.be

Emb.Mong.

Embassy of Mongolia
Avenue Besme 18
1190 Brussel
T 32-2-3446974
F 32-2-3443215

EURASIA

European Institute for Asian Studies (EURASIA)
Rue de Deux Eglises, 35
1000 Brussel
T 32-2-2308122
F 32-2-2305402
100710.323@compuserve.com

JEJ

Japan Economic Journal
Nihon Keizai Shimbun
Bruxelles Bureau
Bd. Charlemagne 1 Bte 42
1040 Brussel
T 32-2-2850966
F 32-2-2306716
naoto.yoshida@pophost.eunet.be

KMKG

Koninklijke Musea voor Kunst en Geschiedenis
(Royal Museums of Art and History)
Jubelpark 10
1000 Brussel
T 32-2-7417211
F 32-2-7337735
Lambrechy@kmkg-mrah.be\
kozyreff@kmkg-mrah.be

KMKG,HCS

Koninklijk Musea voor Kunst en Geschiedenis
Belgisch Instituut voor Hogere Chinese Studien
Jubelpark 10
1000 Brussel
T 32-2-7417342 / 77
F 32-2-7337735

KMKG,IM

Koninklijke Musea voor Kunst en Geschiedenis
Instrumentenmuseum
(Museum of Instruments)
Keilne Zavel 17
B-1000 Brussel
T 32-2-5113595
F 32-2-512-8575

KMP

Kabinet Minister President
Martelaarsplein 19
1000 Brussel
T 32-2-2272911
F 32-2-2272905

KUB, RCC

Katholieke Universiteit Brussel
(Catholic University of Brussels)
Research Centre Communication for Social Change
Vrijheidslaan 17
1081 Brussel
T 32-2-4124247
F 32-2-4124200

KUL, CES

Katholieke Universiteit Leuven
(Catholic University of Leuven)
Centrum voor Economische Studien
(Centre of Economic Studies)
Naamsestraat 69
3000 Leuven
T 32-16-32679025
F 32-16-326796

KUL, FSW

Katholieke Universiteit Leuven
Faculteit der Sociale Wetenschappen
(Faculty of Social Sciences)
E. Van Evenstraat 2C
3000 Leuven
T 32-16-323044
F 32-16-323253

Belgium

KUL,ANTR

Katholieke Universiteit Leuven
ANTR/ESPO/POLS
Place Montesquieu 1/15
1348 Louvain-La-Neuve
T 32-10-474172
F 32-10-474603

KUL,CEAS,JAP

Katholieke Universiteit Leuven
Centre for East Asian Studies
Japan Institute
Blijde-Inkomststraat 21
3000 Leuven
T 32-16-324951
F 32-16-32502

KUL,DAS

Katholieke Universiteit Leuven
Department of Asian Studies
Blijde Inkomststraat 21
3000 Leuven
T 32-16-324945
F 32-16-324932

KUL,DOS

Katholieke Universiteit Leuven
Departement voor Orientalistiek en Slavistiek
(Department of Oriental and Slavic Studies)
P.O.Box 33
3000 Leuven
Visiting Address:
Blijde Inkomststraat 21
T 32-16-324698
F 32-16-324932

KUL,FV

Katholieke Universiteit Leuven
Ferdinand Verbieststichting
P.O. Box 4
3000 Leuven
Visiting Address:
Naamsestraat 63 Leuven
T 32-16-324349
F 32-16-207930
verbiest.foundation@fvf.kuleuven.ac.be

KUL,IO

Katholieke Universiteit Leuven
Institut Orientale
Place Blaise Pascal 1
1348 Louvain-La-Neuve
T 32-10-474958

KUL,OAB

Katholieke Universiteit Leuven
Oost-Aziatische Bibliotheek
(East Asian Library)
Mgr. Ladeuzeplein 21
3000 Leuven
T 32-16-324698
F 32-16-324703

KUL,SIN

Katholieke Universiteit Leuven
Departement Sinologie
(Department of Sinology)
P.O.Box 33
3000 Leuven
Visiting Address:
Blijde Inkomststraat 21
T 32-16-324931
F 32-16-324932
oriental.studies@arts.kuleuven.ac.be

ME

Volkenkundig Museum
(Museum for Ethnography)
Suikerrui 19
2000 Antwerp
T 32-3-2320882
F 32-3-2262516

MFA

Ministry of Foreign Affairs.
Quatre Bras
1000 Brussel
T 32-2-5018259
F 32-2-5018583

MHOV,JS

Mercator Hogeschool Oost-Vlaanderen
Japanse Studies
Meersstraat 138-F
9000 Gent

MROM

Musée Royal de Mariemont
Chausée de Mariemont
7140 Morlanwelz-mariemont
T 32-64-212193
F 32-64-262924

MVG, DGHO

Ministerie van de Vlaamse Gemeenschap
Directoraat-Generaal Hoger Onderwijs en Wetenschappelijk Onderzoek
Koningsstraat 136
1000 Brussel
T 32-2-2114256
F 32-2-2114250

OCCP

Open Cultural Centres Project
Arenbergstraat 28
2000 Brussel
T 32-32024617
F 32-32024600

RUG,SIN

Rijksuniversiteit Gent
(University of Ghent)
Faculteit der Letteren en Wijsbegeerte
Departement Chinese Talen en Culturen
(Department of Sinology)
Blandijnberg 2
9000 Ghent
T 32-92-2644156
F 32-92-2644194

TRO,CD

Culturele en Economische Dienst van Taipei (Taipei Representative Office / Cultural Division)
Kunstlaan 41
1040 Brussel
T 32-2-5110687
F 32-2-5021707

UCL,EU

Université Catholique de Louvain
(Catholic University of Louvain)
Eurasia
Place des Doyens 1
1348 Louvain-La-Neuve
T 32-10-478371
F 32-10-478324
eurasia@espo.ucl.ac.be

UIA, L

Universitaire Instelling Antwerpen
(University of Antwerp)
Linguïstiek
Universiteitsplein 1
2601 Antwerp
T
32-3-8202761
F 32-3-8202762

ULB

Université Libre de Bruxelles
(Free University of Brussels)
Avenue F.D. Roosevelt, 50
1050 Brussel
T 32-2-6503857
F 32-2-6422450

Belgium

ULB, CP

Université Libre de Bruxelles
Center for Politicology
ULB - CP 135
Avenue F.D. Roosevelt, 50
1050 Brussel
T 32-2-6292037
F 32-2-6292282

ULB, FPL

Université Libre de Bruxelles
Faculté de Philosophie et Lettres
(Faculty of Arts and Philosophy)
ULB - CP 175
Avenue F.D. Roosevelt, 50
1050 Brussel
T 32-2-6292577
F 32-2-6293738

ULB,IPOH

Université Libre de Bruxelles
Institut de Philologie et d'Histoire Oriental
(Institute of Philology and Oriental History)
C.P. 133
Aveue F.D. Roosevelt, 50
1050 Brussel
T 32-2-6503990
F 32-2-6503857/3857

ULG,CEC

Université de Liège
(University of Liège)
Centre d'Etudes Chinoises
(Centre for Sinology)
Quai Banning, 6
4000 Liège
T 32-4-3669296

ULG,HPO

Université de Liège
Faculté de Philosophie et Lettres
Département des Sciences de l'Antiquité
Histoire et Philologie Orientales
(Department of Oriental History and Philology)
Place du 20 aout, 32
4000 Liège
T 32-4-3665544
F 32-4-3665655

Bulgaria

BAS, ICSS

Bulgarian Academy of Sciences
Institute for Contemporary Social Science
21 Pionersky Pat Str
1635 Sofia

US,COLC

University of Sofia "St. Kliment Ohridski"
Centre for Oriental Languages and Cultures
Section of Korean Studies
79 Naicho Tsanov Street
1303 Sofia
T 0359-2-200849
F 0359-2-465143

China P.R.

FF, IC

Ford Foundation
International Club
Jianguomenwai Dajie No. 21
100 020 Beijing
T 86-10-6532-6668
F 86-10-6532-5496
ford-beijing@cgnet.com

Croatia

IRMO

Institute for Development and International Relations (IRMO)
Vukotinovica 2
1000 Zagreb
Visiting Address:
Adresw.: 030496.
T 85-1-4554522
F 385-1-444059
ured@mairmo.irmo.hr

Czech Republic

ASCR, IE

Akademie ved Ceské Republiky
(Academy of Sciences of the Czech Republic)
Institute for Ethnology
M chova 7
12000 Prague 2

ASCR,OI

Akademie ved Ceské Republiky
Orientální Ustav
(Academy of Sciences of the Czech Rupublic, Oriental Institute)
Pod Vodárenskou Vezí 4
18208 Prague 8
T 421-2-66052492
F 421-2-6897260
orient@orient.cas.cz

ASCR,OI,BIB

Akademie ved Ceské Republiky
Library
Pod vodárenskou vezí 4
182 08 Prague 8
T 42-2-66052401
F 42-2--6897260

ASCR,OI,DANE

Akademie ved Ceské Republiky
Department of Africa and the Near East
Pod Vodárenskou Vezí 4
182 08 Prague 8
T 42-2-66053521

ASCR,OI,EA

Akademie ved Ceské Republiky
Department of East Asia
Pod Vodárenskou Vezí 4
182 08 Prague 8
T 42-12-66052412
F 42-12-6897260

ASCR,OI,EM

Akademie ved Ceské Republiky
Economic Management
Pod Vodárenskou Vezí 4
182 08 Prague 8
T 42-2-66053713

ASCR,OI,SA

Akademie ved Ceské Republiky
Department of South Asia
Pod Vodárenskou Vezí 4
182 08 Prague 8
T 42-12-66053708
F 42-12-6897260

ASCR,OI,SC

Akademie ved Ceské Republiky
Scientific Council
Pod Vodárenskou Vezí 4
182 08 Prague 8
T 42-2-66052210

CU,FF,DEAS

Univerzita Karlova
(Charles University)
Filozofická Faculta
(Faculty of Philosophy)
Ustav Dálného Vychodu
Department of East Asian Studies
Celetná 20
116 42 Prague 1
T 42-2-24491422
F 42-2-24491423
fareast@ff.cuni.cz

CU,FF,IND

Univerzita Karlova
Indologický Ustav
(Institute of Indology)
Celetná 20
116 42 Prague 1
T 42-2-24491405
indology-l@ff.cuni.cz

Czech Republic

CU,NEA

Univerzita Karlova
Katedra Blìzkeho Vychodu a Afriky
(Department of Near Eastern and African Studies)
Celetná 20
116 42 Prague1
T 42-2-24491220
inea@ff.cuni.cz

IIPE,BIB

Institute of International Politics and Economics
Library and Documentation
Nerudova 3
11850 Prague 1
T 42-2-245 11253
F 42-2-245 11257
umvlibr@iir.cz

MGB

Moravska Galerie V Brno
(Moravian Gallery at Brno)
Husova 14
66226 Brno
T 42-5-4221610406
F 42-5-42213721
m-gal@brno.ies.muni.cz

NGP

National Gallery Prague
(Collection of Asian Art)
Zámek Zbraslav c.p. 2
156 00 Prague 5
T 421-2-57921929
F 421-2-57921639

NMP

National Museum Prague-Naprstek
Betlémské N m 1
110 00 Prague 1
T 42-2-24220899
F 42-2-24214537
ais@nm.anet.cz

PSL,OO

Prague School of Language
Orientalni Odd
(Oriental Languages)
Narodni Tr 20
116 72 Prague 1

PU,FF,JS

Univerzita Palackého
(Palacky University)
Filozofická Fakulta
(Faculty of Philosophy)
Department of Far East Studies
Japanese Section
Krizkovskeho 10
771 80 Olomouc
T 42-68-5224141
F 42-68-26476
skrabi@risc.upol.cz

Denmark

AU, DL

Aarhus University
Department of Linguistics
Nordre Ringgade
8000 Aarhus C

AU, DPS

Aarhus University Department of Political Science
8000 Aarhus C
T 45-89-421341
F 45-86-139839

AU, RCDIR

Aalborg University
Research Centre on Development and International Relations
Fibigerstraede 2
9220 Aalborg
T 45-98-158522
F 45-98-156950

AU,DEAS,OI

Ostasiatisk Institut (Aarhus University Department of East Asian Studies)
Nörrebrogade build. 322
8000 Aarhus C
T 45-89422020
F 45-86184230
ostaaw@hum.aau.dk

CBS, ARU

Copenhagen Business School (CBS)
Asia Research Unit
Nansensgade 19, 7th Floor
1366 Copenhagen K
T 45-38152515
F 45-38152500
inkaren@cbs.dk

CDR

Center for Development Research
Gammel Kongevej 5
1610 Copenhagen K
T 45-33251200
F 45-33258110
cdr@cdr.dk

D,AG

Danchurchaid
Asia Group
Norregade 13
1165 Copenhagen
T 45-33152800
F 45-33911305
danechurchaid@dca.dk

DCHR

The Danish Centre for Human Rights (DCHR)
Studiestraede 38
1455 Copenhagen K
T 45-33-911299
F 45-33-910299

DCM

Department Clinical Microbiology
8800 Viborg Shgehus

DIEM

Department of International Economics and Management
Nansensgade 19
1366 Copenhagen K
T 45-38-152511
F 45-38-152500

DNA

Danish National Archives
Rigsdagsgaarden 9
1218 Copenhagen
T 45-33-923011
reag@sa.dk

DVFA

Denmark Vietnam Friendship Association
Griffenfeldsgade 37-A, 3
2200 Copenhagen N
T 45-35-374717
F 45-35371980
wg@inform.dk

Denmark

ESCAS

European Society for Central Asian Studies (ESCAS)
Taasingevej 19
6710 Esjberg V
T 45-75-468985
F 45-75-156485

FHM

Forhistorisk Museum Moesgård
Moesgård
8270 Hojbjerg
T 45-86-272433
F 45-86-272378

IEA

Institute East Asia
Kejsergade 2-3
1155 Copenhagen

JC,CIBAML,CBS

Institut for Interkulturel Kommunikation og Ledalse (Japan Centre Centre for International Busines Administration and Modern Languages
Copenhagen Business School
Dalgas Have 15
2000 Frederiksberg
T 45-38153815
F 45-38153840

NASA,STM

Nordic Association for South Asian Studies (NASA) Stig Toft Madsen
Strandgade 92 2th
1401 Copenhagen K
T 45-46757781/2932
F 45-46754415
stigtm@mail.ruc.dk

NIAS

Nordic Institute of Asian Studies (NIAS)
Leifsgade 33
2300 Copenhagen S
T 45-31548844
F 45-32962530
sec@nias.ku.dk

NIAS,EUROSEAS

Nordic Institute for Asian Studies (NIAS)\European Association for Southeast Asian Studies (EUROSEAS)
Leifsgade 33
2300 Copenhagen S

NMD

National Museum of Denmark
Ethnographical Dept.
Frederiksholms Kanal 12
1220 Copenhagen K
T 45-33-373208
F 45-33-473320

OW

One World Theater and Art Review Quarterly
Urtehaven 96
2500 Valby
T 45-31-167299/244
F 45-31-167293

RU, DSS

Roskilde University
Department of Social Sciences
House 22.1 P.O. Box 260
4000 Roskilde
T 45-46757781 ext.2507
F 45-46756618 ext.2044

RU,CCAS

Roskilde University Economy and Social Sciences Centre for China and Asian Studies
Villa Europa 3, Tranevej
4050 Gershoj
T 45-47512052
F 45-47512052

RU,IIDS

Roskilde University
Institute for International Development Studies
P.O. Box 260
4000 Roskilde
T 45-46-757781
F 45-46-753705

TLI

Tarab Ladrang Institute St. Sohoj. Horsholm
Konge Wvej 40
2970 Horsholm

TUD, ITSS

Technical University of Denmark
Institute of Technology and Social Sciences
The Library
Building 322, 2
2800 Lyngby

UC, CIG

University of Copenhagen Central Institute of Geography
Oster Voldgade 10
1350 Copenhagen K
T 45-35322500
F 45-35322501

UC, IA

University of Copenhagen Institute of Anthropology
Frederiksholms Kanal 4
1220 Copenhagen K
T 45-35323464/66
F 45-35323465

UC, IH

University of Copenhagen Institute of History
Njalsgade 100
2300 Copenhagen S
T 45-35-328245
F 45-35-328241

UC, IHR

University of Copenhagen Institute of History of Religions
Njalsgade 80
2300 Copenhagen S
T 45-35328957
F 45-35328956

UC, IS

University of Copenhagen Institute Statskundskab
Rosenborggade 15
1130 Copenhagen K

UC,DH

University of Copenhagen Department of History
Njalsgade 102
2300 Copenhagen S

UC,EAI

University of Copenhagen
East Asian Institute
Njalsgade 80
2300 Copenhagen S

UC,FH,DAS

University of Copenhagen Faculty of Humanities Department of Asian Studies
Leifsgade 33
5th floor
2300 Copenhagen S
T 45-3532881/22
F 45-35328835

Denmark

UC,IEH

University of Copenhagen Institute of Economic History
Njalsgade 102
2300 Copenhagen

UC,S

University of Copenhagen Samkvind
Linnésgade 25
1361 Copenhagen K
T 45-35-323502
F 45-32-323506

UC,SSEA,DAS

University of Copenhagen
Department of Asian Studies State and Society in East Asia "Network"
Leifsgade 33
5th floor
2300 Copenhagen S
T 45-35328835
F 45-35328823

UO, IH

University of Odense
Institute of History
Campusvej 55
5230 Odense M

Estonia

AS,EFA

Academy of Sciences
Estonia Folklore Archives
Vanemuise 42
2400 Tartu
T 372-7-420473
F 372-7-420473
ylo@haldjas.folklore.ee

EIH,DOS

Estonian Institute of Humanities
Department of Oriental Studies
Slame 12
Tallinn
T 372-2-601262
F 372-2-601485

UT,DH,COS

University of Tartu
Faculty of Philosophy Department of History
Centre for Oriental Studies
Tähe 4
2400 Tartu
T 372-7-465589
F 372-7-465440/406651

UT,EOS

University of Tartu
Estonia Oriental Society
Tähe 4
2400 Tartu
T 372-7-465589
F 372-7-465440/406651

UT,IE

University of Tartu
Institute of Europe
1 W. Struve Street
2400 Tartu

Ethiopia

ISS

ISS
P.O. Box 31223
Addis Ababa
T 251-1-553900
F 251-1-551499

Finland

AA,CSEAS

Åbo Akademi
(Åbo University)
Centre for South East Asian Studies
Henrikinkatu 7
20500 Åbo
T 358-21-2654806

AA,R

Religionsveenskap
(Department of Comparative Religion and Folkloristics)
Biskopsgatan 10
20500 Åbo
T 358-2-2654398
F 358-2-2654902

AA,S

Språktjänst
(Language Centre)
Domkyrkotorget 3
20500 Åbo
T 358- 2-2654311
F 358-2-2517553

AF

Academy of Finland
(Finlands Akademi)
P.O. Box 99 Vilhonvuorenkatu 6
00501 Heksinki
T 358-9-774881
F 358-9-77488379

EVA

EVA
Centre for Business and Policy Studies
Kirkkot 10
04300 Tuusula
T 358-0-253575
F 358-0-608713

HUT

Helsinki University of Technology
Otakaari 1
02150 Espoo
T 358-0-4514312
F 358-0-4513293

JY,DL

Jyväskylä Yliopiston
University of Jyväskylä
Kirjallisuuden Laitoksen
(Department of Literature)
P.O.Box 35
41400 Jyväskylä
T 358-14-601292,
F 358-14-601291

NACS

Nordic Association for Chinese Studies
Ranta-Nikkiläntie 2
37800 Toijala
T 358-3-5437066
F 358-9-19122094

SP,IO

Satakunta Polytechnic
International Office
Tekniikantie 2
28600 Pori
T 358-39-6272680
F 358-39-6272610
www.spt.fi

UH,HT,AA

Humanistinen Tiedekunta
(Faculty of Arts)
Aasian ja Afrikan kielten ja kulttuurien laitos
(Department of Asian and African Studies)
P.O. Box 13
00014 Helsinki
Visiting Address:
Meritullinkatu 1
T 358-9-19122094
F 358-9-19122094

Finland

UH,HT,E

Folkloristiikan Laitosi
(Department of Ethnology and Cultural Anthropology)
P.O.Box 3
001 70 Helsinki
Visiting Address:
Fabianinkatu 33

T 358-9-19122969

F 358-9-19122970

UH,HT,RI

Renvall-instituutti
(Renvall Institute of Historical Research)
P.O.Box 4
00014 Helsinki
Visiting Address:
Vuorikatu 6 A 4

T 358-9-19123282

F 358-9-191231077

UH,MLT,M

Matemaattis-Luonnontieteellinen Tiedekunta
(Faculty of Science)
Maantieteen Laitos
(Department of Geography)
P.O.Box 4
00100 Helsinki
Visiting Address:
Yliopistonkatu 3

T 358-9-19122130

F 358-9-19122641

UH,TT,U

Teologinen Tiedekunta
(Faculty of Theology)
Uskontotieteen Laitos
(Department of Comparative Religion)
P.O.Box 13
00100 Helsinki
Visiting Address:
Meritullinkatu 1-A

T 358-9-19123583

F 358-9-19123591

UH,VT,KI

Valtiotieteellinen Tiedekunta
(Faculty of Social Science)
Kehitysmaainstituutti
(Institute of Development Studies)
P.O.Box 47
00014 Helsinki
Visiting Address:
Hämmentie 153-B

T 358-9-7084777

F 358-9-7084778

ids-finland@helsinki.fi

UH,VT,S

Sosiologian Laitos
(Department of Sociology)
P.O. Box 18
00014 Helsinki
Visiting Address:
Unioninkatu 35

T 358-9-19123841

F 358-9-19123006

UH,VT,Y

Yleisen Valtio-Opin Laitos
(Department of Political Science)
P.O. Box 54
00014 Helsinki
Visiting Address:
Unioninkatu 37

T 358-9-1918832

F 358-9-1918832

UO,H

Oulun Yliopisto
(University of Oulu)
Historian Laitos
(Department of History)
P.O.Box 111
90571 Oulu
Visiting Address:
Linnanmaa

T 358-81-5533327

F 358-81-5533315

UO,NSG

Maantieteen Laitos
(Departement of Georgraphy)
Linnanmaa
90570 Oulu

T 358-8-5531700

F 358-8-5531693

UTA,PT,NAJAKS

PolitiikanTutkimuksen Laitos
(Department of Political Science and International Relations)
Nordic Association for Japanese and Korean Studies
P.O. Box 607
33101 Tampere

T 358-31-2156552

F 358-31-2156552

ptmime@uta.fi

UTA,PT,PRDS

Unit of Peace Research and Development Studies
P.O. Box 607
33101 Tampere
Visiting Address:
Yliopistonkatu 38
Attila Building

T 358-31-2157017

F 358-31-2156552

UTU

Turun Yliopisto
(University of Turku)
Turun Yliopisto
20500 Turku 50

F 358-2-3336310

UTU,DS

Sosiologia Laitos
(Department of Sociology)
Hämeenkatu 6
20014 Turku

T 358-2-33351

F 358-2-3336270

UTU,SSPH

Poliitisen Historian Laitos
(Department of Political History)
Hämeenkan 6
20014 Turku

T 358-21-3335373

F 358-21-3336585

VU,DEG

Vaasan Ylioposto
(Vaasa University)
Department of Economic Geography
P.O. Box 700
65101 Vaasa
Visiting Address:
Wolffintie 34

T 358-61-3248530

F 358-61-3248251

France

ASEMI,BIB,SL

Fonds Documentaire d'Asie du Sud-Est et le Monde Insulindien
Bibliotheque de l'Université
Section Lettres
100 Boulevard Ed. Herriot
06200 Nice

T 33-4-93375599

F 33-4-93375599

France

ASOM

Academie des Sciences d'Outre-Mer
(Academy of Overseas Studies)
15, Rue la Perouse
75116 Paris

T 33-1-47208793

F 33-1-47208972

ATD

ATD
Fourth World Movement
Hameau de Voux
95540 Mery sur Oise

T 33-1-34216969

F 33-1-34216970

AU,CNRS

Agrégé de l'Université
CNRS
4, Place du Vieux Pré
28100 Dreux

BAMEP

Bibliothèque Asiatique des Missions Etrangères de Paris
(Asian Library of Foreign Missions)
28, Rue de Babylone
75007 Paris

T 33-1-45494234

BILO

Bibliothèque Interuniversitaire des Langues Orientales
(Interuniversity Library of Oriental Languages)
4, Rue de Lille
75007 Paris

T 33-1-44778720

F 33-1-44778730

BML,FC

Bibliothèque Municipale de Lyon
Fonds Chinois
(Municipal Library, China)
30, Boulevard Vivier-Merle
69431 Lyon Cedex 3

BNF,DEE

Bibliothèque Nationale de France
Département des Entrées Etrangères
(National French Library, Foreign Entries)
2, Rue Vivienne
75084 Paris

T 33-1-47038334

BNF,MO

Manuscrits Orientaux
(Oriental Manuscripts)
58, Rue de Richelieu
75002 Paris

T 33-1-47038322

F 33-1-47037666

CDIL

Centre de Documentaion et d'Information sur le Laos
(Documentation and Information Centre - Laos)
14, Rue Dame Genette
57070 Metz

T 33-3-87753783

F 33-3-87372709

cdi@aol.com or guyhan@aol.com

CEPII

Centre d'Études Prospectives et d'Informations Internationales
(Centre for International Prospective Studies and Information)
9, Rue Georges Pitard
75015 Paris

T 33-1-53685500

F 33-1-53685501

CERI

Centre d'Études et du Recherches Internationales
27, Rue Saint-Guillaume
75337 Paris Cedex 7

T 33-1-44108484

F 33-1-44108450

ceri@msh-paris.fr

CERI,FNSP

Fondation Nationale des Sciences Politiques
(Centre for International Research and Study)
27, Rue Saint-Guillaume
75337 Paris Cedex 07

T 33-1-44108484

F 33-1-44108450

CERI@msh-paris.fr

CF

Collège de France
11, Place Marcelin-Berthelot
75005 Paris

T 33-1-44271211

F 33-1-44271109

CF, BIHEC

Bibliothèque de l'IHEC College de France
52, Rue du Cardinal Lemoine
75005 Paris

T 1-44 27 18 54

CF,IEO

Collège de France
Institute d'Extreme Orient
(Institute for the Far East)
52, Rue du Cardinal Lemoine
75005 Paris

T 33-1-39519831

CFJM

CFJM
11, Rue Jean Macé
35700 Rennes

T 33-1-34710083

F 33-1-47257404

CHEAM

Centre des Hautes Études sur l'Afrique et l'Asie Modernes
(Centre for Modern Africa and Asia Studies)
13, Rue du Four
75006 Paris

T 33-1-44413880

F 33-1-40510358

CHEAM,BIB

Bibliothèque
(Library)
13, Rue du Four
75006 Paris

T 33-1-44413880

F 33-1-40510358

CNRS

Centre National de la Recherche Scientifique
(National Centre for Scientific Research)
3, Rue Michel-Ange
75794 Paris Cedex 16

T 33-1-44964000

F 33-1-44965000

CNRS, IPRAUS

Institut Parisien de Recherche: Architecture Urbanistique et Sociale
(Parisian Research Institute: Urban and Social Architecture)
Université de Paris X
École d'Architecture de Paris
78 Rue Rebeval
75019 Paris

T 33-1-42415681

F 33-1-42419149

France

CNRS,AAC

Archéologie d'Asie Centrale
(Central Asian Archaeology)
27, Rue Damesme
75013 Paris
T 33-1-45802777
F 33-1-45801553

CNRS,AOROC

Archéologie d'Orient et d'Occident
(Archaeology of the East and the West)
École Normale Supèrieure Ulm
Laboratoire d' Archéologie
45, Rue d'Ulm
75230 Paris Cedex 6
T 33-1-44323154
F 33-1-44323060

CNRS,APSONAT

Appropriation et Socialisation de la Nature: Pratique, Savoirs et Representations
(Appropriation and Socialisation of Nature: Practice, Knowledge and Representation)
Musée Nationale d'Histoire Naturelle
57, Rue Cuvier
75231 Paris Cedex 5
T 33-1-40793682
F 33-1-40793669
urasecrt@mnhn.fr

CNRS,ARCHIPEL

Archipel
L'Insulinde dans son Contexte Eurasiatique
(Insular Archipelago in its Eurasian Context)
EHESS
Bureaux 731-732
54, Boulevard Raspail
75006 Paris
T 33-1-49542564
F 33-1-45449311
archipel@ehess.fr

CNRS,CASCIP

Centre National de la Recherche Scientifique (Centre for Anthropology on South China an the Indochinese Peninsula)
27 Avenue Damesme
75013 Paris
T 33-1-45802790
F 33-1-45804105

CNRS,CEA

Centre d'Études Africaines
(Centre for African Studies)
EHESS
54 Boulevard Raspail
75006 Paris
T 33-1-49542393
F 33-1-49542692
dozon@ehess.fr

CNRS,CEIAS

Centre d'Études de l'Inde et de l'Asie du Sud
(Centre for Indian and South Asian Studies), EHESS
54, Boulevard Raspail
75006 Paris Cedex 6
T 33-1-49542356
F 33-1-49542676
CEIAS@ehess.fr

CNRS,CJ

CNRS, Equipe de recherche
<Civilisation Japonaise>
(Japanese Studies)
Ihej. Collège de France
52, Rue du Cardinal Lemoine
75231 Paris Cedex 5
T 33-1-44271806
F 33-1-44271854

CNRS,CM

Centre d'Études sur la Chine Moderne et Contemporaine
(Centre for Modern and Contemporary Chinese Studies)
EHESS
54, Boulevard Raspail
75006 Paris
T 33-1-49542089
F 33-1-49542078
all@ehess.fr

CNRS,CM,BIB

Centre d'Études sur la Chine Moderne et Contemporaine
Bibliotheque
(Library)
EHESS
22 Avenue du Président Wilson
75016 Paris
T 33-1-53701813
F 33-1-53701874
rbs@ehess.fr

CNRS,CREDO

Centre de Recherche et de Documentation sur l'Océanie
(Research Centre for the Pacific)
EHESS
2 Rue de la Charité
13002 Marseille
T 33-4-91140785
F 33-4-91140788

CNRS,CRJC

Centre Nationale de la Recherche Scientifique
Centre de Recherches sur le Japon Contemporain
(Research Centre for Contemporary Japan)
EHESS
105, Boulevard Raspail
75006 Paris
T 33-1-45482768
F 33-1-45499443

CNRS,CRLAO

Centre de Recherches Linguistiques sur l'Asie Orientale
(Research Centre for Near Eastern Linguistics)
EHESS
54, Boulevard Raspail
75006 Paris
T 33-1-49542403
F 33-1-49542671
peyraube@ehess.fr

CNRS,DAC

Division des Aires Culturelles
EHESS
54 Boulevard Raspail
75006 Paris

CNRS,EC

Études Coréennes
(Korean Studies)
Université de Paris VII
Asie Orientale
2, Place Jussieu
75005 Paris Cedex 5
T 33-1-44271832
F 33-1-44271854
boulang@ext.jussieu.fr

CNRS,EC

Études Coréennes
(Korean Studies)
Maison de l'Asie
22, Avenue du Président Wilson
75116 Paris Cedex 5
T 33-1-42-799454
F 33-1-42-798147

France

CNRS,EHESS

École des Hautes Études en Sciences Sociales
(School of Social Sciences)
54, Boulevard Raspail
75006 Paris
T 33-1-49542090
F 33-1-45449311

CNRS,EHESS,BIB

École des Hautes Études en Sciences Sociales
Bibliothèque
(Library)
54, Boulevard Raspail
75270 Paris Cedex 6
T 33-1-49542090

CNRS,EHESS,BIB,S

École des Hautes Études en Sciences Sociales
Revue Bibliographique de Sinologie
(Bibliographical Review of Sinology)
22, Avenue du Président Wilson
75116 Paris
T 33-1-53701873
F 33-1-53701874

CNRS,EM

Études d'Ethnomusicologie
(Ethnomusicology)
Musée de l'Homme
Laboratoire d'Ethnomusicologie
7, place du Trocadéro
75116 Paris
T 33-1-47045863
F 33-1-47550547
ethnomus@mnhn.fr

CNRS,EPHE

École Pratique des Hautes Études
(Polytechnic of Higher Education)
52, Rue du Cardinal Lemoine
75005 Paris
T 33-1-44271827
F 33-1-44271854

CNRS,EPHE,CJ

Centre Japon
(Japan Centre)
EPHE
22, Avenue du Président Wilson
75116 Paris
T 33-1-53701877

CNRS,EPHE,SEP

Sciences Economiques et Philosophique
(Economics and Philosophy)
EPHE
45, Rue des Écoles
75005 Paris
T 33-1-61350344

CNRS,EPHE,SHP

Sciences Historiques et Philologiques
(History and Philology)
EPHE
45-47, Rue de Écoles
75005 Paris
T 33-1-53701871
F 33-1-53701872

CNRS,EPHE,SR

Section des Sciences Religieuses
(Religious Studies)
EPHE
45-47, Rue des Écoles
75005 Paris
T 33-1-40463137
F 33-1-40463146

CNRS,EPHE,SR,T

Sciences Religieuses
(Religious Studies)
CDET
(Taoisme)
EPHE
22 Avenue du Président Wilson
75016 Paris
T 33-1-53701865

CNRS,ERASME

Equipe de Recherche d'Anthropologie Sociale: Morphologie Echanges
(Social Anthropology, Morphology)
EHESS
Bureau 13
105, Boulevard Raspail
75006 Paris
T 33-1-45482768
F 33-1-45489443
erasme@msh-paris.fr

CNRS,FNSP

Foundation National des Sciences Politiques
54, Boulevard Raspail
75006 Paris
T 33-69-486245
blanchar@msh.paris.fr

CNRS,IAO

Institut d'Asie Orientale
(Institute of Asian Studies)
Maison Rhône-Alpes des Sciences de l'Homme
14, Avenue Berthelot
69363 Lyon Cedex 7
T 33-4-72726540
F 33-4-72726490
iao@mrash.fr

CNRS,IHEC

Histoire des Techniques et des Science en Chine, au Japon et en Corée
(History of Science and Technology in China, Japan and Korea)
College de France
52, Rue du Cardinal Lemoine
75005 Paris Cedex 5
T 33-1-44271006
F 33-1-44271816

CNRS,IREPD

Institute de Recherche Economie sur la Production et le Development
Centre Asia
(Economic Research Institute for Production and Development)
Université Grenoble II
BP 47
1241, Rue des Résidences
38040 Grenoble Cedex 9
T 33-4-76825423
F 33-4-76228238
jean-raphael.Chaponiere@upmf-grenoble.fr

CNRS,IRSC

Institut de Recherche sur les Sociétés Contemporaines
(Research Institute for Contemporary Societies)
59-61, Rue Pouchet
75849 Paris Cedex 17

CNRS,JAP

Groupe de Recherche sur le Japon: Ethnologie de la Culture Materielle et de la Vie Quotidienne
(Japan Research Group: Ethnology of Material Culture and Contemporary Life)
Collège de France
Intitut d'Extrème Orient
52, Rue de Cardinal Lemoine
75231 Paris
T 33-1-45493237

France

CNRS,LACITO

Langues et Civilisations à Tradition Orale
(Languages and Civilisations in the Oral Tradition)
CNRS
44, Rue de l'Amiral Mouchez
75014 Paris
T 33-1-45809673
F 33-1-45805983
mazaudon@msh-paris.fr

CNRS,LACMI

Langues, Textes, Histoire et Civilisation du Monde Indien
(Languages, Texts, History and Civilisations of the Indian World)
Université Paris III
Bureau 403
13, Rue de Santeuil
75231 Paris Cedex 5
T 33-1-45874138
F 33-1-45874263

CNRS,LASEMA

Laboratoire Asie du Sud-Est et Monde Austronésien
(Southeast Asian and Austronesian Studies)
CNRS
22, Rue d'Athènes
75009 Paris
T 33-1-45261512
F 33-1-44530406

CNRS,LAU

Laboratoire d'Anthropologie Urbaine
(Urban Anthropology)
27, Rue Paul Bert
94204 Ivry sur Seine
T 33-1-49604083
F 33-1-46718496
lau@dr1.cnrs.fr

CNRS,MIDIC

Centre de Recherche sur les Manuscrits Inscriptions et Documents Iconographiques de Chine
(Research Centre for Chinese Manuscripts, Inscriptions and Iconographical Documents)
Collège de France
Institut d'Extrême-Orient
52, Rue du Cardinal Lemoine
75231 Paris Cedex 5
T 33-1-44271833
F 33-1-44271854
drege@ext.jussieu.fr

CNRS,MSCH

Milieux, Societes et Cultures en Himalaya
CNRS
1, Place Aristide Briand
92195 Meudon
T 33-1-45075001
F 33-1-45075872
himal.res@cnrs-bellevue.fr

CNRS,MSH,CAS

Maison des Sciences de l'Homme
Centre Asie du Sud
(South Asian Centre)
22, Rue d'Athène
75009 Paris
T 33-1-49542356
F 33-1-49542676

CNRS,REGARDS

Recherche en Economie, Geographie e Anthropologie sur les Recompositions et le Developpement des Suds
Domaine Universitaire-Maison des Sud
BP 200
Esplanade des Antilles
33405 Talence Cedex
T 33-5-56846852
F 33-5-56846855
deler@regards.cnrs.fr

CNRS,REHSEIS

Recherche Epistomologiques et Historiques sur les Sciences Exactes et les Institutions Scientifique
(Epistomological and Historical Research on the Exact Sciences and Institutions)
CNRS
27, Rue Damesme
75013 Paris
T 33-1-45811485
F 33-1-45807847

CNRS,TC

Techniques et Culture
(Techniques and Culture)
CNRS
27, Rue Paul Bert
94204 Ivry sur Seine
T 33-1-49604036
F 33-1-46718501
upr191@dr1.cnrs.fr

CNSM

Conservatoire Nationale Supérieure de Musique de Paris
(National School of Music)
209, Avenue Jean Jaures
75019 Paris
T 33-1-42801904
F 33-1-40161652

COA

Centre des Archives d'Outre-Mer
(Centre for Overseas Archives)
29, Chemin du Moulin de Testa
13090 Aix-en-Provence
T 33-4-42933850
F 33-4-42933889

CRMJ, EHESS

Centre for Research on Modern Japan\
EHESS
105 Boulevard Raspail
75006 Paris
T 33-1-45482768
F 33-1-45499443

CSI

Cité des Sciences et de l'Industrie
Centre de Recherches en Histoire des Sciences et des Techniques
(Research Centre for the History of Science and Technology)
30, Avenue Corentin Cariou
75930 Paris Cedex 19
T 33-1-45357382
raj@univ-lille3.fr

DPDJ

D.P.D.J. International
77220 Tournan en Brie
T 33-1-64072061
F 33-1-64070247

EACS

European Association of Chinese Studies
92, Boulevard de Port Royal
75005 Paris
T 33-1-43262051
F 33-1-43547202

EFEO

École Française d'Extrême-Orient
22 Avenue du Président Wilson
75116 Paris
T 33-1-53701820
F 33-1-53708760

France

EFEO,BB

École Française d'Extrême-Orient
Buis les Baronnies
La Roche sur les Buis
26170 Buis les Baronnies

EFEO,BIB

Bibliothèque
(Library)
22, Avenue du Président Wilson
75116 Paris
T 33-1-5370 1860
F 33-1-5370 8760

EFEO, UB,DCI

Université de Bordeaux Departement
Civilisation Indonésienne
(Indonesian Civilisations)
41, Cours Pasteur
33000 Bordeaux
T 33-5-56926834

EG

Européen de Géopolitique
(
19 Place Tolozan F.
6900 Lyon
T 33-78920019
F 33-78278730
oeg@univ-lyon2.fr

EH

Economie et Humanisme
(Economics and Humanities)
14 Rue Antoine-Dumont
69372 Lyon Cedex 8
T 33-4-72363278

EIP

European Institute of the Pacific
102 Rue Lourmel
75015 Paris
T 33-1-45779248
F 33-1-45775915

ESEM

European Seminar in Ethnomusicology
29 Rue Roquelaine
31000 Toulouse
T 33-5-61638141
F 33-5-61636730

ESF,SCH

European Science Foundation
Secretary to the Standing Committee fo
the Humanities
1 Quai Lezay-Marnésia
67080 Strasbourg Cedex
T 33-3-88767126/00
F 33-3-88370532
Humanities@esf.c-strasbourg.fr /
www.esf.org

FJ,BP

Fondation du Japon
Bureau de Paris
(Japan Foundation)
42 Avenue Kléber
75116 Paris

FNSP

Fondation Nationale des Sciences
Politiques
(National Foundation of Political
Sciences)
27, Rue Saint-Guillaume
75337 Paris Cedex 7
T 33-1-45495071
F 33-1-42223964

HEC,EI

HEC School of Management
Eurasia Institute
1 Rue de la Libération
78351 Jouy-en Josas Cedex
T 33-1-39677025
F 33-1-39677399

ICP, FA

Institut Catholique de Paris
Faculty of Arts
21, rue d' Assas
75270 Paris

IFRI

Institut François de Rélationes
Internationales
(French Institute of International
Relations)
27, Rue de la Procession
75740 Paris Cedex 15
T 33-1-40616000
F 33-1-40616060

INALCO,CAM

Section d'Études Cambodgiennes
(Cambodian Studies)
Centre Universitaire Dauphine
Place du Maréchal de Lattre de Tassign
75116 Paris

INALCO,CGD

Centre Georges Dumezil d'Études
Comparatives sur le Caucase
(Centre for Comparative Caucasus
Studies)
73, Rue Broca
75013 Paris
T 33-1-44088950
F 33-1-4408979

INALCO,CIV

Institut National des Langues et
Civilisations Orientales (INALCO)
Section Civilisation
(Civilisations)
Centre Universitaire Dauphine
Place du Maréchal de Lattre de Tassign
75016 Paris

INALCO,CRESCIC

Centre for Contemporary Studies in the
Indian Continent
2, Rue de Lille
75007 Paris
T 33-1-49542676

INALCO,CRI

Chargé des Relations Internationales
(International Relations)
2, Rue de Lille
75343 Paris Cedex 7
T 33-1-49264200
F 33-1-49264299
martine.montoya@inalco.fr

INALCO,DAS

Departement Asie du Sud
(South Asian Studies)
2 Rue de Lille
75007 Paris
T 33-1-44054105

INALCO,DASHA

Departement Asie du Sud-Est, Haute-
Asie et Austronesie
(Southeast Asia and Austronesian
Studies)
2, Rue de Lille
75006 Paris

INALCO,JK

Japan - Korea Department
Centre Universitaire Dauphine
Place du Maréchal de Lattre de Tassign
75116 Paris

France

INALCO,LAO

Section d'Études Laotiennes
(Lao Studies)
Centre Universitaire Dauphine
Place du Maréchal de Lattre de Tassign
75116 Paris

INALCO,MKO,CD

Musée Kwok On
Chinese Department
57, Rue du Theatre
75015 Paris
T 33-1-45758575

INALCO,PHIL

Section d'Études Philipino
(Filipino Studies)
Centre Universitaire Dauphine
Place du Maréchal de Lattre de Tassign
75116 Paris

INALCO,RUS

Departement Russia-Eurasia
2, Rue de Lille
75007 Paris
T 33-1-42413229

INALCO,SIN

China Department
Centre Universitaire Dauphin
Place de Maréchal de Lattre de Tassign
75116 Paris

INALCO,THAI

Section d'Études Siamoises
(Thai Studies)
Centre Universitaire Dauphine
Place du Maréchal de Lattre de Tassign
75116 Paris

INALCO,VIET

Section des d'Études Vietnamiennes
(Vietnamese Studies)
Centre Universitaire Dauphine
Place du Maréchal de Lattre de Tassign
75116 Paris

INRA,ES

Institut National de la Recherche Agronomique
(National Research Institute for Agronomy)
Economie et Sociologie
63-65, Boulevard de Brandebourg
94205 Ivry sur Seine
T 33-1-49596900
F 33-1-46704113

INRA,ESR

Unité d'Economie et Sociologie Rurale
(Rural Economy and Sociology)
2, Place Viala
34060 Montpellier
T 33-4-67612551
F 33-4-67545805
chassany@ensam.inra.fr

INSEAD,EAC

INSEAD
Euro-Asia Centre
Boulevard de Constance
77309 Fontainebleau
T 33-1-60724040
F 33-1-60724049
info_eac@insead.fr

INSEAD,EAC,BIB

INSEAD
Euro-Asia Centre
Library
Boulevard de Constance
77309 Fontainebleau Cedex
T 33-1-60724008
F 33-1-60724049
nicolletras@insead.fr

INSERM

Institut National de la Santé et de la Recherche Médicale
8 Rue du General Sarrail
94010 Creteil Cedex
T 33-1-4981 9425
F 33-1-4981 9426

INSERM

Institut National de la Santé et de la Recherche Médicale
(National Institute for Medical Research and Health)
Hôpital des Enfants Malades
149, Rue de Sèvres
75743 Paris Cedex 15
T 33-1-45670811
F 33-1-40569895

IPH

Institut de Paléontologie Humaine
(Institute for Human Paleontology)
1, Rue René Panhard
75013 Paris
T 33-1-43316291
F 33-1-43312279

IR

Institut Ricci
68 Rue de la Tour
75116 Paris
T 33-1-45030004
F 33-1-45042559

LAS

Laboratoire d'Anthropologie Sociale
52 Rue du Cardinal Lemoine
75005 Paris

LBT

Laboratoire de Botanique Tropicale
(Tropical Botany)
163, Rue Broussonet
34000 Montpellier
T 33-4-67041870

LDH

LDH
27 Rue J. Dolent
75014 Paris

LI

Librairie de l'Inde
(Indian Bookshop)
20, Rue Descartes
75005 Paris
T 33-1-43258338
F 33-1-43257952

LP

Laboratoire Phanérogamie
16 Rue Buffon
75005 Paris
T 33-1-40793341
F 33-1-40793342

LPI

Laboratoire Péninsule Indochinoise
(Indochinese Peninsula)
22, Avenue du Président Wilson
75116 Paris
T 33-1-35701871
F 33-1-53701872

MA,CD

Maison de l'Asie
Centre de Documentaion
(Asia House Documentation Centre)
22, Avenue du Président Wilson
75016 Paris
T 33-1-45950769
F 33-1-45959826

France

MAK,DHS

Musée Albert Kahn
Départment des Hauts-de-Seine
14, Rue du Port
92100 Boulogne
T 33-1-4604 5280
F 33-1-4603-8659

MBAA

Musée des Beaux-Arts
1, Rue Friedland
16000 Angoulême
T 33-5-45950769
F 33-5-45959826

MBAB

Musée des Beaux-arts
Jardin de la Mairie 20, cours d'Albret
33000 Bordeaux
T 56 90 91 60

MBACH

Musée des Beaux-Arts de Chartres
29, Cloître Notre-Dame
28000 Chartres
T 33-2-37364139
F 33-2-37234199

MBAHN

Musée des Beaux-Arts et d'Histoire Naturelle
(Museum of Art and Natural History)
3, Rue Toufaire
28200 Chateaudun
T 33- -37455536

MBAPSP

Musée des Beaux-Arts Palais Saint-Pierre
20, Place des Terreaux
69001 Lyon
T 33-4-78280766

MC

Musée Cernuschi
7, Avenue Vélasquez
75008 Paris
T 33-1-45635075
F 33-1-45637816

MD,DAS

Ministère de la Defense
Delegation aux Affaires Stratégiques
(Ministry of Defense, Strategic Affairs)
14, Rue Saint Dominique
00450 Paris, Armées
T 33-1-42193794
F 33-1-42193772

MEUB

Musée d'Ethnographie de l'Université Bordeaux II
(Ethnographical Museum of the University of Bordeaux II)
3 ter, Place de la Victoire
33000 Bordeaux
T 33-5-57571800

MG

Musée Gadagne
14, Rue de Gadagne
69005 Lyon
T 33-4-78420361

MGHN

Musée Guimet d'Histoire Naturelle
(Guimet Museum of Natural History)
28, Boulevard des Belges
69006 Lyon
T 33-4-78932233

MGL

Musée Georges Labit
43, Rue des Martyrs de la Libération
Toulouse
T 33-5-61222175

MH,BIB

Musée de l'Homme
Bibliothèque
(Library)
17 Place du Trocadéro
75116 Paris

MH,LE

Musée de l'Homme
Palais de Chaillot Lab. Ethno
Place de Trocadéro 7 Avenue Vélasque
75116 Paris

MM

Musée de la Musique
(Music Museum)
221 Avenue Jean Jaurès
75019 Paris
T 33-1-44844612
F 33-1-44844601

MNAAG

Musée National des Arts Asiatiques - Guimet
(National Museum of Asian Art - Guimet)
6 Place d'Iena
75116 Paris
T 33-1-47236165
F 33-1-47205750

MNAD

Musée National Adrien-Dubouché
Place Winston Churchill
87000 Limoges
T 33-5-55330850
F 33-5-55330855

MNCE

Musée National de Cèramique
(National Ceramics Museum)
Place de la Manufacture
92310 Sèvre
T 33-1-41140420
F 33-1-45346788

MNCF

Musée National du Château de Fontainbleu
(National Museum of Fontainbleu Castle)
Château du Fontainbleau
77300 Fontainbleau
T 33-1-60715070
F 33-1-60715071

MNCI

Musée Naval de la Compagnie des Inde
(Maritime Museum of the Indian Company)
Citadelle de Port-Louis
Port-Louis
T 33-2-97821914
F 33-2-97824288

MP

Musée Pincé
32 bis, Rue Lenepveu
49100 Angers
T 33-41-889427
F 33-41-860638

MSH

Fondation de la Maison des Sciences de l'Homme
54, Boulevard-Raspail
75270 Paris Cedex 6
T 33-1-49542000
F 33-1-45488353

MTAD

Musée de Tissus
Musée des Arts Décoratifs
30-34, Rue de la Charité
69002 Lyon
T 33-4-78371505
F 33-4-72402512

France

OLO

Oriens Librarie Orientaliste
(Orientalist Library)
10 Boulevard Arago
75013 Paris
T 33-1-45358028
F 33-1-45360150

RCE

Royal Cambodian Embassy
4 Rue Adolphe Yvon
75116 Paris
T 33-1-45034720
F 33-1-45034740

SA

Société Asiatique
(Asian Society)
52, Rue du Cardinal Lemoine
75231 Paris Cedex 05

SA,JA

Société Asiatique
Journal Asiatique
(Asian Journal)
3, Rue Mazarine
75006 Paris

SA,MM

Societé Asiatique
Maison de la Mediterannée
5 Avenue. Pasteur
13100 Aix-en-Provence

TUAC

Advisory Committee to the OECD
26, Avenue de la Grande Armee
75017 Paris

UA, DBIT

Universite d'Avignon
Department of Business and
International Trade
74, Rue Louis Pasteur
84029 Avignon Cedex 1

UA,SIN

Universite d'Artois
Langues
Departement de Chinois
(Sinology)
9, Rue de Temple
BP 665
62030 Arras Cedex
T 33-3-21603700
F 33-3-21603747
delarobertie@univ.artois.fr

UAM,CERSOI

Université d'Aix-Marseille III
Centre d'Études et de Recherches sur les
Sociétés de l'Océan Indien
(Research Centre for the Societies of the
Indian Ocean)
3, Avenue Robert Schuman
13628 Aix-en-Provence Cedex

UAM1,ERLAOS,J

Université de Provence Aix-Marseille I
Études Romanes, Latino-Américaines,
Orientales et Slaves
Departement de Japonais
(Japanology)
29, Avenue Robert Schuman
13100 Aix-en-Provence
T 33-4-42953459
F 33-4-42590496

UAM1,LSH

Université de Provence Aix-Marseille I
Secteur Lettres et Sciences Humaines
(Faculty of Arts and Humanities)
29, Avenue Robert Schumann
13621 Aix-en-Provence Cedex 1
T 33-4-42599930
F 33-4-42594280

UAM1,SLH,DH

Université de Provence Aix-Marseille I
Département d'Histoire
(History)
29, Avenue Robert Schuman
13100 Aix-en-Provence
T 33-4-42-643612
F 33-4-42-208939

UAPV,SLA

Université d'Avignon et des Pays de
Vaucluse
Sciences et Langages Appliqués
(Applied Sciences and Languages)
Rue Saint Jean
84000 Avignon
T 33-1-90858194

UB2

Université Bordeaux II
(University of Bordeaux)
3 ter, Place de la Victoire
33046 Bordeaux Cedex
T 33-5-57571843
F 33-5-57959245

UB2,SSP

Université de Bordeaux II
Sciences Sociales et Psychologiques
(Social Sciences and Psychology)
146, Rue leo Saignat
33076 Bordeaux Cedex
T 33-5-57571010
F 33-5-56990380

UBE

Université Bouddhique Européeene
(European Buddhist University)
26, Rue Véron
75018 Paris
T 33-1-42232317
F 33-1-42232766

UCL,THM

Université Catholique de Lyon
Theologie Histoire et Missiologie
(Catholic University of Lyon, History o
Theology and Missiology)
25 Rue du Plat
69288 Lyon cedex 02
T 33-4-72325042
F 33-4-72326019

UH,FAI

Université du Havre
Faculté des Affaires Internationales
(Faculty of International Affairs)
25, Rue Philippe Lebon
P.O. Box 420
76057 Le Havre
T 33-2-40157150
F 33-2-40157230

UH,FIA,IO

Université du Havre
Faculté des Affaires Internationales
Institute of Oriental Studies
25, Rue Philippe Lebon
76600 Le Havre
T 33-2-35195602
F 33-2-35195606

UJML3,BIBS

Université Jean Moulin-Lyon III
Bibliothèque Sinologique
74, Rue Pasteur
97007 Lyon

UJML3,FL

Université Jean Moulin-Lyon III
Faculté des Langues
74, Rue Pasteur
P.O. Box 0638
69239 Lyon Cedex 2
T 33-4-72722080
F 33-4-72722166

France

UL,FS,ECS

University of Lille
Faculty des Sciences Economiques
Cote Scientifique
Batiment sh2
59655 Villenueve d'Ascq Cedex

UL2,IFC

Université Lyon II
Institut Fernand Courby
Maison de l'Orient Méditerranéen
7, Rue Raulin
69007 Lyon
T 33-4-72715839
F 33-4-72720859
georges.rougemont@mom.fr

UL3,CREO

Université Charles de Gaulle-Lille III
Centre de Recherches sur l'Extrême-Orient
Pont de Bois
59653 Villeneuve d'Ascq, Cedex
T 33-3-20336284
creo@univ-lille3.fr

UL3,ETROM,C

Université Charles de Gaulle Lille III
Étude Romanes, Slaves et Orientales
Departement de Chinoise
(Sinology)
Pont de Bois
P.O. Box 149
59653 Villeneuve d'Ascq
T 33-3-20336284
ufr-etrom@univ-lille3.fr

UL3,ETROM,J

Université de Lille III
Étude Romanes, Slaves et Orientales
Departement de Japonais
(Japanology)
59650 Villeneuve d'Ascq

UMMB,DC

Université Michel de Montaigne
Bordeaux III
Departement de Chinois
(Sinology)
Domaine Universitaire
33405 Talence Cedex

UMMB,DEEO,DU

Université Michel de Montaigne-Bordeaux III
Département d'Études Extrême-Orientales Domaine Universitaire
(Far Eastern Studies)
33405 Talence
T 33-5-56845269
F 33-5-56845090

UMMB3,FL,DOS

Université Michel de Montaigne - Bordeaux III
Faculté de Lettres
Departement Oriental Studies
(Japanology)
33400 Talence

UN,LSH

Université de Nantes
Lettres et de Sciences Humaines
Faculty of Arts and Humanities
P.O. Box 1025
44000 Nantes

UNESCO

UNESCO
World Heritage Centre
7, Place de Fontenoy
75352 Paris 07
T 31-1-45681863
F 31-1-40569570

UNSA,DEG

Université de Nice-Sophia Antipolis
Faculté de Droit, des Sciences Economiques et de Gestion
(Law, Economics and Business Administration)
7, Avenue Robert Schuman
06050 Nice
T 33-4-92157000

UNSA,LSH,E

Université de Nice-Sophia Antipolis
Laboratoire Ethnologie
(Ethnology)
P.O.Box 209
06204 Nice cedex 3
T 33-4-93375353

UNSA,LSH,S

Université de Nice-Sophia Antipolis
Faculté de Lettres & Sciences Humaine
Section de Sociologie
(Sociology)
P.O.Box 209
06204 Nice cedex 3
Visiting Address:
98 Bd. E. Herriot Nice
T 33-4-93375353

UO,FL

Université d'Orléans
Faculté des Lettres
(Humanities)
Rue de Tours
45072 Orléans Cedex 2
T 33-238417101
F 33-238417325

UP,CREOPS,AA

Université Paris-Sorbonne IV
CREOPS Art and Archaeologie
1, Rue Victor-Cousin
75005 Paris
T 33-1-40462211
F 33-1-40462512

UP,G

Université Paris-Sorbonne
U.E.R. Géographie
(Geography)
191 Rue Saint-Jacques
75005 Paris

UP,IAE

Université de Poitiers
Institut d'Administration des Entreprises
(Institute of Business Administration)
P.O. Box 639
20, Rue Guillaume le Troubadour
86022 Poitiers
T 33-5-49454499
F 33-5-49454490

UP,LESC

Université Paris X
Laboratoire d'Ethnologie et de Sociologie Comparative
(Research Unit of Ethnology and Comparaive Sociology)
200 Avenue de la République
92001 Nanterre
T 33-1-40977521
F 33-1-40977117

UP1,CECD,IEDES

Université Paris I
Centre d'Études Comparatives sur le Dévelopement
Institut d'Études du Développement Economique et Social
(Institute for Economic and Social Development)
162, Rue Saint-Charles
75740 Paris Cedex 15

France

UP1,LES

Université Paris I
Laboratoire d'Economie Sociale
(Social Economics)
90 Rue de Tolbiac
75634 Paris Cedex 13
T 33-1-45836444
F 33-1-45866884

UP10,GREC

Université Paris X
Faculty Lettres
Institut Littératures en Philosophie
Departement Lettres Classiques
(Classical Languages)
200, Avenue de l'Université
92001 Nanterre

UP10,LESC

Université Paris X
Laboratoire d'Ethnologie et de Sociologie Comparative
(Research Unit of Ethnology and Comparative Sociology)
200, Avenue de la République
92001 Nanterre Cedex 01
T 33-1-40977551
F 33-1-40977117

UP3,EI

Université de la Sorbonne Nouvelle-Paris III
Études Indiennes
(Indology)
13, Rue de Santeuil
75005 Paris

UP7

Université Paris VII-Denis Diderot
2 Place Jussieu
75005 Paris Cedex 5

UP7, GHSS

Université Paris VII-Denis Diderot
Géographie Histoire et Sciences de la Société
(Historic Geography and Social Sciences)
2, Place Jussieu
75251 Paris Cedex 5
T 33-1-44-277825
F 33-1-44-276964

UP7,BFDEEO

Université Paris VII-Denis Diderot
Bureau de la Formation Doctorale
Études de l'Extrême-Orient
(Doctoral Studies on the Far East)
2, Place Jussiu
75251 Paris cedex 05
T 331--44275781
F 33-1-44277898

UP7,FEG,DEN

Université Paris VII-Denis Diderot
Faculté d'Études Germaniques
Departement d'Études Neerlandaises
(Dutch Studies)
Grand Palais Cours la Reine
75008 Paris
T 33-1-42259640
F 33-1-42894020

UP7,LGSP

Université Paris VII-Denis Diderot
Laboratoire de Geochronologie Science
Physique de la Terre
Physical Science)
2, Place Jussieu
75251 Paris Cedex 5
T 33-1-44-272820
F 33-1-44-278148

UP7,UAO

Université Paris VII-Denis Diderot
Unité Asie Orientale
2, Place Jussieu
75005 Paris Cedex 05
T 33-1-44275781
F 33-1-44277898

UP7,UAO,C

Université Paris VII-Denis Diderot
Unité Asie Orientale
Études Coréennes
(Korean Studies)
2, Place Jussieu
75251 Paris

UP7,UAO,EC

Université Paris VII-Denis Diderot
Unité Asie Orientale
Études Chinoise
(Sinology)
Tour 34-44 2, Place Jussieu
75005 Paris

UP8,

Université Paris VIII-Saint Denis
UFR 5
2, Rue de la Liberté
93200 Saint-Denis
T 33-1--49406669

UP9,DJK

Université Paris IX-Dauphine
Japan-Korea Department
Place du Maréchal de Lattre de Tassign
75116 Paris
T 33-1-44054110
F 33-1-44054107

UPMF,CA

Université Pierre Mendès France
Centre for Emerging Economies
Centre Asie IREPD-CNRS
P.O. Box 47
38040 Grenoble Cedex

UPV

Université Paul Valéry
P.O.Box 5043
34032 Montpellier
T 33-4-67142096
F 33-4-67142062

UPVII, UFRL

Université Paris VII
UFRL-Case 7003
2 Place Jussieu
75005 Paris
T 33-1-44275689
F 33-1-44277919

UR1,IGR

Université de Rennes I
Institut de Gestion de Rennes
(Institute of Business Administration)
P.O. Box 1997
11, Rue Jean Macé
35019 Rennes
T 33-2-99847814
F 33-2-99847800

UR2, LCER

Université de Rennes II
Langues et Cultures Etrangères et Régionales
(Department of Foreign and Regional Languages)
Campus 2 - Villejean
6, Rue Gaston Berger
35043 Rennes
T 33-2-99335252
F 33-2-99335175

USG

Université Stendhal-Grenoble III
P.O. Box 25
38040 Grenoble cedex 09
T 33-76-824300
F 33-76-824335

France

USHS

Université des Sciences Humaines de Strasbourg
(University of the Humanities of Strasbourg)
Place de l'Université
67000 Strasbourg
T 33-3-88-355322
F 33-3-88-250863

USHS,ISESA

Université des Sciences Humaines de Strasbourg
Institut de Sanskrit et d'Études Sud Asiatiques
(Institute of Sanskrit and South Asian Studies)
14, Rue Descartes
67084 Strasbourg cedex
T 33-3-88417832

USHS,LLCE

Université de Sciences Humaines de Strasbourg
Faculté des Langues, Littératures et Civilisations Etrangères
(Faculty of Foreign Languages, Literatures and Cultures)
22, Rue Descartes
67084 Strasbourg
T 33-3-88417402
F 33-3-88417440

UTM,CUP

Université de Toulouse le Mirail Cerpp
UFR Psychologie
5, allée Antonio Machado
31058 Toulouse
T 33-4-61504250

UTM,DJ

Université de Toulouse le Mirail
Departement de Japonais
(Japanology)
5, Allée Antonio Machado
31058 Toulouse

UTM,GA

Université Toulouse-Le Mirail
UFR Géographie et Aménagement
(Geography and Management)
5 Allées Antonio-Machado
31058 Toulouse
T 33-1-40840169

Germany

ALU,HS

Albert-Ludwig-Universität Freiburg
Historisches Seminar
(History)
Werthmannplatz
79085 Freiburg im Breisgau
T 49-761-2033434
F 49-761-2033425

ALU,IVK

Albert-Ludwig-Universität Freiburg
Institut für Völkerkunde
(Etnology)
Werderring 10
79085 Freiburg im Breisgau
T 49-761-2033582/93
F 49-761-2033581
seitz@tuf.uni-freiburg.de

ALU,OS

Albert-Ludwig-Universität Freiburg
Orientalisches Seminar
(Department of Oriental Studies)
Werthmannplatz 3
79085 Freiburg im Breisgau
T 49-761-2033158
F 49-761-2033152

ALU,OS,IND

Albert-Ludwig-Universität Freiburg
Orientalisches Seminar
Indologie
(Indology)
Humboldstrasse 5
79085 Freiburg im Breisgau
T 49-761-2033158
F 49-761-2033152

ASEAN

ASEAN - Institut e.V.
Association of Southeast Asian Nations
P.O.Box 10 1226
69002 Heidelberg

AWL,IK

Akademie der Wissenschaften und der Literatur
Indologische Kommission
(Indology)
Geschwister-Scholl-Strasse 2
55099 Mainz
T 49-6131-57738

BAWS,KZAS

Bayerische Akademie der Wissenschaften
Kommission für Zentralasiatische Studien
(Central Asian Studies)
Marstallplatz 8
80539 Munich
T 49-89-23031194
F 49-89-23031100

BI

Bundes Institut
Lindenbornstrasse 22
50823 Cologne
T 49-221-5747114
F 49-221-5747110

BIBDMIG

Bibliothek der Deutschen Morgenländischen Gesellschaft
August-Bebel-Strasse 13
06099 Halle
T 49-345-8950

BLMK

Badisches Landesmuseum
Schloß
76131 Karlsruhe
T 49-721-9266514/42, 9266594
F 49-721-9266537/ -9266549

BPB

Burma Project Berlin e.V.
Silberhammerweg 78
13503 Berlin
T 49-30-86412630
F 49-30-4310665

BSBIB,AOA

Bayerische Staatsbibliothek
Abteilung Ostasien
(East Asian Department)
P.O. Box 340150
80098 Munich
T 49-89-28638624
F 49-89-26838623

BSBIB,OABT

Bayerische Staatsbibliothek
Orientabteilung
(Middle-Eastern Department)
Ludwigstrasse 16
80539 Munich
T 49-89-28638367
F 49-89-28638293

Germany

CAUK,GA

Christian-Albrechts-Universität Kiel
Historisches Seminar
Lehrstuhl für Geschichte Asiens
(Asian History)
Olshausen Straße 40
24118 Kiel
T 49-431-8802282

CAUK,GI

Christian-Albrechts-Universität Kiel
Geologisches Institut
(Geographical Institute)
Ludewig-Meyn-Str. 14
24098 Kiel
T 49-431-8802941
F 49-431-8804658

CAUK,SO,AI

Christian-Albrechts-Universität Kiel
Seminar für Orientalistik
Abteilung für Indologie
(Indology)
Olshausen Straße 40
24118 Kiel
T 49-431-8803436
F 49-431-8802249

CAUK,SO,AS

Christian-Albrechts-Universität Kiel
Seminar für Orientalistik
Abteilung für Sinologie
(Sinology)
Leibniz Straße 10
24118 Kiel
T 49-431-8801598
F 49-431-8802249

CG

China Galerie
Schwander Straße 46
90596 Schwanstetten
T 49-9170-7454

CI

China Infostelle
(China Study Project)
c/o EMW Normannenweg 17-21
20537 Hamburg
T 49-040-25456149
EMW@Geod.Geonet.De

CMOS

Zentrum Moderner Orient
(Center for Modern Oriental Studies)
Prenzlauer Promenade 149-152
13189 Berlin
T 49-30-4797366
F 49-30-4722023

DFG

Deutsche Forschungsgemeinschaft
(Association of National Research Centres)
Postfach 201448
Ahr Straße 45
53175 Bonn
T 49-228-376741
F 49-228-376744

DGAK

Deutsche Gesellschaft für Asienkunde
(German Association for Asian Studies)
Rhotenbaumchausse 32
T20148 Hamburg
T 49-40-445891
F 49-40-4107945

DOI

Deutsches Orient Institut
Mittelweg 150
20148 Hamburg

DUI

Deutsches Ubersee-Institut
Neuer Jungfernstieg 21
20354 Hamburg
T 49-40-3562598
F 49-40-4107945

DWZP

Deutsche Welle Zentraldienst Politik
50588 Cologne

EACS

European Association for Chinese Studies (EACS) Ruprecht-Karls-Universität Heidelberg
Sinologisches Seminar
Akademie Str. 4-8
69117 Heidelberg
T 49-6221-54265
F 49-6221-542439

EAJS

European Association for Japanese Studies
Gerhard-Mercator-Universität-Gesamthochschule Duisburg
Lothar Str. 65
47048 Duisburg
T 49-203-379 2002
F 49-203-379 2002
eajs@uni-duisburg.de

EASAS,RKU

European Association for South Asian Studies (EASAS)
Ruprecht-Karls-Universität Heidelberg
Südasien-Institut
Im Neuenheimer Feld 330
69120 Heidelberg
T 49-6261-548909
F 49-6221-544998

EJEA

European Japan Experts Association e.V.
c/o Japanese-German Center Berlin
Tiergarten Str. 24-25
Berlin
T 49-30-25006274
F 49-30-25006222
ejea%jdzb@notesgw.compuserve.com

EKO

EKO
Haus der Japanischen Kultur e.V.
Brüggener Weg 6
40547 Düsseldorf
T 49-211-574071
F 49-211-573546

EKUT,BIB

Eberhard-Karls-Universität Tübingen
Universitätsbibliothek
(Library)
Postfach 2620
72016 Tübingen
Visiting Address:
Wilhemstrasse 32
T 49-7071-294030
F 49-7071-293123

EKUT,DOS,BIB

Eberhard-Karls-Universität Tübingen
Department of Oriental Studies Library
Postfach 2620
72016 Tübingen
Visiting Address:
Wilhelmstr. 32
T 49-07071-2972587
F 49-07071-293123

EKUT,IE

Eberhard-Karls-Universität Tübingen
Institut für Völkerkunde
(Institute of Ethnology)
Burgsteige 11
72070 Tübingen
T 49-7071-292402
F 49-7071-294995

Germany

EKUT,JAP

Eberhard-Karls-Universität Tübingen
Seminar für Japanologie
(Faculty of Japanology)
Wilhelm Str. 90
72074 Tübingen
T 49-7071-2976985
F 49-7071-2973989
japanologie@uni.tuebingen.de

EKUT,SIVRW

Eberhard-Karls-Universität Tübingen
Seminar für Indologie und Vergleichende Religionswissenschaften
(Indology and Comparative Religions)
Münzgasse 30
72070 Tübingen
T 49-7071-294005
F 49-7071-292675

EKUT,SSK

Eberhard-Karl-Universität Tübingen
Seminar für Sinologie und Koreanistik
(Sinology and Korean Studies)
Wilhelm Str. 133
72074 Tübingen
T 49-7071-565111
F 49-7071-565100
sinologie@uni-tuebingen.de

FAU

Friedrich-Alexander-Universität Erlangen-Nürnberg
(University of Nürnberg)
Bismarckstr. 1
91054 Erlangen
T 49-9131-852448
F 49-9131-856374

FAU,DG

Friedrich-Alexander-Universität Erlangen-Nürnberg
Department of Geography
Koch Str. 4
91054 Erlangen
T 49-9131-852634

FAU,IASK,SJ

Friedrich-Alexander-Universität Erlangen-Nürnberg
Institut für Ausserauropaïsche Sprachen und Kulturen
Sinologie und Japanologie
(Sinology and Japanology)
Bismarck Straße 1
91054 Erlangen
T 49-9131-856374
F 49-9131-852448

FAU,IPW

Friedrich-Alexander-Universität-Erlangen-Nürnberg
Institut für Politische Wissenschaften
Koch Str. 4
91054 Erlangen

FAU,IS

Friedrich-Alexander-Universität Erlangen-Nürnberg
Institut für Soziologie
(Institute for Sociology)
Kochstrasse 4
91054 Erlangen
T 49-9131-852633
F 49-9131-852013

FAU,IVIS

Friedrich-Alexander-Universität Erlangen-Nürnberg
Institut für Vergleichende Indogermanische Sprachwissenschaft
(Comparative Indo-Germanic Linguistics)
Koch Str. 4
91054 Erlangen
T 49-9131-859376
F 49-9131-856390
p2iasver@phil.uni-erlangen.de

FF,VSIB

Fachhochschule Furtwangen abt. Villingen-Schwenningen Internationale Betriebswirtschaft
Jakob Kienstrasse 17
78054 Villingen-Schwenningen
T 49-7720-307307

FHI

Fritz Haber Institut
Abteilung Physikalische Chemie
Faradayweg 4-6
14195 Berlin
T 49-30-84135408
F 49-30-84133155

FS

Frankesche Stiftungen
Franckeplatz 1/46
4020 Halle
T 345-2127412
F 345-2127433

FSUJ,BOS,IND

Friedrich-Schiller-Universität Jena
Bereich für Orientalistische Sprachwissenschaft
Indonesistik
(Department of Oriental Languages-Indonesian)
Leutragraben 1
07743 Jena
T 49-3641-630682
F 49-3641-632345
xcc@rz.uni-jena.de

FU,ESGW

Fern Universität ESGW/Historisches Institut Aussereuropaeische Geschichte
Feithstrasse 140/II
58084 Hagen
T 49-2331/9872114
F 49-2331/9871921-22
schulzd@f204.fernuni.de

FU,ESWG,DH

Fern Universität ESWG Department of History
Feithstrasse 140
58084 Hagen
T 0049-2331-9872122
F 0049-2331-987192122

FUB,AW,IPKG

Freie Universität Berlin
Altertumswissenschaften Indische Phililogie und Kunstgeschichte
Königin-Luise-Strasse 34a
14195 Berlin
T 49-30-8386240
F 49-30-8384775

FUB,GW,ZELF

Freie Universität Berlin
Geowissenschaften
(Centre for Development Studies)
Grunewald Straße 35
12165 Berlin
T 49-30-8384864
F 49-30-8384987

FUB,IE

Freie Universität Berlin
Philosophie und Sozialwissenschaften
Institut für Ethnologie
(Institute for Ethnology)
Drosselweg 1-3
14195 Berlin
T 49-30-8383598

Germany

FUB,IGS

Freie Universität Berlin
Seminar für Vergleichende und Indogermanische Sprachwissenschaft
Fabeckstrasse 7
14195 Berlin
T 49-30-8326654
F 49-30-8384707

FUB,OS

Freie Universität Berlin
Ostasiatisches Seminar
(Center for East Asian Studies)
Podbielskiallee 42
14195 Berlin
T 49-30-8383857
F 49-30-8313008

FUB,OS,CEAP

Freie Universität Berlin
Otto-Suhr-Institut
Department of Chinese and East Asian Politics
Harnackstrasse 1
14195 Berlin
T 49-30-8382347
F 49-30-8384160
wpfaoso@zedat.fu-berlin.de

FUB,OS,JAP

Freie Universität Berlin
Ostasiatisches Seminar Japanologie
(Japanology)
Podbielskiallee 42
14195 Berlin 33
T 49-30-838 3857/3599

FUB,OS,SIN

Freie Universität Berlin
Ostasiatisches Seminar
Sinologie
Podbielskiallee 42
14195 Berlin
T 49-30-838 6593/3598
F 49-30-831 5317

FUB,PSW,IE,A

Freie Universität Berlin
Philosophie und Sozialwissenschaften
Institut für Ethnologie Regionalbereich Asien
(Institute for Etnology Region Asia)
Drosselweg 1-3
14195 Berlin
T 49-30-8386505
F 49-30-8382382

FUB,W,IW

Freie Universität Berlin
Wirtschaftwissenschaft
Institut für Wirtschaftspolitik
(Institute for Economic Politics)
Boltzmannstr. 20
14195 Berlin
T 49-30-8384040
F 49-30-8384142

GAUG,BIB,IND

Georg-August-Universität Göttingen
Niedersächsische Staats- und Universitätsbibliothek
(Library)
Referat Indologie
Papendiek 14
37070 Göttingen
T 49-551-395283
F 49-551-395384

GAUG,GI

Georg-August-Universität Göttingen
Geographisches Institut
(Geography)
Goldschmidtstr. 3
37077 Göttingen
T 49-551-398094
F 49-551-398055

GAUG,ISV

Georg-August-Universität Göttingen
Institut und Sammlung für Völkerkunde
(Ethnographical Institute and Collection)
Theaterplatz 15
37073 Göttingen
T 49-551-397892
F 49-551-397359

GAUG,IVAA

Georg-August-Universität Göttingen
Seminar für Iranistik und Vorderasiatische Archäologie
(Iranian and Near-Eastern Archaeology
Prinzenstrasse 21
37073 Göttingen
T 49-551-394394

GAUG,OAS,SIN

Georg-August-Universität Göttingen
Ostasiatisches Seminar
Sinologie
(Sinology)
Papendiek 16
37073 Göttingen
T 49-551-397022
F 49-551-397048

GAUG,SIB

Georg-August-Universität Göttingen
Seminar für Indologie und Buddhismuskunde
(Department of Indology and Buddhism Studies)
Hainbund St. 21
37085 Göttingen
T 49-551-57068
F 49-551-48014

GAUG,STZA

Georg-August-Universität Göttingen
Seminar für Turkologie und Zentralasienkunde
(Department of Turkology and Central Asia Studies)
Papendiek 16
37073 Göttingen
T 49-551-394561
F 49-551-399612

GDEV

Gesellschaft für Demokratie und Entwicklung Vietnam
P.O. Box 2526
58595 Iserlon

GI,Z

Goethe-Institut Zentralverwaltung
PF 190419
80604 Munich
T 49-89-15921298
F 49-89-15921608

GMM

Gutenberg-Museum Mainz
Leibfrauenplatz 5
55116 Mainz
T 49-61-31122640
F 49-61-31123488

GMU,EAES

Gerhard-Mercator-Universität-Gesamthochschule Duisburg
East Asian Economic Studies
Postfach 101 503 Lothar Str. 65
47048 Duisburg
T 49-203-3789114
F 49-203-3789157

GMU,FE

Gerhard-Mercator-Universität-Gesamthochschule Duisburg
Faculty of Economics International Economics
Lothar Str. 65
47048 Duisburg
T 49-203-3792357
F 49-203-3792358

Germany

GMU,FJP

Gerhard-Mercator-Universität-Gesamthochschule Duisburg
Research Institute for Economic and Technical Developments in Japan and the Pacific Area
Lothar Str. 65
47048 Duisburg
T 49-203-3792357
F 49-203-3793333

GMU,IO,E

Gerhard-Mercator-Universität-Gesamthochschule Duisburg
Institut für Ostasienwissenschaften
Dept. of Economics
(Centre for East Asian Studies)
Mühlheimer Str. 212
47048 Duisburg
T 49-203-3789367
F 49-203-3789157

GMU,IO,G

Gerhard-Mercator-Universität-Gesamthochschule Duisburg
Institut für Ostasienwissenschaften
Geographie
(Centre for East Asian Studies/Geography)
Mülheimer Str. 212
47057 Duisburg
T 49-203-3794191
F 49-203-3794157
oawiss@uni-duisburg.de

GMU,IO,J

Gerhard-Mercator-Universität-Gesamthochschule Duisburg
Institut für Ostasienwissenschaften
Sprache und Kultur des Modernen Japan
(Japanology)
Gebäude SV (Ostasienvilla)
Mülheimer Str. 212
47048 Duisburg
T 49-203-3794116
F 49-203-3794157

GMU,IO,PS

Gerhard-Mercator-Universität-Gesamthochschule Duisburg
Institut für Ostasienwissenschaften
(Centre for East Asian Studies
Dept. of Political Science
Mühlheimer Str. 212, SV
47048 Duisburg
T 49-203-3789115
F 49-203-3789157
derichs@uni-duisburg.de

H&PWP

Hager & Partner Wirtschaftsberatung Pressedienste
Holz Str. 19
80469 Munich
T 49-89-2603 3183
F 49-89-2602 3184

HAB

Herzog August Bibliothek
Lessingplatz 1
38304 Wolfenbüttel

HAUM

Herzog Anton Ulrich- Museum
Museumstraße 1
38100 Braunschweig
T 49-531-4842400
F 49-531-4842408
H._Ulrich-Museum@magicvillage.de

HB,ABLIM

Hochschule Bremen
Fachbereich Wirtschaft, Fach Wirtschaftssinologie
(Applied Business Languages and International Management)
Werderstrasse 73
28199 Bremen
T 49-421-5905127/123/124
F 49-421-5905140
schaedlr@fbw.hs-bremen.de\dey@fbw.hs-bremen.de

HHU,BIB

Heinrich-Heine-Universität Düsseldorf
Universitäts- und Landes Bibliothek
Universitätsstrasse 1
40225 Düsseldorf
T 49-211-8113072

HHU,GI

Heinrich-Heine-Universität Düsseldorf
Geographsches Institut
Universitätsstrasse 1
50225 Düsseldorf
T 49-211-8112040
F 49-211-812040

HHU,JAP

Heinrich-Heine-Universität Düsseldorf
Philosophische Fakultät Department Modernes Japan
(Modern Japanese Studies)
Gebäude 32.02, Ebene 02
Universitätsstrasse 1
40225 Düsseldorf
T 49-211-8114349
F 49-211-8114714

HKW

Haus der Kulturen der Welt
John Fuster Dulles Alle 10
10099 Berlin
T 49-30-39787160
F 49-30-3948679

HMV

Hamburgisches Museum für Völkerkunde
(Hamburg Museum of Ethnography)
Rothenbaumchaussee 64
20148 Hamburg
T 49-40-44195524
F 49-40-44195524

HMV,SOA

Hamburgisches Museum für Völkerkunde
Abteilung Süd- und Ostasien
(Department of South and East Asia)
Binderstrasse 14
20148 Hamburg 13
T 49-40-44195240
F 49-40-44195242

HPM,IG

Hochschule für Philosophie München
Institut für Gesellschaftspolitik
(Institute of Politics of the Society)
Kaulbachstrasse 31
80539 Munich

HUB, ZAGA

Humboldt Universität zu Berlin
Zentralinstitut für Alte Geschichte und Archäologie
Bereich Alter Orient
Unter den Linden 8
D-10099 Berlin
T 49-30-20370467

HUB, ZSKJ

Humboldt Universität zu Berlin
Zentrum für Sprache und Kultur Japans
Uniter den Linden 6
10099 Berlin

HUB,AA,IJ

Humboldt-Universität zu Berlin
Zentrum für Asien- und Afrikawissenschaften
Institut für Japanologie
(Institute for Japanese Studies)
Johannis Str. 10
10117 Berlin
T 49-30-28397731
F 49-30-28397719

Germany

HUB,AA,IS

Humboldt Universität zu Berlin
Zentrum für Asien- und Afrikawissenschaften
Institut für Sinologie
(Institute of Sinology)
Unter den Linden 6
10099 Berlin
T 49-30-2839770
F 49-30-28397719

HUB,AA,KI

Humboldt-Universität zu Berlin
Zentrum für Asien- und Afrikawissenschaften
Korea-Institut
(Institute for Korean Studies)
Unter den Linden 6
10099 Berlin
T 49-30-20936620
F 49-30-20936666

HUB,AA,SA

Humboldt Universität zu Berlin
Zentrum für Asien-und-Afrikawissenschaften
Südasien-Institut
(South Asia Institute)
Prenzlauer Promenade 149-152
13189 Berlin
T 49-30-479 73 02
F 49-30-479 71 08

HUB,AA,SA,G

Humbolt-Universität zu Berlin
Zentrum für Asien-und-Afrikawissenschaften
Südasien-Institut
Seminar für Geschichte
(Department of History)
Unter den Linden 6
10099 Berlin
T 49-30-20936640
F 49-30-20936666
juergen=luett@asa.hu-berlin.de

HUB,AA,SOA

Humboldt-Universität zu Berlin
Zentrum für Asien- und Afrikawissenschaften Südostasien-Institut
(Institute for Southeast Asian Studies)
Unter den Linden 6
10099 Berlin
T 49-30-28485630/34
F 49-30-28485666
h0198kaq@rz.hu-berlin.de

HUB,AA,SOA,SL

Humboldt-Universität zu Berlin
Zentrum für Asien- und Afrikawissenschaften Südostasien Institut
Abteilung Sprachen und Literaturen
(Institute for Southeast Asian Studies, Department of Language and Literature
Universitätsstrasse 3b
D-10099 Berlin
T 49-30-4229475

HUB,AA,ZA

Humboldt-Universität zu Berlin
Zentrum für Asien- und Afrikawissenschaften Zentralasiatisches Institut
(Central Asia Institute)
Unter den Linden 6
10099 Berlin
T 49-30-10936660
F 49-30-20936666

HUB,IAP

Humboldt-Universität zu Berlin
Institut für Allgemeine Pēdagogik
Abteilung Vergleichende Erziehungswissenschaft
Unter den Linden 6
10099 Berlin
T 49-30-20933331
F 49-30-20933333
juergen=henze@educat.hu-berlin.de

HUB,ITKK

Humboldt-Universität zu Berlin
Institut für Theaterwissenschaft und Kulturelle Kommunikation
Unter den Linden 6
10099 Berlin
T 49-30-30882312
F 49-30-30882231

IAA

Institute of Asian Affairs
Rothenbaumchaussee 32
20148 Hamburg

IFA

Institut für Asienkunde
(Institute for Asian Affairs)
Rothenbaumchaussee 32
20148 Hamburg
T 49-40-443001/03
F 49-40-4107945
ifahn@rrz.uni-hamburg.de

IFA,BIB

Institute für Asienkunde
Bibliothek
(Library)
Rothenbaumchassee 32
20148 Hamburg
T 49-40-443001
F 49-40-4107945

IWZ

Institut für Wissenschaftliche Zusammenarbeit
Vogtshalden Str. 24
72074 Tübingen
T 49-7071-5066
F 49-7071-26753

JFK

Japanisches Kulturinstitut
(Japan Foundation Köln)
Universitätsstrasse 98
50674 Cologne
T 49-221-401071/72
F 49-221-4060897
jki.j@ndh.net

JGU,DG

Johannes-Gutenberg-Universität Mainz
Department of Geography
P.O. Box 3980
55122 Mainz
Visiting Address:
Saar Str. 21
T 49-6131-392154
F 49-6131-394735

JGU,FAS

Johannes-Gutenberg-Universität Mainz
Fachbereich Angewandte Sprachwissenschaft
(Department of Applied Linguistics)
An der Hochschule 2
76711 Germersheim
T 49-7274-5080

JGU,IAVS

Johannes-Gutenberg-Universität Mainz
Institut für Allgemeine und Vergleichende Sprachwissenschaft
(Institute of General and Comparative Linguistics)
Jakob-Welder-weg 18
55099 Mainz
T 49-6131-393080
F 49-6131-393973

Germany

JGU,ICSK

Johannes-Gutenberg-Universität Mainz
Institut für Chinesische Sprache und Kultur
(Institute for Chinese Language and Culture)
An der Hochschule 2
55099 Mainz
T 49-6131-508371/375/374
F 49-6131-508407

JGU,IEAS

Johannes-Gutenberg-Universität Mainz
Institut für Ethnologie und Afrika Studien
(Ethnology and African Studies)
Forum 6
55099 Mainz
T 49-6131-392798
F 49-6131-393730
ifeas@goofy.zdv.uni-mainz.de

JGU,II

Johannes-Gutenberg-Universität Mainz
Institut für Indologie
(Institute for Indology)
Postfach 3980
55099 Mainz
Visiting Address:
Friedrich-von-Pfeiffer-weg 5
T 49-6131-3944553
F 49-6131-394452
meisig@googy.zdv.uni-mainz.de

JGU,IP

Johannes-Gutenberg-Universität Mainz
Institut für Politikwissenschaften
(Iinstitute for Political Science)
Colonel-Kleinmannweg 2
55099 Mainz
T 49-6131-392728
F 49-6131-393328

JGU,MI

Johannes-Gutenberg-Universität Mainz
Musikwissenschaftliches Institut
(Institute of Music Sciences)
Welderweg 18
55099 Mainz
T 49-6131-392589
F 49-6131-392589

JLUG,GI

Justus-Liebig Universität Giessen
Geographisches Institut
(Geographical Institute)
Senckenbergstrasse 1
35390 Giessen
T 49-641-7028210
F 49-641-7028211

JLUG,IO

Justus-Liebig Universität Giessen
Institute for Orientalism
(Oriental Institute)
Otto-Behagel Str. 10-E
35394 Giessen
T 49-641-9931061
F 49-641-9931069

JLUG,ITR

Justus-Liebig Universität Giessen
Institute for Tropical Research
Schott Str. 2
35394 Giessen
T 49-641-9912735
F 49-641-9912729

JLUG,VS

Justus-Liebig Universität Giessen
Vergleichende Sprachwissenschaft
(Comparative Linguistics)
Otto-Behaghel-Strasse 10 Haus G
35394 Giessen
T 49-641-7025615

JWGU,IGSWI

Johann Wolfgang Goethe-Universität Frankfurt
Indogermanische Sprachwissenschaft und Indologie
(Indo-Germanic Linguistics and Indology)
Georg-Voigt-Strasse 8
60054 Frankfurt am Main
T 49-69-7983139

JWGU,IOOP

Johann Wolfgang Goethe-Universität Frankfurt
Institut für Orientalische und Ostasiatische Philologien
(Institute of Oriental Studies and East Asian Languages and Literature)
Dantestrasse 4-6
60325 Frankfurt am Main

JWGU,IOOP,SIN

Johann Wolfgang Goethe-Universität Frankfurt
Institut für Orientalische und Ostasiatische Philologien
Sinologie
P.O. Box 11
60054 Frankfurt am Main
Visiting Address:
Dantestrasse 4-6 60054
T 49-69-7982852

JWGU,IOOP,SOAW

Johann Wolfgang Goethe-Universität Frankfurt
Institut für Orientalische und Ostasiatische Philologien
Südostasienwissenschaften
P.O. Box 11 19 32
60054 Frankfurt am Main
Visiting Address:
Elbingerstrasse 1
T 49-69-79823643
F 49-69-79822873
Nothofer@em.uni-frankfurt.de

JWGU,VK

Johann Wolfgang Goethe-Universität Frankfurt
Völkerkundliche Bibliothek
c/o Frobenius-Institut
Liebig Str. 41
60323 Frankfurt am Main

JWGU,VS

Johann Wolfgang Goethe-Universität Frankfurt
Vergleichende Sprachwissenschaft
(Comparative Linguistics)
Georg-Voigt-Str. 6
P.O.box 111932
60054 Frankfurt am Main
T 49-69-79828591
F 49-69-79822873

KHW

Kirchliche Hochschule Wuppertal
Missions Str. 9B
42285 Wuppertal
T 49-202-28200
F 49-202-2820-101

KI

Kulturwissenschaftliches Institut
Hagmanngarten 5
45259 Essen

Germany

KKF

Korea - Kommunikations - und Forschungszentrum
Korea Vergand e.V.
Asienhaus
Bullmannaue 11
45327 Essen
T 49-201-830 3812
F 49-201-830 3830

KMDE

Kuntsmuseum Düsseldorf im Ehrenhof
Ehrenhof 5
40479 Düsseldorf
T 49-2118992460
F 49-2118929046

KSG

Korea Studien Gesellshaft
(Korea Studies Association)
Nordstrasse 29
40820 Mettman
T 49-2104-971904
F 49-2104-971906

KU,WZBHF

Kassel Universität Wissenschaftliches Zentrum für Berufs- und Hochschol-Forschung
Henschelstrasse 4
34127 Kassel

KUE,KG

Katholische Universität Eichstätt
Mathematisch-Geographische Fakultät
Lehrstuhl für Kulturgeographie
Ostenstrasse 26
85071 Eichstätt
T 49-8421-931304
F 49-8421-935467

LFIK

Ludwig Forum für Internationale Kunst
Jülicher Straße 97-109
52070 Aachen
T 49-241-18070
F 49-241-1807101

LLC

Language Learning Centre
Am Hof 1
53113 Bonn
T 49-228-737248
F 49-228-735678

LMS

Linden-Museum Stuttgart Staatliches Museum für Völkerkunde
Hegelplatz 1
70174 Stuttgart
T 49-711-1231242
F 49-711-297047

LMU,AIS

Ludwig-Maximilians-Universität München
Institut für Allgemeine und Indogermanische Sprachwissenschaft
(Institute for General and Indo-Germanic Linguistic)
Geschwister-Scholl-Platz 1
8000 Munich
T 086-21802485

LMU,GSI

Ludwig-Maximilians-Universität München
Geschwister-Scholl-Institut für Politische Wissenschaft
(Institute of Polictial Science)
Oettingenstr. 67
80538 Munich
T 089-2180-3056
F 089-2180-3054
uf204al@sunmail.lrz-muenchen.de

LMU,II

Ludwig-Maximilians-Universität München
Institut für Indologie und Iranistik
(Indology and Iranian Studies)
Geschwister-Scholl-Platz 1
80539 Munich
T 49-89-21802353

LMU,IOAK

Ludwig-Maximilians-Universität München
Institut für Ostasienkunde
(Institute of East Asia Studies)
Geschwister-Scholl-Platz 1
80539 Munich
T 49-89-21802357
F 49-89-342666

LMU,IOAK,JAP

Ludwig-Maximilians-Universität München
Institut für Ostasienkunde
Japanologie
(Japanology)
Oettingen Str. 67
80538 Munich
T 49-89-21782808
F 49-89-21782801

LMU,IOAK,SIN

Ludwig-Maximilians-Universität München
Institut für Ostasienkunde
Sinologie
(Sinology)
Kaulbach Str. 51A
80539 Munich
T 49-89-21802349
F 49-89-342666
sinologie@lrz.uni.muenchen.de

LMU,IVA

Ludwig Maximilians Universität München
Institute für Völkerkunde und Afrikaistik
(Institute of Ethnology and African Studies)
Oettingen Str. 67
80538 Munich
T 49-89-2178 2601
F 49-89-2178 2602
ethnologie@liz.uni-menchen.de

LMU,JZ

Ludwig-Maximilians-Universität München
Japan-Zentrum
(Centre of Japanese Studies)
Kaiser Str. 9
80801 Munich
T 49-89-211 0630
F 49-89-211 0632

MIKB

Museum für Indische Kunst (Museum of Indian art Berlin)
Takustrasse 40
14195 Berlin
T 49-30-8301361
F 49-308316384

MKF

Museum für Kunsthandwerk
(Museum of Arts and Crafts)
Schaumainkai 17
60594 Frankfurt am Main
T 49-69-21234037
F 49-69-21230703

MLU,ABF

Martin-Luther-Universität Halle-Wittenberg
Arbeitsgemeinschaft für Buddhistische Forschung (Buddhist Centre)
Universitätsplatz 12
4020 Halle
T 046-8950

Germany

MLU,HPS,JAP

Martin-Luther-Universität Halle-Wittenberg
Faculty of History, Philosophy and Sociology
Department of Japanology
Brandberweg 23c
06099 Halle
T 49-345-5524331
F 49-345-5527059
foljanty@japanologie.uni-halle.de

MLU,KAW,II

Martin-Luther-Universität Halle-Wittenberg
Kunst- und Altertumswissenschaften
Institut für Indologie
(indological Institute)
Emil-Abderhalden Strasse 9
06099 Halle
T 49-345-5523652
F 49-345-5527226
slaje@indologie.uni-halle,de

MLU,KAW,OA

Martin-Luther-Universität Halle-Wittenberg
Kunst- und Altertumswissenschaften
Institut für Orientalische Archäologie
(Middle Eastern Archaeology)
Universitätsplatz 12 (Robertinum)
06108 Halle
T 49-46-832356

MOAKB

Museum für Ostasiatsche Kunst
(Museum for East Asian Art)
Lansstraße 8
14195 Berlin
T 49-30-8301382
F 49-30-8316384

MPZ

MPZ
Yorckstr. 2
14467 Potsdam
T 49-331-28998-23
F 49-331-28998-32

MS

Monumenta Serica
Institute.Journal.Library
Arnold-Janssen-Str. 20
53754 Sankt Augustin
T 49-2241-237431
F 49-2241-205841
monumenta.serica@t-online.de

MVB

Museum für Völkerkunde (Museum of Ethnography)
Arnimallee 27
14195 Berlin
T 49-30-8301231/131
F 49-30-8315972

MVF

Museum für Völkerkunde
(Museum of Ethnography)
Schaumainkai 29-37
60594 Frankfurt am Main
T 49-69-21238771
F 49-69-21230704

MVL,IA

Museum für Völkerkunde
Indienabteilung
(Museum of Ethnography, Indian Department)
Täubchenweg 2 (Grassimuseum)
7010 Leipzig
Visiting Address:
P.O. Box 955 04009
T 49-341-21420
F 49-341-2142262

NLM

Niedersächsisches Landemuseum Hannover
Willy-Brandt-Allee 5
30169 Hannover
T 49-511-9807800
F 49-511-9807-810

OAV

Oestasiatischer Verein e.V.
(East Asia Society)
Neuer Jungfernstieg 21
20354 Hamburg

OFU,IR

Otto-Friedrich-Universität Bamberg
Lehrstuhl für Iranistik
(Iranian Studies)
96045 Bamberg
T 49-951-8632178
F 49-951-8632180

OFU,OR

Otto-Friedrich-Universität Bamberg
Orientalistik
(Middle Eastern Studies)
96045 Bamberg

OFU,TUR

Otto-Friedrich-Universität Bamberg
Lehrstuhl für Türkische Sprache
Geschichte und Kultur
(Turkish Studies)
96045 Bamberg
T 49-951-863 2181
F 49-951-863 5182

OWK

Ost-West-Kolleg
Willy Brandtstr. 1
50321 Brühl
T 49-2232-9298240
F 49-2232-9299020

PUM,CJS

Philipps-Universität Marburg
Center for Japanese Studies
Biegenstrasse 9
D-35037 Marburg
T 49-642-128-4527
F 49-642-1288914
is@mailer.uni-marburg.de

PUM,FR

Philipps-Universität Marburg
Religionswissenschaften (Department o Religious Studies)
Liebig Strasse 37
35032 Marburg
T 49-6421-283662
F 49-6421-283944

PUM,ICDC

Philipps -Universität Marburg
Institute for Cooperation in Developing Countries
P.O. Box 1910
35008 Marburg

PUM,IND

Philipps-Universität Marburg
Indologie
Wilhelm-Röpke-Str. 6F
35032 Marburg
T 49-6421-284741
F 49-6421-288913
soni@mailer.uni.marburg.de

PUM,IOAS,ASKU

Philipps-Universität Marburg
Indisch-Ostasiatisches Seminar
Fachbereich Aussereuropäische Sprachen und Kulturen
Wilhelm-Röpke-Strasse 6 F
35032 Marburg
T 49-6421-284741

Germany

PUM,JZ

Philipps-Universität Marburg
Japan-Zentrum
(Centre for Japanese Studies)
Biegenstrasse 9
35032 Marburg
T 49-6421-284627
F 49-6421-288914

PUM,RS

Philipps-Universität Marburg
Religionskundliche Sammlung
Landgraf-Phillip-Strasse 4
35032 Marburg
T 49-6421-282480

PUM,SEM

Philipps-Universität Marburg
Seminar für Semitistik
Wilhelm-Röpke-Strasse 6F
35032 Marburg
T 1-6421-284 794

PUM,SIN

Philipps-Universität Marburg
Sinologie
Wilhelm-Röpke-Strasse 6E
35032 Marburg
T 49-6421-284933
F 49-6421-288913

RKU

Ruprecht-Karls-Universität Heidelberg
Friedrich-Ebertanlage 6-10
69117 Heidelberg
T 49-6221-54 74 66
F 49-6221-54 76 54

RKU, SI

Ruprecht-Karls-Universität Heidelberg
Südasien-Institut
Department of History
Im Neuenheimer Feld 330
69120 Heidelberg
T 49-6221-548942
F 49-6221-544989

RKU,IE

Ruprecht-Karls-Universität Heidelberg
Institut für Ethnologie
(Institute for Ethnology)
Im Neuenheimer Feld 330
69120 Heidelberg
T 49-6221-542236
F 49-6221-543556
ethnologie@urz.uni-heidelberg.de

RKU,KI

Ruprecht-Karls-Universität Heidelberg
Kunsthistorisches Institut
(Art History Institute)
Seminar Str. 4
69117 Heidelberg

RKU,KI,AA

Ruprecht-Karls-Universität Heidelberg
Kunsthistorisches Institut
Department of Asian Art
Seminar Str. 4
69117 Heidelberg
T 49-6221-542352
F 49-6221-543384
oakg@gw.sino.uni-heidelberg.de

RKU,OAW

Ruprecht-Karls-Universität Heidelberg
Orientalistik und Altertumswissenschaf
(Middle Eastern and Early History)
Hauptstrasse 120
69117 Heidelberg

RKU,OAW,JAP

Ruprecht-Karls-Universität Heidelberg
Orientalistik und Altertumswissenschaf
Japanologisches Seminar
(Japanology)
Akademie Str. 4-8
69117 Heidelberg
T 49-6221-547660
F 49-6221-547692
hw3@ix.urz.uni-heidelberg.de

RKU,OAW,SIN

Ruprecht-Karls-Universität Heidelberg
Orientalistik und Altertumswissenschaf
Sinologisches Seminar
(Sinology)
Akademie Str. 4-8
69117 Heidelberg
T 49-6221-547765
F 49-6221-547639

RKU,SI

Ruprecht-Karls-Universität Heidelberg
Südasien-Institut
(South Asia Institute)
Im Neuenheimer Feld 330
69120 Heidelberg
T 49-6221-548900
F 49-6221-544998
Ag5@vm.urz.uni-heidelberg.de

RKU,SI,AG

Ruprecht-Karls-Universität Heidelberg
Südasien-Institut
Abteilung Geographie
(Geography Department)
P.O. Box 103066
69020 Heidelberg
Visiting Address:
Im Neuenheimer Feld 330 69120
Heidelberg
T 49-6221-548951
F 49-6221-545926

RKU,SI,AG

Ruprecht-Karls-Universität Heidelberg
Südasien-Institut
Abteilung für Geschichte
(History)
Im Neuenheimer Feld 330
69120 Heidelberg
T 49-6221-546302
F 49-6221-544998

RKU,SI,BIB

Ruprecht-Karls-Universität Heidelberg
Südasien-Institut
Bibliothek
Im Neuenheimer Feld 330
69120 Heidelberg
T 49-6221-562902
F 49-6221-564998

RKU,SI,DAAE

Ruprecht-Karls-Universität Heidelberg
Südasien-Institut
Department of Applied and Agricultura
Economics
Im Neuenheimer Feld 330
69120 Heidelberg

RKU,SI,DE

Ruprecht-Karls-Universität Heidelberg
Südasien-Institut
Department of Economics
Im Neuenheimer Feld 330
69120 Heidelberg

RKU,SI,DHR

Ruprecht-Karls-Universität Heidelberg
Südasien-Institut
Department of History of Religions
Im Neuenheimer Feld 330
69120 Heidelberg
T 49-6221-402932

Germany

RKU,SI,DI

Ruprecht-Karls-Universität Heidelberg
Südasien-Institut
Department of Indology
Im Neuenheimer Feld 330
69120 Heidelberg
T 49-6221-548916
F 49-6221-544998

RKU,SI,DPS

Ruprecht-Karls-Universität Heidelberg
Südasien-Institut
Department of Political Science
Im Neuenheimer Feld 330
69120 Heidelberg
T 49-06221-548825
F 49-06221-544591

RKU,SI,DTHPH

Ruprecht-Karls-Universität Heidelberg
Südasien-Institut
Department of Tropical Hygiene and Public Health
Im Neuenheimer Feld 330
69120 Heidelberg

RKU,SI,IWE

Ruprecht-Karls-Universität Heidelberg
Südasien-Institut
Internationale Wirtschaft- und Entwicklungspolitik
(International Economic and Development Policy)
Im Neuenheimer Feld 330
69120 Heidelberg
T 49-6221-54 89 13
F 49-6221-54 49 98
H93@urz-mail.urz-uni-heidelberg.de

RKU,SI,KG

Ruprecht-Karls-Universität Heidelberg
Südasien-Institut
Kunstgeschichte
(Art History)
Im Neuenheimer Feld 330
69120 Heidelberg
T 49-6221-54 89 00
F 49-6221-54 49 98

RKU,SI,MSALL

Ruprecht-Karls-Universität Heidelberg
Südasien-Institut
Modern South Asian Languages and Literature
Im Neuenheimer Feld 330
69120 Heidelberg
T 6221-562917
F 6221-544998
fo7@ix.urz.uni-heidelberg.de

RMA

Reiss-Museum Mannheim
(Museum of Anthropology)
Postfach103051
68030 Mannheim
T 49-621-2932081/2082
F 49-621-2933064

RUB,FOAW

Ruhr-Universität Bochum Fakultät für Ostasienwissenschaften
Sektion Wirtschaft Ostasiens
GB 1/159
Postfach 10 21 48
44780 Bochum
Visiting Address:
Universitätstrasse 150 44801
44801 Bochum
T 49-234-7006189
F 49-234-7094265

RUB,FOAW

Ruhr-University of Bochum Fakultät für Ostasienwissenschaften
(Faculty of East Asian Studies)
Universitäts Str. 150\ Postfach 102148
44780 Bochum
T 49-234-7094584
F 49-234-7006189

RUB,FOAW,JAP

Ruhr-Universität Bochum Fakultät für Ostasienwissenschaften Sprache und Literatur Japans
(Japanology)
Postfach 10 21 48
44780 Bochum
T 49-234-700 6252
F 49-234-709 4231

RUB,FOAW,KOR

Ruhr-Universität Bochum Fakultät für Ostasienwissenschaften Koreanistik
(Korean Studies)
Postfach 10 21 48
44721 Bochum

RUB,FOAW,POA

Ruhr-Universität Bochum Fakultät für Ostasienwissenschaften
Lehrstuhl Politik
(Chair of East Asian Politics)
Gebäude GB 1/134 Universitätsstrasse 150
44780 Bochum
T 49-234-7005408
F 49-234-7094585

RUB,GI

Ruhr-Universität Bochum Fakultät für Geowissenschaften
Geographisches Institut
(Gepgraphy)
Universität Str. 150 Geb. NA 7/171
44801 Bochum
T 49-234-7004789
F 49-234-7094484

RUB,SOI

Ruhr-Universität Bochum Seminar für Orientalistik und Indologie
(Middle Eastern and Indian Languages)
Postfach 102148
44780 Bochum
Visiting Address:
Universitätsstr. 150
Geb. GB 2/136
T 49-234-7005125
F 49-234-7094671

RWTH,CF

Rheinisch-Westfälische Technische Hochschule Aachen
China-Forschung
Rochusstrasse 1-14
52056 Aachen
T 49-241-806097
F 49-241-8888160
100271.3215@compuserve.com

SBIBB,OA

Staatsbibliothek zu Berlin
Orientabteilung
Potsdamer Strasse 33
10785 Berlin
T 49-30-2662489
F 49-30-2645955

SCHI,DEA

Schiller Institute
Department East Asia
Postfach 5301
65043 Wiesbaden

SEACC,TC

Southeast Asia Communication Centre
Tai Culture
Tor Str. 40
10119 Berlin
T 49-30-2479458
F 49-30-2479458
taiculture@aol.com

Germany

SEAIC

Southeast Asien Information Centre
Bullmannaue 11
45327 Essen
T 49-201-8303818
F 49-201-8303819
seainfo@geod.geonet.de

SKD,P

Staatliche Kunstammlungen Dresden
Porzellansammlung
Zwinger
010067 Dresden
T 49-351-4914629
F 49-351-4914612

SMB,MFEA

Staatliche Museen zu Berlin
Museum of Far Eastern Art
Takusstrasse 40
14195 Berlin
T 49-30-8301 381
F 49-30-831 59 72

SMVD,DSA

Staatliches Museum für Völkerkunde
Dresden Department of South Asia
Palaisplatz 11
Japanisches Palais
01097 Dresden
T 49-351-814 48 50
F 49-351-814 48 88

SMVM

Staatliches Museum für Völkerkunde
(State Museum of Anthropolgy)
Maximilianstrasse 42
80538 Munich
T 49-89-210136-0
F 49-89-21013647
100275.1130@CompuServe.Com

SW

Sanskrit-Wörterbuch der Turfan-Funde
und Kommission für Buddhistische
Studien der Akademie der
Wissenschaften
Am Reinsgraben 4
3400 Göttingen
T 49-551-58125

SWP,FIPS,A

Stiftung Wissenschaft und Politik
Forschungsinstitut für Internationale
Politik und Sicherheit Asia
Haus Eggenberg Zeller weg 27
82067 Ebenhausen
T 49-8178-70390
F 49-8178-70312

TUB,IEM

Technische Universität Berlin Umwelt-
Sozial- und Planungswissenschaften
Institute of Environmental Managemen
Franklin Str. 28-29
10587 Berlin

TUCW,DR

Technische Universität Carolo-
Wilhelmina zu Braunschweig
George Eckert Institute for Internationa
Textbooks
Department of Research
Celler Str. 3
38114 Braunschweig

TUCW,IGG

Technische Universität Carolo-
Wilhelmina zu Braunschweig
Institut für Geographie & Geoökologie
(Institute of Geography and
Geoecology)
Langer Kamp 19c
38106 Braunschweig
T 49-531-3915625
F 49-531-3918170

TUCW,PS

Technische Universität Carolo-
Wilhelmina zu Braunschweig Seminar
für Politikwissenschaften und Soziologi
(Political Science and Sociology)
Wendenting 1
38114 Braunschweig
T 49-531-3912310
F 49-531-3918211

TUCW,WW

Technische Universität Carolo-
Wilhelmina zu Braunschweig Facultät
Wirtschaftswissenschaften
(Economics)
P.O. Box 3329
38023 Braunschweig

UA,MCH

Universität Augsburg
Modern and Contemporary History
Universitätsstr. 10
86135 Augsburg
T 49-821-5982496
F 49-821-5985501

UB, DH

Universität Bremen
Department of History
Bibliothek Str.
28334 Bremen

UB,ED

Rheinische Friedrich-Wilhelms
Universität Bonn
Economics Development Economics
Adenauerallee 24-42
53113 Bonn
T 49-228-737967
F 49-228-739100

UB,GI

Rheinische Friedrich-Wilhelms
Universität Bonn
Geographisches Institut
(Geography)
Meckenheimer Allee 166
53115 Bonn
T 49-228-737243
F 49-228-737230

UB,IA

Rheinische Friedrich-Wilhelms
Universität Bonn
Institut für Agrarpolitik;
Marktforschung und
Wirtschaftssoziologie
(Institute of Agricultural Policy; Marke
Research and Economic Sociology)
Regina Pacis Weg 3
5300 Bonn
T 49-228-733293
F 49-228-732953

UB,IW

Rheinische Friedrich-Wilhelms-
Universität Bonn
Institut für Wirtschaftsgeographie
(Economic Geography)
Meckenheimer Allee 166
53115 Bonn
T 49-228-737225
F 49-228-595117

UB,JAP

Rheinische Friedrich-Wilhelms
Universität Bonn
Japanologisches Seminar
(Japanology)
Regina Pacis Weg 7
D-53113 Bonn
T 49-228-737223/72247599
F 49-228-737020

Germany

UB,OKG

Rheinische Friedrich-Wilhelms
Universität Bonn
Seminar für Orientalische
Kunstgeschichte
(Middle Eastern Art History)
Regina-Pacis-weg 1
53113 Bonn

T 49-228-737212/13

F 49-288-735579

UB,OS,AI

Rheinische Friedrich-Wilhelms
Universität Bonn
Orientalisches Sprachen
Abteilung für Indonesisch
(Southeast Asian Department)
Adenaueralle 102
53113 Bonn

T 49-228-738432

F 49-228-738415

UB,SI

Rheinische Friedrich-Wilhelms
Universität Bonn
Indologisches Seminar
(Indology)
Regina-Pacis-Weg 7
53113 Bonn

T 49-228-738432

UB,SI

Rheinische Friedrich-Wilhelms
Universität Bonn
Sprachwissenschaftliches Institut
(Linguistic Institute)
An der Schlosskirche 2
53113 Bonn

T 49-228-737692

F 49-228-737696

UB,SO

Rheinische Friedrich-Wilhelms
Universität Bonn
Orientalisches Seminar
(Middle Eastern Studies)
Adenaverallee 102
53113 Bonn

T 49-228-737462

UB,SS

Rheinische Friedrich-Wilhelms
Universität Bonn
Seminar für Sinologie
Regina-Pacis-Weg 7
53113 Bonn

T 49-228-737731

F 49-228-737255

upp800@ibue.n-hn-z.uni-bonn.de

UB,SVR

Rheinische Friedrich-Wilhelms
Universität Bonn
Seminar für Vergleichende
Religionswissenschaft
(Comparative Religions)
Adenauerallee 4-6
53113 Bonn

T 49-228-737324

UB,ZA

Rheinische Friedrich-Wilhelms
Universität Bonn
Seminar für Sprach- und
Kulturwissenschaft Zentralasiens
Regina-Pacis-Weg 7
53113 Bonn

T 49-228-737465

F 49-228-737458

Uzso79@ibm.rhrz.uni-bonn.de

UB,ZA,TB

Rheinische Friedrich-Wilhelms
Universität Bonn
Seminar für Sprach- und
Kulturwissenschaft Zentralasiens
Abteilung Tibet
(Tibetan Studies)
Regina-Pacis-Weg 7
53113 Bonn

T 49-228-737465

F 49-228-737458

UBAY,KW,E

Universität Bayreuth
Kulturwissenschaftliche Fakultät
Abteilung Ethnologie
95440 Bayreuth

T 49-921-555443

F 49-921-555325

UBI,FS

Universität Bielefeld
Fakultät für Soziologie
(Faculty of Sociology)
Postfach 8640
4800 Bielefeld 1
Visiting Address:
Universitätsstr. 25 33615 Bielefeld

T 49-521-1064896

F 49-521-1065844

UBI,FS,SDRC

Universität Bielefeld
Fakultät für Soziologie
Sociology of Development Research
Centre
P.O.Box 100131
33501 Bielefeld

T 49-521-1064650

F 49-521-1062980

hdevers@post.uni-bielefeld.de

UBI,SEAP

Universität Bielefeld
South-East Asia Programme
P.O. Box 8640
33615 Bielefeld

UBI,ZIF

Universität Bielefeld
Zentrum für Interdisziplinäre Forschung
(Centre of Interdisciplinary Research)
Wellenberg 1
33615 Bielefeld

T 49-0521-106 2777

F 49-0521-106 2782

UBR,DCS

Universität Bremen
Department of Cultural Science
P.O.Box 330440
28334 Bremen

T 49-421-2187424

F 49-421-2187574

UBR,DRS

Universität Bremen
Department of Religious Studies
P.O. Box 330440
28334 Bremen

UBR,FW

Universität Bremen
Fachbereich Wirtschaftswissenschaft
World Economics
Postfach 330 440
28334 Bremen

T 49-421-2183011

F 49-421-2184550

UBR,GI

Universität Bremen Geographisches
Institut,
Postfach 33 04 40
28334 Bremen

T 49-421-2183682

F 49-421-2187183

Germany

UFK,FI

Universität Fridericana zu Karlsruhe
Frauenhofer-Institute for Systems and Innovation Research
Breslauerstrasse 48
76139 Karlsruhe
T 44-721-6809141
F 44-721-6809176

UGE,LS

Universität Gesamthochschule Essen
Literatur- und Sprachwissenschaft
(Literature and Linguistics)
Universitätsstrasse 12
45117 Essen
T 49-201-1833375
F 49-201-1832151

UGK,SL

Universität Gesamthochschule Kassel
Abteilung Stadt- und Landschafsplanning
(Urban and Landscape Planning)
Henschel Str. 2
34119 Kassel

UGS,PW

Universität - Gesamthochschule - Siegen
Politikwissenschaft
(Political Science)
Adolf-Reichwein-Str. 2
57068 Siegen

UHAM,G

Gästehaus der Universität Hamburg
Rothenbaumchausse 34
20148 Hamburg

UHAM,IB

Universität Hamburg
Institut für Internationale Beziehungen
(International Relations)
Rothenbaumchaussee 19-23
20148 Hamburg

UHAM,IE

Universität Hamburg
Institut für Ethnologie
(Institute for Ethnology)
Rothenbaumchaussee 64-A
20148 Hamburg
T 49-40-41234182
F 49-40-41236288

UHAM,II

Universität Hamburg
Institut für Indology
Neue Raben Str. 3
20354 Hamburg

UHAM,IIA

Universität Hamburg
Institut für Internationalen Angelegenheiten
(Institute of International Affairs, IIA)
Rothenbaumchaussee 19
20148 Hamburg
T 49-40-41234601
F 49-40-41236263

UHAM,IMOR

Universität Hamburg
Institut für Missions-, Ökumene- und Religionswissenschaften
Sedan Strasse 19
20146 Hamburg

UHAM,IPS

Universität Hamburg
Institute for Political Science
20146 Hamburg

UHAM,JAP

Universität Hamburg
Seminar für Sprache und Kultur Japans
(Department of Japanese Language and Culture)
Von Melle Park 6
20146 Hamburg
T 49-40-41232670
F 49-40-41236200

UHAM,KGIT

Universität Hamburg
Institut für Kultur und Geschichte Indiens und Tibets
(Indian and Tibetan Studies)
Neue Rabenstrasse 3
20345 Hamburg
T 49-40-4123 3385
F 49-40-4123 6267
schmithausen@rrz.uni-hamburg.de

UHAM,SGKVO,AI

Universität Hamburg
Seminar für Geschichte und Kultur des Vorderen Orients Arbeitsbereich Iranistik
(Iranian Studies)
Rothenbaumchaussee 36
Hamburg
T 49-40-41233180
F 49-40-41235674

UHAM,SIS

Universität Hamburg
Seminar für Indonesische und Südseesprachen
(Indonesian and South Sea Languages)
Bogenallee 11
20144 Hamburg
T 49-40-41232696
F 49-40-41236346
indons@phil.philosophie.uni-hamburg.de

UHAM,SKC,AK

Universität Hamburg
Seminar für Sprachen und Kulturen Chinas
(Department of Language and Culture of China)
Abteilung Korea
(Korea Division)
Binder Str. 34
20146 Hamburg
T 49-40-41233296
F 49-40-41236484
or5a007@rrz.uni-hamburg.de

UHAM,SKC,KTV

Universität Hamburg
Seminar für Sprache und Kultur Chinas
Abteilung Korea, Thailand, und Vietnam
Von-Melle-Park 6
20146 Hamburg
T 49-40-41233675/2691
or4a011@rrz-cip-1.rrz.uni-hamburg.de

UHAM,SKC,TBI

Universität Hamburg
Faculty of Orientalistik
Seminar für Sprache und Kultur Chinas
Abt. Thailand, Burma und Indochina
Von-Melle-Park 6
20146 Hamburg
T 49-40-41234878
F 49-40-41236484

UHAM,SKC,VIET

Universität Hamburg
Seminar für Sprache und Kultur Chinas
(Department for Language and Culture of China)
Abteilung Vietnamstudien
(Viet Nam Studies Divison)
Von-Melle-Park 6
20146 Hamburg
T 49-40-41234878
F 49-40-41233106

Germany

UHNV,BP

Universität Hannover
Institut für Berufspädagogik
(Occupational Education)
Wunstofer Str. 14
30453 Hannover

UHNV,EG

Universität Hannover
Abt. Wirtschaftsgeographie
(Economic Geography)
Schneiderberg 50
30167 Hannover
T 49-511-7623310
F 49-511-7623051
Diez@mbox.wigeo.uni-hannover.de

UHOH,IAESST

University Hohenheim
Institute of Agricultural Economics and
Social Sciences in the Tropics
P.O. Box 700562
7000 Stuttgart

UK,AHI,DEAA

Universität zu Köln
Art Historic Institute
Department of East Asian Art
An St. Laurentius 4
50931 Cologne
T 49-221-4704583

UK,IDSL

Universität zu Köln
Institut für Deutsche Sprache und
Literatur
Albert Magnus Platz
50923 Cologne
T 49-221-4702460
F 49-221-4705107

UK,II

Universität zu Köln
Institute for Indology
Pohligstr. 1
50969 Cologne
T 49-221-470-5344
F 49-221-4705151
db.Kapp@uni-Koeln.de

UK,IIFPL

Universität zu Köln
Institute of International and Foreign
Private Law
Gottfried Kelerstrasse 2
50923 Cologne
T 49-221-2057367
F 49-221-4705129

UK,IV

Universität zu Köln
Institut für Völkerkunde
(Institute for Ethnology)
Albertus-Magnus-Platz
50937 Cologne
T 49-221-4702278
F 49-221-4705117

UK,MI

Universität zu Köln
Musikwissenschaftliches Institut
Albertus Magnus-Platz
50923 Cologne
T 49-221-4702249
F 49-221-4704964

UK,OAS,MCS

Universität zu Köln
Ostasiatisches Seminar
(East Asian Department)
Moderne China-Studien
(Modern Chinese Studies)
Dürener Str. 62-67
50923 Cologne
T 49-221-4705401/5402
F 49-221-4705406

UK,OAS,SM

Universität zu Köln
Ostasiatisches Seminar
(East Asian Department)
Abteilung Sinologie und Manjuristik
(Sinology and Manchuria Division)
Albertus-Magnus-platz
50923 Cologne
T 49-0221-4705431/2

UK,OS

Universität zu Köln
Orientalisches Seminar
Albert-Magnus-Platz
50923 Cologne
T 49-221-4705411/5412

UK,OS,AJ

Universität zu Köln
Ostasiatisches Seminar
(East Asia Department)
Abteilung Japanologie
(Japanology Division)
Dürener Str. 56-60
50931 Cologne
T 49-221-4705442
F 49-221-4705448

UK,OS,MA

Universität zu Köln
Orientalisches Seminar Malaiologischer
Apparat
Kerpener str. 30
50923 Cologne
T 49-221-4703470
F 49-221-4705043

UKON,SF,EP

Universität Konstanz
Sozialwissenschaftliche Fakultät
Entwicklungspsychologie
Universitätsstr. 10
78434 Konstanz
T 49-7531-882911
F 49-7531-883039

UKON,SF,KVMJ

Universität Konstanz
Sozialwissenschaftliche Fakultät
Kulturvergleich Gesellschaft und
Kultur des Modernen Japan
(Comparative Cultures and the Culture
of Modern Japan)
Universitätsstr. 10
78434 Konstanz
T 49-7531-882917
F 49-7531-883039

UL,IE

Universität Leipzig
Institut für Ethnologie
Schillerstrasse 6
04109 Leipzig

UL,IIZAW

Universität Leipzig
Institut für Indologie und
Zentralasienwissenschaften
(Indology and Central Asia Studies)
Schillerstrasse 6
D-04109 Leipzig
T 49-341-9737120
F 49-341-9605187

UL,IP

Universität Leipzig
Institut für Politikwissenschaft
Augustusplatz 9
04109 Leipzig
T 49-341-9735630/32
F 49-341-9605003

UL,LFSO

Universität Leipzig
Lehr- und Forschungsbereich Süd-
Ostasien
Augustusplatz 9
04109 Leipzig

Germany

UL,OAI

Universität Leipzig
Ostasiatisches Institut
Schillerstrasse 6
04109 Leipzig
T 49-341-9737150
F 49-341-9737159
ostasien@

UL,OI

Universität Leipzig
Orientalisches Institute
(Middle Eastern Studies)
Schiller Str. 6
04109 Leipzig
T 49-341-9737200
F 49-341-9737219

UMAN,HIS

Universität Mannheim
Historisches Institut
Seminar für Neuere Geschichte
(History)
Schloss EO 210
68131 Mannheim
T 49-621-2925541
F 49-621-2922177

UP,SEAS

Universität Passau
Lehrstuhl für Südostasienkunde
(Department of Southeast Asian Studies
Innstrasse 53
94032 Passau
T 49-851-5092740/1
F 49-851-5092742
seastudies@uni-passau.de/suedostasien

UP,SLTL

Universität Passau
Sprachen und Literaturen von Thailand und Laos
(Language and Literature of Thailand and Laos)
Innstrasse 53
94032 Passau
T 49-851-5092840
F 49-851-5091005
thailaostudies@uni-passau.de

UPOT,LSVROA

Universität Potsdam
Wirtschafts- und
Sozialwissenschaftliche Fakultät
Vergleichende Regierungslehre - Ostasien
(Comparative Governement Studies - East Asia)
P.O. Box 900 327
14439 Potsdam
T 49-331-9770
F 49-331-977-3302

UR,WSF,IPV

Universität Rostock
Wirtschaft- und Sozialwissenschaften
Fakultät Institut für Politik und
Verwaltungswissenshaften
(Political Science)
Vogelsang 14
18055 Rostock
T 49-381-4983323
F 49-381-4983328

URG,AIGS

Universität Regensburg
Institut für Allgemeine und
Indogermanische Sprachwissenschaf
(General and Indo-Germanic Linguistics)
Universitätsstrasse 31
8400 Regensburg
T 0941-9433388

US,DG

Universität des Saarlandes
Department of Geography
6600 Saarbrücken
T 49-681-3022314\914
F 49-681-3022764
j.kubiniok@rz.uni-sb.de

US,IP

Universität des Saarlandes Faculty of Law & Economics Institut für
Politikwissenschaft
(Political Science)
Im Stadtwald, Geb. 31
Postfach 151150
66041 Saarbrücken
T 49-681-3022126
F 49-681-3023186

US,VIGSI

Universität des Saarlandes
Vergleichende Indogermanische
Sprachwissenschaft und Indoiranistik
(Comparative Indo-Germanic
Linguistics and Indo-Iranian Studies)
Postfach 151150
66041 Saarbrücken
T 0681-3023304

UT,CEAPS

Universität Trier
Centre for East Asian and Pacific Studies
Political Science Department
Postfach 3825
54286 Trier
T 49-651-201213
F 49-651-2013917

UT,FAP

Universität Trier
Seminar für Japanologie
(Department of Japanology)
Universitätsring 15
54286 Trier
T 49-651-2012152/62
F 49-651-2013945
japanolo@uni-trier.de\pc-japan@uni-trier.de

UT,SIN

Universität Trier
Seminar für Sinologie
Postfach 3825
54286 Trier
T 49-651-2013203/2
F 49-651-2013944

UU

Universität Ulm
Faculty of Medicine Dept. of Neurology & Psychiatry
Steinh"velstr. 9
89075 Ulm

UW,IOP

Bayerische Julius-Maximilians-
Universität Würzburg
Institut für Orientalische Philologie
(Oriental Philology)
Ludwigstrasse 6
97074 Würzburg
T 49-931-8885571
F 49-931-8884617

Germany

UW,IS

Bayerische Julius-Maximilians-Universität Würzburg
Institüt für Sinologie
(Sinology)
Am Hubland
97074 Würzburg
T 49-931-8885571
F 49-931-8884617
sino001@rzhub.uni-wuerzburg.de

UW,IVS

Bayerische Julius-Maximilians-Universität Würzburg
Institut für Vergleichende Sprachwissenschaft
(Comparative Linguistics)
Residenzplatz 2
970745 Würzburg
T 49-931-34824

UW,RG

Bayerische Julius-Maximilians-Universität Würzburg
Lehrstuhl für Religionsgeschichte
(History of Religion)
Wittelsbacher Platz 1
97074 Würzburg

V-SD

Volkswagen-Stiftung Division Natural and engineering sciences, medicine
Kastanienallee 35
30519 Hannover
T 49-511-8381389
F 49-511-8381344

WHU,KSCM,CJS

WHU-The Koldenz School of Corporate Management Centre for Japanese Studies
Burgplatz 2
56179 Vallendar
T 49-261-6509215
F 49-261-6509111

WWUM,G

Westfälische Wilhelms-Universität Münster
Geschichte
(History Department)
Pferdegasse 1
48143 Münster

WWUM,IE

Westfälische Wilhelms-Universität Münster
Institut für Ethnologie
(Institute for Ethnology)
Stüd Str. 21
48149 Münster
T 49-2-51-834575/54
F 49-2-51-834576

WWUM,IGS

Westfälische Wilhelms-Universität Münster
Seminar für Indogermanische Sprachwissenschaft
(Indo-Germanic Linguistics)
Rothenburg 32/I
4400 Münster
T 0251-834540

WWUM,II

Westfälische Wilhelms-Universität Münster
Insitut für Indologie
(Insitute of Indology)
Salzstrasse 53
48143 Münster
T 49-251-5104711\5104720
F 49-251-5104719

WWUM,IP

Westfälische Wilhelms-Universität Münster
Institut für Politikwissenschaft
(Institute for Political Science)
Scharnhorststr. 100 / Platz der Weissen Rose
48151 Münster
T 49-251-839357
F 49-251-839356

WWUM,ISO

Westfälische Wilhelms-Universität Münster
Institut für Sinology und Ostasienwissenschaften
(Institute for Sinology and East Asian Studies)
Schlaun Str. 2
48143 Münster
T 49-251-824574
F 49-251-834571

WWUM,ISP

Westfälische Wilhelms-Universität Münster
Institut für Sozial Politik Wissenschaften
(Institute for Social-Polictial Studies)
Platz der Weiáen Rose
48151 Münster
T 49-251-839359
F 49-251-839356

ZKM-M

ZKM-Medienmuseum
P.O.Box 6919
76049 Karlsruhe
T 49-721-93400
F 49-721-934019

Greece

BM

Benaki Museum
Koumbari 1
10674 Athens
T 01-3611617
F 01-3622547
mina@ektor.binaki.forthnet.gr

ECCRD

Eurochinese Centre for Research and Development
25 A Voukourestiou St.
10671 Athens
T 30-1-3613312
F 30-1-3616270

NHRF

National Hellenic Research Foundation (NHRF)
48 Vassileos Constantinou Avenue
11635 Athens
T 30-1-7229811
F 30-1-7246618

Hungary

BME,DEE

Budapesti Müszaki Egyetem
(Technical University of Budapest)
Department of Electrical Engineering
Goldmann Gy"rgy ter 3
1521 Budapest
T 36-1-4632740
F 36-1-4634118

ELU,CHL

Eötvös Loránd Tudományegyetem
(Eötvös Loránd University)
Comparative History of law
Egyetem Ter 1-3
1055 Budapest

Hungary

ELU,DJS

Eötvös Loránd Tudományegyetem
(Eötvös Loránd University)
Department of Japanese Studies
Muzeum krt. 4/b
1088 Budapest
T 36-1-2669833/ext.2033
F 36-1-2665699

FHMEAA

F. Hopp Museum of Eastern Asiatic Ar
Andr ssy £t 103
1062 Budapest
T 36-1-3228476
F 36-1-2175838

HAS

Magyar Tudom nyos Akadémia
(Hungarian Academy of Sciences)
Roosevelt tér 9
1051 Budapest
T 36-1-1382344
F 36-1-1172575

HAS,BIB,OC

Hungarian Academy of Sciences
Library
Oriental Collection
P.O.Box 1002
H-1245 Budapest
T 361-3123298
F 361-1316954
apor@vax.mtak.hu

HAS,DT

Hungarian Academy of Sciences
Department for Technology
N dor u. 7 PF 6
1361 Budapest

HAS,EIF

Hungarian Academy of Sciences
Ethnographic Institute Folklore
Orsz gh z utca 30
1250 Budapest
T 361-1759011
F 361-1759764

HAS,IWF,JESRC

Hungarian Academy of Sciences
Institute for World Economics Japan,
East and Southeast Asian Research
Centre
P.O.Box 936
1535 Budapest
T 36-1-3199385
F 36-1-3199386
ahernadi@vki3.vki.hu

HAS,SA

Hungarian Academy of Sciences
Subcommitee of Andragogy
I. Corvin Tér 8
1011 Budapest
T 36-1-201 49 28
F 36-1-201 37 66
esvafhss@attmail.com

IOCFT

Institute for Oriental Communication
and Further Training
Liget Utca 22
1102 Budapest
T 36-1-260-8917
F 36-1-261-4301
h5339hid@ella.hu

JAU,DAS

Józef Attila Todományegyetem
(Józef Attila University)
Department of Altaic Studies
Egyetem u. 2
6722 Szeged
T 36-62-454319
F 36-62-454319

JTHN,ELTE

Japanisztikai Tarsasag Hangari
Nihongakkai
(The Hungarian Society of Japanese
Studies)
c/o ELTE Japanese Studies
Muzeum krt. 4/B
1088 Budapest
T 36-1-2669833 (ext. 2033)
F 36-1-2665699
yamaji@osiris.elte.hu

NETI

Institute of International Technology
(NETI)
P.O. Box 570
1398 Budapest
Visiting Address:
Munk csy Mih ly u 16
T 36-1-301 2030
F 36-1-153 2320

Ireland

RIA,IES

Royal Irish Academy
Indo-European Subcommittee
19 Dawson street
2 Dublin
T 44-3553-1-6762570

Italy

AISTUGIA

Iassociazione Italiana per gli Studi
Giapponesi (AISTUGIA)
Italian Association for Japanese Studies
Via Festa del Perdono 3
20122 Milan
T 39-2-69008517

BIL

Banca Internazionale Lombarda
Via Brera 21
20121 Milan
T 39-2-721221
F 39-2-72022922

CELSO

C.E.L.S.O.
Via di Chiossone 6/10
16123 Geneva
T 39-10-586556

CESMEO

Centro Piemontese di Studi sul Medio e
Estremo Orient (CESMEO)
(International Institute for Advanced
Asian Studies)
Via Cavour 17
10123 Turin
T 39-11-545031
F 39-11-545031/546564

CSFEA

Centre for Study of Far Eastern Art
Via Val d'Aposa 5
40123 Bologna
T 39-51-227975
F 39-51-554592

CTIP,BDFA

CTIP Corporation Business
Development Far East
48, Via Cesare Diulio Viola
00148 Rome

DC

Centro Documentazione
(Documentation Center)
Mondipresa S.c.p.A.
Viale Pasteur, 10
00144 Rome
F 39-6-54954458

DSAAS

Dip. Scienz. Anthr. Arch Stor. Terr. H
150 Univ. Bibl.
Via Gioletti 21/e
10123 Turin
T 39-11-8122702
F 39-11-8174979

Italy

FGC,IVO

Fondazione Giorgio Cini
(Girorgio Cini Foundation)
Istituto Venezia e L'Oriente
(Venice and the Orient Institute)
Isola di san Giorgio Maggiore
30100 Venice

IGCR

Instituto Giapponese di Cultura in Roma
(Japan Cultural Institute in Rome)
Via Antonio Gramsci, 74
00197 Rome
T 39-6-49913562
F 39-6-4451209

IIA

Italian Institute for Asia
Via del Tempio 4
00186 Rome

ISIAO

Instituto Italiano per l'Africa e l'Oriente (Is.I.A.O.) Sezione Lombarda (Italian Institute for Africa and the Orientt\Lombard Section)
Via Festa del Perdono 3
20125 Milan
T 39-2-55212482
F 39-2-58315453

ISLAO

Italian Institute for Africa and the Orient (Islao)
Via Merulana 248 (Palazzo Brancaccio
00185 Rome
T 39-6-4874273
F 39-6-4873138

IUO, ALC

Istituto Universitario Orientale
(University Institute of Orient)
Asian Lexicography Centre
Palazzo Corigliano
Piazza San
Domenico Maggiore 12
80134 Napoli
T 39-81-5517860
F 39-81-5517852

NMOA

National Museum of Oriental Art
Via Merulana 248
00185 Rome

PAV

Pavia Ansaldo & Verusio
Via dell'Annunciata 7
20121 Milan
T 39-2-63381
F 39-2-654051

PI,BANES

Pontificio Instituto
Biblico
Ancient Near Eastern Studies
Via della Pilotta 25
00187 Rome
T 39-6-67016144
F 39-6-67016151

S24O

Il Sole 24 Ore
Via P. Loratto 51
20154 Milan
T 39-2-3103497
F 39-2-3103418

UB,DES

Università degli Studi di Bologna
(University of Bologna)
Department of Educational Science
Via Zamboni 34
40100 Bologna
T 39-51-258458
F 39-51-228847

UB,IG

Università degli Studi di Bologna
Istituto di Glottologia
(Institute of Glottology)
Via Zamboni 16
40100 Bologna
T 39-51-233133

UC, DCP

Università degli Studi Cagliari
(University of Cagliari)
Department of Classic Philology
Loc. 'Sa Duchessa'
09123 Cagliari
T 39-70-2002262
F 39-70-290405

UC,ISESAO

Università Commerciale Luigi Bocconi
Istituto di Studi Economico-Sociali per L'Asia Orientale
(Institute of Economic and Social Studies for East Asia (ISESAO))
Via Sarfatti 25
20136 Milan
T 39-2-58363317
F 39-2-58363309

UCS,ISAO

Università degli Studi Cagliari
(University of Calgliari)
Istituto di Africani e Orientali
(Institute of African and Oriental Studies)
Viale S. Ignazio 78
90123 Cagliari, Sardinia
T 39-70-6753764
F 39-70-6753760

UCSC

Università Cattolica del Sacre Cuore
(Catholic University of the Sacred Heart)
Largo A. Gemelli 1
20123 Milan
T 39-2-723 41
F 39-2-7234 22 10

UF,DSS

Università degli Studi di Firenze
(University of Florence)
Department of State Studies
Via Laura 48
50121 Florence
T 39-55-27571
F 39-55-2345486

UF,IGOLT

Università degli Studi di Firenze
Istituto di Lingue e Letterature Germaniche e Orientali
(Institute of German and Oriental Languages and Literature)
Via di Parione 7
50123 Florence
T 39-55-217704
F 39-55-217704

UG,IMMAH

Università degli Studi di Genova
Istituto di Storia Moderna e Contemporanea e Laboratorio di Storia della Scienza
(Institute of Medieval and Modern Art and History)
Via Balbi 4
16126 Geneva

UIO,DAAS

Istituto Universitario Orientale
(University Institute of Orient)
Department of African and Arabic Studies
Piazza San Giovanni Maggiore 30
80134 Naples

Italy

UIO,DAS

Istituto Universitario Orientale
(University Institute of Orient)
Department of Asian Studies
Palazzo Corigliano
Piazza San Domenico Maggiore 12
80134 Naples

T 39-81-5517860

F 39-81-5517852

UIO,DSO

Istituto Universitario Orientale
(University Institute of Orient)
Department Studi Orientali
Piazza San Domenico Maggiore 19
80134 Napoli

F 39-6-4873138

UM,IFL

Università degli Studi di Milan
(University of Milan)
Istituto di Lingue Staniere (Institute of Foreign Languages, Chinese)
Via del Conservatorio 7
20122 Milan

T 39-2-76074559-562

F 39-2-76013007

UM,IILP

Università degli Studi di Milano
Istituto di Diritto e Politica Internazionale
(Institute of International Law and Politics)
Via Conservatorio 7
20122 Milan

T 39-2-76074401

F 39-2-796146

UN FII,FPS

Università degli Studi di Napoli "Federico II"
(University of Neapel "Federico II")
Faculty of Political Science
Via Guglielmo Sanfelice 47
80134 Napoli

T 39-81-5522928

F 39-81-5522411

UP,CEUP

Università degli Studi di Pavia
(University of Pavia)
Center of Extra European Population "Cesare Bonacossa"
Strada Nuova 65
27100 Pavia

UP,DL

Università degli Studi di Pisa
(University of Pisa)
Department of Linguistics
Via S. Maria 36
56100 Pisa

UP,DLFL

Università degli Studi di Pavia
(University of Pavia)
Dipartimento di Lettere e Filosofia
Linguistics
Strada Nuova 65
27100 Pavia

T 39-382-504484

F 39-382-504487

UP,DMCH

Università degli Studi di Pisa
(University of Pisa)
Department of Modern and Contemporary History
Piazza Torricelli 3/A
56100 Pisa

F 39-50-501017

UP,DPSS

Università degli Studi di Pavia
(University of Pavia)
Department of Political and Social Studies
Strada Nuova 65
27100 Pavia

T 39-382-504446

F 39-382-504446

URLS,DOS

Università degli Studi di Roma "La Sapienza"
(University of Rome " La Sapienza")
Department of Oriental Studies
Piazzale Aldo Moro 5
00185 Rome

T 39-6-49913562

F 39-6-4451209

pcorradini@axrma.uniroma1.it

URS

Università delgi Studi di Roma "La Sapienza"
(University of Rome "La Sapienza)
Dipartment of Economical Science
Via A. Cesalpino 14
00161 Rome

T 39-06-44284200

F 39-06-44044572

UT,DPS

Università degli Studi di Torino
(University of Turin)
Department of Political Studies
Via Maria Vittoria 19
10123 Turin

T 00-39-11-835404

F 00-39-11-882123

UT,IOS

Università degli Studi di Torino
(University of Turin)
Institute of Oriental Studies
Via S. Ottavio 20
10124 Turin

T 39-11-8122211

F 39-11-8171053

piano@cisi.unito.it

UTT,DPS

Università degli Studi di Trieste
(University of Trieste)
Department of Political Science
Piazzale Europa 2
34127 Triest

UTT,HMLIT

Università degli Studi di Trieste
(University of Trieste)
Academyl of Modern Languages for Interpreters and Translators
Via D'Alviano 15/1
34100 Triest

T 39-40-771598

F 39-40-775032

UV,DEAS

Università degli Studi di Venezia
(University of Venice)
Department of European-Asian Studies
San Polo 2035 Palazzo Cappello
30125 Venice

T 39-41-5287220

F 39-41-5241847

UV,DSIEO

Università degli Studi di Venezia
(University of Venice)
Dipartimento di Studi Indologici ed Estremo Orientali
(Department of Indology and Far Eastern Studies)
San Polo 2169
30125 Venice

T 39-41-5285570

F 39-41-720809

Italy

UV,DSIEO,C

Università degli Studi di Venezia
(University of Venice)
Dipartimento de Studi Indologici ed Estremo Orientali
Department of Indian and Far Eastern Studies (Chinese)
Palazzo Soranzo
San Polo 2169
30125 Venice
T 39-41-5285570
F 39-41-720809
sabatti@unive.it

UV,DSIEO,J

Università degli Studi di Venezia
(University of Venice)
Dipartimento di Studi Indologici ed Estremo Orientali
Department of Indian and Far Eastern Studies (Japanese)
Palazzo Cappello
San Polo 2035
30125 Venice
T 39-41-5285801
F 39-41-5242397
boscaro@unive.it

UV,ECSG

Università degli Studi di Venezia
(University of Venice)
Economia e Commercia Scienze
(Economical and Commercial Sciences)
Giuridichi Dorsoduro 3911
30123 Venice
T 39-41-2578155
F 39-41-5242482

Luxemburg

SBI

Skydie Brown International s.a.
Publishing Division-Books on Asia
P.O.Box 66
9001 Ettelbruck

Malaysia

UKM

Universiti Kebangsaan Malaysia
436 000 UKM Bangi, Selangor

Netherlands

AB-DLO

AB-DLO
P.O.Box 14
6700 AA Wageningen

ABN,HA

ABN AMRO Bank NV
Historisch Archief
(Historical Archive)
P.O.Box 283
1000 EA Amsterdam
Visiting Address:
Vijzelstraat 32
T 31-20-6292907
F 31-20-6286314

Adenl

Adenleen B.V.
Abdij van Thornstraat 25
4854 KG Bavel
T 31161-431 390
F 31-161-431 390

AFM

Afrika Museum
Africa Museum
Postweg 6
6571 CS Berg en Dal

AH, AMINDHO

Asia House
Amindho
Amsterdam Indonesia House
WTC-Strawinskylaan 15
1077 XW Amsterdam
T 31-20-6766686
F 31-20-6737801
asia.house@pi.net

AH, TPNAF

Asia House
Trade Promotion the Netherlands - Asia Foundation
WTC -Strawinskylaan 15
1077 XW Amsterdam
T 31-20-676 66 86
F 31-20-673 78 01
Asia.house@pi.net

AH,AMPEK

Asia House
Amsterdam Beijing Association
WTC-Strawinskylaan 15
1077 XW Amsterdam
T 31-20-6766686
F 31-20-6737801
asia.house@pi.net

AH,DKTC

Asia House
Dutch Korean Trade Club
WTC-Strawinskylaan 15
1077 XW Amsterdam
T 31-20-6766686
F 31-20-6737801
asia.house@pi.net

AH,HHG

Asia House
Holland House Guangzhou
WTC-Strawinskylaan 15
1077 XW Amsterdam
T 31-20-6766686
F 31-20-6737801
31-20-6766686

AH,ITC

Asia House
India Trade Council
WTC-Strawinskylaan 15
1077 XW Amsterdam
T 31-20-6766686
F 31-20-6737801
asia.house@pi.net

AH,JTC

Asia House
Japan Trade Club
WTC-Strawinskylaan 15
1077 XW Amsterdam
T 31-20-6766686
F 31-20-6737801
asia.house@pi.net

AH,NTCC

Asia House
Netherlands Thai Chamber of Commerce
WTC-Strawinskylaan 15
1077 XW Amsterdam
T 31-20-6766686
F 31-20-6737801
asia.house@pi.net

AHM

Amsterdam Historisch Museum
(Amsterdam Historical Museum)
Nieuwezijds Voorburgwal 359
1012 LJ Amsterdam
T 31-20-5231822

Netherlands

AHM,BIB

Amsterdam Historisch Museum
(Amsterdam Historical Museum)
Bibliotheek
(Library)
Nieuwezijds Voorburgwal 359
1012 RM Amsterdam
T 31-20-523 18 22
F 31-20-620 77 89
101644@compuserve.com

AKSE

Association for Korean Studies
c/o Leiden University
Centre for Korean Studies
P.O. Box 9515
2300 RA Leiden
T 31-71-5272541
F 31-71-5272215
walraven@rullet.leidenuniv.nl

APAF

Apamana Foundation
P.O. Box 71415
1030 BC Amsterdan
T 31-20-6732268
F 31-20-6732268
idevrie@dds.nl

AR

Algemeen Rijksarchief
(General State Archive)
Prins Willem Alexanderhof 20
2595 BE The Hague
T 31-70-3315400
F 31-70-3805885

ASSR

Amsterdamse School voor Sociaal
Wetenschappelijk Onderzoek
(Institute for Development Research
Amsterdam)
Oude Hoogstraat 24
1012 CE Amsterdam

ASU

Amsterdam Summer University
Kustkanaal Redactie
P.O.Box 53066
1007 RB Amsterdam
T 31-20-6200225
F 31-20-6249368
as4@gn.apc.org

AVRO

AVRO-Televisie
Hoge Naarderweg 3
1217 AB Hilversum
T 31-35-6717 492/911
F 31-35-6717 517/461

BA

Bax Art
Concepts and Series
P.O.Box 18205
1001 ZC Amsterdam
T 31-20-6933601
F 31-20-6933601
baxarts@worldaccess.nl

BIL,AD

Bilance
Asia Department
P.O. Box 77
2341 BV Oegstgeest
Visiting Address:
Rhijngeesterstraatweg 40
T 31-71-5159 500
F 31-71-5175 391
bilance@antenna.nl

BLAAY

De Blaay Adviesgroep B.V.
Raadgevende Ingenieurs Rotterdam -
Jakarta
Vasteland 12-B
3011 BL Rotterdam
T 31-10-413 68 44
F 31-10-412 08 60
deblaayri@ib.com

BLF

Bernard van Leer Foundation
Department of Programme
Development and Management
P.O.Box 82334
2508 EH The Hague

BO

Both Ends
Environmental & Development service
for NGO's
Damrak 28-30
1012 LJ Amsterdam
T 31-20-623 08 23
F 31-20-620 80 49
bothends@gn.apc.org

BOT

Begeleiding en Organisatie van
Tentoonstelingen (B.O.T.)
P.O.Box 10
6663 ZG Lent

BPSC

Bangladesh People's Solidarity Centre
P.O.Box 40066
1009 BB Amsterdam
T 31-20-6937681

Bulaaq Uitg.

Bulaaq Uitgeverij
Recht Boomssloot 88-90
1011 ED Amsterdam
T 31-20-420 22 34
F 31-20-4200744/6319948

BuZa, DAO/ZO

Ministerie van Buitenlandse Zaken
DGRB, Afd. DAO/ZO
P.O.Box 20061
2500 EB The Hague
T 31-70-3484087
F 31-70-3484909

CAC

Child in Art Center
Wallestein 52
1081 BD Amsterdam

CBG

Centraal Bureau voor Genealogie
(Centre for Genealogy)
Pr. Willem-Alexanderhof 26
2502 AT The Hague
T 31-70-3150536

CERES

Research School for Resource Studies
for Human Development (CERES)
P.O.Box 80140
3508 TC Utrecht
Visiting Address:
Heidelberglaan 1 De Uithof
T 31-30-2534815
F 31-30-2537482
ceres@fsw.ruu.nl

CFA

Christie's Fine Art Auctioneers
Corn Schuytstraat 57
1071 JG Amsterdam
T 31-20-5755255
F 31-20-6640899

Netherlands

CHIME

European Foundation for Chinese Music Research
P.O.Box 11092
2301 EB Leiden
Visiting Address:
Gerecht 1 2311 TC Leiden
T 31-71-5133123
F 31-71-5123183
chime@worldaccess.nl

CHKD

China Hong Kong Development B.V.
Exhibition and Training Department
Hongkongstraat 5
3047 BR Rotterdam
T 31-10-4626588
F 31-10-4626598

CHW

Christelijke Hogeschool Winterheim
(Christian School Winterheim)
Campus 2-6
8000 GB Zwolle
T 31-38-4699433
F 31-38-4659268

CIJS

Centrum voor Internationale Juridische Samenwerking
(Centre for International Juridical Co-operation)
Stationsplein 234
2312 AR Leiden

CIP

Chinterpret
De Sitterweg 4
9751 VJ Haren (Gr)
T 31-50-534 84 40
F 31-50-534 11 87

CKE

Centrum Kunsteducatie Apeldoorn
(Centre for Art Education)
Creativiteitscentrum
Craetivity Centre
Nieuwstraat 377
7311 BR Apeldoorn
T 31-55-521 39 67
F 31-55-578 77 56

CNV

C.N.V.
(Christian Employers Organisation, Project Department)
P.O.Box 2475
3500 GL Utrecht
T 31-30-2913681
F 31-30-2933806

CSJN

Culturele Stichting Nippon-Nederland
(Cultural Foundation Japan-Netherlands)
Frans van Mierisstraat 57-hs
1071 RL Amsterdam
T 31-20-6623552
F 31-20-6644993

CVC

Centre for Vietnamese Culture
Brederodegracht 1
1628 LZ Hoorn
T 31-229-239855
F 31-229-217814

D,GKN

Dienstencentrum GKN
P.O.Box 202
3830 AE Leusden

DNB

De Nederlandse Bank
(The Dutch National Bank)
Econometrics S 10-17
P.O. Box 98
1000 AB Amsterdam
T 31-20-5243621
F 31-20-5242529

DNP

Depot van Nederlandse Publicaties
Afd. Abonnementen
P.O.Box 74
2501 AJ The Hague
Visiting Address:
Prins Willem Alexanderhof 5
T 31-70-314 09 11
F 31-70-314 06 54

DOEN

DOEN Foundation
Human rights Division
van Eeghenstraat 70
1070 AP Amsterdam
T 31-20-5737333
F 31-20-6757397

EC,BMB

Euroconsult
BMB
P.O.Box 441
6800 AK Arnhem
Visiting Address:
Beaulieustraat 22
T 31-26-3577111
F 31-26-3577577
euroconsult@heidf.unisource.nl

ECIA

European Club
International Affairs
P.O. Box 59199
3008 PD Rotterdam
T 31-10-4953615
F 31-10-4777835

ESCAS

European Society for Central Asia Studies
Kromme Niewegracht 66
3512 JK Utrecht Utrecht
T 31-30-2536133
F 31-30-2536000

ESCIEP

European Centre on Pacific Issues
(ESCIEP)
Postbus 151
3700 AD Zeist
T 31-30-6927827
F 31-30-6925614
ecsiep@antenna.nl

EUR

Erasmus Universiteit Rotterdam
(Erasmus University Rotterdam)
P.O.Box 1738
3000 DR Rotterdam
Visiting Address:
Burgemeester Oudlaan 50
F 31-10-452 5355

EUR, RSCM,DOPS

Erasmus Universiteit Rotterdam
Rotterdam School of Management
Department of Organization and Personnel Sciences
P.O.Box 1738
3000 DR Rotterdam
Visiting Address:
Burg. Oudlaan 50 3062 PA
(Kamer F3-27)
T 31-10-408 1942/79
F 31-10-452 31 66

Netherlands

EUR, SEO

Erasmus Universiteit
(Erasmus University)
Stichting Economisch Onderzoek
(Economic Research Foundation)
P.O.Box 2638
3000 CP Rotterdam

T 31-10-4082220

F 31-10-2120545

EUR,BIB

Erasmus Universiteit Rotterdam
Bibliotheek
(Library)
P.O.Box 1738
3000 DR Rotterdam
Visiting Address:
Burgemeester Oudlaan 50 3062 PA

T 31-10-408 12 15

EUR,DSVJ

Erasmus Universiteit Rotterdam
Deshima Studievereniging Japankunde
(Deshima Japanological Students Association)
P.O.Box 1738
3000 AD Rotterdam
Visiting Address:
Kamer H 15-13
Burg. Oudlaan 50 3062 PA

T 31-10-4081472

F 31-10-4525436

EUR,EW

Erasmus Universiteit Rotterdam
Faculteit Economie Toegepaste
Economische Wetenschappen (H8-26)
P.O.Box 1738
3000 DR Rotterdam

T 31-10-408 21 72

F 31-10-452 84 68

EUR,EW

Erasmus Universiteit Rotterdam
Faculteit der Economische
Wetenschappen
(Faculty of Economics)
P.O.Box 1738
3000 DR Rotterdam

T 31-10-408 13 77

F 31-10-212 05 47

EUR,EW,BO

Erasmus Universiteit Rotterdam
Faculteit der Economische
Wetenschappen
Department of Business & Organisation
P.O.Box 1738
3000 DR Rotterdam
Visiting Address:
Burgemeester Oudlaan 50
(Kamer H15-14)

EUR,EW,CDP

Erasmus Universiteit Rotterdam
Faculteit der Economische
Wetenschappen
Centre for Development Planning
P.O.Box 1738
3000 DR Rotterdam
Visiting Address:
Burgemeester Oudlaan 50

EUR,EW,EC

Erasmus Universiteit Rotterdam
Faculteit der Economische
Wetenschappen
Erasmus Centre for Economic
Integration Studies
P.O.Box 1738
3000 DR Rotterdam
Visiting Address:
Burgemeester Oudlaan 50

T 31-10-4082171

F 31-10-4527980

EUR,EW,F

Erasmus University Rotterdam
Faculteit der Economische
Wetenschappen (Faculty of Economics)
Department of Finance
P.O.Box 1738
3000 DR Rotterdam

T 31-10-408 14 94

F 31-10-452 63 99

EUR,EW,TE

Erasmus Universiteit Rotterdam
Faculteit der Economische
Wetenschappen (faculty of Economic
Sciences)
Toegepast Economie (Applied
Economics)
P.O.Box 1738
3000 DR Rotterdam
Visiting Address:
Burg. Oudlaan 50 3062 PA

T 31-10-408 14 61

F 31-10-452 70 09

EUR,FR,DSES

Erasmus Universiteit Rotterdam
Faculteit der Rechten
(Faculty of Law)
Department of Social and Economic
Sciences
P.O.Box 1738
3000 DR Rotterdam

T 31-10-408 2663/1617

F 31-10-453 29 27

EUR,HK

Erasmus Universiteit Rotterdam
Faculteit der Historische en
Kunstwetenschappen
(Faculty Historical and Art Studies)
P.O.Box 1738
3000 DR Rotterdam
Visiting Address:
Burgemeester Oudlaan 50 L-gebouw
3062 PA

T 31-10-408 24 86

F 31-10-453 29 22

EUR,HK,G

Erasmus Universiteit Rotterdam
Faculteit der Historische en
Kunstwetenschappen (Faculty of
Historical and Art Sciences
Vakgroep Geschiedenis
(History Department
P.O.Box 1738
3000 DR Rotterdam
Visiting Address:
Burgemeester Oudlaan 50

EUR,HK,KW

Erasmus Universiteit Rotterdam
Faculteit der Historische en
Kunstwetenschappen
Vakgroep Kunst- en
Cultuurwetenschappen
(Art and Culture Studies)
P.O.Box 1738
3000 DR Rotterdam
Visiting Address:
Burgemeester Oudlaan 50 3062 PA
Rotterdam (L-gebouw)

T 31-10-4082487

F 31-10-4532922

EUR,R

Erasmus Universiteit Rotterdam
Faculteit der Rechten
(Faculty of Law)
P.O.Box 1738
3000 DR Rotterdam
Visiting Address:
Burgemeester Oudlaan 50

T 31-10-408 22 74

F 31-10-453 29 20

Netherlands

EUR,VS

Erasmus Universiteit Rotterdam
Vakgroep Sociologie
P.O.Box 1738
3000 DR Rotterdam
Visiting Address:
Burg. Oudlaan 50, 3062 PA
T 31-10-
F 31-10-4525870

EUR,W

Erasmus Universiteit Rotterdam
Faculteit der Wijsbegeerte
(Faculty of Philosophy)
P.O.Box 1738
3000 DR Rotterdam
Visiting Address:
Burgemeester Oudlaan 50 3062 PA N-Gebouw
T 31-10-4081159
F 31-10-2120448

EUROSEAS

European Association for Southeast Asian Studies
c/o Royal Institute of Linguistics and Anthropology
P.O. Box 9515
2300 RA Leiden
Visiting Address:
Reuvensplaats 2
T 31-71-5272295
F 31-71-5272638
euroseas@rullet.leidenuniv.nl

EVD

Etnographische Vereniging Delft
(Ethnographical Society Delft)
Havannastraat1
2622 AH Delft
T 31-15-2566690

FDILA

Foundation for the Development of International Law in Asia
Caesar Franckrode 52
2717 BE Zoetermeer
T 31-79-3211195
F 31-79-3211195

FF

Fundament Foundation
P.O.Box 1068
4801 BB Breda
F 31-76-5200722

FIA

Foundation for Indian Artists
Fokke Simonsstraat 10
1017 TG Amsterdam
T 31-20-6231547
F 31-20-6231547
fia@euronet.nl

FIDOC

Filippijnen Informatie en Documentatie Centrum
(Phillipines Information and Documentation Centre)
Nolensweg 8
3317 LE Dordrecht
T 31-78-6185652

FIO

Foreign Investment Office
Metropol Gesouw
Weesperstraat 89
1018 VN Amsterdam

FIS

Foundation for Indochina Studies
Roetersstraat 11
1018 WB Amsterdam

FN

Filippijnengroep Nederland
(Phillipines Support Group)
Korte Jansstraat 2a
3512 GN Utrecht
T 31-30-2319223

FNI

Forum Nederland-Indonesia
(Netherlands Indonesia Forum)
P.O.Box 95581
2509 CN The Hague
Visiting Address:
Theresiastraat 2 2593 AN The Hague
T 31-70-3352731
F 31-70-3351865
fni@xs4all.nl

G,AB

Gemilang
Antiquariaat Booksellers
P.O.Box 26
7126 ZG Bredevoort
Visiting Address:
Koppelstraat 16
T 31-543-452 325
F 31-543-452 300
booktown@tref.nl

GA,CD,ABI

Gemeente Amsterdam
(Municipality of Amsterdam)
China Desk
Afdeling Buitenlandse Investeringen
(Foreign Investment Department)
Amstel 1
1011 PN Amsterdam

Gal.10&2K

Galerie IO & 2K Kunstproducties
Heemraadssingel 244
3021 DP Rotterdam
T 31-10-4760478
F 31-10-4760478

GDH

Gemeente Den Haag
Chef Kabinet en Protocol
P.O.Box 12600
2500 DJ The Hague
T 31-70-3532083
F 31-70-3533753

GMSL

Groninger Museum voor Stad en Lande
P.O.Box 90
9700 ME Groningen
Visiting Address:
Museumeiland 1
T 31-50-366555
F 31-50-3120815

GO,IP

Gelderse Ontwikkelingsmaatschappij
International Projects
P.O.Box 5215
6802 EE Arnhem

GOA

Stichting Geologisch, Oceanografisch en Atmosferisch Onderzoek (GOA)
P.O.Box 93120
2509 AC The Hague
Visiting Address:
Laan van Nieuw Oost Indi‰ 131

GRA

Groene Amsterdammer
(Weekly Magazine)
P.O.Box 353
1000 AJ Amsterdam
T 31-20-5245518
F 31-20-6221421

Netherlands

HAGAA

House of Asia Gallery for Asian Art
Witte de Withstraat 19 A
3012 BL Rotterdam
T 31-10-213 06 65
F 31-10-411 82 28

HESR

Hogeschool voor Economische Studies Rotterdam
(Rotterdam College for Economics and Business Admininstration)
P.O.Box 4030
3006 AA Rotterdam
Visiting Address:
Kralingse Zoom 91
T 31-10-4536225
F 31-10-4527051
P.Schep@hes-rdam,nl

HESR,ID

HES Rotterdam
Indonesian Department
P.O.Box 4030
3006 AA Rotterdam
Visiting Address:
Kralingse Zoom 91
T 31-10-452 66 63
F 31-10-452 70 51

HGM

Haags Gemeentemuseum (Municipal Museum The Hague)
Stadhouderskade 41
2501 CB The Hague
T 31-70-3381265/1111
F 31-70-3557360

HH

Hogeschool Holland
P.O.Box 261
1110 AG Diemen
T 31-20-560 12 26
F 31-20-560 12 63

HHM,HM

Hoge Hotelschool Maastricht
Hogeschool voor Management
Bethlehemweg 2
6222 BM Maastricht
T 31-43-3687272
F 31-43-3636343

HIS

Institute for Housing and Urban Development Studies
P.O.Box 1935
3000 BX Rotterdam
Visiting Address:
Weena C Point Bldg. Weena 718
3014 DA Rotterdam
T 31-10-402 15 23
F 31-10-404 56 71
wilgenburg@his.nl

HIVOS

Humanistisch Instituut voor Ontwikkelings Samenwerking
(Humanist Institute for Development Co-operation)
Raamweg 16
2596 HL The Hague
T 31-70-3636907
F 31-70-3617447
hivos@tool.nl

HKA,DM

Hogeschool voor de Kunsten Arnhem
(Arnhem School for the Arts)
Department of Music
Onderlangs 9
6812 CE Arnhem
T 31-26-3535635
F 31-26-3535678

HKI,BIB

Hendrik Kraemer Instituut
Bibliotheek
P.O.Box 12
2340 AA Oegstgeest
Visiting Address:
Leidsestraatweg 11
T 31-71-517 79 00

HKU

Hogeschool voor de Kunsten Utrecht
(Utrecht School for the Arts)
P.O.Box 1520
3500 BM Utrecht
Visiting Address:
Lange Viestraat 2-B
T 31-30-233 22 56
F 31-30-233 20 96

HKU,M

Hogeschool voor de Kunsten Utrecht
Department of Music
Mariaplaats 28
3511 LL Utrecht
T 31-30-2314044
F 31-30-2314044
fac.muz@hku.nl / www.hku.nl

HR

Hogeschool Rotterdam
Museumpark 40
3001 HA Rotterdam

IACT

Stichting InterAct
(Interact Foundation)
Wilgenplein 14
2712 XW Zoetermeer
T 31-79-3163674
F 31-79-3163674
iact@worldonline.nl

ICD

International Centre for Development Oriented research in Agriculture
P.O.Box 88
6700 AB Wageningen

ICSA

Instituut voor Culturele en Sociale Antropologie (Institute for Cultural and Social Anthropology)
Postbus 9104
6500 HE Nijmegen
T 31-24-3611945
F 31-24-3612360/1
H.de.Jonge@maw.kun.nl

IGEER

Institute for the History of European Expansion
P.O.Box 9515
2300 RA Leiden
Visiting Address:
Doelensteeg 16
T 31-71-5272768/2765
F 31-71-5272615
Blusse@rullet.leidenuniv.nl

IGV

Indische Genealogische Vereniging
(East en West Indian Genelogical Society)
Fl. Nightingalestr, 83
6543 KV Nijmegen
T 31-24-3771752

II

Inventure India
Paulus Potterstraat 26
1071 DA Amsterdam
T 31-20-6751981
F 31-20-6796348

Netherlands

IIAS

International Institute for Asian Studies (IIAS)
P.O.Box 9515
2300 RA Leiden
Visiting Address:
Nonnensteeg 1-3
T 31-71-5272227
F 31-71-5274162
IIAS@RULLET.LeidenUniv.NL

IIC

Instituut Indonesische Cursussen
(Indonesian Training Institute)
'Princenhof'
Rapenburg 8-10
2311 EV Leiden
T 31-71-5121011
F 31-71-5140347
iic@euronet.nl

IISG,IISH

Internationaal Instituut voor Sociale Geschiedenis (IISG) Asia Department (International Institute of Social History(IISH)/Asia Department)
Cruquiusweg 31
1019 AT Amsterdam
T 31-20-6685866
F 31-20-6654181
inf.gen@iisg.nl

IIUE

International Institute for Urban Environment
Nickersteeg 5
2611 EK Delft
Visiting Address:
Mijnbouwplein 11.
T 31-15-2623279
F 31-15-2624873
urban@theoffice.net

ILRI

International Institute for Land Reclamation and Improvement (ILRI)
P.O.Box 45
6700 AA Wageningen
ilri@ilri.nl

IME

IME Consult
P.O.Box 525
6500 AM Nijmegen
Visiting Address:
Nijmeegsebaan 140 Heilig Landstichting 6500 AM Nijmegen
T 31-24-3228100

INA

Indonesische Nedernlandse Associatie (Indonesian Netherlands Association)
P.O.Box 10
2501 CA The Hague
Visiting Address:
Bezuidenhoutseweg 181
T 31-70-3441582
F 31-70-3853531
ina.netherlands@frs.tool.nl

IndI

India Instituut
(India Institute)
P.O.Box 75861
1070 AW Amsterdam
T 31-20-6626662
F 31-20-6626662
D.PLUKKER@INTER.NL.NET

INDONET

INDONET
P.O.Box 81140
3009 GC Rotterdam
indonet@antenna.nl

ING,GDC

ING Bank
Greater China Desk
P.O.Box 1800
1000 BV Amsterdam

Inst.I

Instituto Italiana
Keizersgracht 564
1017 EM Amsterdam

Int.G

Internationaal Gerechtshof
Carnegieplein 2
2517 KJ The Hague

IPJET

International Platform of Jurists for Eas Timor (IPJET)
Gruttohoek 13
2317 WK Leiden
T 31-71-5221065
F 31-71-5221065
ipjet@antenna.nl

ISRIC

International Soil Reference and Information Centre (ISRIC)
P.O.Box 353
6700 AJ Wageningen
Visiting Address:
Duivendaal 9
T 31-317-471711
F 0317-471700
soil@isric.nl

ISS

Institute of Social Studies
P.O. Box 29776
2502 LT The Hague
Visiting Address:
Kortenaerkade 12 2518 AX The Hague
T 31-70-4260460
F 31-70-4260799
klatter@iss.nl

ISS,BIB

Institute of Social Studies (ISS) Library
P.O. Box 29776
2502 LT The Hague
Visiting Address:
Kortenaerkade 12 2518 AX
T 31-70-426 04 43
F 31-70-426 07 99

ITIM

Institute for Training in Intercultural Management
Celebesstraat 96
2585 TP The Hague
T 31-70-350 50 54
F 31-70-355 20 03

JVBD

Japans (Ver)taalbureau Deshima (Japanese Language School and Translation Bureau)
Prins Hendrikkade 90
1501 AG Zaandam
T 31-75-6177771
F 31-75-6706236
deshima@worldaccess.nl

JvEA

Jan van Eyck Akademie
Academieplein 1
6211 KM Maastricht
T 31-43-3254285
F 31-43-3256474
vaneyck@xs4all.nl

Netherlands

KB, AS

Koninklijke Bibliotheek
Afd. Schatkist
P.O. Box 90407
2509 LK The Hage
Visiting Address:
Prins Willem-Alexanderhof 5.

KI

Komitee Indonesië
(Indonesia Committee)
P.O.Box 92066
1090 AB Amsterdam
Visiting Address:
Minahassastraat 1

T 31-20-6936050

F 31-20-6684085

ki@antenna.nl

KIT

Koninklijk Instituut voor de Tropen
(KIT) (Royal Tropical Institute)
P.O.Box 95001
1090 HA Amsterdam
Visiting Address:
Mauritskade 63 1092 AD

T 31-20-5688454/8711

F 31-20-5688331

BTZ@KIT.support.nl

KIT,BIB

Koninklijk Instituut voor de Tropen
(KIT)
(Royal Tropical Institute)
Library
P.O.Box 95001
1090 HA Amsterdam
Visiting Address:
Mauritskade 63 1092 AD

T 31-20-665 44 23

ibd@support.nl

KIT,TM

Koninklijk Insituut voor de Tropen
(Royal Tropical Institute)
Tropenmuseum
Linnaeusstraat 2
1092 AD Amsterdam

T 31-20-5688200

F 31-20-5688331

KIT,TPM,VIDOC

Koninklijk Instituut voor de Tropen
(KIT)
Tropenmuseum
Visuele Documentatie (VIDOC)
(Visual Documentation)
Mauritskade 63
1093 AD Amsterdam

T 31-20-5688331

F 31-20-5688242

KITLV

Koninklijk Instituut voor Taal-, Land- en Volkenkunde (KITLV) (Royal Institute of Linguistics and Anthropology)
P.O.Box 9515
2300 RA Leiden
Visiting Address:
Reuvensplaats 2 Leiden

T 31-71-5272295

F 31-71-5272638

kitlv@rullet.leidenuniv.nl

KITLV,BIB

Koninklijk Instituut voor Taal-, Land- en Volkenkunde (KITLV)
Bibliotheek (Library)
P.O.Box 9515
2300 RA Leiden
Visiting Address:
Reuvensplaats 2

T 31-71-527 22 95

F 31-71-527 26 38

KITLV,EUROSEAS

Koninklijk Instituut voor Taal-, Land- en Volkenkunde (KITLV) EUROSEAS
P.O.Box 9515
2300 RA Leiden
Visiting Address:
Reuvensplaats 2 2311 BE

T 31-71-527 22 95

F 31-71-527 26 38

euroseas@rullet.leidenuniv.nl

KITLV,Press

KITLV / Koninklijk Instituut voor Taal , Land-, en Volkenkunde Press
P.O.Box 9515
2300 RA Leiden
Visiting Address:
Reuvensplaats 2

KLM

KLM Royal Dutch Airlines
P.O.Box 7700
1117 ZL Schiphol

T 31-20-649 73 37

F 31-20-648 83 10

KMHP

Keramiekmuseum Het Princessehof
(Ceramics Museum Het Proncessehof)
Grote Kerkstraat 11
9811 DZ Leeuwarden

T 31-58-2127438

F 31-58-2122281

KMM

Sectie Militaire Geschiedenis van de Koninklijke Landmacht
(Section of Militairy History of the Royal Army)
P.O.Box 90701 Gebouw 240
2509 LS The Hague
Visiting Address:
Oude Waalsdorperweg 23-35 's-Gravenhage

T 31-70-316 58 46

F 31-70-316 58 51

KNAW

Koninklijke Nederlandse Akademie van Wetenschappen (KNAW) (Netherlands Academy of Arts and Sciences)
P.O.Box 19121
1000 GC Amsterdam
Visiting Address:
Het Trippenhuis
Kloveniersburgwal 29

T 31-20-5510700

F 31-20-6204941

knaw@bureau.knaw.nl

KNAW,IRQA

Koninklijke Nederlandse Akademie van Wetenschappen (KNAW)
(Royal Netherlands Academy of Arts and Sciences)
International Relations and Quality Assessment
P.O.Box 19121
1000 GC Amsterdam
Visiting Address:
Kloverniersburgwal 29 Het Trippenhui

T 31-20-551 07 00

F 31-20-620 49 41

isk@bureau.knaw.nl

KUB, FSW, P

Katholieke Universiteit Brabant
Faculteit der Sociale Wetenschappen
Vakgroep Psychologie
P.O.Box 90153
5000 LE Tilburg
Visiting Address:
Warandelaan 2 5037 AB

T 31-13-466 22 70

F 013-466 23 70

Netherlands

KUB, IVO

Katholieke Universiteit Brabant
(Tilburg University)
Development Research Institute IVO
P.O.Box 90153
5000 LE Tilburg
Visiting Address:
Warandelaan 2

T 31-13-466 22 64

F 013-466 30 15

secr.ivo@kub.nl

KuB, VBSO

Katholieke Universiteit Brabant
Vakgroep Bedrijfskunde Sectie
Ondernemingsfinanciering
P.O.Box 90153
5000 LE Tilburg
Visiting Address:
Warandalaan 2 5037 AB Tilburg

T 31-13-466 20 19

F 013-466 30 72

KUB, VV

Katholieke Universiteit Brabant
(Tilburg University)
Vakgroep Vrijetijdswetenschappen
P.O.Box 90153
5000 LE Tilburg
Visiting Address:
Warandelaan 2 5037 AB

T 31-13-466 22 08

F 013-466 23 70

KUB,VTW

Katholieke Universiteit Brabant
Vakgroep Taal- en
Literatuurwetenschap
P.O.Box 90153
5000 LE Tilburg
Visiting Address:
Warandelaan 2 5037 AB Tilburg

T 31-13-4662568

F 013-4663110

KUN, CvV

Katholieke Universiteit Nijmegen
Centrum voor Vrouwenstudies
P.O.Box 9104
6500 HE Nijmegen
Visiting Address:
Thomas van Aquinostraat 2.

T 31-24-3612339/5461

F 31-24-3611881

KUN, VP

Katholieke Universiteit Nijmegen
Faculteit de Beleidswetenschappen
Vakgroep Politicologie
P.O.Box 9108
6500 HK Nijmegen

T 31-24-3612995

F 31-24-3612379

KUN, VTCMO

Katholieke Universiteit Nijmegen
(University of Nijmegen)
Vakgroep voor Talen en Culturen van
het Midden-Oosten
(Department of Languages and Culture
of the Near East)
P.O.Box 9103
6500 HD Nijmegen
Visiting Address:
Erasmusplein 1 6525 HT
Erasmusgebouw

T 31-24-361 28 92

KUN,ALMB

Katholieke Universiteit Nijmegen
(University of Nijmegen)
Department of ALMB (Applied
Linguistics, Methodology and Business
Comm. Studies)
P.O.Box 9103
6500 HD Nijmegen
Visiting Address:
Erasmusplein 1 6525 HT Nijmegen

T 31-24-361 20 45

F 31-24-361 21 77

KUN,CPS

Katholieke Universiteit Nijmegen
Faculteit der Sociale Wetenschappen
(Faculty of Social Sciences)
Centre for Pacific Studies
P.O.Box 9104
6500 HE Nijmegen
Visiting Address:
Thomas van Aquinostraat 4 6525 GD
Nijmegen

T 31-24-3615579/2361

F 31-24-3611945

csacps@maw.kun.nl or
csacps@baserv.uci.kun.nl

KUN,IDS

Katholieke Universiteit Nijmegen
(University of Nijmegen)
Institute for Development Studies
P.O.Box 9104
6500 HE Nijmegen
Visiting Address:
Thomas van Aquinostr. 4

T 31-24-3613058

F 024-3615957

KUN,IV

Katholieke Universiteit Nijmegen
Instituut voor Volksrecht
P.O.Box 9049
6500 KK Nijmegen
Visiting Address:
Thomas van Aquinostraat 6 Nijmegen

KUN,PW

Katholieke Universiteit Nijmegen
Promotie Werkplaats
P.O. Box 9104
6500 HE Nijmegen

KUN,SES

Katholieke Universiteit Nijmegen
School for Environmental Studies
P.O.Box 9108
6500 HK Nijmegen

T 31-24-361 30 04

KUN,UB

Katholieke Universiteit Nijmegen
Universiteitsbibliotheek
P.O.Box 9100
6500 HA Nijmegen

T 31-24-361 24 40

KUN,VOP

Katholieke Universiteit Nijmegen
Faculteit der Sociale Wetenschappen
Vakgroep Ontwikkelingspsychologie
Montessorilaan 3
6500 HE Nijmegen

KUN,VTER

Katholieke Universiteit Nijmegen
Faculteit der Rechtsgeleerdheid
Vakgroep Theorie en Empirie van het
Recht
Thomas v. Aquinostraat 8
6500 KK Nijmegen

LCM

Louis Couperus Museum
Javastraat 17
2585 AB The Hague

T 31-70-3640653

LGM

Legermuseum
Korte Geer 1
2611 HR Delft

T 31-15-2150500

Netherlands

LIW

Landelijk India Werkgroep
(India Committee of the Netherlands)
Oude Gracht 36
3511 AP Utrecht
T 31-30-2321340
F 31-30-2322246

LSEM

Landelijk Steunpunt Educatie Molukkers
(Institute for Moluccan Education)
P.O.Box 13375
3507 LJ Utrecht
Visiting Address:
Biltstraat 95
3572 AL Utrecht
T 31-30-2333900
F 31-30-2316275

LW,DDE

Landbouwuniversiteit Wageningen
(Agricultural University)
Department of Development Economics
Hollandseweg 1
6706 KN Wageningen
T 31-317-483449
F 31-317-484763

LW,DDE

Landbouwuniversiteit Wageningen
(Wageningen Agricultural University)
Department of Development Economics
P.O.Box 8130
6700 EW Wageningen
T 31-317-489111
F 0317-484037

LW,DHN

Landbouwuniversiteit Wageningen
(Wageningen Agricultural University)
Department of Human Nutrition
P.O.Box 8129
6700 EV Wageningen
Visiting Address:
Bomenweg 2 6703 HD

LW,DISWC

Landbouwuniversiteit Wageningen
(Agricultural University)
Department of Irrigation, Soil and Water Conservation
Nieuwe Kanaal 11
6709 PA Wageningen

LW,DRH

Landbouwuniversiteit Wageningen
(Agricultural University)
Department of Rural History
Hollandseweg 1
6706 KN Wageningen
Visiting Address:
Postbus 9101 6700 HB
T 31-317-482 488
F 0317-484 763

LW,DS

Landbouwuniversiteit Wageningen
(Agricultural University)
Department of Sociology
Section Sociology of Rural Development
P.O.Box 8130
6700 WE Wageningen
Visiting Address:
Costerweg 50 6701 BH
T 31-317-482 075
F 0317-484 037

LW,PR

Landbouwuniversiteit Wageningen
(Wageningen Agricultural University)
Information en PR Office
P.O.Box 9101
6700 HB Wageningen
Visiting Address:
Costerweg 50 6700 BH Wageningen
T 31-317-484472
F 31-317-484884

LW,SS

Landbouwuniversiteit Wageningen
(Agricultural University)
Department of Social Sciences
P.O. Box 8130
6700 EW Wageningen

LW,VAS

Landbouwuniversiteit Wageningen
(Agricultural University)
Vakgroep Agrarische Sociologie
(Department of Agricultural Sociology)
Hollandseweg 1
6707 KN Wageningen

LW,VB

Landbouwuniversiteit Wageningen
(Agricultural University)
Vakgroep Bedrijfskunde
Hollandseweg 1
6706 KN Wageningen
T 31-317-484 035

LW,VE

Landbouwuniversiteit Wageningen
(Agricultural University)
Vakgroep Entomologie
P.O.Box 8031
6700 EH Wageningen
T 31-317-484652
F 31-317-484821

LW,VH

Landbouwuniversiteit Wageningen
(Agricultural University)
Vakgroep Huishoudstudies
P.O.Box 8060
6700 DA Wageningen
Visiting Address:
Ritzema Bosweg 32-A Wageningen
T 31-317-482 088
F 31-317-482 593

MB

Museum Bronbeek
Velperweg 147
6824 MB Arnhem
T 31-26-3840824
F 31-26-3840899
bronbeek@pi.net

MBB

Museum Boymans van Beuningen
P.O.Box 2277
3000 CG Rotterdam
Visiting Address:
Museumpark 18-20 3015 CK Rotterdam
T 31-10-4419400

MCNV

Medisch Comité Nederland-Vietnam
(Netherlands Viet Nam Medical Committee)
P.O.Box 75701
1070 AS Amsterdam
Visiting Address:
Weteringschans 32
T 31-20-627 04 11
F 31-20-625 01 47

MCOOP

Museum 't Coopmanshus
Voorstraat 49-51
8801 LA Franeker
T 31-517-392192

Netherlands

MF

Missieburo Fransiskanen
(Fransican Missionary Office)
P.O.Box 13009
3507 LA Utrecht
T 31-30-2331552
F 31-30-2231441

MGP

Micky Grant Production
Laan van Engelswier 13
3551 XW Utrecht

MH

Medivision Holland
P.O.Box 1552
3600 BN Maarssen
Visiting Address:
Bizonspoor 1233 3605 KZ
Maarssenbroek

MHMSM

Moluks Historisch Museum Sedjarah Maluku
(Moluccan Historical Museum Sedjarah Maluku)
P.O.Box 13379
3507 LJ Utrecht
Visiting Address:
Kruisstraat 313 3581 GK
T 31-30-2367116
F 31-30-232 89 67
mhm@worldonline.nl

MIN,Buza,DGIS

Ministerie van Buitenlandse Zaken
DGIS, Afd. DMO
P.O.Box 20061
2500 EB The Hague

MIN,J

Ministerie van Justitie
P.O.Box 20301
2500 EH The Hague
Visiting Address:
Schedeldoekshaven 100
T 31-70-370 79 11
F 31-70-370 79 00

MIN,OCW,OWB

Ministerie van Onderwijs, Cultuur en Wetenschappen
Directie Onderzoek en Wetenschapsbeleid (OWB)
P.O.Box 25000
2700 LZ Zoetermeer
Visiting Address:
Europaweg 4
T 31-79-3233533
F 31-79-3234816

MIN,VW,RWS

Ministerie van Verkeer en Waterstaat
RWS
P.O.Box 20906
2500 EX The Hague
Visiting Address:
Johan de Wittlaan 3 2517 JR
T 31-70-351 94 49
F 31-70-351 94 44

Min-Buza,DCH/HH

Ministerie van Buitenlandse Zaken
DCH/HH
P.O. Box 20061
2500 EB The Hague

Min.BuZa

Ministerie van Buitenlandse Zaken
DGIS, Afd. DCO
P.O.Box 20061
2500 EB The Hague
Visiting Address:
Bezuidenhoutseweg 67
T 31-70-3484079
F 31-70-3484244

Min.LNV

Ministerie van Landbouw, Natuurbeheer en Visserij Directie I & H
P.O.Box 20401
2500 EK The Hague
Visiting Address:
Bezuidenhoutseweg 73

MLM

Militaire Luchtvaart Museum
(Militairy Aerospace Museum)
Postbus 184
3769 ZK Amsterdam
T 31-346-354518

MMK

Museum voor Moderne Kunst
(Museum of Modern Art)
Utrechtseweg 87
6812 AA Arnhem
T 31-26-3512431

MMS

Missiemuseum Steyl
St. Michaëlstraat 7
5935 BL Steyl/Tegelen
T 31-77-376 82 94

MPIP, CARG

Max-Planck-Instituut voor Psycholinguistiek Cognitive Anthropology Research Group
P.O.Box 310
6500 AH Nijmegen
Visiting Address:
Wundtlaan 1 6525 XD
T 31-24-3521911
F 31-24-3521213
Cogant@mpi.nl

MPV

Marco Polo Vertaalbureau
(Marco Polp Translationbureau)
Milanenhorst 92
2317 CH Leiden
T 31-71-5213688
F 31-71-5213688
marcopol@euronet.nl

MSG

Museum Spaans Gouvernement
Vrijthof 18
6211 LD Maastricht
T 31-43-3211327

MSPE,DOL

Maastricht School of Profesional Education
Department of Oriental Languages
P.O.Box 414
6200 AK Maastricht
Visiting Address:
Brusselseweg 152
T 31-43-3466475
F 31-43-3466490
oriental-room@pi.net

MST

Maritime Systems Technology BV
Surinamestraat 37
2585 GH The Hague
T 31-70-346 95 28
F 31-70-345 71 03
mstnl@pi.net

MULM

Multatuli Museum
Korsjespoortweg 20
1015 AR Amsterdam
T 31-20-6381938

Mus.V

Museum voor Volkenkunde Afdeling PR
Willemskade 25
3016 DM Rotterdam
T 31-10-411 10 55
F 31-10-411 83 31

Netherlands

MUSN

Museon
Stadhouderslaan 41
2517 HV The Hague
T 31-70-3381338
F 31-70-3541820

Muz.Th.

Muziektheater
Waterlooplein 22
1011 PG Amsterdam
T 31-20-5518911

MVROT

Museum voor Volkenkunde (Museum of Ethnology)
Postbus 361
3000 AJ Rotterdam
Visiting Address:
Willemskade 25
3016 DM
T 31-10-4551311/4111055
F 31-10-455 67 01

MVW, BS-G

Ministerie van Verkeer en Waterstaat
Bureau Secretaris-Generaal
P.O.Box 20901
2500 EX The Hague
Visiting Address:
Plesmanlaan 1-6
T 31-70-351 7200/6551
F 31-70-351 7550

ND,LF

Nauta Dutilh
Law Firm
P.O.Box 7113
1007 JC Amsterdam
Visiting Address:
Prinses Irenestraat 59 1077 WV
T 31-20-541 47 47

NF

De Nationale Stichting 'De Nieuwe Kerk'
(National Foundation 'De Nieuwe Kerk')
P.O.Box 3438
1001 AE Amsterdam
Visiting Address:
Gravenstraat 17
T 31-20-626 81 68
F 31-20-622 66 49

NIAS

Netherlands Institute for Advanced Study in the Humanities and Social Sciences (NIAS)
Meijboomlaan 1
2242 PR Wassenaar
T 31-70-512 27 00
F 31-70-511 71 62
nias@nias.knaw.nl

NICCOS

Nijmegen Institute for Comparative Studies in Development and Cultural Change (NICCOS)
P.O.Box 9104
6500 HE Nijmegen
T 31-243613005
F 31-24-3611945

NIDI,BIB

Nederlands Interdisciplinair Demografisch Instituut (NIDI)
(Netherlands Interdisciplinary Demographical Institute)
Library
P.O.Box 11650
2502 AR The Hague
Visiting Address:
Lange Houtstraat 19
T 31-70-356 52 00
F 31-70-364 71 87
siebenga@nidi.nl

NINO

Nederlands Instituut voor het Nabije Oosten
P.O.Box 9515
2300 RA Leiden
Visiting Address:
Witte Singel 25
T 31-71-5272037/2036
F 31-71-5272038

NISAS

Netherlands Institute of South Asian Studies (NISAS)
P.O.Box 58247
1040 HE Amsterdam
Visiting Address:
Oosterpark 40-I
T 31-20-6163371
F 31-20-6811082

NISR

Netherlands Institute for Sea Research
P.O.Box 59
1790 AB Den Burg

NJV

Nederlands-Japanse Vereniging
(Netherlands-Japan Association)
Postbus 9515
2300 RA Leiden
T 31-71-5272215
F 31-71-5272540
Wijsman@Rullet.leidenuniv.nl

NLN B.V.

Nedloyd Lines Nederland B.V.
Boompjes 40
3011 XB Rotterdam
T 31-10-4007666
F 31-10-4006490

NM,STC

NewMetropolis
Science and Technology Center
P.O. Box 421
1000 AK Amsterdam
Visiting Address:
Oosterdok 2, 1011 VX.
T 31-20-570 81 11

NOVIB

Nederlandse Organisatie voor Internationale Ontwikkelingssamenwerking (NOVIB)
(Netherlands Organization for International Development Cooperation
P.O.Box 30919
2500 GX The Hague
Visiting Address:
Mauritskade 9
T 31-70-3421621/1777
F 31-70-3614461
admin@novib.nl

NOW

Nederlandse Organisatie voor Wetenschappelijk Onderzoek (NOW)
(Netherlands Organization for Scientific Research
P.O.Box 93120
2509 AC The Hague
Visiting Address:
Laan van Nieuw Oost Indië131
T 31-70-344 06 40
F 31-70-385 09 71
baaren@nwo.nl

NSMA

Stichting Nederlands Scheepvaartmuseum
(Dutch Maritime Museum)
Kattenburgerplein 1
1018 KK Amsterdam
T 31-20-5232222
F 31-20-5232213

Netherlands

NSMA

Nederlands Scheepvaartmuseum Amsterdam
(Maritime Museum Amsterdam)
Kattenburgerplein 1
1018 KK Amsterdam
T 31-20-5232231/5232222
F 31-20-5232213

NSSEPR

Netherlands School for Social and Economic Policy Research
P.O.Box 80140
3508 TC Utrecht

NTXM

Nederlands Textielmuseum
Goirkestraat 96
5046 GN Tilburg
T 31-13-5367475

NUFFIC, DIAR

NUFFIC
Department International Academical Relations
P.O.Box 29777
2502 LT The Hague
Visiting Address:
Kortnaerkade 11 2518 AX
T 31-70-426 02 60
F 31-70-426 03 99

NUFFIC,DESC

NUFFIC
Nederlandse Organisatie voor Internationale Samenwerking in het Hoger Onderwijs
Netherlands Organization for International Cooperation in Higher Education
Department of Educational Studies and Consultancy
P.O.Box 29777
2502 LT The Hague
Visiting Address:
Kortenaerkade 11
T 31-70-426 02 91
F 31-70-426 02 99
cesosecr@nuffics.nl

NVM

Nijmeegs Volkenkundig Museum
(Nijmegen Ethnographical Museum)
P.O.Box 9104
6500 HE Nijmegen
Visiting Address:
Thomas van Aquinostraat 1
T 31-24-3229193
F 31-24-3611945

NWO, GW

NWO/Nederlandse Organisatie voor Wetenschappelijk Onderzoek
Gebiedbestuur Geesteswetenschappen
Council for the Humanities
P.O.Box 93120
2509 AC The Hague
Visiting Address:
Laan van Nieuw Oost Indë 131
T 31-70-344 08 40
F 31-70-347 16 23
GB-G@NWO.NL

OCD

Organization for Community Development
P.O.Box 65
6460 AB Kerkrade

OHM

Stichting Organisatie voor Hindoe Media (OHM)
(Foundation Organization for Hindu Media)
Koninginneweg 8
1217 KX Hilversum
T 31-35-6248784
F 31-35-6280843

OPWL,LD

OPWL
Legal Division
Laan van Meerdervoort 51
2517 AE The Haque
F 31-70-3671824

PCD

Philips Corporate Design
P.O.Box 218
5600 MD Eindhoven
Visiting Address:
Cederlaan 4 Eindhoven
T 31-40-273 61 90
F 040-273 49 59
c912348@nlccmail.snads.philips.nl

PI,IESG

Posthumus Instituut Postdoctoraal Instituut in de Economische en Sociale Geschiedenis
P.O.Box 1738
3000 DR Rotterdam
Visiting Address:
Burgemeester Oudlaan 50 3062 PA L-gebouw
T 31-10-408 24 79
F 31-10-452 50 71
hwp@mgs.phk.eur.nl

PISW

Postdoctoraal Instituut voor de Sociale Wetenschappen
(Postdoctoral Institute for Social Sciences)
Oude Hoogstraat 24
1012 CE Amsterdam
T 31-20-525 22 62
F 31-20-525 24 46

PMS

Philips Medical systems
P.O.Box 10000
5680 DA Best
T 31-40-762826
F 31-40-762416

PPMH

Poppenspulspelmuseum 't Huis
(Doll's Toys Museum 't Huis)
Kerkweg 38
8193 KL Vorchten
T 31-578-63129

Prolan

Prolan B.V.
Wolfkuilseweg 27
6542 JB Nijmegen
T 31-24-377 08 80
F 31-24-378 09 01

PSO

Personal Service Overseas (PSO)
Willem Witsenplein 2
2590 BK The Hague

RAWOO

Raad van Advies voor het Wetenschappelijk Onderzoek
(RAWOO) (Advisory Council for Scientific Research in Development Problems
P.O.Box 29777
2502 LT The Hague
Visiting Address:
Kortenaerkade 11
T 31-70-426 03 31
F 31-70-426 03 29
rawoosec@nufficcs.nl
nufficcs.nl/ciran/rawoo

RBK

Rijksakademie voor Beeldende Kunsten
Sarphatistraat 470
1018 GW Amsterdam
T 31-20-5270306
F 31-20-5270301

Netherlands

RBK,BIB

Rijksdienst Beeldende Kunst
National Service Visual Arts
Bibliotheek (Library)
P.O.Box 30450
2500 GL The Hague
The hague

RC,VWM

Rotterdams Conservatorium
(Rotterdam Conservatory)
Vakgroep Wereld Muziek
(Department of World Music)
Pieter de Hoochweg 222
3024 BJ Rotterdam
T 31-10-4767399
F 31-10-4253262

RD

Reformatorisch Dagblad
Buitenlandredactie
P.O.Box 670
7300 AR Apeldoorn
Visiting Address:
Laan van Westenenk. 12 7336 AZ
T 31-55-549 52 22
F 31-55-541 22 88
refdag@pi.net

RD

Rotterdams Dagblad
P.O. Box 2999
3000 CZ Rotterdam
T 31-10-4004346

RHM,OT-V

Rijkshogeschool Maastricht Opleiding
Tolk-Vertaler
Sectie Japans
P.O.Box 964
6200 AZ Maastricht

RI

Remedium International bv
Burg. Jansenstraat 39
5037 NB Tilburg

RIOD

Rijksinstituut voor
Oorlogsdocumentatie (RIOD)
(Netherlands State Institute for War
Documentation)
Herengracht 380
1016 CJ Amsterdam
T 31-20-5233800
F 31-20-5233888
riod@xs4all.nl or wardoc@xs4all.nl

RKHD

Rijksbureau voor Kunsthistorische
Documentatie (Netherlands Institute for
Art History)
Postbus 90418
2509 LK The Hague
T 31-70-3471514
F 31-70-3475005

RM,OC&W

Rijksdienst voor de Monumentenzorg
OC&W
P.O.Box 1001
3700 BA Zeist
Visiting Address:
Broederplein 41 3703 CD
T 31-30-6983211
F 31-30-6916189

RMA

Rijksmuseum Amsterdam
(National Museum)
Department of Asiatic Art
P.O.Box 74888
1070 DN Amsterdam
Visiting Address:
Stadhouderskade 42
T 31-20-6672121
F 31-20-6798146
collecties@rijksmuseum.nl

RMKM

Rijksmuseum Kröller-Müller
Houtkampweg 6
6731 AW Otterlo
T 31-318-591241

RMV

Rijksmuseum voor Volkenkunde
(National Museum of Ethnology)
P.O.Box 212
2300 AE Leiden
Visiting Address:
Steenstraat 1 2300 AE
T 31-71-5168800
F 31-71-5128437

RMV, FECC

Rijksmuseum voor Volkenkunde
(National Museum of Ethnology)
The Far Eastern Conservation Centre
P.O.Box 212
2300 AE Leiden
Visiting Address:
Steenstraat 1

RNW

Radio Nederland Wereldomroep
Indonesian Service
P.O.Box 222
1200 JG Hilversum
Visiting Address:
Witte Kruislaan 55
T 31-35-6724347
F 31-35-6724352
ranesi@rnw.nl

RSIA

Ripa School of Indian Arts
Krommewaal 16
1011 BS Amsterdam
T 31-20-6258508

RUG,BAI

Rijksuniversiteit Groningen
(University of Groningen)
Vakgroep Archeologie
(Department of Archaeology)
Biologisch-Archeologisch Instituut
(Biological Archaeological Institute)
Poststraat 6
9712 ER Groningen
T 31-50-3636724

RUG,BIG

Rijksuniversiteit Groningen Faculteit
Bedrijfskunde Stichting B.I.G.
Internationaal Studieproject
(B.I.G. International Study Project)
P.O.Box 800
9700 AV Groningen
Visiting Address:
Landleven 5 9747 AD
T 31-50-3633167
F 050-3633194
i.s.p.@bdk.rug.nl www.bdk.nl

RUG,BU

Rijksuniversiteit Groningen
(University of Groningen)
Bureau van de Universiteit
P.O.Box 72
9700 AB Groningen

RUG,FB

Rijksuniversiteit Groningen
(University of Groningen)
Faculteit Bedrijfskunde
P.O.Box 800
9700 AV Groningen
Visiting Address:
Landleven 5
T 31-50-363 31 67
F 050-363 64 70

Netherlands

RUG,FL

Rijksuniversiteit Groningen
(University of Groningen)
Faculteit der Letteren
P.O.Box 716
9700 AS Groningen
Visiting Address:
Oude Kijk in 't Jatstraat 26 9712 EK
T 31-50-363 59 00

RUG,FPPSW

Rijksuniversiteit Groningen
(University of Groningen)
Faculteit der Psychologische, Pedagogische en Sociologische Wetenschappen
Grote Rozenstraat 31
9712 TG Groningen
T 31-50-3636182
F 31-50-3636844

RUG,FRW

Rijksuniversiteit Groningen
(University of Groningen)
Faculteit der Ruimtelijke Wetenschappen
Population Research Centre
P.O.Box 800
9700 AV Groningen
Visiting Address:
Landleven 5 9747 AD Hoogbouw WSN, Paddepoel
T 31-50-363 38 95
F 050-363 39 01
faculty@frw.rug.nl

RUG,FRW

Rijksuniversiteit Groningen
(University of Groningen)
Faculteit der Ruimtelijke Wetenschappen
P.O.Box 800
9700 AV Groningen
Visiting Address:
Landleven 5 Hoogbouw WSN, Paddepoel
T 31-50-3633895
F 050-3633901

RUG,IIS

Rijksuniversiteit Groningen Institute of Indian Studies
Oude Boteringestraat 23
9712 GC Groningen
T 31-50-3635819
F 31-50-3637263
bakker@let.rug.nl

RUG,VA

Rijksuniversiteit Groningen
(Universtiy of Groningen)
Vakgroep Archeologie
(Department of Archaeology)
P.O.Box 716
9700 AS Groningen
T 31-50-3635900

RUG,VAE

Rijksuniversiteit Groningen
(University of Groningen)
Vakgroep Algemene Economie Sectie Development Economics
P.O.Box 800
9700 AV Groningen
Visiting Address:
Landleven 5
T 31-50-363 7018
F 050-363 7337

RUG,VBB

Rijksuniversiteit Groningen
(University of Groningen)
Vakgroep Bestuursrecht en Bestuurskunde
P.O.Box 176
9700 AS Groningen
Visiting Address:
Oude kijk in 't Jatstraat 26 9712 EK
T 31-50-363 56 74
F 050-363 72 50

RUG,VBE

Rijksuniversiteit Groningen
(University of Groningen)
Vakgroep Bedrijfseconomie
P.O.Box 800
9700 AV Groningen
Visiting Address:
Landleven 5 9747 AD Groningen
T 31-50-3633676
F 050-3637337

RUG,VG

Rijksuniversiteit Groningen
(University of Groningen)
Vakgroep Geschiedenis
(Department of History)
P.O.Box 716
9700 AS Groningen
Visiting Address:
Oude Kijk in 't Jatstraat 26 9712 EK
T 050-363 59 94
F 050-363 72 53
geschied@let.rug.nl

RUG,VKAG

Rijksuniversiteit Groningen
(University of Groningen)
Vakgroep Kunst- en Architectuurgeschiedenis
P.O.Box 716
9700 AS Groningen
T 31-50-3636101
F 050-3637362

RUG,VOTI

Rijksuniversiteit Groningen
(University of Groningen)
Vakgroep Organisatie Technologie en Innovatie
P.O.Box 800
9700 AV Groningen
Visiting Address:
Landleven 5 9747 AD
T 31-50-363 70 20
F 050-363 38 25

RUG,VTCMO

Rijksuniversiteit Groningen
(University of Groningen)
Vakgroep Talen en Culturen van het Midden-Oosten
(Department of Languages and Culture of the Near East)
P.O.Box 716
9700 AS Groningen
Visiting Address:
Oude Kijk in 't Jatstraat 26 9712 EK
T 31-50-363 59 00

RUG,VTW

Rijksuniversiteit Groningen
(University of Groningen)
Vakgroep Taalwetenschappen
P.O.Box 716
9700 AS Groningen
Visiting Address:
Oude Kijk in 't Jatstraat 26 9712 EK
T 31-50-363 5974

RUL, BB

Rijksuniversiteit Leiden
(Leiden University)
Bureau Buitenland
P.O. Box 9500
2300 RA Leiden
Visiting Address:
Stationsweg 2312 AV
T 31-71-5277256
F 31-71-5277257

Netherlands

RUL, JIP

Rijksuniversiteit Leiden
Japan Interuniversity Programme
P.O.Box 9515
2300 RA Leiden
Visiting Address:
Witte Singel 25 Gebouw 1173
T 31-71-5272949
F 31-71-5272991
jip@rullet.leidenuniv.nl

RUL, SAP

Rijksuniversiteit Leiden
Study Abroad Program
P.O.Box 9515
2300 RA Leiden
T 31-71-5272048
F 31-71-5275497
www.leidenuniv.nl/bvdu/pub/sap/abroad.html

RUL, VA/AVMI

Rijksuniversiteit Leiden
(Leiden University)
VA/AVMI
Nonnensteeg 1-3
2311 VJ Leiden

RUL,ASC

Rijksuniversiteit Leiden
Afrika Studiecentrum
P.O.Box 9555
2300 RB Leiden
Visiting Address:
Wassenaarseweg 52 Pieter de la Courtgebouw
T 31-71-527 3372/3354
F 31-71-527 33 44

RUL,ATW

Rijksuniversiteit Leiden
(Leiden University)
Vakgroep Algemene Taalwetenschap (ATW/HIL)
P.O.Box 9515
2300 RA Leiden
Visiting Address:
Cleveringaplaats 1 WSD-Gebouw 1175
T 31-71-527 21 01
F 31-71-527 26 15

RUL,BIB

Rijksuniversiteit Leiden
(Leiden University)
Universiteitsbibliotheek
(Universitylibrary)
P.O.Box 9501
2300 RA Leiden
Visiting Address:
Witte Singel 27 WSD-gebouw 1169
T 31-71-5272832/2800
F 31-71-5272836

RUL,CA/SNWS

Rijksuniversiteit Leiden
Vakgroep CA/SNWS
(Department of Cultural Anthropology and Non-Western Sociology)
P.O.Box 9555
2300 RB Leiden
Visiting Address:
Wassenaarseweg 52 Pieter de la Court gebouw 2333 AK Leiden
T 31-71-5273450/3451
F 31-71-5273619

RUL,CESP

Rijksuniversiteit Leiden
(Leiden University)
Centre of Environmental Science
Programme Environment and Development
P.O.Box 9518
2300 RA Leiden
Visiting Address:
Einsteinweg 2 2333 CC Leiden
T 31-71-527 7486/7461
F 31-71-527 74 96

RUL,CILC

Rijksuniversiteit Leiden
(Leiden University)
Centre for International Legal Cooperation
Stationsplein 240
2312 AR Leiden
T 31-71-5121888
F 31-71-5130160

RUL,CNWS

Rijksuniversiteit Leiden
(Leiden University)
Research School CNWS van Aziatische, Afrikaanse, Amerindische Studies (CNWS)
(Research School CNWS of Asian, African, and Amerindian Studies)
P.O. Box 9515
2300 RA Leiden
Visiting Address:
Nonnensteeg 1-3
2311 VJ Leiden
T 31-71-5272171
F 31-71-5272939
CNWS@Rullet.LeidenUniv.nl

RUL,FG

Rijksuniversiteit Leiden
(Leiden University)
Faculteit der Godgeleerdheid
(Faculty of Theology)
P.O.Box 9515
2300 RA Leiden
Visiting Address:
Matthias de Vrieshof 1 Gebouw 1172
T 31-71-5272570/2572
F 31-71-5272571

RUL,IBR

Rijksuniversiteit Leiden
(Leiden University)
Internships and Business Relations
P.O.Box 9515
2300 RA Leiden
Visiting Address:
P.N. van Eyckhof 1 2311 BV Leiden
T 31-71-527 22 35
F 31-71-527 26 14
stagecoord@rullet.leidenuniv.nl

RUL,ICB

Rijksuniversiteit Leiden
(Leiden University)
Bureau Buitenland
Inter Consultancy Bureau (ICB)
Rapenburg 63
2311 GJ Leiden
T 31-71-527 22 25
F 31-71-527 54 99

Netherlands

RUL,KERN

Rijksuniversiteit Leiden
(Leiden University)
Instituut Kern
Department of Languages and Cultures of South and Central Asia
P.O.Box 9515
2300 RA Leiden
Visiting Address:
Nonnensteeg 1-3
2312 VJ Leiden
T 31-71-5272503
F 31-71-5272615

RUL,KERN,DC

Rijksuniversiteit Leiden
(Leiden University)
Faculty of Arts
Kern Institute,
Documentation Centre on South and Central Asia
P.O.Box 9515
2300 RA Leiden
T 31-71-5272503
F 31-71-5272615

RUL,LISWO

Rijksuniversiteit Leiden
(Leiden University)
Leids Instituut voor Sociaal Wetenschappelijk Onderzoek (LISWO)
P.O.Box 9555
2300 RB Leiden
Visiting Address:
Wassenaarseweg 52 Pieter de la Court gebouw
T 31-71-527 38 45
F 31-71-527 37 88

RUL,OR/HB

Rijksuniversiteit Leiden
(Leiden University)
Onderzoeksinstituut Rijksherbarium/Hortus Botanicus
(Research Institute National Herbarium/Hortus Botanicus)
P.O.Box 9514
2300 RA Leiden
T 31-71-5273515/5144
F 31-71-5273511

RUL,OWZ

Rijksuniversiteit Leiden
(Leiden University)
Coördinaat Onderwijs- en Wetenschapszaken (OWZ)
P.O.Box 9515
2300 RA Leiden
Visiting Address:
Cleveringaplaats 1 WSD-complex,
Centraal Faciliteitengebouw (1175)
T 31-71-527 2318/2404
F 31-71-527 26 15

RUL,PK

Rijksuniversiteit Leiden
(Leiden University)
Prentenkabinet
(Print Room)
Rapenburg 65
2311 GJ Leiden
Visiting Address:
Rapenburg 65
T 31-71-527 27 00
fotohist@RULLET.LeidenUniv.NL

RUL,SI

Rijksuniversiteit Leiden
Sinologisch Instituut
(Sinological Institute)
P.O.Box 9515
2300 RA Leiden
Visiting Address:
Arsenaalstraat 1 WSD-Gebouw 1177
T 31-71-5272524
F 31-71-5272526
SECRCHIN@Rullet.Leiden.Univ.nl

RUL,TCJK

Rijksuniversiteit Leiden
(Leiden University)
Faculty of Arts
Centre for Japanese and Korean Studies
P.O.Box 9515
2300 RA Leiden
Visiting Address:
Arsenaalstraat 1 WSD-gebouw 1177
T 31-71-5272539
F 31-71-5272215
Japanese@rullet.leidenuniv.nl

RUL,TCZOAO

Rijksuniversiteit Leiden
(Leiden University)
Department of Languages and Cultures of Southeast Asia and Oceania (TCZOAO)
P.O.Box 9515
2300 RA Leiden
Visiting Address:
P.N. van Eyckhof 3 WSD-Gebouw 1165
T 31-71-5272418/19
F 31-71-5272632

RUL,TCZOAO,PD

Rijksuniversiteit Leiden
(Leiden University)
Departement of Languages Cultures of Southeast Asia and Oceania\Projects Division
Nonnensteeg 1-3
2311 VJ Leiden
T 31-71-5272416/2419
F 31-71-5272623
projdiv@rullet.leidenuniv.nl

RUL,VA

Rijksuniversiteit Leiden
(Leiden University)
Vakgroep Archeologie
(Department of Archaeology)
P.O.Box 9515
2300 RA Leiden
Visiting Address:
Reuvensplaats 4 WSD-Gebouw 1176
T 31-71-5272411
F 31-71-5272429

RUL,VAILW

Rijksuniversiteit Leiden
(Leiden University)
Vakgroep Algemene en Interculturele Literatuurwetenschap (AILW)
Department of General and Intercultural Literature)
P.O.Box 9515
2300 RA Leiden
Visiting Address:
Van Wijkplaats 2 WSD-Gebouw 1162
T 31-71-527 22 51
F 31-71-527 26 15

Netherlands

RUL,VG

Rijksuniversiteit Leiden
(Leiden University)
Vakgroep Geschiedenis
(Department of History)
P.O.Box 9515
2300 RA Leiden
Visiting Address:
Doelensteeg 16 2311 VL WSD-Gebouw 1174
T 31-71-527 27 68
F 31-71-527 26 52

RUL,VKA

Rijksuniversiteit Leiden
(Leiden University)
Vakgroep Kunstgeschiedenis en Archeologie
P.O.Box 9515
2300 RA Leiden
Visiting Address:
Doelensteeg 16 WSD-Gebouw 1175+1174
T 31-71-527 26 87
F 31-71-527 26 15

RUL,VM

Rijksuniversiteit Leiden
(Leiden University)
Vakgroep Metamedica
P.O.Box 2087
2301 CB Leiden
Visiting Address:
Pathologiegebouw
T 31-71-527 6518/6519
F 31-71-527 53 57

RUL,VN

Rijksuniversiteit Leiden
Vakgroep Nederlandkunde
(Dutch Studies)
P.O.Box 9515
2300 RA Leiden
T 31-71-527 22 33
F 31-71-527 26 15

RUL,VPW

Rijksuniversiteit Leiden
(Leiden University)
Vakgroep Politieke Wetenschappen
P.O.Box 9555
2300 RB Leiden
Visiting Address:
Wassenaarseweg 52 Pieter de la Court gebouw
T 31-71-5273936/3950
F 31-71-5273815

RUL,VRV

Rijksuniversiteit Leiden
(Leiden University)
Vakgroep Rechtshistorische Vakken
Gravensteen Pieterskerkhof 6
2311 SR Leiden
T 31-71-527 74 42
F 31-71-527 74 44

RUL,VTCIMO

Rijksuniversiteit Leiden
(Leiden University)
Vakgroep Talen en Culturen van het Islamitisch Midden-Oosten
P.O.Box 9515
2300 RA Leiden
Visiting Address:
Witte Singel 25 Gebouw 1173
T 31-71-5272253
F 31-71-5272615

RUL,VTW

Rijksuniversiteit Leiden
(Leiden University)
Department of Comparative Linguistics (VTW)
P.O.Box 9515
2300 RA Leiden
Visiting Address:
P.N. van Eyckhof 3 WSD-Gebouw 1165
T 31-71-5272501
F 31-71-5272501
lubotsky@rullet.leidenuniv.nl

RUL,VVI

Rijksuniversiteit Leiden
Van Vollenhoven Instituut voor Recht en Bestuur in Niet-Westerse Landen
(\Van Vollenhoven Institute for Law and Administration in Non-Western Countries)
Rapenburg 33
2311 GG Leiden
T 31-71-5277261
F 31-71-5277760
jfvviad@ruljur.leidenuniv.nl

RvZ

Raad voor de Zending
P.O.Box 12
2340 AA Oegstgeest

SARI

Stichting Arisan Indonesia (Arisan Indonesia Foundation)
Appelternhof 6
6581 GW Malden
T 31-24-3586946/3227623
F 31-24-3227623
sari@mailbox.kun.nl

SAS,OI

Stichting Azië Studies
(Asian Studies Foundation)
Eetfink 540
1103 AE Amsterdam
T 31-20-6906820

SEASP

Southeast Asia Study Project
Jagerwei 9
5551 PW Valkenswaard
T 31-40-2049287
F 31-40-2049287

SEPHIS

SEPHIS
International Institute of Social History
Cruquiusweg 31
1019 AT Amsterdam
T 31-20-4636395
F 31-20--4636385
sephis@iisg.nl

SGO

Sociale Geografie van Ontwikkelingslanden
Nieuwe Prinsengracht 130
1018 VZ Amsterdam

SI,VSW

Sanders Institute
Vakgroep Sociale Wetenschappen
P.O.Box 1738
3000 DR Rotterdam
Visiting Address:
Burgemeester Oudlaan 50
T 31-10-408 26097
F 31-10-452 30 39

SIFO

Stichting voor Internationale Fiscale en Economsiche Ontwikkeling
(Foundation for International Fiscal and Economic Development)
P.O.Box 75338
1070 AH Amsterdam
Visiting Address:
World Trade Centre Strawinskylaan 815 1077 XX
T 31-20-672 24 87
F 31-20-662 80 62

SIKC

Stichting Islamitische Kunst en Cultuur
(Centre of Islamic Art and Culture)
P.O.Box 361
3000 AJ Rotterdam
T 31-10-4111055
F 31-10-4118331

Netherlands

SIM

Studie- en Informatiecentrum
Mensenrechten (SIM)
(Study and Information Centre Human Rights)
Janskerkhof 16
3512 BM Utrecht

T 31-30-253 80 34

F 31-30-253 71 68

sim@pobox.ruu.nl

SISWO

Institute for Coordination of Research in Social Siences
(SISWO)
Redaktie Facta
Plantage Muidergracht 4
1018 TV Amsterdam

T 31-20-5270629

F 31-20-6229430

siswo@siswo.uva.nl

SK

De Schone Kunsten
Zocherstraat 1-d
2021 DG Haarlem

T 31-23-525 80 73

F 31-25-525 49 58

SNB

Stichting Nederland - Bantam
(Netherlands Bantam Foundation)
Stationsweg 56
6711 PT Ede (Gld)

SNSL

Stichting Nederland - Sri Lanka
Netherlands Sri Lanka Foundation)
Rigolettostraat 55
2555 VN The Hague

T 31-70-3252381

F 31-70-3252381

SOJ

Stichting Oud-Jakarta
(Old Jakarta Heritage Foundation)
Fruinlaan 2
2313 ER Leiden

T 31-71-5146090

SOTA

Stichting Onderzoekcentrum Turkistan en Azerbaidzjan (SOTA)
(Foudation Research Centre for Turkestan and Azerbaijan)
P.O.Box 9642
2003 LP Haarlem

T 31-23-529 28 83

F 31-23-529 28 83

sota@euronet.nl / www.euronet.nl\users\sota

STT

Stichting Tong Tong
(Tong Tong Foundation)
Celebesstraat 62
2585 TM The Hague

T 31-70-3540944

F 31-70-3504497

siemboon@worldaccess.nl

SW,A

Stichting Wereldkinderen
Afd. Azië
Riouwstraat 191
2585 HT The Hague

SWPNG

Stichting Werkgroep Papua Nieuw Guinea
(Support Group Papua New Guinea Foundation)
Eekelerweg 7
7102 ES Winterswijk

T 31-543-515610

TAO

TAO
Nieuwe Kanaal 11
6709 PA Wageningen

TF

Strichting Tropenbos
Tropical Forrest Foundation
P.O.Box 232
6700 AE Wageningen

T 31-317-426262

F 31-317-423024

tropenbos@iac.agro.nl

TGD

Theatergroep Delta
Korte Leidsedwarsstraat 12
1017 RC Amsterdam

T 31-20-6261435

F 31-20-4210639

TGF

De Telegraaf
(Dutch daily newspaper)
P.O.Box 376
1000 EB Amsterdam
Visiting Address:
Basisweg 30 1043 AP

THEM

Theatermuseum
Herengracht 168
1016 BP Amsterdam

T 31-20-6235104

TIC

Taipei Information Centre
Burgemeester Haspelslaan 5
1181 NB Amstelveen

T 31-20-641 2536/51470

F 31-20-645 8651

taiinfor@worldonline.nl

TIDC

Tibet Information and Documentation Centre
P.O.Box 1756
1000 BT Amsterdam
Visiting Address:
keizersgracht 302 1016 EX Amsterdam

T 31-20-623 76 99

tibetsg@xs4all.nl

TNO, IAG

Netherlands Institute of Applied Geoscience TNO
P.O.Box 6012
2600 JA Delft
Visiting Address:
Schoemakerstraat 97

T 31-15--269 6900

F 31-15-256 4800

TNO,MP

Nederlandse Organisatie voor Toegepaste Natuurwetenschappelijk Onderzoek (TNO)
Marketing en Programme
P.O.Box 6070
2600 AJ Delft

T 31-15-2694915

F 31-15-2626337

TU

Technische Universiteit Delft
(Delft Techinical University)
Julianalaan 134
2628 BL Delft

T 31-15-2783773

F 31-15-2783100

Netherlands

TU, FT

Tilburg University
Faculty of Theology
P.O.Box 9130
5000 HC Tilburg
Visiting Address:
Academielaan 9 5037 ET Tilburg

TU,CICAT

Technische Universiteit Delft
(Delft University of Technology)
Centre for International Cooperation
and Appropriate Technology (CICAT)
P.O.Box 5048
2600 GA Delft
Visiting Address:
Stevinweg 1
T 31-15-2783612
F 31-15-2781179
cicat@ct.tudelft.nl

TU,FLR

Technische Universiteit Delft
(Delft University of Technology)
Faculteit der Luchtvaart- en
Ruimtevaarttechniek
P.O.Box 5058
2600 GB Delft
Visiting Address:
Kluyverweg 1 2629 HS
T 31-15--278 20 58
F 31-15-278 18 22

TU,FWTMW

Technische Universiteit Delft
(Delft University of Technology)
Faculteit der Wijsbegeerte en
Technische Maatschappijwetenschappe
De Vries v. Heystplantsoen 2
2628 RZ Delft
T 31-15--278 3620
F 31-15-278 7105

TU,MPE

Technische Universiteit Delft
(Delft University of Technology)
Mining and Petroleum Enginering
Mijnboustraat 120
2628 RX Delft

TUE

Technische Universiteit Eindhoven
(Eindhoven University of Technology)
P.O.Box 513
5600 MB Eindhoven

TUE,DTDS

Technische Universiteit Eindhoven
(Eindhoven University of Technology)
Department of Technology and
Development Sciences
P.O.Box 513
5600 MB Eindhoven
Visiting Address:
Den Dolech 2 Dommelgb. kamer 1.25
T 31-40-247 40 21
F 040-244 91 71

TUE,TWIM

Technische Universiteit Eindhoven
(Eindhoven University of Technology)
Faculteit der Wijsbegeerte en
Technische
Maatschappijwetenschappen
Onderzoekscentrum TWIM
P.O.Box 513
5600 MB Eindhoven

TUK

Theologisch Universiteit Kampen
(Kampen Theological University)
P.O.Box 5021
8260 GA Kampen
Visiting Address:
Koornmarkt 1 8261 JX
T 31-38-339 26 66
F 038-339 26 13

TWC

Third World Centre
P.O.Box 91804
6500 HE Nijmegen
Visiting Address:
Thomas van Aquinostraat 4
T 31-24-3613058
F 31-24-3615957
R.Vandalen@MAW.KUN.nl

UeB

Ukiyo-e Books bv.
Breestraat 113-A
2311 CL Leiden
T 31-71-5143552
F 31-71-5141488
ukiyoe@xs4all.nl

UMA

Universiteits Museum Agnietenkapel
Oudezijds Voorburgwal 231
1012 EZ Amsterdam
T 31-20-5253339
agnieten@mail.uba.uva.nl

UNESCO,NC

UNESCO Netherlands Commission
P.O.Box 29777
2502 LT The Hague
Visiting Address:
Schenkkade 50
T 31-70-364 46 55
F 31-70-364 99 17

UT,DTM

Universiteit Twente
(University of Twente)
Department Technology and
Management
P.O.Box 217
7500 AE Enschede
T 31-53-4983541
F 31-53-4893087
r.j.c.vanwaarde@tdg.utwente.nl

UT,FEST

Universiteit Twente
(University of Twente)
Faculty of Educational Science and
Technology
P.O.Box 217
7500 AE Enschede

UT,TDG

Universiteit Twente
(University of Twente)
Technology and Development Group
P.O.Box 217
7500 AE Enschede
T 31-53-489 35 45
F 053-489 30 87

UU,CB

Universiteit Utrecht
(Utrecht University)
College van Bestuur
P.O.Box 80125
3508 TC Utrecht
Visiting Address:
Heidelberglaan 8
T 31-30-253 5150
F 31-30-253 7745

UU,CBM

Universiteit Utrecht
(Utrecht University)
Centre for Policy Studies and
Management (CBM)
Muntstraat 2A
3512 EV Utrecht
T 31-30-253 81 01
F 31-30-253 61 56

Netherlands

UU,DC

Universiteit Utrecht
(Utrecht University)
Department of Cartography
P.O. Box 80115
3508 TC Utrecht

UU,DH

Universiteit Utrecht
(Utrecht University)
Department of History
Muntstraat 4
3512 EV Utrecht
T 31-30-253 82 31
F 31-30-253 83 81

UU,DSG

Universiteit Utrecht
(Utrecht University)
Department of Social Geography of Developing Countries
Transitorium 2 P.O.Box 80115
3508 Utrecht
Visiting Address:
Heidelberglaan 2
T 31-30-253 21 09
F 31-30-254 06 04

UU,FG

Universiteit Utrecht
(Utrecht University)
Faculteit der Godgeleerdheid
P.O.Box 80105
3508 TC Utrecht
Visiting Address:
Heidelberglaan 2 De Uithof
T 31-30-253 18 53
F 31-30-253 32 41
theology@cc.ruu.nl

UU,FL

Universiteit Utrecht
(Utrecht University)
Faculteit der Letteren
Kromme Nieuwegracht 46
3512 HJ Utrecht
T 31-30-253 6105
F 31-30-253 6083
naam@let.ruu.nl

UU,IIMO

Universiteit Utrecht
(Utrecht University)
Interuniversitair Instituut voor Missiologie en Oecumenica (IIMO)
(Interuniversity Institute for Missiological and Ecumenical Research
Transitorium II-Heidelberglaan 2
3584 CS Utrecht
Visiting Address:
Nieuw Adres dd.: 110396
T 31-30-2539412
F 31-30-2539434
iimo@ggl.ruu.nl

UU,OGC

Universiteit Utrecht
(Utrecht University)
Onderzoeksinstituut voor Geschiedenis en Cultuur (OGC)
Trans 10
3512 JK Utrecht
T 31-30-253 82 39
F 31-30-253 60 00
ots@let.ruu.nl

UU,VASW

Universiteit Utrecht
(Utrecht University)
Vakgroep Algemene Sociale Wetenschappen
(Department of Social Sciences)
Transitorium 2 Heidelberglaan 2
3584 CS Utrecht
Visiting Address:
Postbus 80140 3508 TC
T 31-30-253 14 08
F 31-30-253 47 33
aswsecr@fsw.ruu.nl

UU,VCA

Universiteit Utrecht
(Utrecht University)
Vakgroep Culturele Antropologie
(Department of Cultural Anthropology)
Bolognalaan 32
3584 CJ Utrecht
Visiting Address:
Postbus 80140 3508 TC Utrecht
T 31-30-225 3211/1894
F 31-30-225 3466
casecr@fsw.ruu.nl

UU,VG

Universiteit Utrecht
(Utrecht University)
Vakgroep Geschiedenis
(Department of History)
Kromme Nieuwegracht 66
3512 HL Utrecht
T 31-30-253 6222/6153
F 31-30-253 63 91
"user"@let.ruu.nl

UU,VOTC

Universiteit Utrecht
(Utecht University)
Vakgroep Oosterse Talen en Culturen
(Department of Eastern Languages and Cultures)
Drift 15
3512 BR Utrecht
T 31-30-253 61 33
F 31-30-253 61 38
naam@let.ruu.nl

UU,VSGO

Universiteit Utrecht
(Utrecht University)
Vakgroep Sociale Geographie van de Ontwikkelinglanden (Department of Human Geography of Developing Countries)
Postbus 80115
3508 TC Utrecht
Visiting Address:
Heidelberglaan 2
T 31-30-2532350
F 31-30-2540604
vanderlinden@frw.ruu.nl /
l.grunsven@frw.ruu.nl

UvA, ECJK

Universiteit van Amsterdam
(University of Amsterdam)
Etnomusicologisch Centrum 'Jaap Kunst'
Spuistraat 134
1012 VB Amsterdam
T 31-20-5254443
F 31-20-5254429
musica@let.uva.nl

UvA,AHI

Universiteit van Amsterdam
(University of Amsterdam)
Archeologisch-Historisch Instituut
Oude Turfmarkt 129
1012 GC Amsterdam

Netherlands

UvA,ASC

Universiteit van Amsterdam
(University of Amsterdam)
Antropologisch Sociologisch Centrum
Oudezijds Achterburgwal 185
1012 DK Amsterdam

T 31-20-5252614

F 31-20-5253010

UvA,ASC,CASA

Universiteit van Amsterdam
(University of Amsterdam)
Anthropological-Sociological Centre, CASA
Oudezijds Achterburgwal 185
1012 DK Amsterdam

T 31-20-525 25 04

F 31-20-525 30 10

UvA,ASSR

Universiteit van Amsterdam
(University of Amsterdam)
Amsterdam School for Social Science Research (ASSR)
Oude Hoogstraat 24
1012 CE Amsterdam

T 31-20-525 22 62

F 31-20-525 24 46

assr@sara.nl

UvA,ASSR,CASA

Universiteit van Amsterdam\Amsterdam School for Social Science Research (ASSR)\Centre for Asian Studies Amsterdam (CASA)
Oude Hoogstraat 24
1012 CE Amsterdam

T 31-20-5252745/2262

F 31-20-5252446

ASSR@PSCW.UVA.NL or assr@sara.nl

UvA,ATW

Universiteit van Amsterdam
(University of Amsterdam)
Vakgroep Algemene Taalwetenschap
Spuistraat 210
1012 VT Amsterdam

T 31-20-525 38 64

F 31-20-525 30 21

UvA,BASC

Universiteit van Amsterdam\Bibliotheek Antropologisch Sociologisch Centrum
Oudezijds Achterburgwal 185
1012 DK Amsterdam

T 31-20-5252447

UvA,BIB

Universiteit van Amsterdam
(University of Amsterdam)
Universiteitsbibliotheek
(University Library)
P.O.Box 19185
1000 GD Amsterdam
Visiting Address:
Singel 425 1012 WP

UvA,BZI

Universiteit van Amsterdam
(University of Amsterdam)
Belle van Zuylen Instituut
Rokin 84-90
1012 KX Amsterdam

T 31-20-525 21 19

F 31-20-525 22 19

UvA,DA,AI

Universiteit van Amsterdam
(University of Amsterdam) Department of Anthropology
Anthropological Institute
Oudezijds Achterburgwal 185
1012 DK Amsterdam

T 31-20-5253010

F 31-20-5252504

anthropology@pscw.uva.nl

UvA,FEWE

Universiteit van Amsterdam
(University of Amsterdam)
Faculteit der Economische Wetenschappen en Econometrie
P.O.Box 19268
1000 GG Amsterdam
Visiting Address:
Roeterstraat 11 1018 WB

T 31-20-525 41 28

F 31-20-525 41 24

UvA,FPSCW

Universiteit van Amsterdam
(University of Amsterdam)
Faculteit der Politieke en Sociaal-Culturele Wetenschappen
Faculty of Political and Socio-Cultural Sciences)
Binnen Gasthuis
Oudezijds Achterburgwal 237
1012 DL Amsterdam

T 31-20-525 21 47

F 31-20-525 20 86

UvA,FW

Universiteit van Amsterdam
(University of Amsterdam)
Faculteit der Wijsbegeerte
Nieuwe Doelenstraat 15
1012 CP Amsterdam

T 31-20-525 45 00

F 31-20-525 45 03

UvA,GM

Universiteit van Amsterdam
(University of Amsterdam)
Godsdienst en Maatschappij
Oudezijds Achterburgwal 185
1012 DK Amsterdam

T 31-20-525 21 20

F 31-20-525 36 15

UvA,INDRA

Universiteit van Amsterdam
(University of Amsterdam)
Institute for Development Research Amsterdam (INDRA)
Pl. Muidergracht 12
1018 TV Amsterdam

T 31-20-5255050

F 31-20-5255040

UvA,ISA,CC

Universiteit van Amsterdam
International School Amsterdam Center for Comporary European Social Studies Graduate Program in International Relations
Oudezijds Achterburgwal 237
1012 DL Amsterdam

UvA,ISP/ZMA

Universiteit van Amsterdam
(Universiteit van Amsterdam)
Sectie Entomologie, ISP/ZMA
Plantage Middenlaan 64
1018 DH Amsterdam

T 31-20-525 62 45

F 31-20-525 65 28

UvA,IVAM

Universiteit van Amsterdam
(University of Amsterdam)
IVAM Environmental Research
P.O.Box 18180
1001 VZ Amsterdam

F 31-20-5255850

Netherlands

UvA,MAG

Universiteit van Amsterdam
(University of Amsterdam)
Moderne Aziatische Geschiedenis (MAG) (Faculty of Political, Social, and Cultural Sciences)
Oudezijdsachterburgwal 237
1012 DL Amsterdam
T 31-20-5252121/3090
F 31-20-5252100
schultenordholt@pscw.uva.nl

UvA,PSCW,ASiA

Universiteit van Amsterdam\Faculteit der Politieke en Social Wetenschappen (PSCW) Azië Studies in Amsterdam (ASiA) (University of Amsterdam\Department of Political, Social, and Cultural Studies Asian Studies in Amsterdam)
O.Z. Achterburgwal 237
1012 DL Amsterdam
T 31-20-5253090
F 31-20-5252100
schultenordholt@pscw.uva.nl

UvA,SACC

Stichting Asian Cinema Centre
Oudezijds Achterburgwal 185
1012 DK Amsterdam
T 31-20-5252804
F 31-20-5253010
schultenordholt@pscw.uva.nl

UvA,SEFA,CHAIN

University of Amsterdam
Students Association of the University of Amsterdam (SEFA)\China-Amsterdam Interaction (CHAIN)
Roeterstraat 11
1018 WB Amsterdam
T 31-20-6220816
F 31-20-6227882
chain@edufee.fee.uva.nl

UvA,TDI

Universiteit van Amsterdam
(University of Amsterdam) Theology Delenus Institute
Oude Turfmarkt 147
1012 GC Amsterdam
T 31-20-525 20 10
F 31-20-525 20 07
administratie@theo.va.nl

UvA,VCA,SNWV,ZZA

Universiteit van Amsterdam\Vakgroep Culturele Antropologie\Sociologie der Niet-Westerse Volken\Sektie Zuid-en Zuidoost Azië (University of Amsterdam\Cultural Anthropology\Non Western Sociology\South and Southeas Asia Section)
Oudezijds Achterburgwal 185
1012 DK Amsterdam
T 31-20-5252504
F 31-20-5253010
antieman@pscw.uva

UvA,VCW

Universiteit van Amsterdam
(University of Amsterdam)
Vakgroep Communicatiewetenschap
Oude Hoogstraat 24
1012 CE Amsterdam
T 31-20-5253505
F 31-20-5252179

UvA,VHNTL

Universiteit van Amsterdam
(University of Amsterdam)
Vakgroep Historische Nederlandse Taa en Letterkunde
Spuistraat 134
1012 VB Amsterdam
T 31-20-525 46 57
F 31-20-525 44 29

UvA,VISTA

Universiteit van Amsterdam
(University of Amsterdam)
Stichting VISTA (Far Reaching Visuals
Oudezijds Achterburgwal 185
1012 DK Amsterdam
st-vista@dds.nl

UvA,VKG

Universiteit van Amsterdam
(University of Amsterdam)
Vakgroep Kunstgeschiedenis
Herengracht 286
1016 BX Amsterdam
T 31-20-525 30 50
F 31-20-525 30 23

UvA,VMW

Universiteit van Amsterdam
(University of Amsterdam)
Vakgroep Muziekwetenschap
Spuistraat 210
1012 VA Amsterdam
T 31-20-5254443

UvA,VP

Universiteit van Amsterdam
(University of Amsterdam)
Vakgroep Politicologie
(Department of Politicology)
Oude Zijds Achterburgwal 237 Binnen Gasthuis
1012 DL Amsterdam
T 31-20-525 3090

UvA,VPD

Universiteit van Amsterdam
(University of Amsterdam)
Vakgroep Planologie en Demografie
P.O.Box 19268
1000 GG Amsterdam
Visiting Address:
Nieuwe Pringsengracht 130 1018 VZ
T 31-20-525 40 40
F 31-20-525 40 41

UvA,VS

Universiteit van Amsterdam
(University of Amsterdam)
Vakgroep Staatsrecht
P.O.Box 1030
1000 BA Amsterdam
Visiting Address:
Kloveniersburgwal 72
T 31-20-525 39 66
F 31-20-525 34 95

UvA,VSG

Universiteit van Amsterdam
(University of Amsterdam)
Vakgroep Sociale Geografie
Nieuwe Prinsengracht 130
1018 VZ Amsterdam
T 31-20-525 4063

UvA,VVIB

Universiteit van Amsterdam
(University of Amsterdam)
Vakgroep Volkenrecht en Internationale Betrekkingen
P.O.Box 19120
1000 GC Amsterdam
Visiting Address:
Turfdraagsterpad 1 1012 XT Kamer 211
T 31-20-525 26 32
F 31-20-525 29 00

UvA,ZZOAS,EN

Universiteit van Amsterdam
(University of Amsterdam)
Vakgroep Zuid en Zuid-Oost Azië Studies
Oudezijds Achterburgwal 185
1012 DK Amsterdam

Netherlands

VENJB

Vier Eeuwen Nederlands- en Japanse Betrekkingen (Four Centuries of Netherlands and Japanese Relations)
Kloveniersburgwal 55
1011 JX Amsterdam
T 31-20-6274564
F 31-20-6253501

VJK

Vereniging voor Japanse Kunst (Society for Japanese Arts)
Mr Pankenstraat 12
5571 CP Bergeyk
T 31-497-572310
F 31-497-573657

VMGVL

Volkenkundig Museum 'Gerardus van der Leeuw'
(Ethnography Musem `Gerardus van der Leeuw'
Nieuwe Kijk in 't Jatstraat 104
9712 SL Groningen
T 31-50-363 57 91
volkkmus@theol.rug.nl

VMN

Volkenkundig Museum Nusantara
(Ethnography Museum Nusantara)
St. Agathaplein 4
2611 HR Delft
T 31-15-2602358
F 31-15-2138744

VNC

Vriendschapsvereniging Nederland-China (VNC) (Friendship Society Netherlands-China)
P.O.Box 79
3500 AB Utrecht
T 31-30-2611846
F 31-30-2627734

VNHS

Vereniging Nederlands Historisch Scheepvaartmuseum
(Netherlands Association Historical Maritime Museum)
Obrechtlaan 70
3723 KD Bilthoven

VNI

Vereniging Nederland - India
Chrysantenhof 33
2651 XJ Berkel en Rodenrijs
T 31-10-5114400
F 31-10-5121123

VU FPPW

Vrije Universiteit Amsterdam
Faculteit Psychologische en Pedagogische Wetenschappen
Van der Boechorststraat 1
1081 BT Amsterdam
T 31-20-444 88 88
F 31-20-444 88 45

VU, DCA

Vrije Universiteit Amsterdam
Vakgroep Culturele Antropologie
(Department of Cultural Anthropology)
De Boelelaan 1081-C
1081 HV Amsterdam
T 31-20-4446704
F 31-20-4446722

VU, VE

Vrije Universiteit Amsterdam
Vakgroep Engels
(Department of English Languages)
De Boelelaan 1105
1081 HV Amsterdam

VU,CWFS

Vrije Universiteit
Centre for World Food Studies SOW-NL
De Boelelaan 1105
1081 HV Amsterdam
T 31-20-4449321
F 31-20-4449325
pm@sow.econ.vu.nl

VU,DOS,PI

Vrije Universiteit Amsterdam
Dienst Ontwikkelingssamenwerking
(Development Cooperation)
De Boelelaan 1115
1081 HV Amsterdam

VU,FL

Vrije Universiteit
(Free University)
Faculteit der Letteren
Spuistraat 134
1012 VB Amsterdam
T 31-20-5254730
F 31-20-5254429

VU,FR

Vrije Universiteit Amsterdam
Faculteit der Rechtgeleerdheid
(Faculty of Law)
De Boelelaan 1105
1081 HV Amsterdam
T 31-20-444 6250
F 31-20-444 6210

VU,GW

Vrije Universiteit Amsterdam
Godsdienstwetenschappen
De Boelelaan 1105
1081 HV Amsterdam
T 31-20-444 66 20
F 31-20-444 66 35

VU,IM

Vrije Universiteit Amsterdam
Instituut voor Milieuvraagstukken
(Institute for the Environment)
De Boelelaan 1105
1081 HV Amsterdam

VU,MFHC

Vrije Universiteit Amsterdam
Medische Faculteit Health Care in Developing Countries
v/d Boechorststraat 7
1081 BT Amsterdam
T 31-20-444 82 66
F 31-20-444 83 94

VU,VL

Vrije Universiteit Amsterdam
Vakgroep Linguistiek
(Linguistics Department)
De Boelelaan 1105
1081 HV Amsterdam
Visiting Address:
Postbua 7161 1007 MC

VU,VOAE

Vrije Universiteit Amsterdam
Vakgroep Ontwikkelings- en Agrarische Economie
De Boelelaan 1105
1081 HV Amsterdam
T 31-20-444 61 40
F 31-20-444 60 05

VU,VT

Vrije Universiteit Amsterdam
Vakgroep Taalkunde
(Department of Linguistics)
De Boelelaan 1105
1081 HV Amsterdam
T 31-20-444 6440/6430
F 31-20-444 65 00

VU,VTDM

Vrije Universiteit Amsterdam
Vakgroep Theorie en Didactiek Maatschappijleer
De Boelelaan 1081-C
1081 HV Amsterdam
T 31-20-444 68 08
F 31-20-444 68 50

Netherlands

VVIET

Vertaalbureau Vietnam (Translation Bureau Vietnam)
Willemstraat 14
2316 CS Leiden
T 31-71-5226083
F 31-71-5220683
ngo@rullet.leidenuniv.nl

VWS

Ministerie van Volksgezondheid, Welzijn en Sport
P.O.Box 3008
2280 MK Rijswijk

VWU,AR

VWU Publishers B.V.
Azië Redaktie
Groningensingel 96
6803 AE Arnhem
T 31-26-323 11 23
F 31-26-323 04 60

WAU,TE

Landbouwuniversiteit Wageningen (Agricultural University) Department o Terrestrial Ecology & Nature Conservation Tropical Ecology
Bornsesteeg 69
6708 PD Wageningen
T 31-317-48490011
F 31-317-484845
herbert.prins@staf.ton.wau.nl

WM

Westfries Museum
Rode Steen 1
1621 CW Hoorn
T 31-229-280028

Wmag.

Elsevier
(Weekly Magazine)
P.O.Box 152
1000 AD Amsterdam
Visiting Address:
Hoogoorddreef 60

WOTRO

Stichting voor Wetenschappelijk Onderzoek van de Tropen en Ontwikkelingslanden (WOTRO)
(Netherlands Foundation for the Advancement of Tropical Research)
P.O.Box 93138
2509 AC The Hague
Visiting Address:
Laan van Nieuw Oost Indië 131 2593 BM
T 31-70-3440640
F 31-70-3850971
wotro@now.nl

WsM

Werkspoor Museum
Oostenburgergracht 77
1018 NC Amsterdam
T 31-20-6253970
F 31-20-6251035

ZHM

Zaans Historisch Museum
Lagedijk 80
1544 BJ Zaandijk
T 31-75-6217626

Norway

CIC

Center for Intercultural Communication
Misjonsveien 34
4034 Stavanger
T 47-51-516273
F 47-51-516272

CMI,DSHR

Chr. Michelsen Institute
Development Studies and Human Right
Fantoftvegen 38
5036 Fantoft-Bergen
T 47-55-574000
F 47-55-574166

DMA

Department and Museum of Anthropology
P.O. Box 1091 Blindern
0317 Oslo

FNI, NCF

Norwegian China Forum
Fridtjof Nansen Institute
P.O. Box 326
1324 Lysaker
China.Forum@fni.no

HSF

Hogskolen i Sogn og Fjorane
(College of Sogn of Fjorane)
P.O.Box 133
5801 Sogndal
Visiting Address:
Rutlinslid 6
T 47-57-676055
F 47-57-676051

KIMO

Kunstindustrimuseet I Oslo
The Oslo Museum of Applied Arts
St. Olavs Gate 1
0165 Oslo
T 47-22-203578
F 47-22-113971

KTM,IPACH

Kon-Tiki Museum
Institute for Pacific Archaeology and Cultural History
Bygdoynesveien 36
0286 Oslo
T 47-22-438050
F 47-22-445085

NACS

Nordic Association of Chinese Studies Newsletter
P.O. Box 1030 Blindern
0315 Oslo

NI

Nobel Institute
Drammenveien 19
0255 Oslo

NRI

Nordland Research Institute
8002 Bodoe
T 47-75-517610
F 47-75-517234

NSMES

Nordic Society for Middle Eastern Studies
Parkveien 22-A
5007 Bergen
T 47-55-5882647
F 47-55-589891
sylvia.liland@smi.uib.no

NUPI

Norwegian Institute of International Affairs
P.O. Box 8159 dep.
0033 Oslo

Norway

SM

Stavanger Museum
Musegt. 16
N-4005 Stavanger
T 47-45-1526035
F 47-45-1529380

UB,DCP

Universitet i Bergen
Department of Comparative Politics
Christiesgt. 15
5007 Bergen
T 47-55-582175
F 47-55-589425

UB,DHR

Universitet i Bergen
Department of the History of Religions
Sydnesplass 9
5007 Bergen
T 47-55-212449
F 47-55-584742

UB,DLP

Universitet i Bergen
Department of Linguistics and Phonetic
Sydneplass 9
5007 Bergen
T 47-55-212260
F 47-55-231897

UB,DP

Universitet i Bergen
Department of Philosophy
Stonesplassen 7
5007 Bergen
T 47-55-582437
F 47-55-589651

UB,DSA

Universitet i Bergen
Faculty of Social Sciences
Department of Social Anthropology
Fosswinckelsgate 6
5007 Bergen
T 47-55-589250
F 47-55-589260
steinar.vestad@sosanth.uib.no

UO

Universitet i Oslo
(University of Oslo)
P.O.box 1008
0315 Oslo
T 47-22-856877
F 47-22-855278

UO, FSS,ESST

Universitet i Oslo
Faculty of Social Sciences
Education in Society, Science and Technology
P.O. Box 1108 Blindern
0317 Oslo
T 47-22-858962
F 47-22-858960

UO, PS

University of Oslo
Department of Political Science
P.O. Box 1097 Blindern
0317 Oslo

UO,EACS

Universitet i Oslo
European Association of Chinese Studies
P.O. Box 1116 Blindern
0317 Oslo
T 47-22-858900
F 47-22-858920
harald.bockman@sum.uio.no

UO,EAI,BIB

Universitet i Oslo
East Asian Institute
Facultetsbiblioteket
(Library)
Postboks 1009 Blindern
0315 Oslo

UO,FA,CS

Universitet i Oslo
Faculty of Arts
Department of Cultural Studies
P.O. Box 1010 Blindern
0315 Oslo
T 47-22-855943
F 47-22-854828

UO,FA,EOS

Universitet i Oslo
Faculty of Arts
Department of East European and Oriental Studies
P.O. Box 1030
Blindern
0315 Oslo
T 47-22-856778
F 47-22-854140
h.b.eifring@easteur-orient.uio.no

UO,FA,HI

Universitet i Oslo
Faculty of Arts
Department of History
P.O.Box 1008
Blindern
0315 Oslo
T 47-22-856877
F 47-22-855278
p.g.price@hi.uio.no

UO,FSS,EM

Universitet i Oslo
Faculty of Social Sciences
Universitetets Etnografiske Museum
(Ethnological Museum)
Frederiksgate 2
N-0164 Oslo
T 47-22-859300
F 47-22-859960
etnografisk@ima.uio.no

UO,FSS,HG

Universitet i Oslo
Faculty of Social Sciences
Department of Human Geography
P.O. Box 1146 Blindern
0317 Oslo
T 47-22-855952
F 47-22-854828

UO,FSS,SA

Universitet i Oslo
Faculty of Social Sciences
Department of Social Anthropology
P.O. Box 1091 Blindern
0317 Oslo
T 47-22-856526
F 47-22-854502

UO,IGPCM,SM

Universitet i Oslo
Institute of General Practice and Community Medicine
Department of Social Medicine
P.O. Box 1130 Blindern
0317 Oslo
T 47-22-850603
F 47-22-850590

UT,FSS,IA

University Tormsø
Faculty of Social Science
Institute of Anthropology
Saami Studies
9037 Tromsø

Norway

UTR,DG

Universitet i Trondheim
(Norwegian University of Science and Technology)
Department of Geography
7055 Dragvoll Trondheim
T 47-73-591923
F 47-73-591878

UTR,IA

Universitet i Trondheim
Institute of Archaelogy
Institute of Archaeology
The Norwegian University of Science and Technology
7004 Trondheim
T 47-73-592170
F 47-73-592238
anne.larsen@vm.ntnu.no

UTR,SAI

Universitet i Trondheim
Department of Social Anthropology
University Centre
7055 Dragvoll
T 47-73-596552
F 47-73-596555

VKIM

Vestlandske Kunstindustrimuseum
(The West Norway Museum of Decorative Art)
Nordahl Brungsgate 9
N-5014 Bergen
T 47-55-325108
F 47-55-317455

Poland

AMU,COBS

Uniwersytet im Adama Mickiewicza
(Adam Mickiewicz University)
Chair of Oriental and Baltic Studies
Ul. Miedzychodzaka 5
60371 Poznan
T 48-61-616836
F 48-61-616836
Internet: www.orient@hum.amu.edu.pl

MAIP

Muzeum Azji I Pacyfiku
The Asia and Pacific Museum
Ul. Solec 24
00403 Warszawa
T 48-22-6296724
F 48-22-6219470

PAN,CSNEC

Polska Akademia Nauk
(Polish Academy of Sciences)
Centre for Studies on non-European Countries
Palac Staszica Nowy Swiat 72
00330 Warsaw
T 48-22-6566312
F 48-22-6207651

PAN,DAALAS

Polska Akademia Nauk
Institute of History
Department of Asian, African and Latin American Studies
Rynek Starego Miasta 29/31
00272 Warsaw

PAN,IES

Polska Akademia Nauk
Institute of Economic Science
Palac Staszica Nowy Swiat 72
00330 Warsaw
T 48-22-266356
F 48-22-266356

PIIA

Polish Institute of International Affairs
Ul. Warecka 1a
00950 Warsaw

PIIA,DSID

Polish Institute of International Affairs
Department for Scientific Information and Documentation
Ul. Warecka 1a
00950 Warsaw
T 48-22-272826
F 48-22-263026

RCBP,KUI

Regional Consultin Biuro Projektowania
Konsultingu i Ushug Informatycznych
Ul. Sulkowskiego 14
71129 Szczecin
T 48-91-72319

SACCP

The State Ateliers for Conservation of Cultural Property
Ul. Zielna 49
00108 Warsaw
T 48-22-6249481
F 48-22-6207084

UJ,DG

Uniwersytet Jagiellonski
(Jagiellonian University) Department of Geography
Grodzka 64
31044 Kraków
T 48-012-224703
F 48-012-225578

UJ,IOP,CP

Uniwersytet Jagiellonski
(Jagiellonian University)
Institute of Oriental Philology
Collegium Paderevianum
Al. Mickiewicza 9/11
31120 Krakaw
T 48-12-336377/326
F 48-12-226793
Iforien@vela.filg.uj.edu.pl

UL,IH

Uniwersytet Lódzka
(University of Lodz)
Institute of History
Ul. Kaminskiego 27 a
90219 Lodz
T 48-42-785488
F 48-42-785488

UMCS

Uniwersytet Marii Curie-Sklodowskiej
(Marie Curie Sktodowska University)
Pl. M. Curie-Sktodowskiej 5
20 031 Lublin
T 48-81-375349
F 48-81-33669

UW,FGRS,IDC

Uniwersytet Warszawska
(University of Warsaw)
Faculty of Geography and Regional Studies
Institute of Developing Countries
Karowa 20
00324 Warsaw
T 48-22-268547
F 48-22-261965

UW,FJPS,IIR

Uniwersytet Warszawska
Faculty of Journalism and Political Science
Institute of International Relations
Ul. Zurawia 4
00503 Warsaw
T 48-2-6228074
F 48-22-265791
ismn@plearn.edu.pl

Poland

UW,IH

Uniwersytet Warszawska
Institute of History
Krakowskie Przedmiescie 26/28
00927 Warsaw
T 48-22-261988
F 48-22-261988

UW,IOS,DFES

Uniwersytet Warszawska
Institute of Oriental Studies
Department of Far Eastern Studies
Krakowskie Przedmiescie 26/28
00927 Warsaw
F 48-22-263457

UW,IOS,DI

Uniwersytet Warszawska
Institute of Oriental Studies
Department of Indology
Krakowskie Przedmiescie 26/28
00 927 Warsaw
T 48-22-2600381
F 48-22-263683

UW,IOS,DJLC

Uniwersytet Warszawska
Institute of Oriental Studies
Deptartment of Japanese Languages and Culture
Krakowskie Przedmiescie 26/28
00 927 Warsaw
T 48-22-620351
F 48-22-263457

UW,OIS,MS

Uniwersytet Warszawska
Institute of Oriental Studies
Mongolian Studies
Krakowskie Przedmiescie 26/28
00-927 Warsaw
T 48-22-6200381

ZKW

Zamek Królewski na Wawelu
Wawel Royal Castle
Ul. Wawel 5
31-001 Kraków
T 48-12-221950
F 48-12-221950
wawel@cyf.-kr.edu.pl

Portugal

CEHCA

Centro de Estudos de Historia e Cartografia Antiga
(Centre for the Study of History and Antique Cartography)
Rua de Junqueira, 86
1300 Lisbon

EMTG

Escola sec. Manuel Teixeira Gomes
8500 Portimao
T 351-82-26094
F 351-82-415049

FO

Fundaçao Oriente
(Oriental Foundation)
Rua do Salitre, 66-68
1250 Lisbon
T 351-1-5327002
F 351-1-3527042

IICT,CEAA

Instituto de Investigaçao Cient'fica Tropical
(Research Institute for Tropical Sciences)
Centro de Estudos Africanos e Asiticos
(Centre for African and Asian Studies)
Rua de Junqueira, 30
1400 Lisbon
T 351-1-3645071
F 351-1-3631460

IICT,CEU

Instituto de Investigaçao Cient'fica Tropical
Centro de Etnologia Ultramarina Ilha da Madeira
Edif'cio Museu
1400 Lisbon
T 351-1-3645071
F 351-1-3631460

ISCTE,DH,AA

Instituto Superior de Ciências do Trabalho e da Empresa
Department of History
Afro-Asian Unit
Avenida das Forças Armadas
Campus da Cidade Universitária
1600 Lisbon
T 351-1-7903013
F 351-1-7903014

MCG

Museu Calouste Gulbenkian
Ave de Berne 45 A
1067 Lisbon
T 351-1-7935131
F 351-1-7955249

MCT,CCCM

Ministério da Ciência e da Tecnologia
(Ministry of Science and Technology)
Centro Cienfífico e Cultrual de Macau
(Macao Scientific and Cultural Centre)
Avenida Cinco de Outubro, 155-50
1050 Lisbon
T 351-1-797 93 34
F 351-1-797 93 28

UBI,DSCS

Universidade da Beira Interior
(University of Beira Interior)
Departamento de Sociologia e Comunicaçao Social
(Department of Sociology and Social Communication)
Rua Marquês d'Avila e Bolama
6200 Covilha
T 351-75-314207
F 351-75-26198

UE

Universidade de Évora
(University of Évora)
Palaceo do Vihioso
7000 Évora
T 351-66-26589
F 351-66-744677

UL,FF,DH

Universidade de Lisboa
Faculdade de Letras
Departemento de História
(History Department)
Alameda da Universidade
Cidade Universitária
1699 Lisbon
T 351-1-7965162
F 351-1-7960063

UL,FL,CEG

Universidade de Lisboa Faculdade de Letras
Centro Estudos Geograficos
(Department of Geography)
Alameda da Universidade
Cidade Universitária
1699 Lisbon
T 351-1-7965469
F 351-1-7938690

Portugal

UL,FL,TA

Universidade de Lisboa
(University of Lisbon)
Faculdade de Letras
(Faculty of Arts)
Department Timor A'sia
Alameda da Universidade
Cidade Universitária
1699 Lisbon
T 351-1-7965162
F 351-1-7960063

UL,ICS

Universidade de Lisboa
Instituto de Ciências Sociais
(Institute of Social Sciences)
Avenida das Forças Armadas
1600 Lisbon
T 351-1-7932272
F 351-1-7964953
instituto.siencias.sociais@ics.ul.pt

ULHT,CELA

Universidade Lusófona de
Humanidades e Tecnologias
(Lusófona University of Humanities
and Sciences)
Centro de Estudos Luso-Asiáticos
(Centre for Portuguese-Asian Studies)
Campo Grande, 376
1700 Lisbon
T 351-1-7510165
F 351-1-7577006
trdamasio@mail.telepac.pt

ULHT,PP

Universidade Lusófona de
Humanidades e Tecnologias
Faculdade P¢lo de Portimao
Avenida Miguel Bombaroa, 15
8500 Lisbon

ULU,DRI

Universidade Lusíada
(University of Lusíada)
Departemento Relaçoes Internacionais
(Institute of International Relations)
Rua da Jungueira, 188-198
1300 Lisbon
T 351-1-3639944
F 351-1-3638307

UNL,CHAM

Universidade Nova de Lisboa
(The New University of Lisbon)
Faculdade de Ciências Sociais e
Humanas
Centro de Historia de Além-Mar
Avenida de Berna, 26-C
1000 Lisbon
T 351-1-7933519
F 351-1-7977759

UNL,HA,ACP

Universidade Nova de Lisboa
Departamento de Historia de Arte
Arte Colonial Portuguesa
(Art of Colonial Portugal)
Avenida de Berna
1000 Lisbon
T 351-1-7933519
F 351-1-7977759

UNL,IO

Universidade Nova de Lisboa
Instituto Oriental
(Oriental Institute)
Avenida de Berna 24
1000 Lisbon

Republic of Cyprus

AA, FH, DH

American Academy Faculty of
Humanities Department of History
P.O.Box 112
Larnaca
T 357-4052046
F 357-4651046

Romania

MNAR

Muzeul National de Arta al Romaniei
(National Museum of Art of Romania)
Calea Victoriei 49-53
70101 Bucharest
T 40-1-6155193\ 6133030
F 40-1-3124327
brad@art.museum.ro

RA,IWE,EEA

Romanian Academy
Institute of World Economy
East European Affairs and Economics
in Transition
Bulevardul Republicii 12
Sector 3
70384 Bucharest
T 40-1-3125573
F 40-1-3110759

SAGIOS

Sergiu Al-George
Institute of Oriental Studies
P.O. Box 1-822
70700 Bucharest
Visiting Address:
Calea Victoriei 107
T 40-1-3111196
F 40-1-3111196

UB,FL,OL

Universitatea Bucuresti
(University of Bucharest)
Faculty of Foreign Languages
Oriental Languages Department
Strada Pitar Mos 7
Sector 1
Bucharest
T 40-1-2111820
F 40-1-3121313

Russia

BU, FH

Barnaul University
Faculty of History
Molodezhnaya Street 55
656031 Barnaul

IAS

Institute of Asia Studies
Dvortsovaya Nab. 18
199 182 St. Petersburg
T 7-812-3116283
F 7-812-1835381

IL,DEAL

Institute of Linguistics
Department of East Asian Languages
Bolshoi Kislovsky Pereulokeulok 1/12
103009 Moscow
T 7-95-2900528

ILR

Institute of Linguistic Researches
Tuchkov Pereulok. 9
199053 St. Petersburg
T 7-812-2184211
F 7-812-2184611

IMAE

Institute and Museum of Anthropology
and Ethnography
University Embankment 3
199 034 St. Petersburg
T 7-812-2184181
F 7-812-2180811

Russia

IMEMO

IMEMO
Profsoyuznaya 23
118859 Moscow
T 7-95-1208232
F 7-95-3107027

IMLI

IMLI
Ul. Vorovskogo 25A
121069 Moscow
T 7-95-2029433
F 7-95-2003216

IOS, FED

Institute of Oriental Studies
Far Eastern Department
Dvortsovaya nab. 18
199186 St. Petersburg

IOS,DCR

Russian Academy of Sciences
Institute of Oriental Studies
Department for Comparative Religion
Rozdestvenka 12
Moscow

IWEIR

Institute of World Economy and
International Relations
Profsoyuznaya Street 23
117859 Moscow
T 7-95-1205217
F 7-95-3107027

MSIIR

Moscow State Institute of International
Relations
Prospekt Kernadskogo 76
117454 Moscow
T 7-95-4349061/9066

MSIIR,DOS

Moscow State Institute of International
Relations
Department of Oriental Studies
Prospekt Vernadsky 76
117454 Moscow
T 7-95-4349061
F 7-95-4349066

MSU,IAAS,CIBS

Moscow State University
Institute of Asian and African Studies
Centre of Indological and
Buddhological Studies
Mokhovaya 11
103911 Moscow
T 7-95-2036647
F 7-95-4565297/2033647
bivanov@iaas.msu.su

MSU,IAAS,DIP

Moscow State University
Institute of Asian and African Studies
Department of Indian Philology
Mokhovaya 11
103009 Moscow

MSU,IAAS,DSEAP

Moscow State University
Institute of Asian and African Studies
Department of Southeast Asian
Philology
Mokhovaya 11
103 009 Moscow
T 7-95-2032741
F 7-95-2033647

MT,OA

Museum Tsaritsino Oriental Art
Prospekt Dolskaya
115569 Moscow
T 7-95-2454935
F 7-95-2454935

NLR,OD

Rossijskaya Natsionalnaya Biblioteka
Otdel Vostoka
(National Library of Russia Oriental
Department)
Litejnyj Pereulokeulok 49
191104 St. Petersburg
T 7-812-2725776
F 7-812- 3106148
rnb@glas.ape.org

NPH,VJ

Nauka Publication House
Vostok Journal
Spiridonovka 30/1
103001 Moscow
T 7-95-2026650

PGMAE,K

Peter the Great Museum of
Anthropology and Ethnography
Kunstkammer
Universitetskaya Nab. 3
199034 St. Petersburg
T 7-812-2184122
F 7-812-2180811
etn@pcstl/spb.su

PGMAE,OD

Peter-the-Great Museum of
Anthropology and Ethnography
Oriental Department
Universitetskaya Nab. 3
119034 St. Petersburg
T 7-812-2180812 \ 2184377
F 7-812-2180811
etn@pcstl/spb,su

RAS,ICPS

Russian Academy of Sciences
Institute of Comparative Political
Studies
Kolpachny Pereulok 9a
Moscow
T 7-95-2273703

RAS,IEA

Russian Academy of Sciences
Institute of Ethnography and
Anthropology
Dmitriya Ulyanov Street 19
117036 Moscow

RAS,IEA,SEAAO

Russian Academy of Sciences
Institute of Etnography and
Anthropology
Deptartment of South East Asia,
Australia and Oceania
Leninsky Prospekt 32-A
117334 Moscow
T 7-95-9335394
F 7-95-933 06 00
AnthPub@iea.msk.su

RAS,IFES,CRC

Russian Academy of Sciences
Institute of Far Eastern Studies
Centre Russia-China
Krasikova Street 27
117218 Moscow
T 7-95-1240722/0724
F 7-95-3107056

Russia

RAS,IFES,FEB

Russian Academy of Sciences
Institute of Far Eastern Studies
Far Eastern Branch
Krasykova Street 27
117218 Moscow
T 7-95-1290210
F 7-95-3107056

RAS,IFES,FEB,DH

Russian Academy of Sciences
Institute of Far Eastern Studies
Far Eastern Branch
Department of History
Krasikova Street 27
117218 Moscow

RAS,IL

Russian Academy of Sciences
Institute of Linguistics
Semachko Street 1/12
103009 Moscow
F 7-95-2900528

RAS,IOS,AL

Russian Academy of Sciences
Institute of Oriental Studies
Asian Languages
Rozhdestvenka 12
103031 Moscow
T 7-95-9211884
F 7-95-9752396

RAS,IOS,ALD

Russian Academy of Sciences
Institute of Oriental Studies
Asian Literatures Department
Rozhdestvenka 12
103031 Moscow
T 7-95-9236120

RAS,IOS,CIS

Russian Academy of Sciences
Institute of Oriental Studies
Centre for Indian Studies
Rozhdestvenka 12
103759 Moscow
T 7-95-9236282
F 7-95-9752396

RAS,IOS,CJS

Russian Academy of Sciences
Institute of Oriental Studies
Centre for Japanese Studies
Rozhdestvenka 12
103759 Moscow
T 7-95-9289780
F 7-95-9289780

RAS,IOS,DC

Russian Academy of Sciences
Institute of Oriental Studies
Department of China
Rozhdestvenka 12
103753 Moscow
T 7-95-9259568
F 7-95-9752396

RAS,IOS,DHO

Russian Academy of Sciences
Institute of Oriental Studies
Department of History of the Orient
Rozhdestvenka 12
103153 Moscow
T 7-95-9236282
F 7-95-9752396

RAS,IOS,DISA

Russian Academy of Sciences
Institute of Oriental Studies
Department of India and South Asia
Zhdanova Street 12
103031 Moscow

RAS,IOS,DNME

Russian Academy of Sciences
Institute of Oriental Studies
Department of Near and Middle East
Zhdanova Street 12
103031 Moscow

RAS,IOS,DSPS

Russian Academy of Sciences
Institute of Oriental Studies
Department of Social and Political Studies
Rozhdestvenka 12
103031 Moscow
T 7-95-9257384
F 7-95-9752396

RAS,IP,DOP

Russian Academy of Sciences
Institute of Philosophy
Department of Oriental Philosophy
Volkhonka 14
119842 Moscow

RAS,IWL

Russian Academy of Sciences
Institute of World Literature
Povarskaya Street 25A
121069 Moscow
T 7-95-2905030

RASP,IOS

Russian Academy of Sciences
Institute of Oriental Studies
Dvortsovaya Nab. 18
191011 St. Petersburg
T 7-812-3115274
F 7-812-3115101
orient@ieos.spb.su

RASP,IOS,DSSEAS

Russian Academy of Sciences Institute of Oriental Studies
Department of South and South-East Asian Studies
Dvortsovaya Nab. 18
191186 St. Petersburg
T 7-812-3115274

RASV,IHAEP

Russian Academy of Sciences
Institute of History, Archaeology and Ethnography of the People's of the Far East
Far Eastern Branch
Pushkinskaya Street 89
690600 Vladivostok
T 7-4232-220507
F 7-4232-268211
ihae@online.vladivostok.rv

RCSRIS

Russian Centre for Strategic Research and International Studies
Rozhdestvenka 12
103 753 Moscow
T 7-95-9245150
F 7-95-9752396

RME

Russian Museum of Ethnography
Ingenernaya 4/1
191011 St. Petersburg
T 7-812-2191152 / 3158502
7-812-3158502

RPFU,DP

Russian People's Friendship University
Department of Philosophy
Mikluho Maklay Street 6
117198 Moscow
T 7-95-4332000
F 7-95-4337385

Russia

RSUH,IASH

Russian State University for the
Humanities Institute for Advanched
Studies in the Humanities
Miusskaya Square 6
125267 Moscow
T 7-95-2506668
F 7-95-2505109
Sds@rsuh.ru.su

SD,SCIA

State Duma
Staff of the Comittee on International
Affairs
Oktotniyriad
103009 Moscow
T 7-95-2924371
F 7-95-2921081

SHM,OD

Hermitage Museum
Oriental Department
Dvortsovaja Nab. 34
191186 St. Petersburg
T 7-812-2198631

SMOA

State Museum of Oriental Art
Nikitsky Boulevard 12-A
121019 Moskow
T 7-95-2910341
F 7-95-2024846
mliempd@aha.ru

SPCF

St. Petersburg Cultural Foundation
Nevsky Pereulokeulok 31
191011 St. Petersburg

SPU, FOS

St. Petersburg University
Faculty of Oriental Studies
Universitetskaya Nab. 11
199034 St. Petersburg

SPU,FA,DGL

St. Petersburg University
Faculty of Arts
Department of General Linguistics
Universitetskaya Nab. 11
199036 St. Petersburg

SPU,FOS,DAS

St. Petersburg University
Faculty of Oriental Studies
Department of African Studies
Universitetskaya Nab. 11
199034 St. Petersburg

Slovak Republic

SAS,IOAS

Slovak Academy of Sciences
Institute of Oriental and African Studies
Klemensova 19
813 64 Bratislava
T 421-7-326326
F 421-7- 326326
kabinet@ko.savba.sk

Spain

AAC

Asociacion de Amigos de China
(Association of Friends of China)
C/. Francisco Zea, 2-Entreplanta
28028 Madrid
T 34-1-3614573
F 34-1-3615482

ACEF

Centro de Estudios Financieros
Ponzano 15
28010 Madrid

AEEP

Asociacion Espanola de Estudios del
Pacifico
(Spanish Association of Pacific Studies)
Ramiro de Maezto
28040 Madrid

CASESA

Centro ASESA
General Diaz Porlier 57-1§A
28006 Madrid

CEA

Centre d'Estudis Africans
(Centre of African Studies)
Travessera de Gracia 100 Pral. 1a
08012 Barcelona

CERI

Centro Espanol de Relaciones
Internacionales
(Spanish Centre of International
Relations)
C. Hortaleza 104
28004 Madrid
T 34-1-308 6882/2870
F 34-1-319 1584

CSCC,CEHC

Conseso Superior Camaras Comercio
(Chamber of Trade)
Comite Empresarial Hispano-Chino
(Spanish-Sino Business Committee)
Claudio Coello, 19
28001 Madrid

EOI

Escuela Official de Idiomas
(Madrid Offical School of Languages)
Taiwan
Jesus Maestro
Madrid
T 34-1-3781449
F 34-1-7387704

EOIM,DJ

Escuela Oficial de Idiomas de Madrid
(Madrid Offical School of Languages)
Departamento de Japonés
Jesús Maestro
28003 Madrid
T 34-1-5335804/5
F 34-1-5335331

IECE

Instituto de Estudios Coreanos en
Espana
(Institute for Korean Studies in Spain)
Ma Auxiliadora 1, 20B
28040 Madrid
T 34-1-459 43 55
F 34-1-459 43 55

IEdCE

Instituto Espanol de Comercio Exterior
Velázquez, 157
28002 Madrid
T 34-1-5906943/00
F 34-1-5906920/08

IJ

Instituto de Japanologia
Boix y Morer 3,1C
28003 Madrid
T 34-1-5345322
F 34-1-5350197
alisijp@ibm.net

ISJT

Instituto de Secundaria " Joafuin
Turisa"
Guzman el Bueno 92
28003 Madrid

ITR

Instituto Tecnicas Reunidas
Arapiles 13
28016 Madrid
T 34-1-5920319
F 34-1-5920321

MAE

Ministerio de Asuntos Exteriores
(Ministry of Foreign Affairs)
Plaza de la Provincia, 1
28071 Madrid

Spain

MEB

Museu Etnologie de Barcelona
(Museum of Ethnology)
Passeig Santa Madrona Sin
08038 Barcelona

OJM

Organizacion Jetro Madrid
Plaza de Colón, 2
Torres de Colon, I,
28046 Madrid

REMF

Revista "El Mundo Financiero"
Hermosilla, 93
28001 Madrid

UAB,DTI

Universitat Autonoma de Barcelona
(Autonomous University of Barcelona)
Department de Traducci i Interpretaci
(Department of Translation and Interpretation)
Bellatera
08193 Barcelona
T 34-3-5813124
F 34-3-5812762
sgolden@cc.uab.es

UAB,JSC

Universitat Autonoma de Barcelona
Japanese Studies Centre
Campus Universitari Bellaterra
08193 Barcelona

UAM, FFL, DL

Universidad Autonoma de Madrid
Facultad Filosofia y Letras
Departamento Linguistica
(Department of Linguistics)
Canto Blanco
28049 Madrid

UAM,CEAO

Universidad Autonoma de Madrid
Centro de Estudios de Asia Oriental
(Centre for Asian Studies)
Ciudad Universitaria de Cantoblanco
Edificio Rectorado
28049 Madrid
T 34-1-3974695
F 34-1-3974123
tfisac@bosque.sdi.vam.es

UB,DFTP

Universitat de Barcelona
Department de Filosofia Teorética i Practica
(Department of Pure and Practical Philosophy)
Baldini i Reixach
08028 Barcelona
T 34-3-4409200
F 34-3-4498510

UB,FB,DE

Universidad de Barcelona Facultat Biologia
Departamento Ecologia
Av. Diagonal 645
08028 Barcelona
T 34-3-4021086
F 34-3-3307157

UB,FBA,DE

Universidad de Barcelona
Facultad de Bellas Artes
Departamento de Escultura
(Department of Sculpture)
Pau Gargallo 4
08028 Barcelona
T 34-3-333466

UB,FEE, DPEEEM

Universidad de Barcelona
Facultat de Ciènces Economiques i Empresarials
Departamento Politica Economica y Estructura Economia Mundial
(Department of Political Economy)
Av. Diagonal 690
08034 Barcelona
T 34-3-4024575
F 34-3- 4024573
gordillo@riscd2.eco.ub.es

UB,FEE,DEPHP

Universidad de Barcelona
Facultat de Ciènces Economiques i Empresarials
Departamento Economia-Politica y Hacienda Publica
(Department of Economic Politics and Public Housing)
Av. Diagonal 690
08034 Barcelona
Visiting Address:
Torre 4
2a Planta
T 34-3-4021812
F 34-3-4021813

UB,FGH,CEHI

Universidad de Barcelona
Facultad Geografia i Historia
Centro de Estudios Historicos Internationales
(Centre for International History)
Brusi 61
08006 Barcelona
T 34-3-3333466

UC,FEI,DB

Universidad de Cantabria
(University of Cantabria)
Facultad Edificio Interfacultativo
Departamento Biblioteca
(Library)
Avenida de los Castros
39005 Santander
T 34--42-201017

UC,FL,CHA

Universidad de Cordoba
Facultad de Filosofia y Letras
Catedra de Historia de America
(Department of American History)
Plaza del Cardenal Salazar 3
14071 Cordoba
T 957-218762
F 957-218788/8789
hi1gaaba@lucano.uco.es

UCES,DGE

Universidad Consejo Economico y Social
Departamento Gabiete de Estudios
c/ Huertas, 73
28014 Madrid

UCLA,CSH,DF

Universidad de Castilla - La Mancha
(University of Castilla-La Mancha)
Centro Superior de Humanidades
Departamento Filosofia
(Department of Philosophy)
Coberitzo de San Pedro Matir
45071 Toledo

UCM, BA, DD

Universidad Complutense de Madrid
Facultad Bellas Artes
(Faculty of Fine Arts)
Depertamento Dibujo
(Department of Drawing)
Ciudad Universitaria
28040 Madrid
T 34-1-3943656

Spain

UCM, BA, DE

Universidad Complutense de Madrid
Facultad Bellas Artes
Departamento Escultura
(Department of Sculpture)
Ciudad Universitaria
28040 Madrid
T 34-1-3943650

UCM, EEE,DEI

Universidad Complutense de Madrid
Escuela Estudios Empresaliares
(School of Business Administration)
Departamento Estructura e Institucione
Plaza de Espana, 16
28008 Madrid
T 34-1-3946794

UCM, FE, DM

Universidad Complutense de Madrid
Facultad Educacion
Departamento Mide
P° de las Moreras
28015 Madrid

UCM, GH,HAC

Universidad Complutense de Madrid
Facultad de Geografia e Historia
Departemento de Historia del Arte
Contemporaneo
(Department of Contemporary Art
History)
Grupo de Investigacion Asia
(Research Group Asia)
Ciudad Universitaria
28040 Madrid
T 34-1-3945773/3945754/3571862
F 34-1-3945775/3078582

UCM, INE

Universidad Complutense
Instituto Nacional de Empleo
CNFO. INEM
Kmt 64 Conmtr. la Curuna
40400 El Espinar (Segovia)

UCM,FE,DD

Universidad Complutense de Madrid
Facultad de Educación
(Faculty of Education)
Departemento Didactica
(Department of Didactics)
Ciudad Universitaria
28040 Madrid
T 34-1-3946175
F 34-1-3946263

UCM,FEE

Universidad Complutense de Madrid
Facultad de Ciences Economicas y
Empresalriales
(Faculty of Economics and Business
Administration)
Campus de Somosaguas
28223 Madrid
T 34-1-3942546
F 34-1-3942546

UCM,FEE,DDA

Universidad Complutense de Madrid
Facultad Economicas y Empresariales
Departamento Derecho Administrativo
Campus de Somosaguas
28223 Madrid

UCM,FEE,HIE

Universidad Complutense de Madrid
Facultad de Ciences Ecomomicas y
Empresariales
Departamento Historia Instituciones
Economicas
(Department of History and Institutions
of Economy)
Plaza de Espana 16
28008 Madrid
T 34-1-3942446

UCM,FF

Universidad Complutense de Madrid
Facultad de Filiologia
(Faculty of Philology)
Ciudad Universitaria
28040 Madrid
T 34-1-3945831
F 34-1-3945829

UCM,FF,FEI

Universidad Complutense de Madrid
Facultad de Filologia
Departamento de Filologia Espanol I
(Department of Spanish Philology)
Ciudad Universitaria
28040 Madrid
T 34-1-3945831

UCM,GH,DHC

Universidad Complutense de Madrid
Faculdad de Geografia e Historia
Departamento Historia Comtemporanea
(Department of Contemporary History)
Ciudad Universitaria
28040 Madrid
T 34-1-3945905

UCM,GH,DPE

Universidad Complutense de Madrid
Facultad Geografia y Historia
Departamento Prehistoria y Etnologia
(Department of Prehistory and
Ethnology)
Ciudad Universitaria
28040 Madrid
T 34-1-3946010

UCM,GH,GF

Universidad Complutense de Madrid
Facultad Geografia e Historia
Departemento Analisis Geografico
Regional e Geografia Fisica
(Department of Regional and Physical
Geography)
Ciudad Universitaria
28040 Madrid
T 34-1-3945962
F 34-1-3945963

UCM,ICA

Universidad Complutense de Madrid
Instituto Complutense de Asia
(Complutense Institute of Asian Studies
Campus de Somosaguas
28223 Madrid
T 34-1-394 2485/91
F 34-1-394 2488
Iasia02@sis.ucm.es

UCM,PS

Universidad Complutense de Madrid
Facultad de Ciencias Politicas y
Sociologia
(Faculty of Politcal and Social Sciences
Campus de Somosaguas
28223 Madrid
T 34-1-3942754
F 34-1-3942752

UCM,PS,DCPA

Universidad Complutense de Madrid
Facultad de Ciencias Politicas y
Sociologia
Departemento de Ciencia Politica y de
la Administration II
(Department of Political and
Administrative Sciences)
Campus de Somosaguas
28223 Madrid
T 34-1-3942712/2618
F 34-1-3942620

Spain

UCSIC, CEH, DHMC

Universidad Conseso Superior
Investigaciones Cientificas
Centro Estudios Historicos
Departamento Historia Moderna y Contemporanea
Duque de Medinaceli 6
28014 Madrid

UD,SE

University Deusto
School of Economics
Camino de Mundaiz 50
8000 San Sebastian

UE,FL,DH

Universidad Extremaudra
(University of Extremadura)
Facultad de Letras
Departamento de Historia
(Department of History)
Avda de la Universitaria
10071 Caceres
T 34-927-249600

UG,FFL, DLGTL

Universidad Granada
(University of Granada)
Facultad Filosofia y Letras
Departamento Luinguïstico General y Teoria de la Literatura
(Department of General Linguistics and Theory of Literature)
Campus universitario de Cartuja
18071 Granada
T 34-58-243591
F 34-58-243591

UNED,FF,DLE

Universidad National de Educacion a Distancia
Facultad Filologia
(Department of Philology)
Departamento Lengua Espanola
(Spanish Languages Department)
Senda del Rey
Ciudad Universitaria
28040 Madrid
T 34-1-3986810

UNED,FPS,DS

Universidad National de Educacion a Distancia
Facultad Politicas y Sociologia
(Faculty of Political and Social Sciences)
Departamento Sociologica
Senda del Rey
Ciudad Universitaria
28040 Madrid
T 34-1-3987010

UNEDC,FP

Universidad National de Educacion a Distancia
(National Distance Education University)
Centro Asociado di Cordoba
(Study Centre at Cordoba)
Facultad Psycologia
(Faculty of Psychology)
Canto 2
14003 Cordoba
T 34-57-481069
F 34-57-491834

UO,FEII

Universidad de Oviedo
(University of Oviedo)
Facultad Tecnica Superior de Ingenieros Industriales
(Higher Technical School of Industrial Engineering)
Campus de Viesques
33204 Gijon
T 34-8-5182003
F 34-8-5338538

UPF, FEE,DE

Universidad Pompeu Fabra
(Pompeu Fabra University)
Facultad Ciencies Economiques i Empresariales
(Faculty of Economics and Business Administration)
Departamento Economia
(Department of Economics)
Balmes 132
08008 Barcelona

UPF, FH

Universidad Pompeu Fabre
Facultad Humanitas
(Faculty of Humanities)
Balmes 132
08008 Barcelona
T 34-3-5421629
F 34-3-5421620

UPF,FH,EEAO

Universitat Pompeu Fabra
Facultat d'Humanitats
Escola d'Estudis d'Asia Oriental
(School of Oriental Studies)
Ramon Trias Fargas, 25-27
08005 Barcelona

UPF,FPCA,DPE

Universidad Pompeu Fabra
Facultad Periodismo y Comunicacion Audioviual
(Faculty of Journalism and Audiovisual Communication)
Departamento Periodismo Especializad
(Department of Specialised Journalism)
Rbca sta Monica
08002 Barcelona
T 34-3-5422400

URL

Universidad Ramon Llull
Calle Cister
08022 Barcelona

US, II, DJ

Universidad de Sevilla
(University of Sevilla)
Instituto de Idiomas
(Institute for Languages)
Departamento Japones
(Japanese Department)
Palos de la Frontera
21071 Huelva
T 34-955-4218577

US,FF

Universidad de Sevilla
Facultad de Filologia
(Faculty of Philology)
Palos de la Frontera
41004 Sevilla
T 34-955-4551520
F 34-955-4551515

USPC, FCHDC,DH

Universidad San Pablo-Cen
Facultad Ciencias Homands y Dela Comunicacion
Departamento Historia
(Department of History)
Julian Romea 23
Madrid

USTM, IT

Universidad Santo Tomas de Manila
Instituto de Teologia
(Institute of Religious Studies))
Auda de Burgos, 204
28050 Madrid

UV,FGH,DHM

Universidad de Valencia
(University of Valencia)
Facultad de Geografia y Historia
Departamento de Historia Moderna
(Department of Modern History)
AV, de Blasco Ibanez 28
46010 Valencia
T 34-6-3864243

Spain

UVD,JAP

Universidad de Valladolid
(University of Valladolid)
Instituto de Estudios Japoneses
(Institute of Japanese Studies)
Plaza de la Universidad, 1
47002 Valladolid
T 34-83-424268

Sweden

DEPR,SE

Department of Educational &
Psychological
Research School of Education
P.O. Box 23501
200 45 Malmö
T 46-40-325245
F 46-40-325210

GU,ARK

Göteborgs Universitet
Avd. Religionskunskap
Mlndalsvagen 85
412 85 Göteborg

GU,DEH

Göteborgs Universitet
Department of Economic History
Skanstorget 18
41122 Göteborg

GU,DL,C

Göteborgs Universitet
Department of Linguistics
(China)
Renströmsgatan 6
41298 Göteborg
T 46-31-7734186
F 46-31-7734853

GU,DOS

Göteborg University
Department of Oriental Studies
S-41298 Göteborg
T 46-31 7734618
F 46-31-7735270
Noriko.thuman@japan.gu.se

GU,DPDR

Götegorg University
Department of Peace and Development
Research
Brogatan 4
S-41301 Göteborg
T 46-31-7731000
F 46-31-7734910
B.Jorgesnsen@padrigu.gu.se

GU,DSA

Göteborgs Universitet
Department of Social Anthropology
Brogatan 4
41 301 Göteborg
T 46-31-7734303
F 46-31-7734607

GU,GESEAS

Göteborg University
Centre for the East and Southeast
Studies
(GESEAS)
Brogatan 4
41301 Göteborg
T 46-31-7734323
F 46-31-77342505
geseas@gu.se

GU,IASSA

Göteborgs Universitet
IASSA
Pilgatan 19
41122 Göteborg
T 46-31-7734578
F 46-31-7734461

GU,IOL,JS

Göteborg Universitet
Institute of Oriental Languages
Japanese Section
Vstra Hamngatan 3
41298 Göteborg
T 46-31-773 46 18
F 46-31-773 52 70
infor@japco.se

HKR,FH,IH

H"gskolan Karlskrona
Ronneby Faculty Humaniora
Institutionen f'r Humaniora
Karlskrona

JPCAB

Jaakko P"yry Consulting AB
P.O.Box 1130
18122 Liding"
T 46-8-7314500
F 46-8-7676315

KTH,CEE

Kungliga Tekniska Högskolan
(Royal Institute of Technology)
Civil and Environmental Engineering
Dr. Kristanasvag 30
10044 Stockholm

LU,CESEAS

Lunds Universitet
Centre for East and Southeast Asian
Studies
P.O. Box 7083
220 07 Lund
T 46-462223040
F 46-462223041
lu.asiacentre@ekh.lu.se

LU,COHS

Lunds Universitet
Centre for Oral Health Sciences
Carlgustafsväg 34
21421 Malmö

LU,DH

Lunds Universitet
Department of History
P.O. Box 2074
22002 Lund
Visiting Address:
Magle Stora Kyrkogata 12 Lund
T 46-46-2227960
F 46-46-2224207
weng@gemini.ldc.lu.se

LU,DL

Lunds Universitet
Department of Limnology
Ecology Building
223 62 Lund
T 46-46-104453
F 46-46-104536

LU,DLP

Lunds Universitet
Department of Linguistics and Phonetic
Helgonabacken 12
223 62 Lund
T 46-46-2228455
F 46-46-2224210
ling@ling.lu.se

LU,DPS

Lunds Universitet
Department of Political Science
P.O. Box 52
221 00 Lund
T 46-46-2224553
F 46-46-2224006

LU,DS

Lunds Universitet
Department of Sociology
Box 114
221 00 Lund

Sweden

LU,DSEG

Lunds Universitet
Department of Social and Economic Geography
S"lvegatan 13
22362 Lund
T 46-46-2229797
F 46-46-2224913

LU,FA,DEAL

Lunds Universitet
Faculty of Arts
Department of East Asian Languages
P.O. Box 7033
22007 Lund
Visiting Address:
Tunavägen 39-E
T 46-46-222359
F 46-46-222432

LU,ICR,FRS,DI

Lunds Universitet
Institute of Comparative Religion
Faculty of Religious Studies
Deptartment for Islamology
Allhelgona Kyrkogata 8
22221 Lund

LU,IRP

Lunds Universitet
Institute for Research Politics
P.O. Box 2017
S22001 Lund
T 46-46-22276/16
F 46-46-146986
tpi@tpi.lu.se

LU,NCI

Lunds Universitet
Nordic Centre for Innovation
P.O. Box 11004
220 11 Lund
T 46-46-152800
F 46-46-152800
nordiccenter@gemini.ldc.lu.se

LU,PESEAS,IO

Lunds Universitet
Programme for East- and Southeast Asian Studies
International Office
P.O. Box 117
22100 Lund
Visiting Address:
Sandgatan 3
T 46-46-2220000
F 46-46-2224720

LU,PI

Lunds Universitet
Pedagogiska Institutionen
P.O. Box 199
221 00 Lund
T 46-46-108726
F 46-46-104538

LU,RDSSW

Lunds Universitet
Research Department
School of Social Work
Box 23
221 000 Lund
T 46-46-2223161
F 46-46-2229412

MCM

Malmö College of Music
P.O.Box 8203
20041 Malmö
T 46-40-325451
F 46-40-325460

NME

National Museum of Etnography
P.O. Box 27140
10252 Stockholm
Visiting Address:
Djurgardsbrunnsvägen 34
T 46-8-6665000
F 46-8-6665070

NME

The National Museum of Ethnography
P.O. Box 2714
S-102-52 Stockholm
T 46-8-6665000
F 46-8-6665070

NME,BIB

National Museum of Etnography
Library
Skeppsholmen, Box 16176
10324 Stockholm
Visiting Address:
Djurgardsbrunnsvägen 34
T 46-8-6664446
F 46-8-6112845

OCS

Oriental Ceramic Society
Box 19087
40012 Göteborg
T 46-31-167175
F 46-31-167323

OM

Ostasiatiska Museet
(The Museum of Far Eastern Antiquities)
Skeppsholmen
Box 16176
S-10324 Stockholm
T 46-8-6664250
F 46-8-6112845

PG

Padrigu
Brogatan 4
41 301 Göteborg
T 46-31-7731380
F 46-31-7734910

SIDA

Swedish International Development Authority
Birger Jarlsgatan 61
105 25 Stockholm
T 46-8-7285100
F 46-8-6124508

SIDA,AS

Swedish International Development Authority
Asia Secretariat
Birger Jarlsgatan 61
105 25 Stockholm

SIIA

Swedish Institute of International Affair
P.O. Box 1253
11182 Stockholm
Visiting Address:
Lilla Nygatab 23
T 46-8-234060
F 46-8-201049

SJFRD

Sweden-Japan Foundation for Research and Development
P.O. Box 5073
102 42 Stockholm

SSE,ASTRA,EAST

Stockholm School of Economics
ASTRA
East Asia Science & Technology
P.O. Box 6501
113 83 Stockholm
T 46-8-7369360
F 46-8-313017

Sweden

SSE,DE

Stockholm School of Economics
Department of Economics
P.O. Box 6501
113 85 Stockholm

SSE,EIJS

Stockholm School of Economics
The European Institute for Japanese Studies
P.O. BOX 6501
S-11383 Stockholm
Visiting Address:
Sveavägen 65
T 46-8-7369364
F 46-8-313017
ASIA@HHS.SE

SU,CPAS

Stockholm Universitet
Centre for Pacific Asia Studies
S-10691 Stockholm
T 46-8-162897
F 46-8-168810
cpas@orient.su.se

SU,DPS

Stockholms Universitet
Department of Political Science
106 91 Stockholm
T 46-8-163086
F 46-8-152529

SU,DSA

Stockholm University
Department of Social Anthropology
S-10691 Stockholm
T 46-8-162240
F 46-8-158894
ann-charlotte.krus@socant.su.se

SU,IOL

Stockholm Universitet
Institute of Oriental Languages
S-10691 Stockholm
T 46-8-161412
F 46-8-161412
marja.kaikkonen@orient.su.se

SU,IOL,CD

Stockholms Universitet
Institute of Oriental Languages
Chinese Department
Kräftriket
104 05 Stockholm
T 46-8-161412
F 46-8-155464

SU,IOL,DKS

Stockholm Universitet
Institute of Oriental Languages
Department of Korean Studies
Kraftriket 4
10691 Stockholm

SU,IOS,DI

Stockholms Universitet
Institute of Oriental Studies
Department of Indology
Ruslagsvagen 101
106 91 Stockholm
T 46-8-163619
F 46-8-155464

UL,MDAS

Lunds Universitet
Department of Economic History
Master's Degree in East and Southeast Asian Studies
Box 7083
S-22007 Lund
T 46-46-2227485
F 46-46-131585
Ingela.Palmgren@ekh.lu.se

UL,NASEAS

Lunds Universitet
Department of Economic History
Nordic Association for Southeast Asian Studies
P.O. Box 7083
S-22007 Lund
T 46-46-2227485
F 46-46-131585
ingela.palmgren@ehk.lu.se

ULP,DSS

University of Linköping
Department of Social Sciences
58 183 Linkoping

UU,AD

Uppsala Universitet
Aesthetic Department
Slottet S"dra Tornet HO
75237 Uppsala
T 46-18-181583
F 46-18-181589

UU,DA

Uppsala University
Department of Anthropology
Trädgårdsgatan 18
75309 Uppsala
T 46-18-182597
F 46-18-151160

UU,DAAS

Uppsala Universitet
Department of Asian and African Studies
Box 513
751 20 Uppsala

UU,DH

Uppsala Universitet
Department of History
St. Larsgatan 2
75220 Uppsala
T 46-18181528
46-18151536

UU,DI

Uppsala Universitet
Department of Indology
P.O. Box 513
751 20 Uppsala
F 46-18-181094

UU,DPCR

Uppsala Universitet
Department of Peace and Conflict Research
P.O.Box 514
75120 Uppsala
Visiting Address:
Gamla Torget 3 75120 Uppsala Swede
T 46-18-182500
F 46-18-695102

UU,DS,DG

Uppsala Universitet
Development Studies
Department of Government
Box 514
75120 Uppsala
Visiting Address:
Samla Torget 4 Uppsala
F 46-18-181993

UU,TI

Uppsala Universitet
Teologiske Institutionen
P.O.Box 1604
75146 Uppsala
T 46-18-182500
F 46-18-126875

Switzerland

ABD

Asiatica Bücherdienst
Postfach 123
8033 Zürich

Switzerland

BC

Baur Collections
8, Rue Munier-Romilly
1206 Geneve
T 41-22-3461729
F 41-22-7891845

BHM,DV

Bernisches Historisches Museum Abt. Völkerkunde
(Bern Museum of History Dept. of Ethnography)
Helvetiaplatz 5
3000 Bern 6
T 41-31-3507711
F 41-31-3507799

CEDK

Centre d'Etudes et de Documentation sur le Karenni
Case 54 Bergières
1000 Lausanne 22

CS

Caritas-Schweiz
Löwenstrasse 3
6002 Lüzern
T 41-41-4192367
F 41-41-4108258

DOFSBT

Documentation Office for Fundamental Studies in Building Theory (DOFSBT)
Chorgasse 19
8001 Zürich
T 41-1-2516075
F 41-21-3231707

EHT

Eidgenössische Technische Hochschule Zürich
(Swiss Federal Institute of Technology Zürich)
Rämi Str. 101
8092 Zürich
T 41-1-6323219
F 41-1-6321110

EM,A

Ethnography Museum Asia
Carl-Vogt, 65-67
1205 Geneve
T 41-22-4184550
F 41-22-4184551

EPFL,IMT

Ecole Polytechnique Fédérale de Lausanne
Institut de Microtechnique
1015 Lausanne

EPZ,GBI

Ecole Polytechnique de Zürich
Geobotanical Institute
Zürichbergstrasse 38
8044 Zürich
T 49-1-6323877
F 49-1-6321215

EPZ,IAE

Ecole Polytechnique de Zürich Institute for Agricultural Engineering
ETH-Hängerberg
8093 Zürich

EPZ,IPS

Ecole Polytechnique de Zürich
Institute for Plant Sciences
ETH - Zentrum Universitätstrasse 2
8092 Zürich

EPZ,VWHG

Ecole Polytechnique de Zürich
Versuchsanstalt für Wasserbau, Hydrologie und Galziologie
ETH-Zentrum
8092 Zürich

GIIS,IHP

Graduate Institute of International Studies
International History and Politics
132, Rue de Lausanne
1202 Geneve

II

Institut für Indologie
3114 Wichtrach

ILO

International Labour Organisation
P.O. Box 500
1211 Geneve 22
Visiting Address:
4, Route des Morillons
T 41-22-7996418
F 41-22-7997657

IUED

Institut Universitaire d'Etudes du Développement Geève
(Graduate Institute of Development Studies)
P.O. Box 136
1211 Geneve 21
Visiting Address:
24, rue Rothschild
T 41-22-7515940
F 41-22-7384416

ME

Musée d'Ethnographie
4, rue Saint-Nicolas
2006 Neuch/tel
T 038-244120
F 038-213095

MRZ

Museum Rietberg Zürich
Villa Wesendonck Park
Villa Rieter
Gablerstraße 15
8002 Zürich
T 41-1-2024528
F 41-1-2025201

RIIM,USG

Research Institute for International Management
University of St. Gallen
Bodan Str. 6
9000 St. Gallan
T 41-71-224 2448
F 41-71-224 2447

SAS

Swiss Asia Society
Zürichbergstr.4
CH-8032 Zurich
T 41-1-2573181
F 41-1-2615687
oas@unizh.ch

SBA

Stiftung Bibliotheca Afghanica
Benzburweg 5
4410 Liestal
T 41-61-9219838
F 41-61-9219838

SC

Swisscontact
Döltschiweg 39
8055 Zürich

Switzerland

SFITZETH,EAP

Swiss Federal Institute of Technology Zürich
East Asia Programme
Zürichberg Str. 18, BW1 E4
8028 Zürich
T 41-1-6320583
F 41-1-6321048
poa@bwi.bepr.ethz.ch

ST

Schweizerisches Tropeninstitut
(The Swiss Tropical Institute)
Socinstrasse 57
CH-4002 Basel
T 41-61-2848111
F 41-61-2848111/284106
sticourses@ubaclu.unibas.ch

UB,ES

Universität Basel
Ethnologisches Seminar
Münsterplatz 19
4051 Basel
T 41-61-2672745
F 41-61-2672747

UB,GI

Universität Basel
Geopgraphical Institute
Klingelstrasse 16
4056 Basel

UB,GPI

Universität Basel
Geological-Palaeontological Institute
Bernoulli Str. 30-32
4056 Basel

UB,OS

Universität Basel
Orientalisches Seminar
Hirsgässlein 21
4051 Basel

UBE,DLHC

Universität Bern
Department of Linguistics, History and Comparative
Laengass Str. 49
3000 Bern
T 41-31-631 38 98
F 41-31-631 80 05

UBE,IE

Universität Bern
Institut für Ethnologie
Länggasse 49-A
3000 Bern 9
T 41-31-6318995
F 41-31-6314212

UBE,IE

Universität Bern
Interdisziplinäre Einrichtungen
Schlösslistrasse 5
3008 Bern
T 41-31-6318635
F 41-31-6314562

UF,FT,IMSR

Universität Freiburg
Faculty of Theology
Institute for Missiology and Science of Religions
Route du Jura 1
1700 Freiburg

UG,FAH,DOLL

Universite de Genève
Faculty of Arts and Humanities
Department of Oriental Languages and Literature
2, Rue de Candolle
1211 Geneva 4
T 41-22-7057236

UG,FL,DSA

Université de Genève
Faculté des Lettres
Département des Sciences de L'Antiquit
1211 Geneva
T 41-22-7057119

UG,MARC

Université de Genève
The Graduate Institute of Development Studies
Modern Asia Research Centre
P.O. Box 36
CH-1211 Geneva
Visiting Address:
Rue de Lausanne 132
T 41-22-7328310/19
F 41-22-7383996
regnier@uni2a.unige.ch

UL,CDCE

Université de Lausanne
Centre de Droit Comparé et Européen
BFSH 2, Dorigny
1015 Lausanne

UL,DOLC

Université de Lausanne
Faculty of Letters
Department of Oriental Languages and Cultures
B.F.S.H. 2
1015 Lausanne
T 41-21-6922911
F 41-21-6923045
johannes.bronkhorst@orient.unil.ch

UN,IE

Université de Neuchâtel
Institut d'Ethnologie
4, rue St-Nicolas
2006 Neuchâtel
T 41-32-7244122
F 41-32-7241447
raymonde.wicky@lettres.unine.ch

USG,MITM

University of St. Gallen
Management Institute for Technology Management
Unterstrasse 22
9000 St. Gallen
T 41-71-2282492
F 41-71-2282455

UZ,EAI,SINOBIB

Universität Zurich
East Asian Institute
Chinese Library
Zürichbergstrasse 4
8032 Zürich

UZ,ES

Universität Zürich
Ethnologisches Seminar
Freiensteinstrasse 5
8032 Zürich

UZ,IEAS,DJ

Universität Zürich
Institute of East Asian Studies
Deptartment of Japanology
Zürichbergstrasse 4
8032 Zürich
T 41-1-2573181
F 41-1-2615687

UZ,IGS

Universität Zürich Indogermanisches Seminar
Florhofgasse 11
8001 Zürich
T 41-1-2572039

Switzerland

UZ,MCA

Universität Zürich
Museum for Cultural Anthropology
Pelikanstrasse 40
8001 Zürich

UZ,OS

Universität Zürich
Orientalisches Seminar
Beckenhofstrasse 26
8006 Zürich

UZ,SI

University of Zurich
Seminar of Indology
Rämistrasse 68
CH-8001 Zurich
T 41-1-2572057
F 41-1-2576958
indobib@indoger.unizh.ch

UZI,DG

Universität Zürich
Department of Geography
Winterthurerstrasse 190
8057 Zürich
T 41-1-2575111
F 41-1-3625227

VMUZ

Völkerkundemuseum der Universität Zürich
Pelikanstrasse 40
8001 Zürich
T 41-1-6349011
F 41-0-6349050

YB

Yamaichi Bank
Bahnhofstr. 92
8023 Zürich
T 41-1-2286526
F 41-1-2121904

Ukraine

UKMA,DPRS

University of "Kiev-Mohyla Academy"
Department of Philosophy and Religion Studies
2 Skovoroda St.
254070 Kyiv

United Kingdom

ADO

Asia Desk Oxfam
274 Banbury Road
OX2 7D2 Oxford
T 44-1865-313635
F 44-1865-313780
pvalentin@oxfam.org.uk

AHL

Asia House London
39-40 St James's Place
SW1A 1NS London
T 44-1171-4491287
F 44-1171-499 8618

AM,DEA

Ashmolean Museum
Dept. of Eastern Art
The University of Oxford
OX1 2PH Oxford
T 44-1865--278067
F 44-1865-278078
partridge@ashmus.ox.ac.uk

AS

Asia House
105 Picadilly
W1V 9FN London
T 44-1171-4991287
F 44-1171-499-8618
asiahouse@compuserve.com

AU,ABS

Aston University
Aston Business School
Aston Triangle
B4 7ET Birmingham
T 44-1121-3593611
F 44-1121-333 6350
www.aston.ac.uk

AU,DML,JS

Aston University
Department of Modern Languages
Japanese Studies
Aston Triangle
B4 7ET Birmingham

BC,TUEU

Bolton College
Trade Union Education Unit
Rydley Street Centre
BL2 1LD Bolton
T 44-1204-531411
F 44-1204-380004
tued.bolton@mcri.poptel.org.uk

BCHE,SH

Bath College of Higher Education
School of History
Newton Park
BA2 9BN Bath

BCHE,SRD

Bath College of Higher Education
Study of Religions Department
Newton Park
BA2 9BN Bath
T 44-1225-875875/426
F 44-1225-875499
bbocking@bathhe.ac.uk

BGCC

Great Britain-China Centre
15 Belgrave Square
SW1X 8PS London
T 44-1171-2356696
F 44-1171-2456885
gbcc@gn.apc.org

BL,OIOC

British Library
Oriental and India Office Collections
197 Blackfriars Road
SE1 8NG London
T 44-171-4127652/62
F 44-171-4127641
oioc-enquiries@bl.uk

BL,OS,DS

British Library
Oriental Section
Document Supply
Boston Spa Wetherby
LS23 7BQ West Yorkshire

BM

The British Museum
Great Russell Street
WC1B 3DG London
T 44-1171-6361555
F 44-1171-3238561

BM,DCM

British Museum
Department of Coins and Medals
Great Russell street
WC1B 3DG London
T 44-1171-3238172
F 44-1171-3238171

United Kingdom

BM,MM

British Museum
Museum of Mankind
6 Burlington Gardens
W1X 2EX London
T 44-1171-6361555
F 44-1171-232 80 13

BMAG

City of Bristol Museum and Art Gallery
Queen's Road
BS8 1RL Bristol
T 44-1117-9223571
F 44-1117-9222047

BMOA

British Museum
Dept. of Oriental Antiquities
Great Russel Street
WC1B 3DG London
T 44-1171-3238250

BRC,RC

British Refugee Council Resource Centre
3-9 Bondway
SW8 1SJ London
T 44-1171-5826922
F 44-1171-5829929
refcounciluk@gn.apc.org

BVB

Bharatiya Vidya Bhavan
UK Centre
W14 9HQ London
T 44-1171-3813086
F 44-1171-3818758

BVFS

Britain Vietnam Friendship Society
26 Tomlins Grove Flat 2
E3 4NX London
T 44-1181-9807146
F 44-1181-9807146

CAFOD,PDA

Catholic Fund for Overseas Development (CAFOD)
Project Department Asia
2 Romero Close Stockwell Road
SW9 9TY London
T 44-1171-7337900
F 44-1171-2749630
hqcafod@cafod.or.uk

CBTG

China Britain Trade Group
5th F. Abford House 15 Wilton Road
SW1V 1LT London

CCA,KIAD

Canterbury College of Art
Kent Institute of Art and Design
CT1 3AW Canterbury (Kent)

CCAD

Chelsea College of Art and Design
Manresa Road
SW3 6LS London
T 44-1171-5147750
F 44-1171-5147777

CCBI,DCR

Council of Churches for Britain and Ireland
Department of China Relations
Inter-Church House
35-41 Lower Marsh
SE1 7RL London
T 44-1171-6204444
F 44-1171-9280010
ETANG@CIX.CO.UK

CIIR

CIIR
Unit 3, Canonbury Yard 190 A New North Road
N1 7BJ London

CLP,LG,DG,CH

City of London Polytechnic London Guildhall
Department of Geography Calcutta House
Old Castle Street
E1 7NT London
T 44-1171-3201026
F 44-1171-3201117

CLP,LGU,FB

City of London Polytechnics
London Guildhall University Faculty of Business
84 Moorgate
EC2M 6SQ London
T 44-1171-3201600
F 44-1171-3201422

CRIS

Control Risks Information Services
83 Victoria St.
SW1H 0HW London

CS

China Society
16 Bridge Street Christchurch
DH23 1ED Dorset

CSIC,SOC

CSIC
Selly Oakes Colleges
996 Bristol Road
B29 6LQ Birmingham
T 44-1121-4724231
F 44-1121-4728852

CSM

Central St. Martins
Southampton Row
WC1 London
T 44-1171-7539090

CU, KC

Cambridge University
King's College
CB2 1ST Cambridge
T 44-1223-334126
F 44-1223-334126

CU, SBE

Coventry University
School of the Built Environment
Priory Street
CV1 5BF Coventry

CU,BASAS

Cambridge University
British Association for South Asian Studies
Sidgwick Avenue
CBE 9DA Cambridge
T 44-1223-335110
44-1223-335106

CU,CC

Cambridge University
Clare College
CB2 1TL Cambridge
T 44-1223-333239
F 44-1223-333219
ro202@cam.ac.uk

CU,DG

Cambridge University Department of Geography
Downing Place
CB2 2EN Cambridge
T 44-1223-364953
F 44-1223-334748

United Kingdom

CU,DSA

Cambridge University Department of Social Anthropology
Free School Lane
CB2 3RF Cambridge
T 44-1223-334585
F 44-1223-335993

CU,FOS

Cambridge University
Faculty of Oriental Studies
Sidgwick Avenue
CB3 9DA Cambridge
T 44-1223-335106
F 44-1223-335110
PR104@CAM.AC.UK

CU,FSPS

Cambridge University
Faculty of Social and Political Sciences
9 Jesus Lane
CB5 8BA Cambridge
T 44-1223-331874
F 44-1223-314514

CU,PC

Cambridge University
Pembroke College
CB2 1RF Cambridge
T 44-1223-338100
F 44-1223-338163

CUMA

Cambridge University
Museum of Archaeology
Downing Street
CB2 3DZ Cambridge
T 44-1223-333511
F 44-1223-333503
ach13@cus.can.ac.uk

DAJF

Daiwa Anglo-Japanese Foundation
13/14 Cornwall Terrace
Japan House
NW1 4QP London
T 44-1171-4864348
F 44-1171-4862914
c.dillon@mailbox.ulcc.ac.uk

DMU,SH

De Montfort University
School of Humanities
The Gateway
LE1 9BH Leicester
T 44-116-2551551
F 44-1116-2577199

E,IU

Economist
Intelligence Unit
15 Regent Street
SW1Y 4LR London

EC

Embassy of China
5 Birch Grove
W3 9SW London
T 44-1181-9930279
F 44-1181-9932215

EJ

Embassy of Japan
101-104 Piccadilly
W1V 9FN London
T 44-1171-4656592
F 44-1171-4919347
info@ambjapan.org.uk

EUC,SMSS,AA

Edge Hill University College School of Management and Social Sciences
Department of Asian and African Studies
St. Helens Road
L39 4QP Ormskirk
T 44-1695-584387
F 44-1695-579997
cleggje@staff.chche.ac.uk

EUK,P

Embassy of Korea
4 Palace Gate
W8 5NF London
T 44-1171-5810247
F 44-1171-5818076

FCO,NAPRG

Foreign and Commonwealth Office (FCO)
North Asia and Pacific Research Group
Old Admirality Building,Whitehall
SW1 2AF London
T 44-1171-2106213
F 44-1171-2106304
jeh@fcoamru.demm.co.uk

FCO,NAPRG

Foreign and Commonwealth Office (FCO)
North Asia and Pacific Research Group
Old Admirality Building,Whitehall
SW1A 2AH London
T 44-1171-2106213
F 44-1171-2106304
jeh@fcoamru.demm.co.uk

FM

Fitzwilliam Museum
Trumpington Street
CB2 1RB Cambridge
T 44-1223-332900/ 01223
F 44-1223-332923

FOC

Foreign and Commonwealth Office
King Charles Street
SW1A 2AH London
T 44-1301-7236211
F 44-1301-7241872

GCNWA

The Green Centre For Non-Western Ar
The Royal Pavillion, Art Gallery and Museums
BN1 1EE Brighton
T 44-1273-603005
F 44-1273-608202
greencentre@mistral.co.uk

GM,GMA

Glasgow Museum
Gallery of Modern Art
Queen Street
G1 3AZ Glasgow
T 44-1141-3311854
F 44-1141-3329957

GMAM

Glasgow Museum
Glasgow Art Gallery and Museum
The Burrel Collection |St. Mungo
Museum of Religious Life and Art
Art Gallery and Museum, Kelvingrove
G3 8AG Glasgow
T 44-1141-2872000
F 44-1141-2872690

GMCJS

Manchester University
Greater Manchester Centre for Japanese Studies
Humanities Building
Oxford Road
M13 9PL Manchester
T 44-1161-2753255
F 44-1161-2763354
Ann.Smith@man.ac.uk

HG

The Hatton Gallery
The Quandrangle
The University
NE1 7RU Newcastle upon Tyne
T 44-1191-2226000\ 6057
F 44-1191-2611182

United Kingdom

HMC,QH,QC

Historical Manuscripts Commission
Quality house
QualityCourt
Chancery Lane
WC2A 1HP London
T 44-1171-2421198
F 44-1171-8313550
nra@hmc.gov.uk

HOM

Horniman Museum
London Road
Forest Hill
SE23 3PQ London
T 44-1181-1872/ ext. 133
F 44-1181-2915506
birley@horniman.demon.co.uk

IA

Institute of Archaeology.
31-34 Gordon Square
WC1H OPY London
T 44-1171-3877050
F 44-1171-3832572

IBMITS,IFSC

IBM International Treasury Services
International Financial Services Centre
La Touche House Custom House Dock
Dublin 1 (Ireland)

ICS

Institute for Chinese Studies
Walton Street
OX1 2HG Oxford
T 44-1865-280380
F 44-1865-280381

IIED

International Institute for Environment and Development
3 Endsleigh Street
'C1 London

IOLR

India Office Library and Records
197 Blackfriars Road
SE1 8NG London

IOP,EC

Institute of Oriental Philosphy
European Centre
Taplow Court Taplow Maidenhead
SL6 0ER Berkshire
T 44-1628-776719
F 44-1628-773055

IOP,EC

Institute of Oriental Philosphy
European Centre
Taplow Court Taplow Maidenhead
SL6 0ER Berkshire
T 44-1628-776719
F 44-1628-773055
JamieC@compuserve.com

IREES

Institute of Russian and East European Studies
29, Bute Gardens
G12 8RS Glasgow (Scotland)
T 44-1141-3398855
F 44-1141-3305594

JL

Japan Library
Knoll House 35
The Crecent
CT20 3CE Sandgate (Kent)
T 44-1303-220277
F 44-1303-243087

JP

The Japan Foundation
17,old Park Lane
W1Y 3LG London
T 44-1171-4994726
F 44-1171-4951133

KCL,CNR,JNRP

King's College London
School of Humanities
Centre for New Religios Studies
Japanese New Religions Project
Strand
WC2R 2LS London
T 44-1171-8365454
F 44-1171-873 2292
udxa002@kcl.ac.uk\sonia.crivello@kc ac.uk

KCL,DG

King's College London Department of Geography
Strand
WC2R 2LS London
T 44-1171-8732258
F 44-1171-8732287

KCL,MC

King's College Londen
Management Centre
Kensington Campus Campden Hill Road
W8 7AH London

KLI

Kluwer Law International.
Sterling House 66 Wilton Road
SW1V 1DE London

KPIL

Kegan Paul International Ltd.
P.O. Box 256 118 Bedford Court Mansions Bedford Avenue
WC1B 3SW London
Visiting Address:
P.O.Box 256 London
T 44-1171-5805511
F 44-1171-4360899
books@keganpau.demon.cu.uk/bij Hopkins is www

KU, RC

University of Kent at Canterbury
Rutherford College
School of History
CT2 7NX Canterbury (Kent)
T 44-1227-764000
F 44-1227-827258

KU,CBPU

Keele University China Business and Policy Unit
ST5 5BG Keele, Staffordshire
T 44-1782-621111
F 44-1782-613847
POA23@CC.KEELE.AC.UK

KU,DG

Keele University
Department of Geography
ST5 5AY Staffordshire
T 44-1782-621111
F 44-1782-584144

KU,DSSA

Keele University
Department of Sociology and Social Anthropology
ST5 5BG Keele, St
T 44-1782-583203
F 44-1782-583195
niazo@keele.ac.uk

LCU,DS,CRU

London City University
Department of Sociology China Research Unit
Northampton Square
EC1V 0HB London
T 44-1171-4778507
F 44-1171-4778558
S.Feuchtwang@city.ac.uk

United Kingdom

LJMU, DJ

Liverpool John Moores University
Department of Journalism
Dean Walters Bldg.
Rodney Street
L1 7BR Liverpool

LJMU,SSS,CPRS

Liverpool John Moores University
School of Social Sciences Centre for Pacific Rim Studies
Trueman Building
15-21 Webster Street
L3 2ET Liverpool
T 44-1151-2314068
F 44-1151-258-1224
R.Y.LI@LIVJM.AC.UK

LM

National Museums and Galleries at Merseyside Liverpool Museum
William Brown Street
L3 8EN Liverpool
T 44-1151-4784747
F 44-1151-707-9051

LSE,DIR

London School of Economics and political Science
Department of International Relations
Houghton Street
WC2A 2AE London
T 44-1171-9557399
F 44-1171-9557446
M.B.YAHUNDA@lse.ac.uk\M.Leifer@lse.ac.uk

LSEP,STICERD

London School of Economics and Political Science STICERD
Houghton Street
WC2A 2AE London
T 44-1171-9556689
F 44-1171-242-2357
j.e.hunter@lse.ac.uk

LSEPS

London School of Economics and Political Science
Houghton Street
WC2A 2AE London

LSEPS,DA

London School of Economics and Political Science
Department of Anthropology
Houghton Street
WC2A 2AE London
T 44-1171-9557205
F 44-1171-9557603

LSEPS,DDS

London School of Economics and Political Science
Department of Development Studies
Houghton Street
WC2A 2AS London
T 44-1171-9556743
F 44-1171-9556844

LSEPS,DE

London School of Economics and Political Science
Department of Economics
Houghton Street
WC2A 2AE London
T 44-1171-9557489
F 44-1171-9557591

LSEPS,DG

London School of Economics and Political Science
Department of Geography
S504 Graduate Room Houghton Street
WC2A 2AE London
T 44-1171-9557606
F 44-1171-9557412

LSEPS,DPS

London School of Economics and Political Science
Department of Population Studies
Houghton Street
WC2A 2AE London

LSEPS,DS

London School of Economics and Political Science
Department of Sociology
Houghton Street
WC1 2AE London

LSEPS,DSA

London School of Econonomic and Political Sciences Department of Social Anthropology
Houghton Street Aldwych
WC2 2AE London

LSEPS,STICERD

London School of Economics and Political Science
Suntory and Toyota International Centres for Economics and Related Disciplines
Houghton Street
WC2A 2AE London
F 44-1171-2422357
J.RUFF@lse.ac.uk

LSI

Limbless Swimmers International
67 Holiday Village Fairbourne
LL38 2LQ Gwynedd

LSVCHE,SS

LSV College of Higher Education
Social Sciences
The Avenue
S017 1BG Southampton
T 44-1703-228761
F 44-1703-230944

LUI,FA,DH

Liverpool University
Faculty of Arts
Department of History
P.O. Box 147 Roxby Building
L69 3BX Liverpool
Visiting Address:
8 Abercromby Square
T 44-1151-7942394
F 44-1151-7942366

LUI,FSES,DCD

Liverpool University
Faculty of Social and Environmental Studies
Department of Civic Design
P.O.Box 147
L69 3BX Liverpool
T 44-1151-7943121
F 44-1151-7943125

LUI,FSES,DG

Liverpool University
Faculty of Social and Environmental Studies
Department of Geography
Roxby Building P.O.Box 147
L69 3BX Liverpool
T 44-1151-7942835
F 44-1151-7942866

United Kingdom

MCC,IF

Markfiled Conference Centre The Islamic Foundation
Ratby Lane
Markfield
LE67 9RN Leicestershire
T 44-153-024-4944 / 5
F 44-1153-0244946
islamic@islamf.demon.co.uk

MCSI

Muslim Community Studies Institute
P.O.Box 139
LE2 2YH Leicester
T 44-116-2706714
F 44-1116-2706714
asf@volcano.u-net.com

MEAA

Museum of East Asian Art
12 Bennett Street
BA1 2QL Bath

MMAO

Museum of Modern Art Oxford
30, Pembroke Street
OX1 1BP Oxford
T 44-1865-722733
F 44-1865-722573

MMU, DS

Manchester Metropolitan University
Department of Sociology
Rosamund St.
M15 6LL Manchester
T 44-1161-2473009

MMU,FH,DL

Manchester Metropolitan University
Faculty of Humanities Department of Languages
Cavendish Str. Mabel Tylecote Bldg.
M15 6BG Manchester
T 44-1161-2473941
F 44-1161-2476323

MOM

Museum of Mankind Ethnographic Dept. of the British Museum
Burlington Gradens
W1X 2EX London
T 44-1171-6361555
F 44-1171-3238013

MU,SHP

Middlesex University
School of History and Politics
White Hart Lane
N17 8HR London
T 44-1181-3626209

NCOLR,FOS,BIB

National Council on Orientalist Library Resources (NCOLR) Faculty of Oriental Studies Library
Sidgwick Avenue
CB3 9DA Cambridge
T 44-1223-335111
F 44-1223-335110
caa1@cam.ac.uk

NCOLR,OIO,CBL

National Council on Orientalist Library Resources (NCOLR) Oriental and India Office Collection Britisch Library
197 Blackfriars Road
SE1 8NG London
T 44-1171-4127834
F 44-1171-4127834

NCSB

Nene College School of Business
Boughton Green Road
NN2 7AL Northhampton

NIJS

Nissan Institute of Japanese Studies
27 Winchester Road
OX2 6N4 Oxford
T 44-1865-274573
F 44-1865-274574

NM,GM

National Museum
Gallery in Merseyside
William Brown str.
L3 8EN Liverpool
T 44-1151-2070001

NMS,DA

National Museums of Scotland
Department of Archaeology
Chambers street
EH1 1JF Edinburgh (Scotland)
T 44-1131-2257534
F 44-1131-5579498

NRI

Needham Research Institute
8 Sylvester Road
CB3 9AF Cambridge
T 44-1223 311545
F 44-1223 362703

NRI,EAHSL

Needham Research Institute East Asian History of Science Library
8 Sylvester Road
CB3 9AF Cambridge
T 44-1223-311545
F 44-1223-62703
jm10019@cus.cau.ac.uk

NU,DPFT

Napier University
Department of Photography, Film and Television
6-7 Coates Place
EH3 4QD Edinburgh

NUU,CDH

New University of Ulster Department o History
Cromore Road
BT52 1SA Coleraine (N. Ireland)
T 44-1265-44141

OBU,DA

Oxford Brookes University/ Department of Anthropology
Headington
073 OBP Oxford

OBU,SAC

Oxford Brookes University
School of Architecture Cendep
Gipsy Lane Campus
OX3 0BP Oxford
T 44-1865 483413
F 44-1865 48 32 98

OBU,SBMSNFS

Oxford Brookes University
School of Biological Molecular Sciences Nutrition & Food Science
Gypsy Lane Campus
OX3 0BP Headington, Oxford
T 44-1865-483818
F 44-1856-484017

OBU,SSS

Oxford Brookes University
School of Social Sciences
Gipsy Lane
OX3 0BP Oxford
T 44-1865-483750
F 44-1865-483937

United Kingdom

OCIS

Oxford Centre for Islamic Studies
George Street
OX1 2AR Oxford
T 44-1865-278730
F 44-1865-248942
islamic.studies@oxis.ac.uk\oci0001@emine.ox.ac.uk

OMD

Oriental Museum
Elvet Hill, South Road
DH1 3TH Durham
T 44-1191-3747911
F 44-1191-3743242
Oriental.Museum@durham.ac.uk

ONS

Oriental Numismatic Society
30 Warren Road Woodley
RG5 3AR Reading, Berks
T 44-1118-9693528
F 44-1118-9699807

OU,ASC

Oxford University
Asian Studies Centre
St.Antony's College
OX2 6JF Oxford
T 44-1865-274559
F 44-1865-274559
asian@sant.ox.ac.uk\
ST_ANTONYS.OX.AC.UK

OU,BC,MHF

Oxford University
Balliol College
Modern History Faculty
OX1 3BJ Oxford
T 44-1865-277736
F 44-1865-277803
Judith.Brown@history.ox.ac.uk

OU,BL

Oxford University
Bodleian Library
Broad Street
OX1 3BG Oxford
T 44-1865-277180
F 44-1865-277105

OU,FE

Oxford University
Faculty of Economics
Queens Elizabeth House 21 St. Giles
OX1 3LA Oxford
F 44-1865-273607

OU,FI,PS

Oxford University
Forestry Institute
Plant Sciences
South Parks Road
OX1 3RB Oxford
T 44-1865-2750000

OU,FOS,ICS

Oxford University
Faculty of Oriental Studies Institute for Chinese Studies
Walton street
OX1 2HG Oxford
T 44-1865-280387
F 44-1865-280431

OU,IIBIB,BBIB

Oxford University
Indian Institute Library
Bodleian Library
Broad Street
OX1 3BG Oxford
T 44-1865-277083
F 44-1865-277083
indian.institute@bodley.ox.ac.uk

OU,NC

Oxford University
Nuffield College
OX6 6JF Oxford
T 44-1865-278500

OU,OI

Oxford University
Oriental Institute
Pusey Lane
OX1 2LE Oxford
T 44-1865-278200
F 44-1865-278190

OU,PRM

Oxford University
Pitt Rivers Museum
South Parks Road
OX1 3PP Oxford
T 44-1865-270928
F 44-1865-270943

OU,SAME

Oxford University
Institute of Social and Cultural Anthropology
School of Anthropology and Museum Ethnography
51 Banbury Road
OX2 6PE Oxford
T 44-1865-274676
F 44-1865-274630
robert.barnes@anthro.ox.ac.uk

OU,SG

Oxford University
School of Geography
Mansfield Road
OX1 3TB Oxford
T 44-1865-515211

OU,SJC,ICS

Oxford University
St. John's College
Institute for Chinese Studies
OX1 3JP Oxford
T 44-1865-277407
F 44-1865-277421

OU,TC,FMH

Oxford University
Trinity College
Faculty of Modern History
OX1 3BH Oxford
T 44-1865-279867
F 44-1865-279911

OUB,FSS

Open University
Faculty of Social Sciences
Walton Hall Milton Keynes
MK7 6AA Buckinghamshire
T 44-1190-8654439
F 44-1190-8654488
D.R.HUMPHREYS@OPEN.AC.UK

OX,IDC

Oxford University
International Development Centre
Queen Elizabeth House\21 St. Giles
OX1 3LA Oxford
T 44-1865-273600
F 44-1865-273607
geh@geh.ox.ac.uk

PRC

Philippine Resource Centre (PRC)
84 Long Lane
SE1 4AU London

QUB,DSA

Queen's University of Belfast
Department of Social Anthropology
BT7 1NN Belfast (N. Ireland)
T 44-1232-245133
F 44-1232-247895
anthropology2@clio.arts.qub.ac.uk

United Kingdom

QUB,SG,PC

Queen's University of Belfast School of Geosciences Palaeoecology Centre
42 Fitzwilliam Street
BT9 6AX Belfast (N. Ireland)
T 44-1232-245133
F 44-1232-321280

RAD,FCO,FES

Research and Analysis Department
Foreign and Commonwealth Office
(FCO) Far Eastern Section
Whitehall Old Admiralty Building
SW1 2AF London
T 44-1171-2106213
F 44-1171-2106304

RAI

Royal Anthropological Institute
50 Fitzroy Street
W1P 5HS London
T 44-1171-3870455
F 44-1171-3834235
rai@cix.compulink.co.uk

RASGBI

Royal Asiatic Society of Great Britain and Ireland
60 Queen's Gardens
W2 3AF London
T 44-1171-7244742\library:7244741
F 44-1171-7064008

RC,PS

Richmond College
Political Sciences
Queens Road
TW10 6JP Richmond, Surrey
T 44-1181-3328200

RHBNC,DH

Royal Holloway and Bedford New College
Department of History
TW20 0EX Egham, Surrey
T 44-1784-434455
F 44-1784-433032

RSAA

Royal Society for Asian Affairs
2 Belgrave Square
SW1X 8PJ London
T 44-1171-235 5122
F 44-1171-2596771

S,ID

Sotheby's
Islamic Department
34-35 New Bond Street
W1A 2AA London
T 44-1171-4938080
F 44-1171-4093100

SAS,BM

Society for Asian Studies
c/o Department of Oriental Antiquities
The British Museum
W4B 3DG London
T 44-1171-3238844

SCC

St. Catharine's College
CB2 1RL Cambridge
T 44-1223-38321
F 44-1223-38340

SIBF

Southampton Institute Business Finance
East Park Terrace
SO14 0YN Southampton
T 44-1703-332426
1703-319609

SILI

SIL Institute
Horsleys Green, High Wycombe
HP14 3XL Bucks

SOAS

University of London
School of Oriental and African Studies (SOAS)
Thornhaugh Street
Russell Square
WC1H OXG London
T 44-1171-6372388
F 44-1171-436 3844

SOAS,BIB

University of London
SOAS
Library
Thornhaugh Street Russell Square
WC1H OXG London
T 44-1171-6372388
F 44-1171-6362834
Libenquiry@soas.ac.uk (for library enquiries)

SOAS,CARF

University of London
SOAS
Central Asia Research Forum
Thornhaugh Street
Russell Square
WC1H 0XG London
T 44-1171-6372388
F 44-1171-4363844

SOAS,CCI

University of London
SOAS
Contemporary China Institute (CCI)
Thornhaugh Street
Russell Square
WC1H 0XG London
T 44-1171-3236191
F 44-1171-4363844

SOAS,CCS

University of London
SOAS
Centre for Chinese Studies (CCS)
Thornhaugh Street Russell Square
WC1H 0XG London
T 44-1171-3236191
F 44-1171-4353844

SOAS,CEAL

University of London
SOAS
Centre for East Asian Law
Thornhaugh Street
Russell Square
WC1H OXG London
T 44-1171-6372388
F 44-1171-4363844

SOAS,CKS

University of London
SOAS
Centre of Korean Studies
Thornhaugh Street
Russell Square
WC1H 0XG London
T 44-1171-6372388
F 44-1171-4363844

SOAS,CMS

University of London
SOAS
Centre of Music Studies
Thornhaugh Street
Russell Square
WC1H 0XG London
T 44-1171-6376182
F 44-1171-4363844

United Kingdom

SOAS,CSAS

University of London
SOAS
Centre of South Asian Studies
Thornhaugh Street
Russell Square
WC1H 0XG London

T 44-1171-6372388

F 44-1171-4363844

SOAS,CSEAS

University of London
SOAS
Centre of Southeast Asian Studies
Thornhaugh Street
Russell Square
WC1H 0XG London

T 44-1171-6372388

F 44-1171-4363844

SOAS,DAA

University of London
SOAS
Department of Art and Archaeology
Thornhaugh Street Russell Square
WC1H 0XG London

T 44-1171-6372388

F 44-1171-4363844

SOAS,DAS

University of London
SOAS
Department of Anthropology and Sociology
Thornhaugh Street Russell Square
WC1H 0XG London

T 44-1171-3236324

F 44-1171-3236363

SOAS,DE

University of London
SOAS
Department of Economics
Thornhaugh Street Russell Square
WC1H 0XG London

SOAS,DEA

University of London
SOAS
Department of East Asia
Thornhaugh Street Russell Square
WC1H 0XG London

T 44-1171-3236204

F 44-1171-4363844

al3@soas.ac.uk

SOAS,DEPS

University of London
SOAS
Department of Economic and Political Studies
Thornhaugh Street Russell Square
WC1H 0XG London

T 44-1171-3236123

F 44-1171-2326020

SOAS,DH

University of London
SOAS
Department of History
Thornhaugh Street Russell Square
WC1H 0XG London

T 44-1171-3236061

F 44-1171-3236046

SOAS,DHAA

University of London
SOAS
Department of History of Art and Archaeology
Thornhaugh Street Russell Square
WC1H 0XG London

SOAS,DL

University of London
SOAS
Department of Law
Russell Square Thornhaugh Street
WC1H 0XG London

T 44-1171-6372388

F 44-1171-6365615

SOAS,DLCSEA

University of London
SOAS
Department of the Languages and Cultures of Southeast Asia
Thornhaugh Street Russell Square
WC1H 0XG London

T 44-1171-3232416

F 44-1171-4363844

hb3@soas.ac.uk

SOAS,DSA

University of London
SOAS
Department of South Asia
Thornhaugh Street Russell Square
WC1H 0XG London

T 44-1171-3236229

F 44-1171-4363844

SOAS,DSEA

University of London
SOAS
Department of Southeast Asia
Malet Street
WC1E 7HP London

SOAS,JRC

University of London
SOAS
Japan Research Centre (JRC)
Thornhaugh Street
Russell Square
WC1H 0XG London

T 44-1171-3236278

F 44-1171-4363844

jrc@soas.ac.uk

SOC,CISCMR

Selly Oakes Colleges
Centre of Islamic Studies and Christian Muslim Relations
998 Bristol Road
B29 6LE Birmingham

T 44-1121-4724231

F 44-1121-4728852

SSAS

Society for South Asian Studies
Admont, Dander's End, Tring
HP 23 6JY Herts

SU,LPSS

Southbank University
Legal, Political and Social Sciences
Borough Road 103
SE1 0AA London

T 44-1171-2771091

F 44-1171-2526971

TA

Tara Arts
356 Garrattlane
SW18 4ES London

T 44-1181-8711458

F 44-1181-8709540

sheetal@vossnet.co.uk

TOCS

The Oriental Ceramic Society
30B Torrington Square
WC1E 7JL London

T 44-1171-6367985

F 44-1171-580-6749

United Kingdom

TRCM

The Royal Cornwall Museum
River Street
Truro
TR1 2SJ Cornwall
T 44-1872-72205
F 44-1872-40514

TSUK

Tibet Society of the U.K.
114-115 Tottenham Court Road
W1P 9HL London
T 44-1171-3837533
F 44-1171-3837563
members@tibet-society.org.uk

TTI

The Times of India
150 Bramley Road
N14 4HU London
T 44-1181-4470607
F 44-1181-4470913

UA,DPIR

University of Aberdeen Department of Politics and International Relations
Dunbar Street, Edward Wright Bld.
AB9 2TY Aberdeen (Scotland)

UB,DCS

University of Birmingham Department of Cultural Studies
Edgbaston
B15 2TT Birmingham
T 44-1121-4147535
F 44-1121-4146061
R.Kumar@bham.ac.uk

UB,DPS,IS

University of Birmingham Department of Political Science and International Studies
B15 2TT Birmingham
T 44-1121-4146520
F 44-1121-4143496
prestonp@css.bham.ac.uk

UB,ILGS,D,AG

University of Birmingham
Institute of Local Government Studies
Development Administration Group
B15 2TT Birmingham
T 44-1121-4145039
F 44-1121-4145032

UB,ILGS,DLGD

University of Birmingham
Institute of Local Government Studies
Department of Local Government and Development
P.O. Box 363
B15 2TT Birmingham

UB,SPP

University of Birmingham
School of Public Policy
P.O.Box 363
B15 2TT Birmingham
T 44-1121-4145035
F 44-1121-4144989

UBA,SSS

University of Bath
School of Social Sciences
BA2 7AY Bath
T 44-1225-826384
F 44-1225-826381

UBR,DAS

University of Bradford Department of Archaeological Sciences
Richmond Road
BD7 4LY Bradford (W. Yorkshire)
T 44-1274-385430

UBR,DPPC

University of Bradford Development and Project Planning Centre
Pemberton Building
BD7 1DP Bradford (W. Yorkshire)
T 44-1274-383980
F 44-1274-385280

UBR,DPS

University of Bradford Department of Peace Studies
Richmond Road
BD7 1DP Bradford (W. Yorkshire)
T 44-1274-384181
F 44-1274-385235

UBR,DSES

University of Bradford
Department for Social and Economic Studies
Richmond Road
BD7 1DP Bradford, West Yorkshire
T 44-1274-385046
F 44-1274-395295
a.y.samad@bradford.ac.uk

UBR,MC

University of Bradford Management Centre
Emm Lane
BD9 4JL Bradford (W. Yorkshire)
T 44-1274-384393/384389
F 44-1274-546866/385680

UBR,NAS,AS

University of Bradford
Department for Social and Economic Studies
Richmond Road
BD7 1DP Bradford (W. Yorkshire)
T 44-1274-385531/2
F 44-1274-385190

UBRI,DG

University of Bristol
Department of Geography
University Road
BS8 1SS Bristol
T 44-1117-2303754

UBRI,DHS

University of Bristol
Department of Historical Studies
13-15 Woodland Road
BS8 1TB Bristol
T 44-1117 2287933
F 44-1117-2288276

UBRI,DTR,CBS

University of Bristol
Department of Theology and Religious Studies
Centre for Buddhist Studies
3 Woodland Road
BS8 1TB Bristol
T 44-1117-2287760
F 44-1117-9297850
Paul.Williams@bristol.ac.uk

UBRI,DTRS

University of Bristol
Department of Theology and Religious Studies
36 Tyndall's Park Road
BS8 1PL Bristol
T 44-1117-2287760

UC,CH

University of Cambridge
Clare Hall
Herschel Road
CB3 9AL Cambridge
T 44-1223-332360
F 44-1223-332333

United Kingdom

UC,CSAS

University of Cambridge
Centre for South Asian Studies
Laundress Lane
CB2 1SD Cambridge
T 44-1223-338094
F 44-1223-316913
ljc10@cam.ac.uk

UC,IBU

University of Cambridge
Islamic Bibliography Unit Library
West Road
CB3 9DR Cambridge
T 44-1223-333057
F 44-1223-333160
IBU@ULA.CAM.AC.UK

UC,STC

University of Cambridge
St. John's College
CB2 1TP Cambridge

UCL

University College London
Gower Street
WC1E 6BT London
T 44-1171-3877050
F 44-1171-9166985
ucldres@ucl.ac.uk

UCL,DA

University College London Department of Anthropology
Gower Street
WC1E 6BT London
T 44-1171-3807230

UCL,DPU

University College London
Development Planning Unit
9 Endsleigh
WC1H 0ED London
T 44-1171-3887581
F 44-1171-3874541

UCL,FL

University College London Faculty of Laws
Endsleigh Gardens
WC1H 0EG London
T 44-1171-3877050
F 44-1171-3879597

UD,RRC,,SESS

University of Derby
Religious Resource and Research Centre
School of Education and Social Science
Mickleover
DE3 5GX Derby
T 44-1332-622222
F 44-1332-514323
A.Andrews@Derby.Ac.Uk

UDU,BAKS

University of Durcham
Department for East Asian Studies
British Association for Korean Studies (BAKS)
Elvet Hill
DH1 3TH Durham
T 44-1191-3743231
F 44-1191-3743242

UDU,DA

University of Durham
Department of Anthropology
43 Old Elvet
DH1 3HN Durham
T 44-1191-3742840/41
F 44-1191-3742870/7527
Patricia.barber@durcham.ac.uk

UDU,DEAS

University of Durham Department of East Asian Studies
Elvet Hill
DH1 3TH Durham
T 44-1191-3743231
F 44-1191-3743242

UDU,DG

University of Durham
Department of Geography
South Road
DH1 3LE Durham
T 44-1191-3742000
F 44-1191-3742456

UDU,DP

University of Durham
Department of Physics
South Road
DH1 3LE Durham
T 44-1191-3742153
F 44-1191-3743749

UDU,MS

University of Durham
The Music School
Palace Green
DH1 3RL Durham
T 44-1191-3743211
F 44-1191-3743219

UE,DAS

University of Edinburgh Department of Asian Studies
George Square
EH8 9LL Edinburgh (Scotland)
T 44-1131-66 27 87
F 44-1131-6503962
tea@tattoo.ed.ac.uk

UE,DAS

University of Edinburgh Department of Asian Studies
8 Buccleuch Place
EH8 9LW Edinburgh (Scotland)
T 44-1131-6504227
F 44-1131-6511258
Bonnie.S.McDougal@ed.ac.uk

UE,DC

University of Edinburgh Department of Chinese
8 Buccleuch Place
EH8 9LW Edinburgh (Scotland)

UE,DG

University of Edinburgh Department of Geography
Drummond Street
EH8 9XP Edinburgh (Scotland)
T 44-1131-6502565
F 44-1131-5560544
office@uk.ac.ed.geovax

UE,DH

University of Edinburgh Department of History
William Robertson Building 50, George Square
EH8 9JY Edinburgh (Scotland)
F 44-1131-6503784

UE,DS

University of Edinburgh
Department of Sanskrit
7 Buccleuch Place
EH8 9LW Edinburgh (Scotland)
T 44-1131-6504174
F 44-1131-6506804
Sanskrit.Dept@ed.ac.uk\
P.Dundas@ed.ac.uk

United Kingdom

UE,DS

University of Edinburgh Department of Sociology
18 Buccleuch Place
EH8 9LN Edinburgh (Scotland)
T 44-1131-6504001
F 44-1131-6503989

UE,DSA

University of Edinburgh Department of Social Anthropology
40 George Square
EH8 9LL Edinburgh (Scotland)
Visiting Address:
Adam Ferguson Building
T 44-1131-6503941
F 44-1131-6503945

UE,EAS,ACJS

University of Edinburgh
East Asian Studies
Arts Centre for Japanese studies
George Square
EH8 9TX Edinburgh
T 44-1131-6504230
F 44-1131-6506536

UE,IJETS

University of Edinburgh
Institute for Japanese-European Technology Studies
25 Buccleuch Place
EH8 9LN Edinburgh (Scotland)
T 44-1131-6504061
F 44-1131-6674340
L.Dyer@ed.ac.uk

UE,IO

University of Edinburgh International Office
57, George Square
EH8 9JV Edinburgh (Scotland)
T 44-1131-6504301
F 44-1131-6684565
international@ed.ac.uk

UEA,ODG,SDS

University of East Anglia Overseas Development Group School of Development Studies
NR4 7TJ Norwich
T 44-1603-456161
F 44-1603-451999

UEA,SESS

University of East Anglia
School of Economic and Social Studies
NR4 7TJ Norwich
T 44-1603-592714
F 44-1603-250434

UES

University of Essex
Contemporary Japan Centre
Wivenhoe Park
CO4 3SQ Colchester (Essex)
T 44-1206-872543
F 44-1206-873408

UES,DH

University of Essex
Department of History
Wivenhoe Park
CO4 3SQ Colchester (Essex)
T 44-1206-872259
F 44-1206-873598

UES,DS

University of Essex
Department of Sociology
Wivenhoe Park
CO4 3SQ Colchester (Essex)
T 44-1206-873333/3551

UEX,DAL

University of Exeter
Department of Applied Linguistics
EX4 4QJ Exeter
T 44-1392-264303
F 44-1392-264377

UEX,DG

University of Exeter
Department of Geography
Amory Building Rennes Drive
EX4 4RJ Exeter
T 44-1392-263339
F 44-1392-263342

UEX,IPS

University of Exeter
Institute of Population Studies
Hoopern House,
101 Pennsylvania Road
EX4 6DT Exeter, Devon
T 44-1392-57936 / 263800
F 44-1392-490870
ips.director@exeter.ac.uk

UG,DPE

University of Glasgow Department of Political Economy
Adam Smith Building
G12 8RT Glasgow (Scotland)
Visiting Address:
Adam Smith Building
T 44-1141-3305354
F 44-1141-3304946

UG,DS

University of Glasgow Department of Sociology
Adam Smith Building
G12 8RT Glasgow (Scotland)
T 44-1141-3305981
F 44-1141-3308022

UGR,SH

University of Greenwich
School of Humanities
Wellington Street
SE18 6PF London
T 44-1181-3318800
F 44-1181-3318805

UHU,BJL

University of Hull
Brynmor Jones Library
HU6 7RX Hull
T 44-1482-465269
F 44-1482-466205

UHU,CSEAS

University of Hull
Centre for Southeast Asian Studies
2.6 Driffield House Taylor Court,
Salmon Grove
HU6 7RX Hull
T 44-1482-442256

UHU,DSEAS

University of Hull
Department for South-East Asian Studies
Cottingham Road
HU6 7RX Kingston upon Hull
T 44-1482-346311\465758
F 44-1482-465798\465758
S.Rhind@Seas.hull.ac.uk

UHU,IPAS

University of Hull
Institute of Pacific Asia Studies
Cottingham Road
HU6 7RX Hull
T 44-1482-466398
F 44-1482-465758

United Kingdom

UK, DSEAS

University of Kent
Department of South East Asian Studie
CT2 7NZ Danterbury (Kent)

UK,EC

University of Kent Eliot College
(DOSSA)
CT2 7NS Canterbury (Kent)
T 44-1227-764000
F 44-1227-827289

UK,EC,DSSA

University of Kent
Elliot College
Department of Sociology and Social Anthropology
CT2 7NZ Canterbury (Kent)
T 44-1227-764000
F 44-1227-827289

UL,DRS

University of Lancaster
Department of Religious Studies
LA1 4YG Lancaster
T 44-1524-592424
F 44-1524-847039

UL,ICS

University of London
Institute of Commonwealth Studies
(ICS)
28 Russell Square
WC1B 5DS London
T 44-1171-5805876
F 44-1171-2552160
j.manor@sas.ac.uk\icommlib@sas.ac.uk

UL,RHBNC,DH

University of London
Royal Holloway and Bedford New College
Department of History
Egham
TW20 0EX Surrey
T 44-1784-443300
F 44-1784-443032

ULC,DE

University of Lancaster Department of Economics
LA1 4UW Lancaster

ULC,DG

University of Lancaster Department of Geography
LA1 4YB Lancaster
T 44-1524-593742
F 44-1524-847099

ULC,DJS

University of Lancaster Department of Japanese Studies
LA1 4YN Lancaster
T 44-1524-65201
F 44-1524-843934

ULC,SML,DCS

University of Lancaster School of Modern Languages Department of Chinese Studies
LA1 4YN Lancaster
T 44-1524 594465
F 44-1524-84-3934
q.kan@lancaster.ac.uk

ULEED,DEAS

University of Leeds
School of Modern Languages
Department of East Asian Studies
LS2 9JT Leeds
T 44-1113-333460
F 44-1113-336741
f-christiansen@Leeds.ac.uk\
eastasian@leeds.ac.uk

ULEED,DEAS,ACS

University of Leeds
Department of East Asian Studies
British Association for Chinese Studies
LS2 9JT Leeds
T 44-1113 2333460
F 44-1113-2336741

ULEED,DP

University of Leeds
Department of Politics
LS2 9JT Leeds

ULEED,DP

University of Leeds
Department of Philosophy
LS2 9JT Leeds
T 44-1532-333267
phlagd@leeds.ac.uk

ULEED,DTRS

University of Leeds
Department Of Theology and Religious Studies
LS2 9JT Leeds
T 44-1113-2333644
F 44-1113-2333654
k.knott@leeds.ac.uk

ULEED,SE

University of Leeds
School of Education
LS2 9ST Leeds
T 44-1532-431751

ULEED,SG

University of Leeds
School of Geography
LS2 9JT Leeds
T 44-1113-2333308
F 44-1113-2333338

ULEI,DA

University of Leicester Department of Archaeology
University Road
LE1 7RH Leicester

ULEI,DESH

University of Leicester Department of Economic and Social History
University Road
LE1 7RH Leicester

ULU,KLCC

University of Luton
Faculty of Humanities
Ko Luen Chinese Centre
LU1 3AJ Luton, Bedfordshire
T 44-1582-489159
F 44-1582-489014

UM

Ulster Museum
Botanic Gardens
Botanic Gardens
BT9 5AB Belfast (Northern Ireland)
T 44-1232-667769
F 44-1232-681885
winifred.glover.um@nics.gov.uk

UNC,DP,EARC

University of Newcastle upon Tyne
Department of Politics
East Asia Research Centre
NE1 7RU Newcastle upon Tyne
T 44-1191-222-6737
F 44-1191-222-5069

United Kingdom

UNC,DRS

University of Newcastle upon Tyne
Department of Religious Studies
NE1 7RU Newcastle upon Tyne
T 44-1191-2226730
F 44-1191-2225185
d.h.killingley@ncl.ac.uk

UNC,DS

University of Newcastle upon Tyne
Department of Speech
Queen Victoria Road King George VI Building
NE1 7RU Newcastle upon Tyne
T 44-1191-2226000/7388
F 44-1191-2226518

UNC,EAC

University of Newcastle upon Tyne
Department of Speech
NE1 7RU Newcastle upon Tyne
T 44-1191-2228021
F 44-1191-2225069
Shaun.Breslin@ncl.ac.uk

UNL,BS

University of North London Business School
Centre for Leisure and Tourism Studies
227-281 Holloway Road
N7 8HN London

UO, WC, ST

University of Oxford
Westminster College
School of Theology
Westminster College
OX2 9AT Oxford
T 44-1865-247644
F 44-1865-251847

UO,IIL,BL

University of Oxford / Indian Institute Library / Bodleian Library
Broad Street
OX1 3BG Oxford
T 44-1865-277083
F 44-1865-277083
indian.institute@bodley.ox.ac.uk

UO,ISCA

Oxford University
Institute of Social and Cultural Anthropology
51 Banbury Road
OX2 6PE Oxford
T 44-1865-274675
F 44-1865-274630

UO,WC

Oxford University
Wolfson College
OX2 6UD Oxford
T 44-1865-274100
F 44-1865-274125

UR,DAERD

University of Reading
Department of Agricultural Extension and Rural Development
3 Earley Grate Whitekrights Road
RG6 6AL Reading
T 44-1734-875123
F 44-1734-261244

URO,DA

University of Rochester Department of Anthropology
440 Lattimore Hall
NY 14627 Rochester

USA,DE

University of Salford
Department of Economics
M5 4WT Salford
T 44-1617-455000
F 44-1617-455992

USH,CJS

University of Sheffield
Centre for Japanese Studies
S10 2TN Sheffield
T 44-1114-2228400
F 44-1114-2228432
seas@sheffield.ac.uk

USH,CKS

University of Sheffield
School of East Asian Studies
Centre for Korean Studies
Western Bank
S10 2UJ Sheffield
T 44-1114-2768555
F 44-1114-2739826/729479
SEAS@SHEFFIELD.AC.UK

USH,DH

University of Sheffield Department of History
S10 2TN Sheffield

USH,EARS

University of Sheffield
East Asia Research Centre
P.O. Box 595
S10 2UJ Sheffield
T 44-1114-2824854
F 44-1114-2729479

USH,SEAS

University of Sheffield
School of East Asian Studies
P.O.Box: 595.
S10 2UJ Sheffield
T 44-1114-2228421
F 44-1114-2228432
m.weiner@sheffield.ac.uk

USH,SES,EARC

University of Sheffield
School of East Asian Studies East Asia Research Centre
Western Bank
AA Tower, Floor 5
S10 2TN Sheffield
T 44-1114-2228421
F 44-1114-2228432
SEAS@sheffield.ac.uk \
N.Piper@sheffield.ac.uk

USTA,DA

University of St. Andrews Department of Social Anthropology
KY16 9AL Fife (Scotland)
T 44-1334-462978
F 44-1334-462985

USTA,DMH

University of St. Andrews
Faculty of Arts
Department of Modern History
The Scores
KY16 9AL Fife (Scotland)
T 44-1334-462929/2923
F 44-1334-462927
schlhist@st-andrews.ac.uk

USTI,DE

University of Stirling
Department of Economics
FK9 4LA Stirling (Scotland)
T 44-1786-467479
F 44-1786-467469

USTI,SCJS

University of Stirling
Scottish Centre for Japanese Studies
FK9 4LA Stirling (Scotland)
T 44-1786-466080
F 44-1786-466088
ag3@STIRLING.AC.UK

United Kingdom

USTR,DE

University of Strathclyde Department o Economics
100 Cathedral Street Curran Building
G4 0LN Glasgow (Scotland)
T 44-1141-5524400
F 44-1141-5525589
economics@strath.ac.uk

USTR,DH

University of Strathclyde Department o History
McCance Building
16 Richmond Street
G1 1XQ Glasgow (Scotland)
T 44-1141-5524400
F 44-1141-5528509

USUS,AFRAS

University of Sussex
School of African and Asian Studies (AFRAS)
Falmer
BN1 9QN Brighton (E. Sussex)
T 44-1273-678722
F 44-1273-623572
J.A.Brogden@sussex.ac.uk\R.D.Grillo @sussex.ac.uk

USUS,FE

University of Sussex
Faculty of Economies
Falmer
BN1 9QN Brighton (E. Sussex)
T 44-1273-678739
F 44-1273-623572

USUS,FI,SIM

University of Sussex
Faculty of Informatics
School of Information Management
Moulsecoomb
BN2 4GJ Brighton (E. Sussex)

USUS,IDS

University of Sussex
Institute for Development Studies.
Falmer
BN1 9RE Brighton (E. Sussex)
T 44-1273-606261
F 44-1273-621202
ids@sussex.ac.uk

USUS,MS

University of Sussex
Media Studies
Falmer
BN1 9QN Brighton (E. Sussex)
T 44-1273-606755/2095

USUS,SCCS

University of Sussex
School of Cultural and Community Studies Art History
Falmer
BN1 9QN Brighton (E. Sussex)
T 44-1273-606755
F 44-1273-678644

UU,DHPP

University of Ulster
Faculty of Humanities
Dept. of History, Philosophy and Politic
Cromore Road
BT52 1SA Coleraine (Northern Ireland
T 44-1265-44141
F 44-1265-32495

UW,CC,JSC

University of Wales
College of Cardiff
Japanese Studies Centre
Colum Drive
CF1 3EU Cardiff (S. Wales)
T 44-1222-874959
F 44-1222-874419
RICHARDSJL@CARDIFF.AC.UK

UW,UCS,CDS

University of Wales
University College of Swansea
Centre for Development Studies
Singleton Park
SA2 8PP Swansea, Wales
T 44-1792-205678
F 44-1792-295682

UW,UCS,DH

University of Wales
University College of Swansea
Department of History
Singleton Park
SA2 8PP Swansea, Wales

UW,UCS,DSA

University of Wales
University College of Swansea
Department of Sociology and Anthropology
Singleton Park
SA2 8PP Swansea, Wales
T 44-1792-295309
F 44-1792-295750

UW,UCS,DSPASS

University of Wales
University College of Swansea
Department of Social Policy and Applied Social Studies
Singleton Park
SA2 8PP Swansea, Wales
T 44-1792-295317
F 44-1792-295856

UWA,CRER

University of Warwick
Centre for Research in Ethnic Relations
CV4 7AL Coventry
T 44-1203-523-523
F 44-1203-524324

UWA,DE,DERC

University of Warwick Department of Economics Development Economics Research Centre
CV4 7AL Coventry
T 44-1203-524365
F 44-1203-523055

UWA,DPIS

University of Warwick Department of Politics and International Studies
CV4 7AL Coventry
Shirin.Rai@warwick.ac.uk

UWA,DS

University of Warwick Department of Sociology
CV4 7AL Coventry

UWA,SISL

University of Warwick
School of International Studies of Law
Priory Street
CV1 5FB Coventry

UWE,CS

University of Westminster Chinese Section
9-18 Euston Tower
NW1 3EY London
T 44-1171-9115000\extent:4335
F 44-1171-9115001
evansh@wmin.ac.uk

UWE,SL,ECL

University of Westminster
School of Languages
Euston Centre Library
9-18 Euston Centre
NW1 3ET London

United Kingdom

UWL,DTRIS

University of Wales - Lampeter
Department of Theology, Religious and Islamic Studies
SA48 7ED Lampeter
T 44-1570-424708
F 44-1570-423641
g.bunt@lamp.ac.uk

UWO,WBSSC

University of Wolverhampton
Wolverhampton Business School
Shropshire Campus
Shifnal Road
TF2 9NT Shropshire
T 44-1902-323964
F 44-1902-323870

UY,DE

University of York
Department of Economics
Heslington
YO1 5DD York
T 44-1904-433776
F 44-1904-43 37 59

UY,DLLS

University of York
Department of Language and Linguistics Science
YO1 5DD York
T 44-1904-432666
F 44-1904-432673
mkv1@york.ac.uk

UY,DP

University of York
Department of Politics
YO1 5DD York
T 44-1904-433546
F 44-1904-433563

UY,IAAS

University of York
Institute of Advanced Architectural Studies (IoAAS)
Teh Kings Manor
YO1 2EP York
T 44-1904-433964
F 44-1904-433949
rcc1@york.ac.uk

VA

Visiting Arts
11 Portland Place
W1N 4EJ London
T 44-1171-3893018/19
F 44-1171-3893016

VAM

Victoria and Albert Museum
Cromwell Road
South Kensington
SW7 2RL London
T 44-1171-9388500
F 44-1171-9388341/ 8651/8667
far.east@vam.ac.uk

VAM,ISEAD

Victoria and Albert Museum Indian and South-East Asian Department
Cromwell road
South Kensington
SW7 2RL London
T 44-1171-9388290
F 44-1171-9388651

VUM,DH

Victoria University of Manchester
Department of History
Oxford Road
M13 9PL Manchester
T 44-1161-2753120
F 44-1161-2753098

VUM,IDPM

Victoria University of Manchester
Institute for Development Policy and Management
Oxford Road
M13 9PL Manchester
T 44-1161-2752896

WP,IC

Wilton Park
International Conferences
Wilton House Steyning
BN44 3DZ Steynink, W. Sussex
T 44-1903-815020
F 44-1903-815931
wilton@pavilion.co.uk

Vatican City

MME

Museo Missionario Etnologico
Monumenti Musei e Gallerie Pontificie
00120 Citta' del Vaticano
T 39-6-69883293
F 39-6-69885061

DIRECTORY D

NEWSLETTERS

ON ASIA

IN EUROPE

ADiTi News
Organization: The National Organisation of South Asian Dance
Appears: bi-monthly
Price: £ 10 (UK) £ 20 (overseas)
Format: A4 printed
Contact: The National Organisation of South Asian Dance, 3F Oldbourne Mansions, 46/47 Chancery Lane, London WC2A 1JB UK, Tel: +44-171-8315288, Fax: +44-171-831-5299

La Lettre de l'Afrase
Organization: Association Francaise pour la Recherche sur l'Asie du Sud-Est
Editor: Muriel Charras
Appears: 3 x a year
Price: FF.200 (members), FF.100 (students), FF.250 (outside France)
Circulation: 250
Format: A4
Language: French
Contact: Association Francaise pour la Recherche sur l'Asie du Sud-Est, c/o EFEO, 22, Ave du Président Wilson, 75116 Paris, France. Fax: +33-1-46078833. Email: charras@idf.ext.jussieu.fr

AKSE Newsletter
Organization: Association for Korean Studies in Europe
Editor: Koen de Ceuster
Appears: 1 x a year
Price: Free to members or on application
Format: A5
Contact: Centre of Japanese and Korean Studies, Leiden University, P.O. Box 9515, 2300 RA Leiden, the Netherlands. Tel: +31-71-5272539, Fax: +31-71-5272215, E-mail: deceuster@rullet.leidenuniv.nl. http://www.dur.ac.uk/~druOrep/aksepage.htm

ANDA
Organization: Centre d'Edtudes Mongoles et Sibéeriennes, University of Paris X
Editors: M.-D.Even, J. Thevenet, and M.-L.Beffa
Appears: 4 x a year
Price: Annually FF100 or FB 600 or US$ 20
Format: A4
Language: French
Contact: ANDA Secretariat, 10 Blvd A Blanqui, 75013 Paris, France. Fax: +33-1-47028016. E-mail: even@u-parisio.fr

ASEASUK News
Organization: Association for Southeast Asian Studies in the United Kingdom
Editor(s): Pauline Khng and V.T. King
Appears: 2 x a year
Price: Free for members and relevant institutions
Circulation: 400
Format: A4, printed
Contact: Pauline Khng, Centre for Southeast Asian Studies, University of Hull, Hull HU6 7RX, UK. Tel/Fax: +44-482-465758, E-mail: p.khng@seas.hull.ac.uk

Newsletter of the Asia Research Centre of the Copenhagen Business School
Editor(s): Susan Aagaard Petersen
Appears: 2 x a year
Price: Free of Charge
Contact: Susan Aagaard Petersen, Copenhagen Business School, Asia Research Centre, Nansensgade 19,7. DK-1366 Copenhagen K, Denmark. Tel: +45-38152515. Fax: +45-38152500. E-mail: insusan@cbs.dl

La Lettre d'Asie Centrale
Organization: l'Association de Recherche et d'Information sur l'Asie Centrale (ARIAC)
Editors: E. Allès, D. Balland, H. Dawod, G. Dorronsoro, S.A. Dudoignon, G. Jahangiri, C. Poujol, Th. Zarcone
Price: FF.120 (individuals), FF.300 (organizations)
Format: A4, printed
Language: French
Contact: ARIAC, Maison des Sciences de l'Homme, Bureau 108, 54 Boulevard Raspail, 75006 Paris, France. Fax: +33-1-45488353

BAKS Newsletter
Organization: British Association for Korean Studies
Editor: James E. Hoare
Appears: 2 x a year
Price: Free to members
Circulation: To BAKS members
Format: A5
Contact: James E. Hoare, 86 Crescent Lane, London SW4 9PL, UK. Tel: +44-171-2106213, Fax: +44-171-2106304.

Baruga-Sulawesi Research Bulletin
Editors: S. Koolhof; Chr. de Jong; R. van de Berg; A. Lucas
Appears: 1 x a year
Price: Free of charge
Circulation: 300
Format: A4 (30-40 pages)
Contact: S. Koolhof, CNWS, P.O.Box 9515, 2300 RA Leiden, the Netherlands. Tel: +31-71-5272982, Fax: +31-71-5272615

BASAS Bulletin
Organization: British Association for South Asian Studies
Editors: Yunas Samad
Appears: 3 x a year
Format: A4
Contact: Yunas Samad, Dept. of Social and Economic Studies, University of Bradford, Bradford BD7 1DP, UK. Tel: +44-1274-384804, Fax: +44-1274-385295, E-mail: a.y.samad@bradford.ac.uk. Http://www.brad.ac.uk/acad/ses/basasl.html

BITIG
Organization: SOTA, Research Centre for Turkestan and Azerbaijan
Editors: Mehmet Tütüncü
Appears: 4 x a year
Price: Netherlands Dfl. 50, Europe: US$ 50, Overseas US$ 70, per year. Earlier issues on request.
Circulation: 1000 worldwide
Format: A4, printed, 24-30 pg
Language: Dutch, English and Turkish
Contact: SOTA, P.O. Box 9642, 2003 LP Haarlem, The Netherlands. Tel/Fax: +31-23-5292883, E-mail: mtutuncu@inter.nl.net

Boletin de la Asociación Espanola de Estudios del Pacifico
Organization: Asociación Espanola de Estudios del Pacifico
Editors: Florentino Rodao
Appears: 3 x a year
Price: Free of charge
Format: A4
Language: Spanish
Contact: Asociación Espanola de Estudios del Pacifico, Colegio Mayor N.S. Africa, Ramiro de Maeztu s/n, Ciudad Universitaria, 28040 Madrid, Spain. Fax: +34-1-5540401

Nieuwsbrief Burma Centrum Nederland
Organization: Burma Centrum Nederland, BCN
Editors: Gijs Hillenius
Appears: 10 x a year
Price: individuals Dfl 25,-; organizations Dfl.45,- a year
Circulation: 170
Format: A4, b/w, printed
Language: Dutch
Contact: Burma Centrum Nederland, Paulus Potteratraat 20, 1071 DA Amsterdam, the Netherlands. Tel: +31-20-6716952, Fax: +31-20-6713513, Email: bcn@xs4all.nl

Bulletin d'Information du CDIL
Organization: Centre de Documentation d'Information sur le Laos
Editors: G. Crunelle
Appears: 4 x a year
Price: FF 120 (members), FF 150 (subscribers), FF 75 (students)
Format: A4
Language: French
Contact: Centre de Documentation et d'Information sur le Laos, 14 Rue Dame Genette, 57070 Metx, France. Tel: +33-387753783, Fax: +33-387372709

Newsletter of the Canon Foundation
Organization: The Canon Foundation in Europe
Editor: Richard Burke
Appears: 1 x a year
Price: Free of charge
Circulation: 2700
Format: A4, full colour, printed
Contact: The Canon Foundation, Rijnsburgerweg 3, 2334 BA Leiden, the Netherlands. Tel: +31-71-5156555, Fax: +31-71-5157027.

Caraka, 'the Messenger'. A Newsletter for Javanists.
Organization: Dept. of languages and Cultures of Southeast Asia and Oceania, University of Leiden
Editors: Ben Arps, Willem van der Molen, Ignatius Supriyanto, and Jan van den Veerdonk
Appears: 2 x a year
Format: A4, copied
Contact: Caraka, Dept. of Languages and Cultures of Southeast Asia and Oceania, University of Leiden, P.N. van Eyckhof 3, P.O. Box 9515, 2300 RA Leiden, the Netherlands. Fax: +31-71-5272615, Email: CARAKA@RULLET.LeidenUniv.NL

CEAO Newsletter
*Organization:*Centro de Estudio de Asia Oriental Universidad Autonoma de Madrid
*Format:*A4, printed
Language: Spanish and English
Contact: Centro de Estudio de Asia Oriental, Universidad Autónoma de Madrid, Edificio Rectorado, 28049 Madrid, Spain, tel: +34-1-3974695, fax: +34-1-3975278, e-mail: ceao@uam.es

Newsletter of the Center for Pacific Studies, Stockholm University
Appears: 2 x a year
Price: Free of charge
Circulation: 1100
Format: A4
Contact: Katharina Soffronow, Center for Pacific Studies, University of Stockholm, S-10691 Stockholm, Sweden. Tel: +46-8-162897. Fax: +46-8-168810

CERES Newsletter
Organization: Center for Resource Studies of Development (CERES)
Editor: Dr W.E.A. van Beek
Appears: 6 x a year
Format: A4
Contact: CERES Office, P.O. Box 80140, 3508 TC Utrecht, the Netherlands. Tel: +31-30-2534815, Fax: +31-30-2537482, Email: ceres@fsw.ruu.nl

China Information
Organization: Documentation and Research Centre for Contemporary China
Editor: Woei Lien Chong
Appears: 4 x a year
Price: Individuals: Dfl.74,20, Institutions: Dfl.90,-
Circulation: 400
Format: A5
Contact: Documentation and Research Centre for Contemporary China, Arsenaalstraat 1, P.O. Box 9515, 2300 RA Leiden, the Netherlands. Tel: +31-71-5272516, Fax: +31-71-5272615, Email: docchin@rullet.leidenuniv.nl

China Nieuws
Organization: Stichting China Nieuwsbrief
Editor: J.J.P. Kuijper
Appears: 6 x a year
Price: Dfl.125,- a year
Circulation: 450
Format: A4, full colour, printed
Language: Dutch
Contact: Stichting China Nieuwsbrief, AMPEK Secretariat, De Ruyterkade 5, 1013 AA Amsterdam, the Netherlands. Tel: +31-20-5236758, Fax: +31-20-5236732. For subscriptions: Tel: +31-10-4132235/4129097, Fax: +31-10-4139487.

Newsletter of the Circle of Inner Asian Art
Organization: Circle of Inner Asian Art and Archaeology
*Editor:*Arabella Friesen and Lilla B. Russel-Smith
Appears: 2 x a year
Price: Free of Charge
Format: A4
Contact: CIAA, dept. of Art and Archaeology, SOAS, University of London, Thornhaugh Street, Russel Square, London WC1H 0XG, UK. Fax: +44-171-4363844 (state: CIAAA), Email: russellsmith@cix.compulink.co.uk

CNWS Newsletter
Organization: Research School CNWS, School of Asian, African, and Amerindian Studies
Editor: K. Banak
Appears: 2 x a year
Price: Free of Charge
Circulation: 800
Format: A4
Contact: Research School CNWS, P.O. Box 9515, 2300 RA Leiden, the Netherlands. Tel: +31-71-5272171, Fax: +31-71-5272939

'Common Ground', Newsletter on Philippine environment and Development Action
Organization: Philippine Resource Centre, PRC
Appears: 4 x a year.
Price: Annually £2,50
Circulation: 700
Format: A4
Contact: Philippine Resource Centre, 84 Long Lane, London SE1 4AU, UK. Tel: +44-171-3780296, Fax: +44-171-4033997.

DUJAT Nieuwsbrief
Organization: Dutch Japanese Trade Federation
Appears: 6 x a year
Format: A4
Language: Dutch and English
Contact: A.G. Karl (Director DUJAT), P.O. Box 44, 2170 BB Sassenheim, the Netherlands. Tel: +31-252-266344, Fax: +31-252-266202

EAANnouncements
Organization: East Asian Archaeology Network [EAAN]
Editor: Gina Barnes
Appears: 3 x a year
Format: A5
Contact: Ms Amande Cox, Cherry Tree Cottage, 17 Low Road, Burwell, Cambridge, CB5 0EJ England or call Gina Barnes: Tel: +44-191-3743231, Fax: +44-191-3743242. Email: Gina.Barnes@durham.ac.uk

EACS Newsletter
Organization: European Association of Chinese studies
Editor: Marja Kaikkonen
Appears: 4 x a year
Price: Annually DM 30,- (DM 35 for Eurocharges)
Circulation: 700
Format: A5, copied
Contact: Marja Kaikkonen, Institute of Oriental Languages, Stockhlm University, 10691 Stockholm, Sweden. Tel: +46-8-161412, Fax: +46-8-155464, E-mail: Marja.Kaikkonen@orient.su.se

Bulletin of the EAJS
Organization: European Association for Japanese Studies
Appears: 2 x a year
Price: Free to members of the EAJS
Circulation: 600
Format: A5, copied
Contact:EAJS Office, Anja Radegast, Duisburg University FB5, Lotharstr. 65, 47048 Duisburg, Germany, Tel/Fax: +49-203-3792002, Email: eajs@uni.duisburg.de

East and Southeast Asian News
Organization: Lund University Centre for East and Southeast Asian Studies
Editor: Gun Lauritzon
Appears: 6 x a year
Price: Free of Charge
Circulation: 1000
Format: A4
Language: Swedish and English
Contact: Gun Lauritzon, Centre for East and Southeast Asian Studies, Lund University, Box 7083, 22007 Lund, Sweden, Tel: +46-46-2223040. Fax: +46-46-222 3041. E-mail: LU.Asiacentre@ekh.lu.se

ECARDC Network Newsletter
Organization: European Conference on Agriculture and Rural Development,
Editor: A. Bielfeldt
Appears: 6 x a year
Format: A5
Contact: A. Bielfeldt, Justus-Liebig University Giessen, Ludwigstrasse 21, Giessen, Germany.

The European Institute of Japanese Studies Newsletter
Organization: The European Institute of Japanese Studies
Format: A4
Contact: The European Institute of japanese Studies, Stockholm School of Economics, P.P. Box 6501, 11383 Stockholm, Sweden, Tel: +46-8-7369360, Fax: +46-8-313017, E-mail: japan@hhs.se

ESEM Info
Organization: European Seminar in Ethnomusicology
Appears: 3 or 4 x a year
Price: Free to members, membership fee: 25 Ecus per year (students half price)
Format: A5 printed
Contact: ESEM office, 29 Rue Roquelaine, F-31000 Toulouse, France. Tel: +33-6162-3584

ESF Communications
Organization: European Science Foundation
Editor: Sabine Schott
Appears: 2 x a year
Format: A4, printed
Contact: Sabine Schott, European Science Foundation, 1 quai Lezay Marnésia, 67080 Strasbourg Cedex, France. Tel: +33-88-767125, Fax: +33-88-370532.

Lettre d'information Etudes Chinoises
Organization: Association Française d'Études Chinoises, AFEC
Editor: Vincent Goossaert and Anna Ghiglione
Appears: 3 x a year
Price: membership AFEC, FF 250 (EU), FF 150 (EU students), FF 290 (outside EU), FF 315 (outside EU, airmail), FF 350 (institutions)
Format: A5
Language: French
Contact: Vincent Goossaert, 7 rue Franquet, 75015 Paris, France, email: Goossaer@ext.jussiev.fr; Anna Ghiglione, 25 bd de Strasbourg, 75010 Paris, France

Eurasia News
Organization: European Institute for South and South-East Asian Studies, ASBL
Editor: Malcolm Subhan
Appears: 2 x a year
Price: Free of charge
Circulation: 1500
Format: A4, printed
Contact: Deepa Mann-Kler, 35 Rue des Deux Eglises, B-1040 Brussels, Belgium. Tel: +32-2-230 8122, Fax: +32-2-230 5402

European Bulletin of Himalayan Research
Editors: Pascale Dollfus, Martin Gaenszle, András Höfer, Michael Hutt, Corneille Jest, Marie Lecomte-Tilouine, Brigitte Merz, Anne de Sales, Gérard Toffin
Appears: 2 x a year
Price: FF150 (individuals), FF 180 (institutions), FF 45 (students)
Format: A5
Contact: Anne de Sales, CNRS, UPR 299, 1 Place A. Briand, 92195 Meudon Cedex, France. Fax: +33-45075872, E-mail: himal.res@cnrs-bellevue.fr

European Network for Bangladesh Studies
Organization: The European Network for Bangladesh Studies (ENBS)
Editor: Marl Ellison
Price: £80,00
Format: A5
Contact: The European Network for Bangladesh Studies, School of Social Science, University of Bath, Claverton Down, Bath BA2 7AY, UK. Tel: +44-1225-826826, Fax: +44-1225-826381, E-mail: m.a.ellison@bath.ac.uk

European Newsletter of Southeast Asian Studies
Organization: Jointly published by EUROSEAS (European Association for Southeast Asian Studies) and KITLV (Royal Institute for Linguistics and Anthropology)
Editor: Kees van Dijk
Appears: 2 x a year
Price: Dfl.20,- (Netherlands), Dfl.30,- (others) including postage
Circulation: 500
Format: A4
Contact: Kees van Dijk, ENSEAS c/o KITLV, P.O. Box 9515, 2300 RA Leiden, the Netherlands. Tel: +31-71-5272295, Fax: +31-71-5272638

Friends of Bhutan Nieuwsbrief
Organization: Friends of Bhutan Foundation
Appears: 4 x a year
*Price:*Free of charge
Format: A4
Language: Dutch and English
Contact: Harry Zonder, Friends of Bhutan, P.O. Box 31, 7650 AA Tubbergen, the Netherlands. Tel: +31-546 621 261, Fax: +31-546 622 495.

IATS Newsletter
Organization: Finnish Association of East Asian Studies
Editor: Jouko Seppänen
Appears: 1-2 x a year
Price: Membership FAEAS: 30-120 MK
Circulation: 500
Format: A5
Language: English and Finnish
Contact: Jouko Seppänen, Helsinki University of Technology, Otakaari 1, SF-02150 Espoo, Finland. Tel: +358-0-4514312, Fax: +358-0-4513293

ICS Newsletter
Organization: Institute of Commonwealth Studies
Appears: 12 x a year
Format: A4
Contact: Institute of Commonwealth Studies, 28 Russel Square, London WC1B 5DS, UK. Tel: +44-171-5805876, Fax: +44-171-2552160.

IDPAD NewsBrief
Organization: Indo-Dutch Programme on Alternatives in Development
Editor: Anne van Marrewijk
Format: A4
Contact: Anne van Marrewijk, P.O. Box 93138, 2509 AC Den Haag, the Netherlands

IDP News
Organization: The International Dunhuang Project
Editor: Susan Whitfield
Price: Free of Charge
Format: A4
Contact: Susan Whitfield, The International Dunhuang Project, The British Library,
Oriental and India Office Collections, 197 Blackfriars Road, London SE1 8NG, UK. Tel: +44-171-412 7647/7650, Fax: +44-171-4127858, Email: susan.whitfield@bl.uk

IIAS Newsletter
Organization: International Institute for Asian Studies
Editor: Paul van der Velde
Appears: 4 x a year
Circulation: 15,000
Format: A3
Contact: Paul van der Velde, IIAS, P.O. Box 9515, 2300 RA, Leiden, the Netherlands. Tel: +31-71-527 2227, Fax:+31-71-5274162, Email: IIAS@Rullet.Leidenuniv.nl

India Nu
Organization: Landelijke India Werkgroep
Editors: B. Arps, N. Bonouvrié, H. Boon, I. vd Veen, A. Hendricx, M. Koolen, M.Reumers, P. Wolthuis
Appears: 6 x a year
Price: Dfl. 30,- a year
Circulation: 800
Format: A4
Language: Dutch
Contact: Landelijke India Werkgroep, Oude Gracht 36, 3511 AP Utrecht, the Netherlands. Tel: +31-30-2321340, Fax: +31-30-2322246

Indonesian Environmental History Newsletter
Organization: Ecology, Demography and Economy in Nusantara EDEN
Editors: F. Colombijn and D.E.F. Henley
Appears: 2 x a year (Jan/Jun)
Price: Free of Charge
Circulation: 500
Format: A4, copied
Contact:D.E.F. Henley, Tel: +31-71-5272913, E-mail: Henley@rullet.leidenuniv.nl

INIS Newsletter
Organization: Indonesian-Netherlands Cooperation in Islamic Studies INIS
Editor: Dick van der Meij
Appears: 2 x a year
Price: Free of charge
Circulation: 500
Format: A4, printed
Contact: INIS, Dept. of languages and Cultures of Southeast Asia and Oceania, Projects Division, Leiden University, P.O. Box 9515, 2300 RA, Leiden, the Netherlands. Tel; +31-71-5272419, Fax: +31-71-5272632

ISIR Newsletter
Organization: Irian Jaya Studies - a programme for Interdisciplinary Research
Editor: J. Miedema
Appears: 2 x a year
Price: Free of charge
Circulation: 150-200
Format A4 copied
Contact: J. Miedema, Dept. of Southeast Asia and Oceania, Projects Division, Leiden University, Nonnensteeg 1-3, 2311 VJ Leiden, the Netherlands. Tel: +31-71 5272416/2419, Fax: +31-71-5272632, E-mail:projdi@rullet.leidenuniv.nl

Japan Anthropology Workshop Newsletter
Organization: Japan Anthropology Workshop, JAWS
Editor: Roger Goodman
Appears: 2 x a year
Price: Free to members
Circulation: 200
Format: A5, copied
Contact: Roger Goodman, Nissan Institute of Japanese Studies, 27 Winchester Road, Oxford OX2 6NA, UK. Tel: +44-865-274576, Fax: +44-865-274574, E-mail: rgoodman@vax.ox.ac.uk

JRC News
Organization: Japan Research Centre, SOAS
Editors: Japan Research Centre
Appears: 3 x a year

Price: Free of charge
Circulation: 1200 worldwide
Format: A4
Contact: Japan research Centre, School of Oriental and African Studies, University of London, Russel Square, London WC1H 0XG. Tel: +44-171-3236278, Fax: +44-171-4363844, Email: jrc@soas.ac.uk

Kaibauk – Boletin de Informação Timorense
Organization: ALTIC – Associação Luso Timorense de Informação e Cultura
Editors: Crisódio Araújo
Price: Free of charge
Circulation: 600
Format: A4
Language: Portuguese, and sometimes English or Tetum.
Contact: Fátima Cruz, Apartado 22, 2795 Linda a Velha, Portugal, fax: +35-1-14198521.

Kaname Quarterly Bulletin of Japanese Studies
Organization: Instituto de Japonologia, Madrid
Editors: Maria R. del Alisal
Appears: 3 x a year
Contact: Maria R. del Alisal or Pilar Cabanas, Instituto de Japonologia, Boix y Morer 3.3.1.C, 28003 Madrid, Spain, Tel:+34-1-5345322, Fax: +34-1-5350197. Email: alisjip@ibm.net

KIT Newsletter
Organization: Royal Tropical Institute, Amsterdam
Editors: Inge Pit and Anna Maria Doppenberg
Appears: 2 x a year
Price: Free of charge
Circulation: 4500
Format: A4, full colour, printed
Contact: Inge Pit, Royal Tropical Institute (KIT), Mauritskade 63, 1092 AD Amsterdam, the Netherlands. Tel: +31-20-5688296, Fax: +31-20-6684579.

KKTI Bulletin
Organization: Institute for Oriental Communication and Further Training (Külkereskedelmi Föiskola)
Editor: Judit Hidasi
Format: A4
Contact: Dr Judit Hidasi, Institute for oriental Communication and Further Training, Liget u. 22, 1102 Budapest, Hungary. Tel: +36-1-2608917. Fax: +36-1-2614301

Central Asia Quarterly "Labyrinth"
Organization: Central Asian Research Forum
Editor: Dr. Shirin Akiner
Appears: 4 x a year
Price: Annually individuals: £29 (UK and EU), £35 (rest of Europe), £39 (worldwide); institutions: £55 (UK and EU), £60 (rest of Europe), £65 (worldwide)
Contact: Central Asia Quarterly, Central Asia Research Forum, School of Oriental and African Studies, Russel Square, London WC1H 0XG, UK. Tel: +44-71-3236300, Fax: +44-71-4363844, Email: ab8@soas.ac.uk (please designate the subject as labyrinth)

Memoria de Asia
Organization: Instituto Complutense de Asia
Editors: Florentino Rodao and Javier Villalba
Appears: 4 x a year
Price: Free of charge
Circulation: 800
Format: A4
Language: Spanish
Contact: Instituto Complutense de Asia, Mas Ferré, Somosaguas, Universaidad Complutense de Madrid, 28223 Madrid, Spain. Tel: +34-1-3942491, Fax: +34-1-3942488, Email: iasia02@sis.ucm.es

News and Views from Japan
Organization: The Information Centre of the Mission of Japan to the European Communities
Editor: Hajime Tsujimoto
Appears: 2 x a month
Format: A4
Contact: Tsuyoshi Shionoya, Information Centre of the Mission of Japan to the European Communities, 58 Avenue des Arts, 1040 Brussels. Tel: +32-2-5112307

NAJAKS Newsletter
Organization: Nordic Association of Japanese and Korean Studies
Editor: Arne Kalland
Appears: 1-2 x a year
Contact: Arne Kalland, NIAS, Njalsgade 84, DK-2300 Copenhagen, Denmark. Tel: +45-31-548844, Fax: +45-32-962530

NASA Newsletter
Organization: Nordic Association of South Asian Studies
Editor: Hans-Christian Køie Poulsen
Contact: Hans Christian Køie Poulsen, Nordic Institute of Asian Studies, Njalsgade 84, DK-2300 Copenhagen, Denmark. Tel: +45-35-329098/548844, Fax: +45-32-962530, Email: hckoie@nias.ku.dk

Needham Research Institute Newsletter
Organization:The Needham Research Institute
Editor:Michael Loewe
Appears: 2 x a year
Format: A4
Contact: Editor c/o Needham Research Institute, 8 Sylvester Road, Cambridge CB3 9AF, UK.

NIAS Nytt, Nordic Newsletter of Asian Studies
Organization: Nordic Institute for Asian Studies
Editor: Jens-Chr. Sørensen
Appears: 4 x a year
Circulation: 3000
Format: A4
Contact: NIAS Secretariat, Leifsgade 33, DK-2300 Copenhagen S, Denmark. Tel: +45-31548844; Fax: +45-32962530, Email: sec@nias.ku.dk

Nonesa Newsletter
Organization: The Nordic Association for South East Asian Studies, NASEAS
Editor: Ingela Palmgren
Appears: 1-2 x a year
Price: SEK.100 (yearly), Free of charge for NASEAS members
Circulation: 330
Format: A5
Contact: Ingela Palmgren, NASEAS, Dept. of Economic History, P.O. Box 7083, S-22007 Lund, Sweden. Tel: +46-46-104485, Fax: +46-46-131585

Oceania Newsletter
Organization: Centre for Pacific Studies, University of Nijmegen
Editor: Board members
Appears: 2 x a year
Price: Free for members and institutions

focusing on the South Pacific
Format: A5
Contact: Editorial Board of the *Oceania* Newsletter, Centre for Pacific Studies, Universiteit van Nijmegen, P.O. Box 9104, 6500 HE Nijmegen, the Netherlands. Tel: +31-24-3612361, Fax: +31-24-3611945, URL = http://www.kun.nl/cps/cpsindex.html

OCIS Newsletter
Organization: Oxford Centre for Islamic Studies
Appears: 3 x a year
Price: Free of charge
Circulation: 1000
Format: A4
Contact: Mrs Lynn Abdel-Haq, Oxford

OCCN Nieuwsbrief
Organization: Overzeese Chinezen Contact Nederland
Format: A4
Language: Dutch
Contact: Vrije Universiteit Amsterdam, Faculteit Sociaal-Culturele Wetenschappen, Sectie Niet-Westerse Geschiedenis, De Boelelaan 1105, 1081 HV Amsterdam, the Netherlands. Tel: +31-20-4446707, Fax: +31-20-4446722

ONS Newsletter
Organization: Oriental Numismatic Society
Editor: S. Goron
Price: Annually £10, Dfl.35, FF 100, US$20
Format: A4
Contact: Mr S. Goron, 74 Outram Road, Croydon, Surrey, CRO 6XF, UK

Oriental Ceramic Society Newsletter
Organization: Oriental Ceramic Society
Editor: Jean Martin, Carol Michaelson and Rose Kerr
Format: A4
Contact: The Oriental Ceramic Society, 30B Torrington Square, London WC1E 8JL UK, Tel: +44-171-6367985, Fax: +44-171-5806749

Östasiatiska Museets Vänner - Nyhetsbrev
Organization: The Friendship Association of the Museum of Far Eastern Art & Antiquities in Stockholm
Appears: 6 x a year
Price: Free of charge for members of the Museum. Others after agreement.
Circulation: 1200
Format: A4, 4-6 pages
Language: Swedish
Contact: Carin Balfe, Östasiatiska Museets Vänner, Askrikegatan 19, S-115 57 Stockholm, Sweden. Tel/Fax: +46-8-6609351

St.-Petersburg Newsletter on Southeast Asia & Oceania Studies
Organization: University of St.-Petersburg, Oriental faculty
Editor: A.K. Ogloblin
Appears: 2 x a year
Format: A4
*Contact:*Oriental faculty, University of St.-Petersburg, University Quay 11, St.-Petersburg 199034 Russia. Tel: +812-2189517. Fax: +812-2181346, Email: vladimir@orient.lgu.spb.su

Philippines Information Exchange
Organization: Philippine Resource Centre PRC
Appears: 6 x a year
Price: Annually: £5 (individuals), £30 (organizations), free of charge to members of PRC
Circulation: 300
Format: A4
Contact: Philippine Resource Centre, 23 Bevenden Street, London N1 6BH, UK. Tel: +44-171-2515910, Fax: +44-171-2515914, Email: PRC@GEO2.poptel.org.uk

PRUS Newsletter
Organization: Poverty Research Unit at the University of Sussex
Appears: 4 x a year
Format: A4
Contact: Poverty Research Unit, School of African and Asian Studies, University of Sussex, Falmer, Brighton BN1 9QN. Tel: +44-1273-678739, Fax: +44-1273-623572, Email: m.j.farlow@sussex,ac.uk

Punjab Research Group Newslettere
Organization: The Punjab Research Group
Appears: 1 x a year
Contact: Shinder Thandi, Dept. of Economics, Coventry Business School, Coventry University, Coventry CV1 5FB, UK. Tel: +44-203-838238, Fax: +44-203-838251

Science and Empire
Organization: NISTADS (New Delhi) and REHSEIS (Paris)
Editors: Deepak Kumar (NISTADS) and Patrick Petitjean (REHSEIS)
Price: Free of charge
Appears: 2 x a year
Circulation: 650
Format: A4
Contact: Patrick Petitjean, REHSEIS, 27 rue Damesme, 75013 Paris, France. Tel: +33-1-45811485, Fax: +33-1-45807847, Email: ppjean@paris7.jussien.fr *or* Deepak Kumar, NISTADS, Hillside Road, New Delhi, 110012 India. Tel: +91-11-5726406, Fax: +91-11-5754640

SEALG Newsletter
Organization: South East Asia Library group
Editor: Patricia Herbert
Appears: Anually
Price: Two years: $15.00 or £7.50
Circulation: 250 worldwide
Format: A4
Contact: Patricia Herbert, Oriental & India Office Collections, British Library,
197 Blackfriars Road, London SE1 8NG, UK. Tel: +44-171-4127652, Fax: +44-171-4127641.

SEPHIS Newsletter
Organization: South-South Exchange Programme for Research on the History of Development
Editor: Ulbe Bosma
Appears: 2 x a year
Price: Free of Charge
Contact: Ulbe Bosma, Sephis Secretariat, Facultu of History & Art Studies, Erasmus University Rotterdam, P.O. Box 1738, 3000 DR Rotterdam, the netherlands, Tel: +31-10-4082404, Fax: +31-10-4524503, E-mail:bosma@sephis.fhk.eur.nl

Vereinigung für Sozialwissenschaftliche Japanforschung Newsletter
Organization: Vereinigung für Sozialwissenschaftliche Japanforschung
Editor: Angelika Ernst
Appears: 10 x a year
Format: A5
Language: German
Contact: Angelika Ernst, Poessenbachstr. 21, 81479 München, Germany. Fax: +49-89-7902210

Society for Japanese Arts Newsletter
*Organization:*The Society for Japanese Arts
Editor(s): R. Schaap
Appears: 10 x a year
Format: A4
Contact: Society for japanese Arts, Mr Pankenstraat 12, 5571 CP Bergeyk, the Netherlands. Tel: +31-497-572310, Fax: +31-497-573657

South Asia Newsletter
Organization: Centre of South Asian Studies, SOAS
Editor(s): Centre of South Asian Studies, Room 471
Appears: 3 x a year
Price: Free to educational institutions
Circulation: 470
Format: A4
Contact: Centre of South Asian Studies, Room 471, School for Oriental and African Studies, Thornhaugh St., Russell Square, London WC1 0XG, UK. Tel: +44-171-3236353, Fax: +44-171-4363844.

The Newsletter of the "State and Society in East Asia" Network
Editor: Kjeld Erik Brödsgaard
Appears: 2 x a year
Price: Free of Charge
Circulation: 200
Format: A4
Contact: Kjeld Erik Brodsgaard or Mette Mathiasen, East Asian Institute, University of Copenhagen, Njalsgade 80, DK-2300 Copenhagen S, Denmark. Tel: +45-31-542211, Fax: +45-31-546676

Sri Lanka Newsletter
Organization: Stichting Nederland-Sri Lanka
Editor: E. Jongens
Appears: 4 x a year
Price: Members Dfl. 25,-
Circulation: 250-300
Format: A4
Language: Dutch
Contact: Stichting Nederlands-Sri Lanka, Den Haag, the Netherlands. Tel: +31-70 3252381

Südostasien Informationen
Organization: Southeast Asia Information Centre
Editor: Peter Franke
Appears: 4 x a year
Price: (annually) Germany: individuals DM36,-, institutions DM72,-; other countries: individuals DM48,-, institutions DM 96,- (aimail postage + DM15,-)
Circulation: 1200
Format: A4, printed
Language: German
Contact: Southeast Asia Information Centre, Bullmannaue 11, D-45327 Essen, Germany. Tel: +49-201-8303818, Fax: +49-201-8303820. E-mail: seainfo@geod.geonet.de

The Tibet Society of the United Kingdom Newsletter
Editor: Jogn Billington
Appears: 4 x a year
Price: £ 15
Circulation: 2000
Format: A4
Contact: John Billington, The Tibet Society of the UK, 114-115 Tottenham Court Road, London W1P 9HL, UK. Tel: +44-171-3837533. Fax: +44-171-3837563

The Tibet Foundation Newsletter
Editor: Dharmakosha
Price: £ 12
Format: A4
Contact: Tibet Foundation, 10 Bloomsbury Wat, London WC1A 2SH UK, Tel: +44-171-4042889, fax: +44-171-4042366

Ultramarines
Organization: Amis des Archives d'Outre-Mer (AMAROM)
Appears: 2 x a year
Price: Per issue FF.50, annual subscription: FF.90
Circulation: 700
Format: A4
Language: French
Contact: A. Cécile Tizon Germe, AMAROM, 29 Chemin du Moulin Detesta, 13090 Aix-en-Provence, France. Tel: +33-42-264321, Fax: +33-42-268459

BOOKS ON SOUTHEAST ASIA

EMERGING CIVIL SOCIETY IN THE ASIA-PACIFIC COMMUNITY

Edited by Tadashi Yamamoto

This volume lists all major research institutions, foundations, and non-governmental organizations in fifteen Asia-Pacific countries - Australia, Canada, China, Hong Kong, Indonesia, Japan, Korea, Malaysia, New Zealand, the Philippines, Singapore, Taiwan, Thailand, the United States, and Vietnam. The reports on the activities are by leading intellectuals.

Revised edition 1996	776 pages
ISBN 981 3055 06 5 (hard cover)	US$58.00
ISBN 981 3055 05 7 (soft cover)	US$40.00

THE DYNAMICS OF METROPOLITAN MANAGEMENT IN SOUTHEAST ASIA

Edited by Jürgen Rüland

Experiencing unprecedented growth rates, cities in Southeast Asia have faced problems that have threatened to undermine the practice of metropolitan management. Using an interdisciplinary approach, this study evaluates cities in seven countries: Bangkok, Hanoi, Jakarta, Kuala Lumpur, Manila, Singapore and Yangon.

1996	230 pages
ISBN 981 3055 28 6 (soft cover)	US$25.00

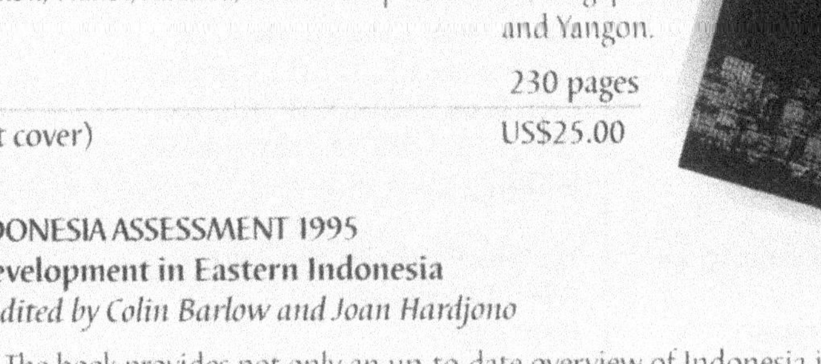

INDONESIA ASSESSMENT 1995

Development in Eastern Indonesia

Edited by Colin Barlow and Joan Hardjono

The book provides not only an up-to-date overview of Indonesia in 1995, but also one of the first comprehensive surveys of Eastern Indonesia, a rapidly growing but little known region of Southeast Asia.

1st Reprint 1997	300 pages
ISBN 981 3055 18 9 (soft cover)	US$25.00

OPEN REGIONALISM AND TRADE LIBERALIZATION

An Asia-Pacific Contribution to the World Trade System

By Ross Garnaut

Open regionalism is regional economic co-operation without discrimination against countries outside the region. This book brings together papers presented over recent years by Professor Ross Garnaut, one of the architects of open regionalism. The papers point to a way forward towards Asia-Pacific and global free trade.

1996	225 pages
ISBN 981 3055 46 4 (hard cover)	US$48.90
ISBN 981 3055 45 6 (soft cover)	US$26.00

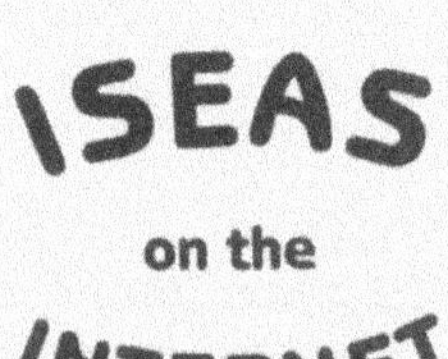

For a listing of ISEAS' recent books and the contents pages of our journals, our World Wide Web server is now on-line. Check out our Home Page on

http://www.iseas.ac.sg/pub.html

Published by
INSTITUTE OF SOUTHEAST ASIAN STUDIES
Heng Mui Keng Terrace, Pasir Panjang, Singapore 119596
Tel: (65) 8702447 • Fax: (65) 7756259
World Wide Web: http://www.iseas.ac.sg/pub.html
Internet e-mail: pubsunit@iseas.ac.sg

WORLD OF INDIAN ACADEMIC/RESEARCH PUBLICATIONS IN ENGLISH, TIBETAN, SANSKRIT, HINDI AND OTHER VERNACULARS

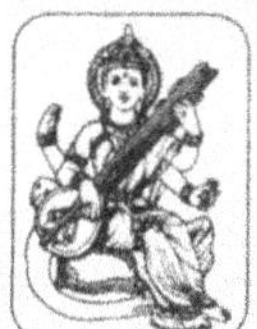

DK AGENCIES (P) LTD.

International Booksellers, Publishers & Subscription Agents
A/15-17, Mohan Garden, Najafgarh Road, NEW DELHI - 110 059 (INDIA)
Phones: (011) 559-8897, 559-8899 **Fax:** (+91-11) 559-8898, (+91-11) 555-8898
E-mail: custserv@dkagencies.com **website** : http://www.dkagencies.com

* **Three decades old name** among book-loving community around the world offering:
  + **Books** + **Back-volumes** + **Subscriptions** + **Multimedia**
* **Cost-free supply** of diverse **Bibliographic Acquisition Profiles** and specialized **Book-catalogues.**
* **Outstanding services to libraries.**
* **Standing Order Service** for serials, periodicals, series and multi-volumes.
* **Blanket Order/Approval Plan Service** offered.
* Meeting on priority the **specific demands of Individual scholars.**
* Present on **INTERNET** with vast automated database.
* For more details visit our **website.**

INDUS BOOKS

OUT OF PRINT BOOKS ON SOUTH ASIA

631 NE 31st Ave, Portland OR 97232 USA
(503) 231-9215 • indus@teleport.com
http://www.teleport.com/~indus/

We specialise in current, out-of-print and rare academic monographs and government documents on India - history, politics, sociology, economics, religions, travelogues, antique maps, prints, etc.

Frequent lists issued.

Prabhu Book Service
PO Box 21
Sadar Bazar
Gurgaon 122001, Haryana
India

Tel. +91 124 320 588
Tel. +91 124 322 836
Fax +91 124 329 805

Gert Jan Bestebreurtje

Antiquarian Bookseller and Print-dealer

Brigittenstraat 2
(Corner Nieuwegracht 42)
Opposite Rijksmuseum
het Catharijneconvent
Postbus 364
3500 AJ Utrecht / Netherlands

Tel.: (0)30-231 92 86 / Fax: (0)30-234 33 62

Specialized in Old & Rare Books on Colonial History and Travel.

Catalogues of books on Asia are to be found as Short List on **Internet:**
http://iias.leidenuniv.nl/books/bestebr/
For more detailed information please fax or write.

We always enjoy meeting our customers personally in Utrecht (35 km *from Amsterdam*) from Monday through Friday, on Saturday by appointment only.
Orders for the book **Haks & Maris, Lexicon of foreign artists who visualized Indonesia (1600-1950)**, may be sent directly to the publisher, see address above.

OLD AND RARE
BOOKS ON ASIA

Booklist from

ASIAN RARE BOOKS

175 W. 93rd street (Suite 16-D)
New York, N.Y. 10025-9344

Fax: (212) 316-3408
Tel: (212) 316-5334
E-mail: ARB@maestro.com
http://www.columbia.edu/cu/ccs/cuwl/clients/arb/

Books Bought
By Appointment

BOOKSTORE "DE VERRE VOLKEN"

(c/o National Museum of Ethnology)

Art Books on Non-Western Civilizations

For our book catalogues please write or fax to:

Steenstraat 1 2312 BS Leiden - The Netherlands
Tel. 31 (0)71-5168706 Fax. 31 (0)348-412838

Open: Tuesday-Sunday

JACKSON, David

A History of Tibetan Painting: The Great Tibetan Painters and Their Traditions

The present book is a first attempt at exploring the sacred painting traditions of Tibet from the mid-15th through 20th centuries on the basis of both the surviving pictorial remains and the extensive written sources that survive in the Tibetan language. The study of this period of Tibetan art history has in effect been neglected in recent years in favor of the earliest periods. Yet the vast majority of extant masterpieces of Tibetan Buddhist painting belong to this more recent period, and the relevant written and pictorial resources now available, though they have never been fully utilized until now, are in fact quite rich.

The present study attempts in the first place to identify the great founders of the main schools of Tibetan painting and to locate references to their surviving works of sacred art. Through recourse to the artists' own writings, if available, to the biographies of their main patrons, and to other contemporaneous or nearly contemporaneous sources, it has been possible to clarify many of the circumstances of the careers of such famous Tibetan painters as sMan-bla-don-grub, mKhyen-brtse-chen-mo and Nam-mkha'-bkra-shis, who were the founders of the sMan-ris, mKhyen-ris and Karma sgar-bris traditions, respectively.

For the convenience of students and researchers, the book includes a survey of the main available Tibetan sources and studies, both traditional and modern, as well as a detailed summary of previous Western research on this subject. It also presents the texts and translations of the most important passages from the main traditional sources. This richly illustrated volume also includes detailed indices, and it will be an indispensable guide and reference work for anyone interested in Tibetan art.

1996, 456 Seiten, 70 Farbabbildungen, 211 Schwarzweiß-Abbildungen, 2 Pläne, 21x29,7 cm, Leinen
ISBN 3-7001-2224-1
ATS 1.400,– DEM 192,– CHF 170,–

WANGDU, Pasang – DIEMBERGER, Hildegard, (coop. G. HAZOD)

Shel dkar chos 'byung. History of the 'White Crystal' Religions and Politics of Southern La stod. Translation and Facsimile Edition of the Tibetan Text

1996, 246 Seiten, 21x29 cm, broschiert, Dph, Band252
Veröffentlichungen zur Sozialantropologie, Band 1
ISBN 3-7001-2597-6
ATS 435,– DEM 59,60 CHF 53,80
Erscheinungstermin: Oktober 1996

BLONDEAU, Anne-Marie – STEINKELLNER, Ernst (Eds.)

Reflections of the Mountain

Essays on the History and Social Meaning of the Mountain Cult in Tibet and the Himalaya

1996, 272 Seiten, 21x29 cm broschiert, Dph, Veröffentlichungen zur Sozialantropologie Band II
ISBN 3-7001-2611-5
ATS 450,– DEM 62,– CHF 56,50
Erscheinungstermin: Dezember 1996

SCHEID, Bernhard

Im Innersten meines Herzens empfinde ich tiefe Scham

Das Alter im Schrifttum des japanischen Mittelalters

1996, 408 Seiten, 15x24 cm, broschiert, Beiträge zur Kultur und Geistesgeschichte Asiens, Band 17
ISBN 3-7001-2474-0
ATS 718,– DEM 98,– CHF 89,–
Erscheinungstermin: Oktober 1996

FORMANEK, Susanne – LINHART, Sepp (Eds.)

Old Age and Aging in Japan and Other Asian Cultures

Spiritual Conditions and Social Reality Past and Present

1997, ca. 400 Seiten, 15x24 cm, broschiert, Beiträge zur Kultur und Geistesgeschichte Asiens, Band 16
ISBN 3-7001-2473-2
ca. ATS 868,– DEM 119,– CHF 105,–
Erscheinungstermin: März 1997

Bestellung und Auslieferung: **Verlag der Österreichischen Akademie der Wissenschaften**
A-1011 Wien, Postfach 471, Postgasse 7/4 , Tel +43-1-515 81/DW 401–406, Fax +43-1-515 81-400
http://www.oeaw.ac.at/einheiten/verlag, e-mail: verlag@oeaw.ac.at

Key CURZON

Asian Studies Books

Alex McKay
Tibet and the British Raj
(London Studies on South Asia)
ISBN 0 7007 0627 5 / £ 35.00

Brian Moeran
A Japanese Advertising Agency
(ConsumAsiaN)
ISBN 0 7007 0503 1 / £ 14.99

Giles Tillotson
Paradigms of Indian Architecture
(Collected Papers on South Asia)
ISBN 0 7007 0628 3 / £ 35.00

Audrey Burton
The Bukharans
(Central Asia Research Forum)
ISBN 0 7007 0417 5 / £ 60.00

Kirsten Refsing
Early European Writings on the Ainu Language
(Ainu Library)
ISBN 0 7007 0400 0 / £ 895.00

Denis Sinor
The Uralic and Altaic Series
ISBN 0 7007 0380 2 / £ 10,500.00

Weng Eang Cheong
The Hong Merchants of Canton
(NIAS Monograph Series 70)
ISBN 0 7007 0361 6 / £ 45.00

Mohammad-R Djalili
Tajikistan
(Central Asia Research Forum)
ISBN 0 7007 0420 5 / £ 40.00

Christine Noelle
State and Tribe in Nineteenth-Century Afghanistan
ISBN 0 7007 0629 1 / £ 40.00

John DeFrancis
ABC Chinese-English Dictionary
ISBN 0 7007 0511 2 / £ 25.00

Michael Dillon
China: A Cultural and Historical Dictionary
(Durham East Asia Series)
ISBN 0 7007 0439 6 / £ 14.99

Brian Moeran
Folk Art Potters of Japan
(Anthropology of Asia Series)
ISBN 0 7007 0605 4 / £ 40.00

Shuichi Kato
A History of Japanese Literature
(Japan Library)
ISBN 1 873410 48 4 / £ 16.99

Donald Wagner
A Classical Chinese Reader
ISBN 0 7007 0961 4 / £ 14.99

Stephen Turnbull
The Kakure Kirishitan of Japan
(Japan Library)
ISBN 1 873410 70 0 / £ 40.00

Walter Maurer
The Sanskrit Language
ISBN 0 7007 0352 7 / £ 60.00

D. Keown & C. Prebish
Buddhism and Human Rights
(Critical Studies in Buddhism)
ISBN 0 7007 0954 1 / £ 40.00

Robert Cribb
An Atlas of Indonesian History
ISBN 0 7007 0985 1 / £ 75.00

Curzon Press Ltd / 15 The Quadrant / Richmond / Surrey TW9 1BP
United Kingdom / Tel: +44-181-9484660 / Fax: +44-181-3326735
E-mail: publish@curzonpress.demon.co.uk

Order Form

Publications of the IIAS

IIAS Lecture Series (Dfl. 10,– unless otherwise stated)

- ☐ Staal, F. – *Concepts of Science in Europe and Asia* – (Leiden, 1993). ISBN 90-74917-01-1.
- ☐ Lombard, D. – *De la vertu des aires culturelles et de celle des aires culturelles asiatiques en particulier* – (Leiden, 1994). ISBN 90-74917-02-X. (*Out of stock*)
- ☐ Kooijmans, P.H. – *Human Rights in an Interdependent World* – (Leiden, 1995). ISBN 90-74917-04-6.
- ☐ Prakash, O. – *Asia and the Pre-modern World Economy* – (Leiden, 1995). ISBN 90-74917-07-0.
- ☐ Mierlo, H. van – *Europe and Asia: Towards a New Partnership* – (Leiden, 1996). ISBN 90-74917-12-7.
- ☐ Wang Gungwu – *The Revival of Chinese Nationalism* – (Leiden, 1996). ISBN 90-74917-16-X.
- ☐ Several authors – *Cultural Rapprochement between Asia and Europe: Five Essays on the Asia-Europe Relationship* – (Leiden / Amsterdam, 1997). ISBN 90-74917-18-6. (Dfl. 20,-)
- ☐ Pronk, J.P. – Asia and Dutch Development Co-operation – *Some Comments from a Student of Asian Development* – (Leiden / Amsterdam, 1997). ISBN 90-74917-20-8.

IIAS Working Papers Series (Dfl. 30,–)

- ☐ Dong Lisheng (ed.) – *Administrative Reform in the People's Republic of China since 1978* – (Leiden, 1994). ISBN 90-74917-03-8.
- ☐ Evers, S.J.Th.M. and M.R. Spindler (eds) – *Civilizations of Madagascar: Ebb and Flow of Influences* – (Leiden, 1995). ISBN 90-74917-11-9.
- ☐ Voogt, A. de (ed.) – *New Approaches to Board Games Research. Asian Origins and Future Perspectives* – (Leiden, 1995). ISBN 90-74917-10-0.
- ☐ Brakel, C. (ed.) – *Performing Arts of Asia. The Performer as (Inter)Cultural Transmitter* – (Leiden, 1996). ISBN 90-74917-15-1.

Other Publications

- ☐ *A Bird's-eye View*– (Leiden, 1995). Free of charge.*
- ☐ *IIAS Internet Guide to Asian Studies.*– (Leiden, 1996). ISBN 90-74917-13-5. Dfl.20,–
- ☐ *IIAS Annual Report 1993. 1994. 1995.* * (*Out of stock*)
- ☐ *IIAS Annual Report 1996* – (Leiden, 1997).*
- ☐ *IIAS Yearbook 1994* – (Leiden, 1995). ISBN 90-74917-08-9. Dfl.35,–
- ☐ *IIAS Yearbook 1995* – (Leiden, 1996). ISBN 90-74917-17-8. Dfl.35,–
- ☐ *Guide to Asian Studies in Europe* – (London, 1998). ISBN 07007-1054-X.
- ☐ *IIAS Guide to Asian Collections in the Netherlands* – (Leiden / Amsterdam). ISBN 90-74917-19-4. Dfl.15,–
- ☐ *IIAS Guide to Asian Collections in Amsterdam* – (Leiden / Amsterdam). ISBN 90-74917-21-6. Dfl.15,–
- ☐ *The Keys to the IIAS, Memobook with useful information for IIAS fellows* – (Leiden, 1995). Dfl.15,–
- ☐ *Brochure European Science Foundation, Asia Committee* – (1995). Free of charge.

*IIAS Newsletter 1 - 12** (*Out of stock*), ☐ 13 (*summer '97*), ☐ 14 (*Autumn '97*). *Free of charge.**

The publications marked *
are available electronically on:
http://iias.leidenuniv.nl
Please mark the (number of) publications you wish to order. We will send you an invoice.

NAME: ______________________

ADDRESS: ______________________

CITY: ______________________

COUNTRY: ______________________

TEL/FAX: ______________________

Signature:

PLEASE RETURN THIS ORDER FORM TO:
International Institute for Asian Studies (IIAS)

For Product Safety Concerns and Information please contact our EU
representative GPSR@taylorandfrancis.com
Taylor & Francis Verlag GmbH, Kaufingerstraße 24, 80331 München, Germany

www.ingramcontent.com/pod-product-compliance
Ingram Content Group UK Ltd.
Pitfield, Milton Keynes, MK11 3LW, UK
UKHW030829080625
459435UK00017B/597